Encyclopedia of Primary Education

Unique in its field, the *Encyclopedia of Primary Education* brings together a wide-ranging body of information relating to current educational practice in a single indispensable volume. This book provides a series of descriptions, definitions and explanations that engage with important practical and conceptual ideas in primary education and contains over 500 entries, incorporating:

- curriculum subjects, themes and topics;
- theories, policies and educational controversies;
- pedagogical terms relating to teaching and learning;
- commentaries on current issues in primary education;
- influential figures in education, both past and present;
- the impact of educational research on policy and practice.

Based on the author's extensive experience in primary education, entries combine an interrogation of educational concepts with the pedagogical and practical implications for classroom practice, children's learning and school management. This handy reference work will be invaluable to anyone currently teaching or training to teach at primary level, teaching assistants, school governors and parents. In fact it is essential reading for anyone with an interest and passion for primary education.

Denis Hayes was Professor of Primary Education at the University of Plymouth. He has extensive experience as a primary teacher, deputy head, head teacher, teacher trainer, academic and researcher.

D1608858

Encyclopedia of Primary Education

Denis Hayes

 Routledge
Taylor & Francis Group

LONDON AND NEW YORK

First published 2010
by Routledge
2 Park Square, Milton Park, Abingdon, Oxon OX14 4RN

Simultaneously published in the USA and Canada
by Routledge
270 Madison Avenue, New York, NY 10016

Routledge is an imprint of the Taylor & Francis Group, an informa business

© 2010 Denis Hayes

Typeset in Galliard by
Taylor & Francis Books
Printed and bound in Great Britain by
CPI Antony Rowe, Chippenham, Wiltshire

British Library Cataloguing in Publication Data
A catalogue record for this book is available from the British Library

Library of Congress Cataloging in Publication Data
Hayes, Denis, 1949–
Encyclopedia of primary education / Denis Hayes.
    p. cm.
  1. Education, Elementary—;Great Britain. 2. Education, Elementary—
Curricula—Great Britain. 3. Education—Terminology. I. Title.
  LB1556.7.G7H39 2009
  372'.941—dc22
                        2009021861

ISBN 10: 0-415-48517-7 (hbk)
ISBN 10: 0-415-48518-5 (pbk)
ISBN 10: 0-203-86460-3 (ebk)

ISBN 13: 978-0-415-48517-3 (hbk)
ISBN 13: 978-0-415-48518-0 (pbk)
ISBN 13: 978-0-203-86460-9 (ebk)

Contents

Foreword

Contrary to the views of some self-styled 'experts' primary education is not just about corralling young children inside classrooms, sitting them down (on the carpet or behind desks) and telling them things which they have to remember. Whatever else this encyclopedia does, it stresses the fact that primary education is an extremely complex enterprise, whether considered in theoretical, practical, research or policy terms.

Scanning the entries alone should be enough to convince the skeptic that educating primary-age children is not just a matter of instructing children in clearly defined 'basic skills' or getting them to acquire the competences necessary to achieve particular levels of performance on tests. It is much more complicated and demanding than that. Like this encyclopedia, primary education is an amalgam of so many different elements – interpersonal, emotional, academic, physical, moral, even aesthetic and spiritual. It involves all sorts of thorny questions which are far from easy to answer and are themselves controversial: ' What is education for? What is "basic" to primary education? What aspects of our culture merit being taught to the young? How should teachers and children treat one another?' This encyclopedia is not afraid to raise such questions, even though it does not claim to provide definitive answers. Throughout it reinforces the powerful notion of primary education as a moral and emotional enterprise, as well as a practical activity – one in which , as the compiler says, 'learning is rooted in relationships, motivation and desire, as much as in methods, structure and equipment'.

Primary education both uses and teaches a multitude of concepts – not just technical ones such as 'ability grouping', 'assessment for learning' or the inevitable and omnipresent 'phonics' but more general, and arguably more fundamental, ones such as 'nurturing', 'caring', 'relationships' and 'emotions'. A multitude of such ideas are discussed here along with the more mundane, but necessary, aspects of primary education such as 'break time', 'desks' and, of perennial concern, dealing with 'naughtiness'!

A variety of other entries capture the realities of everyday teaching – its joys, frustrations, surprises and disappointments. What comes over clearly is the enormous interpersonal complexity involved when twenty-five or more human beings have to interact for five or six hours a day in the confined space called a classroom. Nor does the compiler neglect the uncomfortable dilemmas facing primary teachers – do they stress competition or cooperation, independence or conformity, present or future needs, process or content? Such dilemmas have to be resolved daily but their resolution can never be final or decisive. Readers seeking recipes for sure-fire educational success will not find them here (they cannot be written, let alone acted upon) but they will find insights and information to help them make informed professional decisions, whether they are teachers in training (an unfortunate phrase!), qualified teachers undertaking further study, teaching assistants with aspirations to further their careers or governors trying to grapple with their multiplicity of responsibilities.

Thirty years ago so many books and articles not only failed to add to our understanding of teaching but actually obscured the dilemmas, uncertainties and difficulties which character-ize it. Theirs was a tidy, uncomplicated world where everything fitted neatly into place, where everyone agreed as to children's 'needs', where heads and teachers worked 'harmoniously' towards shared goals and where teachers intuitively 'knew what was best'. It was never so, it is not now – given the contentious nature of education , made more so by a welter of political initiatives in the last two decades. This encyclopedia illus-trates how far writing on primary education has come since then as a result of the work of those featured in the various entries, the work of those mentioned by name in the intro-duction (with one modest exception!), and not least the work of the compiler himself as he has introduced successive cohorts of students to the intricacies and mysteries of primary school teaching.

Writing in 1980 Professor Brian Simon commented that 'primary education has been in a state of almost continuous transition throughout its short history.' It will continue to evolve. As users of this encyclopedia you will play a part in this evolution but hopefully some of you will want to contribute to the future literature of primary education. Who knows? Your insights might well form part of a new encyclopedia of primary education to be published in 2030!

Colin Richards
Emeritus Professor
University of Cumbria and formerly HMI

Acknowledgements

Writing this book did not come solely out of my head and heart; it was created from countless interactions, conversations, fragments of information, attending conferences, hearing lectures, access to books, web sites and other sources of knowledge, as well as my own hard-won experience as a teacher and lecturer in education. It is not possible to thank everyone who has shaped my thinking and influenced my perspectives but I must make particular mention of colleagues on the executive committee of the Association for the Study of Primary Education (ASPE) and those with whom I've served on the Exeter Society for Curriculum Studies, not least its honorary secretary, Michael Golby. I have also been extremely fortunate to be influenced by a number of seminal thinkers, including Jennifer Nias, Peter Woods and Colin Richards.

I want to thank my many colleagues at the former Rolle School of Education in Exmouth, England, for their support, wisdom, insights and willingness to share their understanding of key education issues with me. In particular, I give my unreserved thanks to Ken Lawson and Stephen Howarth for the considerable amount of time that they have spent over the years in discussing education matters and showing me the importance of valuing the person ahead of the achievement. In my role as education tutor and supervisor of trainee teachers on school placement I have gained immeasurably from speaking with hundreds of teachers about the skills, practicalities and emotions attached to the job of teaching. I offer my sincere gratitude to them all for demonstrating such commitment to children and reaffirming my belief that being a primary educator is as much a calling as a profession.

Finally, thanks to my family and friends who have allowed me the space and time to be immersed in writing this book. One of the costs of being an author is the need to become something of a recluse, especially as the deadline for submitting the manuscript approaches. Inevitably, leisure time dissolves and relationships temporarily suffer. Their patience has been greatly appreciated. I trust that I have amply repaid their forbearance.

List of entries

Introduction

I consider it a privilege to have been asked to compile this encyclopedia of primary education and enjoyed immensely the formidable but stimulating task of putting together such a volume. The concept of primary education is wide-ranging and far from easy to pin down, but I've done my best to be faithful to the topic and not be tempted to deviate from the path and indulge my interest in related education matters. One of the challenges of writing an encyclopedia is to provide sufficient information such that each entry can 'stand alone' yet avoid repetition. In doing so I have had to make certain assumptions about the reader's knowledge while adding short explanations and definitions where I consider it to be necessary for clarity. The majority of entries are cross-referenced to provide an indication of where else it is worth looking for information relating to the principal topic.

One of the key factors when writing an encyclopedia is not only deciding which topics to include and exclude but also how much detail to provide for each one. Some subjects are so vast that whole books have been written about them (e.g. bullying); others may seem less important but have great significance for educating and nurturing our children (e.g. friendships). In addition, there is the challenge that every writer faces in keeping pace with current legislation and the latest 'big idea' in education that is often superseded by new initiatives and requirements before the book is even published. Elections sometimes result in a reshaping of the political landscape and a new government or legislature might take a different direction in its education policy from its predecessor, revise old systems and modify existing ones. To offset the impact of these inevitable policy changes, I have avoided focusing too much on legislative matters and tried as far as possible to concentrate on the educational issues that they represent.

I have included some information about influential figures in primary education, past and present. The selection of such 'giants' in the field has been a particularly difficult task, especially deciding who to include from those still living. I could easily have filled the book with details about the impact that many committed and dedicated people have made in the field of education – and primary education in particular – some of whom I've been privileged to meet. The problem is in knowing where to start and where to end such a list. In truth, many of the most powerful education thinkers are found among 'ordinary' primary school teachers and head teachers, who may never have their names in lights but have been a positive influence on thousands of children and practitioners down the years. These are the real heroes, selflessly working for the good of children and trying desperately to maintain their principles in an increasingly politicised system. There are, of course, many politicians who have also genuinely striven for the good of the child but the rapid turnover of government ministers makes it hard to distinguish commitment from ambition.

A few of the entries may surprise you, not least that of Albert Einstein – though his inclusion probably reveals my predilection for people who turn away from the trappings of fame and choose to devote their efforts for the common good. Some of the influential figures operated outside the strict parameters of primary education but have proved to be vastly influential; I refer here to notables such as Bruner, Piaget and Dewey. I have also devoted a number of pages to seminal historical events, such as the Hadow Reports during the early years of the twentieth century and the Plowden Report of 1967, plus a mention of the William Tyndale Junior School debacle in 1974, all of which triggered a rethink of education policy and practice.

Much of the information provided in this encyclopedia is 'generic' in that it pertains to primary education generally; however, some entries are rooted in the education system that operates specifically in the individual countries of England, Wales, Scotland, Northern Ireland and the USA. The political shape of the United Kingdom, with various powers devolved to constituent countries, has made the task of referring to 'the government' much more complicated, as it may refer to the whole of the UK or (increasingly) to an initiative or perspective unique to a particular country (e.g. Scotland). One of the most obvious examples of countries in the UK adopting different approaches to an issue is with respect to testing, where arguments about the value of national curriculum tests ('SATs') has split and riven opinion in England but has largely been resolved elsewhere. In this example, as in many others, the *issues* surrounding testing are endemic but the *practice* varies from place to place.

Like every author, I have tried extremely hard to give credit for every source of information that I have used; in such a complex undertaking, however, there are bound to be occasions when I have inadvertently failed to do so. For any such errors I offer my apologies in advance and welcome clarification. I have freely drawn information from my previous books, notably *Foundations of Primary Teaching* (David Fulton Publishers) and *Primary Education: The key concepts* (Routledge). I must express my indebtedness to general web sites such as Wikipedia for bits of information and links to various sources of data. I have also discovered other snippets of information in long-forgotten files on my computer but their origins remain a mystery.

I agreed to write this encyclopedia because I wanted it to be useful to a wide range of people interested in primary education. Of course the danger of trying to reach such a diverse audience is to end up pleasing no one! However, I trust that I have avoided such a fate and that teachers in training, qualified teachers undertaking further study, teaching assistants with aspirations to further their careers, parents, governors and academics will all find material of value.

Most significantly for me, writing this encyclopedia has reminded me of two fundamental truths: first, how much knowledge I have accumulated about primary education down the years; second, the humbling realisation of how much I still have to learn. In using the book, I hope and anticipate that you will experience something similar.

Primary education

The phrase 'primary education' has been in use since the 1930s to describe the formal phase of schooling for pupils ('students', USA) aged between five and eleven years in the United Kingdom; however, the process of educating children takes place from the moment a child enters the world and even, some would argue, prior to birth. Parents are therefore the first educators; teachers and other professionals contribute to the process and help to structure learning within an educational setting but cannot hope to do the job unaided. Though schools can provide equipment and resources that few parents could ever afford, learning is rooted in relationships, motivation and desire, as much as in methods, structure and equipment.

There have been many changes in the field of primary education over recent years. In fact ever since the incoming British prime minister, Tony Blair, announced as part of the Labour Party's 1997 election manifesto that 'education, education, education' lay at the heart of national policy, huge sums have been invested in the sector. Early years provision for children aged 3–5 years has been expanded considerably; every primary school has teaching assistants to support qualified teachers, some of whom (appointed as higher level teaching assistants) take an active role in supervising and teaching groups of children and whole classes. This particular innovation has been controversial to say the least, viewed by sceptics as a cheap way to provide substitute ('supply') teachers; viewed by supporters as a way to utilise expertise and release teachers to plan lessons and assess pupil progress.

The introduction of government guidelines for literacy and numeracy in the late 1990s – viewed by the vast majority of teachers as requirements – and changes in the structure of lessons as a means of improving standards in English and mathematics, became so embedded in practice across the curriculum that concerns were raised about the repetitious nature of pupils' learning experiences and the accompanying loss of creativity for both teachers and children. A variety of reports and studies were produced in the first decade of the twenty-first century, warning the government of low morale among staff and tedium among pupils (or 'learners' as official documentation increasingly began to describe them), resulting in a series of initiatives to encourage greater flexibility and innovative teaching and learning. The response among primary teachers was mixed: on the one hand, they were pleased, if somewhat suspicious, about the relaxation of external impositions; on the other hand they lacked confidence about changing their teaching approach for fear of adversely affecting test results. In fact, it is fair to say that arguments about the relevance and helpfulness of national tests in literacy, numeracy and science for primary aged children have been a political conundrum and a bane for government. The listing of national test results, school by school in England, has placed considerable pressure on everyone involved in education, and at the time of writing (2009) there appears to be a strong move towards replacing the tests (popularly known as SATs) with a more flexible form of assessment, thereby following the example set by Scotland and Wales.

Other important policy decisions include a renewed emphasis on considering the 'whole child', rather than separating education from welfare. The Every Child Matters initiative has been particularly influential, as the education service provided through local authorities in England have combined forces with social services to try and ensure that children are protected from harm, as well as given every opportunity to succeed academically. Other political initiatives involve additional information for parents about their children's progress, extended school provision beyond the normal working day and a huge expansion in information technology.

Despite the plethora of initiatives and tightening of political control, the heart of primary education remains largely unchanged. In particular, the crucial relationship between teacher and taught; the camaraderie between the many adults working in school on behalf of the children; the dynamic links between home and school; the daily routines; and the thousands of interactions and conversations that take place between adults and children. I try to capture the essence of the intricacies of school life in my book, *Foundations of Primary Education* by focusing on two children's experiences:

Both Monica and Charley enter the school. Both remove their coats, chat to classmates, walk towards the classroom door. They notice teachers, assistants, parents, pictures on walls and familiar objects. Their noses tingle at the intoxicating mixed scents of floor polish, electronic equipment, damp clothing and toilets that greet them. A random set of sounds impinges on their consciousness: chattering voices, clatter and thud of feet, doors creaking and adults talking animatedly. Their eyes light up as they enter the classroom and glimpse the familiar, reassuring sights. They sit down on a carpet or line up at a door, answer to their names, respond to a request or command. The familiar sounds of teachers' voices issue instructions; the children are sensitive to tonal patterns and intonation. They recognise when teachers are cross, sad, bored or pretending, and modify their behaviour accordingly.

The day begins and the bum-numbing effects of registration and, perhaps, class assembly are replaced by work sessions and activities. Playtimes and mealtimes provide relief from their toil. The children disappear into the frantic world of games, chasing, arguments, intensive relationships, erratic behaviours and unpredictable weather. They wonder about the paradoxes of school life: why teachers insist that they wear a coat when it isn't cold or enthuse that going outside is good for them when it is obviously miserable and damp. They see the teachers disappearing into the warmth and security of the staffroom and catch the odd snippet of conversation, wave of laughter, smell of coffee.

As each playtime ends, a few children hanker for a turn to knock on the staffroom door, return a teacup and inform the disappointed teachers that Miss Jenkins says that it's in-time (an expression used only in primary schools). The day continues. A hall-time offers chance for some fun – if teacher allows. Laces are tied, buttons fumbled and socks tugged. The end-of-afternoon story or sharing draws children and teacher together, and soon home-time heralds the end of another school day. Coats are pulled off pegs or scrambled for on the floor; odd gloves mysteriously disappear and reappear; accusations over property and other disputes reverberate down the corridors. Mothers, fathers and grandparents are there to pick up the children, ask brightly about the day, exchange a word with the teacher, flash a smiling 'thank you' and head for home.

Pushchairs and a stream of young mums line up across the front of the building. Parents check lunch boxes, stare at the latest school letter and herd their little flocks towards the exit. Monica skips off happily, keen to tell mother about her successes and show off her new reading book. Charley edges out of the room, casting a hopeful glance at the teacher, before moving away to pick up her younger brothers and sisters, and usher them along the pavements to the local shop to buy them a snack for tea. The teacher gives Charley a reassuring smile and wink: *Take care, Charley. See you tomorrow.* Charley can hardly wait for tomorrow to come.

(pp. 7–8)

A good primary education does not guarantee happiness or success in life but it offers a chance for the Charleys and Monicas of this world to make the best of their abilities and opportunities. Adults in school can only do so much; legislation can only provide a framework and support system; policies can only give an overview; the real hope for children lies in providing the right conditions for learning: (1) knowing they are loved and appreciated; (2) being set a sound moral example by adults; (3) given clear guidelines for behaviour and conduct; (4) provided with knowledge and information; (5) encouraged and trusted; (6) allowed to enjoy learning; (7) shown how knowledge is relevant to life; and (8) led into deep rather than superficial forms of learning.

There are different perspectives on what constitutes an educated child, but a shared belief is that education consists of more than passing examinations and being 'top dog'. It is a continuous life-changing experience that has the potential to benefit all humankind. As such, the affective dimension of education – touching the emotions – is more significant than most politicians and policy-makers seem to appreciate, so you will discover that in addition to the extensive amounts of information in this encyclopedia, the human and personal elements are liberally threaded throughout its pages.

A

ABILITY

See also: creativity, gifted and talented, intelligence, Intelligence Quotient, multiple intelligences, slow learners

Definitions of 'ability' that appear on the Internet include, from Wordnet: 'the quality of being able to perform; a quality that permits or facilitates achievement or accomplishment' and 'possession of the qualities (especially mental qualities) required to do something or get something done'. The 'Wiktionary' definition expands the definition somewhat: 'the quality or state of being able; power to perform, whether physical, moral, intellectual, conventional, or legal; capacity; skill or competence in doing; sufficiency of strength, skill, resources ... '. These wide-ranging definitions contrast rather sharply with the use of ability in educational phrases such as 'high ability' and 'low ability' that signify, in effect, whether or not a child is capable of completing academic work successfully. When educators speak of an 'able child', more often than not they mean that the pupil is fully literate and numerate. When teachers refer to a pupil as 'very able', it is likely that they mean, in the vernacular, that the child is 'top of the class' in that subject (e.g. high ability in mathematics). Pupils at the other end of the spectrum (i.e. not very able) are often spoken of as being 'slow learners'.

Interpretation of ability is significant in educational settings, especially schools, because it is often used to organise children into different groups for learning, especially in English and mathematics. In doing so, teachers have to be aware that able pupils do not necessarily possess the full range of fundamental skills that may be assumed. For instance, Dean (1998) notes that boys, in particular, struggle to keep pace with the demands of writing and sometimes underachieve. Some very able pupils may exhibit odd characteristics that mark them out as being atypical and invite teasing from other children. Others will excel in every curriculum area (including sports) and thereby attract excessive admiration from their peers. Howe (1990) warns that although able children may not react in expected ways, close parental involvement, coupled with high expectations, offers the best way forward.

With the recent resurgence of interest in exceptionally capable pupils, the terms 'gifted' and 'talented' have tended to be used in preference to the descriptor 'very able' to signal that children are in the top 5 per cent of the school population, as measured in formal tests. Indeed, some authors (e.g. Bates and Munday 2005) conflate concepts of ability, giftedness and talent into a single phrase; thus, 'able, gifted and talented'. Educators often make the point that 'ability' should be distinguished from 'capability', which indicates that a child may possess an aptitude that can be developed but is not yet fully formed. Whereas the term 'ability' tends to be used as an intrinsic 'got it' or 'not got it' (rather like

IQ), capability implies that the existing state of affairs can be altered through perseverance, good teaching, opportunity and encouragement. Ability is sometimes used in conjunction with creativity; thus, 'creative ability', signifying the capacity to think in new ways.

Hart *et al.* (2004) rail against the use of ability labelling, arguing that explaining differences in terms of inherent ability is

> not only unjust and untenable but also deprives teachers of the chance to base and develop their practice upon a more complex, multifaceted and infinitely more empowering understanding of teaching and learning processes and of the influences, internal and external to the school, that impinge upon learning and achievement.
>
> (p. 17)

The authors go on to explain that ability labelling is posited on a view that teachers do not make a difference and are therefore powerless to change a child's inherent intellectual limits, 'however lively and inspirational their teaching, however positive their relationships, however illuminating their explanations' (p. 18). They point out that reference to present *attainment* is a more satisfactory way of viewing ability in that it does not preclude future improvement.

The reality is that a teacher's enthusiasm, teaching skills, ability to motivate and close relationship with pupils may expose a larger number of 'able' children than was initially apparent. See Gardner (2005) for a selection of his writing and Schaler (2006) to read thirteen critical essays challenging Gardner's theories of multiple intelligences, ability traits, U-shaped curves in development, and other psychological concepts of spirituality, creativity, and leadership.

Sources

Bates, J. and Munday, S. (2005) *Able, Gifted and Talented*, London: Continuum.
Cooper, C. (1999) *Intelligence and Abilities*, London: Routledge.
Dean, G. (1998) *Challenging the More Able Language User*, London: NACE/David Fulton Publications.
Gardner, H. (2005) *The Development and Education of Mind: The selected works of Howard Gardner*, London: Routledge.
Hart, S., Dixon, A., Drummond, M.J. and McIntyre, D. (2004) *Learning Without Limits*, Maidenhead: Open University Press.
Howe, M.J.A. (1990) *Sense and Nonsense About Hothouse Children*, Leicester: BPS Books.
Schaler, J.A. (2006) *Howard Gardner Under Fire*, Chicago, IL: Open Court Publishing.

ABILITY GROUPS

See also: ability, achievement, core subjects, equal opportunities, gifted and talented, group work, mixed ability teaching, setting and streaming

The practice of grouping pupils by ability in school was popular after the Second World War (which ended in 1945) but became unpopular because of evidence suggesting that it led to low self-esteem for some pupils in the 'bottom' stream, social alienation of lower stream pupils and uncertain impact on academic attainment. These studies coincided with a shift of educational focus towards equality of educational opportunity in the second half of the twentieth century. More recently, ability grouping in mathematics and English has become common in primary schools because it is perceived as a means of raising standards as measured by formal tests; the social and emotional implications for children placed in the lower groups now seem to assume much less importance.

There are two common forms of grouping primary school pupils: (a) *streaming*, in which pupils are separated into groups according to their all-round ability; they remain in these groups for almost all of their curriculum work; and (b) *setting*, in which children are separated into different groups by ability for particular subjects; for example, a child might be in the top set for mathematics and the second set for English. Many teachers of older primary children enjoy teaching pupils who are ability-grouped for mathematics and English because it allows them to focus their planning and teaching more precisely than if they are faced with widely diverse abilities. It is unusual for pupils to be allocated to different groups or class groups for subjects other than these 'core' subjects even though, ironically, the differences in ability can be greater in (say) art and design or physical education.

Studies that consider children's views have found that most pupils want to be in the top group for reading because it confers status and a feeling of superiority; however, with the exception of pupils in the top group, most children prefer all-ability whole class lessons or purely individual work so that they don't feel excluded or 'different'. Furthermore, classes in which there is no ability grouping (i.e. non-streamed classes) seem to show healthier social adjustment and attitudes, especially towards less able classmates. By contrast, where there is an emphasis on streaming, attitudes of those in the lower streams are generally rather negative. Additionally, there is some evidence to suggest that pupils of below average ability in non-streaming schools who are taught by teachers who strongly believe in streaming are disadvantaged, owing to the teacher's unwitting antipathy. However, Condron (2003) found that there is little evidence that ability grouping exacerbates inequality in achievement any more than instruction in situations without ability groups. He argues that variations in achievement increase in much the same way for grouped and for non-grouped pupils during the school year. Furthermore, he claims that grouping does not appear to contribute to class and racial gaps in learning, though in a later paper he notes that there are clear disparities in reading group placement on the basis of special needs, race/ethnicity, gender, and family structure (Condron 2008). The author concludes that most of these inequalities result from the uneven distribution of academic, social, and behavioural skills that matter when teachers make decisions about grouping younger children.

Tach and Farkas (2003) are among educationists who note that ability grouping in primary schools is likely to be the first time that a child is faced with a school-based stratification of learning opportunities based on assessment of his or her academic competence. The impact of ability grouping at a young age on a child's cognitive development is also unclear. There is some evidence to suggest that ability grouping based on reading has an impact upon pupil performance and behaviour. Taken together, reading performance, learning-related behaviour and ability grouping at the beginning of the school year may help to explain, in part, class, race, and gender differences in reading and behaviour at the *end* of the year.

The complexities attached to the appropriateness of grouping by ability are well represented by a study for the Department for Education and Skills by Kutnick et al. (2005) in which the authors concluded that there was no evidence that streamed or set classes produce, on average, higher performance than mixed-ability classes. The research team found that although grouping children within classes has the potential to raise standards, there is no certain way of grouping pupils to be of benefit to all the learners. Findings also indicated that whereas gifted and talented pupils make more progress in a separate ability group, pupils in low-ability groups make less progress when grouped together and become unmotivated owing to poorer teaching and a narrower curriculum. The review concluded that there were no significant differences between setting and mixed-ability teaching in overall attainment but on the whole, low-achieving pupils showed more progress in mixed-ability sets and high-achieving pupils showed more progress in single-ability sets. See also DCSF (2008).

Sources

Condron, D.J. (2003) 'An early start: Effects of ability grouping on reading achievement', Paper presented at the annual meeting of the

American Sociological Association, Atlanta Hilton Hotel, Atlanta GA, on-line at www.allacademic.com/meta/p107314_index.htm

——(2008) 'An early start: Skill grouping and unequal reading gains in the elementary years', *The Sociological Quarterly*, 49 (2), 363–94.

DCSF (2008) *Primary Pupils' Experiences of Different Types of Grouping in School*, on-line at www.standards.dfes.gov.uk/research/themes/pupil_grouping

Kutnick, P., Sebba, P., Blatchford, P., Galton, M. and Thorp, J. (2005) *The Effects of Pupil Grouping: Literature review*, Annesley: DfES Publications, ref. RR688.

Tach, L.M. and Farkas, G. (2003) *Ability Grouping and Educational Stratification in the Early School Years*, on-line at www.allacademic.com/meta/p108028_index.htm

ABSENTEEISM

All children are required to receive a suitable form of education appropriate to their age and abilities; in the UK this ruling applies from the age of five years. The majority of children attend school, though an increasing number are being educated at home. Absence from school is categorised as either authorised (with permission) or unauthorised. Regular school attendance is vital for a number of reasons. First, a lot of juvenile crime is carried out by truants, absent without permission. Second, such children fall behind in their studies and require additional adult support. Third, school absentees usually underachieve in public examinations and are therefore more likely to struggle to find satisfactory and well-remunerated employment. The National Attendance Strategy for England and Wales (2008–9) emphasises the link between children's welfare and school attendance and the importance of ensuring that all children have access to the full time education to which they are entitled.

Such is the political fervour attached to absenteeism that school governors have to set targets for attendance and submit these to the local authority. A number of parents have been taken to court for failing to ensure that their children attend school regularly. Generally, there is a high level of attendance in primary schools where it is not unusual to register attendances in excess of 80 per cent. From September 2007 a new law and revised statutory guidance on exclusions came into force in England. *Improving Behaviour and Attendance: Guidance on exclusion from schools and pupil referral units* gives parents a duty, for the first five days of any exclusion, to ensure that their excluded child is not in a public place during normal school hours. The law also requires schools (for fixed-period exclusions) and local authorities (for permanent exclusions) to provide suitable full-time education from the sixth school day of the exclusion.

ACCELERATED LEARNING

See also: brain function, collaboration in learning, cross-curriculum, deep learning, integrated learning, multiple intelligences

Accelerated learning (AL) is an approach to teaching and training that actively involves the whole person, using music, colour, emotion, play and creativity as part of the training classroom in order to accelerate the learning process. Although the concepts behind AL were developed in the United States during the 1980s and 1990s by (for example) Colin Rose (Rose 1987, 1998) and later developed by enthusiasts such as David Meier (Meier 2000), it wasn't until the late 1990s and beyond that the concept became popular in the UK and spawned a number of texts for teachers (e.g. Smith and Call 2001; Best 2003). The AL approach takes close account of Gardner's theory of multiple intelligences (Gardner 1983, 1993) and puts it into practice to encourage and enable a child to access his or her own preferences rather than assuming that all children learn best in the same way.

When children learn ordinarily with a book or a teacher, it is estimated that they use less than 20 per cent of their brain's capacity. Traditional methods of learning concentrate on the left side of the brain – which controls our powers of language, logic and sequencing – more than the right side – which deals with forms and patterns, rhythm, space and imagination. Through AL, also known as 'super-learning' or 'brain-friendly learning', children (indeed, people of any age) should be able to learn more and retain more by using the whole of the brain. The fact that children can learn many things simultaneously, such as the tune, rhythm and words to a song, while dancing in time to the music, demonstrates that learning is not confined to one part of the brain but can and almost certainly does happen in both parts simultaneously. Studies show that the human brain forgets much of the information it processes if that information isn't reviewed soon after, so to help children remember what they have learned, teachers encourage them to talk about the main points each day and revisit them regularly.

AL programmes are geared towards teaching the whole child: body, mind and spirit, and not merely educating the intellect. Enthusiasts claim that the techniques can be applied in a wide variety of settings and have the potential to enhance knowledge retention and skill acquisition. AL stimulates the brain to work harder by creating new practical learning situations, such as incorporating drama to learn about science or using dance and movement to enhance understanding of mathematics (i.e. cross-curricular or integrated learning). This mode of learning is based on the premise that a 'second hand' experience, that is, an experience which is reported by another person, can never replace a first hand experience involving all the senses, the physical body and, ideally, cooperation with classmates. In addition, working collaboratively (i.e. seeking solutions as a group rather than individually) is used as a strategy to make combined use of pupils' different brainpower and hence make faster progress than in a situation where they work separately.

Smith *et al.* (2005) underline the importance of the teacher in AL in as much as

meaningful learning involves risk and good teachers help learners negotiate it. By contrast, anxiety paralyses performance, so teachers need to provide structured challenges for pupils with suitable adult support. Learning is about seeking and securing connections between areas of knowledge; good teachers take every opportunity to facilitate and promote such links.

Sources

Best, B. (2003) *Accelerated Learning Pocket Book*, Alresford: Management Pocket Books.

Gardner, H. (1983, 1993) *Frames of Mind: The theory of multiple intelligences*, New York: Basic Books.

Meier, D. (2000) *The Accelerated Learning Handbook*, New York: McGraw-Hill Professional.

Rose, C. (1987) *Accelerated Learning*, New York: Dell.

——(1998) *Accelerated Learning for the 21st Century*, New York: Dell.

Smith, A. and Call, N. (2001) *The Alps Approach Resource Book: Accelerated learning in primary schools*, Stafford: Network Educational Press.

Smith, A., Lovatt, M. and Wise, D. (2005) *Accelerated Learning: A user's guide*, Carmarthen: Crown House.

ACHIEVEMENT

See also: rewards, self-esteem, success, tests and testing

Achievement is an important aspect of life and some children obviously achieve more success than others do. It is difficult for grown-ups to remember the thrill and excitement of scoring a goal in a games lesson, winning a prize for a special painting, enjoying a glass of orange after helping the teacher with a job or having a star placed on the chart for finishing another reading book. These are the moments when children's achievements are openly and publicly acknowledged and savoured. A more difficult challenge for adults is to know how to respond to children whose achievements are limited, where success has only ever been partial and exhilaration has

5

depended upon a surrogate basking in the reflected glow from others.

Achievements are sometimes short-lived, and children who depend upon tangible evidence of their own worth can become equally unhappy when achievements remain elusive. A teacher's attitude to achievement influences the creation of a healthy classroom climate and helps children develop a positive attitude towards learning. Teachers who are intolerant of low-achieving or under-achieving children bring about deterioration in self-concept and, consequently, invite even lower achievement or acute anxiety. Achievement is a key ingredient for success, as long as children are also able to use occasional failures and setbacks as a spur to greater effort.

Political pressure has redefined the concept of achievement in terms of success in formal tests and examinations. In England the 'Pupil Achievement Tracker' (PAT) was introduced to track a pupil's performance in tests; in 2008 it was replaced by a system called 'RAISE-online', which provides interactive analysis of school and pupil performance data. RAISE-online also replaces the Ofsted Performance and Assessment (PANDA) reports. Despite the rhetoric about valuing individuality and special educational needs, there lingers a suspicion that the only achievements that politicians consider to be worthy of naming are academic ones and those from exceptionally talented sports and artistic performers.

ACT OF WORSHIP

See *Assembly*

ACTIVE LEARNING

See also: discovery learning, enquiry, intervention, problem solving, think-pair-share

Active learning is closely related to the concept of 'discovery learning' and is used as an overarching term when referring to a number of models of instruction in which the chief responsibility for learning rests with the pupils rather than the teacher. Active methods require children to 'make their own meanings'; that is, to make sense for themselves about what they are learning. Active learning therefore has the potential to develop thinking skills such as analysis, problem solving and evaluation. The noted educationist, Janet Moyles (2007) offers an eight-point approach to promote active learning: (1) An entering strategy, consisting of starting-points and introduction. (2) An exploration mode, where pupils engage with the task supported by adequate resources and directed by adults – see also Johnston (2004). (3) Consideration of content in respect of the subject, processes and skills that the children are intended to learn. (4) Clarification about ownership and responsibility, especially the presence or absence of adult supervision. (5) Adult intervention, interaction and level of support for children. (6) Evaluation and analysis of children's learning. (7) Opportunities for children to reflect on their learning. (8) Justification for the work completed and its outcomes. Failure to provide opportunities for this type of experiential learning can result in pupils who comply with the teacher's wishes but have little understanding of the lesson's purpose or their own responsibilities as learners. Criticisms of active learning include claims that it is inefficient, random and unsustainable without adult guidance, expertise and intervention. However, discussions and 'think-pair-share' approaches to learning (Lyman 1981), in which each child thinks independently before comparing notes with a partner, are seen by most teachers as legitimate learning strategies.

Sources

Johnston, J. (2004) 'The value of exploration and discovery', *Primary Science Review*, 85, 21–23.
Lyman, F.T. (1981) 'The responsive classroom discussion: The inclusion of all students', in Anderson, A. (ed.) *Mainstreaming Digest*, College Park: University of Maryland Press, pp. 109–13.

Moyles, J. (2007) *Beginning Teaching, Beginning Learning in Primary Education*, Maidenhead: Open University Press.

ADMISSIONS CODE

See also: governing body, infant schools, political involvement

School admissions codes are an attempt to ensure a fair and straightforward system that promotes equity and fair access for all pupils. The codes, together with appeal procedures and related legislation have statutory force with which admission authorities, governing bodies, school boards, local authorities, admission forums, schools adjudicators and admission appeal panels must comply. Infant school admissions in England and Wales are constrained by law that classes must not exceed thirty pupils, though exceptions can and increasingly are made to this rule. Primary class sizes in the UK are among the largest in Europe, despite general political consensus that they need to fall. Some educationists complain that political rhetoric about choice and diversity in choosing a school is misleading, as in reality parents can only express a preference.

ADULT BEHAVIOUR

See also: modelling behaviour, relationships, reputation of teachers, teachers' beliefs

Pascal and Bertram (1997) identified key features of adult behaviour that promote good-quality thinking, learning and development in young children. The first attribute is *sensitivity*, such that the adult is aware of the children's feelings and emotional well-being, can empathise and acknowledge children's feelings of insecurity and offer support and encouragement. The second attribute is *stimulation*, reflected in the way an activity or resource is introduced in a positive, exciting and stimulating way; extra information is offered to children; and the adult joins in with children's play in a way that extends their thinking or communication. The third attribute is *autonomy*, in which an adult gives children the freedom to experiment, supports their decisions and judgements, encourages expression of ideas and involves children in rule-making for the benefit of everyone's safety and well-being. Children model themselves on adults and, to an extent, replicate the behaviour that they observe, which places a considerable responsibility on them to act, respond and speak appropriately.

Sources

Pascal, C. and Bertram, A. (1997) *Effective Early Learning: Case studies for improvement*, London: Hodder & Stoughton.

AFFECTIVE DIMENSION OF TEACHING

See also: caring teachers, circle-time, emotional literacy, relationships, self-esteem, social and emotional aspects of learning, teacher role

The curriculum is a formal programme of things that are taught; the element of it that attempts to change, modify or 'affect' pupils' values and behaviour has been labelled *affective education* by educators. Lang *et al.* (1998), who edited a comprehensive book containing a wide-ranging set of European perspectives, define affective education as that part of the educational process concerned with the attitudes, feelings, beliefs and emotions, as well as with the development of interpersonal relationships and social skills. Affective education programmes purport to enhance self-esteem, improve memory, strengthen communication skills, affirm individuality, increase sensitivity to others and teach self-responsibility. In many schools this dimension is promoted in cooperative learning through 'circle-time' sessions, where children sit in a semicircle to discuss and share ideas; important features of this process include taking turns, showing respect to others' viewpoints and being able to see each other's faces.

McNess *et al.* (2003) provide an important reminder that the vast majority of primary educators are deeply committed to the affective dimension of teaching and learning. They argue that in the complex and difficult task of educating children, there are many dimensions for teachers to consider and negotiate. Evidence from talking to primary teachers suggests that from among the wide range of roles they undertake, the social and emotional considerations are greatly significant for them, notably in the ongoing interaction and personal relationship between the teacher and the learner. In other words, part of the skill of good teaching is not only to possess subject knowledge and to be able to put things across systematically and clearly, but also to empathise with children and create effective working conditions.

Attention to the affective domain (area of life) should not be confused with ideas about raising self-esteem through intervention programmes that probe children's deeper consciousnesses and elicit responses that are equivalent to a programme of behaviour modification. Indeed, criticisms of raising a child's self-esteem through the use of such programmes include allegations that they have not been proven to be beneficial to the child either emotionally or academically and that they detract from the time spent on the formal curriculum. A major review of evidence by Strein (1988) in the USA provided little support for the effectiveness of affective education programmes in promoting positive changes in pupils using behavioural or affective measures. More recently, Stilwell and Barclay (2006) concluded that affective education programmes and interventions had an inconsistent impact upon children, teachers and school systems.

Enthusiasts for affective education counter such criticisms by arguing that children benefit from an awareness of other people's feelings and environmental studies where children 'commune with nature' encourage a greater awareness of individual and corporate responsibility. Indeed, the introduction of SEAL (social and emotional aspects of learning) and elements of citizenship education in UK schools is one signal of an acknowledgement that a full education consists of more than passing national tests, though Best (2003) offers a sceptical view of such innovations as being equivalent to 'putting new wine into old bottles'. The key issue emerging from these differing perspectives about affective education is that assisting children to reflect carefully upon the way they behave and act is commendable and should be manifested and modelled by adults working with children; however, evidence about the benefits of formal programmes of study embedded in the curriculum is less compelling.

Sources

Best, R. (2003) 'New bottles for old wine? Affective education and the citizenship revolution in English Schools', *Pastoral Care in Education*, 21 (4), 14–21.

Lang, P., Katz, Y. and Menezes, I. (eds) (1998) *Affective Education: A comparative view*, London: Cassell.

McNess, E., Broadfoot, P. and Osborn, M. (2003) 'Is the effective compromising the affective?' *British Educational Research Journal*, 29 (2), 243–57.

Stilwell, W.E. and Barclay, J.R. (2006) 'Effects of affective education interventions in the elementary school', *Psychology in the Schools*, 16 (1), 80–87.

Strein, W. (1988) 'Classroom-based elementary school affective education programs: A critical review', *Psychology in the Schools*, 25 (3), 288–96.

AIMS OF EDUCATION

See also: child-centred education, Dewey, educated child, Einstein, environmental education

Numerous views have been expressed down the years about the purpose of education. For example, the education philosopher John Dewey (1859–1952), whose name has become synonymous with what is now referred to as 'progressive education', in which children learn to solve problems rather than being told the answers, wrote that education is not merely a preparation for life but is life itself – though perhaps his statement contains rather more rhetoric than enlightenment. The Irish writer William Butler Yeats (1865–1939) claimed that education is not filling a bucket but lighting a fire; his definition touches an emotional nerve but doesn't quite offer the insights to guide educators as to its implementation. The mathematician, physicist and sometime philosopher Albert Einstein (1879–1955) insisted that education is what remains after one has forgotten everything one learned in school, which is amusingly cruel and uncomfortably close to the truth for some pupils. Einstein went on to say that the supreme art of the teacher is to awaken joy in creative expression and knowledge, such that pupils are encouraged to raise questions, see new possibilities and regard old problems from a new perspective.

Many years ago, O'Connor (1957) listed the aims of education as providing people with a minimum of the skills necessary for them to take their place in society and seek further knowledge; provide them with a vocational training that will enable them to be self-supporting; awaken an interest in and a taste for knowledge; make them more critical; put them in touch with and train them to appreciate the cultural and moral achievements of humankind. More recently, Alfie Kohn (educationist and arch-critic of testing) wrote that rather than attempting to define what it means to be well educated, should we instead be asking about the *purposes of education*, which invites us to look beyond academic goals, rejects the deadly notion that the school's first priority should be intellectual development and contends that the main aim of education should be to produce competent, caring, loving and lovable people (Kohn 2003).

While these, and other attempts to define the aims of education, provide us with valuable starting points, they do not define the specific characteristics of primary education

that distinguish them from any other phase of education. A generation ago, Ashton *et al.* (1975) carried out a comprehensive study of primary teacher's priorities in which the authors defined an aim as what a pupil is intended to gain from his or her education; they also noted that teachers gave little thought to their overall aims and were more concerned about what they taught and strategies for doing so.

Shuayb and O'Donnell (2008) note that from their survey of the aims, purposes and values in primary education in England, Germany, the Netherlands, New Zealand, Scotland and Sweden that in the first few years of the twenty-first century they appeared to reflect economic and social imperatives on the one hand and the idea of individualised or personalised teaching and learning on the other. The authors reached a number of broad conclusions, a modified list of which follows (see page 3 of the report):

- The aims, purposes and values of primary education appear to have passed through distinct phases. In the first phase, the child was the main focus and this greatly influenced the aims and values of the curriculum. In the second phase, social and economic concerns began to come to the fore; whilst today's aims focus on raising standards of achievement and preparing children for life in a multicultural society and in an ever-changing economic and work environment.
- There appears to be a belief across countries that in order to achieve excellence – academically, vocationally, economically and socially – education requires a degree of personalisation (though the meaning of the term may vary).
- The aims, values and purposes of primary education today combine the requirement to prepare children for their economic role in society with the need to identify their individual strengths and weaknesses, so as to provide them with the necessary support to achieve targets.
- Governments in the six countries are following Sweden's lead in agreeing that

9

citizenship education is vital as one of the aims of an all-round education.

- There is a growth of interest in healthy, safe and sustainable living and in the primary educator's role in encouraging young children's awareness of such issues.
- The aims, values and purposes of primary education today across the six countries reviewed appear to reflect more similarities than differences, expressed primarily in terms of standards of achievement and of economic and social goals, with only traces of a child-centred philosophy.

From his in-depth study of the aims of primary education, John White (2008) suggests that there has been a lot of emphasis since the turn of the new century towards the promotion of personal well-being as a key aim, this being seen as a more inclusive concept than the personal autonomy that characterised twentieth-century aspirations. He also notes that aims in respect of both 'well-being' and 'autonomy' have also been more explicitly connected to the educational requirements of a liberal democratic society than was formerly the case. Thus, issues associated with the place of civic responsibilities and the rights of religious and other communities found within it have been the focal point for close scrutiny and debate. Contemporary issues have highlighted the importance of education for sustainable development and global awareness, which have strongly influenced the primary school curriculum in the form of environmental education and what are often termed 'green' issues.

Sources

Ashton, P., Kneen, P. and Davies, F. (1975) *Aims into Practice in the Primary School*, London: Hodder and Stoughton.

Kohn, A. (2003) 'What does it mean to be well educated?' *Principal Leadership*, March, 6–9.

O'Connor, D.J. (1957) *An Introduction to the Philosophy of Education*, London: Routledge & Kegan Paul.

Shuayb, M. and O'Donnell, S. (2008) *Aims and Values in Primary Education: England and other countries* (Primary Review Research Survey 1/2), Cambridge: University of Cambridge.

White, J. (2008) *Aims as Policy in English Primary Education* (Primary Review Research Survey 1/1), Cambridge: University of Cambridge.

ALEXANDER, ROBIN

See also: aims of education, curriculum, learning climate, pedagogy, Plowden Report, political involvement

Robin Alexander was born on 26 August 1939 and taught in schools and colleges in various parts of England before moving to the University of Leeds in 1977 where in 1990 he became Professor of Education and Associate Director of the Centre for Policy Studies in Education. In 1995 he moved to Warwick University as Professor of Education, founder Director of the Centre for Research in Elementary and Primary Education and Director of Research at Warwick Institute of Education. Since 2001 he has been based at the University of Cambridge. In 2005 he was elected to the Sir Edward Youde Visiting Professorship at Hong Kong Institute of Education. Robin Alexander has worked consistently to ensure that primary education is taken with the seriousness it deserves.

Alexander has undertaken a succession of studies on various aspects of this phase of education, including teacher thinking and decision-making, local authority administration and influence, the curriculum, assessment, school management, classroom practice, teacher–student interaction and discourse. Information from the studies has fed into national debate and influenced school practice. In 1991, he produced a report on primary education in Leeds, followed a year later by a publication, *Policy and Practice in Primary Education* (1992), which was described by some educationists at the time as the most important document since the Plowden Report of 1967. Alexander's 1991 Leeds report led directly to the then government's commissioning the 'Three Wise Men' primary education enquiry, on which he served with Sir Jim Rose and Chris Woodhead. Alexander has been strongly critical of government policy on primary education, especially during the periods immediately after the 1988 Education Reform Act and the election of the Blair government in 1997.

In the early 1990s, Robin Alexander initiated a substantial piece of research, which involved a comparative study of culture, policy and pedagogy in England, France, India, Russia and the United States conducted at national, school and classroom levels. The study included a detailed analysis of how talk between teacher and learner influenced classroom culture and the nature and quality of children's learning. The resulting book, *Culture and Pedagogy* (2001) won top education book prizes in the United States and Britain.

From 2006 to 2009 Alexander directed *The Primary Review*, an independent enquiry (University of Cambridge) into the condition and future of primary education in England supported by the Esmée Fairbairn Foundation. The study sought to identify the purposes that the primary phase should serve; the values it should espouse; the curriculum and learning environment ('climate') it should provide; and the conditions necessary to ensure the highest quality and address the future needs of children and society. The Cambridge team's wide-ranging research received extensive media coverage, though (apparently) failed to impress government ministers, who sidestepped many of the recommendations, preferring to rely on findings from the 'Rose Report' (Rose 2009) about the primary curriculum. Some of the Alexander study's conclusions include claims that poor academic performance is linked to substandard classrooms; that government policy has created an impersonalised education; and that national testing creates stress for many junior-age children.

Sources

Alexander, R. (1992) *Policy and Practice in Primary Education*, London: Routledge.
——(2001) *Culture and Pedagogy*, London: Blackwell.
——(2009) *The Condition and Future of Primary Education in England* ('The Primary Review'), Cambridge: University of Cambridge/Esmée Fairburn Trust.
Robin Alexander, Research and Evaluation, on-line at www.robinalexander.org.uk/research.htm
Rose, J. for the DCSF (2009) *Primary Curriculum Review*, London: HMSO.
Wilby, P. (2008) 'Jim will fix it', *Guardian*, 5 August.

ALPHABET

See also: capital letters, handwriting, lower case letters, phonics, reading, tactile learning, visual learners, writing

The familiar alphabet in English-speaking countries consists of twenty-six letters. Our alphabet is almost identical to the Roman (or 'Latin') alphabet, which originally appeared in the seventh century BC using just twenty-one letters. The Romans did not use any commas, full stops (USA, 'periods') or spaces but merely wrote each letter one after the other in a continuous line and only used capital letters (A, B, C, etc.). Lowercase letters (a, b, c, etc) were not introduced until after the eighth century AD. It is normal in the UK for children to become familiar with the lower case form of letters initially and only use capitals as the starting letter for proper names, whereas in the USA it is not unusual for children to recognise capital letters of the alphabet at an early stage.

Wasik (2001) advises that a child should be introduced to the alphabet using familiar words – notably the child's name – as a means of building confidence. As children get better at recognising their names they can be encouraged to see similarities between letters in their names and letters in other names and words; for example, a commonly used technique is to help children to find other words that begin with the first letter in their names (such as T in Tom and Tina).

As well as the familiar reciting of the alphabet, teachers find children benefit from knowing how the alphabet works and how it relates to reading and writing. There are literally hundreds of books dedicated to the process of demonstrating that the alphabet is made up of a group of letters with different names and shapes. Children make connections between print and the spoken word when writing letters, so opportunities exist for very young children to express themselves by making scribble marks or marks that look like a letter. Initial attempts to form letters do not require the formal process of handwriting or copying letters from other printed material. However, opportunities for younger children to write or trace letters using a sense of touch can be helpful ('tactile learning'), including writing letters alongside the existing letters; looking at letters and visually remembering their shape before writing; and occasionally tracing the shapes of letters in alphabet books using crayons, pencils, markers or pens.

Mascle (on-line) insists that young children need to experience their world through their senses. Although they learn in the more traditional ways – notably through seeing and hearing – children often prefer the teacher or parent to make the letters of the alphabet 'come alive' for them in a way that utilises their senses. Thus, many teachers of new school entrants provide puzzles containing 3-D alphabet shapes so that children use their fingers to feel the shape of letters; and finger-painting to form large letters on sheets. Capital letters can be used as a basis for visual artwork by constructing a picture from a large version of the letter drawn somewhere on the paper.

Sources

Mascle, D. *Teach Your Child the Alphabet*, on-line at http://TeachYourChildTheAlphabet.com
Wasik, B. (2001) 'Teaching the alphabet to young children', *Young Children*, 56 (1), 34–40.

ANIMALS IN SCHOOL

See also: environmental studies, health and safety, healthy schools

Animals in school provide a source of great interest and stimulation for learners of all ages. However, guidelines stipulate that children must cover cuts before handling the pets, wash their hands thoroughly afterwards and not put fingers or objects in their mouths which might have come into contact with the pets or their cages. In practice, these health and safety precautions have limited the opportunities for teachers to bring in and house mammals in the classroom. Children's direct experiences of creatures is more likely to come from a specialist animal expert visiting the school with a selection of animals or from visits to wildlife centres and zoos. Advocates of animals in the classroom speak of the calming effect it has on children and the talk and creativity that is engendered. Opponents not only express concerns about hazards but also point to the fact that children can be unkind to animals and it is usually the adults that end up taking responsibility for them.

ANNUAL MEETING

See also: governing body, governors, head teacher, parents supporting learning

Each year, a formal meeting of governors and parents is held at which governors produce a report for parents to discuss the manner in which the school has been and is to be conducted, plus any other matters relating to the school raised by parents of registered pupils. Although in practice only a small percentage of parents attend the formal meeting, it serves to highlight the governors' accountability and significance in the life of the school. The performance and success or failings of individual members of staff do not form part of the agenda. Commonly, the head teacher and governors use the evening as a celebration of the school's achievements, as well as fulfilling the formal requirements.

ANSWERING QUESTIONS

See also: closed questions, knowledge, open questions, pupil perspectives, questions and questioning, reflection, thinking

Many teaching techniques rely on children's immediate access to knowledge. A teacher may use a question-and-answer session to draw out what pupils know and understand. One child has her hand flapping in the air every time a question is asked; another remains as still as a statue, eyes lowered, hoping that the teacher does not choose her. It is reasonable to conclude that the enthusiastic child has a higher level of knowledge than her timid classmate, but this is not necessarily the case. The second child may have stored the knowledge and, in the intensity of the moment, been unable to draw it out of her memory bank. She may be weighing up other options rather than the obvious response, or simply hate answering questions publicly for fear of being wrong.

Teachers have to be careful to ask both closed questions that test immediate recall and open questions in which a variety of answers are acceptable. The child who has prompt immediate recall may or may not be able to offer a more considered and thoughtful response. Able children are often the most successful in responding to open questions but all children benefit from being given time to think. The best teachers have fun shooting out closed (single-answer) questions to a class but also ask speculative types of questions that test a child's ability to reflect and perhaps suggest unlikely possibilities and alternatives. It is nearly always the case that if given time to reflect, children will provide surprising and innovative perspectives on what may appear to adults to be plain and straightforward.

ASSESSING PUPILS' PROGRESS

See also: literacy, National Curriculum, numeracy, Primary National Strategy

Assessing Pupils' Progress (APP) is a set of materials introduced through the Primary National Strategy (PNS) to support teachers in making accurate assessments against National Curriculum (NC) levels. It is rooted in the overall strategy of assessment for learning (AFL), one aspect of which is to promote a broad curriculum that relates strongly to the primary framework for literacy and numeracy (mathematics).

APP is based on the principle of teachers gathering a range of evidence about pupils' achievements in reading, writing and mathematics, such that they are able to make and record periodically an assessment of children's academic strengths and areas for development. The assessment criteria are anchored in the NC level descriptions and attempt to represent them in a form that renders them easier for teachers to use when examining a child's performance across an attainment target. The outcome of the assessments is intended to help teachers to plan the next steps in their pupils' learning.

One of the implications of APP is that schools need to have sophisticated systems in place for tracking pupil progress. It is commonly the case that a senior member of staff has responsibility for collating such statistics and presenting them graphically; this task is a complicated and onerous one.

More information about APP is available on-line at www.standards.dfes.gov.uk/primary frameworks.

ARITHMETIC

See also: mathematics, mistakes and misconceptions, numeracy, Office for Standards in Education

Arithmetic is a word that is rarely used in primary schools in the UK today – the preferred term being 'numeracy' – though it is more commonly found in North America. Arithmetic basically deals with handling numbers and includes, for instance, strategies for adding, subtracting, dividing and multiplying numbers (i.e. computations). An important element of arithmetic has been the memorisation of multiplication tables. A report by the Office for Standards in Education

(OFSTED) in 1996 concluded that standards in arithmetic were poor given the time spent teaching this aspect of mathematics. The report highlighted that there was often too much emphasis on repetitive number work that failed to address pupils' fundamental errors or misconceptions. Furthermore, too many pupils lacked fluency in mental calculation and could not tell if their answers were realistic. Such criticisms triggered a national approach to the teaching of mathematics. Angheleri (2001) argues that the teaching of arithmetic in the primary school has traditionally been dominated by a focus on standard algorithms but this approach is now being questioned. (*Note*: an algorithm is a description of a step-by-step procedure that concludes with a result/answer.) An emphasis on promoting the development of mental strategies and providing more opportunities for children to develop their own ways of working is replacing single algorithmic procedures.

Source

Anghileri, J. (2001) *Principles and Practices in Arithmetic Teaching: Innovative approaches for the primary classroom*, Maidenhead: Open University Press.

ART AND DESIGN

See also: arts, citizenship, creativity, information technology, science, tactile learners, visual learners

It is a requirement that children in England and Wales follow the National Curriculum for art and design, and that teachers teach the full programmes of study; respond to the statutory requirements for ICT in art and design; and report progress in the subject each year to parents and colleagues. Art and design has the capacity to stimulate creativity and imagination and provides children with visual, tactile and sensory experiences such that they can communicate what they see, feel and think through the use of colour,

texture, form, pattern and different materials and processes. Children learn to make informed judgements and have opportunity to explore ideas and meanings by studying the work of artists and designers. Opportunities are given for children to work with professional artists, developing personal skills and the ability to work on group and/or individual projects.

Addison and Burgess (2003) explore issues relating to the measuring of artistic performance; visual literacy; the role of art and design in citizenship education; and multicultural art history. Typically in art and design, children are taught how to plan, make and evaluate artefacts and experience projects in textiles, food, wood and recycled materials. Projects are often linked to other subjects; for example, making lighthouses as part of the science curriculum about sources of energy and electricity (Callaway *et al.* 1999).

Sources

Addison, N. and Burgess, L. (2003) *Issues in Art and Design Teaching*, London: Routledge.
Callaway, G., Kear, M. and Leach, A. (1999) *Teaching Art and Design in the Primary School*, London: David Fulton.

ARTS (THE)

See also: art and design, communication, drama, visual learners

The arts in primary school are represented through dance, drama, music and visual arts – including drawing, painting, printmaking, modelling, paper construction, sculpture, digital art/photography, threads and textiles. In the National Curriculum for England and Wales, the drama element was originally a sub-set of the English curriculum. The arts were relegated to a minor position in the curriculum during the late 1990s and into the early years of the twenty-first century as schools focused on teaching literacy and numeracy. Downing *et al.* (2003) in their extensive research about the status and purposes of the arts in primary schools summarised the findings as follows (modified):

- Pressure from national and local government sources to downgrade the importance of the arts.
- Increases in arts provision largely due to staff enthusiasm and skill.
- Deterioration in provision ascribed to external factors, particularly a concentration on the core curriculum.
- Support from parents and governors perceived to be lower than that from within the school but higher than that from local and national government.
- The most highly endorsed purposes for the teaching of the arts are to develop creative and thinking skills, communication and expressive skills.
- Arts contribute to motivation, behaviour, attendance and self-esteem.
- Arts are central to raising standards in school.
- Social benefits of teaching the arts are greatest where large numbers of pupils are eligible for free school meals.

They noted that music, dance and visual arts are taught in the large majority of primary schools as discrete subjects, whereas drama is taught discretely in less than half of the 1,000 or so schools that participated in the survey. Visual Arts was deemed to have more curriculum time dedicated to it than any other arts subject and teachers reported that the visual side of the arts is where they felt most confident in teaching.

One of the most significant contributions and influences in moulding modern thinking about art education is 'The Gulbenkian Report' (Robinson 1982) in which the authors identified six main areas where the arts made important contributions to children's education:

1 Developing the full variety of human intelligence.
2 Developing the ability for creative thought and action.
3 In the education of feeling and sensibility.
4 In the exploration of values.
5 Understanding cultural change and difference.
6 Developing physical and conceptual skills.

Bloomfield (2000) argues that aesthetic and creative education is the entitlement of every child. She presents the arts as the vital fourth 'R', with an integrated mode of learning operating alongside reading, writing and arithmetic, where children can absorb and express ideas, feelings and attitudes. Integrating the arts accords dance, drama, music and visual arts a collective, central and pivotal role in primary education. Bloomfield also claims that immersion in such experiences complements and enriches learning in the humanities, sciences, technology, literacy and numeracy.

Sources

Bloomfield, A. (2000) *Teaching Integrated Arts in the Primary School*, London: David Fulton.
Downing, D., Johnson, F. and Kaur, S. (2003) *Saving a Place for the Arts? A survey of the arts in primary schools in England* (LGA Research Report 41), Slough: NFER.
Robinson, K. (1982) *The Arts in Schools: Principles, practice and provision, the report of a national inquiry*, London: Calouste Gulbenkian Foundation.

ASSEMBLY

See also: aided schools, moral education, religious education, school climate, singing, spiritual education

An assembly takes place when the school community, or a part of it, meets together to share aspects of everyday living and explore issues such as belief, relationships, sharing, tolerance and integrity. It can also act as a medium for communicating matters of significance through stories, illustrations and evidence from people's experiences. In England, an act of collective worship is supposed to be held as part of an assembly as it has been a legal requirement since the 1944 Education Act, though practice varies considerably. To avoid offending parents who hold different religious beliefs or none, the worship element is not normally doctrinal and, in the majority of schools, draws from different faith traditions. Since August 1989 all maintained schools in England and Wales must hold daily Christian Worship (Assembly) and provide Christian religious education according to the Education Reform Act, 1988. As a result, all children in must now attend unless their parents write to the head teacher specifically stating that they do not wish their children to do so. In Scottish schools there are similar arrangements, which rely on traditional practice. Although there is no daily collective worship required by legislation, schools often appoint chaplains from the Church of Scotland and other denominations to lead acts of worship. Schools commonly hold services in the local parish church. There is a requirement for collective worship in all grant-aided schools in Northern Ireland.

Hawkes (2000) notes that the appropriate atmosphere and tone in assemblies is created through the sensitive use of a central focus, such as a display, which also assists in creating a calm and reflective mood. In practice, primary school assemblies tend to be used to celebrate pupil achievement, provide time for reflection by using 'mood music' and conveying messages – and occasionally warnings or guidance about behaviour – from the head teacher or assembly leader. Hawkes also notes that regardless of its format and the type of school concerned, there an assumption that an act of worship experience will be *spiritual* in as much as pupils are given opportunity to explore the 'inner person', associated with feelings, emotions, empathy and a sense of wonder about the world.

In a survey of head teachers in rural Wales, Davies (2000) found a high level of agreement regarding worship, though on certain issues, such as whether teachers should be allowed to exempt themselves from school worship and whether children should sing hymns and say prayers, a range of views prevailed. Schools with a religious foundation, especially those deemed 'aided' have to take closer account of the church leaders' expectations, including 'foundation' governors who represent the church. Inspections of Anglican schools with a religious foundation (Section 48 inspections) include a consideration of the impact of collective worship on the school community.

Organising assemblies has to take account of the physical space available for an all-school sitting; in very large schools it may be impossible to cater for all the children at one time. Schools often get around the space problem by organising classroom-based meetings, with the teacher as leader. In primary schools it is common for children to be actively involved through singing, chanting, echoing what the leader says or contributing ideas and experiences; such involvement is likely to retain their attention and convince children that the assembly is relevant to their needs.

Some schools use the time during assembly to take pupils and offer them additional coaching (in reading, for instance) thus depriving them of the assembly experience; the legalities of such a practice remain unclear, so schools try to ensure that children who are to be withdrawn during assembly time are at least present for part of the assembly, preferably the component where everybody is thinking about an issue together and saying prayers or meditating silently.

There are many books published every year that contain ideas for assembly to satisfy the insatiable demand from teachers for appropriate material. The author of one such book, *Round the Year: Ninety stories for the primary school assembly* (Jackson 2003) writes in the blurb that the collection of stories for assembly includes all kinds of stories – fables and myths, fantasy and folk stories, legends, true stories, stories from the major religions, stories specially written and interactive assemblies – all told in a conversational style. One of the many challenges for assembly leaders when using this type of resource is to clarify what is meant by a fable, myth, legend and (especially) a 'true' story when faced with children of widely differing ages, backgrounds and dispositions. Thus, what to a five-year-old child is true without question may be dismissed as a fantasy by an older sibling. By contrast, authors like Stephen Cottrell (2008) adopt a specifically Christian perspective in *The Adventures of Naughty Nora*, where a mischievous girl gets into all sorts of trouble every day. The stories of her adventures are written for junior children and tease out the message of God's grace in everyday life. Similarly, for younger primary children, *Through the Year with Timothy Bear* by Jeremy Sears (2006) consists of twenty-four short stories devised to help those working with 5–7s to teach biblical and moral truths through storytelling.

Sources

Cottrell, S. (2008) *The Adventures of Naughty Nora*, Abingdon: Barnabas (BRF).

Davies, G. (2000) 'Worship in the primary school: A survey of head teachers' attitudes in rural west Wales', *Research in Education*, 64, 20–35.

Hawkes, N. (2000) *Living Values Education*, on-line at www.livingvalues.net/reference/assembly.html

Jackson, J.L. (2003) *Round the Year: Ninety stories for the primary school assembly*, London: Religious and Moral Education Press.

Sears, J. (2006) *Through the Year with Timothy Bear*, Abingdon: Barnabas (BRF).

ASSESSING CHILDREN'S LEARNING

See also: formative assessment, learning, summative assessment, tests and testing

The assessment of children's learning has assumed considerable importance over recent years, most notably through the national curriculum tests (popularly known as SATs) that have had to be taken by every primary-aged child in England. Systems in Scotland, Wales and Northern Ireland are less centrally administered and have fewer implications for schools and staff. In England the results are compiled into league tables for schools and have been the subject of extensive debate over the impact of assessments on individual children, teachers, parents and schools.

Teachers have long referred to the ongoing assessment of children's learning during lessons as 'formative' and the end product (through marks and grades and comments on work) as 'summative' (see Wiliam and Black 1996). However, in recent years it has become increasingly common for formative assessment to be referred to as 'assessment *for* learning', AFL; and the summative process as 'assessment *of* learning', AOL, with an emphasis on the words 'for' and 'of'. Despite this neat distinction, AFL inevitably overlaps with the AOL and vice versa because an assessment of what a pupil is currently learning inevitably contributes towards an evaluation of what the child *has* learned (end result); likewise, an understanding of what a child has learned must feed into the teacher's planning for what a child needs to learn and consolidate in the future. Evidence to inform assessments can be both direct, such as marking a piece of work, and indirect, such as time on task (Hall 2007).

Primary teachers have historically devised their own models of assessment (Gipps *et al.* 1996) and most schools also have their own 'in-house' tests, from the familiar spelling test or multiplication test through to more sophisticated verbal reasoning tests and problem solving. However, Black and Wiliam (1998, 2006) are among educationists to challenge the notion that assessment and its impact on learning should be the teacher's sole responsibility. They famously refer to treating the classroom as a 'black box', whereby certain external *inputs* are fed in and make particular demands, such as those from pupils; teachers; other resources; management rules and requirements; parental anxieties; and tests, with pressure for children to score highly. The authors completed the model by noting that some *outputs* invariably follow, such as pupils who are more knowledgeable and competent; better test results; teachers who are more or less satisfied and teachers who experience varying degrees of exhaustion.

Since the early forays into ways to improve learning through formative assessment, there have been numerous contributions to the debate including, more recently, the use of electronic systems to track teachers' assessments of pupils. For example Whitelock (2008) argues for the development of new forms of e-assessment but insists that the most important factor is sound pedagogy (act of teaching) rather than introducing state-of-the-art technological wizardry.

The complex process of assessment can be described in terms of three elements: evidence, judgement and outcome (Drummond 2003). Teachers use evidence to make judgements about a child's progress, including weaker and stronger areas of learning, and having made those judgements they have to decide what appropriate action to take ('outcomes'). Establishing causal links between diagnosing areas of a pupil's academic strength and weakness, and adjusting teaching to take account of them, has resulted in a large increase in detailed tabulation of data about pupils' performance in the shape of charts, scattergrams and lists. It is common practice in many primary schools for a senior teacher to take responsibility for compiling such data, using it to evaluate children's progress and by implication the quality of teaching.

In addition to the possible negative effect upon children of 'labelling' them at an early age, some academics challenge the concept of a cyclical pattern of 'teach-learn-assess-teach' at two levels. First, there are concerns about the assumption that it is possible to provide a bespoke teaching programme to 'fit' the needs of each child; second, there are doubts that it is possible to know precisely what children know. The second point about knowledge is significant, for the concept of assessing children is founded on a belief that the extent of a child's knowledge and understanding can be identified and, more significantly, quantified. Those who favour

formal assessments counter-argue that tests provide teachers and parents with crucial insights into children's capabilities that would otherwise remain hidden.

Once the pupils' work is completed, teachers can concentrate on a final assessment of a child's learning, which can take many forms depending on the task or activity pupils were undertaking: written task/speaking and listening/creating something visual, etc. The assessment also has to take into account three additional factors: (1) Whether children worked singly, in pairs or in groups; thus, if children were collaborating on an activity (e.g. a science investigation), the teacher has to be aware of the individual contributions that each child has made towards the end result – a far from easy task. (2) The amount of adult support that was offered in completing the task/doing the activity; thus, if children relied heavily upon support it may signal confusion or low levels of confidence or both. (3) The difficulty and demands of the work.

Teachers draw on artefacts (past examples) of pupils' work that have been collated by or with the children, noting when the work was carried out, how long it took to complete, whether the learner worked unaided and the comment on the work provided by an adult. Older children are sometimes invited or required by the teacher to make a comment on their own work or (less often) on a classmate's work. These artefacts provide concrete evidence of progress and pupils' understanding that cannot be matched by a single grade or mark, including insights into possible *reasons* for children's success or underachievement.

Effective teachers try hard to encourage pupils in directing and assessing their own work, which increases children's sense of ownership of their learning. If dealt with sensitively, this type of ownership tends to raise pupil expectation and motivation for completing tasks, which often leads to an improvement in work quality. However, anticipating what children will learn is an unreliable business because classrooms, children and learning are too complex to accommodate within a simple plan–teach–assess framework (Kelly 2007).

Sources

Black, P. and Wiliam, D. (1998) *Inside the Black Box: Raising standards through classroom assessment*, London: NFER/Nelson.

——(2006) 'Developing a theory of formative assessment', in Gardner, J. (ed.) *Assessment and Learning*, London: Sage.

Drummond, M.J. (2003) *Assessing Children's Learning*, London: David Fulton.

Gipps, C., McCallum, B. and Brown, M. (1996) 'Models of teacher assessment among primary school teachers in England', *The Curriculum Journal*, 7 (2),167–83.

Hall, K. (2007) 'Assessing children's learning', in Moyles, J. (ed.) *Beginning Teaching, Beginning Learning*, Maidenhead: Open University Press.

Kelly, P. (2007) 'The joy of involving pupils in their own assessment', in Hayes, D. (ed.) *Joyful Teaching and Learning in the Primary School*, Exeter: Learning Matters.

Whitelock, D.M. (2008) *Accelerating the Assessment Agenda: Thinking outside the black box*, Luxembourg: Office for Official Publications of the European Communities, Luxembourg.

Wiliam, D and Black, P. (1996) 'Meanings and consequences: A basis for distinguishing formative and summative functions of assessment', *British Educational Research Journal*, 22 (5), 537–48.

ASSESSMENT FOR LEARNING

See also: assessment of learning, mistakes and misconceptions, summative assessment

Assessment for learning (AFL) is a recent phrase used to describe the ongoing involvement of teachers with children's learning during lesson times. Teachers more commonly refer to this form of assessment as 'formative' to indicate that children's ideas and understanding are being shaped.

ASSESSMENT OF LEARNING

See also: assessment for learning, formative assessment, summative assessment, assessment for learning, mistakes and misconceptions

Assessment of learning (AOL) is also referred to as 'summative' assessment, though the former term tends to be used with respect to assessments attached to particular lessons and the latter to assessments that take account of pupil attainment over a longer period of time. AOL takes place when a teacher makes an evaluation of pupils' work based on criteria appropriate to the task being assessed. For instance, a set of arithmetic problems is likely to receive a mark, whereas a written task may receive a grade, a written comment or another indicator of the teacher's assessment (such as a sticker). In an ideal world, AOL should occur with the child present but in practice the teacher might have to evaluate the work independently and later inform the children of the outcome. AOL alerts teachers to specific problems, misconceptions and misunderstandings that can be addressed in future lessons. Assessment of work in art and design is normally verbal and non-judgemental; that is to say, each child's efforts are commended, regardless of the quality of product. There is a greater emphasis on AOL among older primary pupils; teachers spend more time on the more immediate 'formative' assessment ('assessment for learning') with younger pupils.

ASSESSMENT TYPES

See also: assessment for learning, assessment of learning, formative assessment, summative assessment

It is common practice for primary teachers in school to refer to two types of assessment of pupil learning. The first type is known as 'formative' assessment, more recently referred to as 'assessment for learning' (AFL) to describe what takes place during lessons as adults monitor children's progress and provide immediate feedback to guide pupils, redirect their efforts or clarify incorrect thinking. The second broad type of assessment involves 'summative' assessment or 'assessment of learning' (AOL) which is an end-loaded assessment to evaluate and make decisions about children's learning once the tasks and activities have been completed. The two assessment categories overlap in various ways, as it is impossible to offer feedback about learning (AFL) without at the same time making an on-the-spot assessment of the child's present understanding (AOL). Similarly, it would be foolish to conduct an AOL and not to take account of the results when planning future lessons. There are, therefore, some aspects of assessment that overlap the AFL and AOL agendas, which I have referred to as 'assessment of and for learning' or AOFL (Hayes 2009).

Sources

Hayes, D. (2009) *Primary Teaching Today*, London: Routledge.

ASTHMA

See also: health and safety, medication

Asthma in children is a common, chronic illness in childhood, caused by an obstructive respiratory condition that is characterised by recurring attacks of wheezing, shortness of breath, prolonged expiration and an irritated cough. It is a very common condition affecting 1 in 13 adults in the UK, which means that one household out of five has at least one family member affected by asthma. Research by the National Asthma Campaign, NAC (www.asthma.org.uk) concludes that 1 in 8 children are diagnosed as having asthma at some time in their lives. Although the disease can begin in infancy, it is often difficult to diagnose asthma in younger children. An asthma attack can be brief or it can last for several days. Asthma is incurable but can be controlled by taking medication and by avoiding contact with environmental 'triggers', including pollen, cigarette smoke, perfumes and smells from household sprays. General advice from Asthma UK is to make every effort to avoid an attack but in the event of it happening for the sufferer to follow five steps:

1 Take your reliever inhaler (usually blue) immediately.
2 Sit down and ensure that any tight clothing is loosened. Do not lie down.
3 If there is no immediate improvement during an attack, continue to take one puff of your reliever inhaler every minute for five minutes or until symptoms improve.
4 If your symptoms do not improve in five minutes or you are in doubt, call 999 or a doctor urgently.
5 Continue to take one puff of your reliever inhaler every minute until help arrives.

Advice from the Office of Public Services Reform (OPSR 2004) is that teachers should make an effort to find out more about asthma – what it is; what triggers it; and its effects. Adults in school need to learn how to help children by being able to spot the signs of an attack and remind children to use their inhalers when coughing or wheezing, thereby helping to prevent worse attacks. In the case of an asthma attach, they should ask what the person wants but only phone parents or outside medical help if it is serious. Where possible, each child with asthma should be allocated a 'buddy' to accompany them to the first aid room in the case of attack (together with an adult). Teachers sometimes suspect that a child is faking an attack, though experience shows that this behaviour is very rare. In the highly unlikely event that children *are* faking it, however, the incident is taken seriously and referred to the school counsellor or nurse, details recorded in the school logbook and parents informed. Children with asthma may require extra time to change for PE and games, and to be introduced to more challenging physical activity more gradually. Certain weather and environmental conditions may impact upon a child's ability to participate fully in physical activities; for example, newly mown grass or smoke from a nearby bonfire may be detrimental to their well-being.

Asthma News, UK (www.asthma-uk.co.uk) collates up-to-date news and information on asthma in the UK and Ireland. Asthma UK simply claims to be a web site dedicated to the ever increasing number of asthma sufferers (www.asthma.co.uk).

Source

OPSR (2004) *Managing Childhood Asthma in Schools*, London: Cabinet Office.

ATTENDANCE

See *Absenteeism*

ATTENTION-DEFICIT HYPERACTIVITY DISORDER

See also: attention span, behaviour, brain function, distractible children, gender, medication, stereotyping

Attention-deficit hyperactivity disorder (ADHD) is a developmental disorder that is said to affect about 3–5 per cent of the world's population, though Kewley (1999) claims that it is nearer 2 per cent. It often emerges during childhood and is characterised by a persistent pattern of inattention and/or hyperactivity ('excessively active'), as well as forgetfulness, poor impulse control and a tendency to be easily distracted. Kewley defines ADHD as an internationally recognised medical condition of brain dysfunction, in which individuals have problems in inhibiting inappropriate behaviour and controlling impulses, so giving rise to educational, behavioural and other difficulties. ADHD is currently considered to be a persistent and chronic condition for which no medical cure is available, although medication can be prescribed. About 60 per cent of children diagnosed with ADHD retain the condition as adults.

A characteristic of acutely active children is that some of them appear unable to 'switch off' their minds and may need a familiar source of comfort; for example, hugging a soft toy (younger children) or holding a mascot or prized possession (for older children). Additional classroom assistant support is essential under such extreme circumstances – a mature, unflappable assistant who genuinely enjoys the challenge is particularly valuable.

Genuine hyperactivity (as opposed to sheer naughtiness) is not a wilful act; for instance, when a severely hyperactive child becomes exhausted, his or her self-control often breaks down and the hyperactivity may become even more acute. The behaviour cannot be completely eliminated but appropriate strategies and perseverance can help considerably with its management. Methods of treatment might include a combination of medications, behaviour modification programmes, life style changes (e.g. encouraging regular, stable habits) and counselling. It is desirable for adults to help the children understand their own condition and learning needs (see, for instance, Nadeau *et al.* 2004). Sadly, some of the children struggling with ADHD – the majority of whom are boys, though see O'Regan (2002), who dedicates a section of the book to the needs of girls – are treated by being given medical drugs to control their behaviour, though deep concern is now being expressed about the possible long-term damage that such a strategy might be causing.

Not all unsettled pupils have attention deficit *and* hyperactivity: some children struggle to concentrate ('attention deficit'); others are irrepressible ('hyperactivity'); yet others combine the two dimensions, with the inevitable challenging behaviour that follows. It is not uncommon for the fragile world of very unsettled children to collapse under the weight of emotional tensions that they carry but cannot control. If adults make a special effort to be kind and helpful children sometimes take advantage or don't know how to respond appropriately and leave the adult feeling betrayed and disappointed.

21

Hayes (2009) refers to the fact that a lot of adults have to fight an instinctive tendency, occasionally fuelled by colleagues' comments, to label children who struggle to behave and distort situations in the ways described above as 'maladjusted' or 'weird'. It is quite likely and understandable that the child will be labelled by his or her peers and by some adults as a 'nuisance' or 'a trouble-maker'; teachers therefore need to work hard to convince themselves that these pessimistic tags are unhelpful.

Teachers' responsibilities involve structuring life in school and providing a discipline framework within which unsettled children can gradually develop acceptable behaviour. Firm persuasion takes longer than fierce insistence but proves more effective in the long term. See Rief (1993) for practical suggestions about management techniques that promote on-task behaviour. Specific interventions to stretch the child's attention span can be initiated to improve listening and encourage task completion. Thus, a quiet environment encourages thinking and listening; an activity such as silent reading focuses the child's mind; predictable daily events together with constant reassurance are helpful. Nothing helps a hyperactive child more than having a tolerant, patient teacher, with a reservoir of goodwill and humour.

As hyperactive children's pent-up energy cannot be suppressed by applying restrictive measures, the bursts of fervour need an outlet, which in the everyday life of the school may be difficult to discover, though regular outdoor activities such as running, sports and nature walks are beneficial. In free-choice situations, very lively children gain from having a narrow range of choice of activity because too much choice can be hard for them to cope with. Owing to the pupil's rough handling of equipment, items should be safe and relatively unbreakable.

Very active pupils are sometimes desperate to work with one particular classmate and won't settle until they have their 'special friend' as partner. Sadly, the intensive and even obsessive demands that hyperactive children make of a partner can prove overwhelming for the chosen classmate, who looks for a new partner, leaving the hyperactive child even more isolated and desperate for another companion. While it is important to try and eliminate aggressive behaviour, adults have to be wary of imposing unattainable standards, such as insisting that the child sits absolutely still, when such a response exceeds the child's capacity to conform.

In the UK the national Attention Deficit Disorder Information and Support Service (ADDISS) is a national body that provides information and resources about ADHD to sufferers, teachers and health professionals (www.addiss.co.uk). Similarly, in the United States the Attention Deficit Disorder Association (ADDA) is a non-profit making organisation to provide information, resources and networking to adults with ADHD and to the professionals who work with them (www.add.org). Contributors to Lloyd et al. (2006) provide a comprehensive, international perspective on the issues attached to ADHD.

Sources

Hayes, D. (2009) *Primary Teaching Today*, London: Routledge.

Kewley, G.D. (1999) *Attention Deficit Hyperactivity Disorder*, London: David Fulton.

Lloyd, G., Stead, J. and Cohen, D. (eds) (2006) *Critical New Perspectives on ADHD*, London: Routledge.

Nadeau, K.G., Dixon, E.B. and Beyl, C. (2004) *Learning To Slow Down and Pay Attention: A book for kids about ADHD*, Washington DC: Magination Press.

O'Regan, F. (2002) *How to Teach and Manage Children with ADHD*, Whitestone NY: LDA Publishers.

Rief, S.F. (1993) *How to Reach and Teach ADD/ADHD Children*, San Francisco CA: Jossey-Bass.

ATTENTION SPAN

See also: attention-deficit hyperactivity disorder, brain function, distractible children, learning difficulties, motivation for learning, rewards, television

Attention span is the degree to which a child demonstrates sustained focus on designated tasks and activities, especially in school (Gottfried, on-line). Concentration involves the ability to screen out distractions, delay gratification and regulate impulses and emotional responses. An adequate attention span is an important part of learning in a classroom setting, enabling children to organise and consolidate important features of the subjects being studied. Most children develop the expected level of concentration in the course of ordinary school experience but for those with short attention spans, learning problems sometimes develop. Attention span problems are frequently reported in children with learning disabilities, such as those diagnosed with *attention-deficit disorder* (ADD) and *attention-deficit hyperactivity disorder* (ADHD).

Between the age of 9 and 12 years, concentration and brain development continue to progress. Children become more highly motivated and they are able to work through a project, step by step (see Essortment 2002). One of the difficulties children encounter is that they are growing up in a society that is bombarded by rapid visual media with the capacity to reduce healthy attention span development. It is claimed that an extensive exposure to television and computer games develops brain systems that tend to *deflect* attention rather than *focus* it. A small number of children are what is termed hyperactive ('exceedingly active') and may react impulsively to external stimuli, such as a comment from another child, a powerful visual image or an attractive item. It is essential that children receive active practice in thinking and learning to build increasingly stronger neural (brain) connections for the simple reason that a mature attention span comes with a mature brain (Healey 1991).

Attention span is determined in large measure by the type of 'programming' that is received from external stimuli – such as adult talk, picture books and colourful images. Studies suggest that an average child's formal attention span (in minutes) is approximately as long as the age of the child; in other words a five year old can normally only manage five minutes of uninterrupted concentration. Such a claim may surprise parents, who are used to seeing their children immersed in watching TV programmes that are visually compelling. However, the majority of these programmes on TV and electronic games do little to stimulate children's minds, make them think, consider options, make decisions, formulate opinions, evaluate merit and so forth. To maintain interest, programme-makers provide rapid, easily absorbed film extracts, using a range of camera shots, enhanced by multimedia wizardry. Some children become so used to these intensive stimuli that 'one-dimensional' lessons in school that necessitate close attention to a word-dominated content are viewed as uninspiring, with the result that the teacher struggles to keep such children on task. Educators cannot compete with multimedia technology but they can place an emphasis on providing rich and meaningful adult-child verbal interaction. Ruf (2005) reminds us that gifted children are often capable of extended periods of concentration and boys in particular are much more likely to attend carefully to a topic that fascinates them.

It is interesting to contrast the *external* control of visual stimuli used by the media to bombard children's senses with the *internal* control and discipline required by children when participating (for example) in self-directed play or collaborative problem-solving exercise. Under such conditions and within the limits of timetable constraints and teacher direction, the child determines how long he or she will attend to individual tasks, discusses with others the way forward and adjusts to the prevailing social conditions. By contrast, a constant stream of interruptions (especially visually captivating ones) disengages the inner dialogue; that is, the talking that takes place inside the child's head. As a result, concentration and sustained attention become increasingly fragmented; the pupil jumps from one activity to another, restlessly seeking the next stimulus 'fix' and unable or unwilling to persevere to complete a task. Teachers are often hard-pressed to retain the child's interests and have to accept that limited attention may be the result of a disorder and not a behaviour issue.

Sources

Essortment (2002) *Children and Concentration*, on-line at www.essortment.com/all/childandconcen_rzps.htm

Gottfried, N.W. *Attention Span*, on-line at http://social.jrank.org/pages/60/Attention-Span.html

Healy, J. (1991) *Endangered Minds: Why our children don't think and what to do about it*, New York: Simon and Schuster.

Ruf, D.L. (2005) *Losing Our Minds: Gifted children left behind*, Scottsdale AZ: Great Potential Press.

AUDITORY LEARNERS

See also: information technology, kinaesthetic learners, learning styles, listening, speech, speech clarity, visual learners

Children receive information from many different sources, the most significant being auditory sources. Some children learn easily simply by listening, without particular need for visual stimuli or hands-on experience and are sometimes described as 'auditory learners' or, more accurately, as learners with a preference to receive information, guidance and explanation through the ear, as opposed to receiving it through the eye (visual) or fingers (kinaesthetic/tactile) or via investigation. As auditory learners tend to benefit from traditional teaching techniques, many teachers use a lecture-style approach and provide essential information by talking directly to the pupils. Auditory learners benefit when directions and instructions are read aloud, feedback is required or information is presented and requested verbally. To impart meaning to their words, teachers have to consider not only the vocabulary and expressions they use but pay particular attention to the tone, speed and pitch of voice. For example, the simple question, 'What are you doing?' may indicate

fascination or threat, depending on where the emphasis is placed. Teachers sometimes get frustrated that children do not grasp what they are saying when, in fact, they may be more intrigued by the tone of voice than by what the teacher is actually saying. In addition, the rapidity of speech, frequency and length of pauses and number of hesitations can detract from the central message that the words convey. Despite their positive response to the spoken word, auditory learners also benefit from visual aids, opportunities to explore ideas, use of support materials (e.g. mathematical equipment) and information technology. They may or may not be accurate recorders of things they receive from others and discover for themselves; a good listener is not necessarily skilled in summarising points.

AUTISM

See also: attention-deficit hyperactivity disorder, attention span, behaviour, brain function, communication, imagination, misbehaviour

Autism or autism spectrum disorder (ASD) is a lifelong developmental disability that affects the way a person communicates and relates to and interacts with people around them. Autistic spectrum disorder (ASD) is a relatively new term that includes the subgroups within the spectrum of autism. Estimates vary as to the prevalence of ASD in school age children but one estimate is that approximately 8 people in 1,000 (i.e. about 0.8 per cent) are affected by some degree of the disorder. *Asperger's syndrome* is a form of autism, a condition that affects the way a person communicates and relates to others. People with Asperger's syndrome may find difficulty in social relationships and in communicating, and limitations in social imagination and creative play.

For a diagnosis of autism to be made, children with autism must display difficulties in three areas of development: (1) difficulty with language and communication, (2) difficulty in social understanding and interactions, and (3) difficulty with flexibility of thought and imagination. These three elements are sometimes referred to as the 'triad of impairment'. A child with autism can exhibit these difficulties to varying degrees and the condition can encompass a wide spectrum (Wing 2003).

A long list of challenges posed by ASD includes problems in social interaction, responding to verbal and non-verbal cues and using 'social language'. These difficulties may also mean that they do not respond to humour or irony; similarly, the use of sarcasm has no impact. Children may interpret instructions literally, rather than reading between the lines; their behaviour may seem to be subtle manipulation and interpreted by teachers as misbehaviour. They have great trouble grasping the many 'unwritten' school rules.

Unlike children who learn through observation (e.g. when to raise the hand, walk in line), children with autism need direct instruction and specific commands. Choosing between options and events such as riding the bus to school present special challenges for children with autism, who need adult help knowing what kind of behaviour is appropriate and acceptable and numerous reminders about the correct course of action; see advice in Notbohm (2007).

Some educators promote the use of creative means to stimulate children through using art, movement and music. Tubbs (2007) argues that unconventional children require unconventional therapies and that we need to balance the child's body, mind and spirit by providing a wide variety of exercises, activities and games that are both fun and effective. Memorably, the author insists that just because a child may appear stubborn and difficult, it does not necessarily follow that the child isn't intelligent, curious and creative.

Children may develop their own personal agendas during a lesson and pursue a different direction from the one intended by the teacher, some of which may be potentially dangerous. For example, children may deliberately alter the conditions during exploratory work to see 'what happens if' they do something radical. Many pupils exhibit obsessive behaviour and become completely engrossed in a certain topic or line of enquiry.

There are signs that the number of children diagnosed with some form of autism is growing and increasing numbers of children with ASD are diagnosed in the pre-school years. Educational provision is increasingly provided in mainstream schools as part of an inclusion policy. However, even with specialist support, children with severe forms of autism cannot normally receive adequate attention in mainstream school life and require special provision in units or separate schools. Such divergence of opinion about appropriate provision has led to tensions between parents and local authorities about funding priorities and educational establishments.

The Autism Research Institute (ARI, www.autism.com) is a non-profit organisation based in California to conduct and disseminate research on the triggers of autism and methods of diagnosing and treating it. The National Autistic Society in the UK champions the rights and interests of people with autism and aims to provide individuals and their families with help, support and services. Similarly, the Autism Society of America (www.autism-society.org) exists to improve the lives of everyone affected by autism.

Sources

Notbohm, E. (2007) *Ten Things Every Child with Autism Wishes You Knew*, Arlington TX: Future Horizons Incorporated.

Tubbs, J. (2007) *Creative Therapy for Children With Autism, ADD and Asperger's*, New York: Square One Publishers.

Wing, L. (2003) *The Autistic Spectrum: A guide for parents and professionals*, London: Robinson Publishing.

AWE AND WONDER

See also: spiritual education, teaching approach

It is argued that our innate capacity to sense wonder, beauty and awe is what makes the human soul rise above the rest of the creatures. Lerner (2000) insists that awe and wonder should be among the first goals of education. Hart (2003) claims that one of the greatest lessons that children have to teach adults is the power of awe. Thus, 'wonder and awe do not only describe a spiritual experience but a spiritual attitude' (p. 61). Opportunities to pause for the purpose of inculcating a sense of awe and wonder in children and addressing challenging issues have, in some schools, been superseded by routine and repetition. The only regular chance for children to be still, contemplate and (even) meditate is during assembly time when there is an act of worship taking place. In the classroom, primary teachers can be tempted to tell the children what they ought to know instead of allowing them opportunities to enquire, play and investigate; or to prescribe learning so closely that curiosity, the urge to ask questions and take time to consider implications are diminished. However, as Sedgwick (2008) wisely comments about the basis for teaching philosophy and thinking: 'Everyone has to believe that children have that sense of wonder, and also that sense that the unexamined life in not worth living' (Introduction). In a non-stop world, saturated with facts and information from many different sources, the cultivation of awe and wonder – and the sheer joy of being alive – is being increasingly recognised as significant for every child.

Sources

Hart, T. (2003) *The Secret Spiritual World of Children*, San Francisco CA: New World Library.

Lerner, M. (2000) *Spirit Matters*, Charlottesville VA: Hampton Roads Publishing.

Sedgwick, F. (2008) *So You Want to Be a School Teacher?* London: Sage.

B

BASIC SKILLS

See also: English, literacy, mathematics, motor skills, reading, writing

Every primary educator emphasises the importance of children acquiring basic skills but there are various interpretations of the phrase. A commonly held view is that they consist of the ability to read, write (and handwrite) and speak in English (or the indigenous language), compute and solve problems at levels of proficiency necessary to function on the job and in society. The Basic Skills Agency, now called the National Institute of Adult Continuing Education, NIACE, suggests that basic skills simply involve the ability to read, write and speak in English and to use mathematics at a level necessary to function at work and in society in general (NIACE 2008). In a parallel initiative, the Welsh Assembly Government began the work of overseeing the implementation of a 'Words Talk-Numbers Count' basic skills strategy in April 2008.

The acquisition of basic skills' competencies (e.g. how to spell common words correctly; how to count in tens; how to use scissors) needs to be grounded, wherever possible, in pupils' everyday experiences to make learning interesting and relevant. One of the conclusions reached by the Primary Review (Alexander 2009) was that an over-emphasis on teaching the basic skills of literacy and mathematics, together with the national tests in these subjects, had led to weak provision and neglect in other areas of the curriculum.

Sources

Alexander, R. (2009) *The Condition and Future of Primary Education in England* ('The Primary Review'), Cambridge: University of Cambridge/ Esmée Fairburn Trust.

NIACE (2008) *Literacy, Language and Numeracy*, on-line at www.niace.org.uk

BECTA

BECTA stands for British Educational Communications and Technology Agency. It is the government agency leading the national initiative to ensure the effective and innovative use of technology throughout learning. The acronym also stands for 'bringing educational creativity to all'.

BEHAVIOUR

See also: discipline, home background and learning, misbehaviour, rules, sanctions, teacher–pupil interaction

The issue of pupil behaviour is a source of concern for almost every teacher, particularly inexperienced and under-confident ones. With respect to terminology, children's *behaviour* stems from their actions and decisions, whereas adults exert *discipline* as a means of helping children make appropriate decisions about their behaviour. In this regard Dreikurs *et al.* (1998) stress the importance of helping children to take responsibility for their own actions and cite an example of a boy who kept calling out in class. The teacher despaired of finding a solution until she asked the boy himself for his suggestions and he imposed a sanction on himself (the loss of two minutes free time for each transgression) and the problem was cured within a week.

The term 'behaviour' does not simply encompass a child being good or naughty; it includes other manifestations such as exhibiting shyness, withdrawal from mainstream activities and idleness. These, too, are behaviours seen in classrooms with which teachers and increasingly, teaching assistants (Derrington and Groom 2004) have to cope with and, hopefully, help to change for the better. In recent times the concept of teamwork and consistency of approach in implementing behaviour management policies has gained currency (Rogers 2006) with an emphasis on home–school cooperation (Ravet 2007).

Wright (2006) argues that a situation can arise in which a teacher 'seems to be naturally popular or charismatic', with the result that pupils want to please her or him; in doing so, however, the children may 'not assume responsibility for their own behaviour' (p. 53). Consequently, when a different teacher is in charge, pupils who were well behaved with the first teacher fail to be so for the next.

Children need to be provided with an enforceable rule framework, sensibly but consistently applied, within which they can gradually strengthen their own self-control. The need for clarity and patience is most acute when teachers deal with new entrants, some of whom do not possess the self-control or social graces to conform (Roffey and O'Reirden 2001). Newell and Jeffery (2002) emphasise the importance of teachers modelling good behaviour to children. Strategies include being prepared to say sorry; explaining that teachers as well as children have rights; taking a keen interest in learning; demonstrating a strong sense of purpose in teaching; and showing that even difficult behaviour can be overcome. Chaplain (2006) notes, 'Rules alone do not guarantee good behaviour. They need to be linked to consequences – which means *consistently* rewarding pupils who follow the rules and applying sanctions as a deterrent to those who do not' (p. 110, author's emphasis).

Learning to cope with the vagaries of children's behaviour is helped when teachers admit that unacceptable behaviour is sometimes due to an uncertainty in children's minds about where the boundaries lie. Thus, McPhillimy (1996) issues a warning about the need for teachers to examine the *cause* of problems rather than their symptoms: 'Misbehaviour in itself is therefore mainly a symptom of a problem rather than the problem itself. If the underlying problems are dealt with, then the symptom is likely to disappear' (p. 61).

Children who *misbehave* often do so out of choice. They understand the rules but make a decision to disregard them; they are also aware of the likely consequences but hope that they won't get caught or are insufficiently impressed by the sanction to worry if it is applied. Younger children are more likely to misbehave due to a lack of understanding of the rules and school conventions or confusion about adult expectations or an inbuilt naughtiness (not a popular word in education circles but very apt in some situations). Some children *fail to conform*, either because they do not see the need to do so or lack the maturity to comply. In most cases, the situation can be remedied by patient, persistent explanation and use of peer pressure. Children new to school may simply lack awareness of what is required; older ones may be egocentric or come from a family/cultural background that fosters single-mindedness and resistance to rule enforcement, in which case discussions with parents and establishing a home–school agreement about appropriate behaviour is a priority.

Behaviour Matters is a free weekly e-bulletin for classroom management advice under the auspices of 'Teaching Expertise' (www.teachingexpertise.com).

Sources

Chaplain, R. (2006) 'Managing classroom behaviour', in Arthur, J., Grainger, T. and Wray, D. (eds) *Learning to Teach in the Primary School*, London: Routledge.

Derrington, C. and Groom, B. (2004) *A Team Approach to Behaviour Management*, London: Paul Chapman.

Dreikurs, R., Grunwald, B.B. and Pepper, F.C. (1998) *Maintaining Sanity in the Classroom*, New York: HarperCollins.

McPhillimy, B. (1996) *Controlling Your Class*, Chichester: John Wiley.

Newell, S. and Jeffery, D. (2002) *Behaviour Management in the Classroom: A transactional analysis approach*, London: David Fulton.

Ravet, J. (2007) *Are We Listening? Making sense of classroom behaviour with pupils and parents*, Stoke-on-Trent: Trentham.

Roffey, S. and O'Reirden, T. (2001) *Young Children and Classroom Behaviour: Needs, perspectives and strategies*, London: David Fulton.

Rogers, B. (2006) *Classroom Behaviour: A practical guide to effective behaviour management and colleague support*, London: Paul Chapman.

Wright, D. (2006) *Classroom Karma*, London: David Fulton.

BELIEFS, TEACHING AND LEARNING

See also: caring teachers, relationships, teaching approach, teachers' beliefs

A teaching approach consists of the methods and strategies that teachers employ to help pupils learn effectively and reflects the beliefs that they hold about the nature of learning. Thus, one teacher may believe that pupils learn best when they are motivated by opportunities to explore ideas as a group, while another teacher may be convinced that they learn best when working alone with tasks closely targeted to their individual needs. Again, one teacher may employ a considerable amount of direct teaching, utilising question-and-answer supported by repetition of facts, while another teacher employs a problem-solving method in which children are encouraged to raise their own questions and seek their own solutions. One teacher's style may be informal and strongly interactive, using humour and repartee, while another teacher might adopt a more detached approach, eschewing familiarity.

Teaching is not always interactive in the sense described above, as teachers can provide information, explain procedures, give directions, organise work and even use question-and-answer techniques in such a way that the relationship between adult and child is of little consequence. In other words, a complete stranger could come in to the room and manage the process efficiently (rather like an invigilator during examinations) without forming a bond with the pupils. However, teaching primary-age children relies heavily on the creation and maintenance of a bond of trust and mutual respect between adult and child. Educators need to have insight into the things that children find significant if they wish to create effective communication networks that will enhance learning and maintain good relations. Children appreciate adults who are fair, interested in them as individuals, transparent in their dealings, clear about their intentions, helpful in their explanations, non-judgemental in their attitude, yet unflinching in confronting unsatisfactory situations. They benefit from teachers who are prepared to listen carefully to what is said to them, leading to improvements in self-esteem, motivation and academic success.

BEREAVEMENT

See also: children, religious education, spiritual education

Bereavement literally means being robbed and deprived of hope (BBC 2008). Naturally, the death of a close relative has a profound effect upon a child, especially if it is the main carer (normally mum or dad), raising issues about the meaning of death and its implications in the immediate and longer-term (see, for example, Black 1998; Brown 1999). In some cases the impact on children may be far more prolonged than adults realise (Holland 2001). This suffering is more intense when they do not have opportunities to talk or to grieve openly and do not feel that those close to them recognise their feelings.

For very young children, being dead is understood as a long sleep or going on a journey such that death and life overlap and interrelate. As children move through the infant years (5–8 years) death assumes a more frightening presence, such that they believe that unlucky people are 'captured' by it and canny people avoid it. Infant age pupils develop an intense interest in the rituals surrounding death (e.g. the formalities of funeral services and what happens to the dead person). From the age of about nine years onwards, death is interpreted as the perceptible end of bodily life; dead people remain forever dead and death is inevitable, final and universal.

Older primary age children have a view of death that is broadly comparable to that of adults in that they experience shock, confusion, anger and guilt. However, children may not show their feelings openly, leading parents and others to wrongly conclude that they aren't affected by the death. After bereavement, common behaviour changes include becoming withdrawn, bed-wetting, lacking concentration, clinging, bullying, telling lies and being aggressive, all of which may signal their true condition. They may also become tired to the point of exhaustion because so much emotional energy goes into dealing with the loss and the stress of the changes in the family. For some children, there may be additional terrors; for example, if the death has been referred to as 'falling asleep' or 'being taken', then it is sometimes the case that children become afraid of going to bed in case something terrible happens to them (based on BBC 2008). Young children can also experience hallucinations and interpret them as indicating the parent's return 'from the dead' or as evidence of persecution by the

ghost of the dead parent because of imagined shortcomings on the part of the child.

Children who lose one parent often become anxious about the survival of the other; consequently, they may protect that parent from knowing of their distress or 'cling' to the parent or become extremely restless when separated from the parent for any length of time. It is estimated that children have higher levels of emotional disturbance and symptoms than non-bereaved children for up to two years, and up to 40 per cent of bereaved children still show disturbance one year after bereavement.

Any altered behaviour may indicate that children are suffering silently and need special help and acknowledgement of their pain (see Bomber 2007). One of the most significant hurts that bereaved children recall is the feeling that no one acknowledged their loss, as a 'wall of silence' prevents open communication. Duffy (2003) emphasises the seriousness of these issues: 'How we help children during their losses can have a profound effect on the way their own lives will develop in the future and even the way in which they will face their own death' (p. 1). See Killick and Lindeman (1999) for practical advice, guidance and support for those working in school.

Some children need a private place in school as a haven to which they can retreat when grief overtakes them. There are literally dozens of fiction-based books that have been written about death for different ages of children, though teachers have to exercise extreme sensitivity in the use of a book, especially about the possibility of reading it aloud at an inappropriate time so that it triggers uncontrollable distress.

The grief caused by the death of a loved one lasts for a long time, so anniversaries and celebration times are particularly difficult for the child to cope with. It helps if key dates and times are noted and shared with key adults (such as colleagues, family members and even teachers at the next school). Adults also need to bear in mind that close friends of the bereaved boy or girl may also suffer varying emotional reactions (Compassionate Friends 2007).

The Child Bereavement Trust offers confidential telephone support and on-line forums, along with training for professionals working with grieving families and children (www.childbereavement.org.uk).

Sources

BBC (2008) *Coping with Grief: Bereavement*, on-line at www.bbc.co.uk/relationships/coping_with_grief/bereavement_effectschildren.shtml

Black, D. (1998) 'Coping with loss: Bereavement in childhood', *British Medical Journal*, 316, 931–33.

Bomber, L. (2007) *Inside I'm Hurting: Practical strategies for supporting children with attachment difficulties in schools*, Brighton: Worth Publishing.

Brown, E. (1999) *Loss, Change and Grief*, London: David Fulton.

Compassionate Friends (2007) *When a Pupil in your School is Bereaved*, on-line at www.tcf.org.uk/leaflets/leschools.html

Duffy, W. (2003) *Children and Bereavement*, London: Church House Publishing.

Holland, J. (2001) *Understanding Children's Experiences of Parental Bereavement*, London: Jessica Kingsley.

Killick, S. and Lindeman, S. (1999) *Giving Sorrow Words*, London: Paul Chapman/Lucky Duck.

BLOOM'S TAXONOMY

See also: child development, knowledge, learning, understanding

Bloom's Taxonomy is a classification that was developed in the 1950s (Bloom 1956) but experienced a revival at the start of the twenty-first century. It was originally written as a 'taxonomy' of different types of educational objectives but is often seen as a way of considering forms and hierarchies of learning. Benjamin Bloom was one of a team of five principal authors from Chicago who were jointly responsible for developing the classification; Bloom happened to have the surname that came earliest in the alphabet and his name subsequently came to be linked most closely with the taxonomy.

The stated aim of the study was to provide a classification of the goals of the education system on which teachers could build a curriculum. It was a product of its era, when behaviourist psychology was the dominant paradigm ('prevailing theory') and learning objectives had to be specified in terms of measurable end products of the learning process. As well as a framework for testing pupils, one suggested use for the taxonomy was as a tool for analysing a teacher's success in teaching.

Williamson (2001) notes that the team intended that the taxonomy would be devised in three domains: the *cognitive* (about thinking), the *affective* (about emotions) and the *psychomotor* (about movement). However, Bloom *et al.* never completed work on the psychomotor domain, although Dave (1970) proposed a version of it. The *cognitive* domain is that of knowledge and intellectual abilities and skills. It is also said to include the 'behaviours', such as remembering, reasoning, problem solving, concept formation and creative thinking. The *affective* domain includes objectives that describe changes in interest, attitudes, emotions and values, and the development of appreciation and adjustment. In the affective domain, the hierarchy is less clear but runs from an awareness and perception of value issues through responding, then valuing, and then to organising and conceptualising values. The *psychomotor* was less developed but ranges from imitation and reflex movements at a basic level to manipulation and then skilled, articulated and precise movements at the upper level.

The main focus of the team's work was on the cognitive domain. One reason given for this was that the cognitive was said to involve a high level of consciousness and awareness – in contrast to the affective, which was said to involve lower levels of consciousness and awareness. This proposition would be disputed today, with an increased acknowledgement of concepts like emotional intelligence and emotional literacy. The taxonomy in the cognitive domain became a hierarchy of six major classes, supposedly moving from simple to complex, as follows: (1) knowledge,

(2) comprehension, (3) application, (4) analysis, (5) synthesis, and (6) evaluation. Atherton (2005) provides a helpful summary (see amended version below):

Knowledge is mainly about remembering and factual recall: specific terms and facts; ways and means of dealing with specifics through organising, judging, criticising ideas and phenomena; conventions; processes and changes over time; causes and effects; classifications such as genres of literature; criteria for testing or judging; inquiry techniques; principles, laws, explanations and theories.

Comprehension includes summarising ideas; simplifying a problem; expressing things in straightforward language; giving an example or illustration of an abstract idea; interpreting data; distinguishing warranted from unwarranted conclusions from a body of data or evidence; drawing conclusions; making inferences; and predicting trends and consequences.

Application involves applying laws, theories, rules or principles to particular, often practical, situations and solving problems by using acquired skills and knowledge.

Analysis involves activities such as seeing patterns, identifying key components, dissecting arguments; distinguishing facts from hypotheses; analysing relationships between interconnecting ideas; distinguishing cause and effect from other types of relationship; detecting logical fallacies in an argument; analysis of organisational principles (e.g. form and pattern in literary or artistic work); recognising a writer's bias in an historical account or rhetoric in a persuasive account such as an advertisement or political speech.

Synthesis involves integrating ideas, creating novel ideas from old ones, connecting and relating knowledge from different areas, producing conclusions and generalisations.

Evaluation involves assessing, judging, appraising, weighing up, criticising and defending a hypothesis, theory or argument. It is placed at the top of the hierarchy since it is said to involve all the other 'behaviours' outlined above.

It is interesting that this 1950s classification is still used by educators and referred to extensively in discussions about 'higher order thinking'. It has, however, been criticised for its emphasis on measurable outcomes and specific objectives and its lack of focus on the affective domain. There are also valid questions about whether the levels form a genuinely linear progression and are cumulative (i.e. whether a higher level can be reached without the previous levels). Nevertheless, Bloom's Taxonomy has value for teachers when they are considering forms of learning and in specific areas such as lesson planning or assessing pupils' work to see at which level in the hierarchy children are working or are capable of reaching. It is the common experience of many primary teachers that even quite young children are capable of engaging with the more complex elements of the taxonomy (such as analysing and evaluating) if guided in their thinking and encouraged to do so.

Sources

Atherton, J.S. (2005) *Learning and Teaching: Bloom's Taxonomy*, on-line at www.learningandteaching.info/learning/bloomtax.htm

Bloom, B.S. (ed.) (1956) *Taxonomy of Educational Objectives: The classification of educational goals – Handbook I: Cognitive Domain*, New York: McKay.

Dave, R.H. (1970) 'Psychomotor levels', in Armstrong, R.J. (ed.) *Developing and Writing Behavioural Objectives*, Tucson AZ: Educational Innovators Press.

Williamson, D. (2001) *Bloom's Taxonomy of Educational Objectives in the Cognitive Domain*, on-line at www.duncanwil.co.uk/bloomcog_files/frame.html

BODY LANGUAGE

See also: communication, distractible children, interaction, speech, teaching skills

The popular maxim that 'actions speak louder than words' is no less true in primary education than any other area of life. Body language has been described as the gestures, postures and facial expressions by which a person manifests physical, mental and/or emotional states, and communicates nonverbally (without speech) with others; in this case, the adult communicating with the child. Thus, head and hand movements, eye contact, body position and tone of voice express an individual's emotions, feelings, and attitudes (Bolton 1979). However, exaggerated body language can lead to discipline problems if children perceive the way that the adult is behaving as whimsical.

Body language is significant in education because the teacher's non-verbal communication can have an impact on pupil behaviour and conduct and thereby on the quality of learning. In his innovative and visually compelling book, Robertson (1996) argues that a teacher's gestures are valuable unless used to excess, as they constitute an integral part of the adult's relationship with the learner and help to clarify the message being conveyed. The author argues that teachers are performers – not in the same way as a stage artist who aims to receive public acclaim – but rather as a means of improving their teaching. Variations in body language can increase pupil response rate, create enthusiasm and help to excite a more vibrant learning environment. It certainly seems to be true in primary schools that adults with the brightest 'animated' personalities are the most popular with the children.

Studies suggest that when addressing a group of children, communication is enhanced if teachers keep their eyes level (as opposed to staring at the ground or the ceiling) and speak directly ahead as much as possible. Nevertheless, a lot of teachers find that moving the position of the head slightly can be used to good effect; for example, looking down momentarily with arms folded carries the message of being deep in thought and may serve to increase the children's curiosity. Staring straight ahead with a serious face for a few seconds without looking at anyone in particular can be used to convey the fact that the teacher is waiting for the children's close attention. A gentle nodding of the head, with soft eye contact and affirmative sounds, indicates that the teacher is taking an interest in what a pupil is saying and happy to be patient until the child has finished speaking. By contrast, staring up at the ceiling denotes a degree of impatience and unwillingness to tolerate the situation.

Teachers in a variety of teaching situations use their eyes a great deal to bond with the children, transmit unspoken meaning and influence. For instance, wide eyes convey enthusiasm, amazement or incredulity, whereas narrowed eyes suggest concentration or mental interrogation of facts. Many teachers develop what is often known as the 'hard stare' with fixed eyes as a method of discouraging children from unwise behaviour without having to say a word to them. On the other hand, teachers also find that a twinkling eye, a flashed smile and a simple nod of approval can transform a child's attitude and enthusiasm for learning by conveying approval, amusement and affirmation. Since approval by touch has become more problematic in school, affirmation through the use of the eyes has assumed even greater significance and must be fully exploited if teachers want to communicate actively with the class.

Body language transmitted from child to adult is also significant. Children rarely maintain the sort of dignified air that adults learn to develop to conform to cultural courtesies. If children are bored, they look bored; if they cannot concentrate they look distracted; if they dislike something or someone it shows in an instant. Good teachers learn to 'read' these signals, though there are occasions when (say) a child's loud yawn is due to fatigue, not boredom. Distracted behaviour, such as looking around or tipping back on the chair, can be a way of getting ideas, not expressing discontent; a sour face may indicate an upset stomach rather than a miserable disposition. There are also cultural practices that may be misunderstood; for example, it is impolite in some cultures to look into the eyes of the person speaking, so a teacher insisting that the pupil does so might lead to considerable unease on the child's part.

When researching problem-solving situations in classrooms, Cook and Goldin-Meadow (2006) found that when teachers gave instructions using *gesture*, the children were likely to employ a problem-solving strategy using their own gestures. The authors concluded that using gesture during instruction encourages children to produce gestures of their own, which, in turn, leads to more effective learning. They also tentatively claim that children are able to use gesturing with their hands as a means of changing their minds and the direction of their thinking.

Sources

Bolton, R. (1979) *People Skills*, New York: Simon & Schuster.

Cook, S.W. and Goldin-Meadow, S. (2006) 'Role of gesture in learning: Do children use their hands to change their minds?' *Journal of Cognition and Development*, 7 (2), 211–32.

Robertson, J. (1996) *Effective Classroom Control*, London: Hodder and Stoughton.

BOREDOM

See also: behaviour, bullying, discipline, emotions of learning, motivation for learning, playtime

We all remember feeling bored when we were at school and fervently want to avoid our children suffering a similar fate, so educators try hard to ensure that the work is interesting and, as far as possible, enjoyable. As such, there is a high premium on motivation and a love of learning. Kyriacou (2007) suggests that boredom can result from a variety of circumstances, including: (a) the work is inappropriate; (b) the work is too easy or demanding; (c) the children have been expected to concentrate on the same thing for too long; (d) children would prefer to do another activity; and (e) the teacher is bored. Adults need to be aware of such factors and try to provide a more inspirational set of experiences as often as possible. However, one of the challenges of modern-day life is that the race to create increasingly sophisticated and engaging stimuli – whether technological or other forms – means that children may be denied the opportunity to experience and cope with short periods of inactivity.

Although it is advisable to keep children busily engaged with work, there is also a place for silence, where children sit still, reflect on what has been said and control the urge to be active. Stillness is a necessary part of helping children to develop intrinsic ('inner') motivation; tap into their creative potential; develop their ability to concentrate and allow their ingenuity and inventiveness to emerge. Growth and maturation is, by its very nature, slow and steady, and necessitates an ability to cope with periods of inactivity and self-sufficiency. Consequently, educators should not be afraid of insisting on short periods of constructive silence. Experiencing boredom may even motivate children to seek more fulfilling ways of occupying their time. Belton and Priyadharshini (2007) reviewed decades of research and theory on boredom and concluded that it is time that boredom came to be recognised as a legitimate human emotion that can be central to learning and creativity.

An interesting and troubling perspective on the effects of boredom was provided by a report initiated by the Children's Society (Children's Society/Royal Bank of Scotland 2007) in which a study of over 1,000 children indicated that one in four primary school children has been the victim of bullying in the playground, blaming boring break times for the problem. Many schools have increased playground supervision, shortened break times – with the concomitant loss of time to play freely – and provided more constructive equipment to provide pupils with outlets for their pent-up energy, but it appears that problems still remain.

Sources

Belton, T. and Priyadharshini, E. (2007) 'Boredom and schooling: A cross-disciplinary exploration', *Cambridge Journal of Education*, 37 (4), 579–95.

Children's Society/ Royal Bank of Scotland (2007) 'Learning through landscapes', *Good Childhood Inquiry*, Interim Report.

Kyriacou, C. (2007) *Essential Teaching Skills*, London: Nelson Thornes.

BOYS

See *Boys' education*; *Gender (pupils)*

BOYS' EDUCATION

See also: Every Child Matters, failure, feedback, gender, motivation for learning, self-esteem (children), writing

Teachers are generally agreed that boys present a greater challenge in school than girls, both with regard to their academic progress and behaviour. In schools where boys progress well there is a culture where intellectual, cultural and aesthetic accomplishment are valued by them as much as by girls. Academic accomplishment is most pronounced where positive incentives, respect and encouragement exist for boys to pursue their own interests; these elements also help to combat the 'laddish' anti-intellectual culture that can become endemic. Boys who are encouraged to read widely and offered choice about the content of their writing, even when the form or genre is prescribed, and encouraged to write to real audiences where possible, are likely to attain their full potential. Frequent and formative assessment (i.e. an evaluation of progress with constructive feedback and guidance) of boys' work – especially written output – enables them to take pride in the outcome. Teaching and learning is further enhanced when there are opportunities for the boys to tackle non-literary texts, poetry and narrative.

Some boys, capable of communicating effectively through speech and visual means find themselves out of favour with teachers due to their reluctance to commit ideas to paper. Such pupils are often highly motivated and apply themselves wholeheartedly in completing the practical task; however, they then find any excuse to avoid writing or do so casually. Perhaps, unwittingly, these children are conveying the important message that active forms of learning do not *always* have to be accompanied by a literacy task. A report from the Centre for Literacy in Primary Education (www.clpe.co.uk) by Safford et al. (2004) concluded that government policies to help underachieving boys who fall behind in reading and writing at primary school have been influenced by misleading stereotypes, which label them reluctant, resistant or weak and even unteachable. The authors suggest numerous strategies to assist 'marginalised boys' in primary schools improve their literacy skills.

The boy who has experienced constant failure in reading and other aspects of English is marginalised from many of the everyday classroom activities that bring commendation and praise from teachers and peers. Because of his difficulties, he is likely to be offered increasing amounts of support in elementary skills by an adult, usually a teaching assistant, and sometimes at the expense of involvement in the more attractive practical and creative tasks. This double deprivation (loss of approval for academic success, fewer exciting activities) can lead to frustration and resentment and a negative attitude towards school. Teachers, despairing of what to do with these recalcitrant youngsters, sometimes resort to strong control strategies or conclude that they are beyond the school's available expertise and are in need of external specialist expertise. The impact of the *Every Child Matters: Change for children* (DfES 2005a) agenda may assist in offering such children appropriate one to one coaching in areas of weakness and, perhaps, the involvement of parents and external agencies (such as social workers) but should not be seen as a simple solution to a complex problem. Pupils that present the greatest challenge to teachers have to be disciplined when necessary but also understood as to the source of their academic and relational difficulties.

Although school inspections show that girls outperform boys in almost every area of academic work, some schools and teachers seem better able to help boys achieve their potential, especially in the problem area of writing. The issue of schooling boys has assumed a higher profile for teachers in recent years, though 'quick-fix' solutions are unhelpful (Skelton 2001; Epstein *et al.* 1998).

The *Raising Boys' Achievement* project (DfES 2005b) examined exciting and innovative ways of raising achievement across a range of primary, secondary and special schools. By working with over sixty schools across England, the research team identified and evaluated strategies that are particularly helping in motivating boys. Significant factors included a clearly articulated ethos, with a focus on the individual; a friendly, caring environment, culture of equality where no one is allowed to dominate and an emphasis on self-esteem and confidence. There is some evidence to suggest that the use of merit awards, badges, achievement assemblies, 'choosing time' (freedom to select what to do from a range of options), an emphasis on a disciplined environment and giving rewards and praise, with high expectations of each child, also assists achievement. Clear routines seem to provide a sense of security and help to reduce conflict. See Ford (2009) for practical suggestions about inspiring boys.

Sources

DfES (2005a) *Every Child Matters: Change for children*, London: HMSO.
——(2005b) *Raising Boys' Achievements*, on-line at www-rba.educ.cam.ac.uk/report.html
Epstein, D., Elwood, J., Hey, V. and Maw, J. (1998) *Failing Boys? Issues in gender and achievement*, Maidenhead: Open University Press.
Ford, C. (2009) *Practical Advice on How to Inspire Boys*, London: Optimus Education.
Safford, K., O'Sullivan, O. and Barrs, M. (2004) *Boys on the Margin*, London: Centre for Literacy in Primary Education.

Skelton, C. (2001) *Schooling the Boys: Masculinities and primary education*, Maidenhead: Open University Press.

BRAIN FUNCTION

See also: child development, emotional intelligence, learning, motivation for learning, spatial-temporal reasoning

Understanding brain function is an important factor in recognising ways in which children learn and it has become increasingly clear that growth in the womb and the first few years of life are the most critical in terms of development. In most children the process is more or less complete by the age of twelve. Nature seems to give a child's brain a 'second chance' between the ages of about four and twelve years, which means that parents and primary educators bear a significant responsibility to ensure that the brain is given the best possible chance to reach its potential through use of a variety of stimulating and motivating learning opportunities (Call 1999).

Studies strongly suggest that one side of every person's brain is normally dominant. If the left side of the brain dominates, a person is likely to be analytical, whereas if the right side dominates a person is more holistic or global. Thus, a left-brain orientated pupil prefers to learn in a step-by-step sequential format, initially concentrating on the fine details and working towards a broad understanding; such an approach can be described as *inductive*, i.e. evidence is gathered from a lot of detail to create a general principle. By contrast, dominance of the right side of the brain means that the pupil prefers to learn by starting with the general principle and then working out the specific details; such an approach can be described as *deductive*, i.e. knowledge in different contexts is 'deduced' from the key principle. Specifically, a person with a right-sided inclination tends to be more random, intuitive and subjective than the left-sided person, preferring to look at the whole picture rather than the individual parts. The dominance of left or right sides of the brain and their accompanying outcomes suggests that children tend to think and learn in different ways. Consequently, in any group or class of children there will be evidence of a variety of learning characteristics as pupils develop and cultivate ways of responding to their experiences and the information presented to them (Garnett 2005). Although the model of left- and right-side brain dominance is contestable, there is general agreement that it has some validity.

Children are acquiring language before and during the whole of primary school; they benefit from hearing adults talk, sing and read to them during their formative years and affirming children's attempts to use and create different language forms (notably, speaking and writing; see Eke and Lee 2008). *Spatial-temporal reasoning* is the expression used in referring to the brain function controlling difficult, complicated tasks like mathematics or playing chess. Such reasoning allows a person to imagine ratios and proportions; for example, it helps younger children to understand that vessels of different proportions but with the same volume hold the same amount of water.

If children are deprived of an intimate relationship with adults and their peers during the years preceding formal schooling, they will probably struggle later on to form suitable human attachments and may have difficulty in making friends and being part of a group. As the part of the brain that regulates emotion is shaped early on through life experiences and fashioned inside and outside school by regular interaction with others, so-called 'emotional intelligence' – the ability to be at ease with oneself and relate to others appropriately – is critical to life success (Gardner 1983). Ideal learning environments are those that reduce a child's stress level to the absolute minimum, while maintaining high levels of motivation.

Sources

Call, N.J. (1999) *Brain-based Learning in Practice: About the brain*, on-line at www.acceleratedlearning.co.uk

Eke, R. and Lee, J. (2008) *Using Talk Effectively in the Primary School*, London: David Fulton.
Gardner, H. (1983) *Frames of Mind*, New York: Basic Books.
Garnett, S. (2005) *Using Brainpower in the Classroom*, London: Routledge.

BREAK TIME

See also: bullying, free play, gender, playtime, security

Break times consist of formally timetabled periods of about 15 minutes duration during mid-morning and/or mid-afternoon when children are – unless inclement weather prevents it from happening – allowed out of the classroom into a designated outdoor area supervised by adults (teachers or teaching assistants). A break time often coincides with 'playtime' (UK) where children are given opportunity for free play. Teachers regard the break time as an opportunity to draw breath, to liaise with colleagues and to gather resources for the next session. The lunch break is the longest break time spent outside formal lessons, though many schools run clubs and special activities for the children. It is common for someone to act as playground supervisor, normally managing the work of several assistants. In the USA and elsewhere, break times are referred to as 'recess'. Towards the end of the twentieth century, serious concerns were raised about the amount of poor behaviour and bullying that allegedly took place during break times (e.g. Whitney and Smith 1993), which gave rise to some soul-searching on the part of school staffs and educational administrators as to how the experience might be improved.

Based on a longitudinal study of a group of pupils from primary to secondary school, Blatchford (1998) claimed that break times play an important part in children's social development and offer children time to play; to develop friendships; to build social networks; to develop social skills and competence; to be independent from adults; and to learn to manage conflict, aggression and inter-group relations. The author raised the important question about where else children will learn these important skills and what will happen in a society where these skills are not developed, especially in the light of parental concerns about child safety in parks and other outdoor venues.

Blatchford's study revealed that break time and lunchtime take up a surprisingly large part of the school day, such that infant children (pupils up to the age of seven years) spend on average almost one quarter of the school day in break time. Pupils had a predominantly positive view of time away from classes and most of them looked forward to going outside. They were clear that the best thing about break time was, literally, having a break from work, a view that became increasingly strong as children progressed through school. The second best thing identified was the chance to talk to friends and play freely. Unsurprisingly, children's main dislikes were being outside in the cold, not knowing what to do and a fear of physical or verbal aggression from other children.

The Blatchford study also found that, by contrast with pupils' positive assessment of break times, the dominant view of staff was negative, fuelled by concerns about the extent of bullying, racist name-calling and teasing. Teachers also had a perception that children at primary level were not as constructive in their play as they once were, quoting instances of idling in the playground, squabbling and engaging in aggressive TV-based games. At the same time, traditional playground games were seen to be in decline to the extent that school staff felt that they needed to 'teach' such games to pupils. The national survey also revealed the trend of a gradual reduction in time spent at lunchtime and the abolition of the afternoon break. By far the most common reason given for this decision was to increase the amount of time spent on teaching; the pressure to achieve improved test results appears to be contributing to the marginalisation of traditional break times in

school (see University of London 1998). The survey also revealed a trend towards more the deliberate management and closer supervision of break time behaviour.

Bishop and Curtis (2001) in their edited collection of multinational studies from Australia, Canada, France, Israel and Britain, counter the widespread concern about the supposed decline in children's play and provide numerous examples of the vibrancy, creativity and variety of unstructured activities in the school playground. The case studies expose aspects of children's play traditions, including the use of playground space; the ways in which children learn and adapt games and rhymes in multicultural and monocultural settings; children's creativity and subversive use of common objects; and gendered dimensions of play – boys preferring more rough-and-tumble activities.

Sources

Bishop, J.C. and Curtis, M. (eds) (2001) *Play Today in the Primary School Playground*, Maidenhead: Open University Press.

Blatchford, P. (1998) *Social Life in School: Pupils' experiences of break time and recess from 7 to 16*, London: Routledge.

University of London (1998) *Caution Urged Against Further Reductions in Break Time*, Institute of Education, on-line at http://ioewebserver.ioe.ac.uk

Whitney, I. and Smith, P.K. (1993) 'A survey of the nature and extent of bullying in junior/middle and secondary schools', *Educational Research*, 35 (1), 3–25.

BREAKFAST CLUBS

See also: healthy eating, healthy schools

Breakfast clubs are being set up in many schools and seen as a way of increasing the number of children eating breakfast regularly, providing them with a positive social environment and promoting healthy eating. The clubs are intended to involve adults and children and the wider community, involving them in the day-to-day running of the club where possible. The clubs also provide a form of childcare and increase the likelihood that children will arrive on time for regular school. New food-based standards for all school food other than lunches was introduced in September 2007. Breakfast Club Plus is a UK-wide network that supports breakfast clubs by providing guidance for new clubs and information and best practice for established clubs. The Greggs Breakfast Club programme was started in 2000 with the aim of providing a free, nutritious breakfast for primary school children in areas of particular social disadvantage.

BRUNER, JEROME

See also: instruction, learning, learning styles, teaching approach

The education psychologist, Jerome Bruner (born in New York in 1915), proposed three ways in which children learn, namely, through enactive, iconic and symbolic stages (Bruner 1966, 1968). The *enactive* stage is characterised by an active engagement in doing things. The *iconic* stage is characterised by children's use of images and pictures. The *symbolic* stage is one in which children can reason and think abstractly. Even in a single lesson it is sometimes necessary for younger children in particular to pass through the enactive stage before they can cope with the iconic or symbolic stages. For instance, a class of eight-year-olds may require the opportunity to explore randomly the relationship between a series of numbers prior to being taught the mathematical rule that applies. Similarly, ten- and eleven-year-olds may benefit from being given time to create sounds using a variety of musical instruments before receiving specific instruction. Such active engagement assists children in their search for meaning, especially in understanding the meanings behind the symbols they later employ in their work, such as map marks, mathematical nomenclature and figures of speech. Teachers have to decide how long to allow pupils to employ enactive

(exploratory) and iconic (visual representations) strategies before expecting them to engage with an abstract task (without the support of learning aids).

Sources

Bruner, J. (1966) *Toward a Theory of Instruction*, Cambridge MA: Belknap Press of Harvard University Press.
——(1968) *Processes of Cognitive Growth: Infancy*, Worcester MA: Clark University Press.

BULLYING

See also: behaviour, caring teachers, discipline, playgrounds, sanctions

The word 'bullying' is used to describe a range of circumstances in which the child's welfare is at risk. Parents and adults in school therefore need to be alert to common signs that children are victims of bullying; the symptoms include regular headaches, stomach aches, anxiety and puzzling phases of irritability. Parents who suspect that their children are suffering need to contact the school immediately.

Bullying is one of the most difficult experiences of a child's life. The impact of deliberately hurtful behaviour, repeated over a period of time, where it is difficult for those being bullied to defend themselves, rightly concerns all adults and educators. Forms of bullying tend to be described under one or more of three headings: (a) *Physical bullying*, including hitting, kicking and theft; (b) *Verbal bullying*, including name-calling and racist remarks; and (c) *Indirect bullying*, such as spreading rumours. It is sometimes difficult to discriminate between high spirits and bullying and all children have squabbles that to adult eyes look more serious than they are. Within a short time, the animosity is forgotten and the two opponents are the closest of friends! On the other hand, there are situations that can cause long-term distress and unhappiness for children. Rigby (2001) argues that it is important to deal with bullying because it has three potential adverse effects. First, it lowers mental health. Second, it induces social maladjustment. Third, it creates physical illness. Sanders (2004) offers the following observation: 'Most definitions of bullying categorise it as a subset of aggressive behaviour that involves an intention to hurt another person ... Not only can it be displayed physically but it can also be subtle and elusive' (p. 4). Sanders goes on to warn that emotional harassment is much more difficult to identify and prove but should still be included under the definition of bullying. Barton (2006) is more expansive in her definition of bullying as 'any behaviour that results in physical or emotional injury to a person or animal, or one that leads to property damage or destruction. It can be verbal or physical' (p. 6).

Lawson (1994) suggests that there are three types of bullies: aggressive bullies, anxious bullies and passive bullies. The *aggressive bully* is the most serious, as weaker children may be injured. Aggressive bullies are often badly behaved in school and require close supervision and monitoring throughout the day. Controlling aggressive bullying must involve the whole staff to ensure that the malefactors are made to adhere to a strictly enforced set of rules governing their behaviour. Parental involvement is also essential in setting targets for improvement.

Anxious bullies see themselves as failures and vent their frustrations on other children by saying unkind things and undermining their achievements. It is often younger, vulnerable children (unlikely to retaliate) who are subjected to their taunts. This type of bully needs to be helped to gain self-esteem by placing them in a position where they can succeed. Paradoxically, these pupils often relate well to younger children in a structured environment, supervised by an adult who can monitor the situation and offer encouragement and direction. Thankfully, aggressive bullying is rare in primary schools, but the types of behaviour that emerge are likely to be continued once pupils transfer to secondary education and create a climate of fear and uncertainty for the victims.

Passive bullies are the 'support' members of bullying groups but not the principal perpetrators. The term 'passive bully' is not wholly satisfactory as it implies that such types are less guilty than their leaders. Nevertheless, it is probably true to say that many passive bullies do not particularly relish their role and would prefer to spend their time in other ways. Their fear of losing credibility with the aggressors and perhaps becoming victims themselves if they don't go along with the more assertive partner deters them from breaking free. Adults need to help them to develop new friendships by providing them with positive alternatives and ensuring that they have a busy, interesting schedule, especially during break times. Needless to say, the principal characters in any gang need to be dealt with firmly.

According to a *Good Childhood Inquiry* report by the Children's Society/Royal Bank of Scotland (2007), one in four primary school children has been the victim of bullying in the playground, blaming boring break times for the problem. The report also claims much of the bullying in Britain's playgrounds is caused by children simply not being stimulated enough. More than half of mothers worry what will happen to their child out of lesson time and one in ten parents fear dangers existing outside the school gates. While worrying about bullying, parents were also concerned that schools did not allow children to experience old-fashioned fun in the school playground. Well over half of parents interviewed agreed that children were rather overprotected in the playground. Nevertheless, the year-long enquiry showed that bullying is endemic in British schools, affecting children's educational performance and making them feel emotionally, if not physically, ill. Reports of bullying were highest in Wales (47 per cent) and Scotland (34 per cent). Playground bullying seems to peak among eight-year-olds and falls as children get older, but there is still a strong prevalence among the youngest age group surveyed, as 16 per cent of six-year-olds claim to have been bullied. It is fair to add that a young child's definition of being bullied might include experiences that an older child would dismiss as a normal part of everyday life in school.

A new psychodynamic approach to bullying in schools known by the acronym CAPSLE (Creating a Peaceful School Learning Environment) was trialled by UCL (University College London) and US researchers (Fonagy 2009). The research involved more than 1,300 eight-to-eleven year-olds in nine US elementary schools over three years and concluded that encouraging all pupils to reflect on incidents at the end of the day was a more effective way to resolve conflicts. Thus, rather than targeting aggressive children, educationalists developed a programme to develop skills in pupils and staff aimed at preventing a regression into the roles of victim, victimiser and bully. In practice, teachers were discouraged from disciplining the aggressor unless absolutely necessary and 15 minutes at the end of the day was taken to reflect on the day's activities. It was found that pupils were far tougher on themselves than teachers would have been under similar circumstances. The research did not make any attempt to give bullies or victims special treatment, and over time the study found bullies came to be disempowered. The CAPSLE approach was compared with schools that receive no intervention for bullying. Although the study found that bullying increased across all the schools being monitored, the percentage of children victimised was substantially less in CAPSLE schools. See also an on-line summary at www.ucl.ac.uk/media/library/bullying

A study of 663 children from state primary schools in north London and Hertfordshire by Wolke *et al.* (2009) found that girls are tormented by playground bullies for longer than boys; thus, half the number of girls who are bullied between the ages of six and nine are still being bullied aged ten or eleven compared with 30 per cent of boys enduring the same miserable experience. However, boys generally appear more likely to be the victims of bullies, as one in four admitted to being kicked, hit or teased at least once a week, compared with 20 per cent of girls. Male and female bullying took different forms: girl bullies are more likely to spread rumours about their classmates and deliberately ostracise them, while boy bullies tend to use violence or make verbal threats. Wolke also found that children use less physical bullying and more psychological bullying between the ages of eight and eleven. As evidence of this trend, the study discovered that whereas about 10 per cent of the children between six and nine years of age claimed that rumours had been spread about them or that they had been deliberately excluded from social groups, the number had risen to 25 per cent by the time they were ten or eleven years of age.

One of the problems facing teachers is that bullying becomes a learned behaviour that eventually acts like a stimulant; in short, bullying becomes enjoyable for the perpetrator. If bullying is not dealt with sooner rather than later it becomes habit-forming and intervention to stop it being repeated becomes more difficult. Although pernicious bullying and frequent unsatisfactory behaviour which brings distress to others cannot be tolerated, the children concerned must also be shown that there are benefits attached to kindness, consideration and self-sacrifice that cannot be experienced by tormenting someone weaker than themselves. For some bullies, this is a hard lesson to learn.

Racist bullying is an unpleasant area of school life that has received a great deal of attention in recent years. All schools have to demonstrate that they not only have a policy to combat such behaviour but that they are active in ensuring that it is implemented and monitored. Parents have a particularly important role in helping their children to combat bullying and are advised to take action as follows: first, to tell children that there is nothing wrong with them as persons in their own right, as the bully is the one with the problem. Second, to encourage children to inform an adult immediately. If the adult dismisses the complaint (e.g. by saying that he or she should stop telling tales) the child should be encouraged to approach another adult until action is taken. Third, to tell children to avoid places and situations where bullying is more likely, such as hidden areas and isolated pathways. Fourth, to advise that children never placate bullies with offers of goods or money. Finally, if the matter cannot be resolved simply, parents should insist on an interview with the head teacher or senior teacher as soon as possible to work out a plan of action (see Tattum and Herbert 1998).

As teachers become aware of the power of friendships and the fears, frustrations and joys of complex child–child relationships, they discover that it is essential to pay attention to its consequences, for better or worse. Children do not attend school solely for developing friendships, but attention to the implications arising from the quality of relationships is important in the quest for a good teaching and learning environment (Mosley and Sonnet 2006; Hewitt 2007). Bullying is a difficult problem to resolve, not least because children fear that making a fuss will further alienate them from their peers and invite repercussions. Nevertheless, bullied children, whatever the circumstances, will underachieve and be miserable not only in school but in life generally. They deserve, expect and should receive protection from adults, including help in being more assertive.

Sources

Barton, E.A. (2006) *Bully Prevention*, London: Corwin Press.
Children's Society/Royal Bank of Scotland (2007) 'Learning through landscapes', *Good Childhood Inquiry*, Interim Report.
Fonagy, P. (2009) 'A cluster-randomized controlled trial of child-focused psychiatric consultation and a school systems-focused intervention to reduce aggression', *Journal of Child Psychology and Psychiatry*, 32, 159–73.
Hewitt, S. (2007) *Bullying*, London: Franklin Watts.
Lawson, S. (1994) *Helping Children Cope With Bullying*, London: Sheldon Press.
Mosley, J. and Sonnet, H. (2006) *Helping Children deal with Bullying*, Cambridge: LDA.

Rigby, K. (2001) *Stop the Bullying*, London: Jessica Kingsley.
Sanders, C.E. (2004) 'What is bullying?' in Sanders, C.E. and Phye, G.D., *Bullying: Implications for the classroom*, Amsterdam: Elsevier.
Tattum, D.P. and Herbert, G. (1998) *Countering Bullying*, Stoke-on-Trent: Trentham.
Wolke, D., Woods, S. and Samara, M. (2009) 'Who escapes or remains a victim of bullying in primary school?' *British Journal of Developmental Psychology*, on-line at http://dx.doi.org/10.1348/026151008X383003

BUSYNESS

See also: effectiveness, thinking, thinking skills, time management

It is possible to mistake busyness for effectiveness in learning. Smidt (2006) comments: 'We see how children everywhere develop a range of strategies as problem-solvers, and in doing this make hypotheses, try these out, analyse what happens, identify patterns, generate rules, use analogy, come to conclusions and move on' (p. 107). However, in the hurry-scurry of planning, teaching and assessing pupil progress, teachers can be caught on a treadmill of activity and intense concentration, ignore Smidt's shrewd observation and only succeed in exhausting the children and themselves. Although children enjoy sessions that have pace and vitality, they also need opportunities to pause, consider and process the information. In doing so, they have to be given something specific to think about; if children are merely asked to 'think' it is likely that most of them will daydream or sit there blankly. If, on the other hand, they are asked to think about the best option, the way that something might be improved or how the story could end, they have an anchor and focus for their thoughts that allows for inventiveness and imagination. Busyness is then translated into useful learning.

Sources

Smidt, S. (2006) *The Developing Child in the Twenty-first Century*, London: Routledge.

C

CALCULATORS

See also: mathematics, numeracy, special educational needs

Children generally enjoy using calculators, though there is a lingering concern that they are a form of 'cheating' and concerns have been expressed about the way in which they may deter children from working things out in their heads ('mental maths'). In fact calculators offer various functions, including the place value number system (i.e. 'hundreds, tens, units', etc.), signs and symbols and mathematical ideas such as decimal notation and even negative numbers (numbers below nought). In particular, calculators are useful for helping children to explore numbers and number patterns, carry out repeated adding as a means of understanding multiplication, handle very large numbers and confirm their predictions about answers to calculations. There is some evidence to suggest that calculators help children with special educational needs to understand mathematical notation – plus, minus, times and division.

CAPITAL LETTERS

See also: alphabet, lower case letters

Capital letters (ABCDEFGHIJKLMNOPQR STUVWXYZ) are otherwise known as 'upper case' letters. The first word of a sentence begins with a capital letter. The names of the days of the week, and of the months of the year are written with a capital letter. Proper names – an individual person, place, institution or event – are also capitalised. Children tend to be taught 'small case' letters before capitals, though their presence in storybooks (especially from North America) and at the start of each child's name, necessitates that teachers spend time introducing them. Once children begin to write in sentences, the use of capital letters becomes even more significant.

CARETAKERS

See also: janitors, security

Caretaker is a term used widely in British schools to refer to the person who is responsible for the care and upkeep of the school buildings and their grounds. Depending on the nature of the educational establishment, responsibilities include classrooms, corridors, offices, sports facilities and (in the case of residential centres) living accommodation. They unlock buildings in the morning before people arrive, and then lock up at the end of the day. In schools and community centres caretakers will also be in charge of letting people in who have hired rooms for clubs or evening classes. Although a lot of time is spent working alone, caretakers come into contact with a variety of people, including staff, children, teachers, contractors working on the site and visitors. In larger premises, they may also supervise other staff such as assistant caretakers, cleaners and gardeners. All caretakers carry out some general tasks but their exact role depends on the size and type of building they are looking after. Caretakers are responsible for who comes on to the site and the security of the building. This role may involve monitoring CCTV and other surveillance equipment to guard against vandalism and theft, including liaising with the police. The Caretaker's Website (www. thecaretakers.net) is a non-profit making personal web site, started in 2001 to provide a service to school caretakers.

CARING TEACHERS

See also: affective dimension of teaching, fulfilment in teaching, health and safety, motivation for teaching, nurturing, relationships

In its basic form, a caring relationship is a connection or encounter between two people, regardless of age or status, to the benefit of the recipient. In an adult–child relationship, it is almost certainly the case that the adult occupies the role of 'carer' and the child is the recipient of care. Even so, for a genuinely caring relation to exist, both parties must contribute in particular ways: the adult must initially express the care; the child must be willing to accept the care (Noddings 1992). A caring relationship requires that adult and child gradually form an emotional bond, which strengthens as they develop mutual respect and trust.

Every study shows that people become teachers because they love working with children; as such, they are almost invariably very fond of those in their care and, like a responsible parent, want to do everything in their power to ensure each child's welfare. Primary teaching is a female-orientated profession and teachers historically see themselves as substitute parents with moral responsibility for children. The fact that primary teachers care deeply about the pupils for whom they

have responsibility is indicated by the frequent reference they make to 'my' children (Nias 1989). Such care is not confined to the working day but taken home every evening, occupying their minds and actions to such an extent that over time, the emotional demands of caring, coupled with the physical exertion and long working days, can lead to exhaustion. See Nias (1997) for a thought-provoking article about the implications of caring for effective teaching.

Empathy, compassion, commitment, patience, spontaneity and an ability to listen are all closely connected to the trust necessary for creating the conditions for loving relations in the classroom. Consequently, a teacher's love for the subject is not a sufficient factor to make pupils learn, though enthusiasm and fervour is important. Instead, by nurturing what the authors refer to as 'loving recognition and response' rather than thoughtless habits, and by being brave enough to take risks in learning and allow for their own shortcomings and vulnerabilities, teachers can help to develop a tolerant, harmonious and caring society (O'Quinn and Garrison 2004).

In recent times, the concept of 'welfare' has grown beyond the mere *in loco parentis* concept to incorporate issues of law and criminal responsibility. Indeed Nixon (2007) is among many writers who warn that as parents and carers become more aware of their rights under law, teachers, school governors' and local authorities' actions will be tested for negligence should a serious incident occur that results in a pupil's injury or worse. Depending on the age of the children, the person or persons with a primary duty of care must ensure that all reasonable precautions have been taken to protect and safeguard children's welfare, though defining how this concept operates is far from easy.

Sources

Nias, D.J. (1989) *Primary Teachers Talking*, London: Routledge.

Nias, J. (1997) 'Would schools improve if teachers cared less?' *Education 3–13*, 25 (3), 11–22.

Nixon, J. (2007) 'Teachers' legal liabilities and responsibilities', in Cole, M. (ed.) *Professional Attributes and Practice*, London: David Fulton.

Noddings, N. (1992) *The Challenge to Care in Schools*, New York: Teachers College Press.

O'Quinn, E. and Garrison, J. (2004) 'Creating loving relations in the classroom', in Liston, D. and Garrison, J. (eds) *Teaching, Learning and Loving*, London: Routledge.

CENTRE FOR LITERACY IN PRIMARY EDUCATION

See also: literacy, professional development

The Centre for Literacy in Primary Education (CLPE) was founded in 1972 and was originally known as 'The Centre for Language in Primary Education'. It became an independent charitable trust in 2002, at which time it changed its name to CLPE. The CLPE is an educational centre for schools and teachers, parents, teaching assistants and other educators, with a high reputation for its work in the fields of language, literacy and assessment. CLPE is dedicated to the provision of services and training courses and consultancy for schools and teachers, teaching assistants, other educators, and parents and families in London and nationally throughout England (www.clpe.co.uk).

CHILD ADVOCATES

See also: caring teachers, decision-making, health and safety, nurturing

Child advocates have a role in protecting and nurturing children and can be found in many schools and community settings (e.g. churches) in the belief that appreciating the views and feelings of young people helps them to feel involved and make better decisions about their actions and behaviour. The advocacy system is particularly well established in the USA and forms an integral part of child protection measures. Advocacy as a concept is

also concerned with representing the views, wishes and needs of children and young people to decision-makers, and helping them to understand what is possible to achieve. Child advocates are also, within reason, available at any time for children attending the organisations' activities to discuss issues or provide information about a problem or anxiety regarding their relation with a staff member or fellow members of the group (e.g. class or youth club). Child advocates do not, of course, absolve other adults from responsibility to prevent the physical, sexual and emotional abuse of children and young people, and to report any abuse discovered or suspected.

CHILD-CENTRED EDUCATION

See also: basic skills, Dewey, enquiry, Plowden Report, teaching approach

Child-centred education is a broad term, which is often, though perhaps inappropriately, associated with the American philosopher and educationist, John Dewey, to describes a teaching approach in which children actively construct knowledge by exploring the outside world through free-play. Child-centred teachers create an environment that will motivate the children to discover new skills and knowledge for themselves. Teachers do not transfer facts to passive pupils but rather facilitate the discovery of knowledge that is interesting to the children. Teachers may establish areas around the room with different activities for pupils to access or children might be assigned to work together in groups on a chosen project. Relatively little whole-class teaching takes place and there is little systematic direct instruction ('step-by-step') used in helping children to master basic skills. Rather, children discover for themselves through play, investigation and using adults as sources of information and guidance.

The availability of computer technology has – perhaps unintentionally – promoted a child-centred philosophy, as children explore the Internet. Advocates claim that children working in this type of environment show greater social competency and more creativity than those other children. Opponents point out that children need to be taught basic skills before they can employ them creatively and consider child-centred methods to be an unreliable philosophy. Politicians usually deride advocates of a child-centred education as ill informed and being out of touch with research evidence. It is still common to hear sceptics refer to the damage caused by the emphasis on 'child-centred learning' in the Plowden Report, published as long ago as 1967 – though such allegations do not bear close scrutiny.

CHILD DEVELOPMENT THEORIES

See also: behaviour, collaboration in learning, emotions of learning, learning, social development, special educational needs

An understanding of child development that occurs from birth to adulthood was largely ignored throughout much of history. Children were often viewed as small versions of adults and little attention was paid to the many advances in cognitive abilities, language use and physical growth that characterised their maturing. Close interest in the field of child development began early in the twentieth century and tended to concentrate on those exhibiting abnormal behaviour. There were a number of key theories proposed, including those of Sigmund Freud, who stressed the importance of childhood events and experiences but almost exclusively focused on mental disorders rather that normal functioning. By contrast, Erik Erikson believed that each stage of development is focused on overcoming a conflict, such that success or failure in dealing with conflicts can impact overall functioning. Theorists such as Watson, Pavlov, and Skinner dealt only with observable behaviour rather than the thinking

and reasoning that underpinned it; thus, development is considered a reaction to rewards, punishments, stimuli and other reinforcement (such as praise). John Bowlby believed that early relationships with caregivers play a major role in child development and continue to influence social relationships throughout life (About.com, on-line).

Jean Piaget (1896–1980) is, however, probably the one name that most primary educators think of when considering child development. Jean Piaget suggested that children think differently from adults and proposed a stage theory of cognitive development. He was the first to note that children play an active role in gaining knowledge of the world and considered the most critical factor in a child's cognitive development to be interaction with peers. Piaget's approach is central to the school of cognitive theory known as 'cognitive constructivism'. Atherton (2005) notes that although Piaget was a biologist by training, he began to study the development of children's understanding through observing them and talking and listening to them while they worked on exercises he set. Piaget particularly stressed the role of maturation (simply growing up) in children's increasing capacity to understand their world, and proposed that children's thinking does not develop smoothly but rather that there are certain points at which it moves into completely new areas and capabilities, broadly:

- Birth to 18 months/2 years is called the Sensori-motor stage
- 2 years to 7 years, the Pre-operational stage
- 7 years to 11 years, the Concrete Operational
- 11 years and older, the Formal Operational stage.

The theory has been interpreted to mean that before children reach these ages they are not capable of understanding things in certain ways; it has been used as the basis for organising the school curriculum. Also, as Wood

(1998) argues, it follows that the impact of lessons taught by parents or teachers also varies as a function of a child's developmental stage. Thus, 'a major implication of the theory is that the effects and effectiveness of teaching are fundamentally constrained by the structure of the child's intelligence' (p. 38). However, evidence suggests that Piaget's scheme is too rigidly structured because (notably) many children manage concrete operations earlier than the Piagetian model. Similarly, some people never function at the level of formal operations or are not called upon to use them.

While Piaget is associated with constructivism, theorists such as Len Vygotsky (1896–1934) and Jerome Bruner (born 1915) are known as 'social constructivists' because they place more emphasis on the part played by language and the influence of other people in enabling children to learn. Thus, Vygotsky argued that mature mental activity involves 'self-regulation' that develops by means of social interaction. Consequently, instruction and schooling play a central role in helping children to discover how to pay attention, concentrate and learn effectively. Vygotsky's theory presents a view that a more experienced 'partner' – another child or an adult – can provide help to the less knowledgeable partner in the way of an intellectual scaffold, which allows the less experienced learner to accomplish more complex tasks than is possible alone. Like Vygotsky, Bruner asserts that the process of constructing knowledge of the world is not done in isolation but rather within a social context. He argues that 'there is no unique sequence for all learners, and the optimum in any particular case will depend upon a variety of factors, including past learning, stage of development, nature of the material and individual differences' (Bruner 1966, p. 49).

Sources

About.com, *Child Development Theories*, on-line at http://psychology.about.com/od/developmental psychology/a/childdevtheory.htm

Atherton, J. (2005) *Piaget*, on-line at www.learning andteaching.info/learning/piaget.htm
Bruner, J.S. (1966) *Toward a Theory of Instruction*, Cambridge MA: Belknap Press of Harvard University Press.
Wood, D. (1998) *How Children Think and Learn*, London: Wiley-Blackwell.

CHILD WELFARE

See also: bullying, caring teachers, circle-time, Every Child Matters, physical comfort, pupil perspectives, teacher–pupil interaction

All teachers must have a working knowledge and understanding of their professional duties, legal liabilities and responsibilities, together with an awareness of the extent and limits of their duty towards the pupils. Children in the UK are protected by the Children Act (1989, updated in 2004), which requires that adults do not exert unreasonable psychological pressure upon them, such as shouting in their faces, hectoring or using physical chastisement and force. There are obvious exceptions to this rule; for instance, screaming out loud may be the only means of preventing a child running into the road; physical containment may be the only way to prevent one child from injuring another. A further significant intention of the Act was to encourage integrated planning, commissioning and delivery of services to children, as well as improve multi-disciplinary working (notably liaison between Education and Social Services) and to improve the coordination of individual and joint inspections in local authorities. These sentiments are expressed explicitly in the *Every Child Matters* legislation (DfES 2005).

Despite all the efforts to protect children and train teachers to spot 'danger signs', it is a regrettable fact of life that there will always be children whose lives are made miserable or worse by uncaring, ignorant or callous adults. A UNICEF report (2007) accused the UK of failing its children, as it came bottom of a league table for child well-being across twenty-one industrialised countries. UNICEF looked at forty indicators from the years 2000–2003 including poverty, family relationships, and health. One of the report's authors commented that under-investment and a 'dog-eat-dog' society were to blame for Britain's poor performance. No doubt partly in response to the criticism, the updated version of the *Children's Plan: Building brighter futures* (DCSF 2009) was published as a strategy to make England the best place in the world for children and young people to grow up. The plan stresses the importance of children's trust in forging collaborative partnerships, improving integration of services and delivering measurable improvements for all children and young people (see also Roffey 2006a). However, in 2009 a report on young people's well-being by researchers at York University, England, on behalf of the Child Poverty Action Group (CPAG) placed the United Kingdom in twenty-fourth position in a table of twenty-nine European states plus Norway and Iceland.

The Anti-Bullying Alliance (ABA, www. anti-bullyingalliance.org.uk) was founded in 2002 by the National Society for the prevention of Cruelty to Children (NSPCC) and National Children's Bureau. The alliance brings together over fifty organisations into a single network with the aim of reducing bullying and creating safer environments in which children and young people can live, grow, play and learn. The *Good Childhood Study* (published in February 2009, chaired by Lord Layard and commissioned by the Children's Society) reports some stark and telling findings about children's experience of childhood. One of its key findings was that excessive individualism and the aggressive pursuit of personal success needs to be replaced by a value system in which people seek satisfaction from helping others – reflecting the UNICEF criticisms noted above. The development of personal, social and health education (PSHE) and social and emotional aspects of learning (SEAL) in England has helped to develop positive attitudes, address issues of significance to children and stimulate an active interest in society and citizenship.

There are many occasions when a teacher develops a more intimate atmosphere by gathering the children together in a smaller, well-defined area in which they can all sit comfortably. The children sit in a circle with the teacher to discuss key issues, share ideas and celebrate events (e.g. Roffey 2006b). Some teachers stand at the door and say a personal goodbye to each child; others have small rituals, such as using a chant or singing a farewell song before they leave.

Advice from the UK government in its web site 'Directgov' (www.direct.gov.uk) includes first aid, medical needs and security in schools; contacting the school and the complaints procedure; support available if parents are struggling to get their children to school; dealing with bullying; school discipline and exclusions; the school's role in protecting children from abuse; the law concerning school attendance; and the role of schools and local authorities in supporting children with medical needs.

Sources

DCSF (2009) *Children's Plan: Building brighter futures*, London: HMSO.

DfES (2005) *Every Child Matters: Change for children*, London: HMSO.

Roffey, S. (2006a) *School Behaviour and Families: Frameworks for working together*, London: David Fulton.

——(2006b) *Circle time for Emotional Literacy*, London: Paul Chapman.

UNICEF (2007) *The State of the World's Children*, on-line at www.unicef.org/sowc07

CHILDREN

See also: behaviour, child welfare, early years, happiness, memory and memorising, motivation (pupils'), play, pupil perspectives, social development, teachers' beliefs, values

There is a longstanding joke among primary teachers that if it were not for the children the job would be wonderful. In truth, every survey about teacher motivation shows clearly that working with children is at the top of the list, which is good news for every parent and pupil. Although people working with secondary-aged pupils often refer to them as 'kids', adults working with primary pupils prefer the word 'children'. Few teachers opt for the UK government's tendency to refer to all students of whatever age as 'learners'. A generation ago it was common to hear primary teachers say that they taught children, not subjects, though many twenty-first-century education strategists and politicians would react with horror to such a statement. Nevertheless, most of today's primary teachers confide that, secretly, they still adhere to their forebears' axiom of putting the 'whole child' ahead of narrowly focused academic goals.

Smidt (2006) reminds us that 'it was only towards the end of the 20th century that the view of children as social beings – as players in their own life stories – began to be accepted as a principle' (p. 12). She quotes from the UN Convention on the Rights of the Child, which states that children should be encouraged to express their views freely and given the opportunity to be heard, especially in decisions that relate to life decisions. However, experience suggests that this sort of perspective cannot be taken for granted within each home or even within each classroom. The edict that 'children should be seen and not heard' still has many supporters, notably regarding very young children, who are not considered capable of offering a considered opinion. However, from their study of pre-school children, Corriveau et al. (2009) conclude that children as young as age three and four hold opinions and are able to recognise and trust a consensus. Lancaster and Broadbent (2003) note that the importance of listening to children is increasingly being recognised and recent developments across children's services in education, health and social welfare have reinforced the value that government and service providers place on this basic human right. Clark et al. (2005) examine critically how listening to young

children who are in the care of social services is understood and practised. The authors explore how adults listen to young children; the view of the child that different approaches to listening presume; and the risks that listening might entail for young children. However, based on a case study of 'looked after children', Leeson (2007) warns about feelings of helplessness, low self-esteem and poor confidence that follow a lack of opportunities made available to them to make decisions about their own lives.

The vast majority of pupils love being at school. It gives them the opportunity to meet their friends, experience challenges, interact with stimulating equipment, contribute to collaborative ventures and work closely with a range of different adults, all of whom have a concern for them. It is difficult for adults to remember the excitement generated by special school events; the tingling associated with particular smells, sights and sounds; parents coming into school to see the teacher or listen to a presentation; and being made to feel special on a birthday. As we grow older, the imaginings of childhood are replaced by more pragmatic considerations and vain efforts to cram too much into too little time. Yet if teachers want to create a purposeful classroom environment, it is worth recalling some of the emotions, ideals and uncertainties which characterise childhood. Jackson (1987) argues that to make sense of school, children draw on past experiences and their own understandings. She reminds us that these perceptions 'may not necessarily match the perceptions of the teacher, for learning in school can be a very different thing from learning at home' (p. 86).

In Hayes (2009, pp. 92–93) I refer to the way in which children can be wildly enthusiastic for something that touches their hearts and intellects. They have reservoirs of ideas, interests and deep-seated desires that wait to be released. Their heads are full of fantasies, imaginings and extravagant notions about their own and others' lives. They are easily astonished, brimming with wonder and yearning to uncloak the mysteries that surround them. They will chatter incessantly about their hobbies, friends and pastimes. They bicker, dispute what is said, grapple with uncertainty and strive to make sense of their place in the world. The job of every adult is to capture this raw energy, harness the cauldron of fervour that lies quietly simmering in each child and provide the spark that produces motivation for learning.

It is also commonly held by primary educators that their pupils need to be allowed to behave like children and not like mini-adults. Thus, the opportunity to mix with their friends, laugh, sing, play and feel good about themselves is a means of promoting a purposeful learning environment, enhancing creativity and generating a sense of enjoyment (Jones and Wyse 2004). Adults working with children are also conscious of the fact that young lives are directly and significantly affected by their experiences outside the school with parents, siblings, relatives and friends, as well as in it. Children who arrive at school in an emotionally or physically distressed condition are very unlikely to make the most of their opportunities and require sensitive treatment, even when they are uncooperative or behave inappropriately. Similarly, a child who has a birthday or a special event is bound to be more excitable than usual and may behave out of character. Illness and disappointment can also take its toll, as children struggle to concentrate and apply themselves to their work. Sudden dips in performance may be due to children failing to work hard enough but can also be due to extrinsic factors over which they have little control. Wise teachers are alert to such possibilities.

Salo (2002) carried out research into adult's memories of their time in school and discovered that they recalled incidents that may seem trivial to adults but burn deeply into a child's consciousness. Respondents remembered these critical moments in detail, including the teacher's clothes, the expression on their faces and even the teacher's scent. In particular, moments of humiliation and guilt were powerfully engraved into the mind, as were times of delight and shared pleasures.

Teachers bear a heavy responsibility to ensure that pupils are provided with a secure learning climate and, in cases where children have to be disciplined or admonished, it is done so with forbearance and in moderation. Thomas Bray, a seventeenth-century Christian minister, said that we should never fear spoiling children by making them too happy because happiness is the atmosphere in which all good affections grow. Eaude (2006), writing from a child development perspective, emphasises the role of adult language and gesture in encouraging and caring for children. Thus, 'in comforting a child or sharing a moment of significance, unspoken messages, such as touch or a smile, are just as important as overt ones' (p. 94).

Children may not express their views openly to teachers but they do have insights about school life that affect their attitude to work as they interpret and misinterpret situations and circumstances. Cullingford (2008) comments that children prize highly the gift of insight, which is 'the security of understanding, of not having to guess what is required of them, of not being wrong-footed or humiliated by inadvertently doing the wrong thing' (p. 155). Teachers who make a habit of inviting children to express their views are often surprised by the perceptiveness and certainty of their comments.

Every child has moments of anxiety about things that may appear trivial to adults, who have a much fuller grasp of what is going on. Factors such as friendship patterns, anxieties about rougher children, fear of humiliation in front of the rest of the class, embarrassment about getting changed for PE, dread of the water in swimming and being labelled as slow, can all disturb and worry a child. Older children are anxious not to lose face and desperately want to be included with the majority group. This desire to be included explains in part the 'gang' culture that pertains among those of junior age. Younger children nearly always want someone to play with, though occasionally an aloof or an autistic child may be insistent about being left alone.

Regardless of age, all children want to be valued, respected and treated fairly. The UK government has recognised the significance of these social, physical and emotional factors and introduced the *Every Child Matters* (DfES 2005) legislation into schools, whereby every child should be offered the support that they need to be healthy, stay safe, enjoy life and achieve, make a positive contribution and (rather oddly) achieve economic well-being. The emphasis upon recognising 'gifted and talented' children acknowledges the fact that they not only progress at different rates but also possess particular and unique abilities that require exposing and nurturing. Teachers faced with implementing a blanket curriculum have to take account of these variations and anomalies.

It is a sad fact that an increasing number of children suffer from a variety of stressful conditions and a report by the Children's Society in its *Good Childhood Inquiry* – the first independent UK enquiry of its kind – suggested that more than a million children had mental health problems ranging from depression and anxiety to anorexia. The research, conducted between 2006 and 2008 and headed by Stephen Scott, professor of child health and behaviour at the Institute of Psychiatry, King's College London, found that many children felt under pressure to have the latest toys and clothes and were left anxious and depressed if they were unable to keep up with trends. In a subsequent book based on the survey (Layard and Dunn 2009), the authors argue that the greatest threat to children is the present focus on excessive individualism and a belief among adults that individuals should make the most of their own life, rather than contribute to the good of others. The findings broadly coincided with a UNICEF report – *Child Poverty in Perspective: An overview of child wellbeing in rich countries* (UNICEF 2007) that compared the quality of children's lives in twenty-one of the world's richest

countries. Despite its wealth, the UK came out as the worst place to be a child. The report showed that child poverty is a problem in the UK because money isn't distributed fairly, such that many children cannot afford basic things that others take for granted. Young people in the UK came bottom of the league table for relationships with friends and families, and were least likely to find other young people kind and helpful. Thirty-six per cent of young people in the UK said they have been bullied recently and almost 44 per cent had been in a fight at some time during the year. More than 20 per cent of young people claimed that their health was only fair or poor, which was a higher proportion than in any other country.

Sources

Clark, A., Kjorholt, A.T. and Moss, P. (2005) *Beyond Listening: Children's perspectives on early childhood services*, Bristol: Policy Press.

Corriveau, K.H., Fusaro, M. and Harris, P.L. (2009) 'Going with the flow: Preschoolers prefer nondissenters as informants', *Psychological Science*, 20 (3), 372–77.

Cullingford, C. (2008) 'A fleeting history of happiness: Children's perspectives', *Education 3–13*, 36 (2), 153–60.

DfES (2005) *Every Child Matters: Change for children*, London: HMSO.

Eaude, T. (2006) *Children's Spiritual, Moral, Social and Cultural Development*, Exeter: Learning Matters.

Hayes, D. (2009) *Primary Teaching Today*, London: Routledge.

Jackson, M. (1987) 'Making sense of school' in Pollard, A. (ed.) *Children and Their Primary Schools: A new perspective*, Lewes: Falmer Press.

Jones, R. and Wyse, D. (2004) *Creativity in the Primary Curriculum*, London: David Fulton.

Lancaster, Y.P. and Broadbent, V. (2003) *Listening to Young Children*, Maidenhead: Open University Press.

Layard, R. and Dunn, J. (2009) *A Good Childhood: Searching for values in a competitive age*, London: Penguin.

Leeson, C. (2007) 'My life in care: Experiences of non-participation in decision making processes', *Child and Family Social Work*, 12 (3), 268–77.

Salo, U. (2002) 'What a teacher! Students write about teachers', BERA Conference, September 2002, Exeter, England.

Smidt, S. (2006) *The Developing Child in the 21st Century*, London: Routledge.

UNICEF (2007) *Child Poverty in Perspective: An overview of child wellbeing in rich countries*, Innocenti Research Centre, Report Card 7.

CHILDREN AND YOUNG PEOPLE'S WORKFORCE STRATEGY 2020

See also: Every Child Matters, external agencies, life skills

In December 2008 the government in England published its *Children and Young People's Workforce Strategy 2020*, which set out a vision that everybody who works with children and young people should be (a) ambitious for every child and young person, (b) excellent in their practice, (c) committed to partnership and integrated ('inter-agency') working, and (d) respected and valued as professionals. The aim was to ensure that the workforce has the skills and to help children and young people develop and succeed across the five outcomes that define Every Child Matters; that is, being safe, staying healthy, enjoying and achieving, making a positive contribution and achieving economic well-being.

CHILDREN'S QUESTIONS

See also: learning climate, problem solving, pupil perspectives, questions and questioning

All children have an innate capacity for solving problems, part of which involves asking questions. They develop a variety of strategies to make hypotheses, play with ideas, try things out, analyse what happens or fails to happen, identify patterns, generate rules, use analogies, reach conclusions and either try again or attempt something different (Smidt 2006). Problems that intrigue children may not have the same fascination for adults. Children wonder why raindrops don't hurt when they fall such a long way out of the sky, why car brakes squeak and how many apples are on a tree. They also ask profound questions, such as what makes people cry when they are happy. Even quite young children sometimes ask deeply philosophical questions, such as why some people are bad and some are nice.

It is a challenge for early years educators to realise that on starting school, children who have been asking a constant stream of questions at home or in pre-school settings ask very few questions, in the ratio of approximately 10:1 in favour of home (Tizard and Hughes 1984). Furthermore, the questions that children ask adults in school tend to be ones that seek clarification about what should be done or gaining permission for a certain action (such as going to the toilet). By contrast, teachers and assistants ask pupils dozens of questions every day.

Teachers need to create a questioning environment rather than a passive one in which pupils suppress their own burning questions. Children ask more questions when they respect and trust the adults concerned and have been encouraged to take risks in learning. Some teachers organise opportunities for children to talk to their classmates about something of interest to them (such as a hobby) and then receive and answer questions. Regular events of this nature gradually help to increase pupil confidence and create a learning climate in which questioning is seen as an aid to understanding rather than an assessment tool or a source of humiliation (see Baumfield and Mroz 2004).

Sources

Baumfield, V. and Mroz, M. (2004) 'Investigating pupils' questions in the primary classroom', in Wragg, E.C. (ed.) *Reader in Teaching and Learning*, London: Routledge.

Smidt, S. (2006) *The Developing Child in the 21st Century*, London: Routledge.

Tizard, B. and Hughes, M. (1984) *Young Children Learning*, Princeton NJ: Harvard University Press.

CHILDREN AND TESTING

See also: assessment of learning, self-esteem (children), summative assessment, tests and testing

The commitment of the teacher to the pupil rather than merely to the subject being taught is of singular importance (Pollard and Filer 2001) but the commitment of the child to the process of learning is also important. Reay and Wiliam (1999) expose the way in which children respond to the present assessment regime. They point out how the damage to their self-esteem through perceived inadequacy (summarised by one child's negative comment about herself: 'I'll be a nothing') and the unforeseen social consequences of success (notably peer bullying of children deemed to be too capable). Their critique provides a timely reminder that the value of children cannot and should not be determined by their ability to respond to a written test.

Sources

Pollard, A. and Filer, A. (2001) 'Learning and pupil career in a primary school: The case of William', in Collins, J. and Cook, D. (eds) *Understanding Learning: Influences and outcomes*, London: Paul Chapman/Open University.

Reay, D. and Wiliam, D. (1999) 'I'll be a nothing: Structure and construction of identity through assessment', *British Educational Research Journal*, 25 (3), 343–54.

CIRCLE-TIME

See also: bullying, pupil perspectives, self-esteem (pupil), teacher role

Circle-time has its origins in the 'philosophy for children' approach originally advocated by Matthew Lipman to promote questioning, reasoning and dialogue. The circle-time approach, popularised by educationists like Jenny Mosley, involves children sitting in a semicircle to discuss issues, explore ideas, celebrate achievements or make decisions. The teacher is a part of the circle and sits on the same type of chair or cushion as everyone else. This helps to signal that what is happening is a special kind of classroom activity in which the teacher is a facilitator rather than a director. Circle-time depends on everyone

agreeing in advance about procedures (such as only one person speaking at a time) and conduct (such as speaking kindly). The basis of circle-time is that it is non-threatening (children only contribute when they wish to do so) and is intended to increase co-operation and allow for positive reinforcement, thus raising the self-image of every child. On other occasions, the time can be used for book sharing or reading aloud to the class or simply sharing the fun things that children have seen and done. For instance, a recent exciting television programme can stimulate great enthusiasm and promote speaking and listening skills. As with any other approach, the value of circle-time has to be monitored and evaluated to ensure that children are more confident as a result. The Anti-Bullying Network has produced a useful summary of the key aspects and implications of using circle-time (www.antibullying.net/circletimeinfo.htm).

CITIZENSHIP

See also: cross-curriculum, moral development, pupil perspectives, social and emotional aspects of learning, topic work

The introduction of a curriculum for citizenship in England and Wales in September 1992 was contentious, not least because there were suspicions that it was a subtle means of politicising education. However, Professor Bernard Crick, who reported to the government in 1998 on education for citizenship and the teaching of democracy in schools (Crick 1998), defined citizenship education as having three main strands: (1) social and moral responsibility, (2) political literacy, and (3) community involvement.

The citizenship programme for children aged 5–11 years is non-statutory but is incorporated into the programme of nearly all maintained (i.e. 'maintained through general taxation') primary schools. The Teachernet site (DCSF 2007) suggests that citizenship can be taken as a stand-alone subject or, ideally, be incorporated into traditional subjects like history, geography, art and science as well as design, media and ICT as a means of bringing the curriculum to life. Active citizenship at primary level can involve debate on issues such as friendship, loyalty, culture or stereotyping in familiar life contexts. Diane Hinds on the Schoolzone web site (www.schoolzone.co.uk) asserts that citizenship in terms of developing a moral sense in their pupils is simply another term for much of the work that good primary schools have always done, such as encouraging them to take responsibility for their actions and to behave towards others with consideration and respect.

The DCSF (Department for Children, Schools and Families) produced a citizenship scheme based on twelve individual units, including topics as diverse as choices, people who help us, and local democracy for young citizens. Under the banner of PSHE (personal, social and health education) and Citizenship, the NC non-statutory guidelines provide a framework for KS1 and for KS2 divided into twelve units. The guidelines are organised under (a) knowledge, skills and understanding, and (b) breadth of study, the first of which incorporates four sub-areas:

1 developing confidence and responsibility and making the most of their abilities;
2 preparing to play an active role as citizens;
3 developing a healthy, safer lifestyle;
4 developing good relationships and respecting the differences between people.

There are recommended cross-curricular links with other subject areas, such as science, design and technology, information technology, physical education, and history (Claire 2001, 2004). Older primary pupils have opportunities to take responsibility through activities such as assisting with the management of equipment or assisting younger pupils; producing a high quality practical product (in design technology, for instance), and giving a short presentation about an area of interest from outside school. The programme also gives pupils opportunities to make choices and decisions through meeting and talking to invited guests (e.g. older members of the community). Teachers of 10–11 year-old pupils use citizenship lessons to prepare children for significant changes in their lives, including moving to a new school.

Assessment of children's progression in citizenship is in terms of what knowledge and understanding most children should have to become informed citizens. Younger children should be able to respond to simple questions and explain their views and to listen to the views of others. Older children should develop the skills necessary to take part in discussions and debates, talk and write about their opinions, ask and respond to questions and understand different viewpoints.

You could be forgiven for thinking that if the non-statutory guidelines were followed thoroughly there would be little time for anything else to be included in the curriculum. In practice, a number of elements of citizenship are incorporated into assembly times, special projects (such as those dealing with neighbourhood issues, see Hicks 2001) and the warp and weave of daily school life that is governed by behaviour policy and inter-personal relationships. See Alderson (1999) for further insights into issues concerning children's rights.

Contributors to Lee and Fout's 2005 edited collection who employ teachers' perceptions from the USA, Australia, England, Russia and China about education for social citizenship remind us that the things teachers see as important in citizenship education, and how their perceptions facilitate or hinder the preparation of good citizens, varies across the globe according to prevailing social norms and political influences.

The Institute for Citizenship (www.citizen.org.uk/about.html) is an independent charitable trust to promote informed, active citizenship and greater participation in democracy and society through a combination of community projects, research, education, and discussion and debate.

Sources

Alderson, P. (1999) *Young Children's Rights: Beliefs, principles and practice*, London: Save the Children/Jessica Kingsley.

Claire, H. (2001) *Not Aliens: Primary school children and the Citizenship/PSHE curriculum*, Stoke-on-Trent: Trentham.

——(2004) *Teaching Citizenship in Primary Schools*, Exeter: Learning Matters.

Crick, B. (1998) *Education for Citizenship and the Teaching of Democracy in Schools*, London: QCA Publications.

DCSF Standards Site, *Citizenship at Key Stages 1 and 2*, on-line at www.standards.dfes.gov.uk/schemes2/ks1-2citizenship

DCSF Teachernet (2007) *Active Citizenship*, on-line at www.teachernet.gov.uk/teachingandlearning/library/activecitizenship

Hicks, D. (2001) *Citizenship for the Future: A practical classroom guide*, Godalming: World Wildlife Fund.

Hinds, D. in Schoolzone, *Making Good Citizens*, on-line at www.schoolzone.co.uk/resources/articles/Good_citizen.asp

Lee, W.O. and Fouts, J.T. (eds) (2005) *Education for Social Citizenship: Perceptions of teachers in USA, Australia, England, Russia and China*, Hong Kong: Hong Kong University Press.

CLASS CONTROL

See also: behaviour, discipline, expectations

The terminology used for class control issues varies but the word 'behaviour' tends to be used with respect to the child's actions and 'control' and 'discipline' with respect to the teacher's actions. That is, the teacher attempts to influence the child's behaviour through effective discipline in the belief that this is the most effective way of exercising control. In practice, controlling a child or group of children relies on a variety of factors, notably the strength of relationship and mutual respect, but also clarity of expectation, interest level of the work and even the time of day or time of year. Self-control is the aim but in the meantime, adults have to impose rules and enact procedures as a scaffold within which children can gradually learn to behave appropriately.

CLASS MANAGEMENT

See also: discipline, health and safety, organising for learning, physical comfort, planning, rules, time allocation in lessons

If organisation is the structure that facilitates effective teaching and learning, *management* is the means by which it is achieved. The word 'management' is derived from the root 'manage', a word that is used in a variety of expressions that emphasise a variety of outcomes through comments such as, 'If I manage to get there on time', 'She didn't quite manage the second question', and 'He should manage if all goes well'. By using such expressions we mean that a task was completed, not completed or unsatisfactorily completed. Wragg (2001) argues that successful primary teachers operate in many different ways, but the one thing they have in common is an ability to manage their classrooms effectively. Without mastering the skills required to achieve this aim, the most inspiring and knowledgeable teacher will fail. From a US perspective, Evertson *et al.* (2005) stress management of the planning decisions that teachers must make, including arranging the physical space; creating a positive climate; establishing expectations, rules and procedures; planning and conducting instruction; encouraging appropriate behaviour and addressing problems; and using good communication skills.

Teachers take three forms of management into account when they are in charge of a group or class of children: (a) time management, (b) information management, and (c) human management. There are underlying assumptions about each form:

Time management: That the person has taken responsibility to meet the deadline.

Information management: That the person is sufficiently well organised and informed.

Human management: That the person coped with the challenges presented by a class of children.

The significance of these three elements for teachers, who need to meet deadlines (such as finishing lessons on time), to be well informed (in particular, to have good subject knowledge) and cope with pupils (establishing and maintaining order) is considerable. Good *time management* establishes a framework for working, both within individual lessons and across a whole day. It allows for the quirks of classroom life and accommodates the unexpected. This type of flexibility does not mean that every moment is accounted for in the planning process or that pupils have to keep their 'noses to the grindstone', but rather that time is utilised purposefully. Good *information management* ensures that the teacher has a high level of subject knowledge and knows how to access additional sources of information as required (e.g. through the Internet; from colleagues). Teachers who are good at managing information will have the confidence to share ideas with pupils, show interest in their discoveries, monitor their understanding and encourage them to find out more by using their initiative. *Human management* involves finding ways of relating effectively to pupils and other adults and engaging them in the teaching and learning process. Human management is facilitated by clarifying boundaries of behaviour for pupils, using stimulating teaching approaches and presenting ideas in a comprehensible form. Good human managers respect people's genuine concerns and make allowances for their failings, such that the learning environment is characterised by a sense of well-being, mutual respect, high expectation and undisguised celebration of progress.

In designing tasks for groups, teachers must ensure that the children understand what is required of them and that they are offered ownership of ideas and given opportunity to interpret the task. The learning objectives have to be matched to pupils' abilities and the activity has to last sufficiently long to allow them to become fully involved, but not so long that they become discouraged or fed up.

In collaborative enterprises, decisions have to be made about which child from the group handles the resources, takes responsibility for recording results and reports back. In every situation, an essential part of lesson management is to keep noise levels suitably restrained and regulate the children's movements around the room.

Care must be taken over the siting of equipment, safety factors and maintenance of resources; there should be adequate space and light to allow pupils to engage with the task comfortably (Hayes 2003). Attention to practical detail pays dividends in facilitating a smooth-running lesson; for example, a tin full of blunt crayons is only a source of frustration. Systems should also operate in such a way that every child is given an equal opportunity to access equipment and 'have a go' at the exciting elements of the lesson.

At the end of the session, primary teachers are very adept in ensuring that straightforward and efficient procedures are in place to bring things to a smooth close, including clearing up and leaving the room in an orderly fashion. Laslett and Smith (2002) emphasise the four rules of class management: (1) get pupils into the classroom and start the lesson smoothly; (2) look ahead to the end of the lesson and have exit strategies to conclude positively and dismiss pupils in an orderly way; (3) ensure that the lesson is sufficiently varied to maintain interest, curiosity and motivation; and (4) develop mutual trust and respect and awareness of each child as an individual.

Sources

Evertson, C.M., Emmer, E.T. and Worsham, M.E. (2005) *Classroom Management for Elementary Teachers*, Needham Heights MA: Allyn & Bacon.

Hayes, D. (2003) *Planning, Teaching and Class Management*, London: David Fulton.

Laslett, R. and Smith, C. (2002) 'Four rules of class management', in Pollard, A. (ed.) *Readings for Reflective Teaching*, London: Continuum.

Wragg, E.C. (2001) *Class Management in the Primary School*, London: Routledge.

CLEGG, ALEC

See also: eleven–plus, Hadow reports, inclusion, Plowden Report

Alec Clegg (Alexander Bradshaw Clegg) was born on 13 June 1909 and died on 20 January 1986. While still in his forties, Clegg was West Riding's Chief Executive Officer and had served under two great directors of education of the early twentieth century – Sir Peter Innes in Birmingham and F.F. Potter in Cheshire – prior to becoming deputy CEO in Worcestershire and then A.L. Binns' deputy in the West Riding. Such was the reputation of Alec Clegg and his impact on all the educational provision of the West Riding, where he was chief education officer during the late 1950s and throughout the next decade, that teachers elsewhere were known to envy their colleagues in Clegg's county. To be a West Riding teacher, head teacher or local education authority (LEA) adviser was generally acknowledged as being at the forefront of educational practice. Clegg also chronicled the work of Steward Street School, Birmingham, in a Ministry of Education pamphlet 'Story of a school', published in 1949 with ministerial exhortation to primary teachers to imitate the good practice found there. The pamphlet formed a link between the Hadow Report in the 1930s and Plowden Report of 1967 by describing the reality of what the former had dreamt as possible and the latter had celebrated as best practice.

A body of significant educational research confirmed Clegg's own view that eleven–plus selection processes were flawed. An important initiative was the so-called 'Leicestershire experiment', which from 1957 saw the East Midlands area move uncertainly towards a system whereby all children in a locality transferred at age eleven to a three-year 'junior high' school. At fourteen, the brightest and best moved again to two-year Ordinary Level courses in a grammar school while the majority completed one final year of compulsory schooling in the junior high. The rise of middle schools was due in no small part to Clegg's astute understanding, which he transmitted to other local education authorities, that the political imperative of comprehensive reorganisation did not need to be at odds with the educational interests of middle years children.

By the time of Sir Alec Clegg's retirement in 1974, which coincided with the disappearance of the West Riding County Council as a result of local government reorganisation, middle schools still seemed to have a bright future. Many more LEAs were developing plans for three-tier reorganisations and the overall number of English middle schools continued to rise until a peak was reached at the beginning of the 1980s (Crook 2008).

Clegg was never happier than when visiting schools, where he was exceptionally perceptive in recognising genuinely good practice. After receiving his knighthood, he published his best known book, *About Our Schools*, in 1980, in which he made clear that personal relationships and a relevant curriculum was essential if schools were to avoid what he judged to be the 'folly' of concentrating solely on aspects of learning that are easily measurable. For example, he stressed the importance of children expressing their feelings in speech and writing; and he was among the first senior figures to recognise the importance of 'inclusion' (i.e. ensuring that all children were involved, regardless of disability) in subjects such as physical education. He was unimpressed by movement, dance and drama sessions in which children were merely imitating or performing the techniques in which the instructor had drilled them.

Clegg was especially keen that children be able to benefit from outdoor activities and educational visits that 'oiled the wheels of learning' and went 'beyond the textbook' as a means of increasing pupil motivation. Such was his regard for outstanding teaching that nothing pained him more than to observe outstanding teaching that had never been recognised. He encouraged a sense of collaborative creativeness about curriculum and teaching that provided a hallmark of the West Riding.

Sources

Brighouse, T. (2008) 'Sir Alec Clegg', *Education 3–13*, 36 (2), 103–8.

Clegg, A. (1980) *About Our Schools*, London: Blackwell.

Crook, D. (2008) 'The middle school cometh … and goeth: Alec Clegg and the rise and fall of the English middle school', *Education 3–13*, 36 (2), 117–25.

Newsam, P. (2008) 'What price hyacinths? An appreciation of the life and work of Sir Alec Clegg', *Education 3–13*, 36 (2), 109–16.

CLOSED QUESTIONS

See also: failure, open questions, questions and questioning, success, thinking time, understanding

A closed question is one that can be answered with either a single word or a short phrase; that is, there is only one or a very limited number of correct answers. Closed questions generally deal with basic facts rather than inviting opinions to be expressed at length; consequently, they are normally the easiest to ask and straightforward to answer. Teachers often used this questioning style when asking 'quick-fire' questions, such as answers to computations (e.g. multiplications). Where questions are used as a test of children's understanding, the pupil answering the question runs the risk of being wrong, which can discourage less confident children from responding. Closed questions can also be used in situations other than inquisitorial; for instance, questions may be an innocuous enquiry (e.g. 'Do you know where the building blocks were put?') or a confirmation (e.g. 'Is it all right if … ?'). Studies indicate that teachers ask a large number of closed questions, partly to ascertain the level of pupils' understanding, partly to interact with the children and partly to retain control over the proceedings.

COACHING

See *Peer coaching*

CODE OF PRACTICE

See also: assessing children's learning, curriculum, differentiation, inclusion, parental involvement, parents supporting learning, recording, SENCO, special educational needs

The duties of schools and teachers in England are clearly laid out in the special educational needs Code of Practice and the Special Needs and Disability Act or SENDA (2001), effective from January 2002. An equivalent Code operates in Wales but not in Scotland, which has different procedures. The Code outlines the framework for identifying, assessing and making provision for children's needs, though the actual assessment and teaching measures used are left for individual teachers and schools to devise. The Code is only concerned with interventions that are additional to or different from those provided as part of the school's normal differentiated curriculum.

The Code describes two stages at which a more focused assessment and provision operate, referred to as 'School Action' and 'School Action Plus'. At the level of *School Action*, teachers decide on the basis of working closely with a particular pupil and consultation with parents that further support is required for the child to make satisfactory progress in learning (see Beveridge 2004). The special educational needs coordinator (SENCO) in the school may advise that short-term support from outside agencies such as an educational psychologist or speech therapist is appropriate. Information about the child's academic progress is accumulated and evidence collected about previous educational initiatives, all of which is recorded on the child's personal record. Subsequently, an *individual education plan* (IEP) is produced specifying the educational strategy for the next stage of the pupil's education. *School Action Plus* involves a request for longer-term assistance from external agencies following a decision made by the SENCO and colleagues, in consultation with parents. Subsequently, a range of specialists may be approached and involved, depending on the nature of the need, and a new IEP is produced. As the IEP is reviewed and monitored, the school may request a statutory assessment from the local education authority if the pupil has demonstrated a significant cause for concern. This assessment process may lead to a formal statement of special educational needs that will specify the additional support required or, in some cases, a move to specialist provision from outside the school (see Farrell 2003). At this stage it is necessary to define more specifically the nature of the child's special need to facilitate decisions about the most suitable level of provision, though pre-school identification and assessment of children should have alerted teachers to those most at risk (Spencer 2004).

Provision for special educational needs in Northern Ireland has similarities to the system in England, but the Department for Education Northern Ireland (DENI) is the governmental body with responsibility for education policy. In addressing the needs of all pupils who experience learning difficulties, the code for Northern Ireland recognises that there is a continuum of needs and a continuum of provision, which may be manifested in a variety of forms, such that pupils require the greatest possible access to a broad and balanced education including the curriculum. As far as possible it is expected that the needs of most pupils will be met in mainstream schools with or without a statutory assessment, taking into account the wishes of their parents. Procedurally, support for children with SEN in Northern Ireland is subject to a five-stage system in which stages 1–3 are school-based, while at stages 4 and 5 the Board becomes responsible for providing the support. Some children may proceed through all the stages, whereas others may remain at one particular stage. Children can commence receiving help at any point across the stages and may go onto the next stage or revert to a previous stage. There is no specific length of time that a child can spend at any particular stage.

The SEN Code of Practice for Wales emphasises the individuality of each child rather than placing them into rigid categories. Nevertheless, special needs are categorised under one or more of the following four areas:

1 *Communication and interaction*: speech, language and communication difficulties.
2 *Cognition and learning*: learning difficulties which range from moderate to profound.
3 *Behavioural, emotional and social*: this includes a range of different behaviour including things like withdrawal, disruption, hyperactivity, lacking in concentration and social skills.
4 *Sensory, physical or medical*: includes difficulties related to impaired vision or hearing and other physical disabilities.

On 14 November 2005 a new law in Scotland, the Education (Additional Support for Learning) (Scotland) Act 2004, replaced the law relating to special educational needs. The Act introduced *Supporting Children's Learning – Code of Practice 2005* and marked a significant shift in the way children are supported to comply with the purpose of ensuring that all children and young people are provided with the necessary support to help them work towards achieving their fullest potential. It also promotes collaborative working among all those supporting children and young people. Under the new law, any child who needs more or different support from what is normally provided in schools or pre-schools is said to have 'additional support needs'. Even if children are not considered to have special educational needs, they can still obtain additional support if the following issues affect their education:

- social or emotional difficulties;
- behavioural difficulties;
- problems at home;
- bullying;
- being particularly gifted;

- sensory impairment or communication problem;
- physical disability;
- learning difficulty;
- being a young carer;
- moving frequently;
- having English as an additional language (EAL).

Sources

Beveridge, S. (2004) *Children, Families and Schools: Developing partnerships for inclusive education*, London: Routledge.

Farrell, M. (2003) *The Special Education Handbook*, London: David Fulton.

Spencer, C. (2004) *Handbook for Pre-School SEN Provision: The code of practice in relation to the early years*, London: David Fulton.

Talking Point, *SEN Provision in Scotland* and *SEN NI*, both accessed via www.ican.org.uk/talking point

COGNITIVE MAPPING

See also: concepts, cross-curriculum, learning

Concept mapping is a process of visually representing ideas to aid memory and understanding and to help children see that knowledge is linked across subject boundaries. It assists pupils in organising ideas such that they can make better sense of their immediate world. Joseph D. Novak of Cornell University was among the first people to study seriously the concept mapping technique, based on the theories of David Ausubel, who stressed the importance of prior knowledge in being able to learn about new concepts (Ausubel 1963). A concept is here defined as a perceived regularity in events or objects, or records of events or objects that can be designated by the use of a label. Novak, working largely in the field of science (Novak 1991), concluded that meaningful learning involves the assimilation of new concepts and propositions into existing cognitive structures, resulting in a concept map, consisting of a graphical representation where nodes (points or vertices) represent concepts

and links (arcs or lines) represent the relationships between concepts. The links between the concepts can be one-way, two-way or non-directional. The concepts and the links may be categorised, and the concept map may show temporal ('time-related') or causal relationships ('cause and effect') between concepts. Novak provides a helpful summary of key issues on-line at https://www.msu.edu/~luckie/ctools. See also Plotnick (1997).

This type of cognitive mapping is also known as concept mapping, semantic mapping, knowledge mapping, word webbing, networking, clustering, think-links, idea branches, structured overviews and graphic organisers (Fisher, 1995). Graphic organisers include sequences of key words or pictures, Venn diagrams (overlapping circles containing key words, some of which are distinctive and others which are shared); sets of words or pictures; and rank ordering of terms (e.g. with respect to their size, significance or frequency). Cognitive/concept mapping became popular in school through the process of 'brainstorming' – a somewhat discredited term because of possible offence to people with brain-affected conditions, in which children's ideas about a topic or theme are shown diagrammatically with physical links (lines, arrows) between them, gradually generating a spider's web effect.

Sources

Ausubel, D.P. (1963) *The Psychology of Meaningful Verbal Learning*, New York: Grune and Stratton.

Fisher, R. (1995) *Teaching Children to Learn*, Cheltenham: Stanley Thornes.

Novak, J.D. (1991) 'Clarify with concept maps', *The Science Teacher*, 58 (7), 45–49.

Plotnick, E. (1997) *Concept Mapping: A graphical system for understanding the relationship between concepts*, ERIC Identifier: ED407938, on-line at www.ericdigests.org/1998-1/concept.htm

COLLABORATION IN LEARNING

See also: circle-time, constructivism, enquiry, group work, listening, problem solving, talk, thinking skills

Collaboration in learning is the process by which pupils work together to reach a specified and predetermined learning objective, and is rooted in the theory of social constructivism advocated by theorists such as Lev Vygotsky and Jerome Bruner. Collaboration is different from, though closely linked with, co-operation, which is a general term for courtesy and thoughtfulness. Consequently, children may be co-operative while not collaborating, though effective collaboration relies on a high level of co-operation between pupils. However, even collaborative grouping can result in the exclusion of individual children from the process due to their insecurity, lack of experience as a group member or domination by the strongest characters. Collaboration is typically associated with investigative, enquiry-based tasks, whereas co-operation is associated with children working independently or in pairs but being mutually supportive while they do so. The relationship between these elements can be shown as follows:

- Investigative task/collaborative grouping/joint outcome.
- Independent tasks/co-operative grouping/separate outcomes.

There will be occasions when the teacher sets pupils to work in pairs or small groups initially, to report back some time later in the lesson, in which case a spokesperson from each group may be required to summarise ideas. If the purpose is to facilitate free-ranging discussion with children offering their ideas spontaneously, teachers clarify the rules of engagement and then try to enforce them consistently; for example, to wait until someone has finished speaking before offering an alternative perspective.

Fisher (2005, p. 92) suggests that collaborative work gives children the opportunity to benefit in five ways: (1) learning from each other; (2) engaging in exploratory talk to deepen or broaden their understanding; (3) developing problem-solving skills and strategies;

(4) learning to take turns, negotiate with others, see other points of view and argue for their own point of view; and (5) building relationships with a wider circle of people. He adds that it is to be expected that children working together will achieve more than working singly but that for collaborative groups to be successful they have to be planned, monitored and supported. Collaborative tasks require the active involvement of every child to achieve the desired learning outcome. Between them, pupils in a group need to offer a range of skills, principally the ability to speculate, predict, justify, evaluate and generalise. The joint activities do not detract from the principle that each child has a personal responsibility for learning, as no one can learn for somebody else; however, collaborating can assist others to extend and shape their understanding while collaborators reinforce their own learning. This process of engagement is sometimes referred to as a 'learning community' (for example, see Watkins 2005).

Collaborative learning can take a number of forms. The teacher can establish a practical problem-solving situation that relates to the existing curriculum work for the children to resolve; for example, children may be offered three possible ways to improve the tidiness of the playground. Teachers can also establish a theoretical problem-solving situation based on present curriculum work in which the members of the group have to discuss the options and arrive at an agreed solution or position on the matter. In this case, the teacher outlines the issues, invites preliminary comments from the children and presents them with the problem to be discussed in groups of (say) four or five children. For example, in the area of citizenship the issue may relate to an issue of fair distribution. Alternatively, the children can raise an issue about which they feel strongly with the teacher, who then helps them to shape their ideas into a proposition, which each group discusses. For example, children have firm opinions about friendship patterns, school rules, homework, children's television programmes, playground behaviour and associated topics, all of which provide fertile ground for exploring important principles. Teachers also need to consider ways to include children with special educational needs (see Jelly 2000).

One of the most difficult attitudes for children to develop is having an open mind, such that they do not summarily dismiss views, pour scorn on unusual suggestions or marginalise other children in the group. Children need to be shown that having different views about issues is perfectly admissible, providing there is evidence to support their assertions. Teachers have to stress with children the need for careful and respectful listening when working in pairs and in small groups, and as part of this preparation children can be taught to summarise what others have said and ask sensible questions about their ideas. The process of engaging mentally with a subject before offering an opinion or suggestion is a related skill that pupils need to develop before they can make an effective contribution to a collaborative venture. Allowing children opportunities to talk to others enables them to move outside their immediate world, to recognise life's complexities, to gain self-confidence, to learn from sharing ideas, to evaluate opinions and to find ways to offer support to their peers.

Sources

Fisher, R. (2005) *Teaching Children to Learn*, Cheltenham: Stanley Thornes.
Jelly, M. (2000) *Involving Pupils in Practice*, London: David Fulton.
Watkins, C. (2005) *Classrooms as Learning Communities*, London: Routledge.

COLLABORATION (STAFF)

See also: collegiality, curriculum leadership, decision-making, peer coaching

There is an element of collaboration ('working together as a team') built into the work of all teachers, so adeptness in this area is an essential skill as they liaise with colleagues to discuss educational issues and make decisions. Collaboration helps teachers to explore and interrogate taken-for-granted aspects of practice and might provide opportunities for them to challenge the prevailing orthodoxy. On a day-to-day level, teachers liaise constantly about relatively minor procedural matters to ensure the smooth running of their classes and the school in general. During regular team meetings of teachers, decisions are usually made about implementing a decision that impinges on classroom practice and in-service training priorities. Subject leaders and coordinators will usually consult with the head and other colleagues before presenting new ideas (e.g. about use of technology) and organising further training for staff. In recent years the concept of closely involving staff in making decisions has been labelled 'distributed leadership' to underline the point that decision-making does not reside with one person but can involve a number of staff at different times. See, for example, Harris (2008).

Teacher collaboration has to be authentic and not contrived (Hargreaves and Dawe 1990; Hargreaves 1994), conducted within agreed professional boundaries and pedagogically sound; that is, it must be manageable and beneficial for teaching. Much of what passes for collaboration may lack rigour and lapse into low-level debate when it has the potential to enhance the educational provision within the school. It is even possible that a group of teachers' desire to conform or worries about upsetting colleagues or the head teacher or parents may suppress more creative and spontaneous teaching ideas and suggestions for innovative practice that collaborative decision-making could provide. In practice, characteristics of both contrived collegiality and collaborative culture coexist in the majority of schools and other educational settings.

Cranston (2001) tracked two Australian primary schools in which both teachers and parents were closely involved in collaborative forms of decision-making. Despite the relatively positive findings reported for these schools, the evidence could not be used to provide firm assurance that greater collaborative involvement in schools by parents and teachers leads to improvement in learning or the quality of education. Cranston notes that the establishment of such links remains an important issue to pursue in the future, as teachers as well as parents struggle to balance increasing demands on their time and energies.

David (2008) argues that there is a growing body of evidence which suggests that when teachers collaborate to pose and answer questions informed by data from their own pupils, their knowledge grows and their practice changes. The author also insists that teacher collaboration does not occur naturally; it runs against prevailing norms of teacher isolation and individualistic approaches to teaching. Without specific training, teachers often lack the necessary collaboration skills as well as skills in collecting data, making sense of the information and figuring out its implications for action. Despite the validity of such concerns, Harris and Muijs (2004) insist that teachers are uniquely placed to influence the quality of teaching and learning and they are important gatekeepers to development and change. Thus, 'where teachers work together in meaningful partnerships, much can be achieved for the benefit of schools and the young people who learn there' (p. 140). Teacher-to-teacher peer coaching also contributes to the collaborative venture.

Sources

Cranston, N.C. (2001) 'Collaborative decision-making and school-based management: Challenges, rhetoric and reality', *Journal of Educational Enquiry*, 2 (2), 1–24.

David, J.L. (2008) 'What research says about collaborative enquiry', *Educational Leadership*, 66 (4), 87–88.

Hargreaves, A. (1994) *Changing Teachers, Changing Times: Teachers' work and culture in the postmodern age*, London: Cassell.

Hargreaves, A. and Dawe, R. (1990) 'Paths of professional development: Contrived collegiality, collaborative culture, and the case of peer coaching', *Teaching and Teacher Education*, 6, 227–41.

Harris, A. (2008) *Distributed School Leadership: Developing tomorrow's leaders*, London: Routledge.

Harris, A. and Muijs, D. (2004) *Improving Schools Through Teacher Leadership*, Maidenhead: Open University Press.

COLLABORATIVE PROBLEM SOLVING

See also: discussion, group work, problem solving, teaching approach

In organising and managing children's learning, many teachers promote collaborative problem solving and investigations in areas such as science, information technology, mathematics and design technology, and in resolving ethical dilemmas. Teachers sometimes give specific roles to members of the group (such as chairperson, secretary, scribe, time-keeper) though it is normally more successful to allow children to sort themselves out or take turns in the different roles. As with discussion and debate, teachers have a responsibility to encourage all children to participate, to discourage some pupils from dominating the talk and generate sufficient enthusiasm for children to feel that their efforts are worthwhile. Time has to be allowed for feedback from selected children from each group and, where appropriate, questions and comments. The wisdom and efficacy of the moral choices that teachers make to ensure fairness and equity are major factors in determining the quality of a teacher's relationship with pupils.

COLLECTIVE WORSHIP

See *Assembly*

COLLEGIALITY

See also: collaboration, decision-making, effectiveness, head teachers, pupil perspectives

The concept of collegiality, based on the root word 'college' to signify a society of scholars or an association of likeminded people, has become an integral feature of school life. Since the early 1980s the role of parents and school governors/board members in helping to shape priorities and determine the direction of education has been enshrined in legislation. A belief that the head of the school has to take full responsibility for all the decisions that take place in a primary school is an outdated one. In fact, head teachers require and seek as much assistance as possible in the complex task of leading a school and ensuring its success (see, for example, Bragg and Fielding 2005). Effective schools are places where teamwork and staff loyalty are embedded into the fabric of everything that takes place, and teachers therefore need to be as sensitive to corporate endeavour and teamwork as to the technical competence to teach. Adults in school respond to genuine expressions of appreciation and considerateness from colleagues, thereby creating a bank of goodwill and strong feelings of camaraderie that are essential for effective teamwork.

Crucial to the ultimate success of any organisation is the commitment, motivation and satisfaction of the people who work there. In a primary school there are many more adults involved in educational provision than in the past, each person with a stake in its future and a specific contribution to make. The role that teachers have in maintaining staff harmony and promoting collegiality is a key part of their identity, but the busier they become the less time is available to provide support and encouragement for their colleagues. New members and inexperienced members also become part of this company of people and their work is constantly open to scrutiny and evaluation, so they must learn to view colleagues and their advice as a helpful means of improving their overall competence. Nias et al. (1989), Mills and Mills (1995) and Vincett et al. (2005) offer different and useful perspectives on the constructive inclusion of colleagues in school.

Collegiality goes deeper than the mere establishment of systems and hierarchies. It is primarily rooted in the active participation of staff members in such a way that they feel that their views on school priorities are welcome and taken seriously. It is not practical or desirable for every decision to be discussed and affirmed by every member of the staff. However, leaders in primary schools in which collegiality is genuinely espoused ensure that all major decisions are taken with full or majority support. Teachers are comfortable with a collegial approach if they feel that their views are not only sought but also taken into account when decisions are being made. Teachers are unimpressed with a situation in which a head teacher declares an intention to involve everyone but to all intents and purposes makes the decision in isolation. Hargreaves and Dawe (1990) refer to such a situation as 'contrived collegiality'. See also Hayes (1996) for a primary school case study exposing this phenomenon.

Most schools also have methods for canvassing pupils' views about a range of issues affecting them by establishing forums, school councils (composed of pupil representatives) or in-class discussions to provide feedback.

Sources

Bragg, S. and Fielding, M. (2005) 'It's an equal thing – it's about achieving together', in Street, H. and Temperley, J. (eds) *Improving Schools Through Collaborative Enquiry*, London: Continuum International.

Hargreaves, A. and Dawe, R. (1990) 'Paths of professional development: Contrived collegiality, collaborative culture, and the case of peer coaching', *Teaching and Teacher Education*, 6, 227–41.

Hayes, D. (1996) 'Taking nothing for granted: The introduction of collaborative decision-making in a primary school', *Educational Management and Administration*, 24 (3), 291–300.

Mills, J. and Mills, R.W. (1995) *Primary School People: Getting to know your colleagues*, London: Routledge.

Nias, D.J., Southworth, G.W. and Yeomans, R. (1989) *Staff Relationships in the Primary School: A study of school cultures*, London: Cassell.

Vincett, K., Cremin, H. and Thomas, G. (2005) *Teachers and Assistants Working Together*, Maidenhead: Open University Press.

COMMUNICATION

See also: interaction, learning, oracy, Primary National Strategy, speech clarity, teacher role

The development and use of communication and language are at the heart of young children's learning. Learning to listen and speak emerges out of non-verbal communication, which includes body language such as facial expression, eye contact, bending the head to listen, hand gesture and taking turns. These skills develop as babies and young children express their needs and feelings, interact with others and establish their own identities and personalities. As children develop speaking and listening skills, they build the foundations for reading and writing. They need lots of opportunities to interact with others as they develop these skills, to use a wide range of resources for making early progress in reading, mark making and writing.

Every adult working in primary education needs to possess strong interpersonal and communication skills exercised within a climate of patience, flexibility and dependability. Effective communicators are characterised by being able to make decisions with confidence, demonstrate a willingness to ask for help when needed and be open to suggestions and ideas. Adults in school have to persevere to interact with pupils and with one another by using supportive and courteous comments, avoid confrontation by being sensitive to other people's viewpoints and show sympathy for a position even if disagreeing with it, recognising that impressions are constantly being created through use of voice tone, gesture and attitude to what is being said.

One helpful strategy in achieving this aim is for teachers to learn children's names as quickly as possible, as the use of a name is a powerful tool in establishing and maintaining strong links with each individual. In communicating ideas to pupils, teachers have to take account of their age and maturity by using appropriate vocabulary, explaining things calmly and carefully, and encouraging them

to ask questions. The Primary National Strategy in England (DfES 2005) suggests that the underlying principles to effective communication include positive relationships with children; an appreciation of appropriate behaviour and clear unambiguous communication with no 'hidden' messages. The 'language of belonging' and the 'language of choice' are particularly effective when adults are talking with children. Examples of helpful strategies include:

- Praise (sincerely saying well done)
- Affirmations ('You are doing the right thing')
- Positively stated expectations ('I want you to do this')
- Language of belonging ('We all want you to succeed')
- Language of choice ('You take responsibility for your own actions')
- Eye contact (direct but not aggressive)
- Safe physical contact (avoiding inappropriate touching)
- Appropriate body language (stance, gestures, facial expression)
- Voice tone (calm and firm).

Teachers and assistants need to have insight into the things that children find significant if they wish to create effective communication networks that will enhance learning and maintain good relations. Studies have found that there is a tendency for teachers to dominate conversations and neglect to allow pupils to express ideas, ask questions and raise issues. Indeed, one of the pioneers in this field, Douglas Barnes, warned that excesses of what he described as traditional teacher-led discussions 'tend to inhibit many children's active reshaping of knowledge' (Barnes 1975, p. 94). He recommended that pupils should take more control over their talk and writing (including potential audiences), while at the same time being supported by helpful adults.

Whatever the nature or intention of the communicative act, all teachers benefit from giving careful attention to a range of practical considerations, the first of which is audibility, which can be impaired by slurring of words and poor articulation. Teachers have to take account of the speed with which they talk, the frequency and length of pauses and the smoothness of their delivery. In this regard they need to bear in mind the likely significance of, and differences between, fast and confident speech. Fast speech can be used to disguise adult insecurity as it discourages interruptions and overwhelms the pupils with a flow of words; whereas confident speech is steady, rich in character and interesting. Effective teachers vary the speed of their delivery and use deliberate pauses while they establish extended eye contact. These skills are particularly important in communicating with slow learners and younger children; see, for instance, Lathan and Miles (2001) who explore the development of English (communication and literacy) for young children.

A change of pace to emphasise specific points and variations in inflection to indicate a conclusion (downward inflection) or invite speculation (upward inflection) can also be used to good effect. A selective use of pauses offers pupils the opportunity to think and can capture the children's attention if mixed with regular speech. However, the excessive use of pauses and hesitations, such as 'uhm' and 'like er' and 'you know' can irritate children. A further necessary skill is the ability to inject enthusiasm into the proceedings, transmitted through physical and mental energy, accompanied by appropriate gestures and the employment of dynamic verbs. In particular, using 'bright' eye contact engages pupils, indicates a personal interest in them and invites their participation; adopting an upright stance with good posture indicates alertness and a resolute disposition (Hayes 1998).

Communicating with parents is also an essential element of the educator's role, both formally through planned meetings to discuss pupil progress and give information about proposed events; and informally through casual encounters that happen before and after school. Parents, guardians and relatives of younger primary age pupils are most likely

to have regular informal contact with teachers and support staff as they accompany the children to and from school. Parents of older primary age children are more often constrained by their own employment commitments. One measure by which parents judge school staffs is the quality of their receptiveness, pleasant manner and willingness to offer helpful comment about the child's progress.

To explore issues relating to 'communication' as a broader concept, an extensive work edited by Wolfgang Donsbach (2008) covers areas as diverse as communication theory and philosophy; interpersonal communication; journalism; intercultural and inter-group discussions; media effects; strategic communication; media law and policy; media systems in the world; and ICT. In addition, the book by Hargie and Dickson (2004) offers a comprehensive overview about gaining and implementing skills in interpersonal communication.

Sources

Barnes, D. (1975) *From Communication to Curriculum*, Harmondsworth: Penguin.

DfES (2005) *Primary National Strategy: Classroom communication*, London: HMSO.

Donsbach, W. (ed.) (2008) *The International Encyclopaedia of Communication*, London: Blackwell.

Hargie, O. and Dickson, D. (2004) *Skilled Interpersonal Communication: Research, theory and practice*, London: Routledge.

Hayes, D. (1998) *Effective Verbal Communication*, London: Hodder & Stoughton.

Lathan, C. and Miles, A. (2001) *Communications, Curriculum and Classroom*, London: David Fulton.

COMMUNITY COHESION

See also: family and culture, home background and learning, Office for Standards in Education, parental involvement

Since September 2007, schools in England have had a duty to promote community cohesion. As part of their remit to maintain and raise standards in schools, the inspection body, OFSTED (Office for Standards in

Education, Children's Services and Skills), has to report on how they are contributing to community cohesion. The Department for Children, Schools and Families (DCSF) defines the key dimensions of community cohesion as working towards a society in which there is a common vision and sense of belonging by all communities; a society in which the diversity of people's backgrounds and circumstances is appreciated and valued; a society in which similar life opportunities are available to all; and a society in which strong and positive relationships exist and continue to be developed in the workplace, in schools and in the wider community. The Schools Linking Network (SLN) was established as a nationwide network in October 2007 to facilitate school linking and help schools to meet their duty to promote community cohesion (www.schoolslinkingnetwork.org.uk).

COMMUNITY SCHOOLS

A community school in England and Wales is a type of school that is run wholly by the local education authority, which is responsible for the school's admissions, owns the school's estate and employs the staff. In the USA, a community school is a public school (maintained through taxation) that acts as the hub of its community by engaging community resources to offer a range of on-site programmes and services to support the success of its pupils (students) and their families.

COMPASSION

See also: caring teachers, happiness, nurturing

Compassion can usefully be defined as feeling for the suffering of others that leads to sacrificial and selfless action as a means of relieving their condition. However, compassion should not be confused with pity or sympathy – which is an emotion devoid of action – or even with altruism, which is an action of helping others without necessarily feeling

love for them. Helping less fortunate people as a result of guilt or culture (e.g. contributing to a charity at the same time each year because everyone else does) is an act of duty, not compassion. The special significance of compassion in primary education is derived from the fact that studies of teacher motivation show that a desire to help children provides one of the major professional driving forces and is a source of considerable personal satisfaction.

Strategies that parents and educators use to develop compassion in children are based on a combination of information and specific action. Information is likely to include knowledge about the plights of children in poorer areas of the world, discussion about the needs of survivors from natural disasters and, closer to home, contact with local charities. Children benefit from having opportunities to talk about ways in which acts of loving kindness bring joy to the carer as well as the cared for; in doing so, adults provide a role model in demonstrating compassion, such as through involvement in community service. Some years ago, Cleife (1973) argued how 'a sense of obligation must be engendered in children and the kinds of feelings characteristic of mature and rational beings; feelings such as compassion, sympathy, respect for rules and other people' (p. 128). However, the author goes on to admit that these aims, though highly desirable, are not easy to foster in children, especially those deprived of a satisfactory social and moral climate at home.

As part of the curriculum to promote a caring attitude, teachers frequently tell gripping stories and explore folklore that promotes positive values or talk about heroes who were compassionate in their dealings. Teachers often use a contemporary or historically recent figure to illustrate principles about 'compassion in action', but it is likely that they will also include reference to exceptional instances, exemplified through (say) Elizabeth Fry (prison reformer), Florence Nightingale (nursing) and William Wilberforce (politician, abolition of slavery). Drew

(2002) insists that offering compassion is a magnanimous act; it requires us to see beyond our own needs, and open our hearts to another. Beran (2003) summarises the position nicely by saying that the teacher whose vision is sharpened by compassion helps to awaken those processes of self-culture that enable learners to develop their own gifts and aptitudes.

Sources

Beran, M.K. (2003) *Conservative Compassion versus Liberal Pity*, New York: City Journal, The Manhattan Institute.

Cleife, D.H. (1973) 'Authority', in Lloyd, D.I. (ed.) *Philosophy and the Teacher*, London: Routledge.

Drew, N. (2002) *Hope and Healing: Peaceful parenting in an uncertain world*, New York: Kensington.

COMPETITION

See also: parental involvement, rewards, sport, sports days, success, tests and testing

Competition has always existed between pupils in and out of school and will doubtless continue to do so. Parents may contribute to this competitive element when, for example, they ask their children which book they are reading and how it contrasts with other pupils in the class; compare reports with other parents; scan lists to see where a particular school is placed in a league table of performance and urge their children to work harder to gain better grades. During sports' days, parents cheer and urge their children to run faster, jump higher or get ahead of the others – see McMahon 2007 for a critique of the damaging effects of coercive methods to achievement. Older children can become extremely intensive about winning; for example, juniors become animated and exuberant about team games. In a study in which 152 five- to six-year-old children worked alone or in groups over a period of four weeks, both cooperatively and competitively, Lewis *et al.* (1999) noted that individualism versus collectivism

was a key factor. Although competition provides an important element of a pupil's desire to accomplish more and aspire to greater heights of scholastic and sporting achievement, children also need time to relax and have fun. Bigelow *et al.* (2001) stress the importance of allowing children to enjoy themselves while learning sports.

Competition has increased to achieve higher academic results. The introduction of extra classes to refine and rehearse and reinforce knowledge is commonplace in schools, including sessions that are run after hours for children to master weaker areas in English and mathematics and help them to improve their national test results. In addition, most pupils receive regular homework from the time they enter the formal school system. Out of school, some children are encouraged or cajoled by parents to undertake additional academic activities to ensure that they are one step ahead of their classmates and better placed to claim a place in the best schools, colleges and universities. Even very young children soon detect that one way to gain adult approval is to be performing near or at the top of the class. However, while excessive competition may be unsatisfactory, it is equally true that a lack of competitive stimulus often leaves pupils intellectually dissatisfied and underachieving, and can as easily damage their self-esteem as enhance it (Davies 1998). Healthy competition and a desire to win are commendable, as they provide an important training for the realities of life in the adult world. However, excessive competitiveness can be damaging to children's well-being; they need time to run, jump, dance, laugh, play and enjoy being children.

Sources

Bigelow, B., Moroney, T. and Hall, L. (2001) *Just Let The Kids Play: How to stop other adults from ruining your child's fun and success in youth sports*, Deerfield Beach FL: HCI Publishers.

Davies, N. (1998) 'Teaching for self-esteem versus behaviourism and competition', *Prospero*, 4 (1), 18–27.

Lewis, A., Simonds, L. and Maras, P. (1999) 'Elephants, donuts and hamburgers: Young children co-operating to co-operate and co-operating to compete in two primary schools', *Educational Psychology*, 19 (3), 245–58.

McMahon, R. (2007) *Revolution in the Bleachers*, New York: Gotham Books.

COMPLIANCE

See also: discipline, educated child, political involvement, synthetic phonics, teachers' beliefs, teaching profession

The UK government's desire to exercise tight control, not only over what is taught, but *how* it is carried out, has created a situation in which teacher professionalism is being transformed from a condition of autonomy to one of compliance (Hayes 2001). Yet the attempt to telescope all teaching and learning situations into a single model flies in the face of reason. Circumstances from school to school and class to class are so diverse that it is difficult to justify a policy that is so utilitarian that it takes little account of the immediate choices and decisions that all teachers have to make every working day. As Wrigley (2003) notes: 'Improvement by command from above results in the problematic implementation of macro initiatives by teachers who feel unable to question or even fine-tune them' (p. 103). More recently the government established two more working groups to advise on ways to ensure effective discipline in school and whether all primary schools should be 'strongly encouraged' to use an approach to reading known as 'synthetic phonics', which (predictably) has been translated into the new orthodoxy. Glossy pamphlets are issued, conferences organised, trainers mobilised and, within a short period of time, every teacher is inducted into the new approach. Objections are swept aside with reference to the 'extensive consultation', 'expert opinion' and 'education for the twenty-first century'.

It is difficult for schools to avoid being sucked into the compliance vortex that threatens to stifle initiative and restrict professional autonomy by refusing to trust teachers to act in pupils' best interest. Frowe (2005) reasons that while the amount of money invested in education necessitates accountability and monitoring of practice, 'the over-regulation of the profession is corrosive of many of its most valuable elements' (p. 52). Thus, if politicians were more willing to trust the soundness of teachers' professional ideologies, higher educational standards would be achieved than is possible through the present top-down attempts to force an illusion of improvement through unwelcome reforms. Assessments would be used as a means of celebrating success and revelling in the thrill of undiscovered knowledge. Educational progress would not be viewed in terms of children's ability to conform to predetermined learning pathways but as an exploration of territory that would be, for the child concerned, new and undiscovered.

One of the consequences of the move towards compliance has been to stifle open debate about pedagogy. The reason for this is simple. In order to achieve the outcomes that politicians consider a priority, they insist upon a pedagogy that is likely to secure those aims. Unsurprisingly, with the extensive resources that have accompanied their many curriculum innovations, the achievement targets that the government has set for pupils at different stages are generally being met (though there is a concern about reading standards). This success allows the government to claim that their interventionist strategies are effective, increasing the likelihood that it will introduce further reforms and ignore opposing voices. Schools, in the meantime, continue to be judged on the basis of their ability to respond to the government's priorities, as resistance invites tight monitoring by inspectors. If inspection results are unsatisfactory, a school can be deemed unsatisfactory and placed in 'special measures'; in extreme circumstances the school can be closed. Understandably, head teachers and governors are not willing to risk such sanctions and continue to comply with the government's wishes.

There is no doubt that many of the schools that succeed according to government criteria would do well under any circumstances, regardless of the political situation. The key point is, however, that the existence of a system in which schools are struggling to meet and maintain statutory requirements does not foster a climate of innovation and thoughtful debate about educational priorities.

Sources

Frowe, I. (2005) 'Professional trust', *British Journal of Educational Studies*, 53 (1), 34–53.
Hayes, D. (2001) 'Professional status and an emerging culture of conformity amongst teachers in England', *Education 3–13*, 29 (1), 43–49.
Wrigley, T. (2003) 'Is school effectiveness anti-democratic?' *British Journal of Educational Studies*, 51 (2), 89–112.

COMPREHENSION

See *Understanding*

COMPUTER SUITE

See also: computers in learning

Nearly every school in the UK has a computer suite, which is a room or part of a room dedicated to housing this form of technology. A considerable proportion of the national education budget has been used to ensure that all pupils and teachers in schools have access to a suite. Commonly, the computers are situated on worktops at an appropriate height for children, set out symmetrically around the room, thereby allowing supervising adults sufficient space to move about and offer guidance. Children frequently sit in pairs and take turns to use the computer keyboard. In some computer suite systems, the teacher is able to monitor children's use from a 'master' console. Groups and classes of children are allocated timetable space in the suite, which means that in practice the sessions are used to practise computing skills or work with a

specific piece of software, rather than extensive exploratory tasks that are more likely to require extended periods of time.

Computer suites provide only part of the total school computing resources and have some disadvantages compared with computers in or very close to classrooms, which free pupils and teachers to use them when and as needed. By contrast, computer suites are less accessible and can only be used at certain times of the day. Computer suites can also make it difficult for teachers to integrate ICT with other learning activities, as the suite is physically distanced from the immediate classroom resources. Teachers may, however, require access to more technological resources than are available in the average classroom and may not have sufficient space to locate computers properly; in addition, computers quickly become out of date or incompatible with other equipment; software has to be pedagogically sound and there are technical issues with keeping everything in working order.

COMPUTERS IN LEARNING

See also: computer suite, constructivism, creativity, gender, information technology, interactive whiteboard, kinaesthetic learning, literacy, social learning, teachers' beliefs

Computers are such an integral part of modern-day life that it would be astonishing if schools did not reflect the use of this technology in their teaching and learning programmes. A lot of money has been allocated to promote and fund the purchase of computers, and nearly every primary school in the UK has numerous machines and gadgets, and at least one person with special expertise to advise about them (teacher or teaching assistant). The majority of schools also have a purpose-built computer suite with sufficient machines for a large group or a class of children to use.

Enthusiasm among teachers about the appropriateness of computer technology for learning depends to an extent on the age range of pupils that they teach; teachers of younger primary age children who favour a more kinaesthetic ('hands-on') approach are less likely to see the need to incorporate computers into regular teaching than teachers of older age groups. It is also the case, of course, that older pupils have a better grasp of basic computer skills and may even be more competent than those who teach them. Hermans *et al.* (2008) also found that primary teachers' attitudes towards the use of computers in teaching varied considerably, depending on their educational beliefs. The results showed that teachers whose ideas were rooted in constructivism (i.e. that learners have to be helped to make sense of ideas through discussion, reflection, experimenting, sharing, etc.) were more positive about the classroom use of computers than teachers possessing more traditional beliefs (i.e. those who prefer to use more direct 'didactic' methods of teaching).

Computers appeal greatly to certain groups of children and seem to have a particular fascination for boys, pupils with learning difficulties and those who struggle to cope with conventional classroom routines. Although there is a danger of teachers using computers as a 'babysitting service' for unmotivated children, they can provide a powerful incentive and learning tool for them. An article in the *Times Educational Supplement* (TES 2008) reported on the use of a fantasy adventure game that motivated primary pupils, especially reluctant boy writers, and seemed to have a measurable impact on their literacy skills. The game was also used to promote creativity through the media of drawing, writing and discussion. It was reported that pupils were able to write at greater length, exhibited improved vocabularies and used more imaginative styles of writing.

Mumtaz (2001) found from a study of eight-year-old and ten-year-old children that they made more use of the computer at home than at school. The most popular activity on the home computer was playing games, whereas the most frequent activity in school was word-processing, which many pupils considered to be unappealing. Mumtaz also noted interesting gender differences in that boys spent more time playing computer games whereas girls spent more time emailing friends. The study concluded that schools should learn from what works at home and enable children to work on activities they find valuable, motivational and worthwhile.

Concerns have been expressed about the adverse effect on eyesight, social interaction – children, especially boys, may become isolated – and on physical posture. Berns and Klusell (2002) point out that there is a limited ergonomic knowledge among teachers and other responsible people working in schools, leading to two problems in particular. (Ergonomics is the study of ways to improve the relationship between workers and their environment to enhance productivity and minimise fatigue and discomfort.) There were two key factors: first, the physical strain children are exposed to when using computers due to bad workplace design; second, children's lack of awareness about the importance of ergonomic aspects in workplace design. Clearly, educators need to take such matters seriously but cannot legislate for the damage that may be done by children in their own homes.

There is also concern that children read at only half the speed and comprehend less on a standard computer screen compared with same words in traditional paper form. Anecdotal evidence suggests that the large increase in numbers of computers in Welsh schools has not led to improved performance in the classroom, though there were indications that the arrival of interactive whiteboards (IWBs) had helped to motivate disaffected students.

Sources

Berns, T. and Klusell, L. (2002) *Computer Workplaces for Primary School Children: What about ergonomics?* Human Factors and Ergonomics Society Annual Meeting Proceedings, Musculoskeletal Disorders, 415–18.

Hermans, R., Tondeur, J., van Braak, J. and Valcke, M. (2008) 'The impact of primary school teachers' educational beliefs on classroom use of computers', *Computers and Education*, 51 (4), 1499–1509.

Mumtaz, S. (2001) 'Children's enjoyment and perception of computer use in the home and the school', *Computers and Education*, 36 (4), 347–62.

TES (2008) 'Computer game helps to raise primary pupils' literacy skills', 25 April.

CONCEPTS

See also: mistakes and misconceptions, understanding

A concept is a word that has meaning and can be envisaged as a picture in the mind. Children may be asked to select a common concept (e.g. trees) and, singly or in pairs or small groups, think of as many other words that have some connection with it as they can. In time, children provide phrases and sentences to suggest (say) uses for trees, develop stories about them and argue for their preservation. Their ideas are visually represented through a list or chart or pictures or a 'web' diagram, subsequently made more orderly by the adult. A similar procedure can be followed after a teacher has introduced a topic or pupils have engaged in discussion about aspects of the theme to summarise key points. Teachers normally use what the children do to assess their understanding, note inconsistencies in their logic and correct misconceptions.

CONCLUDING LESSONS

See also: cross-curriculum, learning objectives, lesson organisation, lesson planning, lesson plans, lesson review, plenary

Concluding a lesson requires as much attention and careful consideration as any other aspect of the teacher's work and its smooth operation is essential to complete a session successfully. The lesson conclusion – popularly known as 'the plenary' – serves at least four purposes. First, it is used to finish tasks and activities or leave them at a suitable point for further development. It is often the case that the set tasks do not fit neatly into the time allocated for the session and need to reach a suitable point such that the pupils can continue or complete the work in the near future.

Second, the lesson conclusion is an opportunity to draw together the threads of learning. Pupils are encouraged to understand their own learning, see the purpose of the present work and grasp its implications in a wider context. The concluding minutes of the session can be used constructively to talk about such issues, share findings, celebrate successes and get disappointments and setbacks into perspective by emphasising that a lack of success is not the same as a failure.

Third, the conclusion is an opportunity to leave the room in good order. If the lesson is completed in the sense that the subject matter does not require further study or practice, the product of the session (written, numeric, graphic or otherwise) must be handed in for marking. If the lesson is incomplete there are decisions to make about the practicalities of storing the work. If the work is generated through a computer, it pays for the teacher to print it off later when the situation is less pressurised. If delicate 3D items or paintings are involved, storage is obviously more problematic; teachers find that the simple expedient of pupils writing their names on the product or a label to identify to be effective.

Finally, the conclusion offers a chance to look ahead. It is a chance for teachers to review the main learning objectives, the subsidiary objectives and fortuitous ('unanticipated') learning that have taken place with the pupils, but also to think about the next steps in the lesson sequence and where the present learning touches other areas, both in the subject area under consideration and, ideally, the links with other parts of the curriculum (cross-curricular). The more accurately teachers can determine the extent of pupils' learning in the immediate past, the better equipped they are to plan effectively for future sessions.

CONSTRUCTIVISM

See also: didactic teaching, group work, learning, problem solving, teaching approach, understanding, zone of proximal development

The theory of constructivism is associated with the work of Jean Piaget and represents one of the major theories of education, with major implications for how teachers teach and how children learn. Rather than a teacher passing on information and facts directly to pupils through a didactic form of teaching, constructivism suggests that the learner is much more actively involved in a joint enterprise with the teacher of creating ('constructing') understanding. A focus on pupil-centred learning is the most familiar and probably one of the most important contributions of constructivism in the education of primary-age children. Typically, children work in groups, discuss issues, problem-solve and investigate phenomena. *Social* constructivist theory – emerging from the work of Lev Vygotsky and Jerome Bruner – is closely related to constructivism but emphasises the importance of culture and the social context for cognitive development, in which there is a vital role for an active, involved teacher to provide guidance and knowledge. The best-known aspect of social constructivism is Vygotsky's 'zone of proximal development'.

CONSUMABLES

The word 'consumables' is used by teachers when referring to items children need in class that have to be periodically replaced when they are used, damaged or lost. Such items include paper, writing utensils, paint and exercise books. Other resources are normally referred to as 'non-consumables'; for example, games and science equipment.

CONTEXT

See also: learning climate, learning context, physical comfort, school climate

Context refers to the prevailing physical, practical and emotional circumstances that influence pupils' capacity to learn and develop. The most significant contextual factor is the person of the class teacher, whose influence pervades every aspect of classroom life. One teacher's approach inspires and encourages a class, while another teacher can create unease and restless behaviour with the same class in the same room (Kershner and Pointon 2000). Teachers are obviously interested in creating a climate that facilitates learning rather than detracts from it.

Apart from people and facilities, the most important parts of a school system that create the context are its organisation, curriculum and instructional materials and technologies. Decisions about the use of time and the allocation of room space and personnel are made to benefit pupils' learning; however, learning can equally be constrained by their lack of availability. Consequently, the context that an individual teacher tries to establish is directly affected by whole school decisions (how timetables are drawn up, space allotted, policies implemented, etc.) as well as the availability of resources (learning materials and adult assistance) and instructional technology (IT support). Identifying the contextual factors that contribute to, or detract from, effective learning is difficult, owing to the distinctiveness of each situation. The context also incorporates room size and structure, lighting, heating, numbers of pupils in the available space and factors as seemingly mundane as the colour of walls and ceiling height; in fact, anything that has a positive or adverse effect on the quality of learning.

Sources

Kershner, R. and Pointon, P. (2000) 'Making decisions about organising the primary classroom environment as a context for learning: The views of three experienced teachers and their pupils', *Teaching and Teacher Education*, 16 (1), 117–27.

CORE SUBJECTS

See also: curriculum, English, information technology, mathematics, National Curriculum, science

In the National Curriculum for England and Wales, the core subjects consist of English, Mathematics, Science and ICT, though the last of these is intended to be cross–curricular (i.e. spanning several subjects) as well as a subject in its own right. Scotland and Northern Ireland do not have a national curriculum but organise on the basis of broad curriculum areas (see Hamilton and Weiner 2003). Nearly all primary schools timetable the teaching of English, mathematics and science. ICT is both timetabled (to teach computer skills and practise their use) and employed more spontaneously as and when appropriate to support learning. Pupils' knowledge and understanding in the core subjects has been formally tested each year, though it is notable that in 2010 the government in England reverted to teacher assessment for science, leaving only English and mathematics to be externally checked and verified.

In England, the Qualifications and Curriculum Authority 'Primary Dossier' for 2005–6 (QCA 2006) found that there was a general sense that setting out and teaching the curriculum purely in terms of subjects was often unhelpful in promoting pupils' progress. Head teachers and teachers stated that the primary curriculum was overcrowded; the consensus was that the three core subjects occupied about 60 percent of the timetable. Many schools wanted better linkage between subjects in the form of learning areas and felt confident in implementing this themselves.

The Association for Science Education (ASE 2008) in England argues that science,

with its focus on enquiry, objectivity and rigour, provides a unique contribution to the cognitive development of young people, from their early years onwards, and so fully justifies its core subject status within the whole curriculum. Additionally, the association insisted that science is a strong vehicle for the development and application of literacy and numeracy in relevant contexts. Consequently, if the core curriculum is to be maintained, science should have genuine parity in terms of status and weighting, curriculum time, support, access to continuous professional development, and funding.

Each subject lesson requires a considerable investment of a teacher's time for planning, developing teaching strategies, assessing pupil progress and evaluating the quality of learning, plus forging links with other subject and topic areas and out-of-school learning. Useful advice about issues affecting the teaching of core subjects can be found in Hayes (2007) and in Boys and Spink (2008).

Sources

ASE (2008) *Independent Review of the Primary Curriculum*, Submission of Evidence from the Association for Science Education for the 'Primary Review', chaired by Sir Jim Rose.

Boys, R. and Spink, E. (eds) (2008) *Teaching the Core Subjects*, London: Continuum.

Hamilton, D. and Weiner, G. (2003) 'Subject, not subjects: Curriculum, pathways and pedagogy in the UK', in Pinar, W. (ed.) *International Handbook of Curriculum Research*, New York: Lawrence Erlbaum.

Hayes, D. (ed.) (2007) *Joyful Teaching and Learning in the Primary School*, Exeter: Learning Matters.

QCA (2006) 'Monitoring curriculum and assessment: Primary Report 2005–6' *Primary Evidence Dossier Section 5*, Annersley: QCA Publications.

COURAGE (CHILDREN)

See also: child development, children, personal social and health education, self-esteem (children)

Children need to understand what is meant by courage, and although aspects of the topic are covered through personal, social and health education (PSHE) there are distinctive features that require modelling by adults. Schmidt suggests that to strengthen bravery, persistence, integrity and vitality in our children, we must turn discouragement into encouragement ('building courage') in four ways. First, by showing confidence in children by giving them responsibility, asking for their opinions or advice and avoiding the temptation to overprotect or rescue them from difficulties before they have had the opportunity to grapple with the problem. Second, to focus on children's strengths by acknowledging what they do well, redirecting strengths to positive outcomes, concentrating on improvement versus perfection and celebrating as progress is made. Third, to value each child as a unique person on a schedule of development and to separate personal worth from outcomes (successful or otherwise). Fourth, to encourage independence by helping the child to learn to do things for himself or herself.

Primary teachers commonly use examples of outstanding bravery and tenacity to explore the concept of courage, both historical and contemporary. For example, characters from the Bible such as Daniel (in the lions' den) and David (fighting Goliath) are used in religious education to illustrate outstanding bravery; similarly in history, successful generals and monarchs from the distant past frequently figure in the Who's Who of courageous deeds. Contemporary figures might include Neil Armstrong (the first man to set foot on the Moon), Nelson Mandela (political leader) and disabled Olympic athletes. Children are also exposed to instances of people from the past overcoming adversity to achieve fame and success, such as Helen Keller (blind and deaf). In recent years it has been acknowledged that heroes come from every walk of life and every nation; courage is not restricted to people from the Western hemisphere.

Sources

Schmidt, M. (2007) *Teaching Courage*, Welches OR: Kids Talk; on-line at www.shininglightreading.com/kidstalknews

COURAGE (TEACHERS)

See also: learning climate, reputation (teachers), teaching approach, teachers' beliefs, values

Courage may not instantly come to mind when thinking about primary educators but it is, in fact, an essential quality to possess and explore. Courage, as one of the core virtues recognised in the field of positive psychology, incorporates four character strengths – bravery, persistence, integrity and vitality. *Bravery* is the ability to do what you think is right even if it risks personal injury or sacrifice. Every day we practise bravery by living our lives in a manner that reflects our values, character and aspirations. *Persistence* is the ability to get up from being knocked down one more time than anybody else. We have *integrity* when what we say and do is in harmony with our personal beliefs and values. People with integrity take personal responsibility for their lives and don't blame others for disappointments or obstacles. Those with *vitality* bring enthusiasm and energy to whatever task they are doing, however trivial, exuding positive expectations (Schmidt 2007).

Palmer (1990, 2007) argues that poor teaching is not because of poor technique but because teachers allow fear to get the upper hand. Teacher courage is different from the bravery displayed (for instance) by soldiers in battle, a lifeboat crew or an astronaut, where a specific task has to be accomplished at great personal cost. It requires a 'stickability' to persevere when children are restless, face up squarely to one's own shortcomings, refuse to compromise on core beliefs and show a willingness to deviate from the original plans to accommodate pupil interest.

It is easier for teachers to discard their attempts to develop a positive classroom climate by resorting to hectoring, giving an excessive number of 'heads down' tasks and initiative-stifling sanctions than to hone their skills as a mediator and encourager. It is also easier to teach didactically (directly, lecture style) than to provide opportunities for pupils to collaborate, explore and solve problems, with higher risks of task deviation and unanticipated outcomes attached to them. Courage should not, of course, be confused with foolhardiness.

Sources

Palmer, P.J. (1990) *The Active Life: A spirituality of work, creativity and caring*, New York: Harper & Row.
——(2007) *The Courage to Teach: Exploring the inner landscape of a teacher's life*, San Francisco CA: Jossey-Bass.
Schmidt, M. (2007) *Teaching Courage*, Welches OR: Kids Talk; on-line at www.shininglight reading.com/kidstalknews

CREATIVE WRITING

See also: creativity, fantasy, handwriting, imagination, poetry, spelling, writing, writing frames

Creative writing is the phrase used to describe opportunities for pupils to record their ideas (often stories) in written form, which necessarily requires that children are competent in transferring ideas to paper, spelling and handwriting. For younger children, an adult may act as an amanuensis, i.e. the child speaks thoughts aloud and the adult writes down what is said. Inevitably, this procedure is time-consuming and burdensome, so technology is helpful to record the child's words.

As the term 'creative writing' implies, children are encouraged to be creative rather than having a style imposed upon them. In practice, however, most children struggle when asked to write on a blank sheet of paper without guidance, so although the writing may issue from the children's imaginations, it is usually based around a theme given or suggested to them by the teacher. The writing might be almost entirely free or involve modifying a familiar story (e.g. a fairy tale), using poetic language in free verse or creating individual and group poems. The writing may link with a specific subject area; for instance, studies in history may result in pupils using their knowledge to write imaginatively about an event from the perspective of various real or imaginary persons, such as a soldier's perspective of long marches during the Napoleonic Wars or a child's experiences during the Great Plague of London of 1664–66.

Teachers are not only keen to develop their pupils' writing skills but also enhance their composition and dramatising abilities, with the accompanying higher-level thinking involving analysis, interpretation and evaluation. When a teacher provides an environment that promotes writing, pupils have to be given the resources, time and opportunity to create stories, singly and collaboratively. Concern has been expressed that a tightly prescribed curriculum and the use of writing frames in literacy have suppressed opportunity for creative writing and replaced it with a closely regulated system that excludes expansive, imaginative forms of writing.

CREATIVITY

See also: collaboration in learning, collaborative problem solving, imagination, outdoor education, problem solving, thinking skills

Creativity is a slippery term to define. The root of the word means 'to bring into being', encompassing agronomic terms such as germinate, grow, nurture, produce and cultivate; dynamic terms such as construct, experiment and devise; and spiritual terms such as inspiration, spontaneity and revelation. However, as Craft (2005) notes, the most frequent question that she is asked is about the meaning of the word. In response, she proposes that creativity involves people, processes and domains, and suggests that creative processes 'may interrelate together to produce a creative approach to life' (p. 29). Craft's four creative approaches include impulse; unconscious, intuitive, spiritual, emotional; imagination; taking risks and the cycle of creating. Beetlestone (1998) suggests a slightly more elaborate construct of six strands: (1) creativity as a form of learning; (2) using a range of ways to express ideas and feelings; (3) using the imagination; (4) demolishing and creating; (5) problem-solving; and (6) emotional interaction between the individual and the environment.

Fisher (2004) suggests that there are four keys to creativity: motivation, inspiration, gestation and collaboration. Motivation relies on feeling that an endeavour is worthwhile. Inspiration relies on curiosity and getting involved in finding solutions. Gestation allows time for ideas to emerge and think things through consciously and subconsciously. Collaboration involves finding and nurturing partnerships with like-minded people to help them fulfil their potential. The above instances confirm that there is a loose consensus about the factors that characterise creativity, though it is often associated with arts activities (painting, drawing, making models, ceramics and so forth) and the other non-core areas; that is, all subject areas apart from mathematics, English and science. Creativity seems to lend itself more naturally to subjects that are not desk-bound, due to the problem-solving and practical activity that characterises work in these areas. Thus, children express their feelings in drama, experiment with models in technology, work out solutions in PE and pour out their inner consciousness through painting.

There has been a lot of debate about whether creativity is an innate ability that is possessed or not possessed, or a skill that can be developed, caught, taught or wrought. Two key issues underpin a search for answers: first, whether a creative child behaves non-creatively in particular situations and creatively in others. Second, whether an apparently non-creative child can discover a reservoir of creativity that no one (including the child) realised existed until that moment. In answer, Robinson (2001) claims that everyone has the potential to be creative because creativity is possible in any activity in which human intelligence is actively engaged. He asserts that the imposition of government-led initiatives in the areas of numeracy (mathematics) and literacy (English) at the end of the 1990s, together with a 'high stakes' testing regime based on success in national tests in these two subjects, led to many schools developing an almost obsessive approach towards teaching numeracy and literacy at the expense of other imaginative approaches. By contrast, creativity releases pupils from the rigid constraints of a formalised scheme of work to explore and investigate ideas by active participation in genuine events and enterprises that interest them.

Primary children of all ages are stimulated by hearing stories, purely for pleasure, without then having to complete a worksheet or a piece of writing. They prosper when they meet poets and authors instead of just seeing photocopied extracts of their work and hearing about them. Theatre attendance, visits to art galleries, museums, exhibitions and concerts all help to stir pupils' enthusiasm, promote purposeful conversation, excite their emotions and extend their horizons. Primary-aged children develop a sense of wonder by spending regular time outdoors to appreciate seasonal change, by tending a garden and by collaborating on projects. Methods for creative teaching and learning therefore include imaginative use of the school grounds, close involvement with the local community and an emphasis on children gaining direct experience of people, places and events. In short, children learn more when they are enjoying what they do (Jones and Wyse 2004).

It is important that educators are mindful of ways to help pupils to be creative in their work by encouraging diverse thinking, risk-taking and innovative practice (see, for instance, Starbuck 2006; Best and Thomas 2007). Bowkett (2005) argues that creativity 'is as much an attitude as it is a set of mental processes. It incorporates playfulness, curiosity, sensitivity, self-awareness and independence' (p. 3). Inspection reports about creativity in schools seem to agree that it is most likely to be found where teachers do not feel bound by orthodox teaching methods, but make use of cross-curricular themes and spent time developing an enlivened physical environment.

Creativity does not emerge by simply giving children time and space to 'create something', but by generating enthusiasm and offering appropriate adult support within a culture of self-expression where new ideas were actively sought and encouraged. Grainger (2003) argues that teachers should spend more time on discussing literature, oral storytelling, poetry performances and improvised drama if children are to be offered the chance to 'interpret, communicate and create meaning for themselves' (p. 44) in their learning. She stresses that a willingness to take risks with creative and artistic activity enhances teachers' confidence and pupils' imaginative engagement. Teachers who are excited and personally involved with the literacy curriculum are much more likely to communicate its joy and wonder than a plain transmission of facts.

Teachers are sometimes categorised as creative types and non-creative types, but this simple polarity fails to recognise the complexities involved in defining creativity. Teachers may find it easy to introduce creativity into their teaching in one school situation but fail to do so in another owing to the prevailing conditions that release or suppress their creative tendencies. A popular view among education specialists is that creativity in teaching is not a fixed entity but one that relies upon judgement, discernment and confidence to produce new and original ideas. Creativity does not, therefore, occur in a vacuum, but relies upon a framework of understanding, skill acquisition and knowledge that facilitates and supports a climate of problem solving, investigation and experimentation.

True creativity is characterised by teaching that takes account of every child's interests and styles of learning and encourages them to employ their abilities in new contexts. Creativity is therefore closely linked to thinking, which in turn is related to freedom of opportunity, for thinking can start at any time and lead in many directions. It can flourish in any subject area, providing the conditions are suitably unconstrained by external demands and requirements (such as preparing for national tests).

The very best primary education is rooted in maintaining a sensible balance between mastery of essential skills and promoting activities that allow children to explore and interrogate ideas actively. Two of the most influential educationists in the UK with respect to creativity, Anna Craft and Bob Jeffrey, argue that there is not only a need for teaching creatively and teaching for creativity, but also for creative learning (Jeffrey and Craft 2004; Craft and Jeffrey 2008). That is, that children are liberated to engage with learning in such a way that it allows for their proclivities and instincts. This issue is of particular relevance to boys, of which a sizeable minority will happily discuss, experiment and compute, but may show a reluctance to work systematically and provide a written record of their findings.

It is in the day-to-day business of teaching primary mathematics and literacy that the biggest challenge lies for teachers to sponsor and encourage creativity. First and foremost teachers have to ensure that the work is interesting for the children, with the potential to be inspiring. Second, teachers have to offer pupils clear direction in their learning without unduly constraining their enthusiasm and thirst for understanding. Third, teachers open up possibilities for children to think deeply, engage with challenges and use their ingenuity to solve problems. A systematic approach to teaching does not exclude promoting imaginative engagement with the lesson content; on the contrary, it stimulates expressiveness and awareness of possibilities.

In these times of adherence to externally imposed expectations, it is a brave teacher who raises the stakes and deviates from the recommended approach. Yet success as a teacher depends in part on being situated in a school environment where innovation is promoted, for as Jeffrey and Woods (2003) maintain in their graphic description of a vibrant school situation:

> Teaching itself is creative, never formulaic. The aim is creative learning, with children coming to own their own knowledge and skills, being enthused and changed by the process, and having some control of the learning process, but under teacher guidance.
>
> (p. 3)

In a later book, the same authors reveal how pupils act as a powerful resource for creative learning for each other and for their teachers (Jeffrey and Woods 2009). Good teaching, together with opportunities for children to explore and exploit their creative potential, facilitates higher levels of accomplishment. Merely being given opportunity to experiment with ideas without possessing basic skills and devoid of adult intervention has the potential to lead to chaos: too little adult guidance can result in aimlessness; too little opportunity to experiment will almost certainly lead to pupil frustration. However, the position is even more complicated, as too much intervention can reduce self-sufficiency, whereas too much freedom may give children the impression that learning is a random process.

Creativity is normally associated with change for the better, solving problems and the exploration of fresh areas of thinking in a liberated cultural environment. However, the unreserved acclaim that creativity is beneficial is deserving of closer scrutiny. For instance, a surfeit of creativity could, in a team situation, lead to tensions or even disaster. Thus, an over-zealous mountaineer with innovative ideas about tackling a vertical rock face may jeopardise others in the group failing to conform to the agreed procedures. Similarly, a teacher who is highly responsive to pupils' needs and likes to deviate from the planned curriculum to 'go with the flow' of the children's interests may invite criticism from colleagues who teach parallel age groups. If test results prove to be less satisfactory as a result of teachers adopting a more creative teaching and learning style, complaints from parents will undoubtedly follow, despite any other perceived benefits to the children. Creativity, however defined, cannot be isolated from prevailing contextual factors such as stakeholders' expectations, the achievement of established targets and collegial responsibilities. Creativity without discipline may be personally satisfying but counter-productive in other ways.

Sources

Beetlestone, F. (1998) *Creative Children, Imaginative Teaching*, Buckingham: Open University Press.

Best, B. and Thomas, W. (2007) *The Creative Teaching and Learning Toolkit*, London: Continuum.

Bowkett, S. (2005) *100 Ideas for Teaching Creativity*, London: Continuum.

Craft, A. (2005) *Creativity in our Schools: Tensions and dilemmas*, London: Routledge.

Craft, A. and Jeffrey, B. (2008) 'Creativity and performativity in teaching and learning: Tensions, dilemmas, constraints, accommodations and synthesis', *British Journal of Educational Research*, 34 (5), 577–84.

Fisher, R. (2004) 'What is creativity?' in Fisher, R. and Williams, M. (eds) *Unlocking Creativity*, London: David Fulton.

Grainger, T. (2003) 'Creative teachers and the language arts', *Education 3–13*, 31 (1), 43–47.

Jeffrey, B. and Craft, A. (2004) 'Teaching creatively and teaching for creativity: distinctions and relationships', *Educational Studies*, 30 (1), 77–87.

Jeffrey, B. and Woods, P. (2003) *The Creative School*, London: Routledge.

——(2009) *Creative Learning in the Primary School*, London: Routledge.

Jones, R. and Wyse, D. (eds) (2004) *Creativity in the Primary Curriculum*, London: David Fulton.

Robinson, K. (2001) *Out of Our Minds: Learning to be creative*, London: John Wiley.

Starbuck, D. (2006) *Creative Teaching: Getting it right*, London: Continuum.

CROSS-CURRICULUM

See also: constructivism, curriculum, curriculum flows, multiple intelligences, thematic learning

Most definitions of cross-curricular work, also referred to as curriculum integration, emphasise how combinations of subjects are used within project or thematic work, incorporating a wide range of sources, related concepts and flexible schedules. The movement towards an integrated curriculum has its basis in the work of learning theorists who advocate a constructivist view of learning; that is, finding out by experiencing – often jointly with other pupils – rather than by being told. Fogarty (1995) describes ten levels of curricular integration:

1 Fragmented: separate and distinct disciplines.
2 Connected: topics within a discipline are connected.
3 Nested: social, thinking and content skills are targeted within a subject area.
4 Sequenced: similar ideas are taught in concert, although subjects are separate.
5 Shared: team planning and/or teaching that involves two disciplines focuses on shared concepts, skills or attitudes.
6 Webbed: thematic teaching using a theme as a base for instruction in many disciplines.
7 Threaded: thinking skills, social skills, multiple intelligences and study skills are threaded throughout the disciplines.
8 Integrated: priorities that overlap multiple disciplines are examined for common skills, concepts and attitudes.
9 Immersed: learner integrates by viewing all learning through the perspective of one area of interest.
10 Networked: learner directs the integration process through selection of a network of experts and resources.

Cross-curricular work is closely related to interdisciplinary teaching, thematic teaching and synergistic teaching ('synergy' means 'combined interaction'). The integration element emphasises the fusion of ideas and concepts within and across subject areas and broader life experiences in an attempt to make education more relevant and meaningful for children. It is argued that by teaching the curriculum as an integrated whole, pupils' view of learning is likely to be more rounded, whereas if teachers emphasise the separation and discreteness of subjects it can establish artificial barriers in the minds of younger children and they may fail to make secure connections between knowledge components.

Cross-curricular work is seen as a way to establish links between (say) the humanities (history, geography, RE); or between the natural sciences and mathematics; or between music and art (see, for example, Lake 1994). Claire (2004) provides suggestions about ways in which teachers can incorporate citizenship into different subject areas in their planning and teaching.

The idea of integrated curricula has been linked with the theory of multiple intelligences, popularly associated with Howard Gardner (see Fogarty 2007). The knowledge and skills that pupils learn and apply in one area are used to reinforce and expand their learning in other areas, thereby cutting across subject barriers and combining relevant parts of each subject into a composite whole. For example, an understanding of the geography of a region might help to explain the reasons for the location of a key battle in history; again, play activity using building bricks offers opportunities to introduce the names and properties of three-dimensional shapes.

Opponents of cross-curricular approaches warn that learning needs the clearly delineated boundaries provided by single-subject teaching. They argue that it is insufficiently rigorous, especially in ensuring that children have focused and regular opportunities to gain fundamental skills in key subjects, and insist that too much choice allows pupils to avoid areas of learning that they find hard, thereby inculcating poor work habits and attitudes.

It is noteworthy that the Modern Languages in Primary Schools Initiative (MLPSI 2008) in Ireland recommends that as far as possible, links should be made between what occurs in modern language lessons and the curriculum programme in other areas of the curriculum. The thinking behind this belief is that it sends a positive message to the children who are used to subject areas being linked. Such connections result in the language becoming more absorbed into the general curriculum and not being perceived as an unimportant 'extra' subject. Cross-curricular linking gradually becomes more of an instinctive way of thinking for teachers and learners as it is practised.

Sources

Claire, H. (2004) *Teaching Citizenship in Primary Schools*, Exeter: Learning Matters.

Fogarty, R.J. (1995) *The Mindful School: How to integrate the curricula*, French's Forest NSW: James Bennett Publishers.

——(2007) *Integrating Curricula With Multiple Intelligences: Teams, themes, and threads*, Thousand Oaks CA: Corwin Press.

Lake, K. (1994) 'Integrated curriculum', *School Improvement Research Series*, North West Regional Education Laboratory, on-line at www.nwrel.org/scpd/sirs/8/c016.html

MLPSI (2008) *Cross-Curricular Links*, Kildare Education Centre, Ireland, accessible on-line through http://mlpsi.ie

CURIOSITY

See also: drama, outdoor education, science, speculative questions

All children are born with an innate sense of curiosity; indeed, it is fair to claim that it is a pre-requisite for learning. Children's curiosity is best satisfied when learning is presented in the form of issues to be resolved, as well as facts to be stored, so the use of a range of open and speculative questions is essential in opening up children's eyes and minds to other possibilities. Adults have an important role to play by showing amazement when children tell them something about their lives (such as a visit to a friend's house) or show them a precious photograph (of a visit to a theme park, for instance) or a possession (such as a birthday present). In this regard, educators must learn to be childlike and view life from the learner's point of view.

Perry (2001) refers to curiosity as the fuel of development because if children remain curious they will continue to explore and discover. Unfortunately, some children lose their sense of curiosity and desire to discover and as a result make fewer new friends, join fewer social groups, read fewer books and are less inclined to explore the outdoors. In addition, the less-curious children are harder to teach because it becomes more difficult to inspire, enthuse, and motivate them. Perry warns that there are three common ways adults constrain or even crush the enthusiastic exploration of the curious child: (1) fear, (2) disapproval, and (3) absence. By contrast, the presence of a caring, committed and supportive adult provides a platform of security from which children can set out to discover new things and revel in the pleasure and reinforcement that comes from sharing their findings with others.

Primary teachers use curiosity in a number of ways, depending on the age of the children and the subject matter. In outdoor studies, for instance, children might be encouraged to collect samples from nature for closer inspection, description and drawing; these preliminary activities lay the foundation for further investigation using books and electronic sources. Again, reading a story without revealing the ending can generate ideas from the children; the subsequent completion of the tale not only satisfies curiosity but also stimulates discussion about alternatives and options. Many teachers of younger pupils keep special items (such as historical artefacts) concealed during the lesson introduction before revealing them to the delighted children. Similarly, the use of masks and disguises in drama and during play heightens the sense of expectation and excitement and invariably increases motivation for learning.

A report published in 2008, sponsored by the Wellcome Trust and led by Professor Peter Tymms, argued that although the purpose of science in primary schools should be to foster a sense of curiosity and positive attitudes in the young child, the current national approach to science in primary schools is having a negative impact on children's scientific thought and curiosity (Tymms *et al.* 2008).

Sources

Perry, B.D. (2001) 'Curiosity: The fuel of development', *Early Childhood Today*, 15, 22–24.

Tymms, P., Bolden, D. and Merrell, C. (2008) *Science in English Primary Schools: Trends in attainment, attitudes and approaches*, CEM Centre, Durham University.

CURRICULUM

See also: English as an additional language, foundation stage, Hadow reports, inclusion, learning, learning difficulties, organising for learning

It is far from easy to find an agreed definition for 'the curriculum' other than describing the sum total of what pupils need to learn (Ross 2001). A broad-based definition of curriculum would be everything children do, see, hear or feel in their setting, both planned and unplanned. The term derives from a Latin word meaning a racing chariot, based on the notion of a racetrack or course to be run, which gradually came to be understood as referring to a course of study. In fact, over the past century a variety of definitions have been proffered, including one advanced more than a century ago in the 1904 *Suggestions for Teachers Code* that the curriculum of the primary school should provide a training in the English language; handwriting to secure speed as well as legibility; arithmetic, including practical measurements; drawing from objects, memory and brush drawing; geography,

history, music, hygiene and physical training; and moral instruction, given both directly and indirectly.

By 1931 the Hadow Consultative Committee was suggesting that the curriculum should be thought out in terms of activity and experience rather than facts to be stored. Half a century later, in 1985, Her Majesty's Inspectorate of Schools offered a sweeping definition, claiming that a school's curriculum consisted of all those activities designed or encouraged within its organisational framework to promote the intellectual, personal, social and physical development of its pupils. Silcock and Brundrett (2002) claim that 'the school curriculum should aim to promote pupils' spiritual, moral, social and cultural development and prepare all pupils for the opportunities, responsibilities and experiences of life' (p. 19).

A generation ago, teachers were broadly at liberty to make their own decisions about what to teach and how to teach it. In fact, the freedom that teachers enjoyed to organise learning in a way that suited the classroom circumstances was considered to be an essential element of their professional autonomy. Since 1989, a National Curriculum (NC) has operated in all state-maintained schools and many private schools in England, Wales and Northern Ireland (through the Department of Education in Northern Ireland, DENI). In 1999 a Foundation Stage curriculum was published for children aged four and five in nursery and reception classes. National curricula are explicit about the overall aims and values of primary education in that the school curriculum should aim to provide opportunities for all pupils to learn and to achieve, promote pupils' spiritual, moral, social and cultural development, and prepare all pupils for the opportunities, responsibilities and experiences of life.

The curriculum requires teachers to have due regard for inclusion principles that incorporate setting-suitable learning challenges for all pupils so that they can experience success. The process necessitates that teachers respond to children's diverse needs and facilitate learning and assessment for individuals and for groups of pupils. Children with learning difficulties and disabilities, and those for whom English is an additional language, are equally entitled to a relevant, broad and balanced curriculum. Thus, children from all social backgrounds, gender and races must receive a high-quality education, regardless of their physical and mental condition.

Scott (2008) provides an overview of the key critical appreciation of the work of sixteen leading curriculum theorists, thinkers and analysts from the fields of education, philosophy, sociology and psychology to offer a broad perspective with views from the UK, the USA and Europe, and from a range of political stances ranging from radical conservatism through liberalism to socialism and libertarianism. See Blenkin and Kelly's classic work (1983) for valuable insights into the implications of curriculum decisions for classroom practice.

Sources

Blenkin, G.M. and Kelly, A.V. (eds) (1983) *The Primary Curriculum in Action*, London: Paul Chapman.
Ross, A. (2001) 'What is the curriculum?' in Collins, J., Insley K. and Soler J. (eds) *Developing Pedagogy: Researching practice*, London: Paul Chapman/Open University.
Scott, D. (2008) *Critical Essays on Major Curriculum Theorists*, London: Routledge.
Silcock, P. and Brundrett, M. (2002) *Achieving Competence, Success and Excellence in Teaching*, London: Routledge.

CURRICULUM FLOWS

See also: cross-curriculum, curriculum, geography, history, skills

A curriculum structure in which there is an emphasis upon relationships and patterns in knowledge and systems has been referred to as a 'curriculum flow' (see, for example, Cremin *et al.* 2006), whereby pupils draw upon a range of skills from across the curriculum (e.g. map-reading skills from geography; weighing of evidence sources from history) and other experiences to induce deeper learning as they use their knowledge in a variety of situations. Thus, in the geography and history examples noted above, map-reading skills can be used (say) to understand historical battlefields, while evidence sources can be used in discussions about sustainability and energy supplies. In such situations, the teacher becomes less of an instructor and more of a guide and facilitator, providing a focus for learning by suggesting fruitful areas for investigation and fostering links with literacy and numeracy wherever possible. Integrated curriculum flows of this type apply across the school and, while having clear objectives and structures, allow scope for spontaneity, pupil initiative, imagination and creativity to give children more control over their own learning.

Sources

Cremin, T., Burnard, P. and Craft, A. (2006) 'Pedagogy and possibility thinking in the early years', *Thinking Skills and Creativity*, 1 (2), 108–19.

CURRICULUM HISTORY

See also: curriculum, infants, information technology, juniors, key stages, literacy, literacy strategy, National Curriculum, new entrants, numeracy, numeracy strategy, primary reviews, social and emotional aspects of education, teaching methods

Curriculum provision across English and Welsh primary schools in the 1960s and 1970s was inconsistent and depended to a large extent upon the expertise of each teacher, the enthusiasm of a local authority adviser or even upon the availability of a suitable set of published education texts in the school. Only religious education was a compulsory subject (enshrined in the 1944 Education Act). Northern Ireland has followed a similar framework; however, here schools can develop additional curriculum elements to express their particular ethos and meet pupils' individual needs and circumstances; the curriculum also includes the Irish language in Irish-speaking schools. The education system in Scotland has evolved differently from the rest of the UK, as the National Curriculum does not apply and there are no key stages. Compulsory education in Scotland begins in primary schools at the age of five, and the move to secondary school takes place at age twelve.

During the 1970s, serious questions began to be asked about 'value for money' and accountability in education. Some education historians point to the well-balanced and generally conciliatory speech by the then prime minister, James Callaghan, at the foundation stone laying ceremony at Ruskin College, Oxford, on 18 October 1976 at a time when education was publicly politicised. It certainly placed education centre-stage, opened up the so-called 'secret garden' of the curriculum, cast doubt on informal teaching methods and showed that much of the groundwork for creating a national curriculum had already been undertaken behind the scenes.

At the same time, pressure for a standard curriculum (a 'national' curriculum) was gathering support and momentum and the National Curriculum (NC) for England and Wales became law in 1988; it was implemented in all maintained schools over the following two years. MacLure and Elliott (1993) summarised the NC as specifying 'the structure and (partial) contents of a curriculum for all pupils in the state-funded education system in England and Wales (private schools are exempt from its prescriptions), together with a national system of assessment at the ages of 7, 11, 14 and 16' (p. 109). Webb and Vulliamy (1997) argued that the 1988 Education Reform Act ushered in the most profound changes in the English education system since the 1944 Act, which had first established a free national system of primary and secondary schooling.

The 1988 Education Reform Act was designed to provide a minimum educational entitlement for pupils of compulsory school age, to ensure that the curriculum of each school was balanced and broadly based, and to promote the spiritual, moral, cultural, mental and physical opportunities, responsibilities and experiences of adult life. A priority of the NC was to improve national standards of literacy and to give all pupils opportunities, where appropriate, to develop their information technology (IT) capability, applied in a variety of contexts across the newly created key stages. Thus, key stage 1 (KS1) replaced the term 'infant'; KS1 was then defined as reception (new entrants), year 1 and year 2. Similarly, KS2 (years 3 to 6) replaced 'junior'. The later introduction of the Foundation Stage incorporated the reception class, such that the present KS1 now consists only of year 1 and year 2.

Some educators challenged the usefulness and validity of a national curriculum because it limited teacher's autonomy to make decisions about the immediate needs of their pupils and created a state-driven system that was reminiscent, they argued, of totalitarian regimes. Nevertheless, the basic proposition of providing a curriculum that had the potential to eliminate the unhelpful diversity of provision between different schools was initially welcomed by teachers. Only in the years following its introduction – with the accompanying explosion of documentation and impossibly dense syllabuses – did primary teachers become fully aware of its onerous impact, as they laboured long hours to cope with the additional demands. One way and another, from relative obscurity as an election issue in the early 1980s, education would be the barometer for political aspirations and ambitions in the run-up to, and during, the new millennium.

The election campaign of 1992 again saw education at the heart of political debate and reviews of the existing National Curriculum Orders began immediately, with numerous changes to different curriculum subjects and their assessment, which caused confusion and annoyance among primary school practitioners.

Terms like 'curriculum overload', 'innovation fatigue' and 'saturation' became common parlance and well-founded stories of exhaustion and demoralisation among primary teachers became endemic.

The overloaded primary curriculum of the 1990s, together with the associated assessment and recording procedures introduced during the implementation of the National Curriculum, led to serious concerns that children's education, and teachers' well-being, were suffering as a result. In April 1993, the then secretary of state for education established a review of the whole of the National Curriculum, chaired by Sir Ron Dearing, with exceptionally wide terms of reference to evaluate the entire construction and implementation of the National Curriculum (Dearing 1994). By 2000 a revised version of the National Curriculum had been introduced into schools in England and Wales; it was generally held to be more manageable than previous versions. However, other curriculum innovations were rapidly gaining ascendancy, and the introduction of a literacy strategy and numeracy strategy at the end of the 1990s switched attention away from the NC and towards the government's intention to 'boost' standards in English (later, literacy) and mathematics subjects. Time and energy allocated to other curriculum subjects began to erode as teachers implemented the new strategies.

During the early part of the new century, numerous initiatives were promoted by the government, in which the need for the primary education curriculum to incorporate new priorities such as extending creativity, promoting a healthy lifestyle, using the outdoor environment, citizenship and modern foreign language teaching (from 2007–8) and elementary sex education (from 2009) were promoted with great fanfare.

In 2009, two reviews on the state of primary education and recommendations for future policy were published. First, a three-year study known as the 'Primary Review' (PR) and formally entitled *The Condition and Future of Primary Education in England* identified the purposes and values that the primary phase of education should serve to address the needs of children and society (Alexander 2009). Second, the *Primary Curriculum Review* (PCR) advised on how the primary curriculum should change to ensure all children gain a good grounding; offer schools a degree of choice about content and delivery; allow time for a foreign language; emphasise personal development; support the transition from play-based learning to formal learning; and encourage creativity (Rose 2009).

Sources

Alexander, R. (2009) *The Condition and Future of Primary Education in England* ('The Primary Review') Cambridge: University of Cambridge/ Esmée Fairburn Trust.

Dearing, R. (1994) *The National Curriculum and Its Assessment: Final report*, London: SCAA Publications.

MacLure, M. and Elliott, J. (1993) 'Packaging the primary curriculum: Textbooks and the English National Curriculum', *Curriculum Journal*, 4 (1), 91–113.

Rose, J. for the DCSF (2009) *Primary Curriculum Review*, London: HMSO.

Webb, R. and Vulliamy, G. (1997) *A Comparative Analysis of Curriculum Change in Primary Schools in England and Finland: Final report*, York: University of York.

CURRICULUM LEADERSHIP

See also: art and design, collaboration (staff), core subjects, curriculum, design and technology, English, geography, governors, history, information technology, literacy, mathematics, music, religious education, science

Curriculum leadership was once the province of secondary teachers with single-subject responsibilities undertaken as 'heads of departments'. Today, teachers in primary schools are expected to undertake similar roles, many of which are linked to providing leadership in specific curriculum areas; for example, leader for literacy or leader for mathematics. Subject leaders need to possess strong subject knowledge and expertise to advise colleagues, provide ideas and resources for the implementation and teaching of the subject and to document pupil progression in learning across the primary age phase. If leadership is in one of the core subjects (English, mathematics, science), the curriculum leader will also advise colleagues about assessing pupils' attainment and 'tracking' their progress by keeping appropriate records.

Curriculum leadership entails liaising with teachers and assistants, both informally and through staff meetings, to introduce and disseminate information about an aspect of the subject or recent innovations or new requirements. When significant changes are taking place in a curriculum area, the leader normally produces a summary for governors and parents, and may formally present them at organised public meetings for that purpose. The role of curriculum leader also involves coordinating events (such as a whole year or whole school Science Week) and finding time to check equipment, order new or replacement resources and monitor health and safety (especially in practical subjects like design and technology, information technology and physical education, PE).

One of the most challenging roles for a subject leader is to 'model' good teaching for colleagues. It is common for a curriculum leader in a foundation subject (history, geography, PE, music, design and technology, art and design, plus religious education, RE) to take another teacher's class for (notably) PE or music, while the colleague teaches the leader's class. The 'exchange' system allows children to benefit from the curriculum leader's expertise but has timetable and 'continuity in learning' implications if the exchange is irregular. Furthermore, teachers with a curriculum weakness need to improve their knowledge and skills through active teaching and the exchange is unlikely to remedy the position.

Curriculum leadership is also about persuading colleagues about the benefits of a particular teaching approach. In this regard, Day *et al.* (1998) note that professional development is based on the principle that people prefer to be led rather than to be managed and that leadership applies equally to the work of classroom teachers as to senior staff. Excellent leaders are judged not only by outcomes, but also by the quality of their vision, their relationships, plans and policies and their commitment to growth and achievement for children and staff.

Winning over sceptics and those with serious objections to a change of direction requires considerable tact and persuasion. For instance, the curriculum leader for literacy may recommend significant changes in the approach to teaching reading that colleagues find unconvincing. Cardno (2006) notes from her case study of a New Zealand primary school that curriculum leadership does not have to emanate from an individual but may be generated by a senior management team that analyses an ill-defined problem and then designs and implements change strategies that incrementally involve all staff.

Burton and Brundrett (2005) offer suggestions about techniques and strategies of curriculum leadership with regard to the theoretical, practical and technological issues facing primary teachers as they create and manage the curriculum. For the serious reader, Parkay *et al.* (2009) provide a detailed selection of readings that present the knowledge, skills and alternative strategies needed by curriculum planners and teachers at all levels of education, from early childhood through to adulthood.

Sources

Burton, N. and Brundrett, M. (2005) *Leading the Curriculum in the Primary School*, London: Paul Chapman.

Cardno, C. (2006) 'Leading change from within: Action research to strengthen curriculum leadership in a primary school', *School Leadership and Management*, 26 (5), 453–71.

Day, C., Hall, C. and Whitaker, P. (1998) *Developing Leadership in Primary Schools*, London: Sage.

Parkay, F.W., Hass, G. and Anctil, E.J. (2009) *Curriculum Leadership*, London/Upper Saddle River NJ: Pearson Education (US).

CURRICULUM PLANS

See also: curriculum, lesson planning, lesson planning (joint), lesson plans

Schools develop long-, medium- and short-term plans to structure and cover the necessary curriculum content. Long-term plans provide a basic overview of topic areas and units of work across an academic year. Medium-term plans are normally drawn up for each half term and include details of resources, activities and assessment criteria to gauge pupil progress. Short-term plans are the detailed weekly or fortnightly plans completed by individual teachers or small groups of teachers for their groups or classes of children. Depending on the requirements of the head teacher, every teacher also keeps specific plans for each lesson or series of lessons.

D

DANCE

See also: drama, music, physical education, stories

Dance forms part of the physical education (PE) curriculum for primary pupils. It is common for dance to be linked with other elements of the curriculum, notably gymnastics, drama and music. Most dance lessons with younger children are linked to body awareness, co-operation and imaginative stories. Some schools utilise the services of dance specialists to work with juniors in particular. A small number of schools run dance clubs as an extra-curricular activity.

DAYDREAMING

See also: attention span, boredom, brain function, distractible children

Children who are off-task due to daydreaming are usually reprimanded, considered a little eccentric or even labelled as suffering from an 'attention deficit'. However, according to Chang (2006) daydreaming has a number of benefits, such as relaxing; helping to manage personal conflict; thinking positively about others; boosting productivity; cementing beliefs and values; helping achieve goals and relieving boredom. Mason (2007) even claims that daydreaming could be the result of the brain mulling over important but not immediately relevant issues when the external environment ceases to pose interesting and engaging problems. Controversially, the research evidence indicates that it might even be the case that most of the time people are engaged in less directed, unintended thought (i.e. daydreaming) and that this state is routinely interrupted by periods of goal-directed thought (such as completing a task in a lesson), rather than the other way around.

Sources

Chang, L. (2006) 'Why does daydreaming get such a bad rap?' On-line at *WebMD*, www.webmd.com/balance/features/
Mason, M.F. (2007) 'Wandering minds: The default network and stimulus-independent thought', *Science*, 315 (January), 393–95.

DEBATING

See also: discussion, emotional intelligence, homework, information technology, oracy, pupil perspectives, questions and questioning, talk

Debating an issue of relevance to children forms an important part of the speaking and listening agenda in literacy. Debate follows more closely prescribed rules than a conventional discussion and is more carefully structured. It therefore requires formal organisation and tends to be restricted to older primary pupils. Prior to the debate, pupils need time to research the given topic, talk informally to one another and, perhaps, record some of their findings in a form that can be later shared – for example, through the medium of information technology. The search for information can also be extended into homework tasks. During the debate, children who have volunteered to speak are given a period of time (2 minutes, say) in which to do so without interruption. The rest of the class have to sit patiently until the contribution has been concluded before being given about a minute to think about a helpful question or making a comment. A key rule during debates is that no one is allowed to preface their comment with the words 'Yes, but … ' or to employ similar negative overtones. Once the questions and comments are exhausted, another speaker is permitted the same amount of time to present information and ideas. Ideally, speakers should offer contrasting views so that the interactive process of contributing, questioning and commenting is sharper, as pupils grapple with conflicting perspectives and dilemmas. Some teachers use more neutral themes for debating, such as: 'If I were the teacher' or 'What should happen next?' which are also suitable for younger children.

At the end of the session, teachers also have an important function in drawing together the different threads of the arguments, thanking the main participants and reminding the class about the significance of the debate in terms of the overall learning intentions. Although this type of speaking and listening ('oracy') is of itself a valuable means of stimulating interest and inculcating children into mature thinking and a tolerant consideration of differing (or similar) viewpoints, it is doubly worthwhile if it can be seen as directly contributing towards longer-term curriculum goals; for example, the ability to summarise salient points from a body of information. Once teachers have established a relaxed and respectful relationship with and among the children, it is often appropriate to ask the main participants how they felt

before, during and after the session as a means of alerting the children to the significance of emotional factors and their impact on confidence and morale.

DECISION-MAKING

See also: differentiation, discipline, effectiveness, foundation schools, governing body, lesson management, school council, special educational needs, target setting

Teachers make hundreds of decisions every day about how to allocate their time, express ideas to pupils, introduce new concepts and teach fresh skills, to name but a few. They have to decide which teaching strategies to employ; where to store resources; when to assist pupils and when to leave them alone; how to handle a recalcitrant child, and so on. Other decisions involve judgements about the allocation of grades or marks, classroom management, curriculum implementation, task differentiation and pupil assessment.

Decision-making in primary schools tends to fall into one of two broad types; the first concerns how to implement statutory requirements (such as health and safety legislation); the second deals with internal school matters (such as organising the curriculum or the structure of the school day). The governing body/school board and head teacher/school principal, supported by the local authority (LA) or its equivalent – and in the case of church foundation schools, the appointed religious representatives – make most of the major decisions that impact upon the primary school community. Menter *et al.* (2006) note that endorsement for involving teachers in school leadership by contributing to decision-making is evident in Canada, Australia and, particularly, the USA, where leadership programmes have been 'concerned to promote teachers' development and decision making without taking them out of the classroom' (p. 166). Thus, teachers can be leaders of change and recipients at different times, working collaboratively to solve problems and improve effectiveness.

The teacher makes the majority of decisions in the classroom about organising the room; the lesson content; managing learning; and discipline issues, rooted in their beliefs and values about educational provision and professional conduct. First, deciding whether the decision reflects their beliefs about education. Second, whether the decision is pragmatic and results in greater efficiency and effectiveness. Third, whether the decision is supported by empirical evidence; for example, data from tests or children's increased confidence to vindicate a particular teaching approach. Finally, whether the decision takes sufficient account of external requirements, especially government-dictated targets for pupil achievement.

Many primary schools promote the involvement of the children in making procedural and practical decisions that have a direct impact upon their lives, such as where to site a school garden or how to supervise children who come to school early or games suitable for the break time. Establishing a 'school council', which consists of delegates drawn from each class, often facilitates participation (see Deuchar 2004 for a discussion about ethical considerations). In their review of pupil decision-making in England and the Republic of Ireland, Shevlin and Rose (2008) note that educational policy has recognised the desirability of increased pupil involvement and perspectives. The authors provide an overview of the key challenges that face policy-makers and educators in ensuring meaningful participation for children and young people with special educational needs.

Sources

Deuchar, R. (2004) 'Reconciling self-interest and ethics: The role of primary school pupil councils', *Scottish Educational Review*, 36 (2), 159–68.
Menter, I., Mahony, P. and Hextall, I. (2006) 'What a performance! The impact of performance management and threshold assessment on the work and lives of primary teachers', in Webb, R. (ed.) *Changing Teaching and Learning in the Primary School*, Maidenhead: Open University Press.
Shevlin, M. and Rose, R. (2008) 'Pupils as partners in education decision-making: Responding to the legislation in England and Ireland', *European Journal of Special Needs Education*, 23 (4), 423–30.

DEEP LEARNING

See also: attention span, enquiry, memory and memorising, motivation for learning, questions and questioning, superficial learning

Deep learning is said to take place when the learner relates previous knowledge to new knowledge and theoretical ideas to everyday experience; relates and distinguishes evidence and argument; and organises and structures the content into a coherent whole. By contrast, the surface learner is trying to discover and provide what the teacher wants and is likely to be motivated primarily by a fear of failure. Surface ('superficial') learning is associated with memorising unrelated fragments of knowledge; an inability to separate principles from specific examples; and completing a task for approval rather than intrinsic motivation (Atherton 2005, based on Ramsden 1988).

All children need to be given the opportunity to transfer what they have learned to new situations, as this is often the acid test for whether or not deep learning has been achieved. Even if all the group or class appear to have grasped the principles and ideas contained within a particular learning objective, some children will retain what they have learned, while others will require regular reminding and refreshing. However, the more that children see the relevance of their learning, the more likely it is that they will engage enthusiastically with the lesson content and retain what they have learned as they apply it to situations. It is, however, common for children to apparently learn something one day and completely forget it a short time later, especially if the facts are unrelated and detached from their experience.

The teacher has a crucial role to play in creating the conditions under which deep learning is likely to happen. Whether in planning, organising resources, teaching or assessing children's work, teachers have to pay close attention to every detail and its implications for learning. In particular, a teacher's active engagement with learners must be of high quality; thus, picking up on important points raised by the child; offering well-judged comments using suitable vocabulary; and reinforcing children's understanding and knowledge development by repetition, locating the learning in a variety of contexts and asking searching questions.

At all costs, teachers have to avoid the dreary practice of lessons in which there is a 'warm-up' phase that has nothing to do with the main lesson; a question-and-answer session that is little more than allowing the more able children to repeat what they already know; a task phase that is introduced rapidly and concluded prematurely; and a summarising time that consists of nothing more than heartily congratulating a small selection of children while the majority are spectators.

Kelly (2007) suggests that children learn better if they are seen as 'craft apprentices' rather than 'unskilled labourers' and warns against the production line mentality in which the teacher 'controls the transmission of ready-made packages of knowledge by providing appropriate tasks and then monitors and assesses their acquisition' (p. 67). By adopting such an unimaginative approach, children's learning is singly motivated by a desire to complete the work and do well in tests. By contrast, the conditions for deep learning are created by involving children as junior co-participants, teaching them necessary skills to aid independence, promoting intelligent forms of thinking, exploring ideas and allowing them to investigate themes, rather than piling on task after task in a vain hope that some knowledge and understanding will lodge in their minds.

Other strategies for promoting deep learning and include offering choices to pupils; allowing them to make their own decisions; asking them searching questions; providing materials for play and facilitating exploratory activity. Similarly, the use of quizzes, puzzles, team games, walks around the local district and treasure trails, all assist in nurturing the development of a more secure attention span and increased enthusiasm for learning. Even common activities such as dominoes, cards, dice games and matching up pictures are helpful methods to develop a child's memory and concentration. For older primary-age pupils, 'consequence' games such as draughts or chess can be introduced into the classroom, thereby encouraging the child to think ahead and employ effective strategies, rather than relying on instinct.

Sources

Atherton, J.S. (2005) *Learning and Teaching: Deep and surface learning*, on-line at www.learning andteaching.info/learning/deepsurf.htm

Kelly, P. (2007) 'The joy of enhancing children's learning', in Hayes, D. (ed.) *Joyful Teaching and Learning in the Primary School*, Exeter: Learning Matters.

Ramsden, P. (1988) *Improving Learning: New perspectives*, London: Kogan Page.

DESIGN AND TECHNOLOGY

See also: effectiveness, equal opportunities, health and safety, information technology, non-core subject

As design and technology (DT) is a non-core subject, primary schools in England and Wales use guidelines issued by the government, which require that they follow the National Curriculum (NC). The NC programmes of study are divided into twenty-four schemes of work, which can be used at a school's discretion and all schools must show that they are teaching a range of knowledge, skills and concepts appropriate for the subject. The subject is also part of the Northern Ireland curriculum; in Scotland the subject is known as 'Craft and Design'.

Design and technology is essentially a practical subject by which pupils develop skills, nurture their creativity and learn to innovate. DT programmes give children opportunities to acquire and apply knowledge and understanding of materials and components, systems, structures and products; they also have the potential to promote pupils' understanding of technological processes by planning and producing products using materials such as card, wood, textiles and natural resources. Pupils are taught specific skills, such as accurate cutting, fixing of component parts and interpreting plans to employ in practical tasks; children can also be taught to make predictions and conduct what is popularly referred to as 'fair testing'; measure accurately; draw and interpret graphs and bar charts; handle information through the use of a database or spreadsheet using information technology (IT); and investigate texture and colour. As such, design and technology offers numerous cross-curricular and thematic links with subjects such as mathematics, art and science. See Ritchie (2002) for further details. In an older book, Dunn and Larson (1989) emphasise the importance of elements such as co-operative learning; the whole language approach to literacy; and inquiry-based approaches in science and mathematics.

By the age of about seven years, most children should be able to use a range of materials to design and make simple products; select materials, tools and techniques and explain their choices; understand simple mechanisms and structures; measure, assemble, join and combine materials in a variety of ways using basic tools safely; and investigate and evaluate simple products. Most work in the early primary stages involves making a product that has a 'practical' use; for instance, children might design a book cover; make a pencil holder; or construct a kite.

By the age of eleven, most children can use knowledge and understanding of a range of materials, components and techniques to design and make quality products; evaluate work as it develops; and, if necessary, suggest alternatives. They can produce designs and plans that list the stages involved in making a product, and the correct tools and materials to use; accurately measure, mark, cut, join and combine a variety of materials; and work safely by recognising potential hazards to themselves and others. The more capable pupils can also understand the use of electrical and mechanical systems and more complex structures and evaluate what is or is not working well in a product. See DCSF/QCA (2008) for further details.

The use of information technology programmes to aid product design is widespread in primary schools on the planning side of DT. Every school is strongly encouraged to keep a policy for the subject, normally written by the subject leader and/or head teacher, and submitted to the school governing body such that colleagues, parents and inspectors have an overview of relevant activities. As in every curriculum subject, teachers need to monitor, assess and report on children's learning; provide equal opportunities; and meet special educational needs (Hope 2004).

The Design and Technology Association provides advice and guidance in the field of DT: 16 Wellesbourne House, Walton Road, Wellesbourne, Warwicks, CV35 9JB. www. info@data.org.uk

Sources

DCSF/QCA (2008) *Design and Technology at Key Stages 1 and 2*, London: QCA.

Dunn, S. and Larson, L. (1989) *Design Technology: Children's engineering*, London: Routledge.

Hope, G. (2004) *Teaching Design and Technology 3–11*, London: Continuum.

Ritchie, R. (2002) *Primary Design and Technology: A process for learning*, London: David Fulton.

DESKS

See also: physical comfort

A generation ago it was normal for every child to have an individual desk, consisting of a storage area, hinged top and seat. The structure was sturdy, often with an iron framework holding a varnished oak or a similar 'hard' wood. The cost of each desk was high but they were expected to last for a long time. The use of desks accentuated the individual nature of learning and their shape did not allow them to be put together as a means of facilitating cooperative or collaborative work, such as scientific investigations or practical activities. Today, the small proportion of schools in which desks are used (normally for older pupils only) opt for one with a fixed 'table top' and room for resources such as books, paper and writing implements stored in a built-in tray beneath it; there is normally a separate chair rather than one incorporated into the desk structure. In most primary schools today the children sit in pairs at a table with the majority of the regular resources stored in separate trays at the side of the room. This system involves more movement and potential for disruption, as pupils have to get up to access the trays.

DETENTION

See also: head teachers, parent communication, punishment, sanctions

The word 'detention' has its root in 'detain', which means 'to hold back for a period of time'. Detention is not often used in primary schools because the formal act of detention is frequently used after school, with the accompanying logistical problems that it incurs for younger pupils. The most common form of detention in primary schools is in the form of a sanction, such as being made to stay inside during break time by the class teacher. Nevertheless, head teachers have the right to detain pupils – normally older children – at the end of a school session on disciplinary grounds, providing such action is explicitly stated in the school prospectus and discipline policy. As with all punishments, the detention must be reasonable and proportionate to the offence. If it takes place after school, parents

must be given at least 24 hours written notice. The notice to parents should explain why the detention is taking place and details of the practical arrangements (room, supervision, tasks, etc.). Parents have the right to object to the detention. In practice, after-school detentions are extremely rare in primary school settings.

DEWEY, JOHN

See also: child-centred education, morality, pedagogy, reflection, thinking skills

John Dewey (20 October 1859–1 June 1952) was an American philosopher, psychologist, and educational reformer whose ideas have been and continue to be highly influential around the world. Dewey was one of the founders of the branch of psychology that views mental life and behaviour in terms of active adaptation to the environment ('formative psychology') and a leading representative of the progressive movement in school education during the first half of the twentieth century. He is often associated – perhaps unfairly – with child-centred education. Smith (2009) suggests that Dewey's significance for educators is fourfold: (1) education must engage with and enlarge experience; (2) the significance of thinking and reflection; (3) interaction and environments for learning provide a continuing framework for practice; and (4) the centrality of educational democracy. Dewey probably ranks with the greatest thinkers of all time on subjects such as pedagogy, morality, epistemology (study of knowledge), logic, philosophy of science, and social and political theory. Examples of his education publications include:

Dewey, J. (1902) *The Child and the Curriculum*, Chicago: University of Chicago Press.
Dewey, J. and Dewey, E. (1915) *Schools of To-Morrow*, London: Dent.

Sources

Smith, M.K. for *Infed* (2001, 2009), *John Dewey*, on-line at www.infed.org/thinkers/et-dewey.htm

DIALOGUE

See also: debating, dialogue for learning, discussion, oracy, talk

Dialogue involves a conversation between two or more persons in which both make a necessary verbal contribution to maintain the exchanges. In addition to social dialogue ('small talk'), two forms of dialogue are promoted in primary education. The first form is 'critical dialogue', when issues are interrogated. The second is 'creative dialogue', when solutions to problems are being sought. Adult–pupil dialogue forms an essential element of learning, though in the majority of classrooms most talk is initiated by and sustained through the adult, with pupils responding to what the teacher says rather than being an equal participant in the exchanges. In pupil–pupil dialogue, some pupils are naturally garrulous and may dominate conversations to the detriment of more thoughtful children. Other pupils find it difficult to express themselves and yet others prefer to remain silent rather than to expose their inadequate grasp of the subject matter. Teachers have to take all these factors into account when planning their strategies for encouraging talk for learning.

DIALOGUE FOR LEARNING

See also: comprehension, cross-curriculum, dialogue, discussion, group work, learning climate, literacy hour, literacy strategy, oracy, Primary National Strategy, pupil perspectives, reading, writing

There is general agreement among educationists that pupils learn more effectively when they are given the opportunity to talk about their work, express their feelings and offer comment on issues. A study from the USA provides evidence to show that early oral discourse is a predictor of later reading and writing skills. The study by Griffin *et al.*

(2004) investigated relationships between pre-schoolers' oral discourse and their later skill at reading and writing. Thirty-two children participated in oral ('spoken') language tasks at the age of five years, and reading comprehension and writing assessments at the age of eight years. The research found that children's ability to mark the significance of narrated events (i.e. events told to them) at age five predicted reading comprehension skills at age eight. Children's ability to include content in expository talk at age five also predicted their reading comprehension at age eight.

After some years in the doldrums owing to the imposition of the so-called 'literacy hour' in schools in England and Wales after 1999, the concept of learning through dialogue was resurrected in 2006. Official support for teaching through dialogue or 'dialogic talk' as a means of enabling teachers and pupils to share and build on ideas in sustained talk was made explicit in the 'National Literacy Strategy Guidance' (England and Wales) as part of the *Primary National Strategy* (DfES 2006). Alexander (2006) argues that what he refers to as dialogic teaching harnesses the power of talk to stimulate and extend children's thinking, and to advance their learning and understanding. It also enables the teacher more precisely to diagnose and assess.

During a discussion session, teachers typically initiate talk by inviting spoken contributions from pupils on subjects that the teacher introduces. The teacher approves a pupil response and comments further or perhaps asks a question. The children respond again and the teacher confirms or offers perspectives on the different responses. Superficially there appears to be active dialogue, especially if the teacher invites the children to provide alternatives, give another example or offer suggestions. Yet even this apparently rich learning environment may be less efficacious than it seems because it is the teacher who raises all the issues and asks all the questions. It is the teacher who determines the quality of the children's responses. In the practicalities of teaching lessons within a given time frame these practices are almost inevitable if the session is ever to finish. On the other hand, such a strongly teacher-led approach assumes that all ideas must be from adults and that children cannot learn without close adult guidance.

Haynes (2007) comments that although primary schools work with a common curriculum, 'every school is made up of individuals trying to interpret and make sense and meaning of the world through their experience and by talking with one another' (p. 18). Killick (2006) even argues that young children 'can be observed to display a high degree of skill in organising groups, negotiating solutions and to have a high degree of insight into others' feelings, motives and worries' (p. 51). They can provide information, explain how something is done and suggest alternatives. In other words, children's insights and present sources of knowledge are a rich resource waiting to be unearthed. In effect, by a combination of enquiry and dialogue pupils become novice philosophers (see Haynes 2008).

Learning through dialogue does not and will not happen automatically simply because children are split into groups and given something to talk about (Grugeon and Hubbard 2006). It needs to be developed in the same way as any other learning technique, such as scientific enquiry, manipulating mathematical figures or shaping a clay pot. First, a suitably positive learning climate must have been developed such that is supportive and encouraging. Second, children must be inculcated into thinking about their learning rather than passively receiving it from an adult. Third, children must be given strategies for taking turns and offering an opinion. Last, and importantly, children must be taught how to listen to one another. This apparently 'natural' ability is anything but natural for a lot of children; however, the skill can be improved and refined over time.

Despite the growth in interactive teaching involving teacher–pupil exchanges, the incidence of extended dialogue has become less evident in primary teaching because teachers have been encouraged to inject 'pace' into the lessons and plan sessions under specific time constraints, most notably in literacy sessions. As a result, some teachers do not feel comfortable in allowing children room to pursue an argument, explore an issue or express an opinion unless it can be done succinctly and strictly within the constraints of the stated learning target.

A variety of practical considerations have to be taken into account in making the most effective use of time spent on dialogue. First, teachers find it is better to put children into homogeneous groups initially (capable pupils together; less capable pupils together) rather than mixed ones. In mixed groups the dominant children tend to do all the talking and although adults can monitor the situation to some extent, less confident children often merely sit and listen rather than participating. Second, pupils benefit from having a topic to talk about in the early stages. As children grow more experienced and confident, the teacher can allow and encourage them to raise their own topics, but probably within certain boundaries (e.g. relating to the present cross-curricular theme or topic). Sometimes the issue arises naturally from the curriculum work that is being covered with the children. Sometimes a national or international event will trigger considerable interest and the teacher decides to 'catch the moment' (a necessary part of teaching at all times). Third, children respond positively if encouraged to think and organise their thoughts before speaking. Children can jot down a few ideas on paper prior to the main discussion or work in pairs/with an adult to compile a short list of key points. It is particularly helpful for less confident pupils if pupils are urged to say 'in their heads' what they want to speak aloud before opening their mouths.

Sources

Alexander, R.J. (2006) *Towards Dialogic Thinking: Rethinking classroom talk*, York: Dialogos.

DfES (2006) *Primary National Strategy*, London: HMSO.

Griffin, T.M., Hemphill, L., Camp, L. and Palmer Wolf, D. (2004) 'Oral discourse in the pre-school years and later literacy skills', *First Language*, 24, 123–47.

Grugeon, E. and Hubbard, L. (2006) 'Learning through dialogue', in Arthur, J., Grainger, T. and Wray, D. (eds) *Learning to Teach in the Primary School*, London: Routledge.

Haynes, J. (2007) 'Thinking together: Enjoying dialogue with children', in Hayes, D. (ed.) *Joyful Teaching and Learning in the Primary School*, Exeter: Learning Matters.

——(2008) *Children as Philosophers: Learning through enquiry and dialogue in the primary school classroom*, London: Routledge.

Killick, S. (2006) *Emotional Literacy at the Heart of the School Ethos*, London: Paul Chapman.

DIDACTIC TEACHING

See also: constructivism, debating, discussion, memory and memorising, visual aids

The word 'didactic' is used where the teacher presents knowledge and information directly to pupils by using a lecture-style of teaching (adult speaks; children listen). It is the anti-thesis of a 'constructivist' approach to learning in which children work collaboratively to discuss, debate and investigate issues. Didactic teaching particularly benefits children who have the capacity to concentrate on what is being said and can absorb the spoken word without recourse to visual aids or practical activities. In this respect, it is more appropriate for educating older children, who have a greater capacity to concentrate and to retain and memorise information.

DIFFERENTIATION

See also: ability, curriculum, expectations, group work, lesson planning, lesson plans, mathematics, setting and streaming

No matter how carefully pupils are divided on the basis of ability, each group will contain a range of different types of children whose learning and academic needs have to be taken into account during lesson preparation and teaching. Legislation in the UK demands that all children receive a curriculum that is broad, balanced and differentiated. It is, therefore, 'a child's legal right to have a curriculum that is differentiated to meet their needs' (O'Brien and Guiney 2001, p. 4). The concept of dif-ferentiation is based on the belief that pupils differ in the extent to which they can absorb information, grasp ideas and apply themselves to a task, thereby necessitating in the work different demands and teacher expectations.

In the light of the diversity of ability and aptitude for learning that exists in every teaching situation, teachers are faced with a choice about two broad options about the way they differentiate when planning lessons. The first type is differentiation by *outcome* in which all pupils are engaging with similar curriculum material at a variety of conceptual levels. For example, differentiation by out-come may be appropriate when children are working independently or in matching pairs, when they will progress at varying rates, depending on their abilities. In this situation, the teacher's expectations for groups differs according to their academic competence. Second, differentiated *tasks* in which pupils of different ability work with separate curricu-lum material. For example, different groups (or 'sets') in mathematics will attend to tasks that are geared specifically to their compe-tence. In this situation, the activities and tasks involved would differ substantially from group to group so that all the children in the group have a reasonable chance of keeping pace with others in the same group.

For older primary children, organising for learning is frequently selected so that pupils of similar ability across several classes are taught together and placed in groups of similar ability. Whether within a single class or across classes, the ability grouping approach allows the planning to be more specifically targeted towards the academic needs of those particular pupils and requires less differen-tiation, though even within a single ability group there can be considerable variation in ability.

Some teachers believe that there is considerable merit in restoring the system that existed a generation ago (especially in mathematics) whereby each child worked through a series of tasks and problems at his or her own pace, using adult expertise and guidance at key points as necessary. More able children that work fast may be given additional work to be completed in the given time; however, as Davies (2006) advises, the extra task is not there to occupy the pupil but should develop the pupil's learning further and enrich their learning experience (see p. 91).

Medwell (2006) argues that differentiation affects a variety of aspects of planning and teaching, including the following (amended):

- *Presentation*: using a variety of media to present ideas, vocabulary and visual representations, including use of ICT.
- *Content*: ensuring there is content that suits all children and additional content for more capable pupils.
- *Resources*: making use of writing frames ('a blueprint' structure), word banks, alternative and simpler vocabulary for children for whom English is an additional language.
- *Grouping*: putting children of similar ability together or pair a less capable child with a more able child or adult.
- *Task*: match tasks to pupils' abilities (as far as possible).
- *Support*: offer adult support where needed and appropriate.
- *Time*: give more or less time for completion of tasks.

As an individually tailored curriculum is impractical other than for classes numbered in single figures, differentiated planning must rely on a satisfactory grouping of children such that each individual child in the group can cope with the demands of the work provided. See McNamara and Moreton (1997) and Edwards (2003) for practical suggestions and examples.

Sources

Davies, S. (2006) *The Essential Guide to Teaching*, Harlow: Pearson Education.

Edwards, N. (2003) 'Planning for all abilities: Differentiation', in Jacques, K. and Hyland, R. (eds) *Professional Studies*, Exeter: Learning Matters.

McNamara, S. and Moreton, G. (1997) *Understanding Differentiation*, London: David Fulton.

Medwell, J. (2006) 'Approaching short-term planning', in Arthur, J., Grainger, T. and Wray, D. (eds) *Learning to Teach in the Primary School*, London: Routledge.

O'Brien, T. and Guiney, D. (2001) *Differentiation in Teaching and Learning*, London: Continuum.

DILEMMAS FOR TEACHERS

See also: equal opportunity, interaction, morality, passion in teaching, professionalism, relationships, teachers' beliefs

Dilemmas in teaching are nothing new. Many years ago, Evelyn Rogers (Rogers 1946) wrote of the challenge of 'adapting the subject matter' to the needs of forty different children in forty minutes' (p. 178) and the tension between following a prescribed pattern of teaching and responding to pupils' individual interests and enthusiasms. In her article, 'Progressive ideals in practice: The teacher's dilemma', she particularly noted how some less able children are more comfortable with a predictable lesson format, which minimises thinking and emphasises 'doing', while more able children benefited from being forced to engage their minds. Rogers' dilemma and many similar ones will doubtless resonate with modern-day educators.

The *Collins Concise Dictionary* (1991) defines the word 'dilemma' as a position in fact or argument that offers a choice between unwelcome alternatives, in which case primary teachers face a number of them daily. Although impartial decisions are needed as far as possible when dealing with children, teachers need to take account of individual differences while remaining acutely aware of being fair and equitable in their dealings. On the one hand it is necessary for teachers to be consistent in their treatment of children; on the other hand one child will respond to a lighter 'touch' than another. Teachers are not judges in a court of law handing down sentences regardless of whoever stands before them. They must exercise wisdom in the way that they approach all interpersonal encounters. Nevertheless, the need for discernment is far removed from a blanket stereotyping of children on the basis of gender or any other defining characteristic (such as background, sportiness or even physical height). The resolution of the dilemma – in this case, to treat all children 'the same' and neglect individuality; or to treat each child individually and neglect basic tenets about equal opportunity – is to treat every case on its merit and use a large dose of common sense in making decisions, while explaining the reasoning behind the decision to the interested parties.

One of the key skills that teachers have to develop is to evaluate a situation rapidly and make a response that is not only fair but also *seen* to be fair by the children concerned. Tirri (1999) discusses the importance of professional morality in teachers' everyday work by exploring moral dilemmas identified by them and their strategies for resolving them, which were almost invariably case-specific rather than using established or absolute criteria. He found that in virtually all categories of moral dilemmas, teachers used *the best interest of a child* as the key determinant in their thinking and decision-making.

A further dilemma for teachers is that politicians and the media have put forward a weighty agenda about how schools and teachers should respond to the growing demands made by employers and the general public. By accommodating countless reforms and initiatives, primary teachers have demonstrated a healthy and constructive willingness to ensure that the commitment to their profession is seen in the various ways they build on traditions of pedagogy (ways to teach) and altruistic public service. On the other hand, teachers' own priorities and professional

judgements are sometimes at variance with the prescribed edict, thereby creating a tension in the role that can cause consternation, especially as there seems to be an expectation by school inspectors that externally imposed 'recommendations' about practice be enthusiastically embraced.

At the heart of teaching resides a desire to engage positively with the sorts of dilemmas that challenge teachers daily, notably those associated with children's well-being. Fried (1995) describes the concept of the 'passionate teacher' in just these terms:

> To be a passionate teacher is to be someone in love with a field of knowledge, deeply stirred by issues and ideas that challenge our world, *drawn to the dilemmas and potentials of the young people who come into class each day* – or captivated by all of these.
>
> (Prologue, emphasis added)

Sources

Collins Concise Dictionary (1991) London: Harper and Row.
Fried, R. (1995) *The Passionate Teacher: A practical guide*, Boston MA: Beacon Press.
Rogers, E.G. (1946) 'Progressive ideals in practice: The teacher's dilemma', *Educational Research Bulletin*, 25 (7), 178–82.
Tirri, K. (1999) 'Teachers' perceptions of moral dilemmas at school', *Journal of Moral Development*, 28 (1), 31–47.

DISABILITY

See also: learning difficulties, physical comfort

The term 'disability' is most often used to denote that the child suffers from a physical impairment, but it is also used in conjunction with the word 'learning'; thus, *learning disability*. In recent years there have been decisive moves to include children with disabilities in mainstream schools where possible to do so. The term 'handicapped' is now employed to indicate that the prevailing circumstances are hindering pupils from reaching their potential.

The handicap is often linked to resource provision, such that pupils cannot progress in ways of which they are capable because equipment is not available or damaged or inappropriate for use. However, the handicap can also be caused by a lack of time, poor working conditions (such as a stuffy room) or poor teaching. Children have physical disabilities that do not, with appropriate support, unduly handicap their educational opportunities or advancement, while others have congenital ('dating from birth') problems that impact strongly on their capacity to learn and require specialist adult support and intervention.

DISCIPLINE

See also: attention span, behaviour, boredom, fairness, happiness, naughtiness, questions and questioning, sanctions, speech

Responding to unacceptable behaviour is a challenge for all teachers and discipline is the means by which they try to ensure that the environment is orderly and conducive to learning. It requires patient, determined application, particularly in new situations. Strategies that appear to work with one group of pupils may be less successful with a different set of pupils, even in an almost identical situation. The challenges are particularly acute when a teacher begins teaching in a new school, where codes of conduct and accepted procedures are taken for granted by the existing staff and pupils but have yet to be learned by the new teacher (Neill and Caswell 1993). The word 'discipline' is normally reserved for the actions taken by the person in authority (a teacher, parent or helper) to modify the behaviour of the subordinate (the child), especially to teach self-control. However, Nelson (2006) insists that the key to positive discipline is not punishment but mutual respect. The author argues that parents and teachers can be both firm and kind, so that any child from a three-year-old toddler to a rebellious teenager can learn creative

co-operation and self-discipline with no loss of dignity.

Most children enjoy school, behave sensibly for the majority of the time and want to have a positive relationship with adults and other pupils. Some children are unpredictable and restless; others are born wanderers; some seem unable (perhaps, *are* unable) to sit and concentrate for long; a very small number will delight in making life difficult for the teacher, regarding it as a personal challenge to see what they can get away with. It is also true that despite a teacher's best efforts to make lessons relevant and interesting and to create a positive working environment, there may still be children who persist in inappropriate behaviour. For this troublesome minority, there are usually sanctions that can be applied but such procedures are time-consuming and wearisome, though sometimes necessary. Taking suitable action when faced with poor behaviour is one of the challenges that teachers face as they seek to establish a well-controlled yet inspiring classroom environment. Tolerance of minor instances of unacceptable behaviour is counterproductive if it leads to a worsening situation in the long run. On the other hand, teachers have to exercise sound judgement, as early forceful intervention can also be unhelpful if it disrupts the flow of a lesson, sours the atmosphere or creates unease among more timid children.

Some teachers regret that they were 'too soft' early on in their teaching and insufficiently firm in the opening encounters with a new class. Wright (2006) emphasises the concept of passivity, warning that 'the passive teacher is characterised by efforts to be popular that include ingratiating herself. She will have fragile feelings and will take criticism badly' (p. 58). Other teachers employ unnecessarily heavy-handed tactics when a lighter touch would be enough, thereby causing ill feeling and dismay among the children. There is always a danger of developing an impulsive response to every slight breach of the rules that result in stress for both the teacher and the children.

The Hay McBer Report (DfEE 2000) on effective teaching suggested that a lack of disruption and a settled classroom climate were two of the most significant influences on pupils' learning opportunities and progress, and that learning should be enjoyable most of the time and engaging pupils for all of the time. If learning is stale and seen as irrelevant, the children will soon let adults know by their listless attitude, restlessness and, perhaps, expressing their grievance in a variety of undesirable ways, such as yawning loudly, fiddling with their clothes, mouthing words to friends, making silly sounds, staring out of the window, doodling or lolling about. It is not possible to make every learning experience a scintillating one, but by trying to inject a sense of adventure into sessions, explaining the relevance and importance of less-than-thrilling content and maintaining a cheerful demeanour, teachers increase the likelihood that pupils will co-operate and respond positively.

Haydn (2007) argues that attempts by politicians to find straightforward solutions to discipline challenges fail to acknowledge the complexity of the situation; thus, 'The reality is that schools and teachers will always have to work hard, and with considerable initiative and ingenuity, to minimise the problem of disruptive behaviour. The idea that it can be eradicated by a couple of new policies is wishful thinking' (p. 15).

Every teacher wants to be liked by the children, but if this desire becomes obsessive it can detract from being decisive, clear and insistent and leads to a tentative approach to test the children's reactions, rather than saying what needs to be said to maintain classroom order and telling pupils precisely what they must do. Children like adults who are fair-minded, interested in them as people, transparent in their dealings, clear about their intentions, helpful in their explanations, non-judgemental in their words and unflinching in confronting situations when it is necessary. Surveys to determine what type of teacher is most popular nearly always place those with firm but fair approaches near the top. The reason for this rather surprising pupil attitude is simple: children like to know where they stand and who is in charge. They have little time for adults if they perceive that they are unreasonable or nasty or distant; however, a confident 'no nonsense' manner, streaked with humour and a sense of proportion about childish misdemeanours provides a secure learning climate in which children feel free to explore ideas, express opinions and strive for excellence.

Teachers are wise to try and model the behaviour they expect from the children (Newell and Jeffery 2002); if they are bossy, fussy and loud, there is a strong likelihood that it will be reflected in the classroom. If teachers are enthusiastic, level headed and have a smiling disposition, these qualities will become widespread in the same way. In truth, most teachers have no desire to impose a strict regime upon the class if it is possible to avoid it, and would prefer to coax, persuade, encourage and set targets for achievement as a means of keeping children on the straight and narrow. Such action nearly always pays dividends with most children and increases the likelihood that the environment will be relaxed and purposeful, though the rewards are not usually immediate and teachers need to persevere to achieve their aims. The Association of Teachers and Lecturers (ATL, online) offers plenty of realistic advice to novice teachers in particular, including ways to minimise conflict, including:

- Co-operation: helping children and young people to learn to work together and trust, help, and share with each other.
- Communication: helping children to learn to observe carefully, communicate well, and listen to each other.
- Respect: helping children to learn to respect and enjoy people's differences and to understand prejudice and why it is wrong.
- Positive expression: helping children to learn to express their feelings, particularly anger, in ways that are not destructive, and to learn self-control.

- Conflict resolution: helping children learn how to resolve a conflict by talking it through.

Children can be confused if teachers make a statement when they should be giving a command. For example, 'Can you put your books away?' is different in kind from 'Put your books away' and is likely to be interpreted differently by some children. The first utterance is a question (implying a degree of choice); the second is an instruction (communicating insistence). Although the children gradually grow to understand that the question is, in reality, a requirement, it may be some time before vulnerable children grasp this fact, by which time the adult will have had to contend with numerous avoidable incursions of the rule.

Although it is generally wise for teachers to maintain a steady flow of words, delivered in an interesting way, there are numerous occasions when intentional pauses and changes of 'body language' (facial expressions, gesticulations, etc.) are useful. For instance, in the midst of speaking the adult may gaze thoughtfully at the children, make a brief diversionary movement (such as stroking the chin or tapping a pencil on paper) before continuing. This technique has three benefits. First, it allows for some thinking time. Second, it offers a moment of respite from talking so that the children can re-focus their attention. Third, the silence causes the children to gain a sense of anticipation about what follows. The impact of interrupted action is enhanced if the first few words after the pause are spoken deliberately and slowly, as using the opportunity to scan the class and make numerous eye contacts often provides a psychological 'cohesion'. What seems to be a lengthy pause to the teacher feels much shorter to the children and conveys a strong sense of the adult being in command of the situation.

If a punishment or sanction is absolutely necessary, it is best imposed as soon after the behaviour as possible. When the child deliberately continues to break a rule, it may be appropriate to isolate him or her in a chair or a 'time-out' room with loose adult supervision. The time-out lasts about one minute per year of the child's age; for example, an eight-year-old is given up to eight minutes. However, Arnall (2007) insists that discipline should not be confused with punishment and advises parents: 'If you are using time out, grounding, unrelated consequences, spanking, yelling and removal of privileges and it's not achieving the permanent type of relationship you want, this may be the time for a new approach'. She goes on to suggest that 'you can set limits, provide guidance and correct misbehaviour without the use of punishments' (p. 19). One way or another, the good practice that adults employ for restless children and those with limited attention spans is relevant in organising learning for *all* children. In particular, lively children need adult models of control and calmness, so the use of a relaxed tone of voice when it is necessary to exert discipline is invariably beneficial.

Sources

Arnall, J. (2007) *Discipline Without Distress*, Berkley CA: Discipline Without Distress Publishing.

ATL: *Pupil behaviour: Building positive learning relationships with pupils*, on-line at www.new2 teaching.org.uk/tzone/Students/placement/behaviour.asp

DfEE (2000) *Research into Teacher Effectiveness* (Report by Hay McBer to the Department for Education and Employment) London: DfEE Publications.

Haydn, T. (2007) *Managing Pupil Behaviour*, London: Routledge.

Neill, S. and Caswell, C. (1993) *Body Language for Competent Teachers*, London: Routledge.

Nelson, J. (2006) *Positive Discipline*, New York: Ballantine Books.

Newell, S. and Jeffery, D. (2002) *Behaviour Management in the Classroom: A transactional analysis approach*, London: David Fulton.

Wright, D. (2006) *Classroom Karma*, London: David Fulton.

DISCOVERY LEARNING

See also: constructivism, enquiry-based learning, free play, group work, information technology, learning, motivation (pupils), problem solving, thematic learning, topic work

Discovery learning is an open-ended form of problem solving in which the teacher provides an introductory activity or stimulus on a relevant theme or topic to gain the children's interest, stir their natural curiosity and raise the level of enthusiasm and motivation. Children are then permitted considerable latitude to decide how they will proceed and shape the enquiry. When they have found out as much as they can in the allocated time, the children determine how they will present their findings – orally, formally written or presented diagrammatically. With younger children, feedback about their discoveries is normally spoken or presented in the form of a drawing.

Discovery learning is closely related to work by the French psychologist, Jean Piaget, and 'constructivist' theory, in which learners draw on their existing knowledge and past experiences to discover facts and relationships and insights. Robson (2006) refers to Penn (2005) and notes that by the 1950s Piaget's ideas had become known worldwide, especially in the field of early childhood education 'where they were seen as legitimising the idea of learning through "natural" or "free" play [i.e. free from direct adult influence], very much part of the nursery school tradition' (p. 13). Its proponents believe that discovery learning has many advantages, such as encouraging active pupil engagement; promoting autonomy motivation, responsibility and independence; developing creativity and problem solving skills; and offering an individualised learning experience. Critics, on the other hand, have cited disadvantages, such as the creation of cognitive overload (i.e. too much to think about at one time); the possibility of misconceptions (i.e. developing wrong ideas); and teachers failing to detect and correct mistakes and misconceptions (based on the Learning-Theories.com web site).

In primary schools, discovery learning is normally carried out in pairs or small groups and a report of findings is then made to the rest of the class. Resources are provided by the teacher in advance or created by the children as they proceed with their investigations. The use of information technology (notably through computers) is particularly helpful where the discovery is factual, rather than practical knowledge from hands-on application using materials (kinaesthetic learning). Discovery learning has become more difficult to employ in recent years with the onset of timetabling and increases in curriculum content, with its accompanying time pressures. There seems to be a consensus among primary educators that discovery learning is most effective when it is guided by a knowledgeable adult and used in conjunction with the more familiar direct instruction method.

Sources

Learning-Theories.com, *Discovery Learning (Bruner)*, on-line at www.learning-theories.com/discovery-learning-bruner.html

Penn, H. (2005) *Understanding Early Childhood*, Maidenhead: Open University Press.

Robson, S. (2006) *Developing Thinking and Understanding in Young Children*, London: Routledge.

DISCUSSION

See also: circle-time, communication, debating, dialogue for learning, listening, think-pair-share

Discussion takes place when children and adults make verbal contributions that offer perspectives on a topic from a variety of positions. Fisher (2005) suggests that the word discussion has two common uses: A *general* term to cover a wide range of informal situations where talk occurs between people and a *specific* meaning involving a particular form of group interaction where members join together to address an issue of common concern, during which they exchange different points of view in an attempt to reach a better understanding. Fisher refers to this second usage as a 'community of enquiry' and stresses that seven moral principles need to operate to facilitate the discussion: orderliness; reasonableness; truthfulness; freedom of expression; equality of opportunity; respect for others; and open-mindedness.

Pupils' involvement requires that they know enough about an area to offer an opinion, suggest alternatives or summarise a situation. As with all spoken language, discussion necessitates careful listening as well as marshalling and articulation of ideas. Such qualities are not easily acquired but can be shaped and steered by a teacher who is willing to give children the time and opportunity to express their thoughts. One of the challenges for teachers is to help children to understand that discussion is not merely an opportunity to put a point of view but to acknowledge and receive another person's perspective. Even adults find it difficult to be disciplined in discussions, so little wonder that children find it hard. To ensure effective discussion, teachers must ensure that children become competent in (a) expressing their thoughts clearly and listen carefully to one another; (b) responding constructively to what others say; (c) acknowledging that a variety of views exist; and (d) showing determination to learn and understand. Dillon (1994) provides a helpful definition:

> Discussion is a form of group interaction, people talking back-and-forth with one another. What they talk about is an issue, some topic that is in question for them. Their talk consists of advancing and examining different proposals over the issue.
>
> (p. 7)

According to Dillon, the uniqueness of discussion is due to it being disciplined and concerted talk about one issue. Dillon discourages teachers from asking questions during discussion and recommends that teachers use statements, signals, silence, and questions from pupils to stimulate thinking and move the discussion along.

Discussion relies on a dialogical or 'multilogical' approach, in which adult and children's voices are heard and contribute to the betterment of understanding. Black and Varley (2008) noted the responses of primary-age children to discussion opportunities, where a strong sense of affinity with the class was apparent as pupils referred to 'we' instead of using the first person. Whole class discussions provided a communal space and a sense of belonging that reflected the teacher's aim of creating an environment where everybody's ideas are valued.

Pupils are more likely to discuss something if there is something that merits consideration and grabs their interest. For instance, the worthiness of a cause, the correctness of a decision and the ethics of a controversial issue all provide fertile ground for an exchange of views. Younger children may discuss how best to take care of their snacks, ways to share toys or whether it is right to speak to strangers in the street. Older pupils may discuss issues of fairness, equality and classroom sanctions. Children of all ages can contribute to a discussion about local issues (such as a proposed road scheme); national issues (such as how to care for the elderly); and world issues (such as conservation). Opportunities also exist through the formal curriculum offered under the banners of personal, social and health education (PSHE), and citizenship.

Reading aloud an unusual poem, humorous story or intriguing extract can trigger excitement and an exchange of ideas. Flutter and Ruddock (2004) stress the importance of pupils' and teachers' having opportunity to verbalise their perceptions and insights to shed light on school and classroom situations that might otherwise remain undisclosed. Thus:

> When we invite teachers and pupils to give us their accounts of teaching and learning ... we also want to discover more about their perceptions of, and attitudes toward, their experiences in classrooms and schools ... It allows us to identify the things that teachers and young learners consider important

and that make a difference to pupils' opportunities for successful learning.

(p. 2)

Teachers who wish to promote discussion make sure that the context is stress-free and settled but also purposeful; noise and distractions detract from the concentrated attention that discussions need and deserve. With older children, teachers sometimes find it better to split the group or class into smaller units of (say) four or five children or even pairs ('think-pair-share') to discuss the issues, with a subsequent report-back in which summary comments can be made by a child selected from each group. Younger children are usually better off working within a whole-class situation (such as a 'circle-time' arrangement) where the teacher can exercise a more immediate influence upon the proceedings and ensure that timid children are included. A lot depends upon the nature of the discussion as to how intimately the teacher is involved. If the teacher intervenes too much, discussion is stifled; if too little, discussion may stray too far from the intended topic or dissolve into a series of unconnected comments. Experienced teachers find that it pays to be patient before intervening, as children sometimes need short bursts of relaxed talk to 'oil the wheels' before returning to the matter under consideration.

Sources

Black, L. and Varley, D. (2008) 'Young children's perspectives on whole class discussions', *Education 3–13*, 36 (3), 207–21.

Dillon, J.T. (1994) *Using Discussion in Classrooms*, Maidenhead: Open University Press.

Fisher, R. (2005) *Teaching Children to Learn*, Cheltenham: Stanley Thornes.

Flutter, J. and Ruddock, J. (2004) *Consulting Pupils: What's in it for schools?* London: Routledge.

DISPLAYS

See also: learning context, motivation for learning, reputation of teachers, self-esteem, stories, teaching assistants, writing

Despite the objectives-driven nature of modern primary school life, emphasising measurable academic outcomes, many teachers extol the virtues of colourful and well-displayed classrooms and invest a lot of energy into ensuring that pupils' work is visible. Teachers of younger children often establish different areas to stimulate the children's imagination: a *story corner* surrounded by lavishly painted pictures of characters from fairy tales; a *writing corner* separated from the rest of the room by curtains from which hang samples of completed stories and pictures; a *mystery corner* with unusual items of interest; a *home corner* full of household items. The same classroom may have a number of tables with objects collected during outdoor activities, maths equipment and small-scale construction materials to handle, play with and enjoy. Cards with carefully framed questions or challenges are placed alongside the displays, prompting children to extend their thinking by handling the items and talking about them to their friends. The pupils in these classrooms encourage their parents to come and admire their contributions. The teacher is known throughout the school as having a 'fantastic classroom'.

Putting up displays takes a lot of time and effort (Beasley and Moberley 2000) but helps to motivate pupils and enhance self-esteem if children's own work, as opposed to items of interest, is included. Displays also serve as a learning tool (see Cooper *et al.* 1996), notably when they are three-dimensional; for example, combining posters, pictures and written work on a vertical board with an adjacent table containing (say) models, information and questions relating to the theme of the display – to stimulate interest, raise issues and encourage children to talk. Many teachers of younger pupils like to incorporate examples of children's drawings, diagrams and paintings into the display. If the display is sufficiently good, the teacher can use it as a teaching aid and reinforce visual forms of learning. For example, photographs of the children in a variety of formal and informal poses, together with dates of birth and a list of their favourite foods and animals, are arranged on a board, with artefacts from their early lives – feeding cups, christening scrolls, clothing, etc. – on an adjacent table.

Although teaching assistants often take responsibility for organising the displays, teachers have to consider that some assistants do not possess display skills or may not produce the sort of display that the teacher had in mind, so active liaison between adults is essential. Nevertheless, a primary school with colourful, interactive displays, including well-mounted examples of children's work, is still the norm. A classroom of this kind brings prestige to the staff and approval from the people who matter: children, parents, governors and colleagues.

Sources

Beasley, G. and Moberley, A. (2000) *Seasonal Displays*, Pittsburgh PA: Scholastic.

Cooper, H., Hegarty, P. and Simco, N. (1996) *Display in the Classroom: Principles, practice and learning theory*, London: David Fulton.

DISTRACTIBLE CHILDREN

See also: attention-deficit hyperactivity disorder, attention span, behaviour, friendships, homework, rewards

Distractible children have a hard time keeping their minds on a task or activity and may get bored after only a few minutes. However, like all children, if they are doing something they really enjoy they have no trouble paying attention. Homework is particularly hard for these children, as they will forget to write down the details of an assignment or leave it at school or forget to bring a book home or take the wrong one. The homework, if finally finished, is often full of errors and crossings out; as such, it can be a source of frustration for both adult and child. Some children are naturally active and energetic and in all probability will remain so throughout their time in school; however, truly hyperactive children seem to be constantly in motion and are likely to charge around, touching or playing with whatever is in sight and talking incessantly. Sitting still at dinner or during a school lesson or story is a difficult task for most of them; they squirm and fidget in their seats or roam around the room, wiggle their feet, touch surfaces and noisily tap the table with a rule or pencil.

Teachers have to ensure that distractible pupils stay busy but also to be aware that they have a tendency to do several things at once, often superficially and with limited success, resulting in frustration and occasional anger. The more impulsive children seem unable to curb their immediate reactions or think before they act, so they blurt out inappropriate comments, display their emotions with little restraint and act without regard for the later consequences of their conduct. Their impulsivity may make it hard for them to wait for things they want or to take their turn in games; they may therefore grab a favourite toy from another child or even hit classmates when they are upset. Typically, easily distractible children choose to do things that provide an immediate but small reward, rather than engage in activities that may take more effort yet offer the prospect of greater, delayed rewards (see National Institute of Mental Health USA, on-line).

Sources

National Institute of Mental Health (USA), on-line via www.nimh.nih.gov/health/publications

DRAMA

See also: arts, assembly, Bruner, constructivism, creativity, cross-curriculum, English, fantasy, history, inclusion, interaction literacy, numeracy, oracy, science, singing, speech

Drama is located within the English programme in the National Curriculum for England, Wales and for Northern Ireland and is one of the four strands of speaking and listening; it focuses on the processes of *making, performing and appraising.* As part of their work to enhance speaking and listening ('oracy') and participate in drama activities, pupils at key stage 1 (5–7 years) are taught to use language and actions to explore and convey situations, characters and emotions; create and sustain roles; and comment constructively on the drama that they see and experience. At key stage 2 (7–11 years) pupils are taught to create, adapt and sustain different roles; use character action and narrative to convey themes, emotions and ideas in plays they devise and script; use dramatic techniques to explore characters and issues; and evaluate how they and others have contributed to the work in drama.

Younger primary pupils learn to work in role, present drama and stories to other children in their own class and beyond (e.g. as part of an assembly) and respond to performances that they witness by offering comment. Older primary pupils are also encouraged to respond to performances but also to improvise and work in role; subsequently, they may write as if they were a character in role and perform in plays. In Scotland, the National Guidelines for the Expressive Arts 5–14 set out the aims for drama in primary schools. Implicit in the Guidelines is the notion that the four subjects in the expressive arts curriculum are mutually supportive because they share similar principles and engage pupils in similar processes. Aims specific to drama require that pupils should:

- gain understanding of themselves and others through dramatic, imaginative experience;
- communicate ideas and feelings using language, expression and movement in real and imaginary situations;
- develop confidence and self-esteem in their relationships with others and sensitivity towards others;
- develop a range of dramatic skills and techniques.

(See section 2.5)

Drama is an art form and, as such, gives significance to life and relationships. It allows children to explore and understand the significance in order and disorder, harmony and discord, the expected and unexpected, and so forth. Johnson (2004) argues that drama provides a limitless range of contexts, rich with opportunities for developing a deeper understanding of their own creative processes by thinking from within a situation and reflecting on its significance. In the introduction to their book, *Beginning Drama 4–11*, Winston and Tandy (2001) stress its playful orientation. The authors argue that right from when we are very young children we learn to distinguish between the conventions of play and those of everyday life. In addition, 'it is from children's innate capacity for play, and upon the understandings they gain from participating in play, that dramatic activity can be constructed' (p. vii).

Bolton (1992), referring to Bruner (1990), stresses the importance of giving young children opportunities for narrative forms of discourse, for which drama is admirably suited. Bolton emphasises that narrative forms of communication have deep implications for a child's development in making sense ('meaning-making') of situations. Exploring fictitious events such as historical events through drama is a form of make-believe playing; however, to become drama it is necessary for that spontaneous and imaginative play to be translated into a public performance. The author warns, however, that an over-reliance on pleasing an audience and reducing spontaneity is counter-productive.

A constructivist approach to learning is used by teachers when they ask groups of pupils to create 'tableaux' by sub-dividing complex events (e.g. a complete story) into smaller elements, encouraging the children to discuss how they might represent their element and 'freeze-framing' the key moments. For instance, in a depiction of the events relating to the 1666 Great Fire of London, one group might depict a tragic death, another group might depict attempts to escape by boat; and another depict fire-fighters trying to stop fire from spreading.

Dickinson and Neelands (2001) insist that drama is valuable over and beyond its intrinsic value and provides links with other areas of the curriculum ('cross-curricular'). With particular reference to a case study school's approach, the authors suggest a wide range of strategies to show how drama can help with behaviour, inclusion and multicultural issues, improving the whole school ethos and involving parents and governors. Similarly, Ackroyd and Boulton (2001) give numerous practical examples about ways in which drama has a part to play in most curriculum areas, including English (especially speaking and listening), history, science and numeracy.

Sources

Ackroyd, J. and Boulton, J. (2001) *Drama Lessons for Five to Eleven Year Olds*, London: David Fulton.

Bolton, G. (1992) *New Perspectives on Classroom Drama*, Hemel Hempstead: Simon and Schuster.

Bruner, J. (1990) *The Relevance of Meaning*, London: Harvard University Press.

Dickinson, R. and Neelands, J. (2001) *Improve Your Primary School Through Drama*, London: David Fulton.

Johnson, C. (2004) 'Creative drama: Thinking from within', in Fisher, R. and Williams, M. (eds) *Unlocking Creativity*, London: David Fulton.

Winston, J. and Tandy, M. (2001) *Beginning Drama 4–11*, London: David Fulton.

DRESS CODE

See also: decision-making, parents, physical education, professionalism, uniform

Dress codes for pupils normally involve wearing a regulation uniform, though some allowance may be made for younger children with regard to buttons and laces. In the UK there has been a trend towards enforcing a dress code – strengthened by studies (mainly based on secondary education) claiming that a uniform creates a sense of orderliness and reduces class distinction. Some schools, especially in rural areas, take a more liberal view and try to be more accommodating of variations; for example, children may be obliged to wear a particular 'top' with the school logo but have more choice about other clothing. The majority of parents seem to prefer the children to wear a uniform, though the relatively higher cost as compared with regular clothing has produced numerous 'second-hand uniform shops' offering decent quality merchandise at lower prices.

A dress code for adults in school is a more contentious issue, and in the USA it has created a great deal of controversy. Waggoner (2008) explores how decisions about dress code exercise school leaders in balancing reasonable standards of appearance and modelling to pupils, against the right of an individual to select what he or she wears. The sharp divisions of opinion about what constitutes appropriate clothing has led to calls for a more standardised code that will eliminate unnecessary debate and contention. However, reaching any kind of consensus is more difficult to achieve than it may appear, as arguments about professional standards have to be weighed against personal preference.

Teachers involved in physical activities need to wear suitable clothing during sessions but may not have the time, facilities or opportunity to change from formal clothing to sports gear, and back again. In primary schools the tendency is for teachers who normally dress conservatively to wear sports gear when the class is timetabled for games or PE and then throughout the rest of the day.

Adults working with younger children are likely to be involved in physical education activities requiring bending over, floor work and movement; adults working with older primary pupils will be aware of children who are entering early adolescence and more conscious of the human body, so dress accordingly. In the UK it is still unusual for staff to be subjected to a formal dress code; it is much more common for an 'unspoken' code to exist (e.g. men wearing ties; women avoiding high heels) that tends to bring about conformity over a period of time without a policy decision being necessary.

Sources

Waggoner, C. (2008) *What Teachers Wear to School: The administrative dilemma*, on-line at http://cnx.org/content/m15787/latest

DYSLEXIA

See also: brain function, intelligence, intervention, literacy, phonics, reading, special educational needs, writing

Dyslexia comes from the Greek language meaning 'difficulty with words' and is viewed by most educators as a learning disability. About 4 per cent of the population has severe dyslexia, while a further 6 per cent experience mild to moderate problems; in a class of thirty children, this statistic translates into three pupils with dyslexia per class. Evidence suggests that dyslexia results from differences in how the brain processes written and/or spoken language (MacNair 2008). The majority of people who suffer from dyslexia have difficulty with writing, reading and spelling, which are considered to be separate and distinct from difficulties with vision or hearing or from inadequate teaching. Dyslexia cannot be classified as an intellectual disability because it has been diagnosed in people possessing all levels of intelligence, including exceptionally able scholars. Pavey and Harper-Jones (2007) draw definitions from the British Dyslexia Association (BDA, www.bdadyslexia.org.uk) including, 'Dyslexia is evident when accurate and fluent word reading and/or spelling develops very incompletely or with great difficulty. This focuses on literacy learning at the word level, and implies that the problem is severe and persistent despite appropriate learning opportunities'. The authors note that there is an increasing tendency not to view dyslexia as a 'deficit' and emphasise that dealing with the problem requires a whole-school approach and should not be left to individual teachers.

Dyslexia is sometimes used to refer to a child who has an average or above average IQ, with a reading grade some one or more years below the expected level. A common problem for readers is confusing letters like b and d, either when reading or when writing. Sometimes they read (or write) words like 'tar' instead of 'rat' and 'won' instead of 'now'. They may become easily disorientated and struggle to discriminate left and right, east and west. Another frequent sign is elisions; for example, when a child reads or writes 'car' when the word is actually 'care'. Children that read very slowly and hesitantly, without fluency and word by word, or who constantly lose their place in the text, have reading problems associated with dyslexia. A child may try to sound out the letters of the word (i.e. phonetically) but then be unable to say the correct word; for example, sounding the letters 't-a-p' but then be unable to say 'tap'. The child may read or write the letters of a word in the wrong order, such as 'left' for 'felt', or the syllables in the wrong order, such as 'emeny' for 'enemy', or words in the wrong order, such as 'is he' for 'he is'. As a result, children suffering from dyslexia read with poor comprehension or remember little of what they read. Spelling, too, is often a challenge; typically, they spell words as they sound, for example 'rite' instead of 'right'. A further typical characteristic is poor and/or slow handwriting (Audiblox, on-line).

Compensating for dyslexia depends on the severity of difficulty. In cases linked to visual differences, a coloured overlay across the page and tinted lenses can lead to improvement because they can stop the letters from 'dancing on the page' – a common complaint by children with dyslexia. Frost and Emery (2000) suggest that teachers can intervene in a number of ways, a modified version of which appears below:

1 Teach children similarities and differences between how something is said and how it is written.
2 Provide direct instruction in language analysis and the alphabetic code.
3 Give explicit instruction in segmenting and blending speech sounds, helping

children to process progressively larger chunks of words.

4 Use techniques that make phonemes (smallest units of meaningful sounds) more concrete; for example, phonemes and syllables can be represented with blocks where children can be taught how to add, omit, substitute, and rearrange them.

5 Model skills in various reading contexts; review previous reading lessons and relate to current lessons.

6 Discuss the specific purposes and goals of each reading lesson.

7 Provide regular practice with reading materials where the content is located in familiar contexts and include many words that children can decode (to build confidence).

8 As a core sight vocabulary is acquired, expose children to more irregular words to increase reading accuracy.

9 Teach for comprehension by introducing conceptually important vocabulary prior to initial reading and asking children to retell the story and answer questions regarding explicit ('blatant') and implicit ('hidden') content.

10 Teach children the main components of most stories (i.e., character, setting, etc.) and how to identify and use these components to help them remember the story.

11 Teach reading and spelling in conjunction. Teach children the relationship between spelling and reading and how to correctly spell the words they read.

12 Provide positive, explicit and corrective feedback. Praise effort as well as success.

The British Dyslexia Association (BDA) defines its vision as 'a dyslexia friendly society that will enable all dyslexic people to reach their potential'. The BDA promotes early identification and support in schools to ensure opportunity to learn for dyslexic learners. Reid (2007) and Hall (2009) offer practical suggestions about classroom and school implementation.

Sources

Audiblox, *Dyslexia in Children: Symptoms, cause and treatment*, on-line at www.audiblox2000.com/dyslexia_dyslexic/dyslexia015.htm

Frost, J.A. and Emery, M.J. (2000) *Academic Interventions for Children with Dyslexia Who Have Phonological Core Deficits*, on-line at www.kidsource.com/kidsource/content2/dyslexia.html

Hall, W. (2009) *Dyslexia in the Primary Classroom*, Exeter: Learning Matters.

MacNair, T. (2008) *Dyslexia*, BBC Health, on-line at www.bbc.co.uk/health/conditions/dyslexia2.shtml

Pavey, B. and Harper-Jones, G. (2007) *The Dyslexia-friendly Primary School: A practical guide for teachers*, London: Sage.

Reid, G. (2007) *100 Ideas for Supporting Pupils with Dyslexia*, London: Continuum.

DYSPRAXIA

See also: attention-deficit hyperactivity disorder, attention span, bullying, communication, playground, rules, self-esteem

Dyspraxia is a developmental difficulty that can overlap with other conditions such as dyslexia; attention-deficit hyperactivity disorder (ADHD); and social and communication difficulties, including Asperger's syndrome. It affects about 6 per cent of the population and is three times more likely to affect boys than girls. In the past dyspraxia has been referred to as 'clumsy child syndrome' but the reality is considerably more complex. There is no cure for the condition but early diagnosis is essential. In school or when playing with other children, anxiety, concentration and understanding the rules may be a problem; the child is likely to have more difficulty than most in passing a ball or easily trip up when trying to control it. The *Good Schools Guide* (2008) suggests that typical problems in school include:

- difficulties following long instructions, and in planning and organising work and themselves;
- difficulty copying text from book or whiteboard;
- variable ability – better some days than others and may get tired more easily;
- low self-esteem and frustration, which will sometimes result in disruptive behaviour;

- difficulty in ball sports;
- difficulty writing at speed or drawing neatly;
- slower getting changed for games lessons.

Coping with other children's ridicule is an important issue of which parents and adults in school must be aware, as it not only damages the individual's confidence but can also result in bullying and being ostracised. For example, the child may be among the last to be 'chosen' by a classmate for the team in a competitive situation. However, it is perfectly possible for children struggling with dyspraxia to succeed in other areas of life, such as swimming or board games or IT (see Macintyre 2009 for other practical suggestions). The Dyspraxia Foundation (www.dyspraxia foundation.org.uk) provides classroom guidelines for schools and teachers, aimed at helping teachers to make classroom life more comfortable and productive for children in their classes.

Sources

Good Schools Guide (2008) 'Dyspraxia', Liverpool: Lucas Publications.
Macintyre, C. (2009) *Dyspraxia 5–14*, London: David Fulton/NASEN.

E

EARLY YEARS

See also: early years teachers, emotions of learning, Foundation Stage, National Curriculum, observing children, play, Primary National Strategy, stepping stones

Early years is a term used to describe children who are not yet of formal school age (pre-five years in most of the UK) but are receiving a recognised form of education in nurseries, playgroups or pre-school centres. The large majority of staffs working with the youngest children are female. The Early Years Foundation Stage, EYFS (DCSF 2007) is an attempt to build a coherent and flexible approach to care and learning, so that whatever educational setting parents choose for their children, they can be confident that they will receive a good education. The development of an EYFS curriculum for pre-school pupils in most parts of the UK is recognition of the fact that young children require a special type of education that forms the basis for subsequent schooling. The justification for the large amount of funding that has been allocated to this phase of education is underpinned by a belief that pre-school education intervention is amply rewarded by later academic success and increased social stability. Riley (2007) notes how the requirements of the EYFS document relate both to the national curriculum and the Primary National Strategy framework for teaching for literacy and mathematics.

Six developmental 'priming mechanisms' to enhance learning have been suggested for children in the EYFS. First, encouraging them to explore their environment. Second, close involvement of adults to assist with basic intellectual and social training. Third, celebrating new expertise that children acquire. Fourth, rehearsing and expanding new skills. Fifth, protecting children from ridicule for developmental advances. Sixth, stimulating language and communication. The formal early learning goals are set out within six areas of learning, as follows:

1 Personal, social and emotional development
2 Communication, language and literacy
3 Problem solving, reasoning and numeracy
4 Knowledge and understanding of the world
5 Physical development
6 Creative development.

These statutory early learning goals establish expectations for most children to reach by the end of the EYFS. They provide the basis for planning throughout the EYFS, so laying secure foundations for future learning. By the end of the EYFS, some children will have exceeded the goals. Other children, depending on their individual needs, will be working towards some or all of the goals – particularly some younger children, some children with learning difficulties and disabilities and some learning English as an additional language. Detailed guidance on the early learning goals

113

and how to work with children to achieve them is set out in the *Practice Guidance for the Early Years Foundation Stage*. The goals are extensive in scope and create a considerable challenge for teachers and assistants as they attempt to assess and record children's progress. For example, the goals for personal, social and emotional development include:

- Continue to be interested, excited and motivated to learn.
- Be confident to try new activities, initiate ideas and speak in a familiar group.
- Maintain attention, concentrate, and sit quietly when appropriate.
- Respond to significant experiences, showing a range of feelings when appropriate.
- Have a developing awareness of their own needs, views and feelings.
- Be sensitive to the needs, views and feelings of others.
- Have a developing respect for their own cultures and beliefs and those of other people.
- Form good relationships with adults and peers.
- Work as part of a group or class, taking turns and sharing fairly.
- Understand what is right, what is wrong and why.
- Consider the consequences of their words and actions for themselves and others.
- Dress and undress independently and manage their own personal hygiene.
- Select and use activities and resources independently.
- Understand that people have different needs, views, cultures and beliefs that need to be treated with respect.
- Expect others to treat their needs, views, cultures and beliefs with respect.

Equivalent lists refer to aspects of communication, language and literacy; to problem solving, reasoning and numeracy; to knowledge and understanding of the world; and, more briefly, to physical development and creative development. There is also a series of *stepping stones* to show the knowledge, skills

understanding and attitudes that children need in order to achieve the early learning goals. The guidance gives 'examples of what children do' to assist practitioners to identify significant developments and plan the next steps in children's learning. It also gives examples of what the practitioner purportedly needs to do to support and consolidate learning and help children make progress towards the early learning goals.

In an early attempt to grapple with the specific curriculum needs of young children, Blenkin and Whitehead (1987) insisted that an early years programme should include opportunities for showing and telling about feelings aroused when children are unable to complete a task or when they feel fearful of situations. They argue that opportunities to address such emotions can be fostered through talking, drawing, painting, modelling, movement, PE and fantasy play. More recently, Broadhead (2004) presents practitioners with a 'tool-kit' (set of strategies and techniques) for observing and assessing children's play. The author also provides a framework for reflecting on and developing traditional areas of provision across the 3–7 age range, such that links between intellectual development, language growth and emotional well-being are made more explicit.

Readers wishing to explore issues relating to early years education may wish to refer to the series edited by Parker-Rees and Willan (2005) containing an extensive collection of papers for those who wish to ground their own study in wider historical and global discourses about the education of children under eight. In addition, Nutbrown *et al.* (2008) illustrate the fascinating history of early childhood studies by bringing together ideas from the work and writings of major historical figures that have significantly shaped and influenced present-day practice.

Sources

Blenkin, G. and Whitehead, M. (1987) 'Creating a context for development', in Blenkin, G. and

EDUCATED CHILD

Kelly, A.V. (eds) *Early Childhood Education: A developmental curriculum*: London: Paul Chapman.

Broadhead, P. (2004) *Early Years Play and Learning*, London: Routledge.

DCSF, *Sure Start*, on-line at www.surestart.gov.uk

——(2007) *The Early Years Foundation Stage*, London: HMSO.

Nutbrown, C., Clough, P. and Selbie, P. (2008) *Early Childhood Education: History, philosophy and experience*, London: Sage.

Parker-Rees, R. and Willan, J. (eds) (2005) *Early Years Education: Major themes in education*, London: Routledge.

Riley, J. (2007) *Learning in the Early Years*, London: Sage.

EARLY YEARS TEACHERS

See also: communication, early years, Foundation Stage, observing children, social development, social learning, transitions

Early years teachers are sometimes referred to as nursery teachers and work in pre-school, nursery and reception classes with children aged between three and five years. The early years teacher plays an important role in developing a child's enthusiasm for learning and is responsible for developing and implementing work schemes and lesson plans in line with the requirements of the foundation stage curriculum. The teacher will spend most of her or his time with the same group of children. In addition to the more formal aspects of the curriculum, such as developing reading skills, early years teachers foster the children's social and communication skills. In all their work, a lot of emphasis is placed on establishing and maintaining relationships with parents and carers as 'co-educators'. Close observations and recording of children's achievements and development help to prepare them for successful transition to primary school education.

EDUCATED CHILD

See also: interaction, literacy, moral development, numeracy, questions and questioning, relationships, social development, spiritual education, success, tests and testing, thinking, thinking skills

Children receive an education at school but understanding what 'an educated child' means is far from simple. The notion that a good education is to prepare children to pass public tests and examinations has been promoted by politicians but failed to satisfy many educators, who view the task as far greater (see, for example, arguments presented by Kohn 2004). It is, of course, important for children to become both literate and numerate, as this will arm them with the basic skills that give them the confidence to attempt to fulfil their dreams and aspirations, whichever path in life they choose. However, the truly educated child is one who has the skills and ability to continue development or building upon his or her physical, social, mental and emotional well-being in all aspects of life. Such children have a desire to work towards their full potential and an awareness of their own capabilities and limitations, showing a positive attitude to themselves and those around them, which involves building effective relationships and behaving appropriately. Classroom-based knowledge and subject matter provides a basis for prospering in life but truly educated children should want to continue to extend their search for knowledge outside school. They need to understand and be able to apply the knowledge and skills learnt in a classroom environment in a more general social environment.

Fully educated children enjoy and understand the importance of education and are willing to express and share their ideas. They look and delve deeper into lessons and are always willing to do that little bit extra, showing a willing attitude to their school studies, both academically and socially. Such children are able to show their enthusiasm through their work and have the ability to succeed in areas where they are strongest but also to have a positive attitude towards developing in those areas where they are weakest.

115

Educated children can express their thoughts verbally and on paper and are willing to persevere to achieve their goals. In a landmark book edited by Blenkin and Kelly (1983) called *The Primary Curriculum in Action*, the argument was made that to be an educated person is to value things for their own sakes, to think beyond the immediate context, to examine issues critically, to put matters in perspective and, above all, to think independently and question what is taken for granted. Educated people are independent learners who have the confidence to communicate effectively their understanding and awareness of the environment around them and realise that they may not succeed at everything straight away. As part of this search for understanding, children should also realise that it is acceptable to ask thoughtful questions as this will reinforce and deepen learning.

There is also a spiritual element to being truly educated. As children are continually on a self-discovery tour, it is essential for them to know who they are, rather than just knowing they can reach academic targets. The concept of developing 'character' has almost become outmoded in recent years; however, Ryan (2008), writing from a Catholic perspective, makes the point that character development is an essential element of education and that educators have a responsibility to provide guidance and example in helping to shape it. He argues that children do not naturally develop into people of good character; but rather that they need to be educated about what it means to be a good person and, through training and opportunities, to acquire the habits or virtues that mark them out as good people. The corollary to Ryan's argument is that children left to find their own way through life without loving guidance either suffer from physical neglect or develop into self-centred adults. Consequently, it takes time and energy to acquire the habits and dispositions that constitute good character. An educated child therefore needs not only to possess an awareness of how to be fair, respectful, compassionate, trustworthy and trusting, but also to understand different moral approaches and the reasoning behind these, and opportunities to engage with practical ways of putting them into action.

As children move through the primary years they have to learn how to identify specific social situations and consider intuitively how to react and behave, including an ability to establish appropriate and respectful relationships with adults and peers. Hopefully, pupils will recognise how what they are learning in the classroom is relevant to the rest of their lives. They know about the moral values of society and are capable of a holistic approach to the world around them. A comprehensive view of this important area is provided in Peterson and Seligman (2004).

An educated child is, therefore, a highly complex, well-rounded individual with an emotional, intellectual, spiritual and social understanding of themselves and others and able to interact with people of all ages and ethnicities. Such a child can formulate ideas and feelings and communicate these to people, adapt to different environments and accept constructive criticism to be able to reflect on their actions and how their actions affect others. Educated children think about what needs to be done rather than just reacting to situations. They have enquiring minds and a desire to continue learning outside an academic setting.

Sources

Blenkin, G.M. and Kelly, A.V. (1983) *The Primary Curriculum in Action*, London: Paul Chapman.

Kohn, A. (2004) *What Does It Mean to Be Well Educated?* Boston MA: Beacon Press.

Peterson, C. and Seligman, M. (2004) *Character Strengths and Virtues*, New York: Oxford University Press.

Ryan, K. (2008) 'Character education walks again', *Catholic Culture*, Melbourne: New Media Foundation.

EDUCATIONAL VISITS

See also: cross-curriculum, health and safety, medication, outdoor education, planning, relationships, topic work

Children love to go on visits and many claim that it is the most exciting part of the school year for them. Most schools have a well-ordered programme of visits and there are well-trodden paths to museums, landmarks, ancient monuments and adventure courses. Visits are very hard work but immensely rewarding and a means of enhancing the pupils' social development and helping adults to gain insights into each child's disposition, interests, strengths and limitations. Pupils also get to know the adults better and relationships are sealed (or occasionally marred).

School trips, educational visits and other field activities can be great fun but also times of hazard and potential danger, so a lot of planning is required to ensure that a visit is safe and educationally worthwhile (Salaman and Tutchell 2005). In addition to checking that the venue is suitable for the age group and is properly managed, trip organisers have to send letters home detailing the itinerary, receive permission slips from parents, order transport, confirm insurance and liaise with colleagues whose lessons may be affected by the children's absence.

Teachers have to ensure that every element of the visit has been considered in detail. A 'good practice guide' known as *Health and Safety of Pupils on Educational Visits* (DfEE 1998) was designed to help head teachers, teachers, governors in schools and others to ensure that pupils stay safe and healthy on school visits. A supplement to the good practice guide was produced (DfES 2002), as follows:

Standards for Local Authorities sets out the functions of the educational visits co-ordinator in schools and the levels of risk management that local authorities and schools could use.

Standards for Adventure is aimed at the teacher or youth worker who leads young people on adventure activities.

A Handbook for Group Leaders is aimed at anyone who leads groups of young people on any kind of educational visit. It sets out good practice in supervision, ongoing risk assessment and emergency procedures.

Group Safety at the Margins is aimed at anyone who organises learning activities that take place near or in water, such as a walk along a river bank or seashore, collecting samples from ponds or streams, or paddling or walking in gentle, shallow water.

(www.teachernet.gov.uk/wholeschool/healthandsafety)

Comprehensive official guidance containing information and guidelines on all aspects of health and safety that affect schools, including the medical needs of children, emergencies and school security is provided in a document, *Health and Safety: Responsibilities and powers* that was issued to schools in 2001.

Waite and Rea (2007) comment that if suitable clothing is worn and sensible precautions are taken, there is no end to the range of opportunities for outdoor learning at minimal cost. Larger venues (such as zoos) normally have an education department, appropriately staffed and resourced.

Clarifying the role of the different adults involved in the visit is important in making the visit a safe and successful one. Adults are strongly advised to carry a mobile telephone and a list of important contact numbers with them at all times. Teaching assistants have an important role to play in the preparation and monitoring of equipment, supervision of children and support for learning – so time has to be allocated to ensure that they are properly informed. Younger children require more supervision than older ones and under-fives need a large adult presence (one adult per two or three children), but the experience and competence of the adults involved also has to be taken into account.

Educational visits are frequently linked to topic work or a specific area of a subject such as science or history, and result in the production of displays and other artistic outcomes (such as a drama sketch for an assembly). Many teachers use a visit as a starting point for innovative teaching and learning of the cross-curricular kind (touching several distinct subject areas) and the production of stimulating displays and events.

Sources

DfEE (1998) *Health and Safety of Pupils on Educational Visits*, London: HMSO.

DfES (2002) *Health and Safety: Responsibilities and powers*, London: HMSO. On-line at www.teachernet.gov.uk/wholeschool/healthandsafety

Salaman, A. and Tutchell, S. (2005) *Planning Educational Visits for the Early Years*, London: Paul Chapman.

Waite, S. and Rea, T. (2007) 'Enjoying teaching and learning outside the classroom', in Hayes, D. (ed.) *Joyful Teaching and Learning in the Primary School*, Exeter: Learning Matters.

EFFECTIVENESS

See also: achievement, caring teachers, effectiveness, expectations, good teachers, humour, modelling behaviour, motivation for learning, motivation for teaching, observing children, teachers' beliefs

The expressions 'good teacher' and 'effective teacher' are often used interchangeably; however, whereas 'good' has a strongly moral component, effectiveness in education has become equated with practitioners meeting pre-determined performance targets, expressed with regard to pupil performance in formal tests (see Hayes *et al.* 2001; Campion 2004). For qualified teachers, the implications of effectiveness are significant for their salary and promotion prospects; for trainee teachers it is measured by the level of their success on school placements for work experience. Effective teachers have open and accessible communication with colleagues, parents and pupils, and succeed in making each child feel valued, happy and confident. They use techniques that motivate children and maintain discipline while demonstrating genuine care; and adapt their teaching methods to suit and satisfy children's varying needs. See Wong and Wong (2009) for practical advice about classroom organisation and management from a US perspective.

Effective teachers enjoy working with children and have patience to help and encourage them in their learning. They look beyond pupils' immediate abilities and see the potential in every child; observe and listen to children in the class, both as individuals and within a group; assess the academic needs of each one; and organise the learning to give everyone a chance to succeed. They help and encourage the children to become independent thinkers and self-motivated learners, providing the necessary resources and support for learning. The effective teacher needs to possess solid subject knowledge but also to be adept at putting across information in an accessible way such that the child will remember the facts and be enthused to find out more.

Effective teachers make a conscious effort to be liked by the pupils but do not try to ingratiate themselves, as children work better with teachers they admire and respect. Effective teachers have clearly established classroom routines with manageable procedures that make sense to the pupils, who are not afraid to approach them for academic or welfare support. Ultimately, the best teachers succeed in making the children think for themselves and thereby extend their ownership of new learning instead of making them passive recipients of information. They encourage pupil participation, strive to promote a relaxed but purposeful learning environment – where children are given time to think constructively rather than be hurried into providing a 'correct' answer – and aid communication through touches of humour. All adults in school are faced with the challenge of promoting and maintaining group cohesion, while not suppressing genuinely held beliefs and helping children to reconcile their differences. At the same time the adults need to set an example for children by modelling a positive attitude to learning and keeping failure in perspective.

Many educationists have pointed out that a teacher may achieve miracles in motivating a group of underprivileged children who, nonetheless, perform quite poorly in formal tests. Different governments have made a good job of convincing the public that the only success criteria that warrant serious consideration are measurable ones, despite the self-evident truth that (non-measurable) moral and social factors are immensely important in creating a civilised, peaceful society. Parents are interested to know that their children are valued, that teachers are doing their best for them, and that their sons and daughters are happy, well adjusted and fulfilled.

Effectiveness in teaching is ultimately posited on a belief that all children should have the opportunity to succeed at their own level of understanding and feel fulfilled and satisfied. In promoting effective learning, teachers have to be careful not to dismiss underachievement by using tired excuses such as 'boys will be boys' or 'that sort of child never makes an effort' or 'well you cannot expect anything more'. High expectations must be accompanied by adult enthusiasm and belief. Teachers act as guides in as much as they can show pupils that learning is exciting and worthwhile, thereby promoting a spirit of enquiry; offer tantalising glimpses into fresh areas of knowledge; and actively encourage children to think laterally by posing problems and setting up challenges for them to overcome.

Day *et al.* (2007) argue that teacher effectiveness is not simply a consequence of age or experience. First, it is influenced by professional life phases, owing to the fact that older teachers normally have greater responsibility in school and may struggle to maintain a satisfactory work–life balance. Second, effectiveness is influenced by teachers' sense of professional identity, which is affected by the degree of tension they experience between their own educational ideals and those imposed externally by government, advisers, head teacher, colleagues or parents. Third, teachers' ability to handle interactions between personal, work and professional factors impinges strongly upon their effectiveness. In other words, effectiveness resides as much in the heart as in the head.

Sources

Campion, H. (2004) 'Teachers' values and professional practice in primary schools', in Browne, A. and Haylock, D. (eds) *Professional Issues for Primary Teachers*, London: Paul Chapman.
Davis, A. (2001) 'Can we pick out good teachers by discovering what they have taught their pupils?' *Education 3–13*, 29 (3), 33–38.
Day, C., Sammons, P., Stobart, G. Kington, A. and Gu, Q. (2007) *Teachers Matter: Connecting lives, work and effectiveness*, Maidenhead: Open University Press.
Hayes, L., Nikolic, V. and Cabaj, H. (2001) *Am I Teaching Well?* Exeter: Learning Matters.
Wong, H.K. and Wong, R.T. (2009) *The First Days of School: How to be an effective teacher*, Mountain View CA: Harry Wong Publications.

EINSTEIN, ALBERT

See also: discovery learning, educated child, mathematics, science, tests and testing

Einstein may seem an unlikely candidate for inclusion in a reference book about primary education; in fact, he made a number of relevant and significant contributions to our understanding of key philosophical and educational issues. Albert Einstein was born on 14 March 1879 in Ulm, Württemberg, Germany to Jewish parents, Hermann and Pauline. He died on 18 April 1955 in Princeton, New Jersey, USA, aged 76. It is generally accepted that Einstein was one of the greatest scientific minds the world has known and that few people in history have possessed comparable genius. However, Einstein's success was hard-won; he experienced a troubled childhood and became disillusioned with the education system of the day. Despite showing a strong interest in mathematics and science from a young age, he got so bored with his schoolwork that he stopped doing it and was branded an academic failure, including in mathematics! It is widely believed that Einstein's mathematics teacher, Hermann Minkowski, became so exasperated with young Albert's lack of interest in the class that he called him a 'lazy dog'.

In fact a characteristic of Einstein's personality was that he only studied things that interested him and refused to conform to other people's expectations. Even when

119

Einstein was a student in college he used to get upset because the professors only covered what was then known as the 'old physics', when Einstein was desperate to learn about new theories. Einstein's attitude might be considered arrogant and irresponsible by those who deem that effective education depends on learner conformity; but it can also be viewed as courageous and determined by those who value innovativeness and lateral thinking. It is certain that Einstein would not be comfortable in today's education system, in which an objectives-driven curriculum predominates and even opportunities for creativity have to demonstrate that they contribute towards 'raising standards' (i.e. national test scores). Indeed, he once commented that everything that can be counted does not necessarily count; everything that counts cannot necessarily be counted.

Einstein's single-minded approach to learning and refusal to be a passive recipient of information had been a stumbling block in his schooling but now it became an immense asset as he grappled with highly complex phenomena. Einstein envisaged a set of conditions in which space and time are relative and the speed of light is constant. He later wrote a paper called 'On the electrodynamics of moving bodies', later given the name 'Special relativity', published on 30 June 1905.

Einstein spent ten further years of study and experimenting until in 1915 he published another paper called 'General relativity', which created considerably more controversy than 'Special relativity' had done. The opposition to his ideas was such that even when Einstein was awarded the Nobel Prize in Physics it was explicitly stated that the award was for his other contributions to physics and not for the development of the theories. However, during the technological advances in the late 1920s and early 1930s it gradually became accepted that his relativity theory was correct and Einstein earned his place in history.

These accolades proved to be a major turning point in Einstein's life, as shortly after receiving the acclaim he receded from the scientific community and directed his energies towards social reform and issues relating to world order. Thus, in 1931 Einstein published an essay entitled, 'The world as I see it' in *Forum and Century*, vol. 84, pp. 193–94, the thirteenth in the Forum series, 'Living Philosophies'. In the essay he set out his ideas about life, relationships and achieving harmony. The article is particularly noteworthy as it speaks of mystery, marvelling and the need for humility in understanding the world.

By the time of his death in 1955 Einstein had established himself not only as a supreme physicist and intellectual but also as someone who recognised that real achievement was not founded solely in academic distinction. He came to appreciate that a complete 'life education' consists of more than learning what someone else expects you to learn in the way that the teacher expects you to learn it. During the Second World War he was motivated to speak out against the small number of well-educated but deluded scientists had employed their skills to create weapons of mass destruction and inflict pain and suffering on fellow humans.

Sources

Hayes, D. (2007) 'What Einstein can teach us about education', *Education 3–13*, 35 (2), 143–54.

ELEMENTARY EDUCATION

See also: arithmetic, Hadow reports, middle schools, reading, Steiner Waldorf, writing

The Elementary Education Act of 1870 provided education to the British people on an unprecedented scale. School Boards were introduced and given the power to create new schools and pay the fees of the poorest children. Board schools could insist on the attendance of children at elementary schools between the ages of five and thirteen. After the 1931 Hadow Report, the school system was organised on the now-familiar system of primary and secondary education, and elementary schools were phased out.

In North America, 'elementary education' is broadly equivalent to primary education in the UK and refers to formal education for children from kindergarten (age five or six years) until they reach grade 5 (ten to eleven years) or grade 6 (eleven to twelve years). In some states in the USA grade 5 is the first year of junior high school. Traditionally, sixth grade was the final year of elementary school. In the USA and Canada, sixth grade is usually the first year of middle school but sometimes the final year of elementary school; it can sometimes be the second year of middle school. In North America 'primary education' customarily refers to only the first three years of elementary education – that is, from grades 1 to 3. In Waldorf (Waldorf-Steiner) schools, elementary education begins when the child is nearing or already seven years of age.

Elementary education also has a more general definition in being an education in basic subjects – notably reading and writing and arithmetic – provided to young pupils. In this sense, nearly all nations are committed to some form of elementary education, though in many developing countries children are unable to continue full-time studies beyond the primary phase, normally due to lack of available funding.

ELEVEN-PLUS

See also: English, mathematics, parental involvement, tests and testing

The eleven-plus examination is a test given to pupils in their final year of primary school (year 6 in England; year 7 in Northern Ireland) and is normally used for determining whether children are suited to the academic demands of a grammar school education. The format of the examination varies from region to region but normally consists of a verbal reasoning paper, a non-verbal reasoning paper, a mathematics paper and an English

paper – or a selection from these four options. The outcome of the eleven-plus determines whether children will be offered a place in the grammar school of their parent's choice, depending on a child's test score and the availability of places. Since the early 1970s most areas of the United Kingdom have not used the eleven-plus exam and have favoured a non-selective comprehensive education system. Considerable opposition to the eleven-plus has been evident from people who believe that it is socially divisive and wrong to discriminate between children at such an early age. Teachers of final year pupils in primary schools that are located in the same area as a popular grammar school often feel under considerable pressure from parents to coach children for success in the examination.

EMOTIONAL INTELLIGENCE

See also: emotional literacy, intelligence, Intelligence Quotient, success

If asked what they know about intelligence, the average person will probably say something about IQ (Intelligence Quotient) and 'being bright' or 'being dull' or words to that effect. Asked about emotional intelligence (EI), the same person would probably stare blankly. Professional educators would no doubt be familiar with the term but still offer a variety of perspectives and insights. In fact the study of EI evolved from works of such theorists as Gardner (1983) and Williams and Sternberg (1988), who proposed a broader perspective to understanding intelligence. However, Salovey and Mayer are credited with coining 'emotional intelligence' and included Gardner's intrapersonal and interpersonal components in the formulation. In 1990 they published two articles on EI. The first article (Salovey and Mayer 1990) reviewed literature throughout the disciplines of psychology and psychiatry, artificial intelligence and other areas, and concluded that there might exist a human ability fairly called

EI, whereby some people reasoned with emotions better than others. The companion article (Mayer *et al.* 1990) presented a first ability model of EI in which they suggested that EI might exist and could be measured as a genuine form of intelligence. EI can be measured as an Emotional Intelligence Quotient, describing an ability, capacity or skill to perceive, assess and manage the emotions of one's self, of others and of groups. The phrase 'emotional literacy' is used to describe programmes to increase EI – see, for example, Steiner (2000) – though sometimes the terms are used interchangeably.

Goleman popularised EI in the business realm by describing its importance as an ingredient for successful business careers and as a crucial component for effective group performance (e.g. Goleman 2005). It is fair to note that Goleman's theories have not been universally accepted and some educationists in the field regard some of his claims as suspect. For example, Eysenck (2000) argues that Goleman's work on EI exemplifies more clearly than most the fundamental absurdity of the tendency to class almost any type of behaviour as an 'intelligence'. Paul (2000) suggests that Goleman significantly distorted the original Salovey and Mayer model, portraying the emotionally intelligent person as one possessing all the qualities of a *nice* person – kind, warm and friendly – while the originators focused far more on the fluid interplay between emotions and intelligence. Paul also claims that Goleman greatly expanded the boundaries of EI, including qualities such as zeal and persistence, which are not normally associated with emotion. Goleman also equated high EI with maturity and character, a correspondence that Salovey and Mayer had firmly resisted making, and asserted that our EI predicts our success more accurately than IQ.

Sources

Eysenck, H. (2000) *Intelligence: A new look*, Dexter MI: Transaction Publishers.

Gardner, H. (1983) *Frames of Mind*, New York: Basic Books.
Goleman, D. (2005) *Working With Emotional Intelligence*, New York: Bantam Books.
Mayer, J., DiPaolo, M. and Salovey, P. (1990) 'Perceiving affective content in ambiguous visual stimuli: A component of emotional intelligence', *Journal of Personality Assessment*, 54, 772 – 781
Paul, A.M. (2000) *Promotional Intelligence*, Salon Books, www.salon.com
Salovey, P. and Mayer, J.D. (1990) 'Emotional intelligence', *Imagination, Cognition, and Personality*, 9, 185–211.
Steiner, C.M. (2000) *Emotional Literacy: Intelligence with heart*, Fawnskin CA: Personhood Press.
Williams, W.M. and Sternberg, R.J. (1988) 'Group intelligence: Why some groups are better than others', *Intelligence*, 12, 351–77.

EMOTIONAL LITERACY

See also: circle-time, emotional intelligence, relationships, social and emotional aspects of learning, social development

Emotional literacy (EL) is a phrase that was coined by Claude Steiner in the 1970s, defined broadly as, 'you know what emotions you and others have'. He has since gone on to develop his idea of EL, which he later referred to as 'emotional intelligence with a heart' (Steiner 1997, 2000), though EL is a term that is often used interchangeably with EI. (See Mayer *et al.* 1990 for details of the first empirical study of EI that explicitly used the term.)

Hein (2008) simply says that EL is the ability to express feelings with specific feeling words, in three-word sentences; for example, *I feel rejected*. Thus, Hein argues, the purpose for developing our EL is to precisely identify and communicate our feelings. When we do this we are helping nature to fulfil its design for our feelings.

EL has also been described as the practice of interacting with others in ways that build understanding of our own and of their emotions, then using this understanding to inform our actions. It is now common parlance in education circles, though with a variety of usages, including the vernacular form about 'working smarter not harder' (see, for instance, Bocchino 1999). The EL curriculum in school work is intended to help children to forge links between their emotional feelings, their thinking and their behaviour, based on the premise that the way children feel affects the way that they think, and vice versa.

Organisations such as the 'Emotional Literacy Campaign' in the USA (www.feel.org) powerfully advocate the benefits of EL, describing it as the alphabet, grammar and vocabulary of our emotional language and the language of all relationships. Supporters see EL as the antidote to a range of social ills, such as violence, disease, and depression, and the key to healthy and vital relationships. The campaign's blurb asserts that we need to give our children the tools to transform fear into compassion, anger into passion, and loss into love. Similarly, the School of Emotional Literacy based in Kircaldy (Scotland) offers a comparable perspective:

> Emotional literacy involves sensing, understanding and using emotional information from oneself and other people in order to make informed and effective decisions, which then drive our actions. It involves skills training as well as developing personal awareness. Emotional literacy is our ability to read and understand emotional states, and most importantly, to act on them.
>
> (www.schoolofemotional-literacy.com)

In addition to EL and EI, a third expression, 'emotional education' is also in vogue. The Emotional Education web site (www. emotional-education.co.uk) defines emotional education as providing a way of understanding ourselves and others in a deeper way. It notes that the main proponent of EI, Daniel Goleman, a science journalist, was even going to call his first book *Emotional Literacy* until he came across the term EI as defined by Salovey and Mayer (1990; Goleman 1997). There is therefore a degree of confusion around whether EI and EL are in

fact the same concept but called by different names.

In England and Wales, EL is commonly linked with the SEAL initiative (social and emotional aspects of learning) in the belief by assisting children to articulate their feelings and negotiate with peers and adults, they are more likely to embrace learning positively. An in-depth study by a team from the University of Manchester for the DCSF (Humphrey *et al.* 2008) about making brief, early interventions in small groups for children thought to require additional support to develop their social and emotional skills, concluded that it led to a small amount of positive change in pupils. The change appears to be sustained following the end of the intervention if children receive carefully organised support in their everyday classroom settings. With younger primary-aged children the use of 'circle-time' can facilitate such support (Roffey 2006).

Sources

Bocchino, R. (1999) *Emotional Literacy: How to be a different kind of smart*, Thousand Oaks CA: Corwin Press/Sage.

Goleman, D. (1997) *Emotional Intelligence*, New York: Bantam Books.

Hein, S. (2008) *Emotional Literacy*, accessed through http://eqi.org/elit.ht

Humphrey, N., Kalambouka, A., Bolton, J., Lendrum, A., Wigelsworth, M., Lennie, C. and Farrell, P./DCSF (2008) *Primary Social and Emotional Aspects of Learning (SEAL): Evaluation of small group work*, Research Report DCSF-RR064, University of Manchester.

Mayer, J.D., DiPaolo, M.T. and Salovey, P. (1990) 'Perceiving affective content in ambiguous visual stimuli: A component of emotional intelligence', *Journal of Personality Assessment*, 54, 772–81.

Roffey, S. (2006) *Circle Time for Emotional Literacy*, London: Paul Chapman.

Salovey, P. and Mayer, J.D. (1990) 'Emotional intelligence', *Imagination, Cognition, and Personality*, 9, 185–211.

Steiner, C. (1997) *Achieving Emotional Literacy*, London: Bloomsbury.

Steiner, C.M. (2000) *Emotional Literacy: Intelligence with heart*, Fawnskin CA: Personhood Press.

EMOTIONS OF LEARNING

See also: interaction, learning, life skills, motivation for learning, social learning

The impact of emotions has implications for children's learning. Some pupils fear failure and worry about getting things wrong and being in trouble as a result. Other pupils are either unwilling to persevere when faced with challenges because they are unable to cope with the situation, or they avoid making more than a nominal effort to achieve a satisfactory outcome. As these negative responses are the result of emotional insecurity, teachers spend a lot of time seeking to understand the root causes of behaviour and strengthening each child's sense of well-being. Teachers encourage pupils to persevere with work and not be afraid of making genuine errors; they also use mistakes positively by explaining the alternatives and using the opportunity to deepen children's understanding of concepts.

Hyson (2003) suggests that there are six goals in achieving what she describes as an 'emotion-centred curriculum' (see p. 6): (1) creating a secure emotional environment, (2) helping children understand emotions, (3) modelling genuine, appropriate emotional responses, (4) supporting children's regulation of emotions, (5) recognising and honouring children's expressive styles, and (6) uniting children's learning with positive emotions. Hyson goes on to offer evidence of the damage to a child's emotional development when appropriate teaching is lacking. For example, increased instances of stress and anxiety, particularly among boys and low-income black children, when curricula do not adequately address emotional issues.

Macklem (2007) refers to 'emotion regulation' and argues that with targeted training in the classroom, at home and among peers, children can better attain the vital skills they need for a lifetime of social interactions. Teachers whose lives are calm and orderly will carry the associated emotions into the classroom for the benefit of the children for whom they feel responsible in ways that go beyond the academic realm.

Sources

Hyson, M. (2003) *The Emotional Development of Young Children*, New York: Teachers College Press.
Macklem, G.L. (2007) *Practitioner's Guide to Emotion Regulation in School-aged Children*, New York: Springer.

EMOTIONS OF NEW TEACHERS

See also: induction year, probationary year, school climate

Emotions are central to every teacher's work. This fact is especially significant for trainee teachers on work placement and new teachers in school as they enter a situation that is largely unknown to them in respect of the prevailing ethos, interpersonal relationships and patterns of behaviour. As part of the 'rite of passage' (Clandinin 1989), these novice teachers have to cope with adjusting to the prevailing norms; establish and maintain relationships with staff; and learn procedures and adapt to the school's priorities, some of which may be abstruse and difficult to interpret. O'Flynn and Kennedy (2003, pp. 140–45) suggest a number of strategies to survive and prosper in the job, including: (a) build regular physical activity into your routine; (b) plan some quiet relaxation time each day; (c) seek support and help others who need it; (d) conserve energy during the day, remaining calm and pacing yourself; and (e) aim for good enough, not perfect.

An 'induction year' or 'probationary year' exists for newly qualified teachers in most advanced nations, in which the new teacher is mentored by a colleague and inculcated into school practices. However, the emphasis is less on understanding 'the way we do it here' and the subliminal 'unwritten rules' that characterise the particular education establishment and more on enhancing teaching competencies that relate to planning, class management, keeping records and the like.

Sources

Clandinin, D.J. (1989) 'Developing Rhythm in Teaching: The narrative study of a beginning teacher's personal practical knowledge of classrooms', *Curriculum Inquiry*, 19 (2) 122–41.
O'Flynn, S. and Kennedy, H. (2003) *Get Their Attention*, London: David Fulton.

EMOTIONS OF TEACHING

See also: body language, effectiveness, emotional literacy, fulfilment in teaching, Intelligence Quotient, motivation for teaching, reflection, relationships, speech

Primary teachers experience a range of emotions in the job including, at one extreme, powerful sensations of love and a near obsession with personal status and success, while at the other extreme, from an altruistic perspective, a desire to serve the pupils in their care and professionally strive to satisfy the varying expectations of government, colleagues, parents and the local community. Teachers also experience waves of anxiety about their classroom performance, which has gained impetus due to the introduction of 'performance management', in which judgements about their teaching competence and (in some cases) pupils' test results are factors influencing promotion prospects. The emotional *cost* of teaching is mental and emotional exhaustion, constant self-examination and ripples of self-doubt. However, the *rewards* provide high levels of compensation, represented through the reassurance of seeing pupils progress; being an integral part of a community of adults and children in a single endeavour; and opportunities to be creative and fulfilled from being part of a team endeavour (Nias 1989).

Goleman has been instrumental in alerting educationists to the central role played by the emotions in decisions and actions (e.g.

Goleman 2005). He argues that human competencies like self-awareness, self-discipline, persistence and empathy are of greater consequence than IQ (Intelligence Quotient) in much of life, and that we ignore these competencies at our peril. Research about the demands made on teachers suggests that their emotional condition has a major role in the ease with which they handle pressure. It is important, therefore, for teachers and pupils to understand and manage their emotions, learn how to effectively communicate and gain insights from a range of life experiences. The process of becoming more 'emotionally intelligent' is commonly referred to as 'emotional literacy' (EL), which includes listening and reflecting on what is being said by someone; focusing on the non-verbal clues from the speaker ('body language'); understanding the impact of one's words; and clear communication (see Corrie 2003).

It is in the classroom that the impact of a teacher's emotional sensitivity is most readily exposed, as the basis of effective teaching is located in communicating and connecting with pupils through care, trust, mutual respect and establishing a rapport with them. The emotional attachment that exists between teacher and children and the sense that they are in partnership to achieve things of significance, provides a sense of purpose and fulfilment. Teachers enjoy helping children and gain great satisfaction from seeing 'the light go on' as many teachers describe the experience when a child grasps something for the first time. See articles by Nias (1996, 1997), in the second of which she alerts us to the fact that teachers may allow their emotions to dominate at the expense of concentrating on a pupil's academic progress.

Emotionally sensitive teachers make an effort to engage with children at two levels. First, they seek to understand the way children think and thereby demonstrate a genuine interest and concern in their welfare. Second, they offer direction through suggesting possibilities and alternatives in the learning process. Emotional sensitivity also alerts a

125

teacher to the motives that underpin a pupil's behaviour. Thus, a pupil's distorted facial expression may indicate that the child is trying to make sense of a problem. Poor eye contact with adults may mean that the child is feeling alarmed, guilty or under-confident. A pupil's rapid speech can indicate enthusiasm, commitment or confusion, whereas hesitant or slow speech indicates confusion or mental overload and fatigue.

One of the many challenges facing teachers is to make instant decisions about what is genuine and what is contrived emotion. These insights are gained through becoming familiar with the children's dispositions and backgrounds, identifying their individual needs and responding appropriately to their disparate behaviours. The effort involved in making such instant judgements contributes to the emotional demands made of all practitioners. See Hargreaves (2009) for a comprehensive exploration of issues relating to the emotions of teaching.

Sources

Corrie, C. (2003) *Becoming Emotionally Intelligent*, Stafford: Network Educational Press.
Goleman, D. (2005) *Working With Emotional Intelligence*, New York: Bantam Books.
Hargreaves, A. (2009) *Emotions of Teaching*, San Francisco CA: Jossey-Bass.
Nias, D.J. (1989) *Primary Teachers Talking*, London: Routledge.
——(1996) 'Thinking about feeling: The emotions in teaching', *Cambridge Journal of Education*, 26, 293–306.
——(1997) 'Would schools improve if teachers cared less?' *Education 3–13*, 25 (3), 11–22.

ENCOURAGEMENT AND PRAISE

See also: ability, assessment for learning, body language, feedback, formative assessment, rewards, self-esteem

It is helpful to distinguish between *encouragement* and *praise*. Tauber (2007) suggests that whereas praise is a reward given by an adult for completed achievement, encouragement is an acknowledgement of the *effort* made by a child. Praise implies that pupils have fulfilled the adult's expectations, while encouragement helps children to evaluate their own performance and achievements. Encouragement boost pupils' esteem, promotes respect and acceptance and is given without conditions. This final point (encouragement given without conditions) is important because it is common to hear a teacher encouraging or praising a child in one breath, only to point out shortcomings in the next. There is a place and time to offer feedback and guidance to children (referred to as formative assessment or 'assessment for learning', AFL) but encouraging types of comments to celebrate achievement can be separated from the developmental ones.

The most effective teaching takes place in an atmosphere where acknowledgement and praise are offered to all pupils, not only the best-behaved ones. Wise adults catch children doing something praiseworthy (however small) and quietly offer their approval, as the warmth of a teacher's personality and encouragement achieves more than icy threats. Kohn (2004) warns, however, that teachers need to be careful not to create what he describes as 'praise junkies', as a calculated tactic to control children's behaviour rather than as a genuine expression of admiration. Similarly, Australian psychologist Robin Grille is strongly sceptical about the 'praise-reward' mentality that dominates so much of our education systems. Grille (2005) argues that praise is wonderful when it is not used manipulatively but generally recommends that adults praise children less and start *appreciating* them more. Grille goes on to say that children are born with an enormous desire to learn and have an innate capacity for honesty, empathy and considerateness. These qualities come forward as a result of adult guidance, role modelling and our appreciation of children. Rewards and praise for good behaviour or good performance simply get in the way. For fuller details, see also Grille's article,

'Rewards and praise: The poisoned carrot' on The Natural Child web site (www.natural child.com).

Sometimes 'off-task' pupils can be drawn back to the work as they observe an adult's attention to a hard-working classmate (Dix 2007). In this way, encouragement can not only be given to particular children to help them improve on their present efforts, complete a difficult piece of work or concentrate harder in order to achieve a higher standard, but also to act as an incentive for classmates to do likewise. When encouraging children, teachers use a variety of expressions to cajole, chivvy, motivate and offer support, accompanied by sparkling eye contact, clapping, smiles, open faces and close body positions. Praise can later be offered for achievement: good quality work, real effort, instances of sensitivity and responsibility, offered with great enthusiasm, publicly announced.

Children won't accept encouragement or praise from someone they don't respect but will see it rather as a subtle form of coercion. Experienced practitioners find that it is better to bide their time and be gently approving rather than let loose a flood of commendation during the earliest encounters with the class. Less experienced practitioners soon discover that a pupil's efforts and product about which they originally enthused is, in reality, below the child's ability level. As a result, it pays teachers to be cautious in making definite judgements before they have found out about pupils' previous attainments and established an informed view of each child's potential.

When children accept that an adult is trying to understand them rather than looking for things to criticise, they are more likely to confide their reasons for the lower-than-hoped-for quality of the work. A sympathetic but firm approach unlocks doors that remain tightly shut to those adults who adopt a stiffer approach that carries a strong hint of disapproval and reproach. For children who trust and love their teacher, there is no greater source of satisfaction for them and no greater incentive to continue persevering than receiving sincere praise (Kelly and Daniels 1997).

Sources

Dix, P. (2007) *Taking Care of Behaviour*, Harlow: Pearson.

Grille, R. (2005) *Parenting for a Peaceful World*, Sydney: Longueville Media.

Kelly, F.D. and Daniels, J.G. (1997) 'The effects of praise versus encouragement on children's perceptions of teachers', *Journal of Individual Psychology*, 53, 1–11.

Kohn, A. (2004) *What Does It Mean to Be Well Educated?* Boston MA: Beacon Press.

Tauber, R.T. (2007) *Classroom Management: Sound theory and effective practice*, Orlando FL: Harcourt Brace College Publishers.

ENGLISH

See also: communication, creative writing, curriculum, drama, handwriting, literacy, oracy, reading aloud, spelling, stories, writing

English is not only timetabled as a subject in its own right in primary schools but also integral to other curriculum subjects. Broadly, the English curriculum consists of speaking and listening ('oracy'), drama, reading and writing – including spelling, grammar and handwriting. In February 2003 an initiative called 'English 21' was launched in the England by the Qualifications and Curriculum Authority (QCA) to stimulate discussion about the future direction of English in the twenty-first century, which resulted in a raft of proposals, including:

- boosting creativity by bringing poets, writers, actors and journalists into the classroom;
- an increased emphasis on creative writing;
- speaking and listening to be a priority;
- eight and nine year-old pupils to be taught keyboard skills;
- boosting cultural understanding;

127

- using texts from a wide range of cultures;
- reading and writing texts on screen.

Primary school English is intended to develop an awareness of all aspects of language, encourage enjoyment amongst children of the richness and variety of both spoken and written communication, and promote their confidence and competence as speakers, listeners, readers and writers. Pupils are taught the skills of planning, drafting, revising and editing their work and practising writing for a variety of purposes and audiences. Gardner (2009) urges teachers to be adventurous and creative in their teaching, while covering the mains strands of the Primary National Strategy (PNS) for English: narrative, non-fiction and poetry.

Concerns have been expressed that English lessons are being marginalised and replaced by more highly structured 'literacy', such that children no longer have the freedom to read for pleasure or express themselves in writing. The principal accusation is that children are reading too many extracts rather than whole books with the result that the love of reading for its own sake is gradually being lost. Extracts of texts are 'mined' for parts of speech in the belief that once the parts have been named the children can use them independently in their writing. Debate continues about whether the sum of the parts creates the whole; in practice, teachers of older primary children combine a study of different parts of speech with enjoyment of written passages (including reading stories aloud) for their own sake.

Cremin (2009) explores the core elements of creative practice in relation to developing engaged readers, writers, speakers and listeners, together with ways to explore powerful literary, non-fiction, visual and digital texts.

Sources

Cremin, T. (2009) *Teaching English Creatively*, London: Routledge.
Gardner, P. (2009) *Creative English, Creative Curriculum*, London: David Fulton.

ENGLISH AS AN ADDITIONAL LANGUAGE

See also: individual education plans, learning objectives, minority ethnic group under-achievement, problem solving, tactile learners, teaching strategy

English as an additional language (EAL) used to be referred as English as a foreign language (EFL). Gardner (2006) summarises ways to improve the quality of learning for all children, including children for whom English is an additional language. Thus, they should 'encounter an element of problem solving if their learning is to be effective. They need to be able to build on prior knowledge, not to be overloaded in terms of the number of objectives for any one lesson, be able to interact with others and be given time to complete tasks' (p. 78). Gardner goes on to suggest that using puppets, verbal games involving pairs of children, role play, and rhyme and story, and visual tactile resources are strategies likely to enhance learning and create a language-rich environment. Scott (2008) focuses on the needs of newly arrived older children (aged 7–11 years) by providing a structured programme for non-expert teachers and teaching assistants to teach early stage learners of EAL and develop knowledge and understanding of their language development needs.

Children may be highly competent in their own language but struggle when expected to use English. It is possible to lower expectations of the children and assume that they are far less capable than in fact they really are. While it may be tempting to allocate a child with limited English easy tasks to allow for his or her language deficit, teachers have to limit the length of time that this happens, for two reasons. First, the child may become the butt of teasing from classmates owing to the simple nature of the tasks. Second, the child quickly becomes under-stimulated and disillusioned with the undemanding work. The strategies teachers employ to ensure that the child is given appropriate tasks depend upon the extent of the adult language support available and the age of the child. A variety of approaches are commonly used to promote practice that is rooted in positive and high-expectation practice. Thus:

- Taking account of children's special needs in literacy sessions by implementing individual education plans (IEPs) and utilising opportunities to develop language across the curriculum.
- Promoting respect and understanding of diverse cultures, languages, ethnic groups, faith groups, travellers, asylum seekers and refugees in regular interaction with the class and the interest taken in (for example) cultural diversity and special occasions.
- Working with parents from different community groups, both informally and during planned events.
- Ensuring that display work reflects the diversity in ethnicity.
- Discussing issues relating to prejudice with the children, being careful not to unintentionally excite prejudice.

Ideally, children for whom English is an additional language should be assessed by an adult who speaks the same tongue and can therefore provide a better informed picture of their abilities. If such a person is not available, the process will obviously take longer and involvement of a bilingual child is the next best option. In the absence of adult or child to act as interpreter, parental or family help may be called upon, as it is likely that at least one person has a sufficient grasp of English to explain the new child's needs, strengths and limitations.

There are a number of organisations seeking to assist second language users. TESOL (Teachers of English to Speakers of Other Languages, www.tesol.org) was incorporated in 1966; it is a global association for English language teaching professionals headquartered in Alexandria, Virginia, USA.

NALDIC (National Association for Language Development in the Curriculum, www.naldic.org.uk) is a professional body for all those interested in raising the achievement of bilingual pupils with English as an additional language.

Sources

Gardner, J. (2006) 'Children who have English as an additional language', in Knowles, G. (ed.) *Supporting Inclusive Practice*, Exeter: Learning Matters.

Scott, C. (2008) Teaching Children English as an Additional Language: A programme for 7–12 year olds, London: David Fulton.

ENJOYMENT

See also: arts, behaviour, collaboration (staff), EPPE, extra-curricular activities, kinaesthetic learning, learning, motivation for teaching, school secretary, thinking

The government has been so keen to advance the notion that learning can be enjoyable that one of its most influential documents is entitled *Excellence and Enjoyment* (DfES 2003) to promote the idea that high standards and pleasure in learning are compatible. Under such conditions, pupils are seen to engage with their work by learning in such a way that it expands their thinking and promotes their inventiveness. As a result, children are said to relish the diversity of their learning, both in the variety of topics that are presented to them but also in the different ways that they learn, such as in small groups, through the arts, extra-curricular activities (outside the formal curriculum time) and the involvement of parents and friends at home. It is argued that some of the enjoyment is gained from the interactive nature of learning and the excitement that comes from mutual discovery and collaboration, and it is true that all but the very youngest children love to work together on problem-solving and exploratory tasks, both kinaesthetic ('hands-on') and intellectual. By contrast, too much formal work can lead to a stale and lifeless learning environment.

There are two principal forms of enjoyment: enjoyment *of* learning and enjoyment *in* learning. Enjoyment of learning involves a passion for finding out and discovering new things, whereas enjoyment in learning means that the processes used in finding out are satisfying and meaningful. The two forms of enjoyment, though distinctive in character, form two sides of the same coin, as children who enjoy learning for its own sake will find satisfaction in reaching their goal by whatever means is necessary; similarly, children who enjoy what they are doing are likely to learn more.

Enjoyment of learning is not to be confused with casual and random teaching approaches. The belief that children do not come to school to 'have fun' but rather to take their work seriously – a view popular among some politicians and parents – may be borne of such confusion. While a combination of attractive lesson content and a persuasive teaching approach creates the best circumstances for enjoyment, not all content is intrinsically enjoyable, so the challenge for every practitioner is to find ways to present knowledge in ways that inspire and motivate pupils. As Carr (2003) wisely counsels, however, while teachers are keen that their pupils should experience confidence, enjoyment and satisfaction in learning, these outcomes are not the intended aim of teaching. Thus, 'parents would have cause to complain about any teacher who had made his or her pupils happy or confident without teaching them anything' (p. 114).

Results of analyses related to the key stage 2 phase (children aged 7–11 years) of a major longitudinal study by researchers from the University of London investigating the influence of pre-school and primary school on children's cognitive and social/behavioural development in England – referred to as EPPE 3–11 – showed (amongst many other things) that pupils who most enjoyed primary schools were not necessarily those who achieved highly but that their enjoyment was related to the prevailing standard of behaviour (Sammons *et al.* 2008). The quality of enjoyment seemed to be linked to pupils'

perceptions that teachers were interested in them and insisted on good behaviour. The team concluded that feeling safe at school and supported by adults, rather than enjoyment, was the single most important factor that had most effect on children's progress, both academically and socially.

From an adult perspective, all the evidence points to the fact that the majority of school staffs find the work enjoyable and fulfilling, other than when they are faced with what seem to be insurmountable discipline problems or work under an overbearing head teacher. Teachers, administrators (such as the 'school secretary') and ancillary workers agree that their roles are important in society and they enjoy the companionship and sense of mutual endeavour that working in primary schools offers them. Every study of primary teacher motivation concludes that the greatest enjoyment is found in working with a responsive set of children and being an integral part of a team in school with supportive colleagues (Troman and Raggi 2008).

Sources

Carr, D. (2003) *Making Sense of Education*, London: Routledge.

DfES (2003) *Excellence and Enjoyment*, London: HMSO.

Sammons, P., Sylva, K., Melhuish, E., Siraj-Blatchford, I. and Taggart, B. (2008) *The Effective Pre-School and Primary Education 3–11 Project (EPPE 3–11): Influences on children's development and progress in key stage 2*, London: DCSF/Institute of Education, University of London.

Troman, G. and Raggi, A. (2008) 'Primary teacher commitment and the attractions of teaching', *Pedagogy, Culture and Society*, 16 (1), 85–99.

ENQUIRY

See also: deep learning, discovery learning, learning climate, learning objectives, problem solving, topic work

No teaching is wholly teacher-centred or wholly pupil-centred; it is a mixture of different learning experiences located along a continuum between the two types. Enquiry learning involves pupils in an active and careful analysis of a situation or problem in the light of the different sorts of information available to them by using their own thinking skills to empower them to make generalisations or to draw conclusions (Kellett 2004). In this way children are actively involved in generating knowledge in ways and forms that are meaningful to them. See also the UNESCO web site (www.unesco.org). There are many different approaches to enquiry-based learning (or simply 'enquiry learning'), depending upon the subject area or topic, the background skills of the children and the learning objectives set by the teacher.

In enquiry learning, pupils are encouraged to identify their own issues and questions, guided by the teacher as facilitator. Children consider the resources they need to research the topic and acquire the requisite knowledge, which, proponents argue, they retain more readily because it has been gained by first-hand experience and relates to a problem of genuine interest to them. This approach is closely related to the processes of problem solving and investigation, two approaches that involve finding solutions to an aspect of knowledge that is unknown or problematic but can be distinguished on the basis of the methods used to arrive at a result and the diversity of solutions. The term *problem solving* is frequently employed when there is a single solution, whereas *investigation* tends to be used when there are a variety of possible outcomes. Both terms, however, are subsumed within the umbrella term 'enquiry'. Both forms of enquiry typically consist of five steps:

1 Children are presented with the issue or problem to be resolved.
2 Pupils clarify what needs to be investigated, advised by an adult.
3 The enquiry is undertaken.
4 Findings are collated to aid resolution of the issue or problem.
5 The process and what has been achieved is reviewed.

Enquiries can be conducted by individual pupils but are generally more effective as a group effort, as the opportunity for pupils to co-operate in solving problems contributes to academic advancement, social development and increased self-esteem. Interacting with their peers fosters a learning climate in which active discussion about issues is more natural for the pupils concerned. Furthermore, the existence of disagreement forces the children to attend to aspects that they might miss if they worked alone. The search for clarification and truth during enquiry-based learning allows pupils to reconstruct their present understanding and adjust their perspectives on issues.

To value an enquiry-based approach to learning, teachers pose questions that require concentrated thought or even questions for which there is no immediate answer. For instance, it is appropriate to ask children to choose a favourite lunch box motif; but to encourage deeper thinking they need to consider the reasons for the choice, why boys and girls seem to have different preferences and even why the boxes have motifs at all. Deep learning involves less subject content but doing so comprehensively, rather than attempting to cover more content superficially.

Enquiry-based learning is constrained by the need to address stipulated schemes of work and timetable factors. However, the use of unstructured days and an emphasis on topic or 'project' work rather than single-subject work, with timetable barriers relaxed, allows pupils to probe and explore areas of knowledge more freely (Katz and Chard 2000, Chapter 3).

Sources

Katz, L.G. and Chard, S.C. (2000) *Engaging Children's Minds: The project approach*, Stamford CT: Ablex Publishing.

Kellett, M. (2004) 'Just teach us the skills, please, we'll do the rest: Empowering ten-year-olds as active researchers', *Children and Society*, 18 (5), 329–43.

UNESCO, *Approaches to Learning*, accessed on-line via www.unesco.org

ENVIRONMENTAL EDUCATION

See also: environmental studies, nature study

Many of the current debates about environmental education are not new. Much of today's policy and practice can trace its origins back to the Victorian and Edwardian periods (second half of the nineteenth century and first decade of the twentieth century) when organisations such as the School Journey Association were formed and 'nature study' was an essential element of classroom practice. Over the last thirty years or so, environmental education has been increasingly recognised as a crucial component in meeting the challenges associated with sustainable development (NFER, on-line). The Council for Environmental Education (CEE) is a national membership body for organisations and individuals in England committed to environmental education and education for sustainable development (www.cee.org.uk). See further details about the practical outworking of environmental education in schools under *Environmental studies*.

Sources

NFER, *Environmental Education*, on-line at www.nfer.ac.uk/research-areas/environmental-education

ENVIRONMENTAL STUDIES

See also: environmental education, geography, history, humanities, religious education, science

Environmental studies (ES) is, as its name suggests, principally concerned with the study of human interaction with the environment. It is a broad field of interest that includes the natural environment, built environments, social environments (where people congregate), organisational environments (e.g. the workplace) and the connections between them. In the past the subject matter focused almost exclusively on plants and animals,

whereas today issues such as sustainability form a key element of the programme. Thus, schools in England are required to develop pupils' awareness, understanding of, and respect for the environments in which they live and encourage their commitment to sustainable development at a personal, local, national and global level. Subjects under which environmental education can be developed are notably science and geography, but there are opportunities within other subjects and areas of learning, including 'global studies' and 'outdoor education'. Current environmental problems have evolved into a complex set of interdisciplinary issues involving ecological (ecology is the science of plants and animals in relation to their environment, *Collins Dictionary*), political, economic, social, as well as physical and biological considerations. Modern environmental studies include the study of the urban environment ('relating to the town or city') as well as the natural environment. Other definitions emphasise the human role in the management of the environment and the economic, social and health problems that may arise from deterioration of ecosystems.

In most primary education settings, the curriculum content includes a study of animals and their habitats; creating 'wild' and open spaces for natural flora and fauna to flourish (e.g. a cottage garden in the school grounds); study of weather systems (e.g. water cycles and wind speed); care for the planet and conservation (e.g. food chains). ES is normally embedded in the science field of study and educational visits to local sites of interest – including the school grounds – and remote sites, such as a woodland area or farm, form an important element of the learning schedule. Some schools broaden the remit to incorporate history, geography and even religious education (often referred to jointly as 'the humanities') into the programme. Where the work is science-orientated, children focus on aspects such as investigating pond life, looking at very small creatures in their habitats and tree studies (for example, De Boo 2004). Children are also encouraged to find answers to their own questions through scientific investigation of the objects, events or particular part of the environment being studied, either in the field or in the classroom (Elstgeest and Harlen 1990).

Sources

De Boo, M. (2004) *Nature Detectives: Environmental science for primary children*, Hatfield: Association for Science Education/Woodland Trust.

Elstgeest, J. and Harlen, W. (1990) *Environmental Science in the Primary Curriculum*, London: Paul Chapman.

ENVIRONMENTAL STUDIES (SCOTLAND)

See also: citizenship, environmental education, environmental studies, healthy eating, moral education

In Scotland, attitudes to environmental studies relate to key objectives embedded in the Scottish curriculum for all learners aged 3–18 that constitute a commitment to learning, respect and care for self and others, and social and environmental responsibility. A central idea is one of moral and ethical considerations arising from scientific, social and technological change. This way of looking at the world starts with the development of appropriate attitudes, based on a belief that moral and ethical considerations of care for the environment arise out of learning about social, scientific and technological change. It is claimed that such a perspective makes the knowledge and skills focus subordinate to the development of these attitudes. Children primarily acquire knowledge about ES to be more responsible as global citizens, rather than to reach predetermined levels of attainment in specific categories of knowledge (Peacock 2005). More recently, ES has been linked with curriculum areas such as 'healthy eating', safety education and citizenship.

Sources

Peacock, A. (2005) 'Science in the Scottish primary school curriculum', *Primary Science Review*, 87, 30–31.

EPPE 3–11 PROJECT

See also: effectiveness, enjoyment, gender, misbehaviour, singing, tests and testing

The Effective Pre-School and Primary Education (EPPE 3–11) project, 2003–2008, funded by the Department for Children, Schools and Families (DCSF) in the UK, was a five-year extension to Europe's largest longitudinal investigation into the effects of pre-school education on children's developmental outcomes at the start of primary school, called the 'Effective Provision of Pre-School Education'. EPPE 3–11 was managed by the Institute of Education, University of London and tracked 3,000 children from the time they started pre-school until they reached eleven years of age. The project extension was developed to explore four related themes:

1 Do the effects of pre-school continue into key stage 2?
2 What are the characteristics of 'effective' primary classrooms and schools?
3 Who are the resilient and the vulnerable children in the EPPE sample?
4 What is the contribution of 'out-of-school learning' (homes, communities, Internet) to children's development?

The EPPE research provided new evidence concerning the combined effects of pre-school and primary school in shaping children's later development. One unsurprising result was that the better the home learning environment, pre-school and primary school, the better academic results children achieve. The concept of 'better' home environment was defined in terms of ratings for how often parents carried out seven activities with their children: (1) being read to, (2) going to the library, (3) playing with numbers, (4) painting and drawing, (5) being taught letters, (6) being taught numbers, and (7) singing songs. As children grew older, the research team discovered that the home learning environment was not strongly linked to mothers' educational qualifications or to social class – there were some disadvantaged homes that did lots of these activities and some wealthy homes that did far fewer.

As children get older the home learning environment becomes much less significant. In this connection, the study found that boys were more than twice as likely to have a poor home learning environment than girls. At age five, girls are more advanced in reading than boys; but by the age of ten most boys had caught up with the girls, and there were factors other than gender – such as the home and type of school – that seems to have had a powerful influence on attainment.

Children's enjoyment of school related to how well they behaved; however, a perception that adults were interested in them and had control of pupil misbehaviour were also important factors. Feeling safe at school and being supported by staff had the greatest positive impact on children's progress, both academically and socially. The project team concluded that working with parents and providing quality pre-school provision has potential long-term benefits. See the summary of the research provided in the *Times Educational Supplement* (TES 2008); also, for an early childhood perspective, see Siraj-Blatchford *et al.* (2008).

Project findings revealed that once children were in mainstream primary school, the overall quality of teaching affected their social behaviour as well as their intellectual development. In particular, a lot of variation was found in the quality of teaching in year 5 classrooms (ten-year-olds), which seemed to have a more powerful impact on children's academic progress children's than their gender or whether or not they were from economically deprived backgrounds (Sammons *et al.* 2006). One small but interesting practical

point was that the overall quality of teaching tended to be higher in classrooms where teachers used plenary sessions consistently – bringing the whole class together to discuss key characteristics of their learning. Predictably, pupils who attended a more academically effective primary school were found to attain higher national test results and make more progress throughout key stage 2 (ages 7–11 years) than children of equivalent ability in less successful schools, particularly in the case of children with a variety of disadvantages (Sammons *et al.* 2008).

Sources

Sammons, P., Taggart, B., Siraj-Blatchford, I., Sylva, K., Melhuish, E., Barreau, S. and Manni, L. (2006) *Effective Pre-school and Primary Education 3–11 (EPPE 3–11) Summary Report: Variations in teacher and pupil behaviours in Year 5 classes*, Research Report no. 817, Nottingham: DfES Publications.

Sammons, P., Sylva, K., Melhuish, E., Siraj-Blatchford, I. and Taggart, B. (2008) *The Effective Pre-school and Primary Education 3–11 Project (EPPE 3–11: Influences on children's development and progress in key stage 2: social/behavioural outcomes in Year 6*, London: DCSF/Institute of Education, University of London.

Siraj-Blatchford, I., Taggart, B., Sylva, K., Sammons, P. and Melhuish, E. (2008) 'Towards the transformation of practice in early childhood education: The effective provision of pre-school education (EPPE) project', *Cambridge Journal of Education*, 38 (1), 23–36.

TES (2008) article by Helen Ward, 'Preschool learning holds the key to children's success in later life', 5 December. Accessible on-line via www.tes.co.uk

EQUAL OPPORTUNITIES

See also: achievement, body language, bullying, educated child, expectations, gender, home background and learning, special educational needs, stereotyping

Discrimination against a child or adult is not allowed in schools on any basis. Deliberate or unintentional bias towards pupils construed as discriminatory leaves teachers open to charges of unprofessional conduct, so it is important for them to be as impartial as possible at all times when dealing with children. Furthermore, all qualified teachers must recognise and respond effectively to equal opportunities issues, and challenge incidents of bullying and harassment. Not only must all pupils be granted the same opportunities, support and encouragement but it is not appropriate to label children due to circumstances beyond their control, such as home background or physical appearance. A teasing pleasantry about a child's looks or domestic situation may be more hurtful and do greater damage than the adult imagines at the time. It is also the teacher's responsibility to foster an environment in which children treat each other respectfully. The principle that every person deserves to receive a good education is reflected in official documentation. For example, the National Curriculum 2000 for England and Wales states:

> When planning, teachers should set high expectations and provide opportunities for all pupils to achieve, including boys and girls, pupils with special educational needs, pupils with disabilities, pupils from all social and cultural backgrounds, pupils of different ethnic groups including travellers, refugees and asylum seekers, and those from diverse linguistic backgrounds.
>
> (p. 31)

Children like teachers who exercise consistent control and are fair in their dealings with everyone in the class, so fair-mindedness also pays dividends in terms of fostering a settled learning environment. Conscientious teachers regularly interrogate the ways in which their own attitudes towards children might affect learning, such as whether their reactions, body language and voice tone change significantly when dealing with different pupils under similar conditions. A useful antidote to discriminatory attitudes is for adults to develop a positive attitude towards achievement and to adopt a 'you can do it' working atmosphere in which all children can fulfil their potential.

At one time, boys were steered towards the skills and subjects that would provide them with a foundation for working life; girls were expected to become homemakers and were taught accordingly (see Myers 2000 for an historical perspective). Today, teachers have to be aware that both girls and boys have an important role in the workplace and in the home and it is important to treat each child as an individual, rather than make blanket assumptions about temperament, ability and life chances based solely on gender. Teachers also have a considerable responsibility to use teaching approaches that appeal to lively children, as well as to the compliant ones.

Although expectations and role-orientation are woven into the fabric of society and are hard to disentangle, relatively small instances may reveal deeper assumptions about gender roles. For example, grouping all the girls' names beneath the boys' names on a register may simply be a method of organising, or it may reflect a belief that boys are more significant. Similarly, in the choice of team leaders, or allocation of the order in which children take a turn and selection for prestige positions (in a presentation to parents, say), it is necessary to make decisions based on competence, fairness and academic priorities, not gender or assertiveness. Knowles (2006) warns that one 'lingering stereotype about boys is that they are innately clever, but unwilling to work, whereas any success that girls have is frequently put down to hard work and diligence rather than brilliance' (p. 102). Similarly, a sweet smile from a charming girl should not result in a lesser sanction being imposed on her for a misdemeanour compared with that for an untidy boy with a permanent scowl. Knowles argues that it is easy for teachers to fall into the trap of interpreting the same behaviour differently, based on gender. She offers the example of a misbehaving girl being described as 'a bad influence' or 'spiteful little madam', while the boy is simply described as 'mucking about'.

135

Impartial decisions are needed as far as possible when dealing with children, male and female, but should not be confused with a need to take account of individual differences, beginning in the nursery and reception classes. Teachers aim to offer every pupil the opportunity to experience success in learning, setting high but sensible expectations for each boy and girl, pupils who have special educational needs and those with disabilities, pupils from different social and cultural backgrounds, and ethnic groups, refugees and asylum seekers.

The essence of equal opportunity is to provide a more inclusive curriculum, available to as wide a range of children as possible, founded on three tenets: (1) to set pupils suitable and relevant learning challenges, (2) to respond to their diverse learning needs, and (3) to overcome potential barriers to learning that may hinder optimum progress. On the one hand it is necessary for teachers to be consistent in their treatment of children. On the other hand one child will respond to a lighter 'touch' than another child in the same circumstances. Teachers are not judges in a court of law handing down sentences regardless of whoever stands before them; they have to exercise wisdom in the way that they approach all interpersonal encounters. Nevertheless, the need for discernment is different from a blanket stereotyping of children on the basis of gender or any other defining characteristic (such as background, sportiness or even physical height). The key is to treat every case on merit and use a large dose of common sense in making decisions. One of the key skills that every teacher has to develop is to evaluate a situation rapidly and make a response that is not only fair but also seen to be fair by the children.

Stereotyping on the basis of race or religion may be factors on which educators base their expectations for academic achievement or behaviour. For instance, there are various studies showing that black (USA, 'African American') boys in particular may suffer from teachers' low expectations. For example,

Majors (2001) addresses the fact that exclusion and expulsion of black children from schools is endemic in the USA and the UK. However, the issues extend beyond individual teachers or schools; a survey by the *Times Educational Supplement* (TES 2008) noted that expectations about the examination success of minority ethnic groups varied considerably from area to area across English regions.

Sources

Knowles, G. (2006) 'Gifted and talented', in Knowles, G. (ed.) *Supporting Inclusive Practice*, Exeter: Learning Matters.

Majors, R. (2001) *Educating Our Black Children: New directions and radical approaches*, London: Routledge.

Myers, K. (ed.) (2000) *Whatever Happened to Equal Opportunities in Schools?* Maidenhead: Open University Press.

TES (2008) article by Helen Ward and William Stewart, 'Divided on the setting of targets', 27 June.

EVERY CHILD MATTERS

See also: caring teachers, child welfare, children, healthy schools, parents, Sure Start, teaching assistant

The British government has stated its intentions to create 'joined up' provision for children and young people up to the age of nineteen years through its initiative, *Every Child Matters: Change for Children* (DfES 2004), which led to the Children Act (2004). The legislation and subsequent changes have brought about a whole new agenda and philosophy that directly or indirectly involves every school, teacher, teaching assistant, paraprofessional and educational support services. *Every Child Matters* also involved changes in supporting parents and carers, and led to earlier intervention, more accountability and integration between services as well as enhancing workforce reform (Reid 2005; Cheminais 2008). The aim is for all children, regardless of their backgrounds or circumstances, to be supported in staying healthy and safe, achieving success, making a positive contribution to society and learning how to handle their finances. As a result, the organisations involved with providing services to children (hospitals, schools, police, voluntary groups and so on) share information and work together to protect and empower children and young people. The first Children's Commissioner for England was appointed in March 2005 to pay particular attention to gathering and promoting the views of those considered most vulnerable. *Every Child Matters* sets out five outcomes that matter most to children and young people:

1 *Being healthy*: enjoying good physical and mental health and living a healthy lifestyle.
2 *Staying safe*: being protected from harm and neglect.
3 *Enjoying and achieving*: getting the most out of life and developing the skills for adulthood.
4 *Making a positive contribution*: being involved with the community and not engaging in anti-social or offending behaviour.
5 *Economic well-being*: not being prevented by economic disadvantage from achieving their full potential in life.

As part of *Every Child Matters*, 'Sure Start' children's centres provide early education integrated with health and family support services, and 'Removing Barriers to Achievement' sets out the strategy for raising standards of support for children with special educational needs. Restructuring and co-locating the services of extended schools in England, Wales and Northern Ireland ('integrated community schools' in Scotland) are intended to help to improve outcomes for children and young people. In a study by Chamberlain *et al.* (2006) schools were asked to comment on changes that had already taken place in relation to ECM; over 80 per cent of schools responded and the comments typically described improvements or positive developments covering standard aspects of school life. The main changes reported in primary schools

were alterations to the school improvement/ development plan and carrying out a review of the curriculum and current school practices. All primary schools are obliged to offer childcare provision between 8 a.m. and 6 p.m. all year round by 2010, either on-site or in partnership with other schools and local providers. Suggestions about establishing and maintaining effective multi-agency partnerships working in educational settings are explored in Cheminais (2009) and by Knowles (2009).

Sources

Chamberlain, T., Lewis, K., Teeman, D. and Kendall, L. (2006) *Schools' Concerns and their Implications for Local Authorities: Annual survey of trends in education 2006* (LGA Research Report 5/06), Slough: NFER.
Cheminais, R. (2008) *Every Child Matters: A practical guide for teaching assistants*, London: David Fulton.
——(2009) *Effective Multi-Agency Partnerships: Putting every child matters into practice*, London: Sage.
DfES (2004) *Every Child Matters: Change for children*, London: HMSO.
Knowles, G. (2009) *Ensuring Every Child Matters*, London: Sage.
Reid, K. (2005) 'The implications of Every Child Matters and the Children Act for schools', *Pastoral Care in Education*, 23 (1), 12–18.

EXCELLENCE AND ENJOYMENT

See also: creativity, excellent teachers, expectations, parents, Primary National Strategy, success, tests and testing

The then Secretary of State for Education and Skills, Charles Clarke, launched the Primary National Strategy document *Excellence and Enjoyment* for England in May 2003 by asserting that 'excellent teaching gives children the life chances they deserve'. Clarke wrote in the foreword to the document that

our system must not fail any child. High standards – especially in literacy and numeracy – are the backbone of success in learning and in life. Our primary education system must not write off any child through low expectations. Enjoyment is the birthright of every child.

The document was partially a response to teachers' and educators' concerns that teaching and learning had become too systematic and was stifling creativity. *Excellence and Enjoyment* was the backbone of the Primary National Strategy and was intended to re-energise teaching, make learning more fun and promote the rather unrealistic expectation that teachers would tailor-make the curriculum for each child. Schools could build on their existing curriculum strengths and make more use of test data to inform teaching and learning. The importance of engaging parents to learn alongside their children was also emphasised 'to broaden social experiences and increase tolerance of other viewpoints (including different cultures) and family learning'.

EXCELLENCE IN CITIES

See also: attention span, communication, early years, emotional literacy, home background and learning, parental involvement

Children who start primary school with significant disadvantages in areas such as language and communication, attention span, reading and writing, and social finesse, can receive additional support through the UK government's Primary Excellence in Cities project that focuses on working closely with parents. Primary Excellence in Cities has four main objectives:

- To target the most needy children and build on the work of the Sure Start scheme (see below), involving parents as much as possible.
- To bridge the transition from early years settings to primary school, and from the Foundation Stage to key stage 1 (children aged 5-plus to 7 years) by offering needy children extra support.

- To utilise the expertise of experienced teachers in training and equipping other teachers and other staff in early years settings.
- To support parents in developing their children's skills, making packs and videos available for parents to explain what children are learning at school and how they can be helped at home.

Sure Start is a programme that aims to achieve better outcomes for children, parents and communities by increasing the availability of childcare for all children and improving the emotional development of young children. Sure Start also aims to support parents in their aspirations towards employment by the development of helping services in disadvantaged areas, alongside financial help for parents to afford childcare. By 2010 every community should be served by a Sure Start children's centre or its equivalent.

EXCELLENT TEACHERS

See also: basic skills, effectiveness, extracurricular activities, music, physical education, success, teachers' beliefs, tests and testing, zone of proximal development

'Excellent teacher' is a phrase that conjures up many different images in people's minds, most of which are related to teachers who taught them in the past and literally 'excelled'. A conventional view of excellence in teaching is the teacher's ability to help pupils do well in formal tests and examinations. The UK government in England and Wales introduced an 'Excellent Teacher' (ET) scheme in 2004, claiming that ETs have a distinctive role in helping other teachers improve their effectiveness and a major impact on improving pupil attainment across the whole school. Schools can create ET posts at any time but the higher salary attached to the post acts as a disincentive for schools operating on tight budgets. Nevertheless, the principle of using excellent teachers to support and assist colleagues has been formalised (DCSF 2008).

Surveys suggest that outstanding primary teachers allow time to get to know children well and take an interest in their life outside school, their hopes and dreams, hobbies and extra-curricular activities. They are keen that children should do well in the formal part of their education, especially literacy and mathematics, but recognise that a full education consists of more than possessing basic skills and passing examinations. Such teachers encourage pupils to become independent but not aloof, kind but not smothering, assertive and confident but not arrogant. They promote cooperative learning and team membership and reassure children that success is as much about perseverance and determination as it is about the final achievement.

Being an excellent primary teacher also involves exploring ways to present knowledge and explain things to children in a clear and unambiguous way, thus to extend their learning by bridging the gap – the so-called 'zone of proximal development' – between what they presently understand alone and what they are capable of understanding with support. The very best teachers are active in their teaching role and work intensively and with full concentration; they use a range of verbal and demonstrative strategies and techniques to get across a point and help pupils to make sense of work (Gipps *et al.* 2000). Children are encouraged to reflect on their own learning, rehearse ideas and consolidate new knowledge through practising basic skills and applying them to a variety of situations. Excellent teachers show children the connections between different areas of the curriculum, use a range of questions to elicit and test pupils' existing knowledge (closed questions), extend their thinking (open-ended questions) and cause them to make decisions and choices (speculative questions).

Few teachers are excellent in every aspect of their work but they strive to improve. For instance, a teacher may be brilliant when it comes to physical education, but struggle to teach music. A teacher may be outstanding when handling with the whole class during interactive maths, but need advice about helping children to develop advanced reading skills. Although very few primary teachers are exceptional in every area, those who can teach any subject area competently are treasured more highly than those who are exceptional in teaching a few subjects and poor at everything else.

Excellent teachers don't need to brag about their exploits, successes or achievements; they seem more concerned with the welfare of others rather than of themselves. This altruistic attitude is not a clever piece of reverse psychology to fool people into admiring them; rather, it allows their qualities to rise naturally to the surface, rather than publicising them. Such teachers use the talents and abilities they possess to the full and don't hide them away as if they were something shameful, yet avoid giving the impression that they are superior as a result. See an informative paper by Vallance (2000) for a fuller discussion of the issues.

Sources

DCSF (2008) *Excellent Teacher Scheme*, London: HMSO, on-line at www.teachernet.gov.uk
Gipps, C., McCallum, B. and Hargreaves, E. (2000) *What Makes a Good Primary Teacher?* London: Routledge.
Vallance, R. (2000) 'Excellent Teachers: Exploring self-constructs, role, and personal challenges', Paper presented at the Australian Association for Research in Education (AARE) Conference, Sydney, December 2000.

EXERCISE BOOKS

See also: handwriting, homework, learning outcomes, target setting (pupils)

Exercise books were originally designed as booklets that contained problems or written exercises with blank space for writing answers for use by pupils for practising handwriting, spellings and comprehension. In many modern

139

primary schools the exercise book does not contain any pre-printed material and has blank pages into which children write or draw a 'best copy' of their work after completing drafts on spare paper. Exercise books also serve a purpose for recording mathematical computations ('calculating') and diagrams, and as homework diaries and target setting – noting individual learning goals/outcomes for the pupil concerned.

EXPECTATIONS

See also: early years, encouragement and praise, gender, learning climate, motivation for learning, target setting (pupils), writing

Expectation is a more involved concept than it may initially appear to be, consisting of an amalgam of teacher and pupil aspirations, attempts to achieve the lesson purpose, account taken of individual pupil targets for improvement, time constraints, adult support and resource factors. The definition of 'high expectations' is rarely spelled out but reflects a 'can do' rather than a 'doubt you can do' approach to learning; it is not be confused with *unrealistic* expectations in which a child is told that he or she 'can do it' but then allowed to flounder, with the inevitable confusion and loss of motivation that it causes. Educators have to walk a fine line between encouraging ('yes, you can achieve this goal') and smothering ('do what I say') and withdrawing ('try it for yourself') in assisting pupils to reach their potential. Having a high expectation has, of course, to be matched by appropriate action on the teacher's part or it is vacuous.

Learners respond well to teachers' expectations if there is mutual respect, but have little regard for such expectations if the teacher is doubted or disliked. Nevertheless, the phrase 'self-fulfilling prophecy' is often applied to a situation in which teachers' expectations are reflected in what pupils produce (see, for example, chapters 1 and 2 in Tauber 1997).

In other words, if teachers expect little from children, they receive little from them; similarly, if they expect a lot – and providing the learning climate is appropriate – they receive a lot.

One of the requirements for teachers is to demonstrate high expectations of all pupils, to respect their social, cultural, linguistic, religious and ethnic backgrounds and be committed to raising standards. Concerns have been expressed that some teachers have expectations based on gender (e.g. a 'girls are poor at maths' attitude) or ethnic group (e.g. 'parents of Asian descent are keen on education') – see the **Equal opportunities** entry in this book for further details.

Teachers also have to take account of the possibility that a highly demanding expectation for a pupil working alone may become manageable for (say) a pair of children cooperating or a collaborative enterprise involving four or five pupils. Expectations therefore vary depending on the demands of the task, the time available for its completion and the extent of support that is offered or available.

Expectation may relate to a specific aspect of learning, depending on what has been identified by the teacher as particularly significant (the principal learning objective). For instance in a piece of extended writing, the emphasis may be upon developing a storyline, or constructing the piece in a prescribed manner using a predetermined framework, or writing neatly, or inserting a creative element, or enthralling the reader, or accurate grammar, or a combination of several things.

Teachers have a responsibility to clarify their expectations and involve children in determining what is particularly important for each one to promote learning. Thus, in the same piece of writing, a child may have struggled with conveying meaning and the need to concentrate on rectifying the deficit; another child may have lots of good ideas but write incoherently; yet another may need to improve handwriting. Within a single session, therefore, there may be general expectations for all pupils but also a specific target for an individual child to succeed in a particular aspect of the work.

Cassidy (2004, 2005) notes that almost all three- and four-year-olds in Scotland now experience some form of pre-school provision prior to school entry. Consequently, the impact of pre-school experiences on children's readiness for primary school has become an important issue for those involved in the early stages of compulsory schooling. Teachers in early years classes need to be aware of the experiences and achievements of individual children in their pre-school setting to enable each child to transfer into mainstream education with the least amount of disruption to their learning and to have appropriate expectations for their learning.

Expectation does not only apply to academic attainment. For example, Kyriacou (1998) argues that the prevailing discipline in a school will not only be influenced by adults' attitudes and behaviour 'but also by the expectations pupils bring with them' (p. 80) over which educators have little influence. To assist in the process of maintaining a positive ethos, primary schools emphasise the need for pupils to exercise self-discipline and take responsibility for their actions (see Wrigley 2003, chapter 5). Despite the efforts of teachers to impress on pupils the high expectations with respect to behaviour, their quest is sometimes undermined by an increase in the number of emotionally unsettled children in mainstream primary education and the eclectic range of moral norms in society.

Sources

Cassidy, M. (2004) 'Fitting in? Scottish primary teachers' expectations of school entrants', *Scottish Educational Review*, 36 (2), 191–205.

——(2005) 'They do it anyway: A study of Primary 1 teachers' perceptions of children's transition into primary education', *Early Years*, 25 (2), 143–53.

Kyriacou, C. (1998) *Essential Teaching Skills*, London: Nelson Thornes.

Tauber, R.T. (1997) *Self-Fulfilling Prophecy: A practical guide to its use in education*, London: Praeger.

Wrigley, T. (2003) *Schools of Hope*, Stoke-on-Trent: Trentham.

EXTENDED SCHOOLS

See also: child welfare, children, Every Child Matters, homework, inspections, parents supporting learning, sex education, special schools

The concept of extended schools in England, Wales and Northern Ireland – in Scotland they are referred to as 'integrated community schools' – is that they provide a range of services and activities to help meet the needs of children, their families and the wider community (DfES 2005a). Mainstream and special schools are expected to consider providing high-quality 8 a.m. to 6 p.m. childcare throughout the year on school sites, some of which are being developed with this provision in mind (DfES 2006). Activities such as before-school and after-school clubs can also help children develop new interests and skills, and may support parents by providing enhanced childcare options, so allowing them to return to work.

The justification for extended schools relies on evidence that children's early experiences greatly influence their outcomes and life chances in later life and that such provision can help to improve pupil attainment, self-confidence, motivation and attendance; reduce exclusion rates; better enable teachers to focus on teaching and learning; and enhance children's and families access to services. In particular, educational attainment, coupled with security and love, offer a route out of poverty and disadvantage. Children's wider needs can also be addressed through support from multi-agency teams (e.g. social workers, community officers, health workers) working at, or visiting, the school site. There is no one model of what an extended school should be like and each school has to work with the other interested parties (community groups, etc.) to determine what provision is required and to plan how it might best be

141

delivered; however, extended services are likely to include some of the following (OFSTED 2005; DCSF 2008):

- Childcare provision on the school site or through other local providers, available all year round.
- Activities such as homework clubs and study support, sport, music tuition, dance and drama, arts and crafts, chess and first aid courses.
- Parent support including information sessions at key transition points (notably when pupils transfer from primary to secondary education); parenting programmes run with the support of other children's services; and family sessions where children learn with their parents (e.g. about aspects of mathematics).
- Referral to a wide range of specialist support services such as speech therapy, child and adolescent mental health services, family support services, intensive behaviour support.
- Community access to adult learning, ICT, sports and arts facilities.
- Sexual health services, especially for younger people.

Extended schools are at the heart of *Every Child Matters* (DfES 2005b), an initiative that aims to improve outcomes and raise standards of academic achievement for children and young people. An indication of the seriousness with which the British government's views extended schools is that school inspections include an evaluation of how the services are contributing to improved outcomes for children and young people. However, although extended schools are seen as a vehicle for lifting children out of poverty and improving outcomes for them and their families, evidence from the initial phases of the scheme suggest that while liaison between services appears to be improving, poverty remains a serious concern.

The concept of extended schools is not universally welcomed and concerns remain about the impact on family life of having both adults in the household working full-time and

the sense that state provision is becoming a surrogate for proper parenting. Arguments against the scheme revolve about the length of time that parents are apart from their children and issues of affordability. In addition, some schools have struggled to find suitably qualified staff, and the fact that the provision is now included on inspection schedules means that a school can be designated 'failing' even if every other element of the inspection across the school is highly commending.

Sources

DCSF (2008) *Extended Schools*, Teachernet, on-line at www.teachernet.gov.uk/wholeschool/extended schools

DfES (2005a) *Extended Schools: Access to opportunities and services for all*, Nottingham: DfES Publications, on-line at www.teachernet.gov.uk/extendedschools

——(2005b) *Every Child Matters: Change for children*, London: HMSO.

——(2006) *Schools for the Future: Designing schools for extended services*, Nottingham: DfES Publications, on-line at http://publications.teachernet.gov.uk/eOrderingDownload/DFES-2092-2005.pdf

OFSTED (2005) *Inspecting Extended Schools*, London: HMSO.

EXTERNAL AGENCIES

See also: child welfare, Children and Young People's Workforce Strategy 2020, healthy schools, hearing impairment, life education, Office for Standards in Education, physical education, sports

It has always been the case that a small number of children need provision to be made with support/advice from external agencies in order to meet their learning needs (i.e. 'inter-agency work'). The aim of external agencies ('inter-agency working') according to the code of practice for special educational needs ('Working in Partnership with other Agencies') is to provide integrated, high quality, holistic support focused on the needs of the child. In England, the government's decision to combine education and social services provision to facilitate closer cooperation between them has altered the landscape of child welfare. Arrangements through the local or regional authority allow access to health professionals, psychological services, special needs teaching services, early years support teachers and teachers for visually or hearing impaired children. Some schools work actively alongside external agencies to support physical education and school sport. The Office for Standards in Education (OFSTED) reported that schools that contributed well to pupils' health and well-being used external agencies very effectively, especially to teach about drugs, and sex and relationships education. Organisations such as 'Life Education' work with schools and parents to help children develop healthy life choices.

EXTRA-CURRICULAR ACTIVITIES

See also: breakfast clubs, extended schools, health and safety, music, sports

The expression 'extra-curricular' denotes the fact that activities for pupils in school are outside the remit of the prescribed curriculum. Primary teachers have always been involved in providing educational and recreational opportunities for children outside school hours, such that a generation ago extra-curricular activities played an important part in the life of most primary schools. However, the close regulation of teachers' working conditions in recent years and the additional demands made of them to maintain detailed records, carry out extensive assessment procedures and provide justification for every aspect of pupils' learning gradually led to a general curtailment of voluntary activities (Byard 2003). Issues of health and safety, child protection and an increase in litigation have also contributed to a situation where teachers have become more cautious about committing themselves over and above the demands of regular teaching.

In recent years the introduction of financial incentives for teachers to undertake extra duties, increases in the number of ancillary staff, together with the provision of pre-school and after-school opportunities (the 'extended schools' initiative) have helped to halt the decline. Some schools are designated 'community school' owing to their close ties with the neighbourhood and the use of their premises for a variety of activities for local residents. The use of the expression 'extra-curricular' now incorporates a range of activities and opportunities for both children and adults that transcend the more familiar after-school football practice and lunchtime recorder club. Depending on the size of the school, the age of the children and the availability of staff, a range of activities and events covering musical, sporting, academic and more general interests may be offered. The artistic, musical and dramatic talents developed during extra-curricular sessions are sometimes employed for school productions and seasonal celebrations.

Under the extra-curriculum remit, schools run 'booster' classes and additional lessons such as homework clubs for children that take place outside the regular school day to improve pupils' academic performance. All schools are required to develop closer links with the community, opening the school buildings for use and, where possible, providing learning opportunities in conjunction with other social agencies. A proportion of schools open early to provide breakfast for children and continue until early evening by employing ancillary staff to provide childcare facilities, though this facility raises a number of practical issues – not least the fact that formal inspections include an evaluation of learning provision for 3–5 year-olds.

ContinYou is a UK learning charity that has played a role in shaping the out-of-school hours learning and study support movement in education, striving to ensure that extra-curricular activities are kept at the centre of the education and policy agenda. They support and promote out-of-hours opportunities

143

(known as 'Extra Hours') through pro-grammes such as breakfast clubs. Their stated aims are to enrich the lives of children and young people, provide new opportunities for learning, enable them to develop new skills and build on existing provision. Many edu-cationists believe that out-of-hours activities help to raise attainment, improve attendance, increase aspirations, build confidence and re-motivate disaffected pupils.

Sources

Byard, K. (2003) 'Where have all the clubs gone? The decline in extra-curricular activities', *Education 3–13*, 31 (2), 60–63.

ContinYou: on-line at www.continyou.org.uk

F

FAILURE

See also: daydreaming, friendship, learned helplessness, learning climate, motivation for learning, success

Robson (2006), referring to Dweck (2000) points out that children's sense of self-competence begins to develop from an early age and can have a significant impact on their attitude to learning. Dweck suggests that when faced with difficulty or potential failure, children tend to react in one of two ways. The first way is when children display a 'mastery-orientated' attitude, characterised by increased effort; the second set of children display a 'helpless pattern' of behaviour. Mastery-orientated children do not blame themselves for not doing well, whereas helpless children feel personally responsible and are reluctant to persist with the task. According to Dweck, mastery-orientated children engage in self-motivating strategies, self-instruction and self-monitoring; they remain confident of success and learn from their failures rather than allowing them to undermine confidence in their own abilities. By contrast, the helpless type of children denigrate their abilities, quickly lose confidence, focus on failures rather than successes, soon lose heart and even abandon successful strategies (see Robson, pp. 52–53; Dweck, pp. 7–10).

It is important for adults to appreciate what is involved in a child's reaction to a perceived or real failure. It doesn't take too much imagination to grasp what it is like to be constantly coming last; unable to compete with more able classmates; hearing little but criticism from exasperated adults, struggling to make an impression; taken off for 'booster' classes to improve their academic competence in a subject by well-meaning adults; and over time wondering if their academic struggles are a reflection of their inadequacy as a person. After a few years of this type of experience, some children decide that it simply isn't worth any longer making the effort to conform to the demands, so they put their efforts into more rewarding activities like disrupting the class, spoiling someone else's work or finishing the set task in rapid time with minimum effort. Other disillusioned children resort to daydreaming or adopt a detached approach to work and may be diagnosed as having an 'attention deficit'; yet put the same children with so-called attention deficit disorder in an environment of their choosing (e.g. a computer game) and their concentration span is apparently endless.

Most primary children are optimistic about being part of a education system that caters for their individual and friendship needs, supported by adults who spend time and effort in helping them to learn and giving them opportunities to do exciting things. However, if pupils have come from home backgrounds in which schooling is not considered to be a priority it is likely that their brothers and sisters will exhibit similar non-conformist tendencies and staff may refer to the whole family negatively. Many of these unsettled children, though enjoying the companionship and informal opportunities which school provides, are likely to fight shy of the formal learning process and may question the need to complete tasks that appear to have little relevance for them; failure by any definition is an inevitable consequence. A book written some years ago by Pye (1987) called *Invisible Children* provides challenging and readable insights into issues relating to disillusionment with school. See also Makins (1997).

If adults find failure hard to cope with, it is not surprising if children need help if they are to avoid spiralling into an attitude of negativity towards schoolwork and teachers. Dalton and Fairchild (2004) offer helpful comment in respect of maintaining a positive climate:

> Some of your best teaching flows spontaneously from your deepest intuition. At its core, teaching is the artistry of creating experiences that lead people into greater awareness. It's an artistry of knowing the moods, needs and expectations of your pupils, while staying fully aware of your own.
> (p. viii)

By attending to the children's individual needs, perceptive and caring teachers can play a major role in preventing children from becoming despondent and losing motivation for learning. Houghton and McColgan (1995) suggest that adults can help alleviate children's anxieties by being calm when dealing with their fears, trying to avoid giving the impression that the child is somehow to blame and sensitively encouraging them to 'approach what they fear' (p. 41). Grossman (2003) stresses the need for genuineness of character in teachers, arguing that the pupils soon detect whether they can trust a particular adult. The development of trust is more likely if the teacher promotes a view that success is never final and failure is never fatal; it is having the courage to persevere that really matters.

Sources

Dalton, J. and Fairchild, L. (2004) *The Compassionate Classroom: Lessons that nurture wisdom and empathy*, Chicago: Zephyr Press.

Dweck, C.S. (2000) *Self-Theories: Their role in motivation, personality and development*, Hove: Psychology Press.

Grossman, H. (2003) *Classroom Behaviour Management for Diverse and Inclusive Schools*, Lanham MD: Rowman and Littlefield.

Houghton, D. and McColgan, M. (1995) *Working with Children*, London: Collins Educational.

Makins, V. (1997) *The Invisible Children: Nipping failure in the bud*, London: David Fulton.

Pye, J. (1987) *Invisible Children: Who are the real losers at school?* Oxford: Oxford University Press.

Robson, S. (2006) *Developing Thinking and Understanding in Young Children*, London: Routledge.

FAIRNESS

See also: assessing children's learning, equal opportunities, mathematics, misbehaviour, modelling behaviour, pupil perspectives

The most frequently muttered expression issuing from disgruntled children is: *It isn't fair!* (Pelo and Davidson 2000). Although adults cannot hope to, and should not try to pacify children, it is important that they explain why decisions have been taken, console children who don't quite make the grade despite earnest endeavour and hold out the promise of further opportunities for those who are not chosen. Teachers have to strive to ensure that their attitude towards each pupil is constructive, seek to find ways to approve behaviour and commend the work that pupils produce. It is nearly always true that the best-loved teachers make a regular effort to find something endearing in every child and invariably succeed in doing so (see Griffiths and Davies 1995). Consistent fairness does not mean that all children are treated the same but rather that adults model qualities such as helpfulness, a willingness to listen and explain, and a non-discriminatory attitude on the basis of factors like gender, background, race, physical prowess or attractiveness.

Being fair has implications for assessment of children's behaviour and academic work. It is surprisingly easy for an adult to assume that a particular child with a record of poor behaviour is inevitably the guilty party in a dispute between two children. Similarly, when property is damaged or missing, children with a track record tend to be prime suspects. Other children, attempting to be 'helpful' may suggest to the adult that a certain child is responsible, without any proof. Teachers are often faced with making judgements about such situations and have to resist the temptation to be prematurely accusatory or harshly interrogate the child. At the same time, it is also important for adults to avoid adopting a mindset that will not consider the possibility that normally well-behaved children have transgressed or to mete out a milder sanction compared to the one imposed on a regularly naughty child for an identical offence, unless the regular transgressor has already received several warnings.

Pupils' perceptions of adult fairness are highly relevant. The results of a factor analysis of attitudes expressed during group interviews by eleven-year-old pupils by Miller *et al.* (2000) indicated that pupils' attributions for misbehaviour at school were represented by four factors: (1) the fairness of teacher's actions, (2) pupil vulnerability, (3) adverse family circumstances, and (4) strictness of the classroom regime. Pupils in the survey viewed the fairness of teacher's actions and pupil vulnerability as more significant contributors to pupil misbehaviour than adverse family circumstances or strictness of classroom regime. The authors noted that attributions by pupils for difficult classroom behaviour differ markedly from those obtained in studies of teachers.

In evaluating the quality of academic work, too, it is possible for teachers to show unreasonable bias towards conscientious pupils, compared with those who achieve similar results but are less co-operative. Watson (2000) in her study of mathematics teachers found that their views of what constituted

fairness in judgements varied markedly. At one extreme, teachers believed that the only fair assessment would be to administer the same formal test to all pupils of the same age; at the other extreme, teachers believed that the only fair assessment was their own judgement made on the strength of their knowledge of individual pupils and regular observations of them at work. Watson recorded that these checks relied on perspectives from teachers' personal judgements rather than weighing their judgements against evidence from elsewhere. Fairness is an important factor in making academic assessments of this sort – not only from a moral perspective – but also because judgements have implications for pupils' futures, the school's reputation and, in some cases, the teacher's career prospects.

Sources

Griffiths, M. and Davies, C. (1995) *In Fairness to Children: Working for social justice in the primary school*, London: David Fulton.
Miller, A., Ferguson, E. and Byrne, I. (2000) 'Pupils' causal attributions for different classroom behaviour', *British Journal of Educational Psychology*, 70 (1), 85–96.
Pelo, A. and Davidson, A. (2000) *That's Not Fair! A teacher's guide to activism with young children*, St Paul MN: Redleaf Press.
Watson, A. (2000) 'Mathematics teachers acting as informal assessors: Practices, problems and recommendations', *Educational Studies in Mathematics*, 41 (1), 69–91.

FAITH SCHOOLS

See also: English as an additional language, home–school, private schools, religious education

A faith school (or 'parochial' school) is, in its simplest form, a primary or secondary school supported by a religious organisation. Another definition of faith school or religious school is one that provides children with a general education, and was founded or is supported by a religious group (Answers.com, on-line). Approximately one third of the state schools in England are faith schools (90 per cent of which are primary and 10 per cent secondary), the vast majority designated Christian. Of the non-Christian faith schools, the majority (around forty in total) are Jewish, with fewer than ten Muslim schools and a very small number of Sikh schools. In the United States such schools are maintained by a number of religious groups, including Lutherans, Seventh-day Adventists, Orthodox Jews, Muslims, and evangelical Protestant churches; however, the most numerous are those attached to Roman Catholic parishes.

In 2005, a joint declaration by ten faith groups committed to community cohesion agreed to work together to further their shared commitments in four ways:

1 excellence in all our schools;
2 enabling all children to achieve their full potential;
3 celebrating achievement and valuing people;
4 developing effective partnerships between home, school and the wider community.
(Teachernet, on-line)

In 2007, the UK government agreed to work with faith organisations to remove unnecessary barriers to the creation of new faith schools and to encourage independent ('private') schools to enter the maintained sector. Thousands of Muslim children are to be educated in new state faith schools under plans to extend state education to Britain's minority religions amid growing concern that a generation of British Muslim children, whose parents may speak poor English or be poorly integrated in British society, could grow up in segregated communities. The move also gives the government greater control over Muslim schools at a time when questions are being raised about whether some are adequately preparing children for life in Britain. In 2008 the first state-funded Hindu school opened in north London, in an area where almost a third of people are

Hindu, to offer an education based on the religion's values and beliefs, while following the national curriculum. In the UK, almost two thirds of children from Jewish families attend Jewish schools.

Critics of the expansion of faith schools argue that they not only increase segregation of the children who attend them, but also reduce diversity in nearby non-faith schools by attracting away pupils from families with strongly held views about faith (see Times On-line 2007). However, there is fairly convincing evidence to suggest that faith schools have a more settled learning climate, promote positive values that are popular with parents (with and without religious conviction) and achieve better academic results. Opponents of faith schools express concerns over possible divisiveness, dangers of secretarianism (division of society along faith lines) and indoctrination by sectarian groups. Nevertheless, due to their popularity with parents and pressure from religious groups, it is likely that the number of faith schools will increase in coming years. See Cairns *et al.* (2005) for an overview of the debates, issues and practicalities of faith-based education, the challenges and opportunities of different approaches to faith schools and the sorts of choices and decisions faced by parents.

Sources

Answers.com, *Parochial School*, on-line at www.answers.com/topic/parochial-school
Cairns, J., Gardner, R. and Lawton, D. (2005) *Faith Schools: Consensus or conflict?* London: Routledge.
Teachernet, *Faith Schools: Working for cohesion*, on-line at www.teachernet.gov.uk/wholeschool/faithschools/statement
Times On Line (2007): 'More faith schools are planned in an effort to integrate minorities', 8 September, on-line via www.timesonline.co.uk

FALLING OUT

See also: behaviour, body language, friendships, gender, happiness, peer mediation

Despite the best efforts to prevent it happening, there are bound to be times when children fall out with one another and adults have an important role on such occasions to provide a calm and reassuring presence, though this process is far from straightforward, especially when children have become over-excited or intensely angry. Girls tend to have two or three very close friends, while boys tend to have a larger and more fluid group of friends. Whereas disruptions in friendships between boys are normally short and quickly resolved, breakdowns in friendships among girls (especially older ones) tend to be more prolonged owing to the emotional intensity of the relationships; subsequently, such tensions may intrude on their classroom work as the normal cooperation is replaced by animosity. In the most extreme cases, especially if older pupils speak aggressively, walk away when being spoken to or, in rare cases, attack someone, teachers have to rely on exercising rapid and sound judgement. The key is for adults to deal with the 'primary' behaviour (i.e. the first offence) and protect children from injury, and not worry too much about the 'secondary' behaviour (i.e. subsequent behaviour arising from the first offence), such as foul language, abusive remarks or defiant body language. These issues can be addressed later when the situation is calmer. Many schools foster a system of 'peer mediation', consisting of a school-wide system of mutual support where selected pupils are trained to act as peacemakers and arbitrators work alongside adults to help diffuse conflicts and reconcile differences.

FAMILY AND CULTURE

See also: home–school, minority ethnic children, parents

Some cultures emphasise the importance of maintaining close family ties, and several generations may live in the same household or close to each other. As a result, children from certain backgrounds will be used to the continuous presence of family members at home and may have had little experience of separation from them until they enter school. In addition, the concept of complete privacy, so cherished by many in the Western world, is largely unknown to some children from certain backgrounds. Such factors may explain, for instance, why some children are uneasy about going to the toilet on their own or have reservations about changing in the presence of boys. Similarly, different norms and expectations may operate across cultures regarding the roles of men and women, which can lead to the need for discussions with parents about children's attitudes to female members of staff, in particular. Language barriers may necessitate the involvement of intermediaries to translate and minimise misunderstandings. Regardless of school type, locality and the makeup of the indigenous population, cementing ties between home and school has become a more significant element of school life than existed in the past.

FANTASY

See also: children, creativity, imagination

Children usually enter the world of make-believe and fantasy through nursery rhymes, fairy tales and folk tales that are read to them by adults, enabling them to reach beyond their own world and imagine things that otherwise seem impossible. They can travel to faraway lands, meet amazing characters that they never dreamed existed and face their fears head-on by grappling with, and overcoming the 'monsters in their minds'. Gopnik (2005) argues that cognitive science suggests that children love fantasy and have such an affinity for the imaginary because they are so single-mindedly devoted to finding the truth, and because through fantasy their lives are protected in order to allow them to do so. Tyrrell (2001) insists that fantasy and the

149

development of the imagination are an integral part of growing up. Put another way, to be deprived of opportunities to explore areas of fantasy means that children are not receiving their entitlement to a full education. While fantasy is normally associated with younger children, it has the capacity to awaken and stimulate the imagination of every child.

Sources

Gopnik, A. (2005) *The Real Reason Children Love Fantasy*, on-line at www.slate.com/id/2132725

Tyrrell, J. (2001) *The Power of Fantasy in Learning*, London: Routledge.

FEEDBACK

See also: assessment for learning, dialogue for learning, expectations, formative assessment, learning objectives, mathematics, mistakes and misunderstandings, self-esteem, success

The process of evaluating the merits and limitations of pupils' work, in which an informed adult offers constructive comment to a child, is usually referred to as 'feedback' but more recently referred to as 'assessment for learning' (AFL). There is no such thing as unbiased feedback, as each situation demands professional judgement about the nature, content and tone for each piece of feedback. Good quality feedback allows pupils to adjust their priorities, correct misunderstandings and advance their knowledge and thereby continue learning with confidence. Poor quality feedback leaves pupils dissatisfied, unclear about the task requirements and unsure about how to progress. Ways in which pupils are involved in their learning and told what is expected of them, how well they are doing and what to do next, also lie at the heart of effective feedback (Clarke 2003). Marking and other forms of classroom feedback to pupils have the potential to boost self-esteem, motivate and actively promote learning; however, a negative, recriminatory style of feedback can demoralise and alienate children

from learning. The Qualifications and Curriculum Authority (QCA, on-line) offers the following advice (slightly amended) about effective feedback:

- Feedback is most effective when it confirms that pupils are on the right track and stimulates correction or improvement.
- Suggestions for improvement should act to 'scaffold' pupils' learning to help them think things through for themselves, rather than be given the complete solutions as soon as they are uncertain what to do.
- Pupils should be helped to find alternative solutions if repeated explanation of the same solution is ineffective.
- Feedback on progress over a number of attempts is more effective than feedback on one attempt treated in isolation.
- The quality of dialogue in feedback is important.
- Pupils need to have the skills to ask for help and the ethos of the school (and teacher) should encourage them to do so.

The type of feedback given to pupils tends to fall under one of three broad categories: instructional, procedural or advisory. *Instructional* feedback occurs when the adult gives the child unambiguous commands about what needs to be done to improve, remedy or enhance work. *Procedural* feedback clarifies the teacher's expectations about how, why and when the task is done; it does not concern itself with the quality of the work directly. *Advisory* feedback offers suggestions about options and alternatives available to the children; the onus is then placed on pupils to determine the most appropriate course of action. Teachers have to ensure that children are clear about which of the three types of feedback is being given or they may (for example) interpret advice about ways to proceed as an instruction and comply rather than think.

The content of the feedback to pupils from adults therefore depends upon five factors. First, the learning objectives need to act as a touchstone for the advice and guidance that is offered. Second, the relationship between teacher and pupil influences the tone of the feedback, as the closer the relationship, the more relaxed and interactive the exchange is likely to be. Third, the working context is important, as a more formal situation (such as a test or a specific task undertaking requiring silence) will limit the extent of the feedback; such feedback is likely to be more procedural than instructional. Fourth, the nature of the work will have a bearing on the specificity of the feedback: open-ended tasks (especially investigative and problem-solving ones) require the teacher to 'stand back' and allow pupils to persevere without excessive guidance, whereas situations in which there is a defined and single answer or solution require close monitoring to ensure the pupil is following instructions. Fifth, the confidence of pupils and their experience in the area of learning dealt with will affect the composition of the feedback. Thus, confident children with a strong track record in coping with the demands of the work benefit from questions from the teacher that extend their thinking and cause them to reflect more deeply on the issues attached to the work. Timid children or those with little experience in the area of work require more specific direction until they gain confidence. Interestingly, a study of nine-year-old children in mathematics classes by Chalk and Bizo (2004) found that specific praise (i.e. praise that highlighted a specific aspect of a child's work) promoted more on-task behaviour (i.e. concentrating on the work in hand) than positive praise (i.e. general congratulatory praise) and significantly increased pupils' academic self-concept ('feelgood factor').

Where the purpose of the feedback is to help pupils make an evaluation of their own work quality, the child is encouraged to reflect on his or her progress and suggest strategies for improvement. The pupil then becomes supported by, but not dependent on, an adult's direction and approval (Gipps *et al.* 2000). Nevertheless, many teachers commonly find that less confident children prefer

to be told what to do rather than trust their own judgement. Teachers therefore have to exercise fine judgement when offering feedback to children about their work and effort. At one level there is a need for them to explain to children how things can be improved. At another level there is a pressing need, especially with children who have experienced limited academic success in the past, to encourage, praise and celebrate small achievements.

Sources

Chalk, K. and Bizo, L. A. (2004) 'Specific praise improves on-task behaviour and numeracy enjoyment: A study of year four pupils engaged in the numeracy hour', *Educational Psychology in Practice*, 20 (4), 335–51.
Clarke, S. (2003) *Enriching Feedback in the Primary Classroom: Oral and written feedback from teachers and children*, London: Hodder & Stoughton.
Gipps, C., McCallum, B. and Hargreaves, E. (2000) *What Makes a Good Primary Teacher?* London: Routledge.
QCA, *Characteristics of Assessment for Learning (AfL)*, on-line at www.qca.org.uk/qca_4337.aspx#feedback

FESTIVALS

See also: assembly, religious education, thematic learning

The celebration of festivals, especially those with religious significance, forms an important part of primary school life. There are many different resources available to help teachers when they use festivals as a basis for assemblies (e.g. Cox 2007; Peirce 1992) or explore them thematically in subjects such as religious education or cross-curricular themes such as 'world celebrations'.

Sources

Cox, M. (2007) *Assemblies for Autumn Festivals*, Abingdon: Barnabas (BRF).
Peirce, E. (1992) *Active Assemblies for Multiracial Schools*, London: Routledge.

FIRST AND MIDDLE SCHOOLS

See also: primary schools, tests and testing

The first middle schools opened in England in September 1968 to create the middle 'tier' of a three-tier system whereby children attend a 'first' school from the age of 5 years to either 8 or 9 years of age; that is, the schools are either '5–8 first' schools or '5–9 first schools', after which time they transfer to a 'middle' school until they are either 12 or 13 years of age. In other words, the 'middle' school is for pupils between the ages of 8 and 12 years ('8–12 middle schools') or between 9 and 13 years ('9–13 middle schools'), after which they transfer to secondary education. In some parts of the country, middle schools operate for the 10–13 or 10–14 age range (i.e. a '10–13 middle school' or a '10–14 middle school'. A proportion of schools combine the 'first' and 'middle' school components to become 'all through' schools for pupils from the age of 4 or 5 years until they are 12 or 13 years old. A number of local authorities have dismantled the first and middle school system and replaced it with infant schools (for children aged 5–7 years) and junior schools (for children aged 7–11 years) or created single primary schools for children aged 5–11 years. To a large extent the educational arguments about the desirability of one system over another have been overshadowed by the ascendancy of national tests for pupils at age 11 years.

FOREST SCHOOLS

See also: health and safety, nature study, outdoor education, self-esteem (children)

The philosophy of forest schools is to encourage and inspire individuals of any age through positive outdoor experiences. The concept originated in Scandinavia, where there is a strong belief that nature and movement are essential to a child's development. By participating in engaging, motivating and achievable tasks and activities in a woodland environment, each participant has an opportunity to develop intrinsic motivation and enhance their emotional and social skills. Children are taught to observe the natural world closely – what used to be called 'nature study' – but are also taught more risky skills, such as building shelters out of local materials and lighting fires, with suitable care taken about health and safety implications. They also learn about hazards such as stinging nettles, fast-flowing water and overhanging branches. The natural environment is ideal for teaching map reading, tracking and communicating non-verbally. Advocates insist that these experiences can be developed to reach each participant's personal potential, increase self-awareness, boost confidence and generate corporate identity among adults and pupils (www.forestschools.com). Forest schools aim to use accelerated learning techniques to create a learning context that encourages individuals, community groups and larger organisations to utilise their local open space for interactive play, health, recreation and personal development. All organisers of forest schools have to undergo training in outdoor settings; a 'Level 3 Forest School Leaders Award' is also available for people who want to run a forest school. The Forest Education Initiative (FEI) aims to increase the understanding and appreciation of the environmental, social, and economic potential of trees, woodlands and forests, and of the link between the tree and everyday wood products. See perspectives in Knight (2009) and Louv (2006).

Sources

Knight, S. (2009) *Forest Schools and Outdoor Learning in the Early Years*, London: Sage.
Louv, R. (2006) *Last Child in the Woods*, New York: Algonquin Books.

FORMATIVE ASSESSMENT

See also: assessment for learning, motivation for learning, success, summative assessment

Assessment that is ongoing during lessons and helps children to improve the quality of their work is referred to as 'formative assessment' and is found in the warp and weave of classroom life (e.g. Torrance and Pryor 1998; Drummond 2003; Lord and Slinn 2007). In recent years the process of formative assessment has been 're-branded' as 'assessment for learning' (AFL), with an emphasis on the word 'for'. Key features include:

- Learning objectives are made clear to pupils and success criteria are established.
- Learning (as opposed to task outcome) is reviewed at the end of the lesson or lessons.
- Oral and written feedback enables pupils to understand what they have achieved and how to move forward in their learning.
- Pupils are involved through peer and self-assessment.
- Pupils are encouraged (with adult support) to set achievable personal targets.
- Teachers and pupils work together to create a climate of success in the classroom.
  (Based on Bates and Munday 2005, pp. 58–59)

Kirton *et al.* (2007) report from a study about formative assessment in sixteen Scottish primary schools and two junior high schools. They conclude that there is some evidence that use of formative assessment 'led to pupils taking more responsibility for their learning, contributing to improved motivation, confidence and classroom achievement, especially for lower attainers' (p. 605). The authors warn that the tension between constructive formative assessment and summative ('end product') assessment is an uneasy one, for the simple reason that formal assessments through testing assume such significance for teachers and pupils. 'Such a tension between summative and formative assessment needs to be resolved so that the dominance of assessment for accountability does not drive out assessment for learning' (p. 624).

Sources

Bates, J. and Munday, S. (2005) *Able, Gifted and Talented*, London: Continuum.

Drummond, M.J. (2003) *Assessing Children's Learning*, London: David Fulton.

Kirton, A., Hallam, S., Peffers, J., Robertson, P. and Stobart, G. (2007) 'Revolution, evolution or a Trojan Horse? Piloting assessment for learning in some Scottish primary schools', *British Educational Research Journal*, 33 (4), 605–27.

Lord, L. and Slinn, K. (2007) *Curriculum Planning and Assessment for the Foundation Stage*, London: Sage.

Torrance, H. and Pryor, J. (1998) *Investigating Formative Assessment*, Maidenhead: Open University Press.

FOUNDATION SCHOOLS

See also: admissions code, governing bodies, National Curriculum

In England and Wales, a foundation school is a school in which a foundation or trust has a direct influence in the running of the school. Within the maintained sector in England, only about 2 per cent of primary schools are foundation schools and almost all of these are non-faith schools. Foundation schools were set up under the School Standards and Framework Act 1998 to replace grant-maintained schools. Foundation schools are funded by central government via the local education authority but the land and buildings are usually owned by a charitable trust, which can appoint a quarter of the school governors. The governing body employs the staff and has responsibility for admissions to the school. Children must follow the National Curriculum.

FOUNDATION STAGE

See also: assessment of learning, curriculum, literacy, mathematics, National Curriculum, nursery schools, observing children, play, reading, relationships, stepping stones

The Foundation Stage forms the first part of the National Curriculum, focusing on children aged three to the end of the reception year (when they reach the age of five years). The philosophy underpinning the foundation stage curriculum is that learning should be planned and structured with an emphasis on fun, relevant and motivating activities. This stage was introduced as a distinct phase of education in September 2000. Curriculum guidance was distributed in May 2000 to all schools with nursery and reception classes, and to early years settings receiving nursery education grant funding. The guidance set out six areas of learning which form the basis of the foundation stage curriculum:

1 *Personal, social and emotional development.* Children learn to be self-confident, take an interest in things, know what their own needs are, tell the difference between right and wrong, and be able to dress and undress.
2 *Communication, language and literacy.* Children learn to talk confidently and clearly, enjoying stories, songs and poems, hearing and saying sounds, and linking them to the alphabet. They will read and write some familiar words and learn to use a pencil.
3 *Mathematical development.* Children develop an understanding of mathematics through stories, songs, games and imaginative play. They will become comfortable with numbers and with ideas such as 'heavier than' or 'bigger'. They will be aware of shapes and space.
4 *Knowledge and understanding of the world.* Children explore and find out about the world around them, asking questions about it. They will build with different materials, know about everyday technology and learn what it is used for. They will find out about past events in their lives and their families' lives. They will find out about different cultures and beliefs.
5 *Physical development.* Children learn to move confidently, controlling their body and handling equipment.
6 *Creative development.* Children explore colours and shapes, trying out dance, making things, telling stories and making music.

Each area of learning has a set of related early learning goals, and the curriculum guidance is intended to help practitioners plan to meet the diverse needs of all children so that most will achieve and some, where appropriate, will go beyond the early learning goals by the end of the foundation stage. The *stepping stones* (non-statutory) show the kinds of knowledge, skills, understanding and attitudes that children are expected to need if they are to 'achieve' the early learning goals. The *early learning goals*, which are statutory, establish the expectations for most children by the end of the Foundation Stage. The *Education Act 2002* extended the National Curriculum to include the Foundation Stage. The six areas of learning became statutory, and the Act also specified that there should be early learning goals for each of the areas.

A national consultation on the content of the early learning goals was carried out in autumn 2002. Following this consultation the early learning goals, and use of the curriculum guidance became statutory in March 2002. The Act also established a single national assessment system for the Foundation Stage, replacing baseline assessment schemes. The Foundation Stage profile was introduced into schools and settings in 2002–3 with thirteen summary scales covering the six areas of learning, which need to be completed for each child by the end of his or her time in the Foundation Stage. For most children, profiling takes place at the end of the reception year in primary school but profiles based on practitioners' ongoing observations and assessments on all six areas of learning must be completed in any setting where children complete the Foundation Stage. Each child's typical developments and achievements are recorded on assessment scales derived from the stepping stones and the early learning goals.

A revised version of the EYFS Statutory Framework and Practice Guidance document was published in May 2008 with changes intended to clarify areas where feedback indicated it would be helpful (QCA 2008). Four areas were highlighted: (1) *A unique child*: every child is a competent learner from birth who can be resilient, capable, confident and self-assured; (2) *Positive relationships*: children learn to be strong and independent from a base of loving and secure relationships with parents and/or a key person; (3) *Enabling environments*: the environment plays a key role in supporting and extending children's development and learning; (4) *Learning and development*: children develop and learn in different ways and at different rates and all areas of learning and development are equally important and interconnected. See DCSF (2008). Practitioners (teachers and assistants and other helpers) in early years settings normally place strong emphasis on learning through child-initiated and adult-planned play activities, though whole class work – such as singing or counting – and formal group work (with an adult in charge) are increasingly used as children get older. There is also a move towards specific single-subject work (e.g. see Gifford 2005; Haylock and Cockburn 2008 for mathematics; also Browne 2004; Clipson-Boyles 2007; Bradford 2009 for literacy).

Williams and McInnes (2005) describe how young children learn and play differently at various times of day, ways in which fatigue and hunger affect their ability to concentrate and compete tasks, the negative effect when routines of time and place are altered, and the need for flexibility in organising the learning day with such factors in mind. See also Smidt and Green (2009) for insights into planning for early years children.

Sources

Bradford, H. (2009) *Communication, Language and Literacy in the EYFS*, London: David Fulton.

Browne, A. (2004) *Developing Language and Literacy 3–8*, London: Paul Chapman.

Clipson–Boyles, S. (2007) *Supporting Language and Literacy 3–8*, London: David Fulton.

DCSF (2008) *The Early Years Foundation Stage (EYFS)*, Annesley: DCSF Publications, on-line at www.teachernet.gov.uk/teachingandlearning/EYFS

Gifford, S. (2005) *Teaching Mathematics 3–5: Developing learning in the foundation stage*, New York: McGraw-Hill.

Haylock, D. and Cockburn, A. (2008) *Understanding Mathematics for Young Children*, London: Sage.

QCA (2008) *The Foundation Stage: Education for children aged 3 to 5*, London: HMSO, on-line via www.qca.org.uk

Smidt, S. and Green, S. (2009) *Planning for the Early Years Foundation Stage*, London: David Fulton.

Williams, J. and McInnes, K. (2005) *Planning and Using Time in the Foundation Stage*, London: David Fulton.

FOUNDATION STAGE ASSESSMENT

See also: creativity, Foundation Stage, knowledge, literacy, mathematics, personal social and health education, reading, writing

In the UK, discussion about formalising further the assessment of children at the Foundation Stage for children aged 3–5 years is ongoing. Examples include promoting the use of an assessment framework to include personal, social and emotional development, and improvements in young children's language and literacy by stimulating thought, linking sounds and letters, and gaining mastery in reading and writing. Mathematical development includes using numbers as labels for counting, calculating, shape, space and measures, knowledge and understanding of the world, physical development and creative development. Practitioners working with disadvantaged young children have to show their achievements in percentage form, using the following scale ranges: 0–3, working below the goals; 4–7, working within them; 8–9, meeting or exceeding them.

FOUNDATION STAGE PROFILE

See also: assessment of learning, Foundation Stage, Foundation Stage assessment, reception, recording

A Foundation Stage Profile was published in January 2003 to build on the existing curriculum guidance for teachers, emphasising the key role of skilful and well-planned observations in providing reliable assessment information

155

on young children, and setting out a way of summarising young children's achievements at the end of the Foundation Stage. These data provide information for parents and teachers of five-year-olds (reception class). The document contains guidance on how teachers can develop a broad curriculum, respond flexibly to children's needs and track their progress. It also outlines areas of learning, assessment scales and how to record children's development in the form of a profile.

FOUNDATION SUBJECTS

See also: art, curriculum, design and technology, English, geography, mathematics, music, National Curriculum, non-core subjects, religious education

Foundation subjects was the phrase applied to curriculum subject areas in the National Curriculum for England and Wales other than English, mathematics and science and religious education. More recently – and accurately – these subject areas have been described as the 'non-core' subjects. The original nest of six foundation subjects was as follows:

- History
- Geography
- Design technology
- Art
- Music
- Physical education (PE).

Religious education is not listed as a foundation subject but nevertheless has to be taught, though the content, emphasis and programme varies according to the type of school. Art is presently incorporated under 'art and design', whereas design technology is now known as design and technology. Information technology (IT) was a later addition to the foundation subjects but has assumed greater importance in recent years and from 2009 has been included as one of the core subjects.

FREE PLAY

See also: active learning, basic skills, behaviour, discovery learning, early years, enquiry, interaction, play, teaching strategy

Some teachers argue that play is not play unless it is free of adult contrivance, arguing that even if they try to intervene in a play situation they receive short shrift from assertive youngsters. For these teachers, manipulating play situations undermines its purpose and produces an artificial learning environment. They argue that children should be liberated to explore and come to terms with ideas without hindrance. In such classrooms, young children are found busily involved in a variety of activities: sand and water play, construction kits and toys, dressing-up. Noise levels sometimes become high and the teacher, who may be giving an individual pupil close attention or working with a group on basic skills, may choose to ignore the free play activity. Under such conditions, permission for children to spend time in free play can be used as a reward for task completion or good behaviour. Other teachers argue that the extent of the play should be closely controlled and monitored by the teacher. For example, a specific range of games is provided and activities are deliberately limited by the provision of certain resources and the exclusion of others.

Generic play outcomes are those that relate to social harmony, respect for property, tolerance and so forth. Play is seen as an opportunity for children to work through situations, solve problems, employ their imaginative powers to come to terms with new or exciting situations and exercise authority over confusing circumstances, bewildering paradoxes or worrying uncertainties. For these teachers, children use play to confirm ideas, create solutions and extend their thinking. Teachers use the opportunity to interact with the children, listen to their language and questions, and determine the extent of their understanding.

FRIENDSHIP

See also: bullying, caring teachers, competition, fairness, falling out, gender, humour, infants, new entrants, nursery schools, play, teacher–pupil interaction, teaching assistant, transitions

From the most immature nursery child to the boldest adolescent, friendships are a significant element of school life. Young children often feel more secure when sitting by their best friend; older ones like to be accepted as one of the gang. It is often during activities that take place outside the classroom that we see the most obvious examples of close relationships, such as choosing partners or members for a team game or sharing toys. While some children are sought for and cheered enthusiastically when chosen, others are regularly ignored, chosen last or grudgingly accepted into the group. Common challenges for teachers of Foundation Stage children (aged 4–5 years) and of children aged 5–7 years include comforting those who become distressed if separated from a friend on whom they rely or who get upset when someone they want to be their friend chooses not to be. Isolated children sometimes want to use the teacher or teaching assistant as a surrogate friend.

The intensity of friendship patterns and preferences is evident from an early age but intensifies across the primary phase. Teachers of older children face challenges with children who opt to work alone and resist collaborating with others; only select an activity preferred by their friends; become over-reliant on a friend for academic support; try to enter a friendship group and are rejected; or become separated from friends when classes move up at the start of a new academic year. As alliances and rivalries develop over the years, older children can become entrenched in their views of individuals and sometimes the animosity spills over into aggression. Whereas most reception class children will accept their allocated partner, the emergence of prejudice towards children who are 'different' from the majority needs firm, sensitive handling by

adults as children move through the school. Negative racial stereotypes are rare during infant days but can become rampant during the upper stages if left unchecked.

Corsaro (2003) argues that educators should not interpret children's friendships from their own perspectives but try to understand them from the child's point of view. In particular, he insists that there is a need to appreciate the complexities attached to friendship and be aware of the social situations in which friendship knowledge and skills develop. Factors such as gender structure, size of group, amount of time children spend together, the prevailing cultural values within the group, the impact of wider society and even the school curriculum help to shape friendship patterns. The author argues against the notion that children are passive agents that are moulded by adults and interprets that 'being in their own little world' is one that children deliberately choose to create. Cosaro also insists that adults should spend more time watching children as they are interacting and avoid making assumptions without evidence.

Helping children to develop friendships is not the principal purpose of primary education, but attention to the implications arising from good relationships is important in the quest for a positive teaching and learning environment. Paley (2000) describes how very young children can transform themselves and one another by taking in, narrating and acting out tales of kindness and other acts of goodness. She illustrates how children make sense of the unspoken messages articulated to them while they create safe havens for one another where no child is turned away. Children attach great importance to playing with and learning alongside their friends, so teachers have a responsibility to identify and promote such groupings. Woods (1990) noted that friendship and much of the humour and laughter that accompanies it 'has a utilitarian purpose, as well as, in some instances, emotional bonds ... It protects, enhances, shores up the self and is the basic requirement for beginning to cope' (p. 208).

New school entrants in particular need to establish friendships as quickly as possible; it is likely that they know some of their peers from pre-school settings (playgroup; nursery) but the new situation often realigns relationships and can cause a degree of turmoil initially. Nevertheless, as Peters (2003) notes, most children's experiences of friendship when they move to 'proper' school are positive and affirming. Similar challenges face children at any transition point, not least when they transfer from infant to junior school or from primary to secondary education.

There is a growing concern about the loss of childhood, as reflected in the reduced amount of time that children spend with parents, the flood of media images that saturate their minds and the speed with which children are expected to absorb adult perspectives and practices. In this regard Harris (1998) controversially asserts that peer friendship groups – not parents or other adults – are the strongest environmental influence on personality development. Sincere friendships between adults and children can have significant benefits far beyond the immediate situation and offer hope and security for children. While it is not necessary – and probably not desirable – for adults in school to be close friends with pupils, it is essential for them to be friendly, warm and accessible. Teachers work hard to build a rapport with children and thereby place themselves in a much stronger position to influence pupil attitude and behaviour, as the extent of their influence is severely curtailed if they are emotionally detached from the learners. At a time where there is a suspicion of adults who express a loving interest in children's welfare, positive teacher–pupil relationships provide considerable reassurance for those who view compassion as a key dimension of their role.

Sources

Corsaro, W.A. (2003) *We're Friends Right? Inside kids' culture*, Washington DC: Joseph Henry Press.

Harris, J.R. (1998) *The Nurture Assumption: Why children turn out the way they do*, New York: Free Press.

Paley, V.G. (2000) *The Kindness of Children*, Princeton NJ: Harvard University Press.

Peters, S. (2003) 'I didn't expect that I would get tons of friends! Children's experiences of friendship during the transition to school', *Early Years*, 23 (1), 45–53.

Woods, P. (1990) *The Happiest Days?* London: Falmer.

FRIENDSHIP BENCHES

Studies indicate that schools that have transformed their playgrounds have seen bullying fall by up to two thirds, and vandalism fall by more than a quarter. One of the suggested improvements to playgrounds includes so-called 'friendship benches' where lonely children can get help from a playground 'buddy'. Children are taught how to listen to their peers' concerns, identify those who seem unhappy and know what to do if a fight breaks out. It is also helpful if children are taught how or encouraged to play traditional games where every child feels confident to participate. Whether or not these encouraging statistics stay constant over the coming years remains to be seen.

FULFILMENT IN TEACHING

See also: effectiveness, governors, head teacher, inspections, parents, relationships, school climate, teacher–pupil interaction, trainee teachers

People choose to teach for many reasons, not least the pleasure that they gain from being immersed in an environment in which a dedicated group of adults work alongside children with a united, though difficult to define purpose called 'educating'. It is hardly surprising that teachers sometimes feel under the microscope in having to respond to so many different needs to satisfy the expectations of pupils, parents, colleagues, head teacher, governors, as well as the community and education inspectors. When things are going well, the approval from representatives of these groups is exhilarating; by contrast, their disapproval can bring distress and a loss of confidence.

Most of a teacher's fulfilment relies on establishing a secure, harmonious relationship with pupils; it is equally true that a critical comment from a significant person – such as a parent – can upset a teacher's sense of equilibrium and have a detrimental effect on his or her ability to teach and be innovative, as criticism usually produces a 'play safe' approach. Ho and Au (2006) found in a survey of 220 primary and secondary teachers that teaching satisfaction as measured by the 'Teaching Satisfaction Scale' (TSS) correlated positively with self-esteem but negatively with psychological distress and teaching stress. In other words, ease of mind and heart were essential prerequisites for fulfilment. Doubts about personal competence can embed themselves in a teacher's mind, lower morale and constrain innovative practice. For this reason, peace of mind is not a cosy option for inadequate people but a vital necessity to ensure that teachers are operating at optimum efficiency and being daring rather than predictable.

In most jobs, after a stern word from the boss, employees make a more concerted effort to do better and 'move up a gear'; however, improving as a teacher is much more involved. Although there may be a small number of lazy and tardy individuals in school, the vast majority are highly diligent and determined to pour themselves out wholeheartedly for the job (Troman and Raggi 2008). Nothing less is expected from trainee teachers, though inexperience sometimes means that their desire to be conscientious is frustrated by an incomplete understanding of how schools function and

clumsiness with the 'nuts and bolts' of effective teaching and learning.

From a US perspective, Schneider (2003) concluded that school facilities have a direct affect on teaching and learning, such that poor school conditions ('school climate') make it more difficult for teachers to deliver an adequate education to their students, adversely affect teachers' health, and increase the likelihood that teachers will leave their school and the teaching profession. Teachers balance these frustrations with the joys of the job, such as the unmatched satisfaction of seeing a pupil comprehend a difficult concept and the special joy of connecting with children who have resisted the efforts of other adults to establish a bond of trust.

Teachers who elect or have little choice but to teach in challenging situations are likely to find job satisfaction through the sense of camaraderie, they enjoy with colleagues involved in the same 'uphill battle' and the knowledge that they are willing to persevere under adverse conditions to help underprivileged children and make school emotionally safe for them (see Bluestein 2001). For those who stay in the job long enough to cope with the heavy commitments, fulfilment is lasting and real.

Sources

Bluestein, J. (2001) *Creating Emotionally Safe Schools*, Deerfield Beach FL: HCI Books.

Ho, C.L. and Au, W.T. (2006) 'Measuring job satisfaction of teachers', *Educational and Psychological Measurement*, 66 (1), 172–85.

Schneider, M. (2003) *Linking School Facility Conditions to Teacher Satisfaction and Success*, Washington DC: National Clearinghouse, on-line via www.edfacilities.org/pubs

Troman, G. and Raggi, A. (2008) 'Primary teacher commitment and the attractions of teaching', *Pedagogy, Culture and Society*, 16 (1), 85–99.

159

G

GENDER (PUPILS)

See also: behaviour, boys' education, brain function, bullying, child development, communication, competition, early years, failure, memory and memorising, misbehaviour, rewards, social and emotional aspects of learning, social development, talk, writing

The term 'gender' refers to the social and educational aspects of whether a pupil is male or female and relates to the real and perceived biological, genetic, cultural, educational and lifelong implications. Recent evidence indicates that there are common neurological and metabolic differences between boys and girls that affect the rates of their intellectual development in different areas of learning (for example, language) during the early and primary school years, largely to the disadvantage of boys (Westminster Institute of Education 2001; see also Gurian *et al.* 2002). In a study of why men were much more likely to break the law than women, Bennett *et al.* (2005) concluded that one of the reasons females have lower rates of offending is because they acquire social cognitive skills earlier in life than males, influenced by many factors, including better communication between different areas of the brain, fewer frontal lobe deficits (the frontal lobe is located at the front of the brain and associated with reward, attention, long-term memory, planning and drive), greater verbal ability and differential socialisation by parents and peers.

There was a period of time during the later part of the twentieth century when some educationists who were passionate about equal opportunities argued that there was 'no difference' between boys and girls but that girls were disadvantaged educationally because teachers gave them inferior attention and fewer privileges (see, for example, Whyte 1983). A rather more enlightened perspective about the complexity of the issues has been gained through knowledge of the way that male and female foetuses develop in the womb, environmental factors and observations of boys and girls at play. For instance, girls tend to master language more quickly than boys, such that nearly all girls can talk by the age of three but boys take up to 12 months longer.

Garnett (2005) claims that the female brain makes a child more sensitive to nuances of expression and gesture, as well as a better judge of character. Boys tend to be more competitive; written work is sometimes hurried in an effort to finish quickly; they are not known for neatness or accuracy; they are more inclined to be noisy and troublesome. Girls generally enjoy collaborative work and are persevering; they take more care with presentation and are normally more subdued than their male classmates. Boys and girls are not 'the same' by any stretch of the imagination.

It is the experience of primary teachers that girls are less inclined to be disruptive and poorly behaved in class and seem to be more self-conscious than boys when in a group.

The Department for Children, Schools and Families (DCSF) web site 'Gender and Achievement' suggests that part of the explanation for girls' superior achievements lie in the fact that girls normally have greater maturity and more effective learning strategies, together with a prevailing fear of failure in boys. Of course these points are generalisations and there will be exceptions; nevertheless, the fact that boys tend to occupy more space when playing, read later than girls, find it difficult to accommodate newcomers into the group and are often adept at competing practical and spatial activities, has implications for their education. Similarly, the tendency for girls to read early and have refined verbal ability, be more sociable, play fewer competitive games, have longer attention spans and benefit more than boys from auditory learning, means that adults have to take these factors into account when planning, organising and managing learning. Thus, girls may have to be encouraged to be healthily competitive; boys may have to be taught to take more account of the feelings and ideas of other children.

Girls may need to be encouraged to build on their natural literacy strengths and employ them across the curriculum, especially in areas where they may have been traditionally less successful (e.g. problem solving in mathematics); boys may need to be encouraged to develop storylines and verbal sequences as a device for enhancing understanding. Girls may have to be offered support in technological activities, ensuring that they do not allow themselves to be overshadowed by more dominant boys. Boys may have to be taught how to resolve situations of potential conflict and listen carefully to other people's points of view.

Teachers have to be careful that they are not seen to favour the more cooperative girls or pander to the 'boys will be boys' philosophy that tolerates behaviour from them that would be unacceptable from girls. On the other hand, teachers have to be aware that many boys thrive in an active environment where they can use their hands as well as heads and ensure that lessons are not dominated by talk and writing. It is a common experience in classrooms that boys enjoy stimulating interaction with the teacher, contributing ideas and doing the practical tasks but lose their verve for learning during the 'writing up' phase. By contrast, girls may be tentative during the opening lesson phases but come to life when they have to commit something to paper.

Sometimes gender and not ability or potential appears to be the controlling factor in judging academic potential and progress. However, results from national tests indicate that the position is more complex, and girls are forging ahead of boys in most areas of work, especially in language and topic work. The experience of many reception class teachers is that although most girls tend to persevere with reading, take their books home faithfully each night and seem to pick up the necessary skills and strategies with little difficulty, the picture with boys is more varied. Many boys are slower, fail to organise themselves as well as the girls and are attracted more by computer games, construction kits, practical activities and competition than by desk-bound exercises. It is also ironic that despite girls' tendency to socialise more naturally than boys, it is the independent tasks associated with reading that many girls find fulfilling. Paradoxically, the more independent image frequently attached to boys is counteracted by the unease shown by many of them with the solitary work tasks and their preference for collaborative practical work. It is the common experience of teachers that boys who display antisocial behaviour in school often struggle with the basic academic skills. In addition Eaude (2006) suggests that boys find social development especially hard. Thus:

> The reasons are very complicated but because gender identity is, at least in part, socially constructed, both girls and boys experience strong pressure to conform to

the gendered expectations of the family, the peer group and society. Put crudely, boys tend to be encouraged not to express their emotions, to be wary of intimacy and either to interact through emotionally 'safe' activities, such as sport, or to be less dependent on relationships; while girls interact more by developing close relationships.

(p. 46)

When they use the expression 'socially constructed', writers mean that girls and boys behave the way that they do because we ('society') expect it, the implication being that they would behave differently if we held different expectations. Note, however, that Eaude (above) qualifies his statement with the phrase 'in part' because recent research suggests that gendered patterns of achievement might be due to natural differences between the sexes 'as a consequence of hormonal, chromosomal or brain differences' (Francis and Skelton 2005, p. 75). The Francis and Skelton proposition is an interesting case in point, in that while the one author (Skelton) is willing to accept that brain structure research 'offers some potential explanation as to why there are more boys who are autistic, have special needs, or even why boys generally are less adept at literacy than girls', the other author (Francis) 'supports the view that gender is completely socially constructed' (p. 76).

In Northern Ireland, the annual *Kids' Life and Times* survey is an evaluation of all P7 (eleven-year-old) children in Northern Ireland, conducted by Queen's University Belfast and the University of Ulster, about what they think of school and other issues that are of importance to them. The 2008 survey (www.ark.ac.uk/klt) found that just over one quarter (26 per cent) of primary seven boys were completely happy coming to school, compared with 44 per cent of girls. Boys were less happy than girls with writing, reading, spelling, working by themselves and coming to school. The survey also found that just over half of primary seven children think pupils in their school have been bullied.

Sources

Bennett, S., Farrington, D.P. and Huesmann, L.R. (2005) 'Explaining gender differences in crime and violence: The importance of social cognitive skills', *Aggression and Violent Behaviour*, 10 (3), 263–88.

DCSF: *Gender and Achievement*, on-line via http://nationalstrategies.standards.dcsf.gov.uk

Eaude, T. (2006) *Children's Spiritual, Moral, Social and Cultural Development*, Exeter: Learning Matters.

Francis, B. and Skelton, C. (2005) *Gender and Achievement*, London: Routledge.

Garnett, S. (2005) *Using Brainpower in the Classroom*, London: Routledge.

Gurian, M., Henley, P. and Trueman, T. (2002) *Boys and Girls Learn Differently: A guide for teachers and parents*, Hoboken NJ: Wiley.

Queen's University (2008), Kids Life and Times Survey, *Girls Are Happier Than Boys At Primary School*, Science Daily, on-line via www.sciencedaily.com

Westminster Institute of Education (2001) *Primary Launchpad 7: Gender issues*, Oxford: Oxford Brookes University.

Whyte, J. (1983) *Beyond the Wendy House: Sex role stereotyping in primary schools*, York: Longman for Schools Council.

GENDER (STAFF)

See also: mathematics, modelling behaviour, minority ethnic groups, motivation for teaching, professional development, professionalism, teacher–pupil interaction, tests and testing

Primary teaching has long been associated in the public mind as a job for women and a lingering perception that men only become primary teachers if they cannot cope with other forms of employment. The vast majority of primary teachers, both male and female, are from financially secure backgrounds; few come from disadvantaged or straightened circumstances. The number of teachers from most minority ethnic groups is small compared with the overall percentage of population nationally. Figures released by the General Teaching Council for England for 2008 showed that men accounted for only 13 per cent of registered primary school teachers.

Concerns in the UK about the lack of male teachers generally and their complete absence in many schools has led to widespread discussion about ways to enhance the status of primary teaching and provide financial incentives.

A survey of 600 eight- to eleven-year-olds by YouGov for the Training and Development Agency (TDA) in 2008 suggested that many boys would welcome more men in schools. The survey found that 39 per cent of boys did not have any men teaching them and one in twelve had never been taught by a man, 48 per cent of boys believe male teachers set good examples for them and 28 per cent said men understood them better. More than half (51 per cent) of the boys said the presence of a male teacher made them behave better; a good proportion of the boys said men helped them enjoy school more (44 per cent) and feel more confident about themselves (37 per cent). Over recent years the proportion of men teaching infant-age children has increased, though they still account for an extremely low proportion of total staff.

A study by Riddell et al. (2005) in Scotland about gender balance in the teaching workforce found that women students were significantly more likely than men to regard teaching as a good job for people with family responsibilities. A higher proportion of women than men thought that primary teaching a more attractive than secondary teaching. Despite the gloomy view of future career prospects expressed by men in focus groups, the authors note that it is still the case that the majority of promoted posts are occupied by men and, even if their absolute numbers in the profession decline, their chances of promotion compared with those of women are likely to remain good.

Interviews with twenty experienced women teachers in Sweden by Gannerud (2001) identified a number of themes that were significant in their daily work. First, the teachers saw their professional role as gender-neutral but also felt that being female affected their daily work. Second, experiences of motherhood and of teaching as work and the

meaning of a professional attitude were linked. Third, there was a need to balance the demands of private life and work life, in which both spheres are characterised by gender-specific responsibilities and an ethics of care. Fourth, the emotional demands were exhausting and time consuming but also very important for work satisfaction and personal motivation. Fifth, informal collegial ('non-hierarchical') interaction provided a source of emotional support as well as development of professional knowledge. Finally, a perception of teaching as a low-status profession is linked in people's minds with the job being a suitable one for women. Thornton and Bricheno (2000) argue that reasons for limited career development for many women are multi-faceted, but include the disproportionate promotion of men; traditional gender differences in work–home orientation; and expectations about the role of women in school.

Bricheno and Thornton (2002) obtained data for 846 randomly selected primary schools in England regarding the number of males and females teaching in the school and the sex of the head teacher. Results indicated that test results were not particularly affected by whether pupils were taught by a male or female teacher. However, schools with a male head teacher were likely to have more male teachers on the staff. It appeared to be the case that male teachers had a preference to teach in larger schools. In the sample, test results in mathematics were slightly better in primary schools led by a male head teacher.

Debate continues about the extent to which pupils need male as well as female teachers to act as role models, but the soaring incidence of families with only one adult (usually the mother) has added weight to the argument that children benefit from being taught by men as well as women.

Sources

Bricheno, P. and Thornton, M. (2002) 'Staff gender balance in primary schools', *Research in Education*, 68, 57–63.

GENERAL TEACHING COUNCIL (WALES)

Gannerud, E. (2001) 'A gender perspective on the work and lives of women primary school teachers', *Scandinavian Journal of Educational Research*, 45 (1), 55–70.

Riddell, S., Tett, L., Burns, C., Ducklin, A., Ferrie, J., Stafford, A. and Winterton, M. (2005) *Gender Balance of the Teaching Workforce in Publicly Funded Schools*, Moray House School of Education, University of Edinburgh.

Thornton, M. and Bricheno, P. (2000) 'Primary school teachers' careers in England and Wales: The relationship between gender, role, position and promotion aspirations', *Pedagogy, Culture and Society*, 8 (2), 187–206.

GENERAL TEACHING COUNCIL (ENGLAND)

See also: General Teaching Councils, maintained schools, special schools, teaching profession, trainee teachers

The General Teaching Council for England or GTCE (www.gtce.org.uk) is the awarding body for qualified teacher status (QTS) in England and maintains a register of qualified teachers. All teachers in maintained schools and pupil referral units and in non-maintained special schools must be registered with the GTCE; others have a choice whether to register. Since September 2008, provisional registration with the Council has also been a requirement for trainee teachers. The Council's stated aims are to work to improve standards of teaching and the quality of learning in the public interest; that is, working on behalf of children through teachers.

GENERAL TEACHING COUNCIL (NORTHERN IRELAND)

See also: General Teaching Councils, professionalism, teaching profession

The General Teaching Council for Northern Ireland or GTCNI (www.gtcni.org.uk) is the statutory, independent body for the teaching profession, which is dedicated to enhancing the status of teaching and promoting the highest standards of professional conduct and practice. The Council's responsibilities as set out in the Education (Northern Ireland) Order 1998. Articles 34–41 consist of the registration of teachers; the development of a code of professional values and practice for the profession; disciplinary functions relating to professional misconduct; the provision of advice to the Department of Education and employing authorities on a range of issues.

GENERAL TEACHING COUNCIL (SCOTLAND)

See also: General Teaching Councils, professionalism, teaching profession

The General Teaching Council for Scotland or GTCS (www.gtcs.org.uk/Home/home.aspx) is the professional regulatory body for teachers in Scotland, which seeks to maintain and enhance professional standards of Scotland's teachers and support new teachers. It was set up in 1965 under the Teaching Council Scotland Act, following concerns that entry requirements had lowered after the Second World War and unqualified teachers were working in Scottish schools. Its stated aims are to contribute to the development of a world-class educational system in Scotland; to maintain and to enhance professional standards in schools and colleges in collaboration with partners; and to be recognised as an advocate for the teaching profession.

GENERAL TEACHING COUNCIL (WALES)

See also: General Teaching Councils, professionalism, teaching profession

The GTC Wales or GTCW (www.gtcw.org.uk/about.html) is known as Cyngor Addysgu Cyffredinol in the Welsh language and is the statutory self-regulating professional body for the teaching profession in Wales. The Council aspires to contribute to improving standards of teaching and the quality of learning and maintain and improve standards of professional conduct amongst teachers in the interests of the public, as set out in the 'Statement of Professional Values and Practice'. The Council also aims to raise the status of the profession through greater public understanding of what is involved in teaching.

GENERAL TEACHING COUNCILS

See also: governors, governing body, modelling behaviour, planning, professionalism, special educational needs, teaching profession, trainee teachers

To promote a sense of collegiality and consistency across the teaching profession, teachers are bound by formal and implicit codes of ethics that specify how they are to fulfil their duties and obligations with respect to the education they provide. The existence of General Teaching Councils (GTCs), established through the Teaching and Higher Education Act (England and Wales) 1998 largely supersedes previous attempts to define professional behaviour. The GTC for Northern Ireland was established under the auspices of the Education (Northern Ireland) Order 1998. The newly established GTCs are modelled on the Scotland TC that has been in existence since 1965. GTCs are statutory, self-regulating professional bodies for teachers that seek to raise the quality of teaching by maintaining and promoting the highest standards of professional practice and conduct in the interests of teachers, pupils and the general public. It is a legal requirement for qualified teachers to be registered with the respective GTC. Trainee teachers and overseas teachers qualify for provisional registration. Although teaching councils monitor behaviour nationally, it is for school governors/school boards to determine initially whether a teacher's conduct is acceptable and adjudicate in cases where it appears to be unsatisfactory.

One of the functions of a GTC is to investigate and hear cases against registered teachers through its disciplinary committees. Even if they have not been convicted of an offence in court, inappropriate behaviour by teachers in and out of school may constitute unprofessional conduct or incompetence that indicates unfitness of character to be a registered teacher. Teachers can be reported to the Council for offences as diverse as repeatedly failing to hand in planning and assessment files to the head teacher for monitoring; demonstrating overt insensitivity to children with special needs; or using inappropriate language in front of pupils and colleagues. Removal from the register is rare, other than in extreme circumstances. Teachers who are de-registered may ask for reinstatement after an appropriate length of time, though this request is not necessarily acceded to.

GEOGRAPHY

See also: curriculum, discussion, information technology, National Curriculum, science, visual aids

Geography is one of the 'non-core' subjects in the National Curriculum for England and Wales. In 1998 the Qualifications and Curriculum Authority (QCA) produced schemes of work designed to help teachers 'deliver' the programmes of study. Pupils aged 5–7 years investigate their local area and a contrasting area in the United Kingdom or abroad, finding out about the environment in both areas and the people who live there. They also begin to learn about the wider world and conduct geographical enquiries inside and outside the classroom. In doing this children are encouraged to ask geographical questions about people, places and environments, and use geographical skills and resources such as maps and photographs.

Pupils aged 7–11 years investigate a variety of people, places and environments in the United Kingdom and abroad and start to make links between different places in the world. They find out how people affect the environment and how they are affected by it and carry out geographical enquiries inside and outside the classroom. They learn to ask geographical questions and use geographical skills and resources such as maps, atlases, aerial photographs and information technology. The schemes are non-statutory and show one way that the geography programmes of study can be interpreted for the classroom. Teachers are encouraged to adapt ideas from the schemes to meet pupils' needs and the priorities of their school or department. See Martin (2006); Catling and Willy (2009).

Most primary schools are effective in organising studies of the local area of the school and extending this work into investigations of contrasting localities in economically developing countries. The use of fieldwork, teaching of mapwork, weather studies and the examination of aspects of environmental geography are commonly used topics. The best work in geography establishes effective connections with children's daily experiences to enhance their learning, particularly in local studies. This has benefited their understanding of (for instance) maps and environmental issues, particularly where children examine current concerns and issues in the school and locality, such as proposals for new buildings, recycling and signposting.

Geography is, at heart, a visual subject, dependent on images. Such images may be first-hand in the urban or rural environment, townscapes or landscapes. The images may be primary sources (seeing things 'here and now') or secondary sources, such as artefacts, videos, photographs, diagrams and different kinds of maps. Teachers have to assist pupils in 'reading' these visual aids and learn how, through repeated encounters, to interpret and understand them. Children gain great satisfaction from opportunities to talk and discuss about their geographical experiences, rather than being subjected to a curriculum dominated by didactic teaching and two-dimensional activities that involve only task completion and do not raise issues or invite questions. Teachers have the responsibility to provide an appropriate vocabulary for children as they move from describing what they see, feel and hear to comparing examples from two or more localities (Mackintosh 2007).

Some primary teachers have a limited appreciation of the key ideas in geography and find it difficult to engage children in seeking explanations and in making generalisations. There is sometimes a tendency to limit learning to describing what is seen and found out and not to extend it to developing analysis beyond the evidence. This constrained approach reflects the limits of teachers' understanding of geography and is of little surprise given the demands on primary teachers to come to grips with a curriculum that is constantly being updated and modified and emphasises literacy, numeracy and information technology above all other subject areas (Catling 1999).

'Local Studies' is a mapping package that can be used for geographical, historical or environmental mapping projects at key stage 2. The programme allows pupils to draw their own background maps, download them from Internet or use Ordnance Survey maps. Drag and drop map symbols, trace layers, text, pictures and video hot spots all enable the base map to be enhanced for a whole range of projects including the journey to school.

Owing to the need for evidence that they have covered the curriculum and pressure to assess pupil progress using verifiable sources, teachers are tempted to insist that children always maintain a written record of their experiences, knowledge acquired and tasks completed (as opposed to merely discussing or representing them visually). Such procedures may go some way to explaining why, in common with other practical subjects like science, the reduction of geography lessons to a pseudo-literacy session has, regrettably, made it one of the least popular subjects in primary school.

Sources

Catling, S. (1999) 'Geography in primary education in England', *International Research in*

Geographical and Environmental Education, 8 (3), 283–86.

Catling, S. and Willy, T. (2009) *Teaching Primary Geography*, Exeter: Learning Matters.

Mackintosh, M. (2007) 'The joy of teaching and learning geography', in Hayes, D. (ed.) *Joyful Teaching and Learning in the Primary School*, Exeter: Learning Matters.

Martin, F. (2006) *Teaching Geography in Primary Schools*, Cambridge: Chris Kington Publishing.

GIFTED AND TALENTED

See also: ability, art and design, creativity, dance, design and technology, geography, history, imagination, mathematics, music, physical education, religious education, science, slow learners

There are numerous definitions of the terms 'gifted' and 'talented' though it is often employed in a single phrase: 'gifted and talented'. However, a commonly held view is that *gifted* is an exceptional ability in literacy, mathematics, science, history, geography, design and technology, and (rarely) religious education. The word *talented*, on the other hand, tends to be reserved for children who display exceptional ability in other curriculum areas where there is more of a public performance element: art and design, music, physical education, dance and drama. Bates and Munday (2005) define gifted children as 'those who exhibit high ability across one or more academic subject areas', and talented children as 'those who excel in a specific subject area; either socially – in terms of leadership – or in sport, the performing arts or design and technology' (p. 4). However, Knowles (2006, referring to Sternberg and Davidson 2005) offers a different perspective, claiming that giftedness is the potential a child may possess in any particular subject or area of human activity; it is characterised by the child's ability to learn in that area faster than his or her peer group. By contrast, talent is seen by Knowles as 'the *realisation* of that giftedness; in effect, the performance of that giftedness' (p. 150, original emphasis).

Whatever definition we adopt, it is likely that gifted and talented pupils will typically comprise between 5 and 10 per cent of the class. In other words, in a class of thirty children there are likely to be two or three children in that category.

Both talented and gifted children are creative and imaginative, possess keen insight and intuition and can work independently of others. They often have a good, though unconventional sense of humour and are highly motivated (particularly in self-selected tasks), demonstrating exceptional critical thinking skills for problem solving. They will normally have a wide spread of interests, superior powers of reasoning, intellectual curiosity, a broad attention span and a superior vocabulary. Other characteristics include:

- being intensely focused on the task;
- asking insightful questions to probe and clarify concepts;
- seeing possibilities beyond the obvious solution;
- thriving on the challenges and complexity of the problem;
- making abstract connections between pieces of information;
- offering original and unusual solutions;
- posing questions beyond the immediate remit of the task.

Gifted children are capable of employing advanced reading strategies (such as the ability to scan text) and possess strong powers of observation and originality in their approach to solving problems. They tend to respond quickly to new ideas and memorise facts quickly. They may demonstrate maturity beyond their years, expressed by an interest in people and the way that situations interrelate. However, a child who is academically years ahead of someone in the peer group may have the personal maturity of an average child of his or her age and may possess the social skills of an even younger child.

The prominence of gifted or talented ability should not be considered as being either innate or absent; that is, either a child has 'got it' or not. Although it is normally quite easy to distinguish the very able children (i.e. those possessing exceptional innate abilities) from the majority, the learning environment can also have an impact on the *emergence* of the gift or talent (see Hymer and Michel 2002 for practical ideas and suggestions). Bates and Munday (2005) warn that 'children develop at different rates according to their home and school influences, and their potential for achievement may well remain undiscovered and untapped well into their teenage years' (p. 8). Helping gifted children in core subjects, especially mathematics and English, tends to be easier for teachers in that there is a considerable amount of time spent on these areas of the curriculum. Recognising giftedness in science is more complex and may not become evident until secondary school.

Teachers have to be sensitive and flexible in the way that they identify learning outcomes, as a characteristic of gifted and talented children is that they learn things that were unanticipated and unplanned and may be unimpressed with teachers' pre-determined priorities. Teachers are becoming more adept in early intervention and tailoring an education suitable for the needs of the gifted and talented. Ruf (2005) provides a stark reminder that gifted children can get 'left behind' because their uniqueness 'renders them particularly vulnerable and requires modifications in parenting, teaching and counselling in order for them to develop optimally' (p. 31). There is no single curriculum and teaching approach suitable for all gifted children: each case has to be dealt with on its individual merits.

Dickinson (1996) found that very able pupils wanted to find fulfilment through active dialogue with the teacher and to be 'challenged within the curriculum rather than by special provision outside it' (p. 8); that is, able pupils did not want to be isolated from the regular tasks and activities, but rather to be given the opportunity to extend their thinking and be innovative (see, for example, Smith 2005). More able pupils were motivated by teachers' comments more than grades and wanted to receive truthful, realistic and challenging feedback. By contrast, talented children (as defined by exceptional ability in arts or sport) may not shine at (say) mathematics and literacy; as a result they are obliged to spend additional time on these subjects, which reduces the opportunity for them to display their creative abilities in areas where their natural abilities lie. Teachers strive to help children exploit their potential and every school is now required to have a policy covering such matters (see, for example, Eyre and McClure 2001).

Experience suggests that teachers are sometimes tempted to leave bright pupils alone to work independently or simply give them additional work to keep them busy while attention is given to slower learners. In fact, the highest levels of academic performance are achieved when teachers interact with pupils in a way that encourages them to grapple with demanding concepts and levels of understanding. Capable pupils do not benefit from being given 'special treatment' and isolated from the regular tasks and activities but prosper when they are given the opportunity to explore ideas and be innovative.

Sources

Bates, J. and Munday, S. (2005) *Able, Gifted and Talented*, London: Continuum.

Dickinson, C. (1996) *Effective Learning Activities*, Stafford: Network Educational Press.

Eyre, D. and McClure, L. (eds) (2001) *Curriculum Provision for the Gifted and Talented in the Primary School*, London: David Fulton/NACE.

Hymer, B. and Michel, D. (2002) *Gifted and Talented Learners*, London: NACE/David Fulton.

Knowles, G. (2006) 'Gifted and Talented', in Knowles, G. (ed.) *Supporting Inclusive Practice*, Exeter: Learning Matters.

Ruf, D.L. (2005) *Losing Our Minds: Gifted children left behind*, Scottsdale AZ: Great Potential Press.

Smith, C. (2005) *Teaching Gifted and Talented Pupils in the Primary School*, London: Paul Chapman.

Sternberg, R.J. and Davidson, J.E. (2005) *Conceptions of Giftedness*, Cambridge: Cambridge University Press.

169

GIRLS

See *Gender (pupils)*

GOOD TEACHERS

See also: collaboration (staff), communication, effectiveness, excellent teachers, motivation for learning, professionalism, speech, teacher role, teaching profession

Although descriptions of teachers tend to polarise into 'good' or 'useless', the reality is that every teacher excels in certain areas of work and is less effective in others. All successful teachers sound confident, even if they do not feel that way, but good teachers do not allow their confidence to deteriorate into arrogance or a supercilious attitude. Moore (2001) claims that there is a tendency to describe the teacher in terms of personality and charisma; the implication being that good teachers are 'born' rather than 'made'. In a later publication (Moore 2004) the author suggests that the simple use of 'good teacher' is inadequate and offers three descriptions: (1) the competent craftsperson – a concept currently favoured by governments; (2) the reflective practitioner, which continues to get widespread support among teacher trainers and educators; and (3) the charismatic subject, whose popular appeal is evidenced in film and other media representations of teaching. Moore makes the crucial point that reflection can, within certain interpretations, lead not to improvement but to self-blame and advocates a reflexive response (looking at cause and effect) as the way for teachers to move beyond self-blame for their shortcomings towards a recognition of how our lives and experiences shape the way we act. See Darling-Hammond and Baratz-Snowden (2005) for a North American perspective.

The vocabulary used in inspection reports indicates that assessments of teacher competence are based on *efficiency* as much as effectiveness. Thus, teachers are commended for planning thoroughly, structuring their lessons,

differentiating tasks, establishing learning targets, maintaining records, and so forth. There are, however, a number of differences between being a good teacher and an efficient one. Whereas an efficient teacher is diligent, well-organised and able to teach in such a way that targets are met and children are able to achieve what is expected of them, a good teacher is all of these things *together with* an ability to inspire and motivate children into a love of learning. A good teacher relates to pupils in such a way that they feel willing and able to approach with any questions or problems they may have, without hesitation. Good teachers make learning fun and effective, taking into account different children's needs, while maintaining discipline and helping children to achieve high standards of work. They observe children closely and listen carefully to each child, assess the needs of individuals and provide appropriate work for them, helping and encouraging children to become independent thinkers and self-motivated learners.

Director of the Excelsior American School, Shalini Nambiar (2008), argues that good teaching is as much about passion as it is about reason. It is not only about motivating learners but also teaching them *how* to learn, and doing so in a manner that is relevant, meaningful, and memorable. Good teaching is about keeping abreast with recent developments and being at the leading edge of knowledge as much as possible, eliciting responses and developing oral communication skills, especially among quieter pupils. Even in situations dominated by academic priorities, a good teacher's cheerfulness and optimistic approach can transform a child's attitude and offer much-needed hope. Palmer (1998) suggests that 'good teaching is an act of hospitality toward the young and hospitality is always an act that benefits the host even more than the guest' (p. 50).

Good teachers strive to speak clearly and consistently, as young children, slow learners and children for whom English is an additional language particularly benefit from carefully articulated yet natural speech. They slow the rate of speech when saying something important and talk to children using appropriate language for their age and experience, communicating in such a way that each child feels that the teacher is speaking to him or her individually.

Every teacher must be able to work as a team member, both contributing and receiving, because no teacher, however skilled, can succeed in every facet of the job. Good teachers recognise that decisions that draw on collaborative decision-making have a better chance of being right than those that are taken by an individual.

Sources

Darling-Hammond, L. and Baratz-Snowden, J. (2005) *A Good Teacher in Every Classroom: Preparing the highly qualified teachers our children deserve*, San Francisco CA: Jossey-Bass.

Moore, A. (2001) *Teaching and Learning: Pedagogy, curriculum, and culture*, London: Routledge.

——(2004) *The Good Teacher: Dominant discourses in teaching and teacher education*, London: Routledge.

Nambiar, S. (2008) *Teaching is a Passion*, on-line at www.razz-ma-tazz.net/2008/04/09/teaching-is-a-passion

Palmer, P.J. (1998) *The Courage to Teach: Exploring the inner landscape of a teacher's life*, San Francisco CA: Jossey-Bass.

GOVERNING BODY

See also: governors

Every state school in England, Wales and Northern Ireland has a governing body. Governors in primary schools were formerly known as 'managers'. Each governing body consists of a specified number of governors, depending on the type and size of school. All governors are unpaid for their work, though they may receive payment for expenses. Governors are elected as one of the following:

- Parent governors: parents (normally of children at the school)
- Staff governors: members of the school staff
- LA governors: nominated by the local authority
- Community governors: members of the local community (appointed by the rest of the governing body)
- Foundation and sponsor governors: representatives of any sponsoring bodies.

The proportions of governor types vary according to the type of school. However, the minimum number of governors is set at nine and the maximum is set at twenty – though sponsor governors are additional to these numbers. In community schools, which are usually owned by the local authority, parent governors should be at least one third of the governing body, with two places reserved for school staff governors. Local authority governors should constitute 20 per cent of the governing body; and community governors at least 20 per cent. Governors are appointed for a maximum of four years but can be re-elected for a further term of office.

Parent governors can either be elected by parents of children at the school or if insufficient numbers are elected, appointed by the governing body to fill any remaining vacancies. Such appointees can be parents of former pupils or of any child of school age – parents so appointed can be removed from their positions by a majority vote of the governing body. Staff governors (other than the head teacher) are elected by the school staff and must be paid to work at the school, by the school, which excludes external agency workers (e.g. cleaning staff). At least one staff governor must be a teacher, and if there are three or more staff governors, at least one must be a member of the support staff. If no member of the appropriate category stands for election, an elected person from one of the other governor categories can fill the vacant place. *Associate members* may be appointed by the governing body as members of committees, and may include pupils, school staff or anyone else who the governing body feel could usefully contribute to its work.

The full governing body usually meets once every half-term, where the ongoing business of committees, the governing body and the school are discussed, reported on and where decisions are taken, by a majority vote. The head teacher of each school is *ex officio* a staff governor, but he or she can decline to take up the position. Should the head teacher decide not to become a member of the governing body, the place is left vacant.

The equivalent of the governing body in Scotland is the 'board', introduced in 1988 as part of a policy for encouraging parental involvement in schools. The board is responsible for promoting good relationships and a flow of information between the school, parents and community. It comprises parents, teachers and 'co-opted' members from local business or the community, with parents in the majority. The Scottish School Act 2006 resulted in a further strengthening of the role of parent councils.

GOVERNOR SHORTAGE

See also: community cohesion, governing body, governors

In the UK there is a serious national shortage of governors, especially in areas of social deprivation. A research paper for the Department for Children, Schools and Families (DCSF) found that particular groups under-represented as governors include black and minority groups, disabled people, young people, lone parents, those with low incomes, those who are unemployed, and business people (DCSF 2008). Drawing from case studies of three disadvantaged areas, research by Dean *et al.* (2007) found that the governing bodies lacked the capacity to fulfil their managerial role and did not see it as their main function. The composition of governing bodies was not found to be particularly representative of their local communities and were not linked up with local activist groups or local policy partnerships.

Sources

DCSF (2008) *What Does the Evidence Tell Us about School Governors?* DCSF Research Report, London: HMSO.

Dean, C., Dyson, A., Gallannaugh, F., Howes, A. and Raffo, C. (2007) *School, Governors and Disadvantage*, York: Joseph Rowntree Foundation.

GOVERNORS

See also: core subjects, curriculum, head teacher, health and safety, moral development, parents, special educational needs, tests and testing

In England, Wales and Northern Ireland, school governors are members of a school's governing body and form the largest volunteer force in the country. In state schools they have responsibility for raising school standards through their three key roles of (a) setting strategic direction, (b) ensuring accountability, and (c) monitoring and evaluating school performance. Governors in Scottish schools serve on the school board, which has a particular remit to liaise closely with parents and the local community.

The role of school governors has changed considerably in recent years (Doust and Doust 2001; Adams 2002; Adamson 2007). Until the 1980s, primary governors were referred to as school managers; although in theory they had considerable powers, they exercised relatively little influence in schools. The head teacher determined the majority of school policies, and for the most part, teachers decided what and how they taught the children; during this period of time there was no nationally agreed curriculum or externally imposed imperatives steering teachers towards particular teaching approaches. The Education Acts of the 1980s and 1990s drastically altered the responsibilities and status of governing bodies, all of which must now include representatives from the teaching staff, parents and local community. The full composition of a governing body normally includes the following members:

- Local authority governors
- Teachers elected by their colleagues
- A governor elected by support staff
- Parents elected by other parents at the school
- A governor co-opted by other members of the body
- The head teacher (normally)
- Representatives of churches in schools with a religious foundation.

The majority of people become governors because they have a sincere desire to help the school community, though a small number get elected so as to wield influence on behalf of a particular social or religious cause. Although governors may not have a background in education, they normally have other skills and attributes that allow them to offer a variety of perspective on issues. The line between governing bodies offering adequate support to a teaching staff and becoming intrusive is a fine one, but the trend is towards more, rather than less, governor involvement (Dean 2001; Sallis 2007).

Governors are accountable for the performance of the school to parents and the wider community, and help to plan the school's aims and policies and make appointments, including that of head teacher. They have a legal responsibility to ensure the school provides for all its pupils, including those with special educational needs. Governors also make decisions about the school's budget, monitor the curriculum and determine how the school can encourage pupil's spiritual, moral and social development. When school inspectors visit, their report is initially sent to the governors, who are charged with the task of ensuring that the recommendations are followed and shortcomings addressed.

Governors have the somewhat tiresome responsibility for ensuring that school policies and decisions accord with the large number of centrally imposed edicts which have been issued in recent years, including managing the curriculum, publishing an informative school brochure for parents containing test results and other information about the school, staffing, health and safety, special needs provision, employment contracts, disciplinary procedures, buildings and numerous other aspects of school life. In England and Wales, governors are expected to be involved in establishing and monitoring 'target setting' for the national curriculum tests (SATs) in core subjects (English, mathematics, science), which are supposed to improve year upon year.

Governors have the right to enter the school at any time and examine aspects of its life and work, though convention and common courtesy dictate that this should only be done with the permission of the head teacher and, if teaching is to be observed, with the consent of the teachers concerned. Governors are charged with making important decisions about internal promotion, the head teacher's salary and ensuring that teachers are able to enjoy a reasonable balance between work and home commitments. Governors do not have the right to interfere with curriculum planning and implementation, but if they are kept informed about situations they are better able to argue the case for additional resources. All maintained schools should have a governor with a brief for monitoring the implementation of policies for special educational needs (SEN).

Sources

Adams, J.C. (2002) *Local Delivery of a National Agenda: Citizenship, rights and the changing role of school governors in England and Wales*, Hertfordshire: University of Hertfordshire.

Adamson, S. (2007) *Start Here: What new school governors need to know*, Norwich: Adamson Publishing.

Dean, J. (2001) *The Effective School Governor*, London: Routledge.

Doust, S. and Doust, R. (2001) *Governor's Handbook: A comprehensive guide to the duties and responsibilities of school governors in England and Wales*, London: Advisory Centre for Education.

Sallis, J. (2007) *Basics for School Governors*, London: Continuum International.

GROUP WORK

See also: art, collaboration in learning, drama, friendships, interaction, literacy, mathematics, monitoring, numeracy, school climate, science, self-esteem, thematic learning, topic work

Dividing a class into groups is an important part of organising for learning. Grouping pupils is most often based upon the academic ability of the children for mathematics, science and English; friendship groups for creative activities (notably physical education and art); and a mixture of friendship and ability for collaborative work in other subjects. For instance, a teacher might establish three ability groups for mathematics (high, average, low); half a dozen friendship groups for drama; and a mixture of children for project, thematic or topic work in the humanities. A team of researchers led by Peter Kutnick in England found that effective use of pupil groupings within classrooms for pupils at the top end of the primary school and lower secondary school (up to age 14 years) was often limited by conflicts between pupil group size and composition, assigned learning tasks and interpersonal interactions. The study concluded that there was only limited evidence that pupils or teachers had received training or support to work effectively within their classroom groups (Kutnick *et al.* 2005; see also DfES 2006).

In determining the pattern of group work, the demands made of teachers grow in proportion to the number and complexity of groups operating, so handling several groups engaged in similar tasks is easier to cope with than groups working on different topics. In addition, dividing the class into groups has to be considered alongside the challenging process of monitoring, recording of children's progress and bringing the session to a satisfactory conclusion.

Group work does not exist in a vacuum; teachers need to provide relevant knowledge and information before children can purposefully engage with tasks and open-ended problem-solving activities. Thus, an explanation about a computer program system precedes pupils exploring its full potential; similarly, creativity in drama is based on the original example provided by the teacher. Teachers also have to provide the necessary structure and support within which the children can subsequently explore ideas and investigate processes, a function sometimes referred to as 'scaffolding'. Children find out things for themselves and learn more thoroughly if they are given appropriate knowledge, guidance and resources as a foundation on which to build their ideas and innovate. Adults create the secure learning environment and resources; the children explore within the 'space' that has thereby been created.

A key consideration is whether group work is intended to enhance collaboration or used as an organisational tool. That is, whether children sit together in groups to achieve a common learning objective (collaboration) or whether they sit together to make it easier for the teacher to manage proceedings and to share resources. Experience shows that although children sit together they do not necessarily work together, for three reasons: (a) they have a deep-rooted concern that the interaction is a form of cheating, (b) they lack the necessary skills to relate to others in a group, and (c) they prefer to work separately and resent being obliged to take account of other views and preferences.

As children work together they experience a range of emotions and challenges which have as much to do with learning to get along with one another as with solving problems or exploring ideas. Baines *et al.* (2008) emphasise the importance of creating an inclusive and supportive classroom by developing the social, communicative and group working skills of all pupils. Biott and Easen (1994) comment that mixed groups offer opportunities for children to learn social competences in situations where they feel they can act upon shared understandings of how to be both cooperative and assertive. While there is always a danger of friends spending too much time talking about 'off-task' business when they should be concentrating on the work in hand, this risk has to be weighed against the advantages to be gained by mutual support in the pursuit of common aims (Street 2004).

Even with the support of an assistant, control issues can soon emerge if the children are unclear about the work. Consequently, in designing tasks for groups, a number of important considerations have to be taken into account, especially with enquiry-based tasks (both practical and paper-based):

- ensuring that the children understand what is required of them;
- providing the resources and clarifying the extent to which children can be autonomous in their use;
- making decisions about who handles the resources: who takes responsibility for recording results, who reports back and how each child is to be involved;
- matching task to ability and ensure that the activity lasts sufficiently long to allow children to become fully involved but not so long that they suffer from discouragement or task fatigue;
- keeping noise levels suitably restrained;
- regulating pupils' movement around the room.

Hallam *et al.* (2004) conducted a major study into primary school pupils' perceptions of the purposes and practices of ability grouping; their experiences of these practices, and how their attitudes, behaviour, self-esteem, social interaction and feelings towards school were affected. Results showed that pupils were aware of the purposes of ability grouping and most of them were in favour if its use. Children saw the main advantage of ability grouping as having their work set at an appropriate level for them; they saw the main disadvantage as being the stigmatisation of pupils in the lower level groups. Over 40 per cent of pupils reported being teased or having witnessed teasing connected with levels of ability in the classroom. The study's findings suggested that whether or not they were grouped by ability was of less importance to pupils than being in a supportive school ethos.

Sources

Baines, E., Blatchford, P. and Kutnick, P. (2008) *Promoting Effective Group Work in the Classroom*, London: David Fulton.

Biott, C. and Easen, P. (1994) *Collaborative Learning in Staffrooms and Classrooms*, London: David Fulton.

DfES (2006) 'Pupil grouping strategies and practices at key stage 2 and 3', Brief no. RB796, Annesley: DfES Publications.

Hallam, S., Ireson, J. and Davies, J. (2004) 'Grouping practices in the primary school: What influences change?' *British Educational Research Journal*, 30 (1), 117–40.

Kutnick, P., Sebba, J., Blatchford, P., Galton, M. and Thorp, J. (2005) *The Effects of Pupil Grouping: Literature review*, Nottingham: DfES Publications.

Street, J. (2004) *Welcome to Friendship*, Bristol: Sage/Lucky Duck.

HADOW REPORTS

See also: collaboration in learning, curriculum, curriculum history, discovery learning, elementary education, eleven-plus, inclusion, infants, juniors, learning, nursery schools, pedagogy, planning, school library

There are six 'Hadow reports', the best known of which is probably the 1931 report, simply titled *The Primary School*. The other five reports are as follows:

1923   *Differentiation of the Curriculum for Boys and Girls*
1924   *Psychological Tests of Educable Capacity*
1926   *The Education of the Adolescent*
1928   *Books in Public Elementary Schools*
1933   *Infant and Nursery Schools*

The content and recommendations included in these reports has a remarkably contemporary ring, dealing with issues as diverse as providing a relevant curriculum, teaching style, special needs, books and reading, organising for learning, assessment and testing, reporting to parents and the importance of early years provision. The 1926 report was the first official publication to recommend the use of the terms 'primary' and 'secondary', such that primary education should end at the age of eleven and that all 'normal children' should go forward to some form of secondary education. The report stresses the importance of planning the curriculum as a whole and of ensuring that the various subjects are taught in relation to one another.

The 1928 report examines the function of books in schools and assesses the volume, quality and character of the current supply in relation to the various curriculum areas. The report also notes the range of different libraries provided by local authorities and assesses the sources of guidance available for teachers in the choice of books, urging that every school should have a library. The report antedates by some eighty years present-day educational priorities in literacy.

The influential 1931 *Primary School* report focuses on the history of the development of the conception of primary education above the infant stage (post-7 years) and describes the physical and mental development of children between the ages of seven and eleven, which, it concludes, should be the age range (in later years known as the 'junior' phase and, more recently in England and Wales, the soulless tag, key stage 2) for the upper stage of primary education. Although the 1931 report's authors argue for separate infant schools wherever possible, they urge close cooperation between infant and junior schools, stressing that the needs of the specially bright and of retarded children (now referred to as 'slow learners') should be met by appropriate arrangements. The authors suggest that a good school is not a place of compulsory instruction, but a community of old and young, engaged in learning by cooperative experiment and go on to argue, famously, that the curriculum of the primary school is to be thought of in terms of activity and experience rather than knowledge to be acquired and facts to be stored (Gillard, on-line). The emphasis on activity and experience is later echoed in the Plowden Report of 1967. The 1931 Hadow Report favours a 'project' approach to encourage children to solve problems and make discoveries for themselves ('discovery learning'), as opposed to separating primary instruction into subjects, predating the recommendations of the Rose Report (2009). Intriguingly, in the light of continuing debate about the value of testing, the 1931 report suggests that seven-year-old children should be assessed on entry to junior schools but warns that classification should be regarded as provisional and should be subject to frequent revision. In a further parallel with recent developments in education, the authors recommended that continuous records should be kept of each child's progress and parents sent reports of children's progress each term or year.

The last of the six reports, the 1933 Hadow Report, begins with a history of infant education and reviews current knowledge about the physical and mental development of children up to the age of seven. The authors stress that the primary stage of education should be regarded as a continuous whole, a theme that finds an echo in 'continuity of learning' threaded throughout contemporary curriculum guidance. The report also recommends the appropriate use of look and say, phonic, and sentence methods, arguing that each of these methods emphasised important elements in learning to read, and that most teachers borrow something from each of them to meet the need of the moment or the special difficulties of different children. The authors emphasise the importance of detecting early signs of 'retardation' but disapprove of children so identified being taught in separate schools at this early age – another forerunner of modern inclusive practice. The report also urges the provision of an open-air environment to afford children scope for experiment and exploration. Children should be put in the position to teach themselves, gaining knowledge from 'an instructive environment' rather than formal instruction. The authors also urge the provision of nursery education, with relevant training for teachers and the provision of 'helpers'. Forty years later the 1967 Plowden Report pointed out that the under-fives were the only age group for whom no extra educational provision of any kind had been made since 1944 and that nursery education on a large scale remained an unfulfilled promise, a situation largely remedied during the start of the twenty-first century (Kogan 1987).

Many of the committee's recommendations about restructuring the primary curriculum in terms of projects, focusing on children's interests, the use of discovery methods and the importance of collaborative work, would be implemented later in the twentieth century. However, Galton et al. (1980) assert that most schools in the years following the Hadow Report bore all the hallmarks of the elementary system in terms of cheapness, economy, large classes, obsolete, ancient and inadequate buildings, and mind-numbing drill methods – encouraged by the introduction of the eleven-plus examination for selection to secondary school. Today, the report's insistence that the teacher must have freedom in planning and arranging work so as to avoid the danger of a lapse into mechanical routine, has been rejected in favour of an imposed, highly regulated curriculum and closely directed teaching approach ('pedagogy').

Sources

Galton, M., Simon, B. and Croll, P. (1980) *Inside the Primary Classroom* (The ORACLE Report) London: Routledge and Kegan Paul.

Gillard, D. 'The Hadow reports: An introduction', *The Encyclopaedia of Informal Education*, on-line at www.infed.org/schooling/hadow_reports.htm

Kogan, M. (1987) 'The Plowden Report twenty years on', *Oxford Review of Education*, 13 (1), 13–22.

Plowden, B.H. (1967) *Children and their Primary Schools: A report of the Central Advisory Council for*

Education (England) ('The Plowden Report') London: HMSO.

Rose, J. for the DCSF (2009) *Primary Curriculum Review*, London: HMSO.

HANDWRITING

See also: alphabet, basic skills, desks, foundation stage, information technology, left-handedness, literacy, self-esteem, spelling, writing

Handwriting is a basic skill, which affects written communication across the curriculum much like reading and spelling (Tibertius, online). Given effective teaching, handwriting can be mastered by most pupils by the time they are seven or eight years old, enabling them, with practice, to go on to develop a faster and more mature hand ready for secondary school and adult life. Barnett *et al.* (2006) note that handwriting has been the 'Cinderella skill' of literacy for many years, yet unless children are taught to write legibly and at speed their educational achievements may be considerably reduced and their self-esteem affected. The authors argue that an ability to handwrite legibly is not an optional extra but rather an essential skill for every child, even in this age of information technology.

Medwell *et al.* (2007) tested the handwriting speed and ability of almost 200 pupils in three schools. The authors concluded that children who struggle to write fluently devote more brain capacity to getting words onto a page, which often interferes with their ability to generate ideas, select vocabulary or plan what to write. Pupils with average or poor handwriting have only a 40 per cent chance of reaching national standards in tests at the age of 11 years; boys, in particular, are likely to be affected, which may explain why they lag so far behind girls of the same age. Medwell *et al.* insist that handwriting is not just about training the hand but also about training the memory and hand to work together to generate and correct mental images and patterns of letters, and in time to translate these into motor patterns of letters – automatically and without effort.

Learning to handwrite does not follow a prescribed route, though many reception teachers teach letters of the alphabet in formation groups for handwriting; for example, initially teaching *c a d g o s*, as all these letters go back and round, followed by *r n m*, as these letters go down, up and over. Other schools use a teaching pattern similar to the following sequence:

```
c a d g o q
r n m h b k p
i l t u y j
v w x
s f z e
```

To avoid handwriting practice becoming tedious, most teachers have a policy of 'little and often', rather than having fewer prolonged sessions; they may also utilise stories and story characters to represent letter shapes. Whatever approach is adopted, children need to be relaxed yet able to concentrate and (for right-handers) encouraged to hold a pencil between the thumb and forefinger with the pencil resting on the third finger. Whole school policies emphasis a multi-sensory approach in developing handwriting skills for the Foundation Stage (children aged 4–5 years) based on Foundation Stage curriculum guidance:

1 Drawing lines and circles using gross motor movement (e.g. chalk pictures on large paper).
2 Beginning to use anticlockwise movement and retrace vertical lines (e.g. rotational arm movements in physical education sessions).
3 Developing activities that require close hand/eye coordination (e.g. throwing and catching a soft ball).
4 Using tools and equipment that can be controlled with one hand (e.g. rolling a die; picking up small objects with tweezers).
5 Manipulating objects with an increasing level of control (e.g. threading beads).

6 Using correct movements to form recognisable letters (e.g. writing in wet sand).

7 Using a pencil and holding it effectively to form recognisable letters.

As children progress through school (ages 5–7 years) they are encouraged to develop a confident and efficient pencil grip and form lower case letters correctly in a way that will facilitate joining up letters later. Handwriting can be practised in conjunction with spelling and independent writing, with special attention given to ensuring correct letter orientation, formation and proportion. When the teacher judges it suitable, children begin to use and practise the four handwriting 'joins', namely:

1 diagonal joins to letters without ascenders e.g. ai ar un;
2 horizontal joins to letters without ascenders e.g. ou vi wi;
3 diagonal joins to letters with ascenders e.g. ab ul it;
4 horizontal joins to letters with ascenders e.g. ol wh ot.

(See *Developing Early Writing*, DfEE 2001.)

School policies promote the view that handwriting is integral to all activities in the curriculum and children need to be supervised as closely as possible when they are practising, until letter formation is secure, as bad habits are difficult to eradicate later on. Children have to be given time every day to practise concentrating on accuracy, fluency and speed without the distraction of spelling and composing text.

Jarman (2002) claims that there are twelve rules that apply to all linked/joined/cursive handwriting schemes in Western Europe:

1 Good writing is based on a pattern of ovals and parallel lines (e.g. *oioioi*).
2 All small letters start at the top (thus, *abmcs*).
3 All the downstrokes are parallel (thus, *mhnadft*).
4 All similar letters are the same height (thus, *ronceu* and *lhbkd*).

5 All downstrokes are equidistant (e.g. *minimum*).
6 The space between words is the width of the small letter 'o'.
7 Ascenders and descenders are no more than twice the height of small letters, preferably less (e.g. *hglpd*).
8 Capital letters are no higher than the ascenders, preferably less (e.g. *Ch Br Ph*).
9 Lines of writing are far enough apart for ascenders and descenders not to touch.
10 Letters which finish at the top join horizontally (e.g. orvwtf).
11 Letters which finish at the bottom join diagonally (e.g. acdehl).
12 Letters which finish on a stroke moving left, are best left unjoined (thus, bgjpsy).

Left-handed children need special consideration when being taught handwriting. Jean Alston writes for the Left-Handed Club (www.anythingleft-handed.co.uk) and suggests that the three most common problems for left-handed children are:

1 The hand is 'hooked' around the pen and runs above the writing line in an attempt to angle the pen in the same way as a right-hander would, causing the arm and body to be contorted into an awkward position and making handwriting very uncomfortable and slow.
2 Smudged work is caused by the hand pushing the pen across the page.
3 An over-tight grip, which leads to cramped, badly formed letters and an erratic writing style, which is also very tiring for the child.

Alston recommends the following ten guidelines to combat these problems for left-handers (see web site for full details):

● The child should hold the pencil at least 2 cm away from the tip so as not to obscure the writing.
● Younger children should work with a soft pencil that does not stick or tear the paper. Older children should find one that flows smoothly across the page.
● The paper should be placed to the left of the body mid-line and the top tilted

clockwise up to a maximum of 45 degrees to bring the hand into the correct writing position underneath the writing line.

- A coloured star at the left margin helps to remind younger children where to start.
- Children should be seated on the left side of a double desk or next to another left-hander to avoid elbows clashing.
- Children should be able to see the board without twisting round if copying is needed.
- The desk and chair must be at a suitable height for the child.
- Allowance should be made for clumsiness, smudging and untidiness; achievements should receive lots of praise.
- Pencil grips moulded to fit the shape of thumb and finger help children to develop the correct grip.
- Children should be encouraged to write lightly.

Sassoon (2003) covers all aspects of the subject, from whole school planning to classroom management and the teaching of letters in an illustrated and practical sequence; and from initial letterforms through to cursive writing.

Sources

Barnett, A., Stainthorp, R., Henderson, S. and Scheib, B. (2006) *Handwriting Policy and Practice in English Primary Schools*, London: Institute of Education.

DfEE (2001) *Developing Early Writing*, London: HMSO.

Jarman, C. (2002) *Twelve Rules for Good Cursive Handwriting*, on-line at http://quilljar.users.btopenworld.com/rules.html

The Left-Handed Club, www.anythingleft-handed.co.uk

Medwell, J., Strand, S. and Wray, D. (2007) 'The role of handwriting in composing for Year 2 children', *Journal of Reading, Writing and Literacy*, 2 (1), 18–36.

Sassoon, R. (2003) *Handwriting: The way to teach it*, London: Paul Chapman.

Tibertius, S. (on-line) *Developing a Handwriting Policy for the Primary School*, Canterbury: National Handwriting Association, on-line at www.nha-handwriting.org.uk

HAPPINESS

See also: child welfare, children, friendships, interaction, relationships, self-esteem, success, teaching profession

Happiness in life is everybody's ultimate goal and it is hard to imagine any parent or teacher who would not want their children to find it throughout life. Many teachers speak of the joy that they experience seeing pupils enjoying school, making friends and going home with a spring in their step each evening. Seldon (2008) suggests that it is possible for a school to 'teach happiness' by developing the following priorities (amended):

- School should be a place children love to be: they should feel deeply loyal to their school, their fellow pupils and its teachers.
- School should develop all aspects of children's personalities and aptitudes, not just their intellect; they should learn who they are and what they want to do with their lives, both at work and at play.
- They should know how to look after themselves, taking responsibility for their bodies, their emotions and their minds.
- Parents should be fully involved in the whole experience of learning, as should the wider community.
- The teachers at the school should be valued and respected, with the pupils treating them with civility and gratitude, recognising that this is a profession that they should take seriously.

Ivens (2007) has created what he claims to be a psychometrically valid and reliable measure for schoolchildren aged 8–15, piloted and developed against existing measures of self-esteem, affect and depression, which he calls the 'School Children's Happiness Inventory' (SCHI). Ivens argues that the SCHI can be especially useful in assessing the effect of school-based interventions and influences on schoolchildren's well-being.

A three-year study by the Children's Society (2007), *Good Childhood Inquiry: Happiness*, concluded that an aggressive pursuit of personal success by adults is now the greatest threat to the well-being and happiness of children. The research team argued that a preoccupation with self was taking a lot of joy out of children's lives, out of their family lives, out of their school and even out of their leisure life and consumption. It was essential that the next generation of children recognised the importance of contributing to the welfare of others rather than themselves and putting human relationships higher than the accumulation of possessions and acquiring societal status. Noddings (2004) argues that the narrow curriculum found in most classrooms helps shape a culture with misguided priorities, whereas happiness and education not only can but should coexist must be taken seriously by everyone concerned about preparing children and young adults for a truly satisfying life in our democratic society.

MacConville (2008) piloted what she termed 'the happiness curriculum' in West London schools during the autumn of 2007 with classes of 10–13 year-old pupils to help them to negotiate the transition from primary to secondary school. The programme was designed to build resilience, increase optimism, promote adaptive coping skills and teach children effective problem-solving skills. Children were given strategies to demur from negative and unhelpful thinking and experience positive emotions. In all the activities, there was an emphasis on developing thinking and participatory skills. Among other things, children were encouraged to 'stop the gossip in your head' by focusing on the present situation and not being deflected from learning by concerns about the past or future; to be thankful; to have specific and attainable goals of personal significance (i.e. not school 'targets'); to think good, feel good; to accept setbacks; and to take control of their lives to make themselves and school a happier place.

Sources

Children's Society (2007) *Good Childhood Inquiry: Happiness*, London: Church of England Children's Society.

Ivens, J. (2007) 'The development of a happiness measure for schoolchildren', *Educational Psychology in Practice*, 23 (3), 221–39.

MacConville, R. (2008) *Teaching Happiness: A ten-step curriculum for creating positive classrooms*, Milton Keynes: Speechmark Publishing.

Noddings, N. (2004) *Happiness and Education*, Cambridge: Cambridge University Press.

Seldon, A. (2008) 'Teaching happiness', *Ethos*, on-line at www.ethosjournal.com/this_issue/happiness.asp

HEAD TEACHER

See also: assessment of learning, community cohesion, curriculum, faith schools, governors, lessons, parents, professional development, school life

Every report about schools stresses the importance of the head teacher – known as 'the principal' or even 'senior executive' in some schools. The head teacher is responsible for the day-to-day running of the school ('school life') and governors act as an executive. The head teacher has immediate responsibility for achieving agreed aims, safeguarding curriculum entitlement for pupils, maintaining links with the community, involving parents closely in school life, informing parents about their children's progress and establishing appropriate forms of pupil assessment. All these responsibilities are in addition to oversight for staff welfare, training, professional development and appraisal, with a view to making decisions about internal promotions.

With such wide-ranging responsibilities and constant government attention it is unsurprising that recruitment of head teachers in many parts of the UK is problematic. The annual survey of vacancies for 2008 carried out by Professor John Howson of Education Data Services covering England and Wales found that one in three primary schools and one in four secondary schools had to re-advertise head teachers' posts after failing to attract suitable candidates. Analysis of advertisements suggested that primary and faith schools had the biggest problems, but the situation in Wales was less severe, with only 16 per cent of schools needing to re-advertise. From April 2009 in England all first-time head teachers were required to gain the National Professional Qualification for Headship (NPQH). The NPQH is for those who aspire to headship and are no more than 12–18 months from applying for headship posts; it is not for those seeking professional development. The *Head Teachers' Qualifications and Registration (Wales) Regulations 2005* prohibit an individual from serving as a head teacher unless he or she holds the NPQH or a comparable qualification. However, the regulations do not prevent an individual who does not hold the NPQH or equivalent from applying for a headship appointment or being appointed as a head teacher, although the person appointed cannot begin to serve as a head teacher until gaining NPQH or equivalent.

Head teachers work long hours and this exacts a high cost, which is now reflected in enhanced salaries. A large proportion of the head teacher's day is spent dealing with administrative tasks, meeting people and attending meetings. Unless the school is very small, it is unlikely that the head teacher will have a substantial teaching commitment. It is a requirement of the national agreement that all head teachers and teachers enjoy a reasonable work–life balance, enabling them to combine paid employment with their commitments and interests outside work (see Worklife Research Centre, on-line). However, it is generally accepted that, if anything, the workload is increasing, and so unless some adjustments are made to alleviate the problem, the shortage of people wishing to become head teachers seems unlikely to change in the immediate future. In addition, Rutherford (2005) argues that on the basis of interviews with long-serving heads, the role of primary head teacher has changed from one of a sense

of excitement and anticipation to one of increasing disillusionment and frustration.

In their research for the Policy Exchange (2007) the authors argue that head teachers do make a difference but that their influence is almost always indirect, as the vast majority can directly teach only a tiny fraction of the lessons in a school. Their influence is therefore exercised through choice of staff, organisational structure, policies for monitoring of learning, training programmes, the power of persuasion, and by modelling high professional standards for others to emulate (Smith 2002). Head teachers have a vital role in working with governors, parents and inspectors. This 'outward facing' role is an important function and can make a difference between a school being a failed school or not, partly because of the perceptions that are created. The Policy Exchange study concludes that the most important thing in the school is the relationship between the teacher and the pupil. Probably the most important thing that head teachers can do for their pupils is to make sure that there are good teachers in their classrooms.

Sources

Policy Exchange (2007) *The Leadership Effect: Can head teachers make a difference?* London: Policy Exchange Limited /Esmée Fairburn Foundation.

Rutherford, D. (2005) 'Head teachers' reflections on primary headship from 1988–2003', *Journal of Educational Administration*, 43 (3), 278–94.

Smith, R. (2002) *The Primary Headteacher's Handbook*, London: Routledge.

Worklife Research Centre, Middlesex University/ Institute of Education, University of London, on-line at www.workliferesearch.org/wl_site/hp_main.htm

HEALTH AND SAFETY

See also: emotional intelligence, lesson management, lesson organisation, lesson plans, outdoor education, visual aids

Children's safety is a priority for every adult working in school and in recent years there has been a considerable amount of attention given to ensuring that pupils are protected from hazards and avoidable injury, either through carelessness, neglect or ignorance. Sensible health and safety precautions are not intended to limit pupil learning or their participation in practical activities but to liberate the children to work confidently and assuredly. However, the increase in litigation and highly publicised cases of teachers and local education authorities being taken to court by parents over health and safety issues has heightened awareness of the need for increased care. It has also created a climate of extreme caution about pupils undertaking any activity that carries a risk, though the formal accreditation of outdoor centres as 'safe' is diminishing the level of concern.

Most lesson plans used by teachers include a 'risk assessment' category, where potential dangers to pupils have been identified beforehand. These issues are particularly relevant for vulnerable pupils, including the very young, those with disabilities and children with allergies. For very young children, basic cleanliness training may be the priority; for older ones, correct use of tools and equipment may be most important. There are also some common issues such as ensuring that each child is clear about what has to be done and the time constraints involved, has sufficient space to do the task or activity and is aware of others in the vicinity who may be affected by their actions, such as being sprayed by paint. It is also necessary to ensure that there is a minimum of hazards on the floor (such as spilled paste) that might be perilous.

There are at least ten health and safety rules to which teachers are constantly referring. First, people must be able to walk around the room unhindered by obstacles such as poorly positioned furniture or articles lying on the floor. Second, pupils carrying out activities that require large areas must be given the appropriate space in which to work and not be expected to squeeze into a confined spot. Third, equipment and resources have to be stored so that they can be reached without having to stretch or pull items down from the shelf. Fourth, wet activities have to be restricted to a designated area away from main walkways and sink areas kept free from furniture. Fifth, pupils must be taught how and when to wash their hands thoroughly before meals, after messy activities and after contact with soil, flora or fauna. Sixth, teachers need to ensure that pupils' view of the board and other visual aids is unhindered and does not require children to twist unnaturally or squint. Seventh, seating has to be organised in such a way that pupils do not sit next to a draughty window, hot radiator or a tall piece of furniture with free standing objects resting on top. Eighth, pupils must only use specialist equipment with adult supervision and after appropriate training. Ninth, pupils must be regularly reminded not to suck or put small objects in their mouths. Finally, class rules need to stress that pupils must not run in the classroom. If children are involved in any process requiring heat or blades they have to be properly trained and organised to use the equipment. Some practical lessons requiring the use of tools necessitate close adult supervision, which is where the extra pair of hands is invaluable.

Although accidents are rare in primary classrooms, teachers have to know the correct procedures for dealing with casualties. A course of first aid training, regularly updated, gives the confidence they need to act promptly in the case of an emergency, though teachers and assistants are not normally permitted to give medicines in school or carry out procedures which require specialist expertise. Should there be an accident, the responsible adult has to record it in the 'accident book' that is often kept in a school's main office or first-aid room. In situations where a number of different activities are taking place in the room simultaneously, teachers have to ensure that appropriate supervision is available.

Healthy eating, personal hygiene and awareness of the dangers from drugs form an important element of primary pupils' education (McWhirter 2000; Wetton 2003). All children require nutritious food, regular exercise and appropriate amounts of rest and sleep to function efficiently during the day and make the best use of the learning opportunities provided in and out of school. Schools encourage children to eat fruit rather than snacks and pay close attention to the nutritional value of school meals.

School safety programmes tend to reflect adult concerns about children's safety, such as accident prevention, ensuring that pupils are taught about hazards from traffic and roads, trains and railway lines, electricity, fire and heat, machinery, sharp objects, medicines, poisons and so forth. Fears about possible injury to children have also led to the banning of sports day activities once considered perfectly safe, such as the traditional sack race and the three-legged race. Danger from strangers is also commonly emphasised in primary school safety programmes. Children, however, may harbour more concerns about burglars and violence and younger children may be worried by imaginary dangers, especially those that result from exposure to unsuitable television programmes.

Health and safety does not only concern physical well-being, as every adult also has a responsibility to be alert to children's *emotional* condition. Education involves helping children to understand their place in the world, the contribution that they can make to society and their responsibilities to one another. Taking time to listen to children, to understand their needs, hopes and desires is one of the privileges of involvement in primary education (see, for example, Corrie 2003). O'Quinn and Garrison (2004) insist that 'empathy, compassion, commitment, patience, spontaneity and an ability to listen are all closely connected to the trust necessary for creating the conditions for loving relations in the classroom community' (p. 63).

Sources

Corrie, C. (2003) *Becoming Emotionally Intelligent*, Stafford: Network Educational Press.

McWhirter J.M. (2000) 'Evaluating Safe in the Sun: A curriculum programme for primary schools', *Health Education Research*, 15 (2), 203–17.

O'Quinn, E. and Garrison, J. (2004) 'Creating loving relations in the classroom', in Liston, D. and Garrison, J. (eds) *Teaching, Learning and Loving*, London: Routledge.

Wetton, N. (2003) 'Growing up safely in a changing world', *Wired for Health*, NHS Health Development Agency, London: HMSO.

HEALTH AND SAFETY (ADULTS)

See also: displays, health and safety (computers), interactive whiteboard

Adults in school need to make sure they are taking care of their own bodies and general welfare. Work with children is tiring and, with younger children in particular, involves a fair degree of physical movement, including stretching, bending and twisting. Even a simple manoeuvre such as turning back and forth to write on the board then face the class can lead to muscle strain. The use of electronic devices, such as an overhead projector or a computer controlling the interactive whiteboard, can reduce the incidence of back turning, while being aware that the presence of electrical equipment can also be potentially hazardous. A simple exercise to improve neck muscles and head movement is to stand still with feet apart, looking directly forward before gently turning the head over a count of three to the left, holding for a further count of three, before returning slowly to the starting position; then repeating the process by turning the head to the right. Eye strain can be minimised by taking regular breaks from the computer, gentle massaging of each eye and focusing on a far away object from time to time. Only designated persons are allowed to use a ladder in the classroom in order to (say) erect a display or poster.

HEALTH AND SAFETY (COMPUTERS)

See also: computers in school, health and safety (adults)

The use of computer equipment raises specific issues with regard to electrical safety by ensuring that children are properly supervised, liquids are not permitted in the area of the machines and attention is given to the potential hazards from trailing leads and flexes. Teachers are also careful that pupils do not spend an excessive amount of time in front of a computer screen and that chairs are correctly positioned and suitable for the purpose. The danger of repetitive strain injury caused through excessive keyboard work is not normally a serious problem for pupils in school, though it may be a problem in the home if adult supervision is slack. Adults, too, have to be cautious that when they spend time entering data into a computer or (especially) writing reports, they abide by the same safety considerations that they enforce with pupils in the classroom and computer suite. Electrical (mains) equipment of any sort must not be used unless it has been checked by a qualified electrician and labelled safe for use.

HEALTH AND SAFETY (PHYSICAL ACTIVITY)

See also: curriculum, physical education, playground

Of all the subject areas in the primary school curriculum, it is almost certain that the greatest potential source of injury is during physical activities such as gymnastics, dance and games. Normally, all children change into shorts and t-shirts, and have bare feet for indoor activities. If shoes are worn, the grip of the sole rather than the fashionable appearance is the key consideration. The wearing of jewellery is rarely permitted – though occasional exceptions are made on religious grounds – and long hair has to be tied back. Typically, injuries can occur as a result of the following:

- over-exuberant 'warm-up' activities that involve children charging around and the potential for nasty collisions;

- muscle strain caused by unusual body movements attempted before suitable 'warm-up' activities;
- failure to 'warm down' after high-level exertion;
- unstable or damaged equipment;
- hard equipment, especially wooden or solid plastic bats that may hit a child in the face;
- equipment that allows children to climb beyond the limits of their capability;
- long breaks between bouts of physical exertion that result in the body chilling;
- allowing the noise level to rise too high such that the children cannot hear commands.

Adult responsible for supervising children in the playground (US, 'yard') have to strike a balance between allowing children opportunity to run, jump and 'let off steam', while ensuring that collisions, trips and falls are kept to a minimum. It is a demanding task for even the most diligent adult.

HEALTH AND SAFETY (SCIENCE)

See also: science

Most children enjoy the practical aspects of science but can, in their enthusiasm, neglect basic safety considerations. Common examples of potential danger points include:

- hazards of cuts from split plastic and ragged edges;
- water spilled on the floor;
- the need to wash hands thoroughly after contact with soil and outdoor activity;
- cord or wire being wrapped tightly around a wrist or tangled around the neck;
- the effect of bright light on eyes and high-volume sound on eardrums.

HEALTHY EATING

See also: citizenship, early years, personal social and health education, social and emotional aspects of learning

It is estimated that 1 in 10 six-year-olds and 1 in 6 fifteen-year-olds are now obese; that is, weighing more than 20 per cent for males or 25 per cent for females over their ideal weight as determined by height and build. According to the UK government's national diet and nutrition two-part survey in 2000, children were consuming almost double the recommended amount of sugar, saturated fat and salt. The study found that while 92 per cent of children and young people were eating more than adult maximum levels of saturated fat, they were consuming less than half the recommended five portions of fruit and vegetables each day (Office for National Statistics 2000). These findings can be replicated across the Western world and the situation is even more extreme in the USA. National guidance suggests that snacks (e.g. crisps), confectionery such as chocolate bars and chocolate-coated biscuits and meat products such as sausage rolls, pies and sausages are unhelpful if consumed regularly. A study by Alderton and Campell-Barr in 2005 suggested that many early years teachers (for children aged 3–5 years) lacked satisfactory knowledge about food and nutrition issues, leading to less than effective practice. The manual by Brunton and Thornton (2009) offer advice to Foundation Stage practitioners about exercise, healthy eating, staying safe and emotional well-being.

Schools try to contribute to a cohesive approach throughout the school community for the promotion and provision of healthy eating by ensuring that lunches and other food provided in (say) a tuck shop or during an after-school club meet nutrient-based and food-based standards. In many cases, the leader for PSHE (personal, social and health education) or a senior member of staff coordinates the healthy eating programme. Normally, pupils have regular access to fresh drinking water and are encouraged to take fluid after physical activity or during hot weather. Many schools take part in a 'fruit and vegetable' scheme, whereby younger primary aged children receive a free piece of

fruit each day. If children bring a packed lunch, parents are encouraged to ensure that the contents are suitable; some schools do not permit fizzy drinks, chocolate and sweets, and teachers and assistants are discouraged from using them as incentives. A number of schools integrate or link healthy eating education with areas of the curriculum such as citizenship and SEAL (social and emotional aspects of education), drugs education and safety awareness.

Sources

Alderton, T. and Campbell-Barr, V. (2005) 'Quality early education: Quality food and nutrition practices', *International Journal of Early Years Education*, 13 (3), 197–213.

Brunton, P. and Thornton, L. (2009) *Healthy Living in the Early Years Foundation Stage*, London: Optimus Education.

Office for National Statistics (2000) *National Diet and Nutrition Survey (Parts 1 and 2)*, London: HMSO.

HEALTHY SCHOOLS

See also: bullying, Every Child Matters, personal social and health education, physical education, sex education

The 'Healthy Schools' approach is based on evidence that healthier children perform better academically, and that education plays an important role in promoting good health, especially among those who are socially and economically disadvantaged. 'National Healthy School' status is a UK government initiative through the Department for Children, Schools and Families (DCSF) that requires schools to meet criteria in four core themes relating not only to the taught curriculum but also to the emotional, physical and learning environment that the school provides. The themes are as follows:

1 personal, social and health education (PSHE), including sex and relationship education and drug education;
2 healthy eating;

3 physical activity;
4 emotional health and well-being (including bullying).

'Healthy Schools' is part of the government's drive to reduce health inequalities, promote social inclusion and raise educational standards; schools are asked to demonstrate evidence in the core themes using a whole-school approach involving the school community. School inspections will require that healthy schools are making significant contributions to the first two of the national Every Child Matters outcomes for children (DfES 2005), namely: being healthy and staying safe – and also contribute to aspects of the other three outcomes: enjoying and achieving; making a positive contribution; and economic well-being.

Sources

DfES (2005) *Every Child Matters: Change for children*, London: HMSO.

HEARING IMPAIRMENT

See also: body language, class management, inclusion, medication, parental involvement, physical comfort, social development, speech

Although most children's learning is enhanced through auditory means (i.e. speaking and listening) there is always a small proportion of them who struggle due to a hearing impairment that can sometimes go undetected for a long time. A temporary reduction in hearing capacity may result from a cold or virus or 'glue ear'; other children suffer from a chronic (long-term) physical condition that necessitates the use of a hearing aid. Adults working with pupils who have a hearing impairment may be tempted to think of the child first and foremost in terms of 'the deaf child' rather than 'the child who is deaf'. In fact, the terms 'hard of hearing', 'deaf' and 'hearing-impaired' cover a wide range of conditions that often affect a child's listening ability and educational and social development.

Many parents of seriously hearing-impaired children prefer that their children attend the local school rather than go to a school for deaf pupils, not least because they do not want their children to be thought of as 'different' and partly because the children in the mainstream school will live locally, allowing for the growth of natural friendships that can be continued outside school (see Hear-it, online). Beattie (2001) notes that a variety of educational options exist for many children with hearing losses, with options ranging from residential schools to full integration; furthermore, the language and method of instruction is also variable within these educational settings, spanning from auditory/verbal to bilingual and bicultural. Some schools have a special unit for the deaf and hearing-impaired on the same site.

The successful inclusion of deaf or hearing-impaired children in mainstream schools requires close co-operation between the family, audiologists and the school staff in making difficult decisions about appropriate educational and social provision (Marschank 2007). Teachers that work in mainstream schools usually have limited experience with hearing-impaired children, which is why co-operating with specialists is needed to provide the school staff with information and advice. Whatever the particular circumstances, the hearing-impaired child must not feel isolated from the other children because of adverse psychological and social consequences. Consequently, classrooms have to be organised to determine the best possible conditions for audibility. In some instances, an FM system or loop wire system can be installed to amplify the teacher's voice. Children with very poor hearing benefit from being able to look directly at the teacher, a point that is especially significant if the child is learning to lip-read.

Classrooms are not always helpful places for children with sensitive ears, as the noise generated can be a serious problem and adversely affect their concentration level. For instance, children can be confused and unsettled by several children speaking at the same time, the scratching of chairs on the floor and the fidgeting of their classmates. If normal hearing children strain to pick up the voice of the teacher because of background noise, a hearing impaired child finds it virtually impossible. Suggested strategies to reduce noise and improve classroom acoustics include:

- fixing felt pads under table and chair legs;
- maintaining furnishings, such as squeaky drawers and wobbly tables;
- putting up and closing curtains or blinds;
- attaching boarding to classroom walls;
- laying floor carpets.

Australian Hearing (2005) make a wide range of suggestions that are intended to help teachers overcome some of the difficulties hearing-impaired children typically experience in the classroom situation. For example, to seat the pupil close to the teacher for the best sound reception and visual information, but also to allow him or her to move to a better listening position if needed. Similarly, to check that the pupil has a clear view of the whole class to facilitate participation during group activities.

Teachers also need to remember that many deaf children have stronger hearing in one ear than in the other, so a child may need to physically move position as the adult moves around the room. Other factors that enhance the hearing-impaired child's educational opportunities include good lighting on (but not behind) the speaker's face to make lip-reading easier. Lip-reading is also more straightforward when the adult speaking stays in one area while talking, faces the child and, when reading aloud, makes sure that the book is not covering the face. Obviously, it is impossible for a lip-reader if teachers turn their back while talking, though in practice this practice is hard to avoid in the cut and thrust of classroom life. Use of visual aids is particularly valuable for children who rely as much on sight as on sound.

Teachers have to make sure the hearing-impaired child is attending (not just listening)

when they start talking, ask a question or allocate tasks, and understands instructions (e.g. by repeating them). It is sometimes helpful to have a responsible classmate share notes with hearing-impaired classmates about a directive or discussion point. Adults need to be sensitive to the fact that children may be reluctant to admit that they don't understand and need encouragement to be open about such matters. Allowance also has to be made for the fact that hearing-impaired pupils have to work harder to listen than their normal hearing peers and may become rapidly fatigued. Many of the above strategies – speech clarity, ensuring attention, encouraging peer support, and so on – are of general applicability in teaching and therefore serve as models for work with all children.

Sources

Australian Hearing (2005) *Hearing Impairment and School Children*, on-line at www.mydr.com.au/default.asp?article=3207

Beattie, R.G. (2001) *Ethics in Deaf Education: The first six years*, London: Elsevier.

Hear-it, on-line at www.hear-it.org/page.dsp?area=677

Marschark, M. (2007) *Raising and Educating a Deaf Child*, New York: Oxford University Press, USA.

HIGHER-LEVEL TEACHING ASSISTANTS

See also: learning support assistant, teaching assistants

Higher-level teaching assistants (HLTAs) work in the school alongside the teacher, providing support for teaching and learning activities. HLTAs work right across the curriculum, acting as a specialist assistant for a specific subject or department or helping to plan lessons and develop support materials. The main purpose of a HLTA post is to provide a high level of classroom support to help ensure that teachers can focus on the teaching role. The post-holder may be the line-manager for other support staff (e.g. teaching assistants, learning support assistants). A HLTA may undertake some teaching activities within an appropriate system of supervision provided by a teacher. Some HLTAs may well want to work towards qualified teacher status but it is not an expectation. Specific details of the HLTA role are determined by each school.

HISTORY

See also: collaboration in learning, creative writing, discovery learning, enquiry, lessons, poetry, pupil perspectives, questions and questioning, skills, stories, tactile learners, writing

History in the primary phase of education is intended to help children learn about the facts and implications of real events and is principally concerned with enquiring into people, places, times and objects (artefacts). Old objects of historical significance (artefacts) brought into the classroom allow children to understand better life in the past and contrast it with life today. History helps to sharpen a range of skills, notably critical enquiry, investigation, and the evaluation of evidence, together with attitudes that commit to a search for truth (MacIntyre 2002). Cooper (2004) insists that it is the questions that historians ask and the ways in which they answer them that distinguish history as a discipline. She describes the characteristics of history and historians as follows:

> History is concerned with the causes and effects of change over time, with the ways in which and the reasons why societies in the past were different from ours, and what caused them to change. Historians investigate the past by interpreting traces of the past, the evidence.
>
> (p. 2)

Primary teachers in the UK build on children's earlier experiences about the world in which they live, including their families and past and present events in their own lives;

listening and responding to stories, songs, nursery rhymes and poems; taking part in role plays; looking closely at similarities, differences, patterns and change; comparing, sorting, matching, ordering and sequencing everyday objects; talking about their observations and asking questions to gain information about why things happen and how things work. Younger children focus on the lives and lifestyles of familiar people in the recent past and about famous people and events in the more distant past, including those from British history. Older primary children focus on people and important events and developments from recent and more distant times in the locality, in Britain and beyond. Work in history with younger primary children is best carried out at a visual and tangible or tactile ('opportunity to see, touch and feel') level, resulting, for example, in children producing a labelled drawing to indicate how well they have identified the defining qualities of the artefact being observed. Teachers also encourage children to bring family photographs to refine their powers of observation and talk about 'time lines' to represent the sequence of events being represented. In doing so, teachers have to remember that to a five- or six-year-old child, twenty years ago is like ancient history. It is also a well-established part of the history curriculum for pupils aged 5–7 years to pay close attention to the history evident in the locality and district, through walks around the neighbourhood to observe historical markers, such as post-boxes of different ages, and visits to historic houses. As pupils move into the junior phase (key stage 2, ages 7–11 years) they are encouraged to ask questions, speculate and examine evidence as a means of weighing alternative explanations.

Leedham and Murphy (2007) describe the importance of 'getting inside the mind' of historical characters and understanding life as they perceived it at the time, rather than imposing a twenty-first century interpretation on the situation. They point out that the things preoccupying people today will seem strange to a historian in fifty years time.

Although it is common practice for pupils to write about historical events and situations from the perspectives of those that lived at the time, teachers are also aware of the danger posed by allowing children's imagination to dominate at the expense of factual accuracy and for a history session to lapse into an extended writing session.

A framework for teaching history includes a separate subject discipline element ('History' *per se*) and history as part of an inter-related theme or topic incorporating (say) aspects of geography. Through both subject and thematic elements, teachers guide children to understand the chronological location and sequences of major events and the place of personalities in influencing events. For instance, the main purpose may be to inculcate in children the skills of discernment about the value of primary sources as historical evidence. To accomplish this purpose, the teacher may wish to spend the first few sessions introducing the significance of historical evidence to the class through demonstration and transmission teaching, followed by (say) the visit of an expert to the classroom, the use of video material, and so forth. The next session or two might consist of subdividing the class into collaborative groups for the purpose of examining archival items. The following session might involve drawing together the threads of the previous sessions, sharing findings, raising issues, drawing conclusions and recording results. In such a situation, the overall structure of the 'lesson' would cover a number of sessions, as no lesson would be sufficiently long to incorporate all the features needed to achieve the stated purpose.

Depending on the age of the children, the curriculum takes account of national, local and world history, with a particular emphasis on the lives of people during that time period (e.g. military leaders), significant political events (e.g. the abolition of slavery) and economic trends (e.g. trading with the 'New World'). By addressing such issues, history teaching offers opportunities to develop children's sense of identity through learning about the development of Britain or the children's country of origin, Europe and the rest of the world; it also introduces them to the sorts of information needed to understand and interpret the past.

The Historical Association (www.history.org. uk) is an independent UK national charity that has existed since 1906 and publishes the *Primary History* journal three times each year. The charity was granted a Royal Charter in 2007. Its members include teachers, academics, local historians and history enthusiasts.

Sources

Blyth, J. (1989) *History in Primary Schools*, Maidenhead: Open University Press.

Cooper, H. (2004) *The Teaching of History in Primary Schools*, London: David Fulton.

DCSF Standards Site: *History at KS1 and KS2*, on-line at www.standards.dfes.gov.uk/schemes2/history

Leedham, W. and Murphy, M. (2007) 'Joyful history', in Hayes, D. (ed.) *Joyful Teaching and Learning in the Primary School*, Exeter: Learning Matters.

MacIntyre, J. (2002) 'Historical perspectives on the history curriculum', in Johnston, J., Chater, M. and Bell, D. (eds) (2007) *Teaching the Primary Curriculum*, Maidenhead: Open University Press.

HOBBIES AND INTERESTS

See also: discussion, extra-curricular activities, singing

Many parents want their children to develop their experience beyond the realm of academic subjects, which is partly the reason why so many children study dance, singing, piano, painting and so on, even though only a very small number of them will become professional artists or musicians, and so forth. Most teachers encourage children to share their enthusiasms with classmates during 'show and tell' sessions or as the starting point for discussion. Schools offer a range of clubs and extra-curricular activities, such as computer club, different sports and board games to help children satisfy their interests in a relaxed atmosphere.

HOME BACKGROUND AND LEARNING

See also: behaviour, expectations, home–school liaison, mathematics, new entrants, parents, reading, special educational needs, special educational needs coordinator

There can be no doubt that children's home backgrounds markedly affects their ability to learn: some new school entrants may have been discouraged from asking questions by parents and received little stimulation other than from being immersed in television programmes and electronic games. Others will have experienced a rich diet of positive reinforcement and encouragement from adults, and situations that facilitate language acquisition and foster initiative. Studies strongly indicate that pupils from relatively poor home backgrounds and those living in areas of multiple deprivation start school with lower than average reading and mathematics skills. It also shows that there is a contextual effect of attending a school in which a high proportion of pupils come from disadvantaged home backgrounds and this has the effect of reducing the average attainment of pupils on entry to school.

Catering for this wide range of abilities and accommodating children from different backgrounds is one of the major challenges for teachers. Supporting pupils with special educational needs not only necessitates co-operation with parents but also with a range of other professionals from outside the school, such as the educational psychologist and local authority advisory teachers. Specialist expertise is normally available in teaching the hearing-impaired and visually impaired, and a range of other professionals such as speech therapists and physiotherapists, social workers, educational welfare officers and medical services are occasionally involved in providing support to teachers, pupils and their parents. The special educational needs coordinator (SENCO) is often the person in school who liaises with these agencies, as well as providing ongoing support for class teachers.

An interesting study by Galloway (1995) indicated that independent observers did not find that children from poor home backgrounds behaved worse than those from affluent homes. This finding contrasted with the views of the teachers responsible for the same children, who reported a much higher incidence of disruption among them compared with other children. One conclusion from Galloway's research was that teachers can be negatively and irrationally influenced by a child's background and have low expectations of both their behaviour and academic potential.

Sources

Galloway, D. (1995) 'Truancy, delinquency and disruption: Differential school influences', *Education Review (British Psychological Society)*, 19 (2), 49–53.

HOME EDUCATION

See *Home schooling*

HOME–SCHOOL

See also: curriculum, governors, head teachers, home–school agreement, induction of pupils, interaction, parental involvement

Over recent years, legislation has established the rights of parents to be well informed about the curriculum offered by each school and to know about their child's progress through reports and informal access to teachers (Vincent 2000; Beveridge 2004). With each school's budget depending in large measure upon the number of pupils on roll, there is extra incentive for head teachers and governors to ensure that parents are welcomed and made to feel part of the school community. Inevitably, this new relationship has caused schools to re-evaluate their links with parents and establish procedures for responding to and allaying parental concerns.

Designated areas for parents are a common feature of many primary schools and almost every school has regular meetings with groups of parents in a parent–teacher forum, often referred to as the PTA (Parent-Teacher Association) or Friends of the School or a similar title. This forum often provides the impetus for fund-raising, school events and (sometimes) commenting on school policy decisions that have implications for their children's welfare and education.

The greatest level of interaction between parents and school staff is found at nursery, reception and infant level (Fitzgerald 2004; Crozier and Reay 2005) owing to the fact that parents tend to bring their young children into the classroom in the morning and meet them when they leave. As children progress through the school, contact with parents tends to become less regular as older children travel to school on their own or with friends. Parents, freed from the demands of caring for young children, may find a job or decide that they have 'done their stint' as parent-helper and look elsewhere for fulfilment. Junior-aged children sometimes find their parent's regular presence in the school an embarrassment and ask them to stay away. So although it may appear that parents lose interest in their child's education over time, in reality parental interest merely changes perspective (Tizard et al. 1988). Early on, parents are chiefly interested in basic considerations such as:

- Is my child happy in school?
- Is my child being properly cared for?
- Does my child have friends?
- Is my child getting on well with basic skills, especially reading?
- Is my child behaving satisfactorily?

Later, when parents are more likely to concentrate on specific aspects of teaching and learning:

- How is my child progressing in his or her work relative to others in the class?
- Is my child being offered a full range of educational opportunities?

- Is my child excelling or falling behind in any area?
- Does my child have the ability to achieve success in future education?

Parents need reassuring that their children are not disadvantaged at school, that teachers and other pupils treat them fairly and that they are encouraged to do their best. Thus, when adults in school interact with a child, they are not only affecting the child but indirectly influencing the parents, families and friends, too. Although every school has its own particular ideas about establishing and maintaining good quality relationships with parents, contact in the foundation years (for children aged 3–5 years) and at the start of key stage 1 (5–6 years) often includes:

- home visits by the reception class teacher close to the start of a child's formal schooling;
- visits to and from nursery schemes and playgroups by teachers from the mainstream school;
- informal meetings between teacher and parents at the start and end of the day when they are leaving or picking up their children;
- involvement of parents in the classroom, both to assist, and in some cases to help ease the transition of their child from home to school ('induction').

Many head teachers actively promote home–school liaison through invitations to parents and members of the local community to participate in aspects of school life, from practical and mundane tasks such as mending library books, making tea for special events or tidying classroom cupboards, through to an active contribution to teaching and school effectiveness (Wolfendale and Bastiani 2000; Campbell and Fairbairn 2005). All maintained schools in England have to operate a Home–School Agreement (HSA) policy, whereby parents are given details of the school's commitment to the education and welfare of the children and priorities and expectations that are made of parents and pupils. A small percentage of parents are unable or unwilling to participate in a home–school agreement or scheme but cannot be disadvantaged or discriminated against as a result, making the HSA somewhat toothless.

School–Home Support (www.schoolhome support.org.uk) is a national charity that was founded in 1984 in Tower Hamlets, East London. In 2007/8 the charity helped 41,000 children, young people and families in 175 primary and secondary schools, early years se ttings, special schools and pupil referral units. It aims to build bridges between home and school to enable children and young people to make the most of their education. School–Home Support is most active in London, the East Midlands, Northeast England, Yorkshire, Humberside, and Bristol.

Sources

Beveridge, S. (2004) *Children, Families and Schools: Developing partnerships for inclusive education*, London: Routledge.

Campbell, A. and Fairbairn, G. (eds) (2005) *Working with Support in the Classroom*, London: Paul Chapman.

Crozier, G. and Reay, D. (2005) *Activating Participation*, Stoke on Trent: Trentham.

Fitzgerald, D. (2004) *Parent Partnerships in the Early Years*, London: Continuum.

Tizard, B., Blatchford, P., Burke, J., Farquhar, C. and Plewis, I. (1988) *Young Children at School in the Inner City*, London: Erlbaum.

Vincent, C. (2000) *Including Parents? Education, citizenship and parental agency*, Maidenhead: Open University Press.

Wolfendale, S. and Bastiani, J. (eds) (2000) *The Contribution of Parents to School Effectiveness*, London: David Fulton.

HOME–SCHOOL AGREEMENT

See also: absenteeism, behaviour, discipline, governing body, home–school, parents, pupil perspectives

The School Standards and Framework Act 1998 (Section 110) requires the governing bodies of all state-funded schools to adopt a home–school agreement (HSA), through which the rights, responsibilities and expectations of school governors, parents, teachers and children are laid out. The HSA contains expectations about attendance, behaviour and discipline, homework, standards of academic attainment and other issues relating to the school ethos (e.g. dress code). The agreement should be drawn up by the governing body in consultation with the head teacher and set out the school's aims and values, the school's and parents' respective responsibilities and what the school expects of its pupils. These expectations must be broadly in line with legal requirements and specifically in accordance with school policy. Before adopting or reviewing an agreement, the school must consult parents and involve pupils, teachers, other school staff and relevant agencies in the consultation process (Sweeney 1999).

The governing body must take reasonable steps to ensure that all registered parents of pupils aged 5–16 sign the parental declaration and indicate that they understand and accept the agreement. It is sometimes the case that older children or those capable of understanding the implications are also invited to sign. However, it is a rather unsatisfactory condition of the HSA that parental refusal to sign does not result in adverse consequences and cannot be made a condition of entry to the school. This caveat tends to reduce the efficacy of the agreement process, as it is sometimes the parents who would most benefit from close partnership with the school that are reluctant to make a formal commitment.

Sources

DCSF, *Home–School Agreements*, on-line at www.teachernet.gov.uk/management/atoz/h/home-schoolagreements

Sweeney, D. (1999) 'Liaising with parents, carers and agencies', in Cole, M. (ed.) *Professional Issues for Teachers and Student Teachers*, London: David Fulton.

HOME SCHOOLING

See also: active learning, autism, discipline, discovery learning, drama, dyslexia, home–school, minority ethnic groups, music, self-esteem, starting school

Children educated at home or 'home educated children' (referred to as 'home schooling' elsewhere in the world, e.g. the USA and Canada) has become an increasingly popular option with parents in the UK, notably among people designated white British, though religious and cultural reasons prompt a small percentage of Muslim, Christian, Gypsy and Traveller families teach their children at home (Ivatts 2006 for the DfES). A study conducted on behalf of the government (York Consulting 2007) suggested that many of the parents that chose to school their children at home did so because they were worried about bullying and poor discipline in state schools and were generally dissatisfied with the quality of state education. Others thought children were required to start formal schooling too young. There was also a prevailing view that the education system was overly bureaucratic, inflexible and assessment-driven, which acted against the best needs of the children. Some parents considered that their children's special learning needs were not being adequately met in school, including those related to dyslexia, autism and being gifted and talented – see McIntyre-Bhatty (2007) to explore the implications for the home educating community of government involvement through its guidelines, further regulation and legislation.

A number of parents that home school their children use formal and highly structured methods, follow the National Curriculum closely and even hire tutors to teach certain subjects. Other parents espouse more informal practices in response to their children's developing interests, such that children may be encouraged to pursue their passion for (say) music and drama, rather than following an adult agenda. Some parents follow the on-line 'Learnpremium' teaching and learning resource web site provided by the *Guardian* newspaper. In many cases, parents used a mixture of formal and informal methods and educated children in a range of environments, such as trips out to museums.

Parents that espouse home education claim that it leads to higher levels of confidence and self-esteem; creates a close relationship between parent/carer and child; encourages self-directed or active learning ('discovery learning'); and facilitates the development of skills that are equivalent to, or superior to children of similar age in school. Nevertheless, when making a decision about home schooling, parents are advised to take note of a variety of factors:

- the time commitment required to prepare lessons, assess progress, organise field trips, arrange music lessons and so on;
- the fact that parent and child are together almost constantly and therefore have little personal time;
- the financial strain it places on middle-income families, as the parent responsible for the teaching will probably not be earning a regular income;
- the need to ensure that the child has opportunity to meet and play with other children;
- awareness that household organisation will suffer because home education inevitably creates mess and clutter;
- the need to spend time as parents or guardians discussing the issues and practicalities of home schooling before deciding to proceed;
- ensuring the child is committed to the idea and understands the implications;
- taking one year at a time rather than seeing home education as a lifetime commitment;
- the demands made by the process of teaching and the associated knowledge demands, necessitating acquisition of resources and advice as necessary;
- the reasons that other parents began to home school.

(Based on information from
About.com, on-line)

Sources

About.com, *Homeschooling*, on-line at http://homeschooling.about.com

Ivatts, A. (2006) *The Situation Regarding Current Policy, Provision and Practice in Elective Home Education for Gypsy, Roma and Traveller Children*, Annersley: DfES Publications.

McIntyre-Bhatty, K. (2007) 'Interventions and interrogations: An analysis of recent policy imperatives and their rationales in the case of home education', *Education, Knowledge and Economy*, 1 (3), 241–59.

York Consulting, for the DfES (2007) *The Prevalence of Home Education in England: A feasibility study*, Research Report 827, Annersley: DfES Publications.

HOMEWORK

See also: ability, higher-level teaching assistant, home–school, infants, knowledge, learning, parental involvement, reading, reading records, spelling, teaching assistant, understanding

Homework is, as the name suggests, work done by children outside the school day, usually at home. Some schools provide facilities for the work to be done by older pupils immediately after school, with a supervising adult to offer help and support, and with access to basic facilities (reference books, dictionaries, computers, etc.). Each school has a homework policy but teachers have to interpret it in the light of the particular needs of the pupils for whom they have responsibility. Most tasks are used to reinforce existing knowledge (e.g. learning spellings that have formed part of a language activity) but sometimes they extend knowledge (e.g. using the spellings in sentences devised by the child). In setting homework tasks, teachers bear in mind that it has to be just as appropriate to the age and ability of the pupil as the work in school is intended to be (DfEE 1998).

Kidwell (2004) is among those who argue strongly that homework has to be realistic and manageable, as there is little point in having grandiose schemes that are impossible for the children to complete, even with adult support, or that require sophisticated equipment or expensive resources. Some homework consists of 'finishing off' incomplete work from the day; however, this penalises slower workers and does little to extend the more able. Children may be given a number of activities that have to be completed over a period of time (a half term, say). The most straightforward homework is when the same task is given to all children such that they are all able to engage with it at their own level of understanding and experience, and the end product can be marked easily or shared with others in the class. For younger children ('infants' aged 5–7 years), additional reading, supported by an adult if possible, is frequently used as a homework task, with the adult (usually a parent) signing in a 'reading record book' to confirm that it has been done.

Some teachers set homework that draws on pupils' present knowledge; for instance, children may be asked to prepare a three-minute talk about their favourite toy/hobby/day out. Less capable children can base their talk on pictures or visual aids; older ones can use more sophisticated means if they choose to do so. The emphasis of such events is enjoyment and not competitive. Many teachers express their surprise and delight at the depth of knowledge that some children possess, which can act as a platform for further learning.

Formative feedback by teachers (i.e. comments intended to further learning) on homework tasks is not always possible, owing to time constraints and the many other demands placed upon them. However, pupils can be inducted into sharing their work with a classmate, though this apparently simple procedure is more difficult than it sounds, as making fair judgements about quality is demanding. MacGrath (2000) emphasises the importance of acknowledging what a child has accomplished, rather than instantly looking for teaching opportunities to correct mistakes; this positive approach results in 'separating praise from points of instruction, which [can] come later' (p. 25). Teachers sometimes make use of a teaching assistant – especially a higher-level teaching assistant (HLTA) – to check that homework has been completed, offer advice about difficulties and even liaise with parents 'at the classroom door'.

Research published by the University of London's Institute of Education, *Homework: The evidence* (Hallam 2004), found that helping pupils with homework can exacerbate or create family tensions. One of the study's conclusions was that parents might inhibit learning by exercising strict control over the way homework is done, instead of helping the children to interpret it for themselves. The authors conclude that the most effective help that parents can provide is in offering moral support to children, but only helping them directly when specifically asked to do so. The study acknowledges that homework can have modest benefits for academic progress but that brighter pupils and older pupils are the main beneficiaries. The author of the research, Susan Hallam, claims that homework clubs in school are a great advantage to pupils because they have access to resources and informed adults outside the home. Nevertheless, homework can also encourage parental involvement in their children's studies, increase children's independence and provide opportunities for practice and skill development.

Sources

DfEE (1998) *Homework: Guidelines for primary and secondary schools*, Sudbury: DfEE Publications.

Hallam, S. (2004) *Homework: The evidence*, London: University of London, Institute of Education.

Kidwell, V. (2004) *Homework*, London: Continuum.

MacGrath, M. (2000) *The Art of Peaceful Teaching in the Primary School*, London: David Fulton.

HUMANITIES

See also: curriculum, geography, history, religious education, teachers' beliefs, values

In primary schools the core humanities subjects consist of geography, history and, usually to a lesser extent, religious education (RE). Of all the areas in the school curriculum that contribute directly to the development of knowledge and understanding of human behaviour, the humanities are by definition the most significant. When learning in humanities is organised through topic work, it is commonly the case that one of the three subject areas lie at the heart of the planning, with the other two subjects in a supporting role. However, history, geography and RE are often studied individually at the top end of today's primary schools, so the word 'humanities' tends to be used without a capital letter to indicate that it is a general descriptive term rather than a curriculum subject.

Ashley (1999) claims that a 'humanitarian curriculum' should consist of more than allocating a specific number of hours per week to the three basic subjects. Behind the desire to teach the humanities is a belief that children need to be helped to become fully rounded people or 'fully human'. Ashley argues that no part of the curriculum can be value-free and it is a mistake to try and separate facts and knowledge from the values that they represent. Teachers of the humanities must examine their own values and be sensitive to the fact that they directly influence their pupils; as such, teachers have a responsibility to read and interpret the curriculum with such principles in mind.

Without being grounded in the humanities, the development of the primary-age child would be little more than training them in basic techniques of reading, writing and arithmetic because it is the humanities that provide the meaningful context for much worthwhile that is taught and learned (Campbell and Little 1989, preface). The authors go on to say that learning in the humanities has been associated with a focus on children's relationship to society, including those in the past and in other cultural settings. The humanities has also involved learning about values, incorporated in phrases such as respect for people, co-operation and democratising decision-making. Similarly, Kimber *et al.* (1995) stress that it is important to ask how primary school children are best helped to understand what is special about being human, in terms of people, place, events, time, beliefs and values. The authors also invite teachers to consider their own values against a range of case studies of classroom practice.

Sources

Ashley, M. (1999) *Improving Teaching and Learning in the Humanities: Developing primary practice*, London: Routledge.
Campbell, R.J. and Little, V. (1989) *Humanities in the Primary School*, London: Falmer.
Hoodless, P., Bermingham, S. and McCreery, E. (2003) *Teaching Humanities in Primary Schools*, Exeter: Learning Matters.
Kimber, D., Clough, N., Forrest, M., Harnett, P., Menter, I. and Newman, E. (1995) *Humanities in Primary Education: History, geography and religious education in the classroom*, London: David Fulton.

HUMOUR

See also: behaviour, boredom, brain function, happiness, interaction, misbehaviour, relationships, sanctions, teacher role, teaching skills

The importance of using humour in the classroom is significant, especially with older children who are capable of grasping subtleties and enjoy repartee. All emotions are contagious and if adults can gradually create a relaxed but purposeful atmosphere, half the battle is won. Not only are things more enjoyable when the children are smiling and laughing with the teacher (not, of course, *at* the teacher in any malicious sense) but it also puts them in a better frame of mind to learn. Laughing increases brain activity and makes pupils more receptive and tuned in to what is being taught.

Self-deprecating humour from teachers is one of the styles most appreciated by children. Teachers who can laugh at the absurdities that characterise social situations, and admit their part in it, win a lot of children's

hearts. Indeed, Zucker and Parker (1999) emphasise numerous absurdities and ambiguities that characterise teaching – though some of them (such as political interference) have a serious dimension. Second, as teachers become more experienced, they increasingly use humour in more elaborate ways and refine their repartee over time. As part of this process, teachers create a whole series of contrived roles that they bring into play at any given time as a way to engage interest, defuse potentially explosive situations or exert authority.

Woods (1990, chapter 7) describes the various purposes served by humour among older pupils and describes how pupils' humour is closely associated with their personal identity and the social formation of the group to which they belong (e.g. the 'gang'). Sharing a joke can be a joint enterprise in mutual interest, such as offsetting boredom or 'playing up' a teacher to elicit a reaction. Woods also explains ways in which shared humour between pupils and adult can enhance the relationship and serve to 'oil the wheels' of learning.

Lawrence (2006) offers some sensible advice on keeping life in perspective when he suggests that while teachers should be careful to take their work seriously they should never take themselves so seriously that they lose their sense of humour. Life in school relies on every member functioning efficiently, so effort expended in supporting others benefits everyone. Quinn (1997) argues that during deep episodes of interaction between adults and pupils through speaking and listening, 'all can instantly be captivated by a great laugh together' (p. 115). Furthermore, genuinely laughing together not only relieves tension but also brings about increased emotional intimacy between the teacher and learners.

Reception-age children are more inclined to laugh *at* a situation or an individual's unintended humour than to initiate it to create a reaction. Over time, as they better understand the potential of humour for drawing attention to themselves and (perhaps) disadvantaging others, the bolder children may incur adult displeasure by being silly ('misbehaving'). Hobday-Kutsch and McVittie (2002) note that adults and older children use humour as a negotiating tool to determine where power resides in the classroom. They claim on the basis of observations and interviews that most children and adults new to the school realise quite quickly that certain forms of spoken language and discourse are appropriate and others are proscribed. However, a minority of pupils 'feed' off humour with reference to their peer's reactions and, after a time, their expectations. Vulnerable children, who find much of what they do at school to be irrelevant and tedious, use humour as a means of relieving tension and getting through the day, despite the sanctions that fooling around might incur.

Sources

Hobday-Kutsch, J. and McVittie, J. (2002) 'Just clowning around: Classroom perspectives on children's humour', *Canadian Journal of Education*, 27 (2/3), 195–210.

Lawrence, D. (2006) *Enhancing Self-esteem in the Classroom*, London: Paul Chapman.

Quinn, V. (1997) *Critical Thinking in Young Minds*, London: David Fulton.

Woods, P. (1990) *The Happiest Days? How pupils cope with school*, London: Routledge.

Zucker, J. and Parker, D. (1999) *A Class Act*, London: Sapphire Publishers.

I

IMAGINATION

See also: arts, awe and wonder, constructivism, deep learning, fantasy, music, poetry, problem solving, singing, visual aids

Imagination provides pupils with a vehicle to visualise new possibilities. Many teachers see stimulating pupils' imaginations as a pre-requisite to making an activity of educational value. Authentic imagination, which is said to prompt positive action, is different from *hopeful* imagination that is characterised by a passivity that leaves the active work to others. The power of imagination creates vision to empower and motivate children to act resolutely and achieve the desired goal, regardless of setbacks and disappointments. Kieran Egan, a noted education thinker, claims that imagination is not a desirable-but-dispensable frill but should form the heart of any truly educational experience. Consequently, imagination should be integral, not marginal, to basic training or disciplined thought or rational inquiry, as it gives them life meaning. Furthermore, he argues that imagination is not the sole province of the arts in education or a leisure activity but is central to all areas of learning. Egan goes so far as to say that imagination is the hard pragmatic centre of all effective human thought. See, for example, Egan (1992).

The root of the word imagination is, of course, 'imagine', which can be thought of as a mental picture or 'seeing in the mind's eye'. Although the methods by which imagination can be stimulated and heightened vary with age of child, there are a number of common methods that are employed by teachers:

- posing questions that cause the children to think deeply about issues or events ('deep learning');
- offering real-life or fictitious scenarios to highlight key points;
- using familiar objects in unfamiliar ways to offer differing perspectives on a well-known subject or as a source of awe and wonder;
- using powerful music, expressive poems or vivid pictures to evoke an emotional response;
- giving children opportunity to share their experiences with others in the class.

Stimulating children's imaginations through stories, songs, visual resources and other means taps a rich source of learning in primary-age children and, for younger children, creates a fantasy world within which they can gradually come to terms with the realities of the world as it exists. Egan (on-line) notes that historically the connection between memory and imagination is the story. The point about the story's contribution to memorising is that it achieves this aim by making whatever is to be learned into something meaningful. The story invests the material to be learned with the qualities that engage the imagination in the process of learning.

Tyrrell (2001) provides insights into ways in which fantasy can be used in the classroom to stimulate a love for learning and it is

201

noteworthy that the media, especially television and video games, rely on stimulating children's imaginations and creating a comfortable fantasy world for them (see, for example, Belton 2000). From their in-depth study of the relationship existing between computer games, fantasy and learning, Asgari and Kaufman (2005) concluded that fantasy is emotionally appealing, plays a key role in successful computer games and has the potential to increase motivation and learning. The authors suggest that teachers use fantasy to reinforce instructional goals and not compete with them; provide appropriate metaphors and analogies for learning; provide imaginary characters that are familiar to the learner; accommodate gender differences; and relate the fantasy to the content to be learned. The imagination can serve to engage the learner so that other game features can be activated such as interactivity, competition, control, curiosity, challenge and feedback. However, Chudacoff (2007) notes that the toy industry has become closely allied with the television and film industry, based on licensing deals with toy manufacturers, raising concerns that these media-generated toys limit children's imaginations owing to the familiar storylines that are attached to them that children absorb from regularly viewing the programmes.

Hebert (2006) claims that imagination helps school-age children to solve problems by helping them think through different outcomes to various situations and role playing ways to cope with difficult or new circumstances. He insists that imagination helps children to practise and apply new learning and better understand how skills are used 'in the real world'. The author also argues that imagination encourages a rich vocabulary as children listen to real or made-up stories, and helps them to become problem solvers, innovators and creative thinkers. Paley (2005) explores the fascinating and original language of children in their role-playing and storytelling. Drawing from their own words, she explores how this natural mode of learning (i.e. 'left to their own imaginations') allows children to construct meaning in their worlds and claims that what they create is carried into their adult lives.

A concern expressed by many teachers and parents of younger children is that a political climate in which evidence of success relies on measurable outcomes does not encourage teachers or children to use their imaginations because it is a quality that is impossible to quantify. Nevertheless, imagination is increasingly seen as a means of supporting and sustaining the kind of enterprising approach that is needed to invigorate learning and raise standards of achievement. See Greene (2000) for a series of essays about the role of imagination in general education, arts education, aesthetics, literature and the social and multicultural context.

Sources

Asgari, M. and Kaufman, D. (2005) *Relationships Among Computer Games, Fantasy and Learning*, Faculty of Education, Simon Fraser University, Canada.

Belton, T. (2000) 'The face at the window study: A fresh approach to media influence and to investigating the influence of television and videos on children's imagination', *Media, Culture and Society*, 22, 629–43.

Chudacoff, H.P. (2007) *Children at Play: An American history*. New York: NYU Press.

Egan, K. (1992) *Imagination in Teaching and Learning: The middle school years*, Chicago IL: University of Chicago Press.

——(undated) *Memory, Imagination and Learning: Connected by the story*, on-line at www.educ.sfu.ca/kegan/MemoryIm.html

Greene, M. (2000) *Releasing the Imagination: Essays on education, the arts and social change*, San Francisco CA: Jossey-Bass.

Hebert, J.L. (2006) *Imagination in Kids Is Important*, on-line via http://primaryschool.suite101.com

Paley, V.G. (2005) *A Child's Work: The importance of fantasy play*, Chicago IL: University of Chicago Press.

Tyrrell, J. (2001) *The Power of Fantasy in Early Learning*, London: Routledge.

INCLUSION

See also: arithmetic, behaviour, drama, equal opportunities, fairness, happiness, learning and teacher influence, learning climate, numeracy, physical comfort, physical education, special educational needs, teaching approach

It is a universal principle among educators that every child deserves a fair chance to learn and enjoy social interaction, to be treated with appropriate kindness and consistency, to be happy and to satisfy his or her aspirations. Inclusive education is concerned with minimising barriers to learning and participation in educational settings, both in terms of the adequacy of provision and issues of equity (Nind 2005). Schools are charged with offering an education to all pupils by modifying the way that practitioners approach their work such that no child is excluded who could, with appropriate human and practical resources, be incorporated into the warp and weave of regular school life (DfES 2001). Schools that formerly excluded pupils with particular disabilities and special learning needs (including children with emotional vulnerabilities) are now obliged to include them whenever resources are available to make it possible. It is therefore no longer acceptable that children with disabilities who have the intellectual capacity to learn are hindered from doing so on the basis of their physical limitations (see, for example, Thomas 1998 regarding whole-school issues; Jones 2004 for practitioner advice; and Fox *et al.* 2004 for issues relating to children with Down's Syndrome).

Whereas the majority of physically disabled pupils can be comfortably incorporated within mainstream activities, teachers usually find the presence of emotionally vulnerable children to be a much greater challenge. There is an increasing body of evidence to show that disruptive pupils tend to adversely affect the education of other children, even with the presence and involvement of an assistant to provide learning support (though see Florian *et al.* 2006 for a contrary view). Although the pupils that experience the greatest difficulties in learning and conforming to behavioural norms provide a useful

barometer for teachers about the quality of their organisation, clarity of explanations and relevance of lessons, they also absorb a considerable amount of time and energy.

Reid (2005) notes that full inclusion must be also be reflected in the teaching approach employed by the teacher to provide a diverse, individually structured, meaningful learning experience for everyone, regardless of ability. Three principles underpin the provision of effective learning opportunities for all children in school. The first is that teachers are required to set suitable challenges for all pupils, including less able and more able ones. The second is for teachers to respond to pupils' diverse needs by creating a productive learning environment ('climate'), offer all children an equal opportunity to access resources and participate in activities, assess their progress and set them suitable challenges. The third is for teachers, in conjunction with other colleagues where necessary, to combat potential barriers to learning for individuals and groups of pupils with disabilities and those for whom English is an additional language (EAL). Pupils for whom English is not a first language may learn to speak and write but not possess the cultural insights that make learning meaningful (Gregory 2008). Some children who struggle with English (including language-impoverished indigenous pupils for whom English is the first language) may excel in an area that does not depend as heavily on the written or spoken word, such as arithmetic ('numeracy'), drama or physical activity. Other children are not used to listening or simply cannot absorb what an adult says because of communication difficulties.

All adults in school have to be alert to ways in which they are able to assist in servicing an inclusion policy, not only for pupils' benefit but also to ensure that every adult in school feels significant and valued by being 'included'. Nutbrown and Clough (2006) engage with issues relating to the everyday experiences of young children, parents and practitioners in relation to educational theory.

Sources

DfES (2001) *Inclusive Schooling*, London: HMSO.

Florian, L., Rouse, M. and Hawkins, K.B. (2006) *Achievement and Inclusion in Schools*, London: Routledge.

Fox, S., Farrell, P. and Davis, P. (2004) 'Factors associated with the effective inclusion of primary-aged pupils with Down's Syndrome', *British Journal of Special Education*, 31 (4), 184–90.

Gregory, E. (2008) *Learning to Read in a New Language: Making sense of words and worlds*, London: Paul Chapman.

Jones, C. (2004) *Supporting Inclusion in the Early Years*, Maidenhead: Open University Press.

Nind, M. (2005) 'Inclusive education: Discourse and action', *British Educational Research Journal*, 31 (2), 269–75.

Nutbrown, C. and Clough, P. (2006) *Inclusion in the Early Years*, London: Sage.

Reid, G. (2005) *Learning Styles and Inclusion*, London: Paul Chapman.

Thomas, G. (1998) *The Making of the Inclusive School*, London: Routledge.

INDIVIDUAL EDUCATION PLAN

See also: communication, life skills, parental involvement, special educational needs, target setting (pupils)

An individual education plan (IEP) is drawn up by the class teacher to help the parent and the school identify a child's special educational needs and to target areas of particular difficulty. The targets are related to the pupil's particular difficulty – learning, communication, behavioural or sensory/physical disability. It shows the steps to be taken to support the child's learning and also set a date for reviewing progress. The IEP lists details of learning targets for the child to reach in a given time; the allocated person who will support the child and how it will be organised; and the resources to be utilised. In addition, the plan has to show how success in the target will be measured and the parental contribution to the process. Provision might include involvement of a specialist teacher (e.g. for speech training) or teaching assistant; working in a small group; and alternative activities such as speech and language support, mentoring, life skills teaching and anger management. The targets set on an IEP should be SMART, an acronym composed of the initial letters of specific, measurable, attainable, realistic and time-related. The plan should be discussed with the child and a copy of it given to the parents, who will be invited to give their views at the meeting held to review the progress made under the current plan and set targets for the subsequent one.

INDUCTION OF PUPILS

See also: behaviour, curriculum, friendships, home background and learning, infants, juniors, new entrants, parental involvement, playground, reception, sports, transitions

Induction refers to the process by which pupils are inculcated into the working practices of a school and become, through structured support and guidance, better able to understand and cope with the procedures, routines and covert agendas that exist there. For children who have never been to school it can be a shock for them to discover that the freedom and spontaneity of pre-school is curtailed and they have to conform to specified practices. To reduce the impact of the change there is normally close liaison between reception teachers (who teach new school entrants), pre-school workers and parents. A similar arrangement exists between teachers teaching pupils in their final year at primary school and staff in the receiving secondary school during the transition period.

Davies (2006, chapter 19) suggests that the aim of transition at any stage is to build bridges between pupils, schools and parents, of which there are three types. First, the 'pastoral bridge', such that schools want to ensure that pupils transfer feeling safe and secure, confidently knowing where they are going and who will be there for them, as well as what they will be doing. Second, the 'curriculum bridge', whereby learning that has taken place in the former setting is built upon in the new one. Third, the 'loyalty bridge', as schools try to ensure that there is a bond of built-in loyalty between the parents and the new school. Davies acknowledges that no matter how well primary schools induct pupils there will always be those who find it difficult to settle. A few children find the move from primary to secondary school quite traumatic; such anxiety can be reduced by close liaison between staff; notice boards in the primary school with information about the secondary school(s); availability of leaflets and newsletters from the new school; involvement of the primary pupils with events in the secondary school (e.g. a sports event); use of a 'buddy' scheme, whereby volunteers from the secondary school visit the 'feeder' primary school and meet the children who are about to transfer. Specialist staff from the secondary school can also assist with some teaching of the primary children and provide access to resources that the smaller school is unable to afford.

Regardless of background, all children are gradually inducted, both by peers and teachers, into patterns of behaviour and understanding that reflect and maintain school life. It is hard to come to a school for the very first time and have to learn unfamiliar and sometimes baffling procedures, routines and rituals. After all, where else but in school do you need to stick your arm up in the air before being allowed to speak or to sit still for half an hour on an uncomfortable wooden floor listening to a grown-up reading stories? Only in a classroom do you have to ask for permission to leave the room, get dressed and undressed with lots of other children before going to clamber over large apparatus in a hall or endure the windy conditions of an exposed tarmac playground. Little wonder that children who are new to school take time to settle, sometimes become confused, make mistakes, and find the experience unsettling. In particular, children whose families are highly mobile (e.g. travellers) have the considerable challenge of adjusting to new

situations quite regularly. These children do not have the luxury of building friendships over a lengthy period of time. Similarly, children who arrive from overseas with a limited knowledge of English require close support and attention to prevent isolation and under-achievement.

Over the weeks and months, the unfamiliarity fades and is normally replaced by a healthy adjustment to the vagaries of school life (Brooker 2002; Smith and Lynch 2005). Indeed, a reluctance to conform sometimes evolves into a zealous eagerness to defend the status quo. Older infants and younger juniors vie with one another to see who can most vigorously uphold justice with crossly disputed versions of the truth, accusations and counteraccusations. There is also a need to consider the plight of insecure younger children, who hold back when there's a scramble for the best equipment or place in the queue, passively accepting their lowly position and storing up a growing belief that they will never be able to compete with their stronger, more assertive peers.

As they witness classroom and school encounters, children gain a view of what is important and what is trivial, and of adult status and tolerance (Charlton et al. 1996; Cullingford 2002). With the passage of time, their intuition and familiarity with school routines and relationships alert them to the teacher's apprehension when certain significant adults enter the room – especially if they are wearing smart suits and carrying a clipboard. In the playground ('yard') they are keenly aware of who dominates and who submits; which children are most popular and which are the target of derisive comment; who are the rough and noisy ones and who always gets told off. They make a mental note that such-and-such a child can usually be blamed for misdemeanours, regardless of the truth, and occasionally prey upon the fact to divert attention from their own naughty behaviour. Some children discover how to approach a teacher in such a way as to gain sympathy or favour. A few soon take delight in finding every opportunity to take advantage of grown-ups and luxuriate in the excitement of undetected disobedience.

The more comfortable and relaxed children feel in the new situation, the more likely the boundaries between home and school will become blurred. The teacher who admonishes a child, 'Don't do that, you're not at home now', may be failing to recognise that such behaviour is often a sign that the induction process has successfully been completed.

Sources

Brooker, L. (2002) *Starting School: Young children learning cultures*, Maidenhead: Open University Press.

Charlton, T., Jones, K. and Flores-Hole, H. (1996) 'The effects of teacher behaviour upon pupil behaviour', in Charlton, T. Jones, K. and Cummings, M. (eds) *Pupil Needs and Classroom Practices*, Cheltenham: Park Published Papers.

Cullingford, C. (2002) *The Best Years of their Lives? Pupils' experience of school*, London: Kogan Page.

Davies, S. (2006) *The Essential Guide to Teaching*, Harlow: Pearson Education.

Smith, J. and Lynch, J. (eds) (2005) *The Primary School Year*, London: Routledge.

INDUCTION OF NEW TEACHERS

See also: assessing children's learning, behaviour, bullying, class management, effectiveness, monitoring, parent communication, parents' evening, planning, probationary year, professional development, recording, reporting

To improve the experience and provide a bridge from initial teacher training to regular teaching, arrangements exist to support newly qualified teachers (NQTs) during the first year of qualified teaching through an induction programme. The programme is intended provide well-targeted monitoring and support within the framework of a reduced timetable (around 90 per cent) and to help embed an ethos of continuing professional development and career development. When working efficiently, the induction process helps new teachers to find their feet, show their potential, make rapid progress in becoming effective practitioners and exert an impact on the school's overall development and progress (Hayes 2000). A new framework of professional standards for teachers in England came into effect from September 2007, which includes core standards, which an NQT will be required to meet fully by the end of the induction period.

There is mutual recognition of QTS between Wales and England, such that the QTS gained in Wales is fully recognised in England and beyond. If QTS is acquired in England, the person can teach in Wales. Similarly, if QTS is acquired via an employment-based training scheme it is recognised in both countries. All newly qualified teachers in Scotland are required to complete a period of probationary teaching service before being awarded full registration as a teacher with the General Teaching Council for Scotland (GTCS), implemented for the first time in August 2002 as a result of recommendations made in the McCrone Report ('A Teaching Profession for the 21st Century'). Research by the Professional Association of Teachers (PAT) notes that the induction system provides for a guaranteed one-year training place for probationary teachers in Scotland, which brings peace of mind and assurance of continued work in the profession for many new teachers; for others, there remains the challenge of obtaining a permanent post at the end of the induction year. Currently, no such agreement is in place for NQTs in England and Wales. However, there is anecdotal evidence indicating that a guaranteed induction year in Scotland is not necessarily good for the profession overall as it provides a 'back door route' into a permanent job for some who may not succeed through the usual recruitment process. By contrast, in order to gain some teaching experience, many NQTs in Wales and England take on supply work, without any assurance from their school or local authority that this work will contribute to their induction period (PAT 2007). In Northern Ireland, an NQT is assessed by his or her mentor/head of department or possibly by the head teacher. In Northern Ireland, arrangements are made for 'beginning teachers' to undertake a one-year induction period at the start of their careers. The induction year and early professional development are essential phases of the integrated, competence-based approach of initial and early teacher education.

To successfully complete the induction year standards, new teachers must seek and use opportunities to work collaboratively with colleagues to raise standards by sharing effective practice in the school; show a commitment to their professional development by identifying areas in which they need to improve their professional knowledge, understanding and practice in order to teach more effectively in their current post; and demonstrate increasing responsibility and professional competence in their teaching and when working with other adults, including parents. A new teacher needs to be able to demonstrate competence in planning, teaching, class management, monitoring, assessing, recording and reporting, and take close account of the needs of individual children. There are also demands made of new teachers with regard to implementing school policies (such as dealing with bullying and racial harassment) and taking responsibility for their own professional development.

As part of a new teacher's development, a fellow staff member is allocated as mentor (officially known as the *induction tutor* or *teacher tutor* in Northern Ireland). Jonson (2008) emphasises that the tutor must possess high-quality mentoring skills, such as demonstration teaching, positive observation and feedback, informal communication, role modelling and providing direct assistance. In a larger primary school the induction tutor is likely to be a senior teacher; in a smaller school it may be the deputy head or head teacher. In addition to offering general advice and encouragement, the tutor encourages the new teacher to contribute to working parties and visit other local schools to enhance his or her experience of primary education. The induction tutor is also available to offer advice about diverse aspects of school life, such as time management, handling paperwork, dealing with troublesome children, relating to parents and maintaining a reasonable work/home balance (see Bubb 2007).

NQTs will not normally be expected to endure excessive demands by (say) having to take a very large class or a group of particularly difficult pupils. They should be given opportunities to gain wider experience by working alongside colleagues, observing successful teachers at work and attending courses to enhance their knowledge and understanding of primary education issues and practices. Jacklin *et al.* (2006) note that new teachers have particular concerns about dealing with parents and deep anxieties about the possibility that a parent might complain about the quality of their teaching. However, many of these concerns fade during the year as the new teacher gains confidence and learns from the emotional and psychological demands attached to experience of parents' evenings.

Sources

Bubb, S. (2007) *Successful Induction for New Teachers*, London: Paul Chapman.

Hayes, D. (2000) *The Handbook for NQTs (Primary)*, London: David Fulton.

Jacklin, A., Griffiths, V. and Robinson, C. (2006) *Beginning Primary Teaching: Moving beyond survival*, Maidenhead: Open University Press.

Jonson, K.F. (2008) *Being an Effective Mentor: How to help beginning teachers succeed*, London: Corwin Press.

PAT (2007) *Comparative Study of the Induction Period Placements for Newly Qualified Teachers in England, Scotland and Wales*, Derby: Professional Association of Teachers.

INFANTS

See also: juniors, key stages, reception

An infant school is a British school for children between the ages of five and seven years, after which they transfer to the 'juniors'. The first year of infant school for children aged five years of age is called the reception year. In recent years the use of 'infant' to describe a child attending an infant school has been largely superseded by the use of 'key stage 1 pupil'. Although most schools in England and Wales are primary schools for children from five to eleven years, larger schools are sometimes divided into infant and junior departments for organisational purposes. Where separate infant and junior schools exist in close proximity, there is normally close liaison between staff in the two schools to try and ensure continuity of learning when children transfer from the one school to the other.

INFORMATION TECHNOLOGY

See also: collaboration in learning, computer suite, core subjects, cross-curriculum, curriculum, geography, interactive whiteboard, literacy, mathematics, reporting, writing

Information and communication technology (ICT) is now an integral part of the curriculum and considered one of the core subjects. At one time it was restricted to secondary schools as an element of what was termed 'computer studies'; however, ICT is now taught to children from the reception class (five-year-olds) onwards. In ICT, educators view the 'technology' aspect as relatively less important than the 'information and communication' side. Whereas, technology changes over time, the concepts of handling data and converting it into information are largely constant. The main thrust of the learning is finding things out; developing ideas and making things happen; exchanging and sharing information; and reviewing, modifying and evaluating work as it progresses.

In addition to a desktop computer, teaching areas in nearly all schools contain an interactive whiteboard (IWB) that is, in effect, a computerised screen that can be operated from the computer or by physically touching the board. Many teachers also keep a digital camera and DVD recorder in the classroom. Most primary schools also have a dedicated room for ICT, usually known as the ICT or computer 'suite' where the whole class can be taught how to master basic skills, utilise software programs and network their computers. In addition, some schools have wireless 'hotspots' that can be used throughout the school, thereby allowing greater flexibility in using the equipment at various points in the building. It is normal in all but the smallest schools to have a member of staff with the expertise and time to deal with technical problems as they arise. See BECTA (2007) for more information about policy development.

During the early stages of primary education, the emphasis is on getting children familiar with the technology, handling the equipment, becoming comfortable with its use by following a specific scheme of work and using dedicated software for completing particular tasks. As they move through primary school, pupils are taught how to use various programs for a particular task and given opportunities to practice. They may, for instance, present their findings from an investigation using several forms of information, such as pictures, graphics and text. Extensive use is made of basic software packages with sounds and animation for story writing, sharing research and presenting information (see Loveless 2009). Staff and pupils might work collaboratively on a variety of challenging multimedia projects, such as creating an animated film or using spreadsheets to enter data emerging from a numeracy project. More ambitious schools promote links with pupils from neighbouring schools or further afield and train children to establish their own web sites. Teachers and administrative staff use ICT to record pupil progress, complete reports to parents, monitor attendance and summarise test results diagrammatically.

In planning how to teach ICT, some schools opt for a cross-curricular delivery model, whereby the subject leaders integrate the ICT learning objectives into the schemes of work for each subject (e.g. geography) – an

208

option that requires teachers to identify and assess learning objectives for ICT in addition to the single-subject ones. From a single-subject perspective, ICT is most frequently used to enhance literacy and mathematics teaching (see Rudd and Tyldesley 2006; English 2006).

Sources

BECTA (2007) *How to Develop a Primary School ICT policy*, on-line at http://schools.becta.org.uk

English, R. (2006) *Mathematics and ICT in the Primary School*, London: David Fulton.

Loveless, A. (2009) *ICT in the Primary School*, Maidenhead: Open University Press.

Rudd, A. and Tyldesley, A. (2006) *Literacy and ICT in the Primary School*, London: David Fulton.

INITIAL TEACHING ALPHABET

See also: alphabet, capital letters, dyslexia, lower case letters, spelling

The Initial Teaching Alphabet (ITA) was designed by Sir James Pitman, the grandson of the man who devised Pitman's shorthand, to help young children learn to read more quickly. It was introduced into a number of English schools in 1961. The system was soon adopted by some schools in the United States and Australia. ITA uses the twenty-six letters of the standard Roman alphabet plus a further fourteen characters to represent sounds such as 'oo' and 'th'. In total it has forty-four lower case letters, each with one sound value. Sentences written in ITA are all in lower case. As about 13 per cent of English words are not spelt the way they sound, the system purported to aid children – especially those with dyslexia – and end illiteracy by providing children with a logical spelling system in which words were made up of speech sounds. Once children reach seven years old they have to revert to the standard alphabet and conventional spellings.

A key problem in using ITA proved to be the fact that it is based on 'received pronunciation' (sometimes referred to as 'the queen's English') so people with accents and dialects find it difficult to decipher. The lack of published material using ITA, together with difficulties in making the transition to the traditional orthography at age seven, created severe problems in reading and spelling, and was a principal reason for rejection of the system by the vast majority of educators during the late 1970s. It is interesting to note that an ITA Association existed in Australia until the mid-1990s.

Sources

Omniglot, *Pitman Initial Teaching Alphabet*, on-line at www.omniglot.com/writing/ita.htm

INSPECTIONS

See also: English as an additional language, equal opportunities, minority ethnic groups, new entrants, nursery schools, Office for Standards in Education, special educational needs

In the United Kingdom, government inspections regulate education provision in all settings from child-minding through nursery, school and eventually to higher forms of education at colleges and universities, aiming to help learners of all ages to achieve the highest possible standards. In England and Wales, the formal mechanism for externally imposed inspections is through OFSTED (known as 'Office for Standards in Education', though in fact renamed 'Office for Standards in Education, Children's Services and Skills' in 2008) whose purpose is to raise the aspirations of teachers and learners and contribute to the long-term achievement of providing better life chances for all concerned, in the belief that educational, economic and social well-being is a necessary prerequisite for success nationally. OFSTED pledges to report fairly and truthfully, listen to service users and providers, and communicate its findings with service providers through to policy-makers. It reports directly to Parliament and to the Lord Chancellor about children and family courts administration; it does not, however, formally report directly to government ministers, though they certainly use the results of its reports for political ends. In Scotland, a similar role is provided by HM Inspectorate; and in Northern Ireland by the Department of Education's Education and Training Inspectorate, commonly referred to as 'The Inspectorate'. OFSTED inspectors use a four-point grading system for all inspection grades:

Grade 1 outstanding
Grade 2 good
Grade 3 satisfactory
Grade 4 inadequate

In addition to grading the teaching and learning sessions that are observed, the four-point grading scale is used for all grades that are given during inspection, including those for areas of learning, contributory areas of learning, all leadership and management grades, and the grade for overall effectiveness. The use of 'satisfactory' has gradually and rather oddly become interpreted as 'not very satisfactory'; only the top two grades constitute a truly successful outcome.

Although the main function of every school inspection is to judge the quality of teaching and learning, it also gathers statistics about levels of pupil mobility, the identity and proportion of minority ethnic groups represented in the school – including pupils from refugee and Gypsy or traveller families – and the number of pupils for whom English is an additional language or are still at an early stage of learning English. Inspectors evaluate how teachers promote equality of opportunity by finding out if the children are treated with respect and their contributions are valued and encouraged, and if teaching methods and resources are without bias and are properly matched to meeting the needs of all pupils.

Inspectors are also interested in the effectiveness of the arrangements that a school makes for inducting new children into the procedures and working habits of the school (especially brand new entrants). The curriculum has to ensure equality of access and opportunity for all pupils and take account of pupils' cultural and religious beliefs, diverse ethnic backgrounds, special educational needs, disabilities; and of gifted and talented children. Inspectors also ascertain how a school will seek, value and act upon pupils' views and how well it works in partnership with parents, other schools and the community.

The nature of school inspection has inevitably been the focal point for considerable debate and scrutiny. Fielding (2002) described the then inspection arrangements as a betrayal of democracy and pointed out the differences between the inspectoral perspective of 'schooling as performance' and the need for agenda that emphasised the 'education as exploration' agenda. A report by the independent think-tank, Civitas, the institute for the study of civil society, cast doubts over the reliability of the verdicts handed down by OFSTED (Civitas 2008). The report claimed that inspectors relied too heavily on test and exam performance data to make judgements and claimed that some inspectors were using out-of-date information. A primary head teacher from East London was quoted as saying that inspections 'currently help to create a culture of fear in our most vulnerable schools: the very schools that need the most encouragement and support'.

Owing to complaints that inspections were causing too much stress among staff due to the length of time between receiving news of the pending inspection and its taking place – often running into many months – notice times were shortened considerably. A criticism of inspections, whatever the notice given or duration, is that there appears to be a tendency that the most efficient schools (e.g. paperwork in order; procedurally exact; precision in following the curriculum) are necessarily deemed the most effective. There is also some annoyance that an improving school that is 'in transition' is allocated grades without adequate acknowledgement of its progress. On the other hand, inspections are an opportunity to commend publicly successful schools and their staffs. It is fair to claim that most teachers would happily forgo the official praise if they could be spared the stress of inspections (see Jeffrey and Woods 1997; Troman and Woods 2001).

Sources

Civitas (2008) *Inspecting the Inspectorate*, London: Civitas.

Fielding, M. (2002) 'OFSTED, inspection and the betrayal of democracy', *Journal of Philosophy of Education*, 35 (4), 695–709.

Jeffrey, B. and Woods, P. (1997) *Testing Teachers: The effects of inspections on primary teachers*, London: Routledge.

QCA: *What School Inspectors Look For*, on-line at www.qca.org.uk/qca_7283.aspx

Troman, G. and Woods, P. (2001) *Primary Teachers' Stress*, London: Routledge.

INSTRUCTION

See also: computers in school, discipline, effectiveness, information technology, interactive whiteboard, questions and questioning, teaching methods

The word 'instruction' is not often used in primary education because of its negative association with formality and regimented learning. Nevertheless, instruction is an essential component of effective teaching and a necessary skill for every teacher, both in learning and in maintaining discipline. As a component of learning, instruction takes a variety of forms: explanation, exposition and demonstration. *Explanation* is a method by which a teacher offers information, explores situations and justifies decisions or positions in a rational, structured manner. It is a technique that frequently employs examples to illustrate key points. Explanations take account of the age of the children and teachers adjust their language and terminology accordingly, such that children are given time to absorb what is

said, think about the implications and ask questions of clarification. Like all good teaching, explanations build on the children's existing knowledge and understanding.

Exposition is a more complex form of explanation, involving graphic illustrations, critique or commentary on an aspect of work or a specific occurrence. Exposition is literally 'exposing' or revealing a situation or value position as viewed from a variety of perspectives. During exposition, teachers use persuasion, project their personalities into what they say and often exhibit a little flamboyance. For instance, an exposition to older primary children might highlight the harmful exploitation of indigenous populations. In this case, illustrations may include statistical details of economies before and after foreign intervention and a critique of the benefits and losses that accrued. The teacher might encourage the children to raise their own questions after carefully considering the issues. With younger children, an exposition might deal with issues of road safety, healthy eating or moral issues such as kindness.

Demonstration includes elements of exposition but makes use of more varied resources and equipment, together with presentations of the techniques, skills or procedures associated with the task. For instance, a teacher may demonstrate the correct handling and techniques associated with a variety of percussion instruments or the way to access an index or employ strategies in a sport. Demonstration depends on the teacher having a firm grasp of the processes and able to show them to the pupil audience at the same time as talking to them about the conceptual or practical procedures involved.

Pupils need help from adults to distinguish between instructional and invitational comments. Thus, the instructional comment anticipates compliance, whereas the invitational comment is a recommendation rather than a command. Inexperienced teachers sometimes present children with a choice when they intend to project a command and find that they have to revert to a formal instruction after initially using an invitation. It is possible for what is intended as a command to end up sounding like a choice or an aspiration. For example, there is a significant difference between statements such as 'Can you sit still, please?' (choice) and 'I would be pleased if you sat still' (aspiration) and 'Please put your pencil down and sit still' (command).

Primary teachers make increasing use of information technology to aid instruction, notably *interactive whiteboards* that provide access to the Internet and in-school computer systems. The technology allows teachers to draw from a wide range of information, including charts, diagrams, photographs and other data, and also to display an example of a pupil's work on screen for the attention of the whole class (by employing a digital camera). Children's work that would have been erased using a conventional board can be saved on the computer for future use.

INTEGRATED DAY

See also: English, enquiry, instruction, mathematics, monitoring, National Curriculum, recording, tests and testing, time allocation in lessons, topic work

An integrated day is a way of structuring learning with few timetable constraints, minimal didactic teaching and opportunity for groups of children to pursue different activities concurrently, though mathematics, English and physical education are still taught as separate subjects. The integrated day is commonly associated with topic work and at one time was commonly used by primary teachers; however, the demands of a national curriculum and associated testing now limit it to work among the very youngest pupils. Unlike formal teaching situations that are dominated by systematic instruction and where teachers make the vast majority of decisions about lesson content, tasks and learning outcomes, an integrated day permits

pupils more choice about what they learn and how they learn it. Instead of the closely monitored lessons with a prescribed internal lesson structure and specified learning objectives, the loosely organised system allows pupils to follow a variety of lines of enquiry across different subject areas. The teacher establishes the broad parameters of study in advance, but children's spontaneous interests and 'need to know' are accommodated and encouraged. The advantages associated with the integrated day include the chance to give pupils sufficient time to explore issues, to work at their own pace and pursue more directly what interests them about the topic ('enquiry-based learning'). Because teachers do not lead through the lesson step by step, they are free to monitor pupil progress, offer advice and concentrate on individual needs. The disadvantages associated with an integrated day include ensuring that resources are available to meet every contingency, the need to maintain detailed records to keep track of pupil progress, and checking that during the day (or days) a child is experiencing a wide range of learning opportunities in sufficient depth.

INTEGRATED LEARNING

See also: creativity, cross-curriculum, curriculum, knowledge, learning objectives, thematic learning

Most primary school timetables, especially for older children, are organised along subject-specific lines. However, over recent years there has been a gradual but perceptible move towards organising the curriculum along thematically integrated lines; that is, with reference to specific themes that incorporate two or more subject areas (e.g. art & design and geography). This trend has generally been more evident in Scotland and Northern Ireland than in England and Wales, though an emphasis on 'creativity' in teaching and learning has facilitated re-engagement with cross-curricular practices that were commonplace before the introduction of the National Curriculum. In doing so, a number of issues have had to be considered by primary educators, not least the tension between offering pupils freedom to roam across subject boundaries, and imposing a curriculum structure to ensure consistency and compliance with government requirements. Teachers find that an ideal situation is one in which there is equilibrium between two things; first, establishing predetermined learning objectives (what the teacher hopes the children will learn); second, permitting pupil initiatives and preferences that may lead to unanticipated learning outcomes.

Curriculum integration has been criticised as resulting in more random learning associated with the heady days of the topic and project work era during the 1960s and 1970s, but experience shows that children respond positively to a 'connected' approach, not least because it allows them to view learning as a whole and not as isolated, unrelated components. Indeed, Lipson *et al.* (1993) argue that an integrated knowledge base (i.e. spanning subjects) leads to faster retrieval of information and multiple perspectives lead to a more integrated knowledge base, encourage depth and breadth in learning, promote positive attitudes and provide more quality time for curriculum exploration. Similarly, Lake (2001) points to the many examples of teachers who link subject areas and provide meaningful learning experiences that develop skills and knowledge, while leading to an understanding of conceptual relationships between the different curriculum elements.

Sources

Lake, K. (2001) *Integrated Curriculum*, School Improvement Research Series, issue 16, on-line at www.nwrel.org/scpd/sirs/8/c016.html
Lipson, M., Valencia, S., Wixson, K. and Peters, C. (1993) 'Integration and thematic teaching: Integration to improve teaching and learning', *Language Arts*, 70 (4), 252–64.

INTELLIGENCE

See also: art, communication, Intelligence Quotient, kinaesthetic learning, multiple intelligences, music, oracy, outdoor education, philosophy for children, stereotyping

For many years the notion of 'intelligence' was dominated by the Intelligence Quotient (IQ) and it is still commonplace to hear reference to people as having a high or low IQ as an indicator of their brainpower and general competence. The work of Howard Gardner has been influential in alerting educators that it is unwise to use a single measure of intelligence from which to draw conclusions about an individual's competence and potential, but rather to think of a range of 'intelligences'; that is, *multiple intelligences* (Gardner 1983, 1991; 1993; 1999). Gardner views intelligence as the capacity to solve problems or to fashion products that are valued in one or more cultural settings (Gardner and Hatch 1989) and initially formulated a list of seven intelligences (an eighth category, Naturalistic Intelligence was added later). The first two categories, especially, have been incorporated into school education; the next three are usually associated with the more creative arts; and the final two are what Gardner referred to as 'personal intelligences'. Thus:

Linguistic intelligence that involves sensitivity to spoken and written language, the ability to learn languages and the capacity to use language to accomplish certain goals.

Logical-mathematical intelligence that consists of the capacity to analyse problems logically, carry out mathematical operations and investigate issues scientifically.

Musical intelligence runs almost parallel to linguistic intelligence and involves skill in the performance, composition and appreciation of musical patterns. It encompasses the capacity to recognise and compose musical pitches, tones and rhythms.

Bodily-kinaesthetic intelligence entails the potential of using one's whole body or parts of the body to solve problems and use mental abilities to coordinate bodily movements.

Spatial intelligence involves the potential to recognise and use the patterns of wide space and more confined areas.

Interpersonal intelligence is concerned with the capacity to understand the intentions, motivations and desires of other people, facilitating the ability to work effectively with others.

Intrapersonal intelligence entails the capacity to understand oneself, to appreciate one's feelings, fears and motivations.

Most theories of intelligence assume that intelligences simply exist in the head and in the brain and can be measured reliably, independent of context. It has become increasingly evident, however, that intelligence cannot be understood or measured with accuracy while it is considered independent of the particular contexts in which an individual lives, works and plays; and also of the opportunities and values provided by that situation.

Garnett (2005) interprets the original seven forms of intelligence as described by Gardner (Naturalistic Intelligence and Existential/Philosophical Intelligence were added to the list later) with regard to the ways in which the possession of such an 'intelligence' can assist pupils' learning as follows:

Verbal/Linguistic intelligence: Helps pupils to communicate and make sense of the world through language.

Musical/Rhythmic intelligence: Helps pupils to create, communicate and understand meanings made out of sound.

Logical/Mathematical intelligence: Helps pupils to appreciate abstract relations, use deductive and inductive reasoning and critical thinking.

Visual/Spatial intelligence: Helps pupils perceive visual or spatial information and to create visual images from memory.

Body/Kinaesthetic intelligence: Helps pupils to use all or parts of the body to create or solve problems.

Interpersonal intelligence: Helps pupils to make and see distinctions in other people's feelings and intentions.

Intrapersonal intelligence: Helps pupils to distinguish among their own moods and feelings

Garnett goes on to offer fuller descriptions for each of the above categories, a selection from which include:

Verbal/Linguistic – reading, writing, listening and speaking ('oracy') … creating stories, using metaphors and similes, symbolism and conceptual patterning … humour, jokes, puns, play on words and the ability to quickly acquire other languages.

Musical/Rhythmic – tapping out intricate rhythms … [Pupils] might like to have soft music in the background to help them concentrate.

Logical/Mathematical – pupils with a strong leaning to this intelligence may like to develop strategies, perform experiments, reason things out, work with numbers, and explore patterns and relationships.

Visual/Spatial – pupils tend to have active imaginations and are good at expressing their ideas and thoughts through drawings, paintings, sculpture, patterns and colour schemes.

Body/Kinaesthetic – pupils like to learn through touching, physical movement, manipulating concrete objects, interacting with their environment and 'making and doing'.

Interpersonal – pupils like organising, collaborating and solving problems between people. They notice and react well to the moods of their friends.

Intrapersonal – pupils are good at taking responsibility for their own learning. They typically enjoy working alone and are more uncomfortable in groups and will not usually volunteer to make whole class contributions.

Fisher (2005) reasons that the eighth intelligence (Naturalistic) can be defined as our capacity to investigate the physical world, which enables us to find out more about the outside world in a systematic way. The ninth intelligence, which Gardner calls 'Existential Intelligence', Fisher refers to as 'Philosophical', and states that: 'It expresses itself in the ability to ask deep questions about human existence, such as the meaning of life and why we die' (p. 12). (See also under **Philosophy for children** in this book.) Fisher agrees that the concept of multiple intelligences is a contested one but that it seems to fit how humans respond to the world. He also makes the point that there may be other forms of intelligence, such as Spiritual Intelligence (a concept rejected by Gardner) that have not yet been defined. Furthermore, intelligences do not have to stand alone but can and do combine in different ways.

Gardner's work has value because it encourages us to identify a child's special capability and build on natural strengths. However, in attempting to move away from the concept of a single intelligence (the Intelligence Quotient, IQ) towards multiple intelligences, the Gardner categorisation could become equally unhelpful if it is used as an alternative labelling system for children ('stereotyping') – an approach that is quite contrary to Gardner's intentions. It is quite possible to predict a scenario in which a child will simply refuse to try in the mistaken belief that *I don't have such and such intelligence*. There is the world of difference between identifying natural strengths and ignoring the fact that weaker areas can become stronger with perseverance and application.

The theory of multiple intelligences implies that a major transformation may be required in the way schools are run and learning is organised. It suggests that teachers be trained to present their lessons in a wide variety of ways by using music, co-operative learning, art activities, role-play, multimedia, outdoor education, and promoting inner reflection, though good teachers have always employed such diversity of method.

Sources

Fisher, R. (2005) *Teaching Children to Learn*, Cheltenham: Stanley Thornes.
Gardner, H. (1983, 1993) *Frames of Mind: The theory of multiple intelligences*, New York: Basic Books.
——(1991) *The Unschooled Mind: How children think and how schools should teach*, New York: Basic Books.
——(1999) *Intelligence Reframed: Multiple intelligences for the 21st century*, New York: Basic Books.
Gardner, H. and Hatch, T. (1989) 'Multiple intelligences go to school: Educational implications of the theory of multiple intelligences', *Educational Researcher*, 18 (8), 4–9.
Garnett, S. (2005) *Using Brainpower in the Classroom*, London: Routledge.
Smith, M.K. (2002, 2008) 'Howard Gardner and multiple intelligences', *The Encyclopaedia of Informal Education*, on-line at www.infed.org/thinkers/gardner.htm

INTELLIGENCE QUOTIENT

See also: ability, differentiation, expectations, gifted and talented, intelligence, nature–nurture, personalised learning, tests and testing

In the early years of the twentieth century a French psychologist, Albert Binet, together with Theodore Simon, designed a test – to be known as the *Intelligence Quotient* – to distinguish and protect children who were deemed mentally defective, eventually published in 1904. It is claimed that IQ scores reflect general capacity for performing intellectual tasks, such as solving verbal and mathematical problems, and the average score is 100. Furthermore, about two thirds of people have about average IQ; roughly 13 per cent have what is deemed low intelligence and about 13 per cent what is deemed to be high intelligence. By the IQ measure, a very small percentage of people with an IQ below 70 (some 2.5 per cent of the population) are classified as mentally deficient and 2.5 per cent have an IQ over 140 and are classified as genius or near genius. See entry under **Gifted and talented** in this book.

Since the introduction of IQ, a view of ability as *inborn intelligence* (as opposed to acquired intelligence) has been deeply influential in education, the so-called 'nature' rather than 'nurture' view of development. According to the 'nature' view, ability is seen as a genetic inheritance: a specific amount of innate, general, cognitive power distributed across the population, which is assumed to drive learning. In other words, when a group of pupils of similar age put all their efforts into learning, differences of attainment will result according to their innate ability. According to IQ proponents, these ability labels therefore not only explain differences in outcomes but also can be used as predictors of success. As a result the notion of 'less able' and 'more able' emerge, with the inevitable result that adult expectations of the children in their care vary according to their perceived 'ability' (Hart *et al.* 2004).

Confidence in the IQ test as a reliable predictor of competence led to an artificial distinction between so-called 'academic' children and 'non-academic' children, which has tended to marginalise pupils who do not gain average or above average scores. The notion that a single test can achieve such an ambitious aim is highly suspect, to say the least, yet even today members of the public tend to use it as a yardstick to measure potential, explain inadequacy and value individuals. Indeed, Lucas (2001) even argues that all that is 'uncreative' in school can be traced back to Binet's work on IQ; thus, 'the existence of IQ tests as the benchmark for

intelligence has led to an unhelpful distinction between academic and creative arts due to the difficulty of assessing the latter' (p. 37). It is fair to say, however, that teachers in primary schools prefer to focus on each child's potential, rather than make predictions about what each child is capable of doing. In support of this eclectic position, Howard Gardner is probably foremost in claiming that until relatively recently (and to some extent even today) the word 'intelligence' has been used primarily to describe mental powers, such that individuals living in the West were referred to as intelligent if they were quick or eloquent or scientifically astute or wise (see for example Gardner 1991).

Primary educators focus much of their attention on language development and logic, sometimes at the expense of other areas, such that we greatly esteem the articulate and mathematically inclined people in our culture. However, Gardner argues that we should give equal attention to individuals who learn better by other means – for example, artists, architects, musicians, naturalists, designers, dancers, therapists, entrepreneurs, and others who may not be recognised as high achievers by traditional measures but greatly enrich the world. Gardner (1999) also points out that in other cultures, the individual who was obedient, well-behaved, quiet or equipped with magical powers may well have been referred to as intelligent.

Most primary teachers are rather suspicious of testing generally – and IQ tests in particular – because of the negative effect that low scores have on expectations of pupil achievement and the negative impact it can have on children's sense of self-worth. Nevertheless, organising for learning in most primary classrooms is based, howbeit unintentionally, on a belief that teaching can be 'bespoke tailored' to the needs of each children (see 'personalised learning'). In practice, if children are deemed to be of 'low ability', they are given specific tasks and activities appropriate to their competence; by contrast, a child deemed to be of high ability is designated more demanding work accordingly. While this practice – commonly referred to as differentiation – has a great deal of merit from an organisational perspective, teachers have to be careful that they do not classify children with labels that declare, in effect, that such-and-such a dull child will never achieve anything much, whereas the bright (gifted/talented) will achieve a lot. There is a growing body of evidence to show that intelligence can, with appropriate teaching and learning opportunities, grow and develop – a theory that directly opposes a fixed view of intelligence and 'snapshots' of progress by means of a single formal examination.

Sources

Gardner, H. (1991) *The Unschooled Mind: How children think and how schools should teach*, New York: Basic Books.

——(1999) *Intelligence in Seven Steps*, accessible on-line via New Horizons for Learning, on-line at www.newhorizons.org

Hart, S., Dixon, A., Drummond, M.J. and McIntyre, D. (2004) *Learning Without Limits*, Maidenhead: Open University Press.

Lucas, B. (2001) 'Creative teaching, teaching creatively and creative learning', in Craft, A., Jeffrey, B. and Leibling, M. (eds) *Creativity in Education*, London: Continuum.

INTERACTION

See also: body language, collaboration, communication, discipline, discussion, interactive teaching, knowledge, learning (teacher influence), literacy, mathematics, skills, understanding, visual aids

It is no exaggeration to claim that effective interaction lies at the heart of primary education and has been highlighted through approaches to teaching English (literacy) and mathematics (numeracy) by the British government during the late 1990s; see, for example, Hardman *et al.* 2003; Smith *et al.* 2004; Pratt 2006. Interaction is a broad term used to describe the numerous instances when adults in the classroom make some form of verbal or non-verbal connection ('body language') with pupils, or pupils with adults or their peers. The formality or informality varies as the circumstances dictate; for example, in a teacher-led lesson phase the interaction is normally initiated and closely controlled by the adult. By contrast, out-of-lesson interactions are frequently informal (unless firm discipline needs to be exerted) and may be initiated by adult or child. In Moyles *et al.* (2003) the authors examine the practical and theoretical aspects that are key to understanding and undertaking interactive teaching in primary classrooms. They interrogate three questions in particular: (a) What is 'interactive teaching' in primary classrooms? (b) What do primary teachers and children do to interact effectively? (c) Are there benefits in such interactions to both teaching and learning?

Johnston (2002) stresses the importance of adult–child and child–child interaction as the basis for effective early learning. She suggests that adults affect children's learning through interacting with them in two principal ways. First, an adult provides a role model for the children and shows them by example, such as demonstrating enthusiasm for a task. Second, an adult can focus the children's attention and raise issues by asking questions. Johnston underlines that by interacting with children, adults should learn alongside them, as it is important that children do not see adults as having a complete set of knowledge, understandings and skills.

The provision of direct information and instructions to children forms a key part of the interaction process. To ensure that pupils hear and understand what is said, teachers have to be clear about the information and knowledge they want to convey and to engage the children's interest as they do so. Careful sequencing of points is important, especially for less able pupils and younger children, as it offers them a framework within which they can build their understanding. There is also a limit to the amount of information that children can hold in their minds at one time; so visual aids such as a picture, chart or summary sheet are often used as memory aids.

Teachers commonly interact with pupils by asking a question, affirming the response, commenting further on the points that have been raised or alerting the children to the errors in their reasoning. Sometimes a teacher asks another child to provide an answer or offer a perspective. In the richest form of interaction, children are given an opportunity to ask questions, both to clarify what has been said and to expand the scope of their ideas.

The need to teach lessons within a given time frame means that there is often a limited amount of opportunity for child-initiated conversations; the effect of this time limitation is that adults initiate nearly all the verbal exchanges and restrict pupils' opportunities to respond. In addition, teachers have been encouraged to inject 'pace' into the sessions, reducing the opportunities for prolonged thinking. Some younger children speak slowly; others need to ponder, pause and retrace the steps of their thinking, requiring even more time to complete what they want to say. If time is absorbed by a child's extended verbal contribution, the squeeze on the remaining lesson phases becomes a serious factor in fulfilling the intended learning outcomes. Consequently, teachers do not always feel comfortable in allowing children room to pursue an argument, explore an issue or express an opinion unless it can be done succinctly, owing to the amount of curriculum content to be covered in a given time.

Teachers of younger children, in particular, often employ a 'circle-time' approach in which every child has a chance to speak and contribute in an affirming (i.e. uncritical) atmosphere. Teachers wishing to develop children's verbal competence sometimes use the strategy of 'tell a friend what you think before you tell an adult' during interactive sessions or make stronger use of collaborative work, whereby a number of children work together initially to discuss ideas and formulate suggestions that are then explored (see, for example, Johnston

2004). Hart *et al.* (2004) conclude from a series of classroom case studies that young people can constantly surprise educators by their understanding, skills and seriousness of purpose. Thus, 'given the right conditions, all young people can, with time, be enlisted as co-agents in their own learning' (p. 265).

Sources

Hardman, F., Smith, F. and Wall, K. (2003) 'Interactive whole class teaching in the National Literacy Strategy', *Cambridge Journal of Education*, 33 (2), 197–215.

Hart, S., Dixon, A., Drummond, M.J. and McIntyre, D. (2004) *Learning Without Limits*, Maidenhead: Open University Press.

Johnston, J. (2002) 'Teaching and learning in the early years', in Johnston, J., Chater, D. and Bell, D. (eds) *Teaching the Primary Curriculum*, Maidenhead: Open University.

——(2004) 'The value of exploration and discovery', *Primary Science Review*, 85, 21–23.

Moyles, J., Hargreaves, L., Merry, R., Paterson, F. and Esarte-Sarries, V. (2003) *Interactive Teaching in the Primary School*, Maidenhead: Open University Press.

Pratt, N. (2006) *Interactive Maths Teaching in the Primary School*, London: Paul Chapman.

Smith, F., Hardman, F., Wall, K. and Mroz, M. (2004) 'Interactive whole class teaching in the National Literacy and Numeracy Strategies', *British Educational Research Journal*, 30 (3), 395–411.

INTERACTIVE TEACHING

See also: answering questions, dialogue for learning, didactic teaching, discussion, literacy strategy, political involvement, scaffolding

'Interactive teaching' is a widely used, but loosely defined term, which is presented in official documents as an example of a good teaching strategy, though educators have pointed to the detrimental effects if teachers feel obliged to embrace a particular approach because it is politically derived (e.g. Merry 2004). The word 'interactive' is made up of two elements: 'inter' and 'active'. The 'inter' part represents the direct contact that takes place between two subjects (in this case, between the teacher and child); the 'active' infers that the contact involves a dynamic relationship between personalities. Interactive whole class teaching is seen as an active teaching model in which high-quality dialogue and discussion between teachers and pupils is promoted. Pupils are expected to contribute by asking questions, suggesting ideas and explaining their thinking to the rest of the group or class and demonstrating how an idea might work in practice.

High levels of interaction can place considerable strain on maintaining an orderly environment. Teachers have to strike a balance between eliciting responses and ensuring that the situation does not become disrupting. Most teachers are keen to exploit the advantages gained through interactive whole class (or large group) teaching but find it advisable to begin by using a more didactic approach and only gradually invite participation as and when they have established full authority in the situation.

Pollard (2005) suggested that the characteristics and qualities of interaction between teachers and learners can be represented in terms of a continuum of high to low adult involvement, and low to high pupil initiative. Thus:

(a) High adult involvement, low pupil initiative is 'teacher-driven', in which an adult manages pupil learning.
(b) High adult involvement, high pupil initiative is 'learning-driven', in which learning processes are highlighted.
(c) Low adult involvement, low pupil initiative is 'resource-driven', in which learning is managed through resources.
(d) Low adult involvement, high pupil initiative is 'child-driven', in which pupils take a substantial amount of responsibility for their learning.

By contrast, Kennewell and Beauchamp (2007) conceptualise interactivity in whole class teaching on a continuum depending on threee factors:

1 the degree of teacher/pupil control;
2 the nature of the interaction;

3 the nature of the scaffolding provided through dialogue.

The authors claim that the greater the degree of interactivity, the more likely are practices such as collective reflection; reflective scaffolding characterised by two-way dialogue; and active participation where there exist more opportunities for pupils to influence the direction and content of lessons.

As teachers become more confident in their teaching and get to know the children's competence and responses more completely, they adapt their approach such that across a series of sessions they increase the level of interactivity. Thus, in their first few encounters with the group or class, teachers maintain a firm grip on the proceedings, whereby children 'speak when they are spoken to', answer questions when chosen and respond to invitations for a simple acknowledgement from them (hands-up, nods, yes and no). As the teacher learns more about pupils' knowledge, capability and personalities, they invite pupil participation while still retaining a strong grip on proceedings. The degree of pupil freedom to respond and initiate is increased until the teacher has achieved a harmony between adult and pupil contributions. Some teachers worry that they might lose control or that pupils' verbal contributions will be too diverse and lose sight of the principal learning objectives. However, high pupil initiative in a whole class/large group teaching situation is not to be confused with unfettered freedom. The adult acts as moderator in monitoring the children's contributions and 'steering' the direction of learning.

It is frequently the case that inexperienced or less confident teachers, who yearn for a more egalitarian learning climate, find the practical challenge of exercising control over lively and eager youngsters too much to cope with and revert to a more teacher-directed approach ('didactic'). However, Brown and Leibling (2005), writing from a mathematics perspective, suggest that teachers should experiment with their teaching, create rather than react, and take risks rather than play safe with traditional methods.

There are occasions when a designated child is given responsibility to take a leading role in the interactive process. For instance, a chosen child answers questions from the other children about an interest, hobby or experience. In such case, the chosen child chooses on the basis of 'hands-up'. Another variation is for a chosen child to select a classmate to answer a question; once the answer is given, the child who asked the question selects another child to ask the chosen child a question, and so on.

A high level of pupil initiative makes heavy demands on a teacher but can be extremely rewarding, both in terms of the learning that takes place and also the social benefits, as children learn to take turns, listen to other points of view, evaluate comments, ask questions and enthuse about ideas. These skills do not come naturally to most children, so the teacher has to spend time beforehand and during the interaction in spelling out the rules. For a fuller discussion about teachers' understanding and professional insights about interactive teaching, see Moyles *et al.* (2003).

Sources

Brown, T. and Leibling, H. (2005) *The Really Useful Maths Book: A guide to interactive teaching*, London: Routledge.

Kennewell, S. and Beauchamp, G. (2007) 'Features of interactive whiteboards', *Learning, Media and Technology*, 32 (3), 227–41.

Merry, R. (2004) 'Are we allowed to … ? Teacher autonomy and interactive teaching in the Literacy Hour', *Education 3–13*, 32 (3), 19–23; 31.

Moyles, J., Hargreaves, L., Merry, R., Paterson, A. and Esarte-Sarries, V. (2003) *Interactive Teaching in the Primary School*, Maidenhead: Open University Press.

Pollard, A. (2005) *Reflective Teaching*, London: Continuum.

INTERACTIVE WHITEBOARD

See also: attention span, computers in school, didactic teaching, motivation for learning, teaching methods

Gage (2004) describes the interactive whiteboard (IWB) as a mix of a computer, an overhead projector and a whiteboard (or chalkboard). She describes how a computer – normally controlled by the teacher – runs an IWB and displays the same image on its large screen that appears on the computer screen. Special pens that act like a computer mouse can be used with the IWB, though a finger on the screen can also be used to operate the system. The boards have onscreen keyboards such that text can be typed directly. As IWBs link with the Internet, teachers can show information to the whole class at the same time. Many primary teachers use an IWB in conjunction with a digital camera to take pictures of children's work and show examples of these on the screen; it is also common practice to amend and annotate existing drafts of written work.

Advantages of the IWB over conventional overhead projectors include the facility to reveal portions of text piece by piece, highlight key words, and import and incorporate images, which can be saved and viewed at any time. Barber *et al.* (2007) note that IWBs are becoming increasingly common in schools and in early years settings and it is important for new teachers – indeed, all teachers – to be equipped with the necessary skills and understanding to use them effectively to enhance learning.

There are conflicting views about the value of the IWB for teaching and learning. From his extensive survey of the literature, Rudd (2008) writes that it is undoubtedly true that IWBs have been used to significantly improve and extend teaching and learning practices, through aspects such as better display facilities; better clarification and visual representation; modelling and explanation of 'difficult' concepts; engaging and motivating pupils more effectively; and helping increase attention spans and improve focus. Rudd quotes Wallace (2007) who suggests that IWBs and associated software have enabled a better connection between learners and the learning content, and enabled modelling and simulation activities to be presented more readily, with the use of boards also adding to the 'theatrical tension' within the classroom which creates a more captivating learning environment. He also refers to work by Moss et al. (2007) by claiming that their use can also support the immediate collection and analysis of pupil inputs in ways that were not previously possible.

On the other hand, Rudd's research suggests that the mere introduction of such technologies is insufficient to promote greater interactivity in the classroom and that their use may even have detrimental effects. In particular, there are concerns that some teachers who favour a didactic ('direct teaching') approach use the IWB to increase teacher control and ownership of classroom interactions and thereby as a tool for maintaining classroom order. One of Rudd's key findings is that as a presentational device, and when well used, IWBs offer a versatile and dynamic teaching and learning tool, with relative ease of use, storage and retrieval of work by teachers, which can have a potentially positive impact on teacher workloads (quoting Glover and Miller 2001 from a secondary school perspective). However, it is clear that the introduction of an IWB does not in and of itself transform existing teaching methods.

Sources

Barber, D., Cooper, L. and Meeson, G. (2007) *Learning and Teaching with Interactive Whiteboards: Primary and early years*, Exeter: Learning Matters.

Gage, J. (2004) *How to Use an Interactive Whiteboard Really Effectively in Your Primary Classroom*, London: David Fulton.

Glover, D. and Miller, D. (2001) 'Running with technology: The pedagogic impact of the large-scale introduction of interactive whiteboards in one secondary school', *Journal of Information Technology for Teacher Education*, 10 (3), 257–76.

Moss, G., Jewitt, C., Levaãiç, R., Armstrong, V., Cardini, A. and Castle, F. (2007) *The Interactive Whiteboards, Pedagogy and Pupil Performance Evaluation: An evaluation of the Schools Whiteboard Expansion (SWE) project* (London Challenge), London: Institute of Education, University of London/DfES.

Rudd, T. (2008) *Interactive Whiteboards in the Classroom*, Futurelab, on-line at www.futurelab.org.uk/events/listing/whiteboards/report

Wallace, A. (2007) Presentation at: 'Do IWBs Have a Future in the UK Classroom?', Promethean/Futurelab debate, London, 24 May.

INTERVENTION

See also: ability, attention span, classroom climate, learned helplessness, lesson organisation, monitoring, reading, teaching strategies

An integral part of a teacher's classroom work is monitoring pupil progress by keenly observing how the children are coping with the set tasks and activities, and then intervening by offering appropriate support to them. Teacher intervention in pupils' learning is necessary for any one of at least five reasons. First, the teacher's poor initial lesson introduction, organisation or resources means that further explanation is necessary. Second, poor matching between the child's ability and task difficulty results in confusion or uncertainty. Third, the child's lack of confidence creates tentativeness. Fourth, a child's failure to grasp what is required results in uncertainty about how to go about the task. Fifth, the child's lack of concentration ('attention span') necessitates regular reminders from teachers about remaining on task. The majority of pupils let a teacher know if they have concerns or questions about what they are doing. However, teachers and assistants have to develop the skill of monitoring that consists of scanning the room to gain clues about the way that children are attending to their work and the level of adult support that needs to be provided. In short, to create a caring environment and establish, maintain and evaluate a classroom climate that helps children adapt and thrive (Brehm et al. 2004).

The relationship between monitoring and intervening is fluid. Sometimes a teacher may be aware that a child is struggling but decide to delay intervening to allow opportunity for the child to think and engage with the problem. On other occasions the teacher may decide to be highly specific and tell the child precisely what must be done. Awareness of children's progress through observation of behaviour and information from their written work provide numerous insights into a child's conceptual grasp of the task, confidence in tackling the set work and, ultimately, the nature of their achievements. In this regard, all primary teachers need to be skilled observers of children and keen judges of how much support to offer.

The extent of adult intervention depends on the specificity or flexibility within the task, the teacher's knowledge of the child's willingness to persevere and how much the work has been understood. If the pupil is unwilling to persevere, it may signal a poor attitude or a weak aptitude towards learning. If pupils lack understanding, it may be that the teacher has assumed too much or failed to explain adequately. If the pupil lacks confidence, adults have a significant part in helping to build self-esteem by using praise and encouragement. If the end product is still disappointing, teachers have to give serious attention to issues of task clarity, lack of understanding, poor attitude and lack of self-confidence as they make instant judgements about the type and quality of their intervention.

Unless the occasion is a formal test in which assistance is not permitted, every teacher has to balance the importance of offering guidance to children against intervening to such an extent that the child loses ownership of the task. Consequently, part of a teacher's skill in knowing when to intervene is discerning when it is better *not* to intervene. Experienced teachers develop an aptitude for spotting events and noting pupils' comments and behaviours that require immediate attention, those that can be left for a while and those that are best ignored. Sometimes teachers find it useful to allow time for the pupil to self-correct rather than rushing in immediately, particularly if the lesson purpose is principally about allowing pupils to grapple with problems rather than providing immediate

solutions. Myhill and Warren (2005) warn that many teaching strategies or teacher–pupil interactions act as a heavy prompt or even as what they refer to as a straitjacket upon pupil learning. In particular, the teacher's emphasis upon ensuring that children are introduced to key concepts or topics sometimes means that the movement to independent learning is not achieved and the 'scaffold' becomes a means of control rather than of temporary guidance. The principle underpinning 'standing off' from children as they struggle is that they need to be taught self-sufficiency rather than promoting their over-reliance on a teacher.

Some children are happy to be told the answer by an adult instead of putting their minds to a problem. A pattern of behaviour can emerge whereby the child engages with a task, encounters difficulty and immediately asks for assistance and advice, which the teacher dutifully provides. Such dependence has been referred to as 'learned helplessness' (Seligman 1975). However, the behaviour pattern can be gradually changed, such that the child engages with the task, encounters a difficulty, thinks intently about solutions, seeks advice from a friend and only as a last resort seeks advice from an adult. However, leaving a child to flounder for too long without adult help is counter-productive if it leads to disillusionment and creates restless behaviour (Roffey and O'Reirdan 2003).

A variety of national programmes have been developed to 'intervene' if pupils are deemed to be lagging behind their peers or failing to achieve the progress of which they seem capable. Reading is especially targeted using programmes such as 'Reading Recovery' or more generally under the theme of 'reading intervention'.

Sources

Brehm, K., Doll, B. and Zucker, S. (2004) *Resilient Classrooms: Creating healthy environments for learning*, New York: Guilford Press.

Myhill, D. and Warren, P. (2005) 'Scaffolds or straitjackets? Critical moments in classroom discourse', *Educational Review*, 57 (1), 55–69.

Roffey, S. and O'Reirdan, T. (2003) *Plans for Better Behaviour in the Primary School*, London: David Fulton.

Seligman, M. (1975) *Helplessness: On depression, development and death*, San Francisco CA: Freeman Press.

INVISIBLE CHILDREN

When given a choice, it is nearly always the case that a few children will regularly choose to sit as far away from the adult in charge as they can manage; others will sit to one side, out of regular eye-line. Pye (1989) noted that in imagining an invisible triangle with the teacher located at one apex and children at the furthest corners of the carpet or room marking the other two points, those within the triangle lie in the teacher's immediate range of vision, while those outside the triangle are least visible. In practice, this means that children sitting near to the front but to each side of the teacher (and therefore out of the 'triangle') are less visible than the other pupils. Pye called children who deliberately use such strategies to keep a low profile and remain as aloof as possible from proceedings as 'invisible children'.

Sources

Pye, J. (1989) *Invisible Children*, Oxford: Oxford University Press.

ISAACS, SUSAN

See also: affective dimensions of teaching, child development, curiosity, discovery learning, early years, environmental studies, nature study, recording

Susan Isaacs (1885–1948), née Fairhurst, was an entrepreneurial infant school teacher, a philosopher, a psychologist and a practising psychoanalyst. All of these perspectives contributed to the sharpness of her perceptions about young children's behaviour and the way they learn and understand. She started her own psychoanalysis practice in 1923, being an advocate for the theories of the psychologist Sigmund Freud, and of John Dewey. Isaacs was one of the first critics of Jean Piaget's stages of child development. From 1933 to 1943 she taught at the Institute of Education, University of London.

Isaacs ran an experimental progressive school, Malting House, in Cambridge from 1924 to 1927 after answering an advertisement placed by the wealthy eccentric Englishman Geoffrey Pyke, who intended his son, David, to have a childhood and an education free of trauma and based on self-discovery and scientific enquiry. The school emphasised direct instruction and had no established curriculum. Isaacs began work at the Malting House School, located in a spacious house beside the River Cam in the centre of Cambridge, in the autumn of 1924 and stayed there until the end of 1927, when she returned to London. In the first term, there was a group of ten boys, ranging in age from 2 years 8 months to 4 years 10 months. In 1926–27, the age range was 3 years to 10 years 5 months, and in the last term covered by Isaacs' own records, there were twenty children in the group, ranging in age from 2 years 7 months to 8 years 6 months. After Pyke experienced a severe financial setback, the school finally closed at the end of 1929.

The conditions of relative freedom at Malting House took the form of an all-round lessening of the degree of inhibition of children's impulses compared to other schools or family groups. Some practical considerations, particularly for the children's safety, set a number of limits on their behaviour, but there were very few limits on physical activities and virtually no constraint on the children's verbal expression, feelings, views and questions. Children were encouraged to be more active, curious, creative, exploratory and inventive than they could have been in an ordinary school, moving freely between a large hall, four small rooms (one used largely as a science laboratory) and a large garden with animals and a fresh water aquarium (for 'environmental studies'). Isaacs and her assistants accumulated numerous anecdotal records about children's activities, language and responses during the first two years of the school's existence. These notes formed the basis for the two substantial volumes in which Isaacs documented the work of the Malting House School: *Intellectual Growth in Young Children* (1930) and *Social Development of Young Children* (1933).

In the 1930 book, Isaacs describes children's powers of discovery, reason, and thought. In the 1933 sequel, she gives a comprehensive account of their social relations: hostility and aggression, friendliness and cooperation, love and hate, guilt and shame, and their capacity for compassion and reparation. In another book, *The Children We Teach* (1932) she emphasises the interconnectedness of affect and cognition, on the supposition that children cannot be really emotionally satisfied unless they can also learn, nor really learn unless their emotional needs are met.

Sources

Drummond, M. (2000) 'Comparisons in early years education: History, fact, and fiction', *Early Childhood Research and Practice*, 2 (1), http://ecrp.uiuc.edu/v2n1/drummond.html

Gardner, D.E.M. (1969) *Susan Isaacs*, London: Methuen.

Institute of Education, London, *Isaacs, Susan Sutherland (1885–1948)*, Reference code GB 0366 SI, www.aim25.ac.uk/cgi-bin/search2?coll_id=2316&inst_id=5

Isaacs, S. (1930) *Intellectual Growth in Young Children*, London: Routledge.

——(1932) *The Children We Teach: Seven to eleven years*, University of London, Institute of Education.

——(1933) *Social Development of Young Children*, London: Routledge & Kegan Paul.

J

JANITORS

See also: caretakers

The specific definition of janitor will differ from country to country but is broadly defined as someone employed to clean and maintain a building or area. In North America a janitorial job might include the role of a building superintendent or maintenance engineer (residential building or apartment block) responsible for all aspects of keeping the building in order. In the UK, the word 'caretaker' is normally used in preference to 'janitor'.

JOB INTERVIEWS

See also: communication, class control, head teacher, information technology, motivating for learning, professional development, teaching assistants, trainee teachers

In their survey of what primary head teachers and trainee (student) teachers considered the most important characteristics exhibited by candidates on interview for a teaching post, Newton and Newton (2001) found considerable agreement between the two groups. Both the head teachers and student teachers believed that enthusiasm, interpersonal communication, and oral communication and listening skills were most significant. In addition, a good reference, the ability to write well and competence in a specialist subject were also rated highly. However, supremely, the single most important characteristic of prospective effective teachers was their ability to motivate and involve children. The head teachers also considered good class control to be very important. Knowledge of information technology was significant but less important than the other qualities that teachers need to possess to ensure that knowledge is successfully transmitted.

In the years since Newton and Newton's 2001 study, the significance of information technology has increased. Although these authors found a close match between head teachers' and student teachers' beliefs about the basic qualities needed by effective teachers, they point out that opinions about details may vary. For instance, a school may have a behaviour management policy with which the candidate, while keen on discipline, is uneasy about. In the same way, views about the best way to motivate and involve children can differ markedly. Despite these anomalies, the principle is clear. The best hope of gaining employment is for prospective primary teachers to show that they are enthusiastic about teaching, good communicators, careful listeners, knowledgeable about their subjects and how to teach them, and clear about discipline and control strategies. Prior to the job interview it is necessary for candidates to read the school prospectus carefully to understand the school's 'inner world' and priorities.

Candidates need to look carefully at their application letters because the interviewing panel nearly always ask for clarification about some points, especially about issues such as classroom environment, pupil independence, differentiation and response to individual needs and unexpected learning priorities that emerge during sessions. It is common for the panel to ask about setting pupil targets, assessing progress and recording outcomes. The candidate's attitude to other adults – assistants, colleagues and parents – is also likely to be probed to ensure that issues of partnership in learning are understood.

A panel will want to know how a candidate will ensure that children achieve their potential in learning and foster co-operation, kindness, good habits, self-discipline and creativity. The school will also have a policy or may be under pressure to incorporate a wider range of children into mainstream classrooms and the panel hopes to hear candidates being positive about the right for all children to be valued and receive the best education; the need for properly trained teaching assistants; and the provision of appropriate resources and professional development for teachers. Even with recently qualified teachers, the panel is as interested in what has already been achieved in practice, so candidates are wise to refer to instances of their classroom practice in support of their claims. Kizlik (2008) offers a range of advice about the sorts of things that new teachers should pay heed to when they are interviewed, including:

- Dressing appropriately to make a good first impression, as choice of clothing tells a lot about the person.
- Pronouncing words correctly, speaking at a sensible rate (not too fast) and avoiding the ubiquitous *like* as a form of punctuation.
- Bringing a well-organised portfolio that documents classroom work, having carefully checked all spelling and grammar.
- Being sure of what they believe about education and why they believe it.

- Having appropriate samples of technology skills, such as graphic designs, presentation software and word processing available for scrutiny if requested by the panel.
- Conveying a sense of mastery of subject content and its place in the curriculum.
- Having a discipline/classroom management system and being ready to justify it.
- Speaking clearly and directly, looking panel members in the eyes, asking relevant questions and thanking them for the opportunity to be interviewed.

The panel likes to believe that each candidate is genuinely keen to work at the school and not merely interested in getting any job in any school. A parent governor may ask about attitudes towards parents, developing contacts with them and the relationships that will be established. An older governor may ask about control and discipline or the candidate's attitude to spiritual and moral issues. If it is a religious foundation school, there are bound to be questions about life issues, personal faith commitment and willingness to embrace the school ethos.

Candidates are normally asked to teach a lesson to a group or whole class of children. If so, they will have been informed about this in advance. Observers look for good interactive skills, sound subject knowledge, a confident manner and a positive attitude. Wise candidates rehearse their teaching beforehand, either to a group of children, a sympathetic friend or 'inside the head'. The candidate is occasionally expected to give a short presentation in advance of the interview on a given education topic (e.g. fostering a love of reading; influencing colleagues to adopt a particular teaching approach; assessment for learning). The panel is not looking for an educational genius and will not be impressed by a plethora of technical terms and academic arguments. The members appreciate hearing a well-structured talk in plain language, with clear links to the implications for practice.

At one time all candidates were 'held' together in the same room and the head teacher or a designated governor would announce the panel's decision after all the interviews were concluded. In recent years it has become normal practice for each candidate to leave after the interview process is concluded and to be contacted later in the day and informed of the panel's decision. Owing to the high percentage of internal candidates appointed to vacancies, there can be a feeling among the unsuccessful candidates that the decision was a foregone conclusion; in fact, the head teacher and governors invariably select the best person for the job. See also DCSF (on-line) for further information about preparing for interviews.

Sources

DCSF, *Preparing for Interviews*, Teachernet, on-line at www.teachernet.gov.uk/teachingandlearning/library/prepforinterviews

Kizlik, B. (2008) *Things to Say and Do at that First Teaching Interview*, ADPRIMA, on-line at www.adprima.com/interview.htm

Newton, D.P. and Newton, L.D. (2001) 'Choosing and judging teachers: What heads and student teachers think matters', *Research in Education*, 66, 54–64.

JOB INTERVIEWS (LEADERSHIP POSTS)

See also: governing bodies, skills, tests and testing, workforce reforms

Candidates being interviewed for a leadership position need to prepare for questions that might arise about national testing and league tables; the relationship between senior leadership, management teams and governing bodies; workforce reform; leadership skills; and ideas about how the department, key phase or whole school can develop and prosper. Although true for all interview situations, it is essential for a leadership position to 'read' the members of the governing body panel as quickly and as accurately as possible to understand the rationale for their questions and what is dear to their hearts. Interviews are intended to identify weaknesses or shortcomings in personality, skills and achievements, and interviewers press candidates on perceived flaws and ask questions in such a way as to probe those areas. However, interviews are also a time for candidates to highlight their skills and achievements, strengths and ambitions (see DCSF on-line, *Preparing for Interviews*).

Sources

DCSF, *Preparing for Interviews*, Teachernet, on-line at www.teachernet.gov.uk/teachingandlearning/library/prepforinterviews

JOB SATISFACTION

See also: caring teachers, children, communication, curriculum, educated child, effectiveness, governors, happiness, head teacher, inspections, motivation for teaching, organising for learning, parents, pedagogy and practice, teachers' beliefs, trainee teachers

People choose to teach for many reasons, not least the pleasure that they gain from being immersed in an environment in which a dedicated group of adults work alongside children with a united, though difficult to define purpose called 'educating'. Indeed, contributors to Hayes (2007) provide convincing evidence that teaching and learning in different subject areas can be described as 'joyful'. Most of a teacher's fulfilment relies on establishing a secure, harmonious relationship with pupils; it is equally true that a critical comment from a significant person – such as a parent – can upset a teacher's sense of equilibrium and have a detrimental effect on his or her ability to teach and be innovative, as criticism usually evokes a 'play safe' approach. It is hardly surprising that teachers sometimes feel under the microscope in having to respond to so many different needs to satisfy the expectations of pupils, parents, colleagues, head teacher, governors, the community, and education inspectors. When things are going well, the approval from representatives of these groups is exhilarating; by contrast, their disapproval can bring distress and a loss of confidence. Doubts about personal competence can embed themselves in a teacher's mind, lower morale and constrain innovative practice. For this reason, peace of mind is not a cosy option for inadequate people but a vital necessity to ensure that teachers are operating at optimum efficiency and being daring rather than mundane practitioners. For trainee teachers, the same sort of factors influences their state of mind, but the class teacher and tutor (rather than the head teacher, parents and inspectors) tend to be the touchstones for reassurance.

A lot of effort has been expended in determining the reasons that lie behind people's decision to undertake a course of teacher training. A comprehensive survey by Spear *et al.* (2000) of the factors that motivate teachers found that those associated with job satisfaction were (in order of priority) the chance to work with children, relate to colleagues and develop close relations with pupils. Similarly, Shann (1998) interviewed ninety-two teachers and discovered that their relations with pupils ranked highest in terms of importance and job satisfaction. A poll by the largest teaching union in the UK, the National Union of Teachers, discovered that 97 per cent of primary teachers considered that working with children was a positive aspect of their job (Mansell 2000). Similar conclusions were reached by Tirri (1999), who found that the best interests of the child were the prevalent determinant in all categories of moral dilemmas that teachers in England faced in school. Oberski (1999) argued that newly qualified teachers were 'not so much motivated by a desire to teach as by a desire to have positive relationships with pupils' (p. 148). Some of the most recent data confirm previous research that many of the key factors that provide the initial spur to becoming and remaining as a primary teacher are rooted in caring, fulfilment and impact upon society (Moran *et al.* 2001; Hammond 2002; Thornton *et al.* 2002; Hayes 2004).

The findings referred to above are only a selection of studies demonstrating that teachers are among the groups of professions that 'identify the goals of their work with the good of humanity at large' (Katz 1995, p. 223). Indeed, Nias (1996) argues that without personal commitment teaching becomes 'unbalanced, meagre, lacking fire and in the end, therefore, unsuccessful' (p. 306) and that to take close account of its impact on staff is ultimately to safeguard children's education. In similar vein, Acker (1999) comments that 'the unguarded demonstration of a child's affection for the teacher, the emotional attachment between teacher and class, the sense that one is doing a job that counts, give teachers a sense of purpose to sustain them' (p. 4). Woods and Jeffrey (1996) explore the heart of effective teaching and conclude that 'Teaching is a matter of communicating and connecting, through the emotions, through care, trust, respect, rapport. It features a great deal of fun, excitement and enthusiasm' (p. 72).

McNess *et al.* (2003) provide an important reminder that teachers are deeply committed to the affective dimension of teaching and learning. They argue that, in the complex and difficult task that teachers undertake, there are many dimensions for practitioners to consider and negotiate. These include mastery of a curriculum area, the organisational and pedagogic skills needed to plan and assess children's learning and, crucially, social and emotional factors. Evidence from the primary assessment, curriculum and experience (PACE) project referred to by McNess and colleagues suggests that social and emotional factors have great significance for teachers. Thus, the affective dimension of teaching 'relied heavily upon joint negotiation and a close personal relationship between the teacher and the learner' (p. 248). In other words, part of the joy of good teaching is not rooted only in good subject knowledge, or even in being able to put things across systematically and clearly to the pupils, but also in empathising with learners and building effective working relations. See also Hayes (2009, part 1), for a fuller description of teacher attributes and job fulfilment.

Sources

Acker, S. (1999) *The Realities of Teachers' Work*, London: Cassell.

Hammond, M. (2002) 'Why teach? A case study investigating the decision to train to teach ICT', *Journal of Education for Teaching*, 28 (2), 135–48.

Hayes, D. (2004) 'Recruitment and retention: Insights into the motivation of primary trainee teachers in England', *Research in Education*, 71, 37–49.

——(ed.) (2007) *Joyful Teaching and Learning in the Primary School*, Exeter: Learning Matters.

——(2009) *Primary Teaching Today*, London: Routledge.

Katz, L.G. (1995) *Talks with Teachers of Young Children*, Norwood NJ: Ablex.

Mansell, W. (2000) 'Teachers feel literacy strain', *Times Educational Supplement*, 7 January.

McNess, E., Broadfoot, P. and Osborn, M. (2003), 'Is the effective compromising the affective?' *British Educational Research Journal*, 29 (2), 243–57.

Moran, A., Kilpatrick, R., Abbott, J., Dallat, J. and McClune, B. (2001), 'Training to teach: Motivating factors and implications for recruitment' *Research in Education*, 15 (1), 17–32.

Nias, J. (1996) 'Thinking about feeling', *Cambridge Journal of Education*, 26 (3), 296–306.

Oberski, L, Ford, K., Higgins, S., and Fisher, P. (1999) 'The importance of relationships in teacher education', *Journal of Education for Teaching*, 25 (2), 135–50.

Shann, M.H. (1998), 'Professional commitment and satisfaction among teachers in urban middle schools', *Journal of Educational Research*, 92 (2), 67–74.

Spear, M., Gould, K. and Lee, B. (2000) *Who Would be a Teacher?* Slough: NFER.

Thornton, M., Bricheno, P. and Reid, I. (2002) 'Students' reasons for wanting to teach in primary school', *Research in Education*, 67, 33–43.

Tirri, K. (1999) 'Teachers' perceptions of moral dilemmas at school', *Journal of Moral Education*, 28 (1), 31–47.

Woods, P. and Jeffrey, B. (1996) *Teachable Moments: The art of teaching in primary schools*, Buckingham: Open University Press.

JUNIORS

See also: infants, key stages

A junior school is the name given to the majority of schools in the UK for children between the ages of seven and eleven years, after which pupils transfer to secondary education. The word 'junior' used to apply to children attending junior schools or in the upper end of a primary school but has largely been superseded by the more formal 'key stage 2 pupil'.

K

KEY STAGES

See also: infants, juniors, National Curriculum

Since the introduction of the National Curriculum in England and Wales, coverage of the curriculum has been divided into four key stages (KS). Key stage 1 (KS1) is designed for children aged 5–7 and follows on directly after the foundation stage for children aged 3–5 years, which terminates at the end of the reception year. KS1 applies to pupils in school year 1 (5–6 years of age) and year 2 (6–7 years). The whole age range from 5–7 years – consisting of reception, year 1, year 2 – was formerly referred to as 'infants'.

Key stage 2 (KS2) is designed for children aged 7–11 years and follows KS1. The curriculum content in KS2 applies to pupils in year 3 (7–8 years), year 4 (8–9 years), year 5 (9–10 years) and year 6 (10–11 years). Children in KS2 (years 3, 4, 5, 6) were formerly referred to as 'juniors'. Most primary schools accommodate children aged between 4/5 and 11 years; a smaller percentage are infant schools for children aged between 4/5 and 7 years and separate junior schools for children aged between 7 and 11 years. Key stage 3 (KS3) and key stage 4 (KS4) are the curricula for secondary-aged pupils – KS3 for pupils aged 11–14 and KS4 for pupils aged 14–16.

Statutory examinations exist for pupils at the end of each key stage (in England), popularly known as SATs (after the original nomenclature, standard assessment tasks/tests) but more correctly referred to as National Curriculum tests. Wales, Scotland and Northern Ireland have slightly different systems but the concept of a key stage is implicit throughout the United Kingdom education system.

KINAESTHETIC LEARNERS

See also: active learning, design and technology, discovery learning, lesson organisation, mathematics, memory and memorising, nursery schools, tactile learners

It is claimed that every child learns differently and has a unique 'learning style'. All pupils are exposed to a lot of auditory (hearing) and visual (seeing) experiences, allied with an emphasis on written forms of recording (manual or computer). However, in addition to these learning preferences, most children benefit from kinaesthetic means ('pertaining to muscles and movement'): touching, feeling and experiencing the material at hand. Kinaesthetic learners learn best by moving their bodies and activating their large or small muscles; such children are the hands-on learners or 'doers' that concentrate better and learn more easily when movement is incorporated into the process. Typically, kinaesthetic learners wiggle, tap their feet and move their legs when they are sitting and often do well as performers, such as athletes, actors, or dancers.

Kinaesthetic learning and tactile learning are often viewed as being identical, though a useful distinction is to think of the tactile as involving more constrained fine-motor skills ('finger touch') and less gross-motor actions than the kinaesthetic. As kinaesthetic learners remember what they do and what they experience with their hands or bodies (movement and touch) they enjoy using tools or lessons that involve active/practical participation and can recall how to do things after they have done them once (motor memory).

It is estimated that over one third of all children are strongly kinaesthetic learners and benefit from action games, finger rhymes, role play, drama, puppets, re-arranging, cutting and pasting, lacing, card games, board games, learning activities involving clapping, tapping, hopping, jumping and nodding. Experience shows that the vast majority of children enter nursery education as kinaesthetic and tactile learners, moving and touching everything as they learn. Midway through primary school, some pupils show a tendency to learn best by reference to visual stimuli. In the upper end of the primary phase, some pupils, especially girls, become more strongly auditory learners. However, many males maintain an orientation towards kinaesthetic and tactile strengths throughout their adult years.

Kinaesthetic learners are most successful when totally engaged with the learning ('active learning'), so acquire information fastest when participating in a construction activity, drama presentation, field trip, games or other physical activity. Children with a strong kinaesthetic orientation are also the ones who may be wrongly diagnosed as suffering from attention-deficit hyperactivity disorder (ADHD). The reason for being labelled in this way is that their method of focusing on the task is often mistaken for not paying attention. These children like getting up and acting something out rather than explaining it verbally or committing it to paper; they also need to move their bodies or move around the room while thinking something through – a practice that can be distracting to everyone else. The children are perceived by adults as exhibiting bad behaviour and get into trouble as a result.

Owing to the high numbers of kinaesthetic learners, many teachers argue for more 'hands-on' learning opportunities across the curriculum, not merely in the 'practical' subjects like design and technology (Glynn 2001). Thus, the lesson introduction might involve an action game or physical responses from pupils, so that in addition to the usual 'raise a hand', children may be asked to touch their noses if they know the answer or roll their shoulders to indicate that they are still thinking. The tasks that pupils undertake can be orientated towards more discovery learning ('finding out') and investigation, as opposed to systematic paper-and-pencil exercises or discussion.

As with all 'learning styles', a kinaesthetic orientation is a preferred means and does not preclude learning through auditory, visual or any other methods. It is therefore unhelpful to label a child as a 'kinaesthetic learner' or any other single appellation but rather to note the tendency and respond accordingly. In fact, there are very few children who don't respond well to practical, participative, bodily active activities with clear verbal and/or written explanation. Walling (2006) offers suggestions about teaching writing to different kinds of learners, including those orientated towards a kinaesthetic style. Clausen-May (2005) deals with similar issues in mathematics across all age ranges.

Sources

Clausen-May, T. (2005) *Teaching Maths to Pupils with Different Learning Styles*, London: Paul Chapman.

Glynn, C. (2001) *Learning on Their Feet: A sourcebook for kinaesthetic learning across the curriculum*, Shoreham VT: Discover Writing Press.

Walling, D.R. (2006) *Teaching Writing to Visual, Auditory and Kinaesthetic Learners*, Thousand Oaks CA: Corwin Press.

KNOWLEDGE

See also: child development, dilemmas, effectiveness, learning, learning context, multiplication tables, rote learning, spelling, understanding

Knowledge has a safe ring to it but is far from easy to define. There are many different forms of knowledge, including knowledge of facts, of controversies, of situations, of procedures and of people. Knowledge of facts involves more than memorising; it needs to take account of new understanding – for instance, we now know that the earth is more or less round, not flat. Knowledge of controversies requires an awareness of the disputed information; for instance, whether or not Columbus discovered America. Knowledge of moral dilemmas demands a wide view of the relevant factors and an ability to make judgements about their significance. Knowledge of procedures is necessary when a task has to be completed or decisions made about effectiveness. Knowledge of people is needed to prosper in social situations, and so forth.

There is a lot more information available to pupils today than a generation ago, so they face both immense opportunities and challenges in negotiating the available knowledge. The fact that the amount of information in the world is estimated to double approximately every seven years has implications for curriculum content and selection. Children gradually need to gain wisdom about the use of knowledge, its appropriateness, its relevance and its application and teachers have the task of helping children to locate what they learn in social contexts or at least using case studies to exemplify the principles involved.

Although at one stage of a child's development it may be sufficient to 'know' something to be 'true', it may subsequently be appropriate to point out that things are not as straightforward as they appear. For example, seven-year-old children can be told that all objects fall towards the ground at the same rate, but eleven-year-olds also need to be aware that the principle only holds for objects over a certain density and under normal atmospheric conditions. A fifteen-year-old may be interested in the variations according to air pressure, the effect of a vacuum, and so forth. Knowledge therefore evolves and deepens with age, experience and a greater facility with language use.

Knowledge may also be thought of in terms of being transitory, such as remembering a telephone number for as long as it takes to dial it but no longer. It can be accessible, such as recalling a spelling rule for use when writing but not holding the knowledge at the forefront of thinking for regular use. It can be immediate, such as knowing a friend's name or the route to school without needing to think actively about it. Most knowledge needs to be immediately accessible, such as remembering a multiplication table to employ in solving a problem, but children sometimes remain locked in the transitory knowledge zone; they appear to have learned something during the morning lesson but cannot remember it after lunch. Sometimes the knowledge is locked into a child's recall system but cannot be accessed, either because it is too deeply stored or the child is tired or circumstances (such as stress) create a barrier to remembering. Knowledge that does not relate to previous learning is no more than mechanical repetition or 'rote learning'. For instance, a child could learn a list of Latin names off by heart and get full marks in a test, but have no idea about their meaning or significance.

Writing from an early years perspective, English (2002) notes that teachers' knowledge of children's understanding is informed by a variety of theories of cognitive development. She points to the work of the Russian psychologist Len Vygotsky, as helping us to appreciate that changes in a child's understanding are more dependent on experience than on developmental stages. Thus, children move 'from an initial understanding, which is rather vague, to a level where the learner attempts to make sense of new knowledge, connecting it with prior learning' (p. 82).

When working with children, it is helpful to think of knowledge from their perspective:

Received knowledge I know because I can repeat what you have told me.

Descriptive knowledge I know because I can tell you about it.

Explanatory knowledge I know because I can explain why it happened.

Applied knowledge I know because I can understand the implications for its use.

Walker and Soltis (1992) use the term 'knowledge in use' and identify three forms: associative, applicative and replicative. *Associative* knowledge allows links to be made with previous learning. *Replicative* knowledge is being able to remember and reproduce facts when required. *Applicative* knowledge is for use in solving questions. The authors argue that applicative knowledge is the most significant of the three because 'it requires seeing the connection between what one knows and what one wants to achieve' (p. 41). Thinking about how knowledge is used allows pupils to move from basic comprehension to being able to analyse and evaluate situations. The most powerful forms of knowledge involve higher levels of understanding that permit its use in a variety of contexts. Knowledge without understanding is merely information.

The most powerful forms of knowledge facilitate understanding across a variety of contexts rather than being restricted to the understanding that is attached to it by the learner in the present situation. For example, McKeon (2004) notes that the National Primary Strategy (DfES 2004) is encouraging schools to design broad and rich curricula that make the most of links between different areas, building on literacy and numeracy and developing speaking and listening skills and incorporating subjects such as science. Primary teachers that espouse the integrated nature of knowledge are likely to promote enquiry-based learning in which children have to apply their knowledge to solve genuine problems.

The most effective teaching incorporates both the transmission of knowledge and its application. Poulson (2001) commends the fact that numerous policies have attempted to strengthen the subject knowledge of primary teachers in Britain. However, she suggests that policy-makers should give a higher priority to developing an understanding of the relationship between tacit ('implied') and formal knowledge, and of how teachers learn.

Sources

DfES (2004) *The National Primary Strategy*, London: HMSO.

English, E. (2002) 'Teaching for understanding: Curriculum guidance for the Foundation Stage', in Newton, L.D. (ed.) *Teaching for Understanding Across the Primary Curriculum*, Clevedon: Multilingual Matters.

McKeon, F. (2004) 'Teacher autonomy and subject knowledge', *Education 3–13*, 32 (3), 32–37.

Poulson, L. (2001) 'Paradigm lost? Subject knowledge, primary teachers and education policy', *British Journal of Education Studies*, 49 (1), 40–55.

Walker, D.F. and Soltis, J.F. (1992) *Curriculum and Aims*, New York: Teachers College Press.

L

LARGE SPACE ACTIVITIES

See also: dance, design and technology, drama, organising for learning, physical education

Large space activities, such as those for physical education, dance, drama, and design and technology tasks, carry significant resource implications: adhesive tape and pots have to be distributed in advance; clay has to be accessible; tables have to be relocated, and so on. Similarly, equipment has to be checked in advance of PE lessons for safety and availability; drama properties ('props') have to be put in position; the floor space has to be cleared before a dance session; computers have to be switched on, programs set up and paper trays filled for printing. If arrangements are not in hand, the lesson stutters because the process of organising resources absorbs the time and effort that would have gone into active teaching, the exception being when the involvement of the children in the organisation forms an important part of the lesson. For example, pupils may be asked to arrange equipment or furniture as a component of their play or sort out games' resources for team activities.

LEARNED HELPLESSNESS

See also: behaviour, caring teachers, failure, friendships, gender, mealtime assistants, nurturing, pupil personality, pupil perspectives, trainee teachers

It is important for children to know that their teachers and helpers want the best for them and will do all they can to assist them in achieving it. This is different from mollycoddling children or preventing them from gaining independence and the ability to make decisions for themselves. There is often a fine line between supporting children and smothering them with kindness. To assist a child at a moment in time has the ultimate purpose of fostering independence, whereas excessive attention makes the adult feel good but does not help children to become self-sufficient. The end result of making children over-reliant on adults and negative about their own abilities is often referred to as 'learned helplessness' (LH), a term attributed to Martin Seligman (1975). The concept of 'locus of control' is important in understanding learned helplessness and relates to whether an individual believes that events depend on his or her behaviour and personality – so-called 'internal locus of control' – or on luck, chance, fate or the actions of other people – so-called 'external locus of control' (Rotter 1975). Children who are 'helpless' believe that they are powerless to prevent failure and subject to the decisions and actions of others. Gordon (2006) grimly summarises the child's condition as 'it hurts too much to try'.

McLeod (on-line) describes the purpose of a family and a sensitive school environment as a means of providing a nurturing environment that protects the children from the vicissitudes of the world while they are developing the physical, emotional and intellectual abilities to function on their own. McLeod goes on to argue that love, compassion, joy and equanimity are vital: love, so that the child opens to the world; compassion, so that the child learns not to fear suffering; joy, so that the child feels confident in his or her own abilities; and equanimity, so that the child can be free to go when he or she has matured. By contrast, if the child experiences qualified love it can trigger a fear of consequences instead of compassion; derision instead of joy; and judgement instead of equanimity. Under such circumstances, self-doubt takes hold and the child's confidence gradually collapses.

Learned helplessness leads to a reluctance in tackling challenging tasks and tentativeness at solving problems. Failure reinforces children's negative self-image and leads to passivity and an unwillingness to try again or persevere. Consequently, these 'helpless' children fall behind in academic work and often struggle with social skills and developing relationships. They feel incompetent and are convinced that they are unable to master new material or successfully revisit areas in which they previously experienced difficulty. Once this attitude becomes prevalent in a child (or adult) it is extremely difficult to change it to a more hopeful and positive one. In short, learned helplessness constrains learning and leads to passivity. In more chronic situations it can also lead to depression and deep pessimism (Howe 1999, see chapter 7).

If adults hear a child constantly asking for their approval and advice about every tiny nuance of the work, it can reasonably be concluded that LH has taken hold. It then takes take time, lots of reassurance and a gradual severing of the reliance link before the child is released from the effects of this suffocating condition. Remedying learned helplessness involves three strategies. First, gaining a thorough understanding of the nature and depth of the problem through talking to the child and developing trust. Second, helping children to discover the root beliefs that cause their self-defeating strategies and the distorted perceptions these beliefs create. Third, giving children the tools to change and refute the distorted beliefs and thereby reduce the emotional, motivational and learning deficits. Although there should be an emphasis on positive aspects of the work or situation and not on the errors, children need to know how to handle mistakes in a positive manner – a behaviour that adults can model for them. The outcome need not be perfect by adult standards but should satisfy the child concerned.

A critical part of the adult role is to provide reassurance for children, giving a clear message to them that everything is under control and that adults can be relied upon to be fair, supportive and firm. Such a positive picture may not be every child's experience of adults outside school and it may be a little time before some of them are convinced. Perversely, some older children seem to feel that certain adults, particularly those whom they perceive as powerless (notably mealtime assistants, cleaners and some trainee teachers) can be treated casually, and mischievous youngsters find great pleasure in pushing their patience to the limit. Thankfully, the majority of primary-age children are willing to trust adults, enthusiastically enjoy school and do their best. For the adults concerned, this is a privilege and a joy.

Sources

Gordon, M. (2006) 'The turned off child', Oregon LDA, on-line at www.ldaor.org/Newsletter-Fall 2006.html

Howe, M.J.A. (1999) *A Teacher's Guide to the Psychology of Learning*, London: Blackwell.

McLeod, K. 'Learned Helplessness', on-line at www.unfetteredmind.com/articles/helplessness.php

Rotter, J. (1975) 'Some problems and misconceptions related to the construct of internal versus external control of reinforcement', Journal of *Consulting and Clinical Psychology*, 43, 56–67.

Seligman, M. (1975) *Helplessness: On depression, development and death*, San Francisco CA: Freeman.

LEARNING

See also: brain function, enquiry, General Teaching Councils, imagination, information, knowledge, learning context, learning (teacher influence), lesson plans, memory and memorising, meta-learning, motivation for learning, pupil perspectives, retention in learning, skills, special educational needs, tests and testing, understanding

Learning is a word that rolls easily off the tongue but it is difficult to define and explain the processes that combine to produce a learning outcome (i.e. to say that a thing has been learned). Indeed, one of the main challenges for primary educators is to know when it is appropriate to claim that a child has 'fully' learned something. Children take differing amounts of time to grasp concepts and remember facts, and most children do not learn in a smooth, uninterrupted way but are like the tide moving up the beach in a series of waves; sometimes gaining ground, sometimes slipping back, occasionally surging forward. Learning can be variously described as the process that helps the learner to make sense of information and create something new from it; transform current understanding into a more elucidated form; utilise the knowledge and insights gained from earlier experiences to respond effectively to new ones; and move away from the security of certain knowledge to explore less well familiar areas. Robson (2006) argues that it is difficult to differentiate between learning and thinking, though she claims that learning is a consequence of thinking. She also suggests that it is necessary to take a broad view of learning, 'which includes use of the imagination, a playful disposition, persistence and the ability to learn with and from others' (p. 3). Children are not merely recipients of learning but active partners and initiators of it.

Human learning is therefore highly complex and comes in a variety of forms, sometimes involving the intellect, sometimes the emotions, and sometimes both. There is, however, general agreement that the process benefits from well-informed and capable teaching. Although it is natural to emphasise the importance of making sure that children have learned something after exposure to a planned educational experience, the nature of learning can vary considerably from child to child. For instance:

- learned for now but likely to be forgotten very soon;
- learned, never to be forgotten;
- learned within defined limits;
- learned but requiring updating and reinforcement to be secure;
- learned and understood so thoroughly that the learning can be used successfully in different situations.

Thus it is possible for children to learn how to use a piece of computer software early in the school year but without regular practice they are likely to forget the procedure quite quickly. In this case, the learning has been temporary and functional and the fourth of the above statements is relevant. Again, a child may learn how to multiply two numbers by using a certain technique but flounder when given the same problem in a different format. In this case, the third of the statements is relevant. The ideal is for children to have such a grasp of knowledge, skills and understanding that they can use their existing abilities to forge ahead confidently into new areas of learning, as noted in the final option above. This type of pervasive learning moves beyond the boundaries artificially imposed by the task or activity, and can be applied more widely.

Learning may be broadly described as the restricted type (functional, short-term) or the transferable type (usable in different contexts). Take, for instance, the example in which children learn to use a software program. Some children will doubtless become adept at using the program and may even be called upon by the teacher to tutor other children about its functioning. However, only a proportion of the same group of well-informed children will make connections with the implications for using other, similar programs. Again, children who learn a set of spellings for a test may get them all correct, yet misspell some of the words in free writing. The aim is, of course, to ensure that children not only master the word list but can also utilise their learning in a variety of active, writing situations where spelling is only one of the required skills.

Some learning is short-term; other forms need to become embedded and for all practical purposes permanently etched in the mind (long-term memory). The child who learns lines for a drama sketch in front of the school will memorise them carefully, prompted no doubt by an anxious parent who is keen for the child to do well. This sort of learning may require repetition, frequent reminders, and a move from artificial to more natural speech as the words become familiar. A few months after the performance, the words may be largely forgotten, though odd phrases spring to mind. Contrast this temporary memorising with the ability to interpret words on a page for the purpose of reading, in which the regular use of the words in a variety of contexts (books, work sheets, text on a whiteboard, screen) will more or less ensure that they are never forgotten and can be produced at any time.

Many educators have pointed out that learning encompasses more than children satisfying the designated lesson objective (Fisher 2005). Just as children can convince themselves that they must have learned something if they get the right answer by an approved method, so teachers can slip into the same way of thinking and believe that task-completion is the primary learning goal. In fact, finishing a task may or may not involve deep learning. Too many so-called experiential lessons (enquiry-based) – notably in science – consist of little more than mechanically 'predicting' and 'testing' and 'recording' without properly engaging with the principles underpinning the work or employing problem-solving skills. MacGilchrist

(2003) makes five important points about the nature of learning that have implications for classroom practice:

1 Learning is an active process of meaning-making. Learners construct and integrate new knowledge in a way that makes sense to them.

2 Learning about learning (meta-learning) and making sense of experience is a hallmark of effective learners. Learners become increasingly aware of the thinking and learning processes that are taking place and thereby assume greater control over them.

3 The relationship between learning and performance is complex and is influenced by motivation and self-image. Some children are capable of completing tasks ('performance orientation') without thinking hard about the implications of the work and gaining personal satisfaction other than through a tick at the bottom of the page.

4 Learning involves the understanding and mastery of emotions, both personal and viewing things from other people's perspectives. Learning can be enhanced through developing a variety of social skills and a willingness to persevere and stay on task.

5 Learning is situational. The social contexts of the school and classroom are significant in promoting or inhibiting learning.

To explain the functions of learning, Bloom and his colleagues developed what came to be known as Bloom's Taxonomy in the 1950s (Bloom 1956), whereby they suggested a hierarchy of six major classes of learning, supposedly moving from simple to complex, as follows: (1) knowledge, (2) comprehension, (3) application, (4) analysis, (5) synthesis, and (6) evaluation. Despite its somewhat elementary and linear form, the taxonomy is of interest to educators when planning and teaching learning programmes or evaluating work because it offers them a rough yardstick against which to monitor the

238

level of demands that are being placed on children.

One explanation about learning that receives support from medical evidence is that different types of learning are associated with the right and left parts of the brain. The left part deals principally with language acquisition, sequences, analysis and number; it works to analyse information and responds best to structured and sequenced learning. The right hand part of the brain interprets images, looks for patterns, creates metaphors and strives to synthesise and consolidate information. Interplay between the two parts of the brain appears to be necessary for the development of deep understanding, creative expression and problem solving.

Pupil learning that consists of memory without understanding has limited value. For example, children might be systematically taught to read words correctly, recite multiplication tables or chant a religious creed, but unless they grasp their meaning and significance the depth of learning remains shallow. Learning that is purely functional, such as knowing how to subtract two numbers, has limited usefulness unless it can be employed in a genuine life situation (such as shopping). Watkins (2003) argues that characteristics of effective learning imply that the learner is (a) active and strategic; (b) skilled in cooperation, dialogue and creating knowledge with others; (c) able to develop goals and plans; and (d) monitors his or her own learning and is versatile across contexts ('different life situations'). Consequently, pupils need to reflect on their own learning as an essential ingredient in their development, assisted by talking to peers or adults. Schools that promote effective learning emphasise intrinsic (self-initiated) motivation, social relationships and an overall learning culture, in which it becomes natural to talk about learning. Watkins also argues against a 'quick fix' culture and use of instrumental strategies that merely exacerbate an already unsatisfactory situation. Instead, a more human and future-orientated approach involves substituting the word 'work' for 'learning' and considering what is worth working on.

Educators have also given a lot of attention to so-called 'learning styles' or 'learning modes' in recent years, whereby every individual is said to learn best in one of three, four or five ways, depending on different models. The interpretation involves three styles, often referred to as VAK, standing for visual learning, auditory learning and kinaesthetic learning. Visual learners are those who learn best by seeing (e.g. pictures, graphs and diagrams). Auditory learners learn best by hearing (e.g. listening to a poem). Kinaesthetic learners learn best by handling things. Some educationists separate kinaesthetic from tactile: the former referring to 'constructing' (e.g. building kits; using computer programs) and the latter emphasising 'touch' (e.g. work with clay). Yet others include a category of written learning style, in which pupils learn through expressing themselves through literacy. None of the definitions is watertight and there is a degree of overlap between them, but the basic principle is for teachers to take account of individual learning preferences.

Children learn best when they are given opportunity to use a combination of tactile senses, visual stimuli, careful listening, enquiry-based activities, conversation and paper-and-pencil exercises, supported by teacher explanation and reinforced through individual or group activities. Innovative and imaginative learners learn particularly effectively when they have opportunity to use the full range of their senses and ask questions about why things happen. Learners who are more analytical tend to process information by studying a range of possibilities closely, thinking deeply and reflecting on the issues involved, before developing their own ideas and comparing them with what they observe happening. Pragmatic learners first speculate and make suggestions before finding out if their ideas work in practice, then adjust their ideas accordingly. Dynamic learners learn best when they have a chance to experiment with ways in which they can use their present level of information and surmise about other possibilities. Teachers have to take account of these different learning preferences when they plan lessons, such that there is sufficient freedom to satisfy the innovative pupil, sufficient intellectual challenge to satisfy the analytical pupil, sufficient opportunity for practice to satisfy the pragmatic pupil and sufficient investigation to satisfy the inquisitive pupil. Teachers also have to take account of the needs of children with special educational needs (SEN) and those for whom English is not the primary tongue.

Every group of contains people with different learning preferences and teachers cannot possibly hope to recognise, process and deliver them all. They can only organise learning situations in which there is an informed diversity; that is, by varying groups, types of stimuli and challenges. For example, the stimuli can include pictures, discussions, making, doing, saying and hearing (Garnett 2005). Children then need to be given the opportunity to transfer what they have learned to new situations; this is often the acid test for whether or not deep learning has been achieved. Even if all the group or class appear to have grasped the principles and ideas, some children will retain what they have learned; others will require regular reminding and updating. However, the more that children can see the relevance and usefulness of their learning, the more likely it is that they will engage enthusiastically with the lesson content and retain what they need to know. Jeffrey and Woods (2003) enthusiastically declare that 'real learning and children's personal knowledge are encouraged through hand-on, active engagements, through role play and through generating positive feelings about learning. Learning is exciting, fun, inspiring, rewarding and motivating' (p. 8). Teachers gain this information when they get alongside children, converse with them, ask questions, allow them to respond, offer advice and explanation, and discuss the next steps in the learning process. See information from the General Teaching Council, England (GTC 2003).

Most learning is gained or enhanced by 'experiencing', for which no amount of direct teaching will substitute, such as exploring a woodland copse and absorbing its sights, scents and sounds; or a visit to a working museum. Similarly, listening to poets and authors read from their own work, enjoying practical drama, playing with construction materials, touching unusual objects and buying vegetables from a market stall, all help children to understand the world better. Children's learning is also improved through investigations in which the outcome is uncertain. For instance, science experiments, paint mixing, library searches and computer simulations all involve investigations that assist conceptual understanding, skills acquisition and factual knowledge. Some forms of pupil learning relate to the acquisition of practical skills, such as the correct use of equipment, utilising technology or accessing resource books. Other types of learning involve understanding procedures and require practice in following a sequence, such as manipulating computer software. Yet other forms of learning relate to solving problems, such as in design and technology, requiring time for ideas to be explored and practically put to use.

Learning is principally for the purpose of empowering pupils to live their lives more productively and successfully. Examination success is likely to assist this process of self-fulfilment but there is a danger that anxious teachers may see scores gained during a test as the sole yardstick of achievement. Williams and Ryan (2000) argue that teachers should view tests as an opportunity to gain information that will help to improve their teaching and raise standards; however, a wide range of other eminent educationists disagree with test results as the chief purpose of learning. For instance, Kohn (2004) argues from a US context that twenty-first century children are tested to an unprecedented extent, yet standardised test scores may even be correlated with shallow forms of learning, as pupils focus entirely on the curriculum content for the examination and neglect other learning possibilities. Smith (2006) argues that pupil empowerment is a crucial factor in learning, such that all children, including those with a special need, should be involved in decision-making at two levels. First, and principally, by contributing to decisions about the effectiveness of their own provision. Second, pupils 'can also participate in decision-making at a wider level and thus influence school policy' (p. 146).

Sources

Bloom, B.S. (ed.) (1956) *Taxonomy of Educational Objectives, the Classification of Educational Goals – Handbook I: Cognitive domain*, New York: McKay.
Fisher, R. (2005) *Teaching Children to Learn*, Cheltenham: Stanley Thornes.
Garnett, S. (2005) *Using Brainpower in the Classroom*, London: Routledge.
GTC (2003) 'Social interaction as a means of constructing learning: The impact of Lev Vygotsky's ideas on teaching and learning', on-line at www.gtce.org.uk/research/vygotskyhome.asp
Jeffrey, B. and Woods, P. (2003) *The Creative School: A framework for success, quality and effectiveness*, London: Routledge.
Kohn, A. (2004) *What Does It Mean to Be Well Educated?* Boston MA: Beacon Press.
MacGilchrist, B. (2003) 'Primary learners of the future', *Education 3–13*, 31 (3), 58–65.
Robson, S. (2006) *Developing Thinking and Understanding in Young Children*, London: Routledge.
Smith, C. (2006) 'From special needs to inclusive education', in Sharp, J., Ward, S. and Hankin, L. (eds) *Education Studies: An issues-based approach*, Exeter: Learning Matters.
Watkins, C. (2003) *Learning: A sense-maker's guide*, London: Association for Teachers and Lecturers.
Williams, J. and Ryan, J. (2000) 'National testing and the improvement of classroom teaching: Can they co-exist?' *British Educational Research Journal*, 26 (1), 49–73.

LEARNING AND TEACHER INFLUENCE

See also: discussion, encouragement and praise, interactive whiteboard, motivation for learning, thinking, visual aids

The way children learn in school is to a large extent influenced by the person and competence of the teacher. Pupils learn more productively when teachers adopt a positive attitude towards them and acknowledge that in searching for creative solutions there will be setbacks and need to be times of consolidation through repeated practice. All children benefit from being given opportunity to discuss what they are doing and where it fits into their present understanding, as regardless of how carefully presented and interesting teachers make the lesson material, little learning of note takes place unless pupils engage mentally with the subject matter and make sense of things for themselves. To do so requires that the teacher is willing to spend time teaching and encouraging children to think for themselves and does not rely too heavily on adult knowledge (Wallace and Bentley 2004). Pupils will often complete their tasks simply because they are given them to do by a teacher; but the mere completion of tasks to occupy the space of a lesson does not ensure thorough learning has occurred. The teacher's role in the process is to provide the resources, guidance and wisdom that facilitate the learning. Such teaching recognises that learning does not consist merely of the linear transfer of an adult's superior intellect to a less knowledgeable pupil, but rather children's accommodation of fresh understanding into their existing knowledge.

Learning is more likely to take place when the teacher makes expectations about the lesson clear. Children make most progress when the challenges they face are manageable and allow them to use their knowledge, skills and understanding to achieve the lesson targets and, ideally, to use their initiative to explore further. They are likely to learn best when sessions are fun and relevant. They like working with their friends where possible and respond well to an enthusiastic, committed teacher who introduces ideas in an original way through a variety of visual aids (not just the interactive whiteboard), drama, poetry, telling a story, asking a question, and so on. At the risk of being simplistic, it is fair to say that learning takes place most effectively

241

when pupils are motivated by the teacher and lesson content; and least effectively when they do not (see Howe 1999, chapter 7).

Sources

Howe, M.J.A. (1999) *A Teacher's Guide to the Psychology of Learning*, Oxford: Blackwell.
Wallace, B. and Bentley, R. (eds) (2004) *Teaching Thinking Skills Across the Middle Years*, London: David Fulton/National Association for Able Children in Education.

LEARNING CLIMATE

See also: active learning, behaviour, collaboration in learning, desks, displays, inclusion, interaction, learning context, mistakes, motivation for learning, relationships, teaching approaches

A high-quality learning climate/environment describes a situation in which motivation to learn is high, influenced by positive adult attitudes and learner disposition, and resulting in high levels of attainment. To make optimum progress, a learning climate has to be created in which mistakes are used constructively, children are encouraged to discuss their learning with adults and other pupils, and opportunities are afforded for them to explore challenging forms of learning. The highest levels of performance are achieved when teachers interact with pupils in a way that encourages them to grapple with more demanding concepts and levels of understanding than other children. By contrast, the imposition of artificial ceilings in tasks result in pupil frustration. In this regard, it is important to give close attention to pupil perspectives about the working environment (Pointon and Kershner 2000).

Le Cornu and Collins (2004) argue that pupils' participation and inclusion is related to their perceptions of themselves, the quality of their relationships in school and their feelings about the culture of the classrooms in which they work. For example, a child in class A with teacher X may do better or worse than in class B with teacher Y depending on the nature of the work and, crucially, the adult–pupil relationship. Gardner (2006) suggests ways to improve the quality of learning for all children: strategies include using puppets, verbal games involving pairs of children, role-play, rhyme and story, and visual tactile resources to create a language-rich environment and enhance learning.

When the relationship between adults and children is mutually respectful and everyone knows where the boundaries of appropriate behaviour lie, it saves having to waste time on constantly exploring what is and is not acceptable behaviour. Where children can take risks without fear of being censured and ideas can be exchanged in the certainty that they will be treated seriously, a fertile environment for innovation exists and creativity flourishes. By contrast, a learning climate where mistakes are not tolerated and boundaries are blurred leaves children feeling vulnerable and restricts their curiosity and imagination, as they spend their time acting defensively to avoid blame or recrimination (see McGrath 2000, chapter 1).

The bedrock of academic success is found in creating a learning climate in which pupils have self-confidence, feel relaxed in the company of other children in the class and enjoy an easy relationship with the teacher. Teachers facilitate positive experiences by establishing and maintaining a calm and expectant climate, within which a variety of learning approaches is encouraged. Pupils help themselves by being taught the skills of conflict resolution, collaborating, reflecting, discriminating, listening and sitting quietly. Teachers promote pupil satisfaction by ensuring that lessons are relevant, accessible, engaging and interesting, and organising the classroom such that children are so engrossed in the tasks that they have no desire to be mischievous.

A thoughtfully arranged and clean classroom in which children are helped to value the physical environment is more inviting than one with an air of disarray and dowdiness. Rooms that look cared for and give the impression that they are places where everyone can work safely and efficiently and with a sense of purpose are likely to be enhanced by interactive displays and models, with examples of good quality children's work on the walls. Some corridors are festooned with colourful motifs and stimulating pictures, all of which take considerable time and energy to produce, mount and maintain (Cooper *et al.* 1996). The vast majority of primary schools promote active learning for all pupils in a caring environment and are committed to equity, empowerment of pupils in their learning, independent thinking, high standards of work and individuality.

Sources

Cooper, H., Hegarty, P. and Simco, N. (1996) *Display in the Classroom: Principles, practice and learning theory*, London: David Fulton.

MacGrath, M. (2000) *The Art of Peaceful Teaching*, London: David Fulton.

Gardner, J. (2006) 'Children who have English as an additional language', in Knowles, G. (ed.) *Supporting Inclusive Practice*, Exeter: Learning Matters.

Le Cornu, R. and Collins, J. (2004) 'Re-emphasizing the role of affect in learning and teaching', *Pastoral Care in Education*, 22 (4), 27–33.

Pointon, P. and Kershner, R. (2000) 'Children's views of the primary classroom as an environment for working and learning', *Research in Education*, 64, 64–77.

LEARNING CONTEXT

See also: communicating, expectations, interaction, learning climate, motivation for learning, play, questions and questioning, reading, success

It is clear to anyone who works in school that learning is powerfully influenced by three factors: situation, motivation and emotion. If it were not so, we could dispense with schools and teachers and send 'electronic teaching machines' to do the job. Every learning experience is 'situational' in that it is influenced and affected by the physical and social context. For example, Clarke (2008) advises that for younger children each area of the classroom should have a purpose, so that children know where to go when they want to plan, discover, answer questions or gather information. These areas may be play-based – such as role play, small world, creative workshop, investigate, malleable play – or they may be curriculum-based; for example, writing, science, mathematics, book corner, art and craft. Thus, within the physical environment, the numerous interactions that take place daily between child and adult, and between different children, impact upon the quality of learning because (a) we learn from one another; (b) energy is generated through human interaction; and (c) mutual endeavour leads to a sense of team work and raises aspirations, sometimes through competition. Certainly, all children have the right to enjoy a rich, complex environment and one that provides a wealth of sensory experiences (Thornton and Brunton 2005).

Turner-Bisset (2003) argues that classrooms must move with the times and consider the teaching and learning needs of primary education in this century rather than those that existed in the last. On the other hand, there are some teaching and learning needs that remain unchanged across the generations, not least the need for security, affirmation and respect, set within a framework of fundamental skill acquisition (such as reading and communicating effectively) and mutually beneficial ethical and moral boundaries.

The depth of a teacher's motivation and expectations about pupil achievement make a profound difference to the way in which children approach the work. Children respond well to an adult who displays a positive attitude and belief about attainment and celebrates small successes rather than highlighting minor errors. Anning and Edwards (2003) make a direct link between children's learning and adult's learning, in that 'children learn to love learning through being with adults who also love to learn, and are themselves in context that encourage their learning' (p. 145).

Pupils' attitudes towards themselves influence the quality of learning and the impact of these emotional factors on learning is increasingly viewed as being of crucial importance. Although a degree of anticipatory tension can spur children to success, too much anxiety hinders learning. It is a common experience in classrooms that some children adopt a very positive attitude despite their limitations, while others are doubtful despite their obvious ability. There are three sets of conditions that assist the promotion of pupil confidence in learning: to feel secure; to know the rules; and to be clear about the lesson intention. The fact that children need to feel secure is particularly important when teachers are asking questions or inviting responses from the class. Timid children are unlikely to risk answering if by doing so they are met by a teacher's exasperated rebuke. Teachers who treat all answers seriously (including incorrect ones) and encourage those who try hard soon have pupils clamouring to participate; patience and understanding can transform a timid child's tentativeness into boldness. The maxim to 'have a go and find out what happens', promoted and practised within a safe environment, acts as a springboard for progress. See the contributors to Freiberg (1999) for a fuller understanding of the components of a healthy learning environment and the tools needed to improve that environment.

Sources

Anning, A. and Edwards, A. (2003) *Promoting Children's Learning from Birth to Five*, Maidenhead: Open University Press.

Clarke, J. (2008) 'Learning and thinking', *Early Years Update* (April), on-line via www.teachingexpertise.com

Freiberg, H.J. (ed.) (1999) *School Climate: Measuring, improving and sustaining healthy learning environments*, London: Routledge.

Thornton, L. and Brunton, P. (2005) *Understanding the Reggio Approach*, London: David Fulton.

Turner-Bisset, R. (2003) 'On the carpet: Changing primary teacher contexts', *Education 3–13*, 31 (3), 4–10.

LEARNING DIFFICULTIES (ORIGINS)

See also: friendships, home background and learning, motivation for learning, play, social and emotional aspects of education, special educational needs

Although learning comes relatively easy to many children, others find that they have to work hard over a long period of time before things make sense to them. Some children seem unable to master quite elementary principles and are adjudged to have special educational needs and require a considerable amount of adult help in coping with regular class work. Most playgroup leaders and nursery workers claim that they can spot children at risk early on, as judged by their poor vocabulary, difficulty socialising and solitary forms of play. It is not unusual for children who struggle academically to exhibit lack of motivation and general dissatisfaction with life. Some of these children have few friends and a tendency to exhibit erratic behaviour. In addition to academic achievement, therefore, the learning process has implications for children's emotional and social well-being. Involvement of parents is important, though a parent may struggle with similar issues to the child and require support and advice.

LEARNING OBJECTIVES

See also: discovery learning, lesson planning, motivation for learning, success

The term 'objective' in the phrase 'learning objective' derives from the root word 'object', one definition of which is an intention or target. In education parlance it has come to mean the product or outcome of a learning experience. Thus, a learning objective represents the focal point of teaching, by which the teacher organises and manages pupils' learning in such a way that they gain new or deeper levels of insight in the aspect of the subject area studied. The learning objectives form an integral part of the formal lesson planning, though in practice learning is far more sophisticated than is represented by a linear model of (a) establishing an objective, (b) teaching towards that objective, and (c) assessing how much children have learned. Popham (2004) alerts us to the fact that the terms 'goal' and 'objective' are used interchangeably, as well as synonyms like 'aims' and 'intents'. He also advises that some educators employ a much more distinctive meaning of the terms, using goal as a broad term of intent and objective to denote specific aspects of that goal.

Much of mainstream primary teaching today is underpinned by the process of identifying pupils' present state of knowledge, teaching and setting tasks with a view to improving their learning and evaluating the outcomes. However, primary education that is based on this objectives-led model of teaching and learning has to be reconciled with the well-established fact that children learn best when motivated, given some choice about their activities, encouraged to explore and investigate phenomena and use spoken language in natural settings. As a result, objectives-led teaching and the need for flexibility in learning sit uneasily together. Concerns are rooted in a belief that too much precision about the things pupils must learn leads to an unmanageable number of objectives that creates a pedestrian approach to learning if pursued laboriously.

There are three specific concerns attached to reservations about the efficacy of learning objectives. First, many objectives can only be loosely described. For instance, the intended learning outcome may be for children to understand how to employ adjectives as a means of describing nouns with greater accuracy. However, the understanding may reside at the level of knowing that adjectives are also known as add-nouns (adding to the meaning of the noun) or may involve familiarity with a range of adjectives to provide a choice when describing the noun, or may incorporate subject-specific adjectives (e.g. the *evaporating* liquid) or colloquialisms (such as 'the *cool* attitude'). Again, the concept of 'greater accuracy' in writing is a subjective judgement, requiring an understanding of audience and the meaning that is being conveyed. Consequently, what appears to be a straightforward learning objective is, in fact, sophisticated and diverse, and requires considerable skill in interpreting and managing.

The second concern associated with the identification of specific learning objectives is that it is difficult for teachers to quantify pupils' existing learning, as all tests and measures are subject to the limitations of the measure being employed. There are also many aspects of learning that defy straightforward evaluation, such as innovation, insight, wisdom and team membership. Objectives-driven learning is based on an assumption that it is not only possible to specify what children presently know but also to direct their learning so precisely that they will learn exactly what the teacher intends. The implication is that if teachers fail to discern pupils' needs precisely, they cannot possibly provide a matching set of tasks and activities to promote their learning. In fact, such precision between needs and tasks is difficult to achieve.

The third issue raised by an objectives-driven process is the fact that children are capable of learning many things over and above the intended outcomes that have not been anticipated by the teacher. By strict adherence to the approach of establishing objectives, designing work through which children attain them and monitoring their progress towards the narrowly stated objectives, teachers may inadvertently suppress or restrict unforeseen learning opportunities. Using mathematics as the example, Pratt and Berry (2007) insist that sharing the learning objectives in too much detail with children can be counterproductive, as it reduces the joy of discovery. A lot depends on the lesson purpose: if it is dominated by information and factual knowledge that can easily be defined and assessed (such as memorising key events in history) then a fixed learning objective is more relevant than if the purpose is exploratory and involves play, investigation or problem-solving, in which case the final outcome is likely to be more diverse.

The majority of children and adults have a 'product' attitude to learning. Pupils are set tasks for completion or activities to perform, and they strive to finish the work to the teacher's satisfaction. The children soon become aware that they will be rewarded with praise and approving comments from adults if they accomplish precisely what is expected of them. If children deviate from the set task, they are guided back onto the right path or scolded if they insist on pursuing their own preferences. Fisher (2005) argues that if children become obsessed with an objectives-driven agenda, they tend to display some of the following characteristics:

- Success is viewed as absolute, being either achieved totally or missed completely. There is no halfway position for such children and they become upset if they do not fulfil or exceed expectations.
- Excuses are given to explain away shortcomings in their work. Children view anything less than perfect or below the achievements of their rivals as a personal affront.
- Ability to learn certain things is seen as fixed rather than something to be improved. Children will say that they are 'no good' at some things and brilliant at others. In response to a teacher's prompting they will resist being coached or trained to get better at something.
- Difficulties dominate their thinking rather than possibilities and solutions.
- Initial failure or problems result in depression. Children with a product orientation evaluate success only in terms of achieving the objective. They do not regard the process as significant; only the end result matters.

The establishment of learning objectives offer teachers a useful means of controlling lesson content, covering the curriculum and focusing pupils' thinking on an identified area of knowledge and understanding. Objectives also facilitate closer monitoring of the curriculum because they provide a straightforward means of checking what children have learned and what remains to be learned. However, strict adherence to this approach tends to over-simplify the complex nature of learning. See Hughes (2008) for details about classroom implementation.

Sources

Fisher, R. (2005) *Teaching Children to Think*, London: Nelson Thornes.

Hughes, P. (2008) *Principles of Primary Education Study Guide*, London: David Fulton.

Popham, W.J. (2004) 'Objectives', in Flinders, D.J. and Thornton S.J. (eds) *The Curriculum Studies Reader*, London: Routledge.

Pratt, N. and Berry, J. (2007) 'The joy of mathematics', in Hayes, D. (ed.) *Joyful Teaching and Learning in the Primary School*, Exeter: Learning Matters.

LEARNING OUTCOMES

See also: assessing children's learning, curriculum, knowledge, problem solving, skills, success, understanding

A learning outcome can be defined as what is achieved by pupils, either intentionally or unintentionally, during a period of time dedicated to learning a specified curriculum content. Unless there is a specific and easily measured lesson outcome – such as whether the children can recognise a letter shape, count in tens or spell particular words – it is usually not possible or desirable to try and 'achieve' learning objectives through single sessions. Deep learning is best achieved in stages by being initiated during one lesson, developed in a subsequent lesson or lessons and concluded at a later stage after a lot of rehearsal, practice, discussion, problem solving and investigation. Evidence for success in achieving learning outcomes is provided through assessment of children's knowledge, understanding and skill acquisition, either through completion of set tasks, a formal test, questioning, observations of them at work or a combination of approaches.

LEARNING STYLES

See also: child development, discussion, dyslexia, gender, learning, reading, television, visual aids, visual auditory and kinaesthetic learning

The concept of 'learning styles', whereby every person learns best by exposure to different forms of teaching and learning opportunities, existed for some years but gained considerable impetus after David Kolb published his *Learning Styles Model* (Kolb 1984), which in turn gave rise to the experiential learning theory (ELT) and learning styles inventory (LSI). Kolb's learning styles model and experiential learning theory are recognised as fundamental concepts towards our understanding and explaining human learning behaviour, and towards helping others to learn. Kolb's learning theory sets out four distinct learning styles (or preferences), which are based on a four-stage learning cycle: (1) concrete experience, CE; (2) reflective observation, RO; (3) abstract conceptualisation, AC; (4) active experimentation, AE. The theory holds that this cycle leads to a four-type definition of learning styles, each representing the combination of two preferred styles: diverging (CE/RO); assimilating (AC/RO); converging (AC/AE); accommodating (CE/AE). Furthermore, Kolb argues that people have a preference for a certain single learning style, influenced as they pass through three stages of development: *acquisition* – birth to adolescence; *specialisation* – school and early adulthood; *integration* – mid-career to later life. He also suggests that our propensity to reconcile and successfully integrate the four

different learning styles improves as we mature through our development stages. See Given (2000) for an historical overview of learning styles.

Although in formal education it has become popular in recent years to think of learning in terms of three styles: visual, auditory and kinaesthetic (using the acronym VAK), Cook (2008) argues that there are in fact four main ways in which children learn: visual, auditory, kinaesthetic and also *tactile* (relying on touch). He claims that all children learn best – though not exclusively – through one or more of these learning channels and adults can help them to be successful by teaching each child through his or her primary learning style or learning styles. A teaching approach can be described as 'multisensory' if the method of instruction utilises all or most of these channels in each lesson. Cook describes each learning preference in terms of the characteristics listed below (slightly modified), noting that some descriptors (e.g. 'field trips') apply to more than one category. Thus:

Auditory: reading aloud; debates; panel discussions; informal discussions; interviews; lectures and speeches; recorded books; text-to-speech; plays; radio broadcasts; music and songs. In the typical classroom, auditory activities that involve reading, listening and hearing tend to dominate proceedings. Reading is classified as an auditory activity because it involves the language centre of the brain and language processing skills, which are auditory in nature. Thus, when people read, they 'hear' the words in their minds.

Visual: films, movies, DVDs and videos; television; pictures; posters; murals; maps, charts, graphs; field trips; computer software; demonstrations; drama; experiments. Cook also claims that although not all visual learners have dyslexia, all children with dyslexia are strong visual learners and will therefore learn better if the teacher uses visual teaching tools rather than relying on lecture, reading and writing. Children with dyslexia take in information through watching videos, films/movies, plays and demonstrations, and also pick up a great deal of information from their daily environment. Children with dyslexia may enter school as bright and eager learners but soon get labelled as failing because they are being taught using a preponderance of auditory methods; that is, a heavy emphasis on the printed word.

Kinaesthetic: for example, games; models; letter tiles, computer software; arts and crafts; hands-on practice; experiments; field trips.

Tactile: for example, arts and crafts; clay modelling; gardening; dressing-up; painting; sewing.

After the age of about four children take in most 'school' information through three of their senses: eyes, ears and touch. Children who prefer auditory learning usually do quite well in the school system because teacher talk is still the most prevalent form of imparting information. Children who prefer visual learning tend to do quite well in primary school, as there is an emphasis on pictures, drawing and images. The children that are most disadvantaged are the ones who prefer to learn kinaesthetically, which encompasses sense of touch and the need to move about and respond emotionally. It is no accident that the words 'touched' and 'emotions' both refer to an emotional reaction as well as to something physical. Children who swing on their chairs, fidget and are always jumping up to fetch things are not normally doing it to be naughty but rather as a necessary part of their learning. Clausen-May (2005) also points out that pupils with visual and kinaesthetic learning styles often struggle with a school curriculum that is largely based on print. In particular, children may be put off mathematics owing to the heavy reliance placed on interpreting the printed page (words, diagrams). A greater emphasis on practical work and discussion can help to alleviate some of these disadvantages.

In a consideration of learning styles, teachers have to take account of the fact that girls (usually) possess stronger verbal skills and mature more quickly than boys, who tend to have more sophisticated spatial skills. There are also differences in boys' and girls' responses to stressful situations; girls often seek support from their peers, whereas boys 'stand and fight' (see James 2007 for a full account of these and other factors). It has also been suggested that a teacher's own learning style may influence how he or she teaches, which may not be readily compatible with some pupils' learning styles. For instance, most teachers are highly literate and able to absorb the spoken word easily, whereas the pupils may or may not be so inclined.

Sources

Clausen-May, T. (2005) *Teaching Maths to Pupils with Different Learning Styles*, London: Sage.

Cook, S.L. (2008) *Learning Styles*, on-line at www.learningabledkids.com/home_school_info/learning_styles.html

Given, B.K. (2000) *Learning Styles*, Fairfax VA: Learning Forum Publications.

James, A.N. (2007) *Teaching the Male Brain: How boys think, feel and learn in school*, New York: Corwin Press.

Kolb, D. (1984) *Experiential Learning: Experience as the source of learning and development*, Englewood Cliffs NJ: Prentice Hall.

Norman, S. 'Learning and Thinking', *KVA – How Children Learn*, on-line at www.teachingexpertise.com/articles/kva-how-children-learn-621

Pritchard, A. (2005) *Ways of Learning: Learning theories and learning styles in the classroom*, London: David Fulton.

LEARNING STYLES AND TEACHING APPROACH

See also: coaching, home background and learning, home–school agreement, learning styles, teaching approach

Although VAK stands for the three 'learning styles' of visual, auditory and kinaesthetic modes, it is also helpful to consider the three as representing *teaching* approaches that must be used to exploit pupils' propensity for one form of learning or another. In so doing, teachers can plan any phase of their teaching (e.g. the introduction, task management, review of lesson, etc.) to emphasise one or more of the VAK modes, as follows:

1 The adult talks all the time and the children sit and listen (auditory).
2 The adult talks but also uses visual aids to explain or illustrate a point (auditory, visual).
3 The adult uses visual aids as the basis for teaching and refers to them regularly when talking (visual, auditory).
4 The adult talks or demonstrates a technique and invites different children to offer their ideas (interactive auditory).
5 The adult demonstrates a technique, explains its significance and invites children to step forward and assist with its working (visual, auditory, kinaesthetic).
6 The adult spends a short time explaining a task and allows maximum time for children to actively explore (auditory, kinaesthetic).
7 The adult explains the task, allows children time to actively explore it, and encourages feedback from them (auditory, kinaesthetic, auditory).

Some subject areas lend themselves to one approach more than to another; for example, science, design and technology, craft and 'shape-and-space' aspects of mathematics will normally require the application of practical skills (kinaesthetic). A teacher may want children to actively explore a theme through play or use a variety of materials in craft and provide them with considerable freedom to do so. On the other hand the teacher may organise practical activities, select the equipment and strictly define the procedures. In both cases the children would have exposure to kinaesthetic learning but their experiences would differ considerably with respect to the degree of freedom of choice and their autonomy in decision-making. Again, the study of artistic form based a well-known artist's

paintings would emphasise the visual dimension. However, a lot of teaching is dominated by an auditory teaching style – explanations, presentation of facts and questions – regardless of the subject area, to the disadvantage of children for whom this mode is less appropriate.

Teachers have to be cognisant of how 'learning styles' impinge upon the way in which teaching and learning are organised and managed. If, as claimed by some educationists, children have different styles of learning, teachers have to (a) discern the nature of this preferred style, and (b) adjust their approach to take account of the different styles. However, Franklin (2006) argues that a moment's thought shows the impossibility of organising teaching in such a way that different groups of children are divided on the basis of a preferred learning style. A more realistic approach is to enrich all the pupils' learning experiences through rehearsal and reinforcement. Bird (2006) notes the conceptual and practical difficulties facing teachers when they attempt to accommodate pupils' learning styles into classroom practice. He cites five different ways in which learning styles are categorised:

- visual, auditory, kinaesthetic/tactile;
- reflectors, activists, theorists and pragmatists;
- innovative, analytic, common sense and dynamic;
- field-dependent and field-independent;
- sequential/global; visual/verbal; sensory/intuitive; active/reflective.

Bird suggests that the implications for teachers are fourfold:

1 Using strategies to identify learning needs and subsequently provide adult assistance for children with similar needs in small groups or individually coached.
2 Ensuring that exceptionally able pupils (sometimes referred to as 'gifted and talented') are given opportunity to engage with more demanding tasks in

that subject area that stretch their capabilities.

3 Considering more imaginative ways of setting and grouping pupils; for instance, rotating pairs for different activities and intensive coaching for clusters of pupils who struggle with the same learning.

4 Paying particular attention to pupils from home backgrounds where they may not receive adequate support and encouragement.

The fourth element of provision noted above has to be handled very sensitively and may involve nothing more than a teaching assistant 'looking out' for the child and offering discrete support to complete tasks and praise to provide security and encouragement. Most schools have close links with parents whose children require special assistance in their learning or behaviour or both, and there are usually agreed policies in place for contacting and working with them, including partnership 'contracts' between home and school.

Sources

Bird, R. (2006) 'Personalised learning', *Secondary Headship*, November, 11–20.
Franklin, S. (2006) 'VAKing out learning styles', *Education 3–13*, 34 (1), 81–87.

LEARNING SUPPORT ASSISTANTS

See also: attention-deficit hyperactivity disorder, attention span, intervention, learned helplessness, literacy, numeracy, slow learners, teaching assistants

The term LSA is widely used for teaching assistants (TAs) who work in classrooms with teachers to support children with special needs, notably those with formal learning 'statements'. The needs can include specifically academic ones ('slow learners') or emotional ones (behavioural) or physical disabilities or a combination. LSAs might work with an individual child or with small groups of children – often to help them develop and strengthen their basic skills in literacy and numeracy – but in some schools they are given a wider brief. In a one-to-one situation there is a risk of the child becoming too dependent on the assistant ('learned helplessness') or, especially in the case of older primary children, feeling resentful about the constant close attention they receive that highlights their 'different' status. To combat the 'exclusive attention' factor, an LSA is sometimes deployed to oversee the work of a group of pupils, of which the special needs child is one. Pupils are most likely to require additional support at the beginning of lessons and when they move away from whole class to small group situations. Intervention is also necessary to redirect children's attention and energies when they are wandering off task, especially pupils diagnosed with attention deficit disorders and/or hyperactivity disorders.

LEFT-HANDEDNESS

See also: intelligence, Intelligence Quotient, tests and testing, writing

Teachers need to be aware of how many left-handed children there are in the class and how to help them. Resources include the availability of softer-leaded pencils, left-handed scissors, a left-handed ruler, an ergonomic left-handed mouse or a mouse set up for left-handers and a sloping board beneath paper to assist correct writing and drawing. If children sit 'side on' it may indicate that one eye is weaker than the other or that the child has a particular spatial preference. Left-handed children tend to write 'into' their bodies and may develop an awkward posture. A study by the University of Bristol (UK) of children from the University of Bristol's 'Children of the 90s' project found that left-handed children score lower in intelligence tests and about 1 per cent lower in tests throughout their school career than right-handed children (Gregg *et al.* 2008). The team compared data on each child's performance in school tests at the end of key stage 1 (age 7 years), key stage 2 (age 11 years) and key stage 3 (age 14 years) tests, as well as an Intelligence Quotient (IQ) test. Slower development is more highlighted in children for whom neither hand is dominant (so-called 'mixed-handedness'), particularly in girls. While left-handedness is no longer seen as peculiar, having to function in a world that caters principally for right-handed people still leaves left-handers handicapped in the national literacy and numeracy tests; these gaps do not diminish as children get older. Nevertheless, an interesting footnote is that in adulthood the average earnings of left-handed people are higher than for right-handed people.

Sources

Gregg, P., Propper, C. and Janke, K. (2008) *Handedness and Child Development*, Bristol: University of Bristol/ESRC/Leverhulme Trust, Working Paper 08/198.

LESSON CONTINUITY

See also: learning objectives, lesson management, lesson planning, teaching methods

Although the process of introducing the lesson, allocating tasks and evaluating outcomes during each teaching session is a necessary discipline, it is also important for teachers to take a longer-term view of the learning process. Lessons do not always fit neatly into a time slot (one hour, say) and the lesson purpose often requires more time to fulfil than a single timetabled session allows, other than at a superficial level. Continuity refers to the close relationship required between the learning objectives/intentions from lesson to lesson, when there is a discernible thread of knowledge, skills and understanding running through a series of lessons. Each new session begins by rehearsing some of the key points from the previous one. Assessment of what took place in one lesson enables the next one to be planned more accurately by using evidence about the

way that the children responded to the tasks, answered questions and completed the work. Consequently, progress in learning is reinforced from one session to the next as the threads of learning are woven together and teaching becomes more sensitive to children's needs.

Three factors have to be taken into account when planning lessons that span several sessions. First, short-term lesson objectives (per single session) have to be subsumed within the longer-term learning intentions. Second, the linked sessions must be reasonably close together to facilitate continuity – younger children in particular need regular and rapid reinforcement. Third, children who have been absent from an earlier session need opportunity to catch up. The introduction of tightly defined teaching sessions and the strong advice from school inspection reports about the importance of systematic lesson structures can deter teachers from thinking more imaginatively about the ways that learning can be organised. However, lessons that straddle a number of sessions provide the opportunity to explore ideas within a more natural and less rigid framework than attempting to cram every element into a single, artificially designated period of time.

The second type of continuity concerns 'curriculum continuity' between primary and secondary schools to minimise disruption in learning as children make the transition. Teachers in the receiving secondary school benefit from knowing what topics and texts have been covered in the 'feeder' primary schools; the skills and understanding that pupils possess; and the style of previous lessons in the subject. In theory, secondary teachers can use this knowledge to organise and present education programmes in a way that will revise previous material and take children's learning forward smoothly. Experience shows, however, that regardless of the effort that teachers at feeder and receiving schools make to ensure a seamless transition, there is an inevitable hiatus in learning as the pupils adjust to the new school situation and different teaching methods.

LESSON MANAGEMENT

See also: concluding lessons, encouragement and praise, health and safety, learning climate, lesson organisation, rewards, sanctions, success, teaching skills, time management

The concept of class management has been a consideration for teachers across generations; see, for example, Arnold (1902). If organisation is the structure that facilitates effective teaching and learning, management is the means by which it is achieved. Dean (2001) rightly insists that every teacher is a manager of learning and how teachers discharge this responsibility not only depends on what each teacher is like as a person and the relationships that are built with colleagues and children. Wragg (2001) insists that there are certain skills that teachers possess that are of paramount importance, of which class management is certainly one. Effective classroom management can be the single most influential factor in succeeding as a teacher, and is a core teaching skill that both trainee and experienced teachers should constantly be improving. The word 'management' is derived from the root 'manage', a word we use in a variety of expressions that emphasise a successful outcome. Examples of how the word is used include:

I managed to get it in on time. That is, I succeeded in meeting the deadline.

She managed the final question. That is, she had sufficient knowledge to ensure success.

He managed to control the class. That is, he had the ability to exert effective discipline in the situation.

The use of such expressions points to three different aspects of management that teachers need to take into account in their daily work: (a) time management, (b) information management, and (c) human management. The most familiar management situation for teachers is with respect to the regular organisation,

provision of resources and negotiating the direction of pupil learning during lessons. Effective lesson management ensures that pupils understand the procedures attached to the process of learning, which is made more likely when teachers are explicit with their instructions, explain precisely what is expected of the children and involve them in decisions where appropriate (Hayes 2003). Teachers improve the effectiveness of their management by starting lessons promptly, showing enthusiasm for its content, checking that pupils have the necessary information to cope with the work tasks and making resources easily available to every child. Good class management is enhanced when the lesson is appropriately paced and teachers insist upon careful work and enthuse about children's effort and successes.

Effective managing also involves taking practical considerations carefully into account, such as not keeping children sitting for too long on the carpet at the start of the lesson or organising too many messy activities at one time or working up to the last moment, thereby failing to leave sufficient time to clear up and discuss the lesson content. During the session teachers also have to ensure that they do not give too much time or attention to one group of pupils and neglect others. Although some tasks require more adult involvement than others, smooth management necessitates that teachers don't become indispensable to pupils, but rather encourage them to be independent thinkers.

Issues centred upon behaviour management are always at the top of a teacher's agenda; attention to the other aspects of lesson management mentioned above decrease the likelihood of disruption and facilitate an orderly learning climate (see Newell and Jeffery 2002; Nelson 2006; Haydn 2007). Effective lesson management therefore concerns itself with prevention of problems rather than solving them; employing appropriate teaching skills to support learning; the use of praise, rewards and sanctions; and the ongoing issue that teachers always have with determining what constitutes a suitable noise level (Barnes 2006). Management is particularly important towards the end of the lesson, as poor use of time may mean that the lesson over-runs and children have to leave the room before it is tidy or are delayed from going out to the playground or late starting the next lesson. A managed and orderly exit is essential, both from a discipline and a health and safety perspective.

Sources

Arnold, F. (1902) *Text Book of School and Class Management*, London: The Macmillan Company.

Barnes, R. (2006) *The Practical Guide to Primary Classroom Management*, London: Paul Chapman.

Dean, J. (2001) *Organising Learning in the Primary School Classroom*, London: Routledge.

Haydn, T. (2007) *Managing Pupil Behaviour*, London: Routledge.

Hayes, D. (2003) *Planning, Teaching and Class Management*, London: David Fulton.

Nelson, J. (2006) *Positive Discipline*, New York: Ballantine Books.

Newell, S. and Jeffery, D. (2002) *Behaviour Management in the Classroom: A transactional analysis approach*, London: David Fulton.

Wragg, E.C. (2001) *Class Management in the Primary School*, London: Routledge.

LESSON ORGANISATION

See also: differentiation, festivals, group work, learning climate, lessons, literacy, new entrants, numeracy, seating arrangements, teaching skills

Dean (2001) argues that children achieving their potential depends on the teacher's ability to organise children's learning; the teaching skills possessed; the ability to observe, select and present material and lead discussion; to assess and evaluate; and to reflect on one's own performance. Kelly (2006) asserts that how teachers organise their classrooms says a great deal about the way that they view children's learning:

> Colleagues, parents and, perhaps most importantly, children will read much about

what you value from those features of class-room life for which you are responsible: the areas of the curriculum you choose to link and focus on, the lessons and activities you plan, the roles you ascribe to other adults in your classroom, how you group and seat the children, the decisions you allow children to take, the resources you provide and the ways in which you make them available, your use of display and of opportunities to learn outside the classroom and school.

(p. 137)

Well-organised teaching leads to a settled learning environment ('climate') and thereby improves the learning experience for pupils and also for adults. In particular, there is a need for teachers to establish strategies for establishing clear classroom procedures and building a foundation for a successful first year with new entrants (Moran *et al.* 2009). Whole-class lessons are often associated with the formal structure of literacy or numeracy; however there are a number of other variations in organising lessons, of which six approaches are seen in primary schools. For ease of reference, these forms of organisation will be referred to as (1) linear, (2) circular, (3) staged, (4) spoked, (5) single task, and (6) stepped.

Linear organisation consists of a single whole-class introduction followed by tasks that gradually increase in difficulty as pupils work their way through them.

Circular organisation differs from linear in two important respects: (a) it relies solely on group work, and (b) it requires synchronised completion. The circular approach is used where groups are involved in working on different tasks from the same curriculum area (say, history) or tasks from different subject areas within a common theme (e.g. festivals). It is most commonly used in science or other enquiry-based sessions.

Staged organisation children is when children are grouped on the basis of academic ability for different subject activities at the

253

same time and offers an exciting alternative approach for confident and ambitious teachers. For example, one group may be working on an aspect of mathematics, another group on written English, a third group on artwork. If the groups consist of children with varying academic ability, then within each of these broad groupings, differentiation takes place *within* a single group rather than across groups.

Spoked organisation is probably the most common form of managing learning through organising children into ability groups and providing a separate but related task for each of the groups. The introductory phase of the lesson brings all the children together for the purpose of explaining and exploring the topic, raising issues, asking questions and so forth, before sending them to do their activities.

Single task organisation option is used when every group is engaged on a similar task in a particular curriculum subject or area but the teacher has different expectations for each group, depending upon their ability and previous experience of the work. Following the introduction and explanation of the task, each group is allocated the same resources and given a similar length of time to complete the problem, investigation, experiment or research.

Stepped organisation is most commonly used in organising and managing large-space lessons (gymnastics, games and drama) and requires specific and detailed explanations/demonstrations by the teacher, followed by more independent activities undertaken by pupils. In the stepped approach, all the children are introduced to an elementary task, which they then explore or practise for a given length of time, followed by teacher introductions to increasingly complex tasks, each of which the children engage with as individuals, pairs or small groups.

Most teachers have a basic pattern of organisation but vary the set-up according to the circumstances. For instance, tables may be placed together for the purpose of sharing resources for a large-scale project. Children may need to move around the room if there is a 'circus' of various tasks to be completed in a given time (in science, say), each task in a different area of the room. There are also practical factors to be taken into account if children have special learning needs and, for example, require more space for wheelchair access or specially adapted working surfaces for those with limited upper-body mobility.

Inexperienced teachers sometimes leave insufficient time during one lesson to achieve all that they planned, or fail to sort out in advance the activities that different children will be involved in doing. More experienced teachers know that there are likely to be interruptions during the lesson that need to be taken into account in the planning and that lessons immediately before or after any events (such as assembly or singing practice) might affect the time available or pupils' concentration levels. It is unrealistic to think that because the classroom organisation has been carried out efficiently in advance of the lesson, everything will proceed without a hitch. The best teachers not only organise but also ensure that they manage classroom affairs (monitoring, intervening, guiding, assessing) so as to ensure the most favourable conditions for learning.

Sources

Dean, J. (2001) *Organising Learning in the Primary School Classroom*, London: Routledge.

Kelly, P. (2006) 'Organising your classroom for learning', in Arthur, J., Grainger, T. and Wray, D. (eds) *Learning to Teach in the Primary School*, London: Routledge.

Moran, C., Stobbe, J., Baron, W., Miller, J. and Moir, E. (2009) *Keys to the Elementary Classroom*, Thousand Oaks CA: Corwin Press.

LESSON PACE

See also: closed questions, information, interactive whiteboard, lesson management, reflection, teaching approach

Pace is associated with a fast-moving, productive session in which pupils are asked to work hard with unbroken concentration. It is an important feature of a well-disciplined lesson because if pupils are kept suitably busy there is little time for inappropriate off-task behaviour. Pace is particularly important with groups of high-achieving pupils, who are more than able to cope with extended periods of rigorous challenge. Such children thrive on the demands of a lively teaching approach that moves them rapidly through the early lesson phases to allow them ample time to grapple with challenging activities. Experienced teachers tend to begin a session steadily and gradually increase the pace, being especially careful to control the flow of words and not allowing them to tumble out too quickly. The best technique seems to be to say fewer and more interesting things to begin, thereby capturing children's interest and sparking their imagination before building up the speed and intensity. In determining suitable pace, a lot depends on the lesson content; for instance, providing new information normally requires a steadier, more considered pace than (say) an interactive phase consisting of numerous questions and a high level of teacher–pupil engagement.

Teachers in full flow strive to maintain a brisk pace without leaving children stranded in the wake; they also have to be careful that such a forceful approach does not prevent children from having time to think and reflect on the lesson content. There is a tendency for teachers who utilise a rapid pace to employ large numbers of closed questions (with a single correct answer), which appeal to confident and capable children but overwhelm slower learners. Introducing moments of 'suspended silence', while the teacher 'freezes the moment', and varying use of tone, volume and emphasis, all help to draw the children into the lesson and heighten their anticipation about what might follow.

To maintain pace and stretch the brains of the most able without leaving the teacher and pupils mentally exhausted at the end of the time, the following suggestions for teachers (based on Smith 2007) are relevant:

- Plan lessons thinking about what pupils will be asked to do, not what adults will be doing.
- Be at the front of the classroom, waiting to begin and expect your pupils to mirror that attention.
- Write lesson aims on the board and a quick task to get pupils down to work immediately.
- Tell pupils to tell their interesting bits of news later, rather than delaying the start.
- Plan a starter activity that doesn't need lengthy introduction but is a quick and focused.
- Have the necessary resources out on tables or ask early arrivals to do this.
- Don't get sidetracked by pupil requests, off-task enquiries, or administration tasks.

Smith also advises that during a lesson or learning experience, teachers can help to maintain momentum and keep the session moving along by preparing for the next activity via writing on the board; distributing the next resources; giving instructions for the main activity or key learning points verbally and visually; having a clock in the room that all can see; making the circumstances of learning clear and enforcing them; using the timer on the interactive whiteboard (IWB) to enforce time limits or asking a pupil to be a timekeeper and announce the end of the time allocated. Other helpful strategies to keep the lesson moving include a competitive element; fast-paced music; tasks that require pupil feedback; ascribing roles within collaborative groups (e.g. chairperson, scribe); and ending the lesson promptly so that the next one can begin on time. Medwell *et al.* (1998) noted that with regard to literacy teaching, the most effective lessons were conducted at a brisk pace: 'They regularly refocused children's attention on the task in hand and used clear time frames to keep children on task' (p. 78).

Sources

Medwell, J., Wray, D., Poulson, L. and Fox, R. (1998) *Effective Teachers of Literacy*, Final report, School of Education, University of Exeter.

Smith, J. (2007) 'Injecting pace into lessons', *Learning and Thinking*, on-line at www.teaching expertise.com/articles/injecting-pace-into-lessons-2055

LESSON PLANNING

See also: assessment of learning, curriculum plans, inclusion, learning context, learning objectives, lesson continuity, lesson planning (joint), progression in learning, schemes of work, summative assessment

The purpose of lesson planning is to produce plans that facilitate the implementation of a systematic teaching programme over a given period of time (e.g. one hour). The process of lesson planning requires teachers to give careful thought to the pupils' specific learning needs and the context in which learning happens, taking into consideration factors such as resources, size of room, numbers of children, ability levels, availability of adult support staff and time allocation. Lesson planning is an active process, requiring some knowledge of the school's existing plans and schemes of work (see, for instance, Butt 2006). In drawing up successful lesson plans, teachers have to do so in accordance with the school's medium-term school curriculum plans (often spanning half a term) and to collaborate with other teachers who have responsibility for the same age group or subject – often formally done weekly or fortnightly, alongside the more regular informal liaison. Although all teachers are pleased to have 'ready-made' lesson ideas, the planning process is the opportunity to adapt them to the particular situation and, where the plan fits into the longer-term learning objectives, what it assumes about children's existing knowledge and the modifications that are necessary to meet the needs of individual pupils, including slow and fast learners. Even

tried and tested lesson formats have to be modified for different groups of children. As Hart (2000) reminds us 'Classroom dynamics are so complex that it is impossible to predict or fully control what will happen when decisions made at the point of planning are translated into practice' (p. 7). Nevertheless, careful and detailed thought about the practicalities of lesson implementation prior to the commencement of the session (expressed in terms of lesson organisation), as well as during it (expressed in terms of lesson management), increases the likelihood of success.

A lot of the preparation that contributes towards effective teaching happens away from the classroom, which can make it appear to an observer that the teacher has some innate qualities that make things run smoothly with minimum effort. In reality, lesson planning is an active process, requiring a familiarity with the school's broader educational priorities and children's learning needs (see, for example, Walker 2008). The inclusion of each child is an essential factor for teachers to consider when planning a lesson or session, which might entail preparing separate tasks for the less able children or modifying the lesson so that they are able to find success in an elementary task, while the more confident pupils extend their learning through more challenging activities. If less able children are extracted from the lesson for tuition purposes, teachers have to take account of the way in which they will be incorporated into the lesson on their return. Planning for learning involves much more than finding appropriate activities for the pupils, though children are usually much more interested in *what* they are doing than why.

An evaluation of one lesson enables teachers to plan the next one more accurately by using evidence about the way that the children responded to the tasks, answered questions and completed the activities. Assessment criteria, linked closely to learning objectives, are considered in the planning to provide indicators by which pupil progress and attainment can be judged. Although it is impossible to observe every child closely during each lesson, teachers often employ a straightforward categorisation to indicate how pupils engaged with the knowledge demands, such as 'coped comfortably', 'struggled to cope' or 'requires more challenge'. The three categories provide a starting point for a more sophisticated evaluation of progress, which normally relies on an assessment of children's written output after they have handed in the work (sometimes referred to as 'summative' assessment or assessment of learning, AOL). The planning process supports progression in learning through continuity from one session to the next as the threads of learning are woven together and teaching is targeted using information from previous lessons. Contributors to Hughes (1995) offer insights into the short-term and long-term changes that take place as children progress through various domains of learning.

Sources

Butt, G. (2006) *Lesson Planning*, London: Continuum.

Hart, S. (2000) *Thinking Through Teaching*, London: David Fulton.

Hughes, M. (ed.) (1995) *Progression in Learning: BERA dialogues 11*, Bristol: Multilingual Matters.

Walker, L. (2008) *The Essential Guide to Lesson Planning*, London: Longman.

LESSON PLANNING (JOINT)

See also: curriculum plans, lesson planning

In drawing up lesson plans, teachers do so with reference to the school's existing medium-term curriculum plans (often spanning half a term) and working closely with other teachers who have responsibility for the same age group or subject (often meeting fortnightly to formulate plans and share ideas). Keeping 'in step' with colleagues in this way provides stability and a framework for progression but may also act to constrain and limit opportunities for innovation.

LESSON PLANS

See also: ability, answering questions, assessment of learning, differentiation, learning objectives, lesson planning, plenary, teaching assistant

A lesson plan can be compared with a map of an underground railway system that offers guidance about going from one place to another with minimum delay by using a net of coloured lines between stations. The map does not give or intend to give any information about the state of the trains, the exact distance between stations or the air quality in the tunnels; it simply points the way to get from the start to the finish most efficiently. A lesson plan parallels the principle of a tube train map by setting out the chronological steps in such a way that the session runs smoothly. It does not contain details of how the children will behave, make predictions about whether the equipment will prove to be satisfactory or describe the nature of the classroom climate, and is not intended to do so. Nevertheless, if the 'journey' through the lesson is to be a success, the planning must take account of time constraints and anticipate factors that may detract from learning or enhance it.

Every lesson plan is based on specified learning objectives, though learning *intentions* is sometimes a preferred term, as it not always possible to predict precisely what children will learn and sometimes the same objectives apply to several consecutive sessions, requiring only minor adjustments in the focus of teaching. Although the objectives apply to every child in general terms, the specific needs of particular children have to be taken into account through differentiation of the vocabulary, questions and tasks that are used to reinforce learning. The learning objectives are linked to assessment criteria, as a way of monitoring the effectiveness of the lesson in achieving the stated aims. Careful observation of the way that children answer questions and go about their tasks provide teachers with a lot of information about how well they have understood the work.

Lessons do not take place in isolation and a lesson plan has to indicate the links with previous lessons to strengthen continuity and the developmental nature of learning. Lesson plans make allowance for faster and slower workers, less able and more able pupils, and the vagaries of classroom life. A short lesson at the end of the day following an exciting drama session requires a different approach from one of normal length during the early part of the day. Pupils are not involved in lesson preparation, so teachers have to explain to them what is happening in the lesson if the children are to engage fully with it.

Resources consist of practical items and human assistance, so lesson plan details include: (a) a list of the equipment needed to teach and for the children to aid their task completion; and (b) the role of the adult helper (teaching assistant or parent). Lesson plan details have to include a list of the equipment needed both to teach and for the children to aid their task completion, and specific details about the role of the adult helper. If equipment requires special training or there are health and safety factors to consider, these must, of course, be taken into account when planning the lesson, as even commonly used resources can pose dangers if procedures are not correctly followed. For example, using PE equipment that has loose parts would clearly be reckless.

Less able and more able children may be given different tasks from the majority of children such that the less able are able to find success in the elementary component tasks and the more able can extend their learning through open-ended activities that require higher-level thinking skills, such as speculating, drawing comparisons and evaluating. If less able children are extracted from the lesson for tuition purposes, teachers need to take account of the way in which they will be incorporated back into the lesson on their return. In addition, it has become increasingly important to be sensitive to the individual needs of each child, which may, for instance, involve 'booster' sessions or intensive 'coaching' through after-school classes and computer-assisted learning.

Lesson plans often contain a list of significant words and expressions, especially subject-related ones. The extent to which key spellings are made available to pupils and the extent to which they try to spell the words unaided or with the aid of a word bank is a decision that has to be made by each teacher. The majority of teachers encourage children to try and spell words for themselves before asking an adult. Subject-related terms require special explanation. Significant words and expressions, especially subject-related ones, are noted on lesson plans. Some teachers write down examples of sentences containing the key words to use as part of the teaching, as this strategy reinforces pupil learning.

The final phase of a lesson (the 'lesson review' or 'plenary') allows the teacher to summarise what has been achieved, draws together the threads of learning that have characterised the lesson, including mistakes and misconceptions, offers pupils the opportunity to share with others in the class what they have done and achieved, and indicates what will follow in the next lesson.

LESSON REVIEW

See also: assessment of learning, encouragement and praise, lessons, mistakes and misconceptions, oracy, plenary

The process of lesson review is an important part of the learning process, as it gives opportunity for the teacher to encourage pupils to talk about the work they have done, draw together the key points from the lesson and point out mistakes, misconceptions and errors. If the whole class or group is present and involved in the review procedure, the process is often referred to as a 'plenary'. Sometimes a review simply requires the teacher to spend a minute or two summarising what has just taken place. Sometimes it involves the teacher selecting children at random to tell the rest of the class what they have found out or done. Occasionally it involves one child speaking on behalf of the collaborating group to explain what they have discovered from working together. Other strategies include children showing or reading aloud their work to everybody; saying what surprised or pleased them about their work; voting on which idea or approach they preferred; telling someone other than their partner about what they did. In these various ways a teacher can use the review phase to help ascertain what children have learned, a process referred to as assessment of learning (AOL).

Children normally love the opportunity to talk about their work and show off their models, charts, pictures and drawings. Teachers have a vital role to play in the process of gathering the class together and enthusing about pupils' achievements. Whichever method (or combination of methods) is used to involve pupils, it is important for teachers to ensure that they receive every contribution enthusiastically. Even comments from children that are self-evident or replicating what has already been said will merit, and normally receive, praise and commendation. Very young or shy children also need to feel that they have contributed towards this phase of the lesson, even if they have not actually spoken; this aim is often achieved by asking for a show of hands about different aspects of the lesson, to which all children can contribute, or finding a child who has done well and letting all the children bask in the reflected glory. Other plenary approaches include children saying what surprised or pleased them about what they have done, what problems they encountered, or reading an extract from a piece of written work.

The last moments of a lesson can also be used to remind the children of what is coming after the break or during the next lesson in that subject. Teachers have a key role in bringing to a halt the work being undertaken by the children, gathering the class together

with minimum disruption and highlighting pupils' achievements. In addition to ending positively by celebrating all that has been achieved, there are many occasions when the final moments of a lesson are used to remind the children of what follows the break or happens during the next lesson. In these ways, a lesson review not only reinforces learning but also provides the whole class with a sense of fulfilment and security. See Petty (2004, chapter 40).

Sources

Petty, G. (2004) *Teaching Today*, Cheltenham: Stanley Thornes.

LESSONS

See also: cross-curriculum, curriculum, differentiation, English, good teachers, lesson management, lesson objectives, lesson plans, learning styles, literacy, mathematics, numeracy, thematic learning, topic work

A generation ago, the word 'lesson' tended to apply to secondary education where different subjects were taught within an allocated time frame. Until towards the end of the twentieth century, the primary education curriculum was based largely on integrating subjects within a 'topic' (topic work) or 'thematic' framework (laying the stress on one particular subject above others) that emphasised the interconnectivity of learning through a cross-curricular approach. Nevertheless, mathematics and English were taught separately as well as being incorporated into the topic. In recent years, the emphasis upon literacy and numeracy (and to a lesser extent, science) as subjects in their own right has given rise to the term 'lesson' being applied to distinct subject sessions. A lesson has thereby acquired dual meaning: (1) the subject content covered over a given period of time; (2) the time allocation for content coverage specified within a set timetable. All lessons are based on a curriculum, broadly defined as what the teacher intends that pupils learn. The curriculum may reflect (a) intended learning outcomes that are processes, like learning to research a topic or learning to divide numbers; (b) learning outcomes relating to memorising information, such as multiplication tables; (c) learning outcomes that form a basis for judgements, like the qualities of being a good friend; and (d) learning outcomes that relate to applying knowledge and skills, like writing a story, analysing and solving problems through investigation and use of the Internet (see Kizlik, on-line).

Lesson content is determined by what the teacher intends that pupils should learn and understand, and must be straightforward to teach, allowing the teacher to introduce the aspect of learning, supply children with tasks to complete and rapidly evaluate their progress. Lesson structure has to take account of the pace at which pupils learn and the manner in which they do so, as some children work quickly and efficiently, while others work laboriously. Some children like to think deeply before proceeding, others are spontaneous and eager to complete the work as fast as possible. Some pupils can think abstractly (i.e. they can figure things out in their heads); other children require visual, verbal or even kinaesthetic resources (such as materials of different textures to assist partially sighted children) to assist them in their work. Teachers also have to ensure that the tasks and activities undertaken by pupils are properly differentiated to allow children to finish the allocated work within the lesson time frame.

Lessons have to be managed, with clearly identified learning objectives that are normally linked to the requirements of a nationally monitored system. Most teachers share the intended learning intentions with the pupils, either verbally or through a written reminder or both, so that pupils are aware that lesson tasks and activities do not constitute a final product but are part of a larger educational endeavour.

The concept of a lesson is not only based on the assumption that teaching should focus on identifiable learning outcomes during the period allotted to it, but also that the process can be precisely planned, organised and monitored to correspond precisely with the allocated time period (Butt 2003). Research by McCallum et al. (2001) showed that good primary teachers had a repertoire of at least six lesson structures, though not all of the teachers drew upon the full repertoire regularly. The three-stage lesson (teacher input, pupil activities, plenary/lesson review) was commonly used. The introductory phase was sometimes up to 20 minutes long and used for relaying knowledge, demonstrating, linking new knowledge to past experience and giving and repeating instructions. Good teachers sometimes repeated a lesson structure that 'worked for them'; sometimes they varied the structure to 'best fit' the subject being taught. The research team found that both approaches, if done well, had pace, pupil engagement and intellectually challenging teaching.

The most productive lessons seem to be those in which teachers have high (but sensible) expectations of the children; offer clear instructions; help them to identify their own learning targets and encourage an active, purposeful dialogue about the content. By contrast, weaker lessons are vague, teacher-dominated, routine or repetitive and badly paced. The best lessons are those in which the teacher uses an appropriate range of teaching strategies (giving information directly, using IT resources, employing question-and-answer, making children think and reflect); sets appropriate challenges with respect to the ability range of children; monitors progress; and intervenes sensitively to guide children's learning.

Sources

Butt, G. (2003) *Lesson Planning*, London: Continuum.
Kizlik, S. 'Lesson plans the easy way', *Adprima*, on-line at www.adprima.com/easyless.htm
McCallum, B., Gipps, C. and Hargreaves, E. (2001) 'The structure of lessons', *Education 3–13*, 29 (1), 33–37

LIFE EDUCATION

See also: Every Child Matters, healthy schools

Life Education (www.lifeeducation.org.uk) is an organisation whose main work is with primary schools and parents, delivered through local trusts, to ensure that children develop the knowledge, skills and attitudes they need to make informed choices about health to enhance and enrich their lives. Life Education works collaboratively with organisations and agencies within 'Every Child Matters', the national 'Healthy Schools' framework, and with children and parent organisations.

LIFE SKILLS

See also: free play, health and safety, motor skills, parents, skills

Concerns have been expressed about the way in which overprotected children are being deprived of 'life skills' experiences. Anxious teachers and parents are said to be breeding a generation of 'cotton wool kids' who are too afraid to climb trees, ride their bicycles or even cross the road unsupervised and thereby failing to acquire basic survival skills (*Daily Telegraph* 2008). Some parents are actively discouraging their children from playing sport because they are worried about injury. Alarm over danger from strangers and traffic has led to a reduction in opportunities for children to leave the confines of home and move freely. As a result of these concerns, some children are missing out on simple pleasures that former generations took for granted, and restrictions on children's freedom appear to be linked to increased rates of anxiety disorders in even the very young. At the same time, reducing time for spontaneous ('free') play is denying children the chance to perfect fundamental motor skills, such as balance and coordination, which are normally developed through play. In addition, a lot of imaginative play equipment has been removed from parks because of fears about litigation if an accident were to occur.

Sources

Daily Telegraph (2008) 'Cotton wool kids losing basic skills', on-line at www.news.com.au

LISTENING

See also: attention span, body language, communication, oracy, teacher–pupil interaction, television

Real listening is an active process that has three basic steps: hearing what is said, understanding what the speaker is trying to convey and evaluating the implications of what has been said. Children in school are often encouraged by their teachers to 'listen more carefully'; thus, if pupils misinterpret the instruction or fail to grasp the task, they are rebuked. In fact, listening requires mastery of many different elements, for instance: physically 'tuning in'; paying attention for the whole time the speaker is talking; noting voice intonation, emphases and phrasing; watching for body language clues (such as eye movements); distinguishing between genuine and rhetorical questions; incorporating innuendo, humour and metaphor; and understanding the vocabulary used by the speaker. In addition, the listener himself or herself brings previous experiences, emotions and predispositions that all affect the way in which the speaker's words are heard and interpreted. Listeners should place their full attention on the person who is speaking; concentrate on the words being said; let the speaker finish; think before responding; listen for main ideas; ask questions to clarify points; and give helpful feedback (Info Homework Centre, on-line). The skill of listening is described by Bocchino (1999) as the foundation communication skill because everyone needs to verbalise what they are thinking in such a way that the hearer can understand; equally, the hearer needs to receive and

261

understand what others are saying. The cycle of communication therefore consists of expression and interpretation. The higher the quality of the expression, the more likely that the words will be correctly interpreted; more careful listening increases the likelihood of correct interpretation.

Nelson-Jones (2007) stresses the importance of non-verbal signals in establishing a suitable climate for listening through so-called 'attending behaviour'. Thus, a good listener gives the strong impression of being available and not in too much of a hurry to take time or too distracted to concentrate. In the rush and hurry of classroom life, such conditions are not easily achieved but necessary for effective communication. An adult who is a good listener will adopt a relaxed but alert posture and avoid giving out signals that indicate tension, such as arms wrapped around the body, drumming fingers and swaying. Bolton (1986) describes this relaxed alertness as a 'posture of involvement' because, he claims, body language often speaks louder than words. Communication is enhanced through physical openness, leaning forward slightly, maintaining soft eye contact, a facial expression that reflects the tone of the speaker's conversation (smiling is normally appropriate unless the speaker is agitated or upset) and frequent head nods.

Listening within the formal organisation of the curriculum is normally listed in conjunction with 'speaking'; thus: 'speaking and listening' ('oracy'). It has been estimated that the average primary school pupil is expected to listen to adults for at least half of their time in class, amounting to some two and a half hours daily, so it is little wonder that some children lose concentration. On the other hand, children are capable of listening attentively and continuously to a favourite television programme or film for a long period of time; the difference between listening to a teacher and listening to the TV is that the latter can be done passively, whereas the former requires a response and action.

Listening also has close links with reading because both are means of receiving communications and require the interpretation of symbols: hearing in the case of the words used; seeing in the case of reading the print on a page. In addition, both listening and reading require interpretation of main ideas, relationships, sequences, sensing the mood and intent of the speaker or writer and evaluating his or her ideas. Children have to be taught to give their full attention to the speaker and not to allow their minds to wander. They also need to let the speaker finish before they begin to talk – something that many children find extremely hard to do. Children have to be trained to finish listening before they begin speaking because it is impossible for them to give proper attention if they are busy thinking about what they want to say next and then blurt it out.

Considering the complexity that attends listening, it is little wonder that some children struggle to make sense of what is said to them. Some teachers employ creative approaches to teaching and learning communication skills, such as using 'talking' puppets with younger pupils. As well as their visual attraction, the benefit of using puppets is that the children 'channel' their speaking and listening through them, thereby deflecting attention; shy pupils are especially helped through such innovative means. Teachers also have a responsibility to make their intentions and expectations clear to pupils by using unambiguous language, issuing specific commands and offering opportunities for children to ask questions of clarification without fear of being chastised for doing so. Many studies show that pupils regard a willingness to listen patiently as one of the most important attributes in a teacher.

Sources

Bocchino, R. (1999) *Emotional Literacy: To be a different kind of smart*, London: Sage.

Bolton, R. (1986) *People Skills*, New York: Simon and Schuster.

Info Homework Centre, *Speaking and Listening Skills*, on-line at www.infoplease.com/homework

Nelson-Jones, R. (2007) *Basic Counselling Skills*, London: Sage.

LITERACY

See also: communication, English, English as an additional language, handwriting, literacy hour, Primary National Strategy, primary reviews, reading, teaching assistant, writing

Fundamentally, a literate person is someone who is able to read and write. The term 'literacy' largely replaced the more general word 'English' in primary schools around the end of the twentieth century to describe the process by which children become literate. The teaching of literacy has always been a priority in primary schools but in recent years this priority has been given additional impetus through a large number of government-initiated curriculum reforms and the use of national testing as a crucial indicator for school success, especially in England. In the UK, probably the most influential educational organisation concerned with the teaching of literacy is the United Kingdom Literacy Association (UKLA, www.ukla.org).

The more opportunity that children have to communicate verbally and make use of well-informed adults, who will inspire and motivate them, the faster is their progress towards linguistic competence. Research into the literacy development of young primary children has focused on the important contribution made by the school and the home and confirmed the importance of spoken language as a prerequisite to proficiency in written language. See Morrow (2005) and Latham (2002) for information about helping young children to read and write.

Young children are faced with the considerable challenge of grasping the concept that printed text is the means of representing recorded speech; they must also understand that writing provides the vehicle by which the conversion from spoken to written form takes place. Some pupils face considerable difficulties in comprehending the connections

between spoken and written language. Statistically, these difficulties are more prevalent in boys than in girls (Bearne and Grainger 2004).

Within any class of children there will be considerable variation in their previous experience of the spoken and written word. Some children come from linguistically rich homes, in which there are active verbal exchanges promoted by loquacious adults. Other children come from homes where there is little emphasis on reading and adults employ a restricted vocabulary range. Some children speak a different first language from English; in such instances English is referred to as an additional language (EAL). Studies suggest that many EAL children are effective decoders of print but may struggle with the rhythm of words and find it hard to grasp the deeper meanings of text. Teachers have to take close account of pupils' different language experiences when planning and teaching. The Primary National Strategy (PNS) framework for literacy in England has twelve strands of literacy:

1 Speaking
2 Listening and responding
3 Group discussion, interaction
4 Drama
5 Word recognition
6 Word structure and spelling
7 Understand and interpret texts
8 Engage with, respond to texts
9 Creating and shaping texts
10 Text structure and organisation
11 Sentence structure, punctuation
12 Presentation

The PNS also incorporates recommendations from the Rose Review (Rose 2009) that the most effective teaching of early reading builds on high-quality speaking and listening, using systematic high-quality phonics teaching as main first strategy based on synthetic phonics (based on a phonetic system; e.g. c-a-t, d-o-g, etc.).

In order to give all children the best opportunities for effective development and learning in communication, language and literacy, practitioners have to give particular attention to providing opportunities for children to communicate thoughts, ideas and feelings, and build up relationships with adults and each other (Hancock and Mansfield 2001). It is recommended that children should experience a rich literacy experience, including drama, stories, speaking and listening around this. Attention to children with English as an additional language and to the needs of boys remain high.

Teachers give children opportunities to share and enjoy a wide range of rhymes, music, songs, poetry, stories and non-fiction books; linking language with physical movement in action songs and rhymes; role-play and practical experiences such as cookery and gardening. The learning environment reflects the importance of language through the use of signs, notices and books, providing opportunities for children to see adults writing and to experiment with writing for themselves through making marks, personal writing symbols and conventional script. In practice, teachers have to give time to develop spoken language through conversations between children and adults, both one-to-one and in small groups, to enhance their phonological awareness.

Even a carefully designed programme can be uninspiring for children unless the teaching environment emphasises the usefulness and enjoyment to be gained from the endeavour. Children who have been under-stimulated at home or who struggle constantly with learning to read and write take a lot of persuading that the effort is worthwhile. Unlike some other aspects of learning, children cannot easily conceal weaknesses in literacy and if problems persist they quickly become demoralised. The considerable challenge for teachers of younger pupils is that if children are still finding difficulty by the age of seven, they will probably continue to be academically handicapped throughout their primary schooling and beyond. McBride-Chang (2004) provides a detailed description of how children learn to read and critically analyses

research and theory on literacy acquisition from an ecological perspective. Geekie *et al.* (1999) offer an account of literacy learning based on what effective teachers and learners actually do, and demonstrate how literacy develops in social and communicative exchanges.

Teaching assistants exercise an important role in supporting the needs of children who struggle with literacy. Pupils who are deemed to be underachieving are sometimes given additional 'booster' classes as a means of enhancing their competence and gaining better results in national tests. Early identification of, and response to, any particular difficulties in children's language development through liaison between bilingual workers, speech therapists and practitioners may be necessary. Particular attention also has to be paid to children who use alternative communication systems, such as Braille or sign language.

Sources

Bearne, E. and Grainger, T. (2004) 'Raising boys' achievement in writing', *Literacy*, 38 (3), 156–58.

Geekie, P., Cambourne, B. and Fitzsimmons, P. (1999) *Understanding Literacy Development*, Stoke-on-Trent: Trentham.

Hancock, R. and Mansfield, M. (2001) 'The literacy hour: A case for listening to children', in J. Collins, K. Insley and J. Soler (eds) *Developing Pedagogy: Researching practice*, London: Paul Chapman/Open University.

Latham, D. (2002) *How Children Learn to Write*, London: Paul Chapman.

McBride-Chang, C. (2004) *Children's Literacy Development*, London: Hodder Education.

Morrow, L. (2005) *Literacy Development in the Early Years: Helping children read and write*, Needham Heights MA: Allyn & Bacon.

Rose, J. for the DCSF (2009) *Primary Curriculum Review*, London: HMSO.

LITERACY HOUR

See also: ability, ability groups, English, literacy, reading, teaching assistants, writing

Since September 1998, all primary schools in England have been expected to implement the 'literacy hour' as laid down in the National Literacy Strategy (NLS) as described in the 'framework for teaching'. The lesson should begin with the teacher sharing the learning objectives with the class, followed by about fifteen minutes in which the teacher models with the whole class, reading using an enlarged text, or describing in writing what the pupils have to do. During the next fifteen minutes, the teacher focuses on specific words or sentences with the whole class. The children then work for about twenty minutes in groups or individually on tasks linked to aspects of reading, writing or word and sentence work, while the teacher works specifically with one or more ability groups (so-called 'guided work'). Younger children often have a teaching assistant to provide support and guidance. The final ten minutes of the lesson concludes with feedback from the children on what they have been doing in relation to the objectives of the lesson.

Although schools were not required to implement the literacy hour, the vast majority did so out of fear that they would disadvantage their pupils and be seen as unwilling to embrace change. After a few years it became evident that the structure was acting as a constraint for teachers who wanted to adopt a more imaginative and creative approach to teaching literacy. It is noteworthy that the basic structure of the literacy hour – sharing learning intentions for the lesson; whole-class teacher input; group or independent work; and lesson review (plenary) – has provided a pattern in primary education for many lessons other than literacy.

LITERACY STRATEGY (THE NATIONAL)

See also: literacy, literacy hour, numeracy strategy, Primary National Strategy

Following a pilot project in 1996, which involved schools in fourteen local education authorities, the National Literacy Strategy (NLS) was introduced to all primary schools in England in September 1998. The strategy was planned for teachers to teach a daily 'literacy hour' to consist of thirty minutes whole class teaching, about twenty minutes of work in groups and a plenary session to review and summarise the lesson. Initially, teachers conformed closely to the prescribed format but it quickly became clear that a more flexible approach was needed. In 2003, the NLS and the related numeracy strategy became part of the Primary National Strategy (PNS).

LOOKED-AFTER CHILDREN

See also: Every Child Matters, personal education plan

The term 'looked after children' (LAC) refers to children in public care who are placed with foster carers, in residential homes or with parents or other relatives. The children will usually attend the local school in the normal way, though they tend to underachieve (Cairns and Stanway 2004). Emanating from the 'Every Child Matters' (ECM) initiative (DfES 2005) there are significant differences in the types of schools that prioritise looked after children in their support arrangements. Large primary schools and primary schools in more challenging circumstances are more likely to prioritise LAC, but schools with low proportions of pupils eligible for free school meals (England and Wales) and schools with high levels of academic attainment are less likely to do so. Government guidance expects that children living in care will have a personal education plan (PEP) by their first review. It is a statutory part of the care plan and should be monitored and reviewed every six months and after any change of school.

Sources

Cairns, K. and Stanway, C. (2004) *Learn the Child: Helping looked after children to learn*, London: British Association for Adoption and Fostering.

DfES (2005) *Every Child Matters: Change for children*, London: HMSO.

LOWER CASE LETTERS

See also: alphabet, capital letters, handwriting

Lower case letters (a b c d e f g, etc.) are the letters of the alphabet that are not written in capitals. They are also known as 'small case' or 'minuscule' letters. Children generally learn to recognise and write lower case letters before upper case (capital) letters.

M

MAINTAINED SCHOOLS

A maintained school in a local authority (LA) in England or Wales is one that is funded through taxation. All maintained schools are described in one of the following ways:

- A *Foundation* school
- A *Community* school
- A *Voluntary Controlled* school
- A *Voluntary Aided* school
- A *Nursery* school
- A *Special* school.

MARSHALL, SYBIL

See also: arts, child-centred education, cross-curriculum, enquiry, integrated day, Plowden Report, trainee teachers

Sybil Marshall was born on 26 November 1913 and died on 29 August 2005. She enjoyed three distinct career phases, the first being as a Fenland primary school teacher, in which she ran single-handed a one-room school of twenty-six children, aged 4–11 years, from the early 1930s until 1962. She published an account of her experiences in *An Experiment In Education* (1963).

Marshall was keen to explore and exploit the connections between the experiences of everyday life and the process of education, establishing her reputation in advance of the Plowden Committee's report on primary education in 1967, for which it was one of the influential texts in shaping a positive

response to the 'progressive' ideas being espoused. It is generally agreed that the driving force in Marshall's educational philosophy was conviction rather than a sentimental hankering for an unattainable ideal. It is said that Sybil Marshall was never limited by the strictures of what was needed but rather saw the greatness of human potential.

Marshall became a reader in primary education at Sussex University from 1967 until she retired in 1976, during which time she was involved in a second education experiment by creating an education area where postgraduate student (trainee) teachers reflected on what they had experienced on their primary school placements (then known as 'teaching practice', now commonly referred to as 'school experience'). It is important to note that hitherto, the only 'areas' of study were traditional subject areas, such as English and mathematics, so a course dedicated to reviewing and evaluating classroom practice was wholly innovative. Marshall selected themes that were cross-curricular in scope (i.e. crossing subject boundaries) rather than based on discrete subject areas.

Sybil demonstrated how children could produce highly creative work if given the right stimuli and resources, but programmes of work were exhaustively prepared and drew upon her own cultural legacy; she expected her teachers to do no less. Marshall famously claimed that she did not want an integrated day or an integrated curriculum, but rather an 'integrated person'. The curriculum was

267

child-centred in the sense of engaging with things that children found interesting but, contrary to critical caricatures of her work, it was very much teacher-led.

Marshall published an amusing account of head teachers on secondment in *Adventure in Creative Education* (1968). It is claimed that the head teachers concerned had been taken aback, as they came under Marshall's unique tutorage in a disused Rotherham workhouse. Her methods reached a wider audience still with the highly successful programme for Granada TV, *Picture Box*, with about 324 million children viewing it over a period of some 23 years. Marshall won the Angel Prize for Literature for her publication, *Everyman's Book of English Folk Tales* in 1981.

Retirement prompted her third career phase of writing a series of novels, the first of which she completed at the age of eighty. The trilogy, published by Penguin Books, consists of *A Nest of Magpies* (1993), *Sharp Through the Hawthorn* (1994) and *Strip the Willow* (1996), and represent a fictionalised autobiography. Marshall's contributions to education were acknowledged in the latter part of her life as the castaway on the famous BBC radio programme, *Desert Island Discs*.

Sources

Lamont, W. (2005) 'Obituary: Sybil Marshall', *Guardian*, Wednesday 31 August.
Marshall, S. (1963) *An Experiment In Education*, Cambridge: Cambridge University Press.
——(1981) *Everyman's Book of English Folk Tales*, London: Everyman Publications.
——(1993) *A Nest of Magpies*, London: Penguin Books.
——(1994) *Sharp Through the Hawthorn*, London: Penguin Books.
——(1996) *Strip the Willow*, London: Penguin Books.
The Oakeshott Institute USA, on-line at www.oakeshott.org/SMBio.html

MATHEMATICS

See also: gender, home background and learning, numeracy, reading, understanding, writing

There are few subjects that polarise the population in the same way as mathematics does; a few people express great enthusiasm whenever the subject is mentioned; many adults claim to dislike it intensely. Even some qualified teachers struggle to move beyond the mechanics of teaching the subject, have low confidence and need support in developing mathematical understanding (Haylock 2005). It is a strange phenomenon that being poor at maths does not bring the ignominy that accompanies being poor at reading and writing (Pratt and Berry 2007). The adult acceptance that 'I am useless at maths' has undoubtedly had an impact of children's attitudes towards the subject, notably among girls. Street *et al.* (2009) focus on numeracy ('numbers') as a social practice and report on their investigations into the meanings and uses of numeracy in school and home and community contexts. The authors note considerable variation in what they refer to as the 'cultural resources' available in different homes and the way it appears to impact on children's achievements in numeracy, such that the closer the 'match' between home and school resources, the more likely that the child will do well in the subject.

The Renewed Framework for Mathematics was introduced for teachers in England (DfES 2006) and centres around five main themes: (1) encouraging flexibility, (2) a more structured teaching and learning programme, (3) more effective use of assessment, (4) raising expectations, and (5) broadening and strengthening the pedagogy. The new objectives for mathematics are organised in seven core strands:

1 Using and applying mathematics
2 Counting and understanding number
3 Knowing and using number facts
4 Calculating
5 Understanding shape
6 Measuring
7 Handling data.

Thus, compared with the original National Numeracy Strategy, NNS, introduced by the

British government in 1999 to shape the teaching of mathematics (DfEE 1999), the Renewed Framework places more emphasis on speaking and listening, tied in with further investigative and exploratory approaches. It stresses the importance of creative teaching and of understanding and reviewing each child's progress throughout each topic.

Mathematical development in young children is influenced by social and contextual factors. For instance, parental attitudes towards the subject and the general absence of mathematics featuring in conversations at home, other than those involving basic counting, mean that many children come to pre-schooling and the reception class with an underdeveloped sense of the subject. Other children view mathematics as being detached from real life. Despite these reservations, however, children entering school may also bring with them a fund of insight into different aspects of mathematics, such as numeral recognition, simple addition, subtraction and sharing. Teachers encourage pupils to explore the implications of their existing knowledge through play and shared experiences. Although older primary-age children may be able to work out computations correctly and score good marks in national tests, they are not necessarily able to apply their mathematics to problems and investigate unfamiliar situations that would provide evidence of deeper understanding.

Children seem to enjoy maths best when they are required to use their mathematical knowledge actively, rather than merely completing lists of sums. Although pupils need to master basic skills attached to the four rules of mathematics (adding, subtracting, dividing and multiplying) they also benefit from seeing how mathematical ways of thinking can be empowering and creative. Teachers find that lessons that maintain an air of mystery and encourage children to employ their knowledge to find solutions are a means of stimulating children and raising interest levels. The high-stakes significance of national test results in mathematics has led to a situation in which whole-class didactic teaching ('instructing') and

highly systematic and regulated forms of learning has dominated to such an extent that the more imaginative expressions of mathematical working have tended to be marginalised.

Haylock and Cockburn (2008) emphasise the connections that can be made that relate language, symbols, concrete materials and pictures to the key ideas that are central to learning. The authors emphasise that children should be helped to develop an understanding of mathematics for themselves, rather than just learning recipes and routines with little meaning. Mathematical understanding can also be developed through use of stories, songs, games and imaginative play. To give all children the best opportunities for effective mathematical development, teachers give attention to activities such as observing numbers and patterns in the environment and in daily routines; practical activities that require communication skills; activities that are imaginative and enjoyable; and real-life problems. Teachers employ mathematical vocabulary during the daily routines and activities and encourage pupils to employ subject-specific words.

Sources

DfEE (1999) *National Numeracy Strategy*, London: HMSO.

DfES (2006) *Primary Framework for Literacy and Mathematics*, on-line at www.standards.dfes.gov.uk/primaryframework/mathematics

Haylock, D. (2005) *Mathematics Explained for Primary Teachers*, London: Sage.

Haylock, D. and Cockburn, A. (2008) *Understanding Mathematics for Young Children*, London: Sage.

Pratt, N. and Berry, J. (2007) 'The joy of mathematics', in Hayes, D. (ed.) *Joyful Teaching and Learning in the Primary School*, Exeter: Learning Matters.

Street, B., Baker, D. and Tomlin, A. (2009) *Navigating Numeracies: Home-school numeracy practices*, New York: Springer.

MATHEMATICS PRIMARY FRAMEWORK

See also: mathematics, National Curriculum, numeracy, problem solving, progression in learning, talk

In 2006 the Revised Primary Framework for the teaching of mathematics in England and Wales was launched in electronic form on the government's Standards web site (DfES 2006). Although schools were encouraged to move towards implementing the revised version rather than continuing to rely upon the original 1999 framework, guidance materials emphasised the need for teachers to begin the transition by reviewing their current work and priorities in mathematics and using elements of the renewed framework that reflected the priorities arising from the review. This emphasis reinforced the message that the purpose of the renewed framework was to build on positive aspects of the original National Numeracy Strategy (DfEE 1999), rather than to replace it.

The original 1999 framework for teaching mathematics was focused on number and calculations, and its teaching objectives tended to address the learning of mathematical content rather than mathematical process. This was in contrast to the original National Curriculum for England and Wales, which gave more attention to the using and applying of mathematics and required teachers to teach children to 'use and apply' their mathematics by involving them in problem solving, communicating and reasoning. These three process strands were embedded within the three programmes of study of the National Curriculum; number, shape and space and handling data suggesting that mathematical content should be taught through practical, problem-based tasks for children. One of the main strengths of the original 1999 framework was the range of different mental calculation strategies included and examples of how these might be recorded.

An aim of the renewed framework was to give greater attention to using and applying mathematics by employing five inter-linked themes: (a) solve problems; (b) represent – analyse, record, do, check, confirm; (c) enquire – plan, decide, organise, interpret, reason, justify; (d) communicate – describe, create, apply, explore, predict, hypothesise,

test; and (e) communicate – explain solutions, choices, decisions, reasoning. When solving problems or following a line of enquiry, children can represent their ideas using pictures, objects, numbers, symbols or diagrams; reason and predict; and communicate their results in written or oral form.

The Revised Framework is also different from the 1999 framework in being in the form of an electronic version that allows teachers to link quickly to a wide range of teaching and learning resources, so that they are able to customise more easily their planning, teaching and assessment. To simplify the structure of the objectives, seven strands of learning are identified, which offer a broad overview of the mathematics curriculum in the primary phase. The objectives are aligned to the seven strands to demonstrate progression in each strand. Thus:

1 Using and applying mathematics
2 Counting and understanding number
3 Knowing and using number facts
4 Calculating
5 Understanding shape
6 Measuring
7 Handling data

In constructing the strands, knowledge of number facts has been separated from calculation; methods of calculation have been unified; measures have been kept separate from shape and space; and problem solving has been embedded into the broader strand of using and applying mathematics. Teachers also support children in developing their understanding of problem solving, reasoning and numeracy in a broad range of contexts in which they can explore, practise and talk about their developing understanding. Pupils may be guided to find patterns; make connections; recognise relationships; work with numbers, shapes, space and measures; and count, sort and match. Teachers of younger children promote mathematical ideas, concepts and language during child-initiated play and assisting them to explore problems. See

Hansen (2008) for practical examples that correspond to the different strands of the primary framework.

In the renewed framework there is an emphasis on the need for teachers to make and use connections between different mathematical ideas and use natural cross-curricular links in their planning and teaching. Teachers are advised to take into account the inter-relatedness of different mathematical ideas so that children have a coherent learning experience. Although examples of activities and a wide range of easily accessed teaching and learning resources are provided on the web site, they need to be adapted to suit individual circumstances and children's needs.

There are concerns that the renewed framework presents a more rigid approach to the teaching of calculation by advising that all children should be using traditional standard methods of calculation for the four basic operations before they leave primary school. This recommendation contrasts with the original 1999 framework, which put great emphasis on the need for children to learn more easily understandable methods of calculation, based on flexible mental strategies, and to have some choice over which method they chose to use in a particular situation.

Sources

DfEE (1999) *National Numeracy Strategy*, London: HMSO.

DfES (2006) *Primary Framework for Literacy and Mathematics*, on-line at www.standards.dfes.gov.uk/primaryframework/mathematics

Hansen, A. (2008) *Primary Mathematics: Extending knowledge in practice*, Exeter: Learning Matters.

MEALTIME ASSISTANTS

See also: behaviour, governors, head teachers, humour, relationships

Many people feel that mealtime assistants (MTAs) – still commonly but inaccurately referred to as 'dinner ladies' – have the least enviable job in schools. Although the majority of MTAs are dedicated and conscientious, their lack of authority can cause them to struggle with uncooperative children, and the sound of strained adult voices is a familiar one in some schools. An increasing number of head teachers and governors have come to recognise that as MTAs play an important role in the life of the school, and it is worth investing time in the provision of training and guidance. As a result, issues such as behaviour management, assertiveness, interpersonal relationships and first-aid are addressed through regular sessions. MTAs need to have a good sense of humour, plenty of stamina and a strong personality. Due to the low wages, most of them will be local parents and a number of them may have a second job. When MTAs are seen leaving school the moment the dinner break is over, they are likely to have other responsibilities or are (understandably) refusing to do unpaid overtime. Certain MTAs may be allocated to a child with special needs, and most of them are encouraged or trained to learn more about the value of play and handling potentially combustible situations.

In the case of younger children, it is likely that an MTA will come to the classroom a few minutes before the official end of the morning to take responsibility for the children who stay for lunch. If it is a wet day, the MTAs will be trying to look after the children all together in the school hall or flitting from classroom to classroom attempting to entertain and subdue the restless children. MTAs are only responsible for children who remain at school to eat their lunch, not for children who go home. Younger children who are going home for lunch have to be supervised by the teacher until an adult collects them. If children return to school too early from lunch, they are not, strictly speaking, the responsibility of MTAs.

MEDICATION

See also: caring teachers, health and safety, home–school

It is well understood by everyone involved in primary education that the majority of pupils will at some time have a medical condition that affects their participation in school activities. However, parents and/or carers are responsible for ensuring the child is well enough to attend school and medication must only be taken there when it is absolutely essential. If children are unwell they must, of course, be kept at home, as there is no legal duty to require a school staff to administer medication to pupils and it is done on a voluntary basis. Where the school agrees to administer medicines, parents and/or carers have to complete a consent form, which also incorporates indemnity for school staff administering medicines or medical procedures. A positive response by a school to a pupil's medical needs not only benefits the pupil concerned but also positively influences the attitude of the whole class/school, as adults are perceived as caring and interested in pupil welfare. The medication required by pupils varies from being short term to requiring regular daily administration over a lengthy period of time in order that pupils can attend school regularly. All schools have a clear written policy on managing medication in school and systems to support individual pupils with medical needs. The medication is often supervised by the head teacher or delegated to a member of the support staff – preferably someone with medical knowledge and first-aid training.

MEMORY AND MEMORISING

See also: attention-deficit hyperactivity disorder, brain function, information, information technology, intelligence, kinaesthetic learners, learning styles, motivation for learning, poetry, stories, tactile learners, teaching strategies

Memorising is a complex phenomenon, the most familiar aspect being an *active working memory* that pupils use immediately after they see or hear something, a term that is widely used to refer to a memory system that provides a mental 'jotting pad' to store information necessary for everyday activities such as remembering telephone numbers, following directions and instructions and keeping track of shopping list items. A working memory allows children to hold information in their heads and manipulate it mentally, such as by adding up numbers without using pen and paper or a calculator. The majority of children with poor working memory are slow to learn in the areas of reading, mathematics and science, across both primary and secondary school years (Gathercole and Alloway 2008). Some psychologists refer to the active working memory as a temporary storage facility where information is located until the brain can process the information into what is commonly referred to as *short-term memory*, which is effective for brief periods of time but does not accommodate complete retention. Thus, children may appear to learn something one day but forget it by the next and have difficulty transferring the information to the second type of memory, known as *long-term memory* (permanently stored). In extreme cases a child will have difficulty grasping information for long enough in the active working memory to transfer it to the short-term memory. However, when memory works well, knowledge will be transferred from the active to the short-term and eventually to the long-term memory with minimum intellectual effort. It is generally accepted that brain development and memory are closely related to the amount and quality of sleep that children get each night.

Both 'episodic' memory (memory for events) and 'semantic' memory (memory for facts) are significant for young learners. Some children who are brain-damaged at birth struggle to recall episodic events from their everyday life with any reliability but are still capable of gaining average grades in work that relies on semantic memory, particularly in speech and language, reading and writing and recall of well-ordered facts. A poor working memory, rather than low intelligence, is the reason for under-performance in school, say researchers who claim to have developed a tool to assess memory capacity. Durham University researchers, led by Tracy Alloway (2008) found that a tenth of more 3,000 school children in Britain across all ages suffer from poor working memory, which has a more detrimental effect on their learning abilities than intelligence measures. Teachers don't tend to identify memory as a source of difficulty in children with working memory problems, despite their poor classroom functioning, but rather tend to describe them as inattentive.

The Working Memory Rating Scale (WMRS) was developed by Alloway and her team on the basis of interviews with teachers to provide a quick way for early identification of working memory problems that will impair learning. The assessment of children through use of a WMRS is said to allow educators to draw on their classroom expertise in early detection of children with memory failures and modify their teaching accordingly.

Children with memory strengths are easy to identify because they can accommodate large amounts of information and retain it effortlessly from a variety of sources. While such children may participate well in class discussions and offer interesting perspectives on complex issues, they don't necessarily do well in tests, especially if it involves writing answers down. These pupils – more often boys than girls – present a considerable challenge for teachers and may require additional adult support or regular access to information technology support materials. By contrast, children who struggle with memory weaknesses may appear to understand a concept, yet need a considerable amount of repetition, careful explanation and opportunities to explore ideas through problem-solving and investigations.

A common way in which teachers are alerted to a pupil's weak memory is when the child's written work is characterised by poor sequencing, missing words and inadequate grammar, despite the fact that they can articulate their ideas. If pupils have problems in absorbing information that is communicated verbally or are simply poor listeners they need to have directions explained and visually reinforced (with a diagram, for instance). If children have poor visual recall they may forget what they have read or been shown and need to have their learning supported through careful explanation and 'hands-on' (kinaesthetic/tactile) experiences.

Teachers are regularly faced with determining whether children cannot remember because they are unable to do so or because they are unwilling to give the subject sufficient attention and persevere to master information and skills. Problems can also be created by the teacher's inadequacy to explain clearly, use appropriate vocabulary and inspire children, which in turn leads to a low-key learning climate, tedium and reduced motivation. Children are more likely to remember and understand when the topic is interesting and relevant to them, so teachers are constantly seeking ways to enliven repetitive lessons through creative and interactive means, such as role play, stories and use of visual images.

There are a number of strategies that teachers use to build memory in primary-aged children. The first is to offer children opportunities for regular practice (for instance, in learning sets of numbers or lists of spellings). Second, teachers utilise spare moments to remind the children about key facts and engage them in a simple activity to reinforce the concepts. Third, reading well-loved books serves as a memory tool for pupils; in particular, reading aloud exposes them to language that will be of long-term benefit in tackling problems, discussing decisions and understanding instructions. When younger children ask the teacher to read a book again and again, the repetition assists memory of the story, sequencing of events and the satisfaction that they receive from grasping the plot. Fourth, teachers stimulate children's memories by enquiring what happens next or asking them to summarise what has happened so far and making a game of retelling the whole story by moving from child to child, each one making a small contribution. In this way, pupils remain involved without feeling under excessive pressure, thereby relaxing their minds and facilitating clearer thinking.

Burden (2005) found that children with attention-deficit hyperactivity disorder (ADHD) and non-ADHD groups performed similarly on tests of *explicit* memory (recall and recognition) and on *perceptual* aspects of implicit memory (word stem completion and picture fragment identification) as a function of age, retention interval and the stimulus used (i.e., using a picture or word). However, boys diagnosed with ADHD seemed to struggle with a unique memory deficit associated with the condition.

Rhyming and teaching letter sounds are important language skills that encourage memory growth and are commonly employed in verse and poetry. Well-written prose, especially amusing pieces, is greatly enjoyed by primary pupils and can also be memorised for single or choral speaking. Once mastered by the majority, speaking the passage in unison allows less confident children to be included within the group enterprise and conceal individual shortcomings. Using multiple and entertaining ways to study enhances learning for all children, but especially for those with poor recall, as the combination of different and captivating approaches literally makes the work 'memorable'. Highly motivated children are also more likely to share what they have done in school with family and friends, thereby further reinforcing learning.

Sources

Alloway, T.P., Gathercole, S.E. and Kirkwood, H. (2008) *The Working Memory Rating Scale*, London: Pearson Assessment.
Burden, M.J. (2005) 'Implicit memory development in school-age children with ADHD', *Developmental Neuropsychology*, 28 (3), 779–807.
Gathercole, S.E. and Alloway, T.P. (2008) Working Memory and Learning: A practical guide for teachers, London: Sage.

META-LEARNING

See also: collaboration in learning, learning

Over the past few years a lot of emphasis has been placed on what is sometimes referred to as 'meta-learning', which is a sophisticated way of saying, 'learning how to learn', a term coined by John Biggs of the University of Hong Kong in 1985 to show how we can take control of our own learning. The prefix 'meta' is derived from the Latin and means 'after, along-with and beyond'. One of the key principles is that learning is a skill to be acquired, mastered and improved, not a once-for-all 'hard-wired' trait that pupils (and adults) possess or do not possess. Meta-learning begins with raising awareness of learning in a child's mind, praising advancement and offering the child numerous opportunities to practise. It also embraces a variety of conditions that may interfere with the learning process, such as immaturity, stress and poor health (Cross 2006, chapter 6). Further, by learning about learning, children find out about themselves: their preferences, desires and the things that enthuse and motivate them. If the concept is extended to collaborative settings, it offers children insights into how others in the group learn, too.

Source

Cross, J. (2006) *Informal Learning*, Pfeiffer e-Books, on-line at www.pfeiffer.com

METACOGNITION

See also: learning styles, reflection

The term 'metacognition' refers to an individual's own awareness and consideration of his or her cognitive processes and strategies (Flavell 1979). Metacognition means, broadly, thinking about one's thinking processes and signifies people's ability to be self-reflexive; that is, to undergo a higher form of reflection than would normally be experienced (Fisher

1998). In school, children are encouraged to take conscious control of their learning rather than have it 'imposed' on them by adults. Teachers use a variety of strategies to achieve this aim, including sharing with children the learning objectives at the commencement of the lesson and asking them to say or write about what they think they have learned at the end. There has also been a surge of interest in 'learning styles' and the extent to which different children benefit most from the spoken word, the use of visual images and undertaking practical activities. Metacognition is known to be an important factor in academic achievement; however, it is also important in a wider life context. Encouraging children to reflect upon their thinking can help them to make wiser decisions in all aspects of their lives (Larkin 2009).

Sources

Fisher, R. (1998) 'Thinking about thinking: Developing metacognition in children', *Early Child Development and Care*, 141, 1–15.
Flavell J. (1979) 'Metacognition and cognitive monitoring: A new area of cognitive-developmental enquiry', *American Psychologist*, 34, 906–11.
Larkin, M. (2009) *Metacognition in Young Children*, London: Routledge.

MIDDLE SCHOOLS

See *First and middle schools*

MINORITY ETHNIC CHILDREN

See also: English as an additional language, expectations, home background and learning, parents, peer coaching, special educational needs

In recent years there has been a large influx of immigrants (now commonly referred to as 'migrants') to the UK from the European Union and Commonwealth countries, together with asylum seekers from many different places in the world. Their arrival has strengthened the diversity of cultures, knowledge and expertise in the country but also created some serious challenges for the communities in which they are located. Particular pressures have fallen upon the education system and social services as children arrive in school with little understanding of the indigenous norms and, in most cases, with English as an additional language (EAL). Once in school, most children quickly pick up the language but their parents – especially mothers – may only speak their first language and struggle to adjust to the indigenous culture. Teachers have had to confront issues about contacting parents, providing information and maintaining other forms of regular communication (Gardner 2006).

There is a considerable amount of advice available from different groups with an interest in the welfare of immigrants (e.g. Joint Council for the Welfare of Immigrants, JCWI, www.jcwi.org.uk) but it is far from easy and probably unwise to generalise, as each class contains such an exclusive range of pupil needs. Sometimes only one child from a particular country of origin will be in the class and receive individual attention; sometimes a number of pupils of similar origin will be in the class but vary in their grasp of English; again, there will sometimes be a large proportion of pupils speaking the same language, allowing for the formation of groups to receive targeted teaching or coaching in reading and writing. Perhaps the greatest challenge for a new teacher is to coordinate the many activities and adults involved in the special educational provision.

National surveys reveal a complex picture of minority ethnic attainment and participation, suggesting that the involvement of parents and the community in the life and development of the school is highly significant. One of the major issues facing teachers concerns the variation in achievement across ethnic minority groups, though they are committed to operate an agreed strategy to ensure effective learning and teaching for bilingual pupils and promote an ethos of mutual respect and tolerance. Generally, it appears that a large proportion of Black, Bangladeshi and Pakistani pupils perform less well than other ethnic groups during the period of compulsory schooling and are recorded as having special educational needs, though there are notable exceptions in individual schools. By contrast, Indian and Chinese pupils tend to perform better than other ethnic groups. Nevertheless, Beveridge (2005) notes that 'there remains a dispropor- tionate representation of particular minority ethnic groups among children with special educational needs and among those formally excluded from school' (p. 50). Explanations about the reasons for underachievement of certain minority groups are partly explained by the social and material deprivation that characterises those groups. However, there isn't a simple relationship between these fig- ures and academic achievement, as the biggest gap in attainment is across the full range of White pupils. Clearly, then, there are other factors that need to be taken into account when addressing issues of under-performance.

The most successful schools in raising eth- nic minority academic attainment have high expectations of staff and pupils, and ensure that they initiate and maintain close links with parents. Every teacher and trainee has to ask a number of important questions about their teaching approach and attitude towards all pupils, including:

- Are all children achieving their potential and gaining individual benefit from their education?
- If some children appear to be under- achieving, what factors seem to be contributing to this state of affairs?
- Are some children underachieving because of lack of access to curriculum opportunities?
- What steps can/should be taken to address the unsatisfactory situation?
- Would some identifiable groups of children benefit from exclusive attention from an adult or a modified curriculum?

One of the keys to successfully integrating all new children into the classroom is to assess their academic competence as accurately and swiftly as possible. In her work as a teacher of younger children, the American author Heyda (2002) describes the strategies she employs when dealing with the arrival of new children in the class who speak little or no English:

- Welcome the child with a big smile and a warm friendly voice.
- Assign a 'buddy', preferably someone who speaks the language, to accompany the child throughout the day.
- Take care not to use 'baby talk' that might embarrass the child or speak too loudly as if the child has a hearing impairment.
- Utilise support staff at an early stage.
- Be encouraging and positive.
- Use the child's mistakes as starting points for progress.
- Use lots of visual aids to get across con- cepts, such as drawing pictures next to vocabulary and using photographs and diagrams to explain things.
- Give the child plenty of hands-on experiences.
- Label the room with key words.

In a multilingual situation in which there are numerous children who speak the same first language, the challenges of incorporating a newcomer into the class are usually less severe than if the child is the only pupil who speaks the language. In such circumstances the school is likely to have additional adult support for EAL, though the proliferation of different languages in the school and the involvement of various language assistants present formidable organisation and management issues.

The Commission for Racial Equality (CRE) web site (www.cre.gov.uk) contains a useful, though extremely detailed set of guidelines for schools in the form of two audits to monitor whether the curriculum, teaching and assessment, and pupils' personal development, attainment and progress are sensitive to ethnic diversity and cultural fac- tors. The *curriculum audit* contains fourteen statements for the staff and governors of schools to consider and the *personal development audit* emphasises caring for and valuing individuals so that they can make the best use of their educational experiences.

Sources

Beveridge, S. (2005) *Children, Families and Schools: Developing partnerships for inclusive education*, London: Routledge.

Gardner, J. (2006) 'Children who have English as an additional language', in Knowles, G. (ed.) *Supporting Inclusive Practice*, Exeter: Learning Matters.

Heyda, P.A. (2002) *The Primary Teacher's Survival Guide*, Portsmouth NH: Heinemann.

MINORITY ETHNIC GROUP UNDERACHIEVEMENT

See also: communication, English as an additional language, equal opportunities, minority ethnic children

The reason for the underachievement of some minority groups is partly explained by the social and material deprivation that characterises those groups. However, the relationship between economic deprivation and academic progress is far from simple, so school-related factors also have to be considered when addressing issues of under-performance.

Three characteristics have been identified as significant for helping children from ethnic minority groups to improve their educational attainment: (1) to agree a strategy that applies across the whole school; (2) to strive for effective learning and teaching, including support for bilingual pupils; and (3) to create an ethos of respect, with a clear approach to issues relating to racism and behaviour. In addition, parents and the community are encouraged to undertake a full part in the life and development of the school.

Teachers have to exercise special attention when communicating effectively with children for whom English is an additional language. In such cases, strategies include the use of steady, well-articulated speech, a good range of tactile ('opportunities to touch and feel') experiences for the children and making a special effort to involve all the children in creative activities where spoken language is not necessarily essential to complete the work. In the UK on 1 October 2007, the Commission for Racial Equality (CRE), the Disability Rights Commission (DRC) and the Equal Opportunities Commission (EOC) were merged into the new Equality and Human Rights Commission. The web sites of these commissions have also been incorporated into the new Equality and Human Rights Commission web site (www.equalityhumanrights. com). Multiverse (www.multiverse.ac.uk) is a web site for teacher educators and trainee teachers addressing the educational achievement of pupils from diverse backgrounds.

MISBEHAVIOUR

See also: attention span, behaviour, home–school, life skills, parents, sanctions, teacher–pupil interaction

Classroom misbehaviour or 'inappropriate behaviour' is many teachers' secret dread. The prospect of indiscipline affects adults and children: adults, because they want to avoid being humiliated and remain 'in control'; children, because they do not always possess the life skills or strategies to avoid confrontation, steer clear of trouble or helpfully influence the behaviour of their peers. This last point is particularly important, for although a teacher may speak of a class of children as being 'difficult', it is often the case that the problems are confined to a very small number whose influence in the classroom gradually becomes pervasive. While it is true that a minority of children are reluctant to obey, won't listen to adults and prefer to antagonise other children rather than conform to the rhythm of classroom life, the vast majority of children are desperate for the security that comes through effective discipline. The term 'misbehaviour' is often preferred to 'bad behaviour' because the latter involves a moral judgement about the individual concerned, whereas the former is a simple descriptor.

Some children are unpredictable and restless; others are born wanderers; some seem unable (perhaps, *are* unable) to sit and concentrate for long; a very small number will delight in making life difficult for the teacher, regarding it as a personal challenge to see what they can get away with. As James and Brownsword (1994) rightly remind us, not all children know *how* to behave; so positive reinforcement of the appropriate behaviour by brief, sincere words of praise can also guide other children and spur them to adjust and improve their own behaviour. The authors argue that if these acts or 'types' of good and sensible behaviour are recorded and praised, it increases the likelihood that they will reoccur and inform the children what is expected of them in future.

Medhus (2001) stresses the importance of parent–teacher liaison and the need for children to be allocated roles in the class, as behaviour improves when children feel as if they have something to contribute. Where possible, the role should tie in with the nature of their behavioural problem; thus, a child that has a problem talking in class can assist the teacher in keeping order; a child that wanders about when the class walks in line can be made the line leader for a few days. Social successes and responsible behaviour are every bit as much a significant part of a child's education as academic achievement.

It is also true that despite a teacher's best efforts to make lessons relevant and interesting and to create a positive working environment, there may still be children who persist in inappropriate behaviour. For this troublesome minority, there are usually sanctions that can be applied, varying from school to school, but such procedures can be time-consuming and wearisome (though sometimes necessary). In truth, most teachers have no desire to impose a strict regime upon the class if it is possible to avoid it, and would prefer to coax, persuade, encourage and set targets for achievement as a means of keeping children on the straight and narrow.

Even one disruptive child can make life extremely uncomfortable for a teacher and the rest of the class. However, it is likely that the child is used to different codes of behaviour outside school, where the degree of strictness employed, use of threats, loudness of verbal exchanges and imposition of sanctions may be far more severe. The accumulation of these emotions, experiences and expectations from home are brought into school and a child may find it genuinely difficult to adjust and conform. Charlton and David (2003) usefully deal with the theoretical background of developing, assessing and understanding children's behaviour; the relationship between learning and behaviour problems; and the dynamics of emotional and behavioural difficulties. In exploring strategies to influence pupil behaviour, the authors also underline the importance of pastoral care, liaison with outside agencies and work with parents.

Explaining children's behaviour is not the same as the adults concerned employing a weak and passive approach to their misdirected energies, but looking at the reasons underlying the behaviour and acknowledging the factors contributing to it before deciding upon appropriate action. Teachers have to take account of, and make allowance for particular times of the week such as Monday morning (when the children are still adjusting to school after two days of relative freedom); the end of the week (when children become tired and eager for the weekend); and of periods prior to major events (such as half-term break, school concerts and the like). Despite the temptation to become gloomy about the attitude and behaviour of a minority, wise adults try to stress positive aspects of children's actions whenever possible.

Sources

Charlton, T. and David, K. (eds) (2003) *Managing Misbehaviour in Schools*, London: Routledge.

James, F. and Brownsword, K. (1994) *A Positive Approach*, Twickenham: Belair Publications.

Medhus, E. (2001) *Raising Children Who Think for Themselves*, New York: Atria Books (Simon & Schuster).

MISTAKES AND MISCONCEPTIONS

See also: communication, knowledge, mathematics, plenary, relationships

The Victorian politician E.J. Phelps is credited with coining the maxim: 'the man who makes no mistakes does not usually make anything' in a speech at Mansion House, 24 January 1899 (*Penguin Dictionary of Quotations*). There is, of course, a difference between genuine errors made in the legitimate pursuit of a goal and errors that result from weak application to the task. Mistakes can be categorised under four broad headings: slips, misunderstandings, misconceptions and misapplication. Slips result from a lack of concentration and momentary lapses. For example, a young child might reverse letters or numbers. Misunderstandings lead to adopting an incorrect approach and, as a result, an inappropriate outcome. For example, a child may confuse numbers on the x- and y-axis of a graph (see Spooner 2004). Misconceptions lead to confusion, as the insights and grasp of basic principles that are necessary for completion are inadequate. For example, a child may not understand the relationship between heat loss and the materials used for insulation. Misapplication occurs when, despite possessing the knowledge and practical strategies, they are not employed correctly. For example, a child may know how to use a dictionary but always start the search at the beginning instead of estimating the position of the word and turning to approximately the area in which it is located. It is easy for teachers to spend more of their time dealing with relatively minor slips and misunderstandings, rather than the more profound misconceptions and misapplications.

To teach in a way that prevents pupils from developing any misconceptions (sometimes called 'faultless communication') is desirable but extremely difficult in practice, and teachers have to accept that pupils will make some generalisations that are not necessarily precise or correct. On occasions, pupil misconceptions remain hidden unless teachers make a specific effort to disclose them, so a style of teaching that seeks to expose and rectify misconceptions through careful questioning and encouraging pupils to share their concerns openly is essential. At the same time, teachers need to engender an attitude among their pupils that it is preferable to try and found to be wrong than to hesitate to try for fear of being wrong. Hart *et al.* (2004) insist that building confidence and emotional security is essential for learning; thus: 'One central priority for teachers is to try to increase the extent to which young people feel emotionally safe, comfortable and positive about their participation in learning activities' (p. 173).

Results from the Diagnosis Teaching Project, conducted at Nottingham University's Shell Centre for Mathematical Education by Mike Askew and Dylan Wiliam indicate that learning is more effective when common misconceptions are addressed in teaching (Askew and Wiliam 2004). The first significant issue they raised was that addressing misconceptions during teaching improves pupils' achievements and long-term retention of mathematical concepts. Allowing the children to make their mistakes and then clarifying the position through constructive discussion seems to be more effective than drawing attention to a misconception before giving the examples. The second issue is that the intensity and degree of engagement with a task that pupils demonstrate in a collaborative group discussion is much more of an important influence on their learning than the amount of time spent on the task. Intensive discussions usually involve spending much longer on small but important teaching points, but this approach results in a much higher level of long-term retention than in situations where more curriculum content is covered superficially over the same period of time.

During the final phase of the lesson it is normal for primary teachers to bring the whole class together (sometimes referred to as the 'plenary' session) to celebrate achievements but also to correct misconceptions, summarise key facts and ideas, identify links to other areas of work, discuss what learning is likely to follow and, where appropriate, set homework tasks.

Sources

Askew, M. and Wiliam, D. (2004) for the DfES, *Guide for Your Professional Development: Unit 2 appendices*, London: HMSO.

Hart, S., Dixon, A., Drummond, M.J. and McIntyre, D. (2004) *Learning Without Limits*, Maidenhead: Open University Press.

Spooner, M. (2004) *Errors and Misconceptions in Mathematics at Key Stage 2*, London: David Fulton.

MIXED ABILITY TEACHING

See also: decision-making, early years, literacy, mathematics, motivation, organising for learning, reading, topic work, writing

Mixed ability teaching or 'non-graded education' is defined as the practice of teaching children of different ability levels together in the same classroom, and has been common practice in primary schools for fifty years or more. Within these non-graded structures, children progress along a continuum of simple through more complex material at their own rates (Cotton 1993). A generation ago, A.V. Kelly, a strong advocate of this approach, argued that the 'first and most fundamental requirement of all teachers in catering for mixed ability classes is a deep understanding of the educative process' (Kelly 1975, p. 14) as more responsibility for decision-making fell to the teacher than working through a set syllabus. However, Kelly also acknowledged that the then familiar use of 'topic work' approaches to accommodate the wide range of abilities could lead to some

children wasting time rather than working purposefully; he therefore advocated the keeping of full and adequate records of each child's work to monitor progress. It is worth noting that the difference between Kelly's reasons for recording progress – as confirmation of achievement to enhance motivation and encourage further effort – and the modern advocacy of the approach (as evidence to level and grade of children as a means of evaluating teacher competence) could hardly be more stark. It is also a fact that in reality, no two children are of identical ability so any grouping on this basis relies on teachers' assessment of pupils' competence in specific and identifiable ways, notably in reading, writing, comprehension and mathematics.

Organising mixed ability teaching is more challenging for teachers, as it requires decisions about grouping and catering for the range of understanding and insight possessed by the pupils in each group or class. In the majority of early years situations, children are placed in mixed ability groups to work on tasks and activities initiated by the teacher; in the case of younger pupils a teaching assistant is present with the group for all or most of the time to teach, guide and encourage them. However, as pupils move towards the top of the primary school there is more likelihood that they will be allocated a group based on assessments of their progress in mathematics and literacy, with a subsequent narrowing of ability breadth.

Sources

Cotton, K. (1993) *Nongraded Primary Education*, on-line at www.nwrel.org/scpd/sirs/7/cu14.html

Kelly, A.V. (1975) 'Mixed ability groups – the key issues', in Kelly, A.V. (ed.) *Case Studies in Mixed Ability Teaching*, London: Harper and Row.

MODELLING BEHAVIOUR

See also: behaviour, learning climate, learning (teacher influence), mistakes, teacher role, teachers' beliefs, thinking

Children are close observers of all adults, including parents, relatives, teachers and support staff, and pick up on any inconsistencies they see. Children learn what is acceptable behaviour by watching and imitating the behaviour of others, so when grown-ups set a good example they are helping to establish a foundation for young people to behave responsibly. It is particularly important that adults demonstrate consistency between what they say and what they do, as even very young children are quick to point out any obvious mismatches. Hallam and Rogers (2008) advise that policy-makers should encourage society and the media to create role models who will have a positive influence on young people's attitudes and behaviour, rather than many of today's role models, who are frequently rewarded in terms of celebrity for behaving badly. Modelling can take place at a number of levels, such as the degree of warmth and approachability; concern for the needs of others; active caring; dedication and perseverance; patience; priorities; and so forth.

Nelson-Jones (2003) suggests from a counselling perspective that modelling not only involves demonstrating behaviour but also involves *thinking*. That is, one person's behaviour acts as a stimulus for similar thoughts, attitudes or behaviours on the part of another individual. Consequently, modelling may focus on action skills, thinking skills or a mixture of the two (see pp. 179–83). To use Carl Rogers' argument, adults must help children to strive to live life to its maximum potential, with an emphasis on establishing sincere relationships (Rogers 2004).

Fenstermacher (2004) describes modelling as a form of *manner* defined as conduct that expresses highly regarded moral and intellectual traits. A teacher may, for instance, exhibit characteristics such as being fair, caring, brave and persevering; or may be unreliable, biased, patronising and selfish; or a mixture of commendable and undesirable behaviour. There may be a tension between the adult manner at home and at school, such that children are uncertain about which type of behaviour is acceptable. For instance, parents may casually use obscene language, whereas a teacher would be reprimanded for doing so; children therefore have to discern and judge how certain behaviour is admissible in one context but not in another. Again, children see and hear adults on television and films behaving in a variety of ways, some of which would be wholly unsuitable in everyday life.

A child's regular class teacher's manner is particularly important, not only because it offers the pupils a model to emulate (or reject) but also because it impinges on the way that adults and children interact in school. Thus, a classroom setting in which the teacher welcomes questions, responds to children's news with enthusiasm, encourages discussion and does not dwell on mistakes is different in kind from a setting in which the teacher concentrates on the formal, individual work and places a strong emphasis on accuracy rather than enterprise. While the former situation is likely to be buzzing with conversation, smiles and enthusiasm, the latter will probably be subdued.

There are other ways in which teachers model behaviour they want to see reflected in their pupils. For instance, by arriving on time for sessions, being properly prepared and enthusiastic about the lesson content and concealing negative emotions when confronting unsatisfactory behaviour, combating rudeness and dealing with incivility. Instead, they have the challenging task of firmly but courteously reminding children about appropriate speech and actions (Dix 2007). Teachers therefore seek to provide children with an environment ('learning climate') in which they are safe to explore, discover new things and make genuine mistakes without the fear of humiliation.

Sources

Dix, P. (2007) *Taking Care of Behaviour*, Harlow: Pearson.

Fenstermacher, G.D. (2004) 'On the concept of manner and its visibility in teaching practice', in

Wragg, E.C. (ed.) *Reader in Teaching and Learning*, London: Routledge.

Hallam, S. and Rogers, L. (2008) *Improving Behaviour and Attendance at School*, Maidenhead: Open University Press.

Nelson-Jones, R. (2003) *Practical Counselling and Helping Skills*, London: Cassell.

Rogers, C. (2004) *On Becoming a Person*, London: Constable.

MODERN FOREIGN LANGUAGES

Modern foreign languages (MFL) is not a compulsory National Curriculum subject for primary aged children in England, but by 2010 every child in key stage 2 (juniors, 7–11 years) in maintained schools will have an entitlement to learn a language other than English. In Scotland the term 'modern languages' is preferred and the framework for 5–14 modern languages provides a means of organising what pupils should know and be able to do as a result of their learning. There are four attainment outcomes within the framework: listening; speaking; reading; and writing.

MONITORING

See also: assessing children's learning, assessment for learning, feedback, formative assessment, intervention, Primary National Strategy, rewards, special educational needs

Monitoring pupil progress is a procedure by which children's work is regulated through close and active attention from teachers and support staff. Monitoring is closely associated with intervention, a process that follows monitoring, by which teachers offer specific guidance and direction to pupils to correct errors, challenge their thinking and focus their attention on a specific area of work. Those seeking qualified teacher status need to demonstrate competence in monitoring, assessment, recording, reporting and accountability to pupils, colleagues and parents, compositely referred to as MARRA (Headington 2000). Perceptive monitoring of pupil

progress is an essential component of teaching, as there is a close correlation between how well it is carried out and the quality of children's learning. Knowledge that teachers and their assistants build up through regular contact with pupils, together with information from a variety of other sources as necessary – parents, staff, external agencies and the children themselves – provides valuable insights into pupil learning needs. All schools hold regular review meetings to discuss progress with adults who are involved with the children's education; for children with special learning needs, the range of adults is likely to be wide; for children progressing satisfactorily, the review will normally only involve the regular staff.

An essential element of the monitoring and intervening agenda is for teachers to be keenly aware of the critical moments when pupils demonstrate through their words or actions that they have grasped a concept, developed a skill or gained some knowledge that assists their fuller understanding of a topic or theme. These assessment opportunities ('assessment for learning' or 'formative assessment') tend to be exposed through four pupil actions: (a) when they answer questions, (b) when they complete a piece of work, (c) when they explain something to an adult, and (d) when they share findings from a collaborative (team) exercise.

Monitoring and intervening allows teachers to offer feedback that will assist children in formulating ideas, understanding the work they are engaged in, and helping them to make sense of their learning (Angelle 2004). Fostering intrinsic rewards (self-satisfaction) as well as extrinsic rewards (based on adult satisfaction) impresses upon pupils that work is worthwhile for its own sake and not merely to please and satisfy others. Monitoring is also a means by which teachers ensure that pupils concentrate on the task they are undertaking and behave appropriately during lessons.

Under formal test conditions, the process of monitoring consists of ensuring that pupils conform to the required conditions (silence, individual working, co-operating, etc.). However, in the vast majority of primary classroom learning situations, monitoring involves close observation of children as they grapple with tasks and respond to the demands made of them. Monitoring of work in response to children's requests for clarification leads to active intervention and the provision of appropriate advice to them about the direction and quality of their work. Monitoring is more straightforward when teachers have clarified the expectations for pupils in advance of starting the tasks or activities, and explained what constitutes satisfactory work, so that both teacher and learners have shared aims.

When adults and children enjoy a comfortable working relationship, the constructive and sensitive criticism that results from monitoring acts as an encouragement and stimulus to pupils as they grapple with concepts and master practical challenges. If the monitoring is perceived by pupils as an attempt to 'catch them out' it leads to defensiveness and resentment. Many teachers invite pupils to be self-critical and evaluate their own or other pupil's work ('peer assessment') as an important contribution to the sense of shared endeavour. The Primary National Strategy in England promotes the regular use of pupil progress review meetings, at which the following agenda is likely to be used (DCSF 2007):

- to have an open discussion about the progress children are making and to value teacher judgement;
- to identify progress of individual children;
- to identify cohort progress;
- to focus specifically on the target group but to also identify children at risk due to additional circumstances;
- to identify progress of groups within the cohort – gender, special educational needs (SEN) and ethnicity;
- to look at the impact of the intervention programmes;
- to identify action points.

The above agenda leads to a raft of questions that schools have to address about the extent to which teacher assessment and national test results match; whether a particular cohort is 'on target' to achieve the results predicted by the school; the performance of boys, girls, children with English as an additional language (EAL) and children with special educational needs; successful strategies and barriers in the drive to raise attainment; and (in England) whether results show improvement between tests at age seven and eleven.

Computer software is now used extensively in schools to track, plot and systematically record individual pupil progress. The concept of monitoring has thereby shifted from a process in which each teacher observes and mentally or physically notes pupil progress and makes necessary adjustments to planning and teaching, to one in which statistical data are used to 'personalise' learning, set targets for pupil achievement and provide evidence that schools are succeeding in raising attainment. One consequence of the move towards such detailed forms of accounting is that senior teachers and subject leaders spend a larger proportion of their time on such matters and less time actively teaching – a situation which leads to concerns about over-regulation and unnecessary bureaucracy.

Sources

Angelle P. (2004) 'Monitoring progress through feedback', *School Effectiveness and School Improvement*, 15 (1), 115–20.
DCSF Standards Site (2007) *Pupil Progress Meetings: Prompts and guidance*, London: HMSO. www.standards.dfes.gov.uk
Headington, R. (2000) *Monitoring, Assessment, Recording, Reporting and Accountability*, London: David Fulton.

MORAL CHOICES

See also: behaviour, moral development, punishment, relationships, rewards, rules

The American psychologist Lawrence Kohlberg was interested in children's reasons for making moral choices and established a theory based

283

on six stages, the first four of which apply most directly to primary children (see, for example, Kohlberg 1981):

1 *Obedience and punishment*: The earliest stage of moral development is especially common in young children, who see rules as fixed and absolute. Obeying the rules is important because it is a means to avoid punishment.

2 *Individualism and exchange*: At this stage of moral development, children account for individual points of view and judge actions based on how they serve individual needs.

3 *Interpersonal relationships*: This stage of moral development is focused on living up to social expectations and roles with an emphasis on conformity, being nice and how choices influence relationships.

4 *Maintaining social order*: The focus is on maintaining law and order by following the rules, doing one's duty, and respecting authority.

5 *Social contract and individual rights*: People begin to account for the differing values, opinions, and beliefs of other people.

6 *Universal principles*: People follow their own principles of justice, even if they conflict with laws and rules.

Source

Kohlberg, L. (1981) *Essays on Moral Development 1*, San Francisco CA: Harper & Row.

MORAL DEVELOPMENT

See also: caring teachers, citizenship, moral choices, morality, parental involvement, spiritual development, teachers' beliefs

The well-known psychologist, Sigmund Freud, claimed that the quality of relationship the child has with his or her parents greatly affects the way a child develops morally. *Social learning theories*, on the other hand, state that children initially learn how to behave morally through modelling or imitating appropriate adult behaviour (not necessarily parents). By

contrast, *cognitive developmental theories* claim that a child's ability to reason morally depends on his or her general thinking abilities. All of the theories, although somewhat different from each other, offer some insight into moral development. See Sanger and Osguthorpe (2005) for an analysis of some basic challenges in making sense of approaches to moral education and the development of a framework to meet these challenges.

In curriculum terms, moral development is closely related to 'ethics' and forms part of the (non-statutory) citizenship curriculum in primary education in England, Wales and Northern Ireland. In Scotland, religious and moral education (RME) are linked; Government guidelines recommend that in primary schools RME is allocated 15 per cent of the curriculum, along with Health Education and Personal and Social Development, although it is recognised that RME does not have the monopoly on moral education and that some aspects of moral education will fall within other areas of the curriculum. All programmes recognise that children's needs are not purely academic but also social, spiritual and emotional. There are strong indications that while examination results are improving, there is a concomitant increase in drug dependency, sexually transmitted diseases, self-harm, dissatisfaction with school among sections of the community, and an expanding group of disaffected young people who resort to extreme forms of behaviour. Even children of primary school age are not immune from the impact of social division and strife. One of the aims of primary education is to help pupils to understand their place in society and encourage them to empathise with the views of others. Children can also be enthused to discover their own strengths, passions and gifting.

The notion that a moral development programme will succeed in creating 'morally upright' people has been the subject of intense debate. People who are capable of talking at a high moral level may not behave accordingly. There is general agreement that valuing the self, valuing others, valuing society and valuing the environment provide a helpful framework within which issues of morality can be presented and discussed. However, such statements do not necessarily achieve the intended goal for a number of reasons. First, parents may hold particular views that are not fully in accord with those promoted by the school. Second, issues are rarely clear-cut; for instance, when children are encouraged to be truthful yet tactful – a balance that even adults find tricky to maintain.

People working in primary schools are more likely to base their approach on what have been called the 'five Es' (Lickona 1999), thus: Example; Exhortation ('it is good to'); Explanation ('I want you to do this because'); Experience; and an Environment providing stability and love. Day (2004, see chapter 2) puts the matter succinctly: 'Moral purposes are at the heart of every teacher's work. They underpin their sense of commitment to their pupils, which includes but goes beyond the instrumental policy agendas of governments' (p. 24). Chater (2002) is even more direct in interrogating how young people develop morally, and poses a variety of possibilities: being told what is right and wrong; discovering pleasure, meaning and intellectual and emotional satisfaction in doing right; or through being encouraged to discover right and wrong for themselves. He also poses a blunt question for all parents and educators: 'Would moral development happen anyway, regardless of adult intervention?' (p. 44).

One of the UK government slogans to recruit teachers, 'Use your head, teach', is one indicator of a move towards teaching as being, first and foremost, a profession requiring intelligent and knowledgeable members. However, there is unease among primary practitioners that the emphasis on academic attainment may be viewed by the public and politicians as incompatible with demonstrating and practising a caring and nurturing attitude towards children. For primary educators, pressure to achieve standards means that there is sometimes a tension between the time and effort expended in striving for higher test results and the attention paid to moral and ethical issues. Osguthorpe (2008) argues that we need to produce teachers of good disposition and moral characters for the sake of teaching that accords with what is good, right, and virtuous, as these qualities impact upon all aspects of classroom life and teacher effectiveness. Adults who work in schools are not directly responsible for children's moral development and every primary teacher is conscious about trespassing on areas that are rightly the business of parents. Nevertheless, each time a child is admonished by a teacher, told how to behave or presented with choices, an ethical position is being established and a moral statement is being made. One way and another, deliberately or incidentally, teachers have an influence on the development of children's characters and are therefore locked into a position in which they exercise moral authority. Parents appear to recognise increasingly that children need and benefit from spiritual influences, as manifested through the popularity of schools with a religious foundation or strong moral ethic.

Primary educators grapple with questions about what forms of education will help to develop young people, forms that are not only academically sound but also wise and morally discerning in their decisions. In doing so they have to balance curriculum demands with the requirement to promote acceptable standards of behaviour. The imposition of a code of conduct shaped by a school discipline policy may bring about positive changes in pupil behaviour while constraints are in place, but fail to provide the moral certainty that will lead to appropriate choices about lifestyle when children move outside the school influence. No teacher wishes to educate young people to be reckless and foolish, yet recklessness and foolishness have become all too familiar in society. It is clear that knowledge, examination success or even an intelligent understanding of issues cannot create a civilised and just society unless they are underpinned by more deeply seated moral imperatives. Adults that work in primary

285

schools care deeply for the pupils they consider to be 'their' children and want them to do well in their studies, to prosper in their relationships and to be satisfied with their successes and endeavours. Educators want to use their influence to reveal something profound to children about life and meaning, helping them to appreciate that with perseverance and determination they can not only achieve commendable academic standards but also discover something about their own worth and the worth of others.

Sources

Chater, M. (2002) 'The child as spiritual citizen', in Johnston, J., Chater, M. and Bell, D. (eds) *Teaching the Primary Curriculum*, Maidenhead: Open University Press.

Day, C. (2004) *A Passion for Teaching*, London: Routledge.

Lickona, T. (1999) *Educating for Character*, New York: Bantam Press.

Osguthorpe, R.D. (2008) 'On the reasons we want teachers of good disposition and moral character', *Journal of Teacher Education*, 59 (4), 288–99.

Sanger, M. and Osguthorpe, R.D. (2005) 'Making sense of approaches to moral education', *Journal of Moral Education*, 34 (1), 57–71.

MORALITY

See also: behaviour, moral choices, moral development, rules

Morality is a term applied to issues about caring relationships, universal principles that regulate forms of behaviour, right (virtuous) and wrong (inappropriate) conduct, and character. As children develop their general thinking skills, they are also expected to start to conform to the moral rules that bond society. Piaget studied many aspects of moral judgement, and most of his findings fit into a two-stage theory, whereby children younger than 10 or 11 years think about moral dilemmas in terms of consequences; older children tend to base their judgements on intentions. Thus, younger children regard rules as fixed and absolute, handed down by adults or by God, whereas the older child understands that it is permissible to change rules if everyone agrees, such that rules are not sacred and absolute but are devices that humans use to get along co-operatively (Crain 1985).

Source

Crain, W.C. (1985) *Theories of Development*, London: Prentice Hall.

MOTIVATION FOR LEARNING

See also: curiosity, encouragement and praise, learning, learning (teacher influence), modelling behaviour, pupil perspectives, recording, rewards, success, target setting (pupils)

Children are not born with a particular view of themselves or their level of self-worth; it is something that they develop over the years, shaped through their relationships with family and friends and their wider social experiences. Although teachers cannot alter directly the way that children in their class have been or are treated by adults outside school, they can make a significant contribution to their wellbeing by concentrating their efforts in six areas. First, finding out what children already know and understand. This process necessitates talking to the children, listening to what they say, checking previous school records, and observing how they approach tasks and use their existing knowledge and understanding. Second, modelling a positive attitude towards learning by celebrating success, commiserating with failure, being enthusiastic about discovering new facts, specifying alternatives and offering help and guidance whenever possible. Third, giving close personal attention to children who are struggling, restless or bored, remembering that most disaffection is caused by the perceived irrelevance of the work or fear of failure. Fourth, involving children in learning by discussing the lesson purpose, establishing manageable learning targets and inviting them to comment on the quality of their work and effort. Fifth, acknowledging pupils' points of view and feelings. Finally, emphasising that success is attainable and worth cherishing.

Studies suggest that the extent of children's satisfaction with their education experience decreases with age and drops considerably when they reach secondary school (see, for example, the classic study by Woods 1990; Cullingford 2002). Thus, a large majority of primary pupils think that school is a positive experience; this contrasts with about one quarter in secondary schools who feel similarly enthusiastic. When measuring pupils' views about the relevance of what they learn and retain while in school, the motivation gap between the primary and secondary phases is even more pronounced. As pupils who retain a sense of curiosity and are at ease about their lives in school are more likely to be strongly motivated, teachers and assistants have a significant responsibility to create a dynamic learning environment in which children can prosper and enjoy what they are doing. In top-performing primary schools there is a serious effort to achieve academic success without sacrificing an investigative spirit and spontaneity. In stressing the importance of supporting children's learning and harnessing their eagerness, Ellis (2007) advises teachers:

> We need to be creative to maintain their enthusiasm and flexible to meet their immediate needs. We want to light a fire in these children's lives for learning, to set them on a course, which will motivate them to keep learning throughout their lives.
>
> (p. 25)

Katz and Chard (2000) remind us that from a child's point of view, school is real life, not contrived or pretend, so children need to make learning an adventure that is sometimes challenging, sometimes perplexing but always motivating. Although some parts of the curriculum are less appealing than others, teachers should strive to create a learning environment that offers diverse experiences,

excites children's interest and, wherever possible, builds on their enthusiasm. Learning becomes worthwhile when the content is interesting and relevant; the lesson is presented imaginatively; the tasks associated with the lesson present a reasonable challenge; the learning climate is lively and encouraging. Teachers have a vital role to play in:

- explaining the usefulness of the lesson;
- stirring children's imaginations through tone of voice, passion of delivery and the incorporation of visual material, story, verbal exchanges and collaborative activity;
- enhancing pupil self-image and motivation by differentiating tasks so that each child can succeed and feel pleased with her or his efforts;
- transforming the climate from one of stale conformity to energetic vibrancy by a friendly but purposeful approach to teaching, patient explanations and an emphasis on positive aspects of learning.

Unease about a lesson's relevance is sometimes expressed by younger children through their superficial commitment to the task, yawning or restless behaviour. Older children will also exhibit these tendencies but will often be more assertive and even ask directly about why an activity is necessary or its purpose. Hallam and Rogers (2008) recommend that teachers emphasise praise-and-reward systems, rather than punishments, ensuring that pupils understand any sanctions applied and acknowledge them as fair; the authors also stress the importance of pupils taking responsibility for their own behaviour.

Motivating a child to do well does not, of itself, produce a sudden transformation from uncertainty to optimism. However, a positive approach, coupled with appropriate support and direction allows a child to persevere in the certain knowledge that there is an adult 'safety net' underneath. Over time the buoyant and upbeat mood spreads throughout the class and, coupled with a small number of external rewards (such as stickers and merit

287

cards) positively influences the children's expectations and sense of determination. If the classroom exudes a 'we can' approach to learning, the increase in self-esteem, work of high quality and co-operation soon becomes tangible. Motivation is not only important for academic work but also in preparing children to cope with the social demands of everyday life and when they move on to secondary school.

Sources

Cullingford, C. (2002) *The Best Years of their Lives? Pupils' experiences of school*, London: Kogan Page.
Ellis, N. (2007) 'Foundation Stage: Expectations and vision', in Moyles, J. (ed.) *Beginning Teaching, Beginning Learning in Primary Education*, Maidenhead: Open University.
Hallam, S. and Rogers, L. (2008) *Improving Behaviour and Attendance at School*, Maidenhead: Open University Press.
Katz, L.G. and Chard, S.C. (2000) *Engaging Children's Minds: The project approach*, Stamford CT: Ablex Publishing.
Woods, P. (1990) *The Happiest Days?* London: Falmer.

MOTIVATION FOR TEACHING

See also: aims of education, beliefs teaching and learning, caring teachers, moral development, nurturing, relationships, workforce reforms

Surveys about motivation for teaching conclude that altruism, a love for children, a desire to help pupils learn and the pleasure associated with the job are highly significant factors for new recruits to the profession. People decide to become primary school teachers because they feel that it is a useful and worthwhile way to spend their working lives through making a positive contribution to the well-being of society. Research shows that many of the key factors that provide the initial spur for becoming a primary teacher are rooted in caring, self-fulfilment and the positive impact it has on young people's lives (e.g. Spear *et al.* 2000). Studies based on the views

of trainee teachers reveal that their motivation rests on a belief that they can not only contribute to children's academic progress but also influence their social and moral development (Moran *et al.* 2001; Thornton *et al.* 2002). In their study of teacher commitment in six primary schools, Troman and Raggi (2008) found that the mission to teach is still strongly evident, together with a desire to nurture expressed as 'love' and 'caring'. These altruistic desires do not mean that teachers are uninterested in good working conditions, a respectable salary and opportunities for career enhancement, but that nothing can match the satisfaction that comes from making a significant difference to the life of each child.

One of the challenges associated with an educational climate in which success is largely measured through quantitative test results is that it may be at the expense of the caring and nurturing atmosphere that many primary educators extol. Advocates of this 'child-centred' approach to education claim that the principle of caring for all of a child's development needs forms the bedrock of a successful education. Child-centred educators argue that when teachers' practice is based on an ethic of care it provides the motivation and commitment for them to persevere and helps to compensate for the exhausting effects that the intensification of their work has created in recent years.

In an attempt to recruit a larger number of teachers, the web site of the teacher Training and Development Agency, TDA (the government body responsible for monitoring the recruitment and training of teachers in England, formerly known as the Teacher Training Agency, TTA) is now replete with stimulating statements such as 'Teaching is like no other job. It is as inspiring, challenging and unique as each child you teach' and 'Talk to teachers, pick up the exhilaration they feel' and 'You will be working ... with other intelligent and like-minded people'. This emphasis is a response to concerns that the previous recruitment campaign relied too heavily on the belief that altruism was the principal motivating factor for aspiring teachers and deterred potential applicants who were seeking a career that offered intellectual satisfaction, good conditions of service and personal fulfilment. Based on the responses of 241 recently graduated teachers Cooman (2007) concluded that teachers consider intrinsic, altruistic and interpersonal features as strong job-specific motivators, while non-teachers are more attracted by individualistic work values such as career opportunities and executive power.

According to a Department for Children, Schools and Families (DCSF) research report published in late 2007, entitled Newly Qualified Teachers' Experiences of Their First Year of Teaching, the high points experienced by newly qualified teachers tended to be associated with positive relationships with pupils and colleagues, their increased sense of professional autonomy over the first year, and their perceptions of achievement and change over the same period. The low points included the extreme demands of their role, workload and the ever-present battle with disaffected pupils. These results contrast rather starkly with a more recent school inspection report (October 2007), which claimed that schools had used workforce reforms to improve teachers' lives, though not necessarily to improve standards of education. Writing from a US perspective, Kozol (2007) says that the best veteran teachers bring a sense of personal stability and of assimilated self-lessness, as well as all the 'nuts and bolts' of classroom management and good instructional approaches they have acquired and developed. They are therefore able to assist younger colleagues in dealing with parents and the local community, having known generations of families who have passed through the school.

Sources

Cooman, R.D. (2007) 'Graduate teacher motivation for choosing a job in education', International Journal for Educational and Vocational Guidance, 7 (2), 123–36.
DCSF (2007) Newly Qualified Teachers' Experiences of their First Year of Teaching, London: HMSO.
Kozol, J. (2007) Letters to a Young Teacher, New York: Random House.
Moran, A., Kilpatrick, R., Abbott, J., Dallat, J. and McClune, B. (2001) 'Training to teach: Motivating factors and implications for recruitment', Evaluation and Research in Education, 15 (1), 17–32.
Spear, M., Gould, K. and Lee, B. (2000) 'Who Would be a Teacher? A review of factors motivating and demotivating prospective and practising teachers', Slough: National Foundation for Educational Research.
Thornton, M., Bricheno, P. and Reid, I. (2002) 'Students' reasons for wanting to teach in primary school', Research in Education, 67, 33–43.
Troman, G. and Raggi, A. (2008) 'Primary teacher commitment and the attractions of teaching', Pedagogy, Culture and Society, 16 (1), 85–99.

MOTOR SKILLS

See also: skills

A motor skill is a learned skill that involves voluntary muscular movement to complete a task (as opposed to spontaneous or involuntary movements). Motor skills range from habitual tasks, such as walking or chewing, to perceptual tasks, like playing an instrument or using a computer keyboard, to the use of 'fine' movements, such as handling a pencil when writing.

MULTIPLE INTELLIGENCES

See also: ability, intelligence, Intelligence Quotient, problem solving

The theory of multiple intelligences was developed in 1983 by Dr Howard Gardner, professor of education at Harvard University, who suggested that the traditional notion of intelligence based on Intelligence Quotient (IQ) testing is far too limiting. Instead, Gardner proposed first seven and then eight different intelligences to account for a broader range of human potential in children and adults (Gardner 1983, 1993):

1 Linguistic intelligence, also known as 'word smart'.
2 Logical-mathematical intelligence, also known as 'number/reasoning smart'.
3 Spatial intelligence, also known as 'picture smart'.
4 Bodily-kinaesthetic intelligence, also known as 'body smart'.
5 Musical intelligence, also known as 'music smart'.
6 Interpersonal intelligence, also known as 'people smart'.
7 Intrapersonal intelligence, also known as 'self smart'.
8 Naturalist intelligence, also known as 'nature smart'.

Armstrong (1999, 2000) suggests that the theory provides eight different potential pathways to learning, simply described as (1) *words* – linguistic intelligence; (2) *numbers or logic* – logical-mathematical intelligence; (3) *pictures* – spatial intelligence; (4) *music* – musical intelligence; (5) *self-reflection* – intrapersonal intelligence; (6) *a physical experience* – bodily-kinaesthetic intelligence; (7) *a social experience* – interpersonal intelligence; and (8) *an experience in the natural world* – naturalist intelligence.

Gardner surmised that an extraterrestrial visitor would be more interested to know how humans performed exceptionally well in particular fields, such as the chess master, the orchestral conductor or the accomplished athlete, rather than enquiring about their individual IQs. This perspective gains support from the fact that many accomplished people are undoubtedly talented and intelligent, yet traditional methods of assessing intelligence fail to identify them as such. In the business world, people of high IQ sometimes find themselves subordinate to people of much lower IQ, so this single measure is clearly not adequate to explain why some people succeed more than others of similar stature. Gardner famously coined the maxim: *It is not how smart you are but how you are smart.* Human beings all have a repertoire of skills for solving different kinds of problems, so intelligence is

more helpfully thought of as an ability to solve a problem or fashion a product that is valued in different cultural settings; for example, in a rural setting the ability to select the right time to sow and harvest crops would be considered a great asset, whereas in a city culture trading stock market shares would be prized. Thus, the notion of multiple intelligences (plural) took shape and influenced the way that educators viewed learners and modes of learning.

Sources

Armstrong, T. (1999) *7 Kinds of Smart: Identifying and developing your many intelligences*, New York: Plume.
——(2000) *Multiple Intelligences in the Classroom*, Alexandria VA: Association for Supervision and Curriculum Development.
Gardner, H. (1983, 1993) *Frames of Mind: The theory of multiple intelligences*, New York: Basic Books.

MULTIPLICATION TABLES

See also: mathematics, memory and memorisation, numeracy

Multiplication of numbers is a short-cut method to achieve repeated addition. For instance, $5+5+5+5$ (= 20) can be worked put by adding $5+5$ (= 10) add 5 (= 15) add 5 = 20. This method is manageable with smaller numbers but soon becomes unwieldy with larger ones; for instance, imagine trying to work out 25×34 by repeated addition. Using multiplication avoids the complications and potential for error that using repeated addition entails. One of the more helpful definitions of 'multiplication table' according to the 'Answers.com' web dictionary (www.answers.com) is 'a table, used as an aid in memorisation, that lists the products of certain numbers multiplied together, typically the numbers 1 to 12'.

In past generations it was commonplace for pupils to learn their multiplication tables (e.g. one times three is three; two times three is six; three times three is nine, etc.) from an early age by reciting them repeatedly and being tested to ensure that they had firmly grasped them. Today, teachers try to ensure that children understand the concept of addition (and subtraction) of numbers before being introduced to multiplication; although chanting of tables is still a regular feature of many mathematics programmes, they are not learnt in isolation, as was once the case. Hermitt (on-line) offers the following advice (amended version; see web site for detailed information) for teaching children tables, including

- Teach the 1 times tables and the 10 times tables first.
- Teach skipping and catchy songs to learn the 2, 3 and 5 times table.
- Teach the 4, 6 and 8 times tables using logic. For example, in learning the 4 times tables, double-double the number. Thus, 4×7 is $2 \times 2 \times 7$, so 7 is doubled to make 14, which is doubled again to make 28.
- Use reversals of numbers to use an easier multiplier; for example, 2×8 (using the 8 times table) becomes 8×2 (using the better known 2 times table).
- Use rhymes; for example, to remember that 7×7 is 49, say: 'Chris remembered just in time that seven times seven is forty-nine'.

During the latter part of the twentieth century the received wisdom about teaching tables was that it was not worth spending much time doing it. The availability of calculators meant that pupils could discover the answer at the click of a button and did not need to hold information in their heads. However, the introduction in schools (England and Wales) during the late 1990s of what was popularly known as the 'numeracy hour' emphasised the importance of the oddly termed 'mental maths' phase – working out computations 'in the head' rather than using calculators or printed charts. Consequently, knowledge of tables 'off-by-heart' assumed greater importance again, though it is fair to

say that it has never reached its former level of significance as an integral element of primary education.

Sources

Hermitt, A. *How to Teach the Multiplication Tables to Your Child*, on-line at www.ehow.com/how_2283448_teach-multiplication-tables-child.html

MUSIC

See also: art and design, attention span, creativity, dance, drama, excellence and enjoyment, memory and memorising, spatial-temporal reasoning

Music forms part of the fabric of society, such that the intrinsic value of music for each individual is widely recognised in the diverse cultures that contribute to the world as children experience it. The prospect of music, and classical music in particular, as a device for enhancing intellect and stimulating young children's development, fascinates educators and parents and there have been numerous claims over recent years in support of its positive effects. Studies in the early 1990s suggested that pupil scores on spatial-temporal reasoning tests improved by up to one third after listening to classical music, notably from composers like Mozart. Although these claims are not universally recognised, it is certainly true that music provides opportunity for children to be liberated from their immediate situations and employ their imaginations to enter brighter realms of joy and contentment. It can also serve to inspire, uplift and release creativity.

It is also possible that background music assists in *developing memory*, as memory recall tends to improve when the music played during learning is then played when trying to remember the relevant facts. This phenomenon is based on the principle that knowledge is associated with forms of music in much the same way that a scent will trigger memories of particular events or occasions. The benefit

291

of listening to music for a pupil's attention span is unclear. However, Hallam *et al.* (2002) found in a study of 10–12 year-old children in class that calming music led to better performance on both tasks when compared with a no-music condition. Music perceived as arousing, aggressive and unpleasant disrupted performance on the memory task and led to a lower level of reported altruistic behaviour by the children.

The primary schools strategy document, *Excellence and Enjoyment* (DfES 2004) states that all children in England and Wales should have access to instrumental and vocal tuition, but reports about the standard of music education suggest that although the quality of teaching is good in most schools, fewer than half gave pupils any opportunity to practise their musical skills. A scheme commenced in January 2007 to devote more school time to music in the hope that it would encourage pupils to become more self-assured, and in 2007 Howard Goodall was appointed as a national singing ambassador for England.

From the age of five to fourteen music forms part of the Scottish curriculum called 'expressive arts', which also includes PE, drama, and art and design. The curriculum in Wales states that music should enhance pupils' communication, information technology, creative and personal and social skills and understanding of the Welsh Foundation Stage Curriculum, the *Curriculum Cymreig*. All pupils, age 5–14 have a statutory entitlement to music education in class. The main aim of the music curriculum in Northern Ireland is to develop pupils' musical ability, with children experiencing making and responding to music. Children study music as a compulsory subject from the age of five to fourteen years.

Less than an hour a week is devoted to music in most primary schools, and it has been estimated that only 13 per cent of primary pupils learn to play an instrument. Many primary teachers feel ill equipped and

insecure at the prospect of having to teach the subject. However, the use of music in the classroom can be enhanced if children:

- dance and express themselves physically by stomping, marching, swaying, jumping and shaking;
- hum and sing along with music to enhance their language development skills;
- invent their own instruments from classroom materials or recycled objects and perform for or with the rest of the class.

Teachers also highlight a composer each month by providing brief biographical information and playing extracts from his or her work. See Jones and Robson (2008) for more detailed suggestions about classroom practice.

The fact that children have different musical preferences can act as a prompt for analysing likes and dislikes; some pupils have very strong and entrenched feelings about their favourite pieces. Some teachers have some 'music magic' every day lasting for a few minutes during registration or after lunch, the purpose of which is not to analyse the music but to ask children to rate their enjoyment under simple headings, such as, 'it made me sad; it made me feel glad; it did not make me feel anything special' or to finish the sentence *The music makes me think about ...* Alternatively, teachers use music as a 2-minute stimulus for stretching, moving or dancing, referring to the time as 'mad music' or 'wacky wiggles' or 'bounce to the beat' to emphasise its fun side.

Sources

DfES (2004) *Excellence and Enjoyment: A strategy for primary schools*, London: HMSO.

Hallam, S., Price, J. and Katsarou, G. (2002) 'The effects of background music on primary school pupils' task performance, *Educational Studies*, 28 (2), 111–22.

Jones, P. and Robson, C. (2008) *Teaching Music in Primary Schools*, Exeter: Learning Matters.

N

NATIONAL CURRICULUM

See also: assessing children's learning, communication, core subjects, information technology, key stages, moral development, personal social and health education, religious education, Scottish curriculum, spiritual development

The word 'curriculum' in 'national curriculum' refers to the subjects that pupils have to study at school. Until 1988 in the UK, teachers were largely free to decide what they taught their pupils and religious education (RE) was the only compulsory subject on the timetable. This led to a great deal of variety of practice between schools, but also allowed teachers to adjust the curriculum to suit the specific needs of children in that educational setting. To ensure all pupils received what was referred to as 'a balanced education', the National Curriculum (NC) was developed at the end of the 1980s for England and Wales, defining four key stages of education:

- Key stage 1: up to age seven (Years 1 and 2).
- Key stage 2: age seven to eleven (Years 3, 4, 5 and 6).
- Key stage 3: age eleven to fourteen (Years 7, 8 and 9).
- Key stage 4: age fourteen to sixteen (Years 10 and 11).

The first two stages cover the primary stage; the second two stages cover the secondary stage. The NC lists the subjects to be taught and details the content. It also states the standards or levels that pupils are expected to attain at ages 7, 11 and 14. Other than a very small percentage of exceptional cases, all pupils aged 5–16, except those at private schools, must follow the National Curriculum, which consists of the following: (a) Three core subjects: English, mathematics and science; (b) Nine foundation (non-core) subjects – design and technology (DT), information and communication technology (ICT), history, geography, art and design, music, physical education (PE), modern foreign languages and citizenship (not compulsory at primary level); and (c) Religious education, which is taught according to a locally agreed syllabus. Parents may choose to withdraw their children from these sessions. The Welsh language is a core subject in Welsh-speaking schools. Several other modified versions of the NC have been published since the first version, with a considerable slimming of content. Children learn a wide range of specific skills in each subject and broader skills that can help them in any area of school, work or life: communication; application of number; information technology; working with others; improving own learning and performance; and problem solving. Schools must also promote children's spiritual, moral, social and cultural development.

All schools in Northern Ireland follow the Northern Ireland Curriculum, which is based on a similar framework to the NC used in

England and Wales, though schools can develop additional curriculum elements to express their particular ethos and meet pupils rsquo; individual needs and circumstances. In Irish-speaking schools, the curriculum also includes the Irish language. Scotland has its own qualification framework that is separate from that in England, Wales and Northern Ireland. There is no national curriculum in Scotland; breadth, balance and progression are achieved through broad curriculum areas, not subjects. The areas are (1) language, (2) mathematics, (3) environmental studies, (4) expressive arts, and (5) religious, moral and social education. By contrast, pupils in Northern Ireland study five broad areas: (1) English, (2) mathematics, (3) science and technology, (4) creative and expressive studies, and (5) language studies; and there are four cross-curricular themes in primary education: education for culture; understanding cultural heritage; health education; and information technology (IT) – see Hamilton and Weiner 2003, p. 627.

In the UK (with the exception of Scotland) the curriculum contains a common structure and design for all subjects divided into key stages, for which there is a programme of study that sets out what has to be taught in the subject. Together with the programmes of study, notes of guidance, definitions and links with ICT and with other subject areas are appended. In addition there are attainment targets for each subject, setting out all that pupils of different abilities and maturity are expected to have gained by the end of each key stage. At the primary phase, each attainment target consists of six level descriptions of increasing difficulty; at secondary school level the number increases to eight. English has three attainment targets for children at key stages 1 and 2: speaking and listening; reading; writing. Each level description describes the types and range of understanding that pupils working at that level should demonstrate. On the basis of children's attainments, teachers have to decide which description best fits their performance.

It is anticipated that the majority of seven-year-old children will reach level 2 and the majority of eleven-year-olds will reach level 4 in English and mathematics, though there is considerable government pressure (in England) for children to attain higher grades. Many primary teachers complain that an emphasis on improved test scores narrows the curriculum at the expense of the more creative elements such as drama and art.

Of the core subjects, mathematics has three elements for pupils aged five to seven years: (1) using and applying mathematics, (2) number and algebra, and (3) shape, space and measures. In addition, children aged seven to eleven have to study a fourth element: handling data. There are also four elements in science: scientific enquiry, life processes and living things, materials and their properties, physical processes. Literacy (referred to as English in the NC) has been the focus of greatest attention nationally and in individual schools; the most effective method for teaching reading has been at the forefront of debate and prompted a great deal of discussion and controversy. All other non-core subjects have a single element. Guidelines about personal, social and health education (PSHE), and about citizenship, are also provided in the NC document. The primary school curriculum in England must also include a modern foreign language and sex education.

Assessment arrangements for seven-year-olds at key stage 1 (KS1) combine NC test results with continuous teacher assessment. The arrangement for KS1 tests allows schools more flexibility over how and when they are administered and form part of one single overall assessment of each pupil. At age 5 years, the teacher carries out an assessment of children's all-round development, using their knowledge of the work pupils have done throughout the year in class to judge each pupil's progress. At age 7 years, teachers mark the national tests in English and mathematics in school. At age 11 years, the national tests in English, mathematics and science are marked externally and the school's results are published nationally in England but not in other parts of the UK.

Sources

BBC: 'What is the National Curriculum: Parents help' (based on an article by Judith Puddic), on-line at www.bbc.co.uk/schools/parents/work/curriculum_guide/national_curriculum.shtml

Hamilton, D. and Weiner, G. (2003) 'Subject, not subjects: Curriculum, pathways and pedagogy in the UK', in Pinar, W. (ed.) *International Handbook of Curriculum Research*, New York: Lawrence Erlbaum.

NATIONAL GOVERNORS' ASSOCIATION

See also: governors

The National Governors' Association (NGA, www.nga.org.uk/index.aspx) is the repre-sentative body for school governors in Eng-land and works for governors by supporting local governor associations and governing bodies; lobbying ministers and policy-makers; producing guidance and information; and organising events and conferences Governors can join the NGA as individuals, as members of a governing body or through their local governors' association. Local authorities, edu-cation organisations and education businesses can support the work of the NGA as corporate partners.

NATIONAL PRIMARY STRATEGY

See also: early years, Every Child Matters, excellence and enjoyment, Foundation Stage, literacy, mathematics, reading, Rose Review

The National Primary Strategy or NPS is the UK government's main lever for raising stan-dards of education for children aged 5–7 years in England. Its aim is to embed effective teaching and learning in all schools and early years settings through a mix of training and materials, comprehensive development pro-grammes for teachers and the provision of support from local consultants. At the heart of the Strategy are the *Early Years Foundation Stage Framework* and the *Primary Framework*, containing core guidance on how to teach the curriculum in settings and schools, with an emphasis on planning and assessment. The primary framework was designed to support teachers and schools to deliver high-quality learning and teaching for all children. It con-tains detailed guidance and materials to sup-port literacy and mathematics in primary schools and settings. The renewed primary framework is intended to offer everyone involved in teaching children aged from 3 to 11 an opportunity to embed the principles of *Every Child Matters* (DfES 2005) and *Excellence and Enjoyment* (DfES 2003) into practice. Thus: 'Excellent teaching gives children the life chances they deserve … Enjoyment is the birthright of every child. But the most pow-erful mix is the one that brings the two together. Children learn better when they are excited and engaged … ' (NPS, ref. 0377/2003).

The stated aim of the *Primary Framework for Literacy and Mathematics* is to support and increase all children's access to excellent teaching, leading to exciting and successful learning. The renewed framework builds on the learning that has taken place since the original frameworks for teaching literacy and mathematics were introduced in 1998 and 1999. The framework was developed to bring new impetus and structures for teaching and learning in literacy and mathematics, rather than repackaging the existing guidance. Schools and other education settings are encouraged to understand the changes and to move towards implementation rather than to rely upon the original framework.

Significant developments in the teaching of early reading have been incorporated as a consequence of both research and the find-ings of the independent review of the teach-ing of early reading – the Rose Report (Rose 2006). The report provided recommendations on what constitutes high-quality phonics work. These recommendations were summarised in a core position paper, 'Phonics and early reading: an overview for head teachers, literacy leaders and teachers in schools, and managers and practitioners in Early Years settings'. All principles underpinning these recommendations were incorporated into the revised *Primary Framework for Literacy and Mathematics* (DCSF 2008) and the new *Early Years Foundation Stage*, a revised version of which was published on 19 May 2008. The structure of the electronic version of the *Primary Framework for Literacy and Mathematics* aims to provide practitioners with ready access to a broad range of appropriate guidance and resources to ensure that the needs of all children are met. It is probable that the Primary National Strategy for Literacy will be superseded in 2011.

Sources

DCSF Standards Site (2008) *Primary Framework for Literacy and Mathematics*, on-line at www.standards. dfes.gov.uk/primaryframeworks
DfES (2003) *Excellence and Enjoyment*, London: HMSO.
——(2005) *Every Child Matters: Change for children*, London: HMSO.
Rose, J. for the DCSF (2007) 'Independent review of the teaching of early reading', London: HMSO, on-line at www.standards.dcsf.gov.uk/phonics/rosereview

NATURE–NURTURE

See also: attention span, behaviour, child development, instruction, nurturing children, parental involvement

The nature versus nurture debate concerns the relative importance of an individual's innate 'nature' (what a person seems to be disposed towards) versus 'nurture' (the accumulation of personal experiences) in determining or causing individual differences in physical and behavioural traits. There is general agreement that both factors are significant, though opinions differ about which influence is the more powerful. The 'nurture' school of thought was championed by American psychologists, who argued that behaviour is learned and modifiable through experience. The 'nature' school of thought came to the forefront in the early to mid-twentieth century among European biologists such as Konrad Lorenz, best known for his pioneering work on imprinting in young animals. The controversial aspect of nature theory is the claim that behavioural tendencies are instinctive and cannot be changed by life experience. The implication of this claim for parents and teachers is that children are predisposed to particular actions and attitudes that cannot easily be remedied through intervention. Unfortunately, this argument has been used to argue that certain races are inferior, and to justify certain types of anti-social behaviour by arguing that it is merely a reflection of what comes naturally to the people concerned.

The view that humans acquire all or almost all their behavioural traits from nurture is sometimes known as the tabula rasa ('blank slate') theory. Powell (2006) notes that whereas we know that genetics determines where we get our facial features, such as eye colour, it cannot fully explain where we get our personality, sense of adventure and talents (such as being able to sing) that may differ markedly from (say) brothers and sisters brought up in the same family environment. She argues that while it is clear that physical characteristics are hereditary, the genetic argument is less straightforward when it comes to explaining an individual's behaviour. Nature–nurture was once considered to be an appropriate division of developmental influences, but as both types of factors are known to play such interacting roles in human development, many modern psychologists consider that the polarisation represents an outdated state of knowledge.

Compared to animals, du Plessis (2000) argues that humans enter the world very poorly equipped to cope with life, in that children must learn to know and do everything other than use natural body functions, such as breathing and the use of reflexes.

Consequently, all children must learn to walk erect, to talk, to eat with a knife and fork, to catch a ball, to ride a bicycle, to swim and so forth. Children must also learn to sustain attention, listen when spoken to, follow instructions and conform to societal norms. The author also claims that the same principle applies to qualities such as friendliness, thankfulness, honesty, truthfulness, unselfishness and respect for authority, all of which must be learned for the child to lead a happy and successful adult life. Schools are especially responsible for the formal aspects of education to provide society with an able workforce. Parents are, however, the primary educators of their child and, as such, have the greatest responsibility to nurture and direct their children to adulthood.

Silcock (2008) agrees that both nature and nurture have a bearing upon learner success in and out of school but claims that the particular ways in which gene-determined inheritance systems ('nature') interact with circumstances ('nurture') to affect learning is not easily interpreted. He proposes that genes not only make experience possible by scaffolding the biological mechanisms by which we learn, think and perceive, but they they also affect the moment-to-moment experiences themselves. The ability to read, write, solve mathematical puzzles, pose scientific hypotheses, use computers or play musical instruments have to be taught and learned, so cannot be ascribed purely to innate ability. Equally, however, cultural customs may inhibit as well as aid progress: for instance, adults can underestimate children's potentialities on the basis of low expectation and hinder children from achieving their full capabilities. Silcock goes on to object to the tendency for some curricular initiatives in England to be based so completely on environmental input ('nurture') that they totally ignore biological evidence and predetermined competence ('nature'). Much educational assumes that all pupils can reach high standards in key studies if they and their teachers work hard enough and impress what adults

most wish to teach on pupils' minds regardless of 'nature' factors. As a result, politicians and education advisers make wholesale recommendations of ways that all pupils to learn and become independent problem-solvers, creative, empathetic, enterprising and so forth. In an educational setting it is of considerable importance for educators to know what can be changed with relative ease because it comes naturally to the child concerned; and what can only altered with dedicated effort because it does not come naturally.

Sources

Du Plessis, S. (2000) 'Child development: Nurtured by love or matured by nature?' On-line at www.audiblox2000.com/early_childhood/child_development.htm

Powell, K. (2006) 'Nature versus nurture: Are we really born that way?' On-line at http://genealogy.about.com/cs/geneticgenealogy/a/nature_nurture.htm

Silcock, P.J. (2008) 'Towards a biologically-informed primary school practice', *Education 3–13*, 36 (2), 161–69.

NATURE STUDY

See also: environmental education, environmental studies

The Nature Study Movement was founded in the USA at the end of the nineteenth century by Anna Comstock and Liberty Bailey. The idea was simply to encourage children (and adults) to look closely at the world around them, make detailed observations of natural life and draw conclusions about its significance – rather than sitting in a classroom poring over books. By so doing, it was reasoned that children would be educated to think in terms of the environment and how to safeguard it. Typically, teachers would take children on a 'nature walk' to observe the local surroundings, collect samples for the 'nature table' and, perhaps, examine samples of soil, water from a stream and various flora that had been collected. In recent years, the concept of nature study has been gradually superseded by environmental education. A copy of Comstock's original 1911 book, *Handbook of Nature Study* was revised and reissued by Cornell University Press in 1986.

NAUGHTINESS

See also: behaviour, caring teachers, discipline, misbehaviour, nurturing, parental involvement, social and emotional aspects of learning

Naughtiness is a controversial concept that divides people in education, some of whom argue against using the word in any context; others believe that it is acceptable providing it refers to the act and is not a label for the perpetrator; a minority feel that naughtiness can and should be attached to the child as a means of conveying an important message about acceptable behaviour. It is also a truism that children's growing desire to express themselves and have control over their environment, coupled with external pressures over which they have no control, often trigger uncharacteristic patterns of behaviour. It is therefore preferable to talk about 'naughty behaviour' rather than 'naughty children' to avoid talking about them negatively, as a child is never 'all naughty' or 'all nice'.

Whether or not a naughty child is considered to be mischievous or disobedient, it is preferable to start by trying to understand rather than passing judgement. According to a document published by the National Union of Teachers (NUT) in the UK in August 2008 called *Teachers Under Pressure*, classroom disruption in primary schools in England is a significant problem for teachers (Galton and Macbeath 2008). The study found that many teachers blamed their pupils' unruly behaviour on the inability of parents to control them at home (see also Garner 2008). Many pupils lacked the social skills required to get on in class owing to highly permissive parents who admitted to indulging their children,

often for the sake of peace or simply because they had run out of alternative incentives and sanctions. The Galton and Macbeath report claims that schools face formidable challenges, particularly in poor areas where there has been an increase in the incidence of confrontation and conflict.

An article in Minti – a site for parents (2006) – suggests that labels, like stereotypes, can lead to limiting children to certain roles in the family and at school. Thus, the naughty boy in the class becomes the scapegoat and receives very close attention from adults, who watch closely for his or her unacceptable behaviour in a way that does not happen for the other children. An alternative perspective is to view children as the 'unfinished product', full of potential and not always responsible for their actions or aware of the consequences. All children go through phases as they grow up, with associated challenges, frustrations and issues that need to be resolved. Typically, they grow tired of the same routines, of adults or older siblings making all the decisions or their sister or brother getting more attention than they do. They also experiment, explore the unknown, push the boundaries of acceptability and wrestle to understand their place in the world.

If adults actively look for reasons why children are naughty and disobedient, it is easy to overlook the many commendable things that they do and achieve. Consequently, a policy of noting and rewarding children for doing good and worthy things is preferable to constantly admonishing them for poor behaviour. When children are wilfully naughty it is possible that they are unclear about what is acceptable, anxious about their position in the social order or otherwise lacking security. On the other hand, every teacher and many parents will be aware that some children are just plain naughty, regardless of context, upbringing or attempts to manage their behaviour. Most of them grow out of it in time if provided with firm and loving guidance from caring adults.

Sources

Galton, M. and Macbeath, J. (2008) 'Teachers under pressure', National Union of Teachers, on-line via www.teachers.org.uk

Garner, R. (2008) 'Parents get the blame for naughty children', *Independent*, 24 November.

Minti (2006) 'Being naughty is not the same as being a naughty boy', on-line at www.minti.com/parenting-advice/516

NEW ENTRANTS

See *Starting school*

NON-CORE SUBJECTS

See also: core subjects, foundation subjects, National Curriculum, religious education

Non-core subjects are the subjects of the National Curriculum (England and Wales) other than the 'core' subjects of English (literacy), mathematics, science, information and communication technology (ICT), and religious education – which stands alone. The non-core subjects were formerly and unhelpfully referred to as 'foundation' subjects.

NON-VERBAL COMMUNICATION

See *Body language*

NUMERACY

See also: arithmetic, collaboration in learning, interactive teaching, learning objectives, mathematics, numeracy strategy, plenary, problem solving, teaching assistant

The UK Committee on Education, presided over by Sir Geoffrey Crowther, coined the word 'numeracy' in 1959. Numeracy refers to the process of dealing with numbers and related mathematical concepts, and a numerate person is someone who is efficient in numeracy. Another common definition of numeracy is the ability to use number in calculations, including counting. The introduction of the 1996 *Framework for Teaching Mathematics* (DfES 1996) was popular with teachers, as it focused their attention on key learning objectives with a range of extremely helpful examples that teachers could access when they were unsure of how to approach the teaching of a particular strand of mathematics (see also Suggate *et al.* 2001). Since the introduction of a national strategy for numeracy (National Numeracy Strategy or NNS) in primary schools in England in 1999, some teachers incorrectly use 'numeracy' as shorthand for all work in mathematics. See Thompson (1999) for studies of effective teachers of numeracy and information and communication technology (ICT); an evaluation of international primary textbooks; assessment; using and applying mathematics; and family numeracy – together with suggestions for helping teachers develop aspects of their numeracy teaching skills.

The two main aims of the NNS were to improve the teaching of mathematics in the classroom and to improve the management of numeracy at school level. Teachers are provided with yearly teaching programmes to help them set appropriate expectations for their pupils and understand how pupils should make progress through the primary years. See also Askew and Wiliam (2004). In 2006, the NNS was superseded by the *Primary Framework for Literacy and Mathematics* – specifically the 'Renewed Framework for Mathematics' – that contains detailed guidance and materials to support literacy and mathematics in primary schools and other settings (e.g. nurseries). The electronic version of the primary framework with its descriptors and examples is on-line at www.standards.dfes.gov.uk/primaryframeworks

Numeracy lessons are often based on a three-part framework beginning with oral work and mental calculation using whole class teaching that is sometimes referred to as the 'mental-oral phase', often consisting of interactive, fast-moving questions or mathematical games to make children think hard, 'engage' their minds and orientate them to the topic that forms the heart of the lesson (see Pratt 2006 for insights into interactive teaching). The second part – or central lesson phase – is used to introduce new topics or consolidate previous work and offer opportunity for pupils to implement their knowledge and rehearse their understanding by practising mathematical examples through tasks and activities (popularly known as 'doing sums'). In the case of younger primary pupils, this activity phase frequently involves the sub-division of children into groups with a super-vising adult – normally a teaching assistant (TA); see Compton *et al.* 2007.

The final lesson phase – referred to as the plenary or 'coming together' – is to allow teachers to draw out what children have learned and to deal with any misconceptions or misunderstandings that may have emerged during the lesson. Most teachers use these final few minutes of a session as an opportunity to celebrate success, identify areas of confusion and indicate the direction of future learning.

Teachers pay close attention to a number of issues when planning for and teaching numeracy. First, recognising that the time they spend in eliciting existing pupils' knowledge and understanding helps to clarify future learning needs. Second, being sensitive to the fact that the children may have a dearth of experience in using mathematical language and must be exposed gradually to key voca-bulary with careful explanation and practical involvement to reinforce concepts. Third, ensuring that the emphasis on formal teaching of number is not at the expense of investiga-tive work and does not deprive children of opportunities to find out things through direct experience. Fourth, offering younger pupils a chance to explore ideas, sensitive to the fact that without active teacher involve-ment this opportunity does not in itself guarantee understanding. Fifth, translating perceptions into mathematical notation and symbols, which is a major challenge for many pupils. Sixth, talking to children about work in mathematics to foster interest and learning.

Finally, using mathematics to solve genuine problems and promote a belief in children that the subject has relevance for everyday living.

Studies indicate that primary teachers who are prepared to spend time dwelling on key areas of understanding and exploring the implications of numeracy are more successful than those that speed along in a vain attempt to 'cover' the curriculum content. Teachers who ask challenging questions, give pupils time to think and offer their own insights, and use a variety of reinforcing strategies (repetition, worked examples, collaboration and problem solving) tend to cultivate the most highly motivated and mathematically astute children.

Sources

Askew, M. and Wiliam, D. for the DfES (2004) *Guide For Your Professional Development: Unit 2 appendices*, London: HMSO.

Compton, A., Fielding, H. and Scott, M. (2007) *Supporting Numeracy: A guide for school support staff*, London: Paul Chapman.

DfES (1996) *Framework for Teaching Mathematics*, London: HMSO.

Pratt, N. (2006) *Interactive Maths Teaching in the Primary School*, London: Paul Chapman.

Suggate, J., Davis, A. and Goulding, M. (2001) *Mathematical Knowledge for Primary Teachers*, London: David Fulton.

Thompson, I. (1999) *Issues in Teaching Numeracy in Primary Schools*, Maidenhead: Open University Press.

NUMERACY HOUR

See also: homework, lesson review, mistakes and misconceptions, numeracy strategy, plenary, Primary National Strategy

In 1998 the National Numeracy Strategy in England provided a framework for the teaching of mathematics in primary schools in England, including the non-statutory 'numeracy hour'. The numeracy hour consists of three parts: (1) about five to ten minutes of oral work and mental calculation with the whole class – sometimes oddly referred to as the 'mental-oral' component; (2) the main teaching activity for about thirty to forty minutes, with teacher input and pupil tasks and activities as a whole class, in groups, in pairs or individually; and (3) a plenary ('lesson review') to round off the lesson for the final ten or fifteen minutes to clarify mistakes and misconceptions, identify progress, summarise key facts and ideas, make links with other work, discuss the next steps and (sometimes) set homework. The strategy was incorporated into the Primary National Strategy in 2003. The framework for teaching mathematics was updated in 2006.

NUMERACY STRATEGY (NATIONAL)

See also: arithmetic, mistakes and misconceptions, numeracy hour, Primary National Strategy

The origins of the National Numeracy Strategy (NNS) were in the National Numeracy Project (1996) led by a 'numeracy task force' to address perceived weaknesses in the teaching of mathematics, notably in primary schools. Particular emphasis was placed on the teaching of number ('arithmetic') through calculation and computation. In 1998 a framework was introduced in primary schools in England, including the non-statutory 'numeracy hour'. The strategy included a clear term-by-term outline of expected teaching in mathematics for all pupils from new entrants to the end of primary schooling (ten- and eleven-year-olds, year 6). In 2003, the strategy was absorbed into the broader Primary National Strategy and the framework for teaching was updated in 2006.

NURSERY SCHOOL

See also: early years, early years teachers

A nursery school is for children, usually between the ages of three and five, who are not old enough to attend regular day school. The first nursery schools were opened in London in 1907. Nursery teachers are sometimes called early years teachers.

NURTURING CHILDREN

See also: adult behaviour, breakfast clubs, caring teachers, health and safety, learning climate, morality, motivation for teaching, nature–nurture debate, spiritual education

Marjorie Boxall pioneered the setting up of nurture groups in the London Borough of Enfield in the early 1970s as a response to social deprivation and its consequences for children in school. Boxall argued that without adequate nurturing, the fabric of society is at risk, for with each generation there are fewer people to provide good nurturing and more children who have been deprived of it. She has been particularly keen to promote nurture groups that provide children with social and emotional experiences as a prerequisite for formal school learning. In support of Boxall's view, school inspectors increasingly acknowledge that formal education is enhanced when schools provide a high-quality 'nurturing' environment. Nurture groups are increasingly recognised as an effective method for schools needing to help children who show emotional, behavioural and learning difficulties. It is claimed that the groups are particularly effective for children whose early development has been hindered by adverse circumstances, providing the learning experiences are bound into a close relationship with an attentive and responsive parent or carer (Boxall 2002).

Foster (2004, on-line) is among those who argue that children's spiritual development can be affected by nurturing. Proponents insist that children are born into this world with a divine sense of purpose, such that they are open, accepting, non-judgemental, curious and sensitive to everything around them. Foster offers a view that adults play a vital role in such development. Thus, children need to see us enjoying the wonder of the world: walking in the rain, drawing angels in the snow, constructing secret dens out of sheets and a clothes horse, celebrating the miracle of a rainbow, blowing bubbles and watching their changing colours, watching the sun go down and the moon come up, lying in bed and listening to a wind chime, waking up with a smile to welcome the new day.

Nurturing children's spirituality has the potential to develop their sense of personal value; their belonging in the world; and the belief that they have the capacity for joy and fulfilment. Jacobs and Crowley (2007) focus on nurturing as a means of enhancing young children's sense of wonder and joy in learning. Other authors write from a specific moral perspective; see, for example, Catterton Allen (2008).

Teachers view their relationships with pupils as very important in maintaining good discipline and ensuring high achievement (see, for example, Oberski et al. 1999). The majority of primary teachers, especially those working with young children, are comfortable with the nurture theory, pointing out that there appears to be a causal link between weak progress, poor behaviour and troubled family backgrounds. Fostering a nurturing environment depends upon a welcoming and warm atmosphere ('climate'), where the academic, developmental, behavioural and emotional needs of each pupil are all considered to be important. At the same time, work patterns for pupils need to be set at an appropriate level and the work content meaningful and presented creatively, so that children find the work satisfying and enjoyable. Nearly every primary teacher is highly motivated by the responsibility for children's welfare that is attached to the job.

Nurturing has health and safety implications. For instance, some children come to school with little or no breakfast, and the availability of food through pre-school 'breakfast clubs' and the like, is shown to lead to an improvement in behaviour and concentration.

Similarly, the development of homework clubs and childcare facilities after school can provide security for otherwise vulnerable children. An important aspect of nurturing is respecting pupils' right to privacy and opportunity to sit quietly and undisturbed where practical to do so. The fostering of mutual respect between adults and children has been shown to lead to an improvement in behaviour and a more purposeful learning climate.

Sources

Boxall, M. (2002) Nurture Groups in School: Principles and practice, London: Paul Chapman.
Catterton Allen, H. (ed.) (2008) Nurturing Children's Spirituality: Christian perspectives and best practices, Brockton MA: Cascade Books.
Foster, H. (2004) 'Nurturing children's spirituality', Families South West, on-line at www.families online.co.uk/article/articleview/477/1/19
Jacobs, G. and Crowley, K. (2007) Play Projects and Preschool Standards: Nurturing children's sense of wonder and joy in learning, Thousand Oaks CA: Corwin Press.
Oberski, I., Ford, K., Higgins, S. and Fiher, P. (1999) 'The importance of relationships in teacher education', Journal of Education for Teaching, 25 (2), 135–50.

NURTURING ADULTS

See also: caring teachers, effectiveness, parents, primary schools

Nurturing extends to a concern for adult colleagues and associates (e.g. administrative staff, parents). A supportive pastoral climate for all members of the school community is an essential characteristic of primary schools. A distinctive feature of effective schools is the quality of relationships between teachers, support staff, parents and visitors. This caring attitude provides an example and role model for the children in which they can be immersed and, hopefully, learn to emulate. In such circumstances, every aspect of school life exudes purpose and celebration of genuine effort and success, with the concomitant high morale and enthusiasm that is engendered.

302

OBSERVING CHILDREN

See also: answering questions, attention span, daydreaming, intervention, questions and questioning, recording

All teachers and teaching assistants have to become expert observers of children in school, for at least four reasons. First, it provides insights into pupils' patterns of behaviour and especially their socialising. Second, during lessons it indicates their attention span and concentration level. Third, it allows the adult to see if a child is anxious, guilty, uncertain, bold, assertive, tentative or lackadaisical at that moment in time. Fourth, it facilitates eye contact, warm smiles and nods of encouragement from the adult to the child. During question and answer sessions, adults observe which children contribute answers, which ones never respond and which ones rely on their friends. Some teachers associate observation of classroom practice with the formal procedures attached to inspections, in which particular behaviours and decisions are deemed to be good, bad or indifferent (Hargreaves and Wolfe 2007). By contrast, child observation is non-judgemental and serves to provide descriptions to inform teaching.

Teachers have to decide why the observation is necessary, who to observe and when to do it. They also have to consider practicalities of how to organise the observation time without interruption, something that is far from easy in a busy classroom. Decisions also have to be made about how to record the observations: note form, checklist, diagram, photographs, audio and video. If visual forms of evidence are collected, the teacher has to take account of sensitivities associated with taking pictures of children. See Sharman *et al.* (2001); Hobart and Frankel (2004); Riddall-Leech (2005) for practical suggestions about strategies for observing younger children.

It is sometimes possible to carry out a systematic observation of a child over a given period of time (e.g. ten minutes) and note the child's actions every thirty seconds (say). The adult writes some general comments about the child: played alone; concentrated on the task; liaised with a partner; daydreamed; spoke to an adult; asked another child a question, and so forth. A more sophisticated form of this open approach is to note the length of time that the child spent performing the action. In practice, a child may be doing several things at once, making it harder to record the detail. It is not possible, of course, for the adult to 'see inside the child's head', so apparent daydreaming may, in reality, be careful reflection; informal chatter may, in fact, be the child's way of ascertaining what is happening or confirming an idea. Teachers can adopt a similar approach when pupils are working in a group to ascertain which child is most assertive, passive, confident, and so forth. Teachers are reluctant to intervene too quickly as they prefer that children resolve issues amongst themselves rather than rely too much on adults to sort the matter. If, however, there is a suspicion of coercion or bullying, an adult has to step in and take appropriate action.

Sources

Hargreaves, L. and Wolfe, S. (2007) 'Observing closely to see more clearly: Observation in the primary classroom', in Moyles, J. (ed.) *Beginning Teaching Beginning Learning in Primary Education*, Maidenhead: Open University.

Hobart, C. and Frankel, J. (2004) *A Practical Guide to Child Observation and Assessment*, London: Nelson Thornes.

Riddall-Leech, S. (2005) *How to Observe Children*, London: Heinemann.

Sharman, C., Cross, W. and Vennis, D. (2001) *Observing Children: A practical guide*, London: Continuum.

OFFICE FOR STANDARDS IN EDUCATION

See also: inspections, self-esteem

In September 1993 a new independent inspectorate was established to inspect standards of education in every maintained school under the control of the Office for Standards in Education (OFSTED). The inspection team, including at least one person from outside the education field, would hold open meetings for parents, produce a report setting out the school's strengths and weaknesses, and make a copy of their report available for public scrutiny. A summary of the inspectors' findings, and the resulting action plan, were now to be included in the school's prospectus, obliging schools to examine carefully their curriculum programmes of study and teaching methods. Critics of the system have expressed concerns that important aspects of school life that are not easily measurable or instantly observable are given insufficient weight, yet play a key part in shaping motivation and raising self-esteem, such as tolerance, sportsmanship, co-operation, determination, flair, creativity, perseverance and other personal and social qualities.

OFFICE FOR STANDARDS IN EDUCATION, CHILDREN'S SERVICES AND SKILLS

The new OFSTED was constituted on 1 April 2007 and is now called the 'Office for Standards in Education, Children's Services and Skills'. It brings together the experience of four formerly separate inspectorates to inspect and regulate the provision of care for children and young people; and to inspect education and training for learners of all ages.

OPEN EVENING

See *Parents' evening*

OPEN QUESTIONS

See also: closed questions, questions and questioning, speculative questions

Teachers use open questions on occasions when children's opinions and feelings about issues are being actively sought; frequently, the first word in the question is 'why' or 'how'; for example, 'Why do you think we need to save water?' or 'How can we save water?' Sometimes an open question is used immediately after a closed question (which requires a single answer) as a means of exploring further the original reply. Open questions place a responsibility on the recipients to explain and justify their answers and children need a little time to order their thoughts before responding. A well-framed open question requires a more expansive reply than a simple 'yes' or 'no' and can often be used as a precursor to asking a speculative question; for example, 'What might happen if we don't save water?'

ORACY

See also: body language, collaboration in learning, communication, cross-curriculum, literacy, literacy strategy, reading, teacher role

Oracy is based on the root word 'oral', which is shorthand for the speaking and listening that takes place during verbal interaction. Its educational value is predicated on a belief that allowing children the space and time to talk together about a topic of common interest, and thereby combining their knowledge, understanding and wisdom leads to a more satisfactory outcome than would occur with one person working alone. Speaking and listening forms an integral element of communicating with others and is a fundamental part of literacy education because research shows that exploratory talk is an effective way of using language to *think*, which forms one of the principal building blocks of literacy.

Haworth (2001) traces the gradual erosion of the cross-curricular function of oracy during the 1980s and 1990s in favour of a centralised oracy, controlled by the teacher and related, in complex but subordinate ways, to literacy. For information about the National Oracy Project see Johnson (1993). Subsequently, a number of government publications have offered support in the area of speaking and listening to complement the objectives for reading and writing set out in the national literacy strategy introduced in the UK in 1998. The materials reflect the requirements for teachers to extend and reinforce speaking and listening in every subject area, building on and extending the approach outlined in *Teaching Speaking and Listening in Key Stages 1 and 2* (QCA 1999). The document places a lot of emphasis on the potential for learning when children are given properly constructed opportunities to explore issues, make decisions, experiment with ideas and draw conclusions through working together rather than singly.

Oracy has a more prominent place in language learning than in other areas of the curriculum, being both the medium of communication and the message it conveys. Oracy is especially important for young learners, so they need regular and frequent opportunities to listen to the language – described as 'educating the ear' – so that they are able to identify and distinguish new sounds, reproduce and re-use them and then make links between the sounds and written form of the language. In their study of 159 pupils aged 6–13 years, Macleod *et al.* (2007) found that there was a link between children's exposure to hearing their own voices and word recognition ability in reading.

To promote listening, teachers encourage children to wait their turn while another child is speaking and carefully attend to what others are saying. However, effective listening involves more than hearing the words and understanding their meaning. It also entails observation of the speaker's body language, registering the feelings and perceptions that lie behind the words, being sensitive to verbal clues and making inferences from the tone of voice. The skill can be improved and refined by the teacher repeating or summarising for the benefit of the whole class what a child has said and giving selected children an opportunity to do the same. Primary teachers use a variety of engaging techniques to improve pupils' listening skills, such as the 'repeat after me' game where the children echoes the leader's statements using the same tone of voice.

In addition to organising pupils in pairs or groups to assist their oracy development, teachers perform one or more of three teaching roles during speaking and listening sessions: as a facilitator, as a participant, and as an expert. As a *facilitator*, teachers ensure that they have prepared the ground by explaining the purpose of the exercise, reminding children of the rules and steering them towards reaching a conclusion. As a *participant*, teachers are involved as a temporary member of the group, contributing ideas and suggestions. As an *expert*, teachers provide insights and advice while the children discuss matters.

Sources

Haworth, A. (2001) 'The re-positioning of oracy: A millennium project', *Cambridge Journal of Education*, 31, 11–23.

305

Johnson, J. (1993) 'The National Oracy Project', *Spoken English*, 26 (1), 25–38.

Macleod, F.J., Macmillan, P. and Norwich, B. (2007) 'Listening to myself: Improving oracy and literacy among children who fall behind', *Early Child Development and Care*, 177 (6/7), 633–44.

QCA (1999) *Teaching Speaking and Listening in Key Stages 1 and 2*, London: HMSO.

ORGANISING FOR LEARNING

See also: behaviour, collaboration in learning, friendships, health and safety, interactive whiteboard, lesson management, lesson planning, physical comfort, seating arrangements, time management

It is almost impossible to be an effective teacher without being well organised at every level and able to answer fundamental questions: What am I doing? Why am I doing it? What is the best way to achieve it? Disorientated, muddled teachers usually create messy, disorganised pupils; the opposite is also true. Hastings and Chantrey Wood (2002) insist that children's attention and behaviour benefit from creating a better match between working contexts and the tasks that they are asked to undertake. Organising for learning involves teachers preparing for lessons, ensuring that appropriate resources are available and setting out the classroom so that children can work efficiently. Whereas the *management* of learning is confined to the period of active teaching, the majority of organising happens before lessons commence and facilitates their smooth operation.

Dean (2008) suggests that teachers need to look closely at their 'organisational preferences' and lists fourteen significant areas: (1) pattern of daily programme, (2) teacher's use of time, (3) children's use of time, (4) choice of activity, (5) curriculum content, (6) use of competition and cooperation, (7) grouping of children, (8) use of space, (9) use of furniture, (10) use of resources, (11) records and assessment, (12) work with other teachers, (13) work with parents, and (14) equal opportunities. For each area, Dean offers a spectrum of possible views to align with a teacher's ideas, preferences and skills.

One of the issues identified by Dean is time management. Teachers have to 'think ahead' by deciding in advance what is essential, what is necessary and what is non-essential. They then decide what is urgent and what can wait. Obviously the combination of 'essential' and 'urgent' has to be tackled first; all else can wait. However, if too many tasks become essential and urgent, it acts as a warning to teachers that they are failing to plan sufficiently far in advance, though in the intensity of school life there are occasions when unexpected events conspire to upset the most carefully laid plans.

Whether a classroom is brand new or a Victorian edifice, the children need to be able to move around comfortably and safely. Teachers eliminate the majority of hazards by ensuring that the room is orderly and having a place for every item, seeing the classroom as a workshop rather than a lounge or an office. Most teachers allocate children a specific place for the majority of lessons unless they are moved for a particular purpose such as working collaboratively on an art project or collaborative craft activity. There are some advantages in creating a horseshoe pattern of seating, as this design allows every child to see every other child during class discussions or question-and-answer sessions, though few primary school classrooms are sufficiently large to allow for such a configuration. If teachers use a board or visual forms of technology to illustrate what they are teaching, children have to be seated in such a way that they can see and hear clearly. Although a seating arrangement where friends sit together is popular with children, it can create organisational complications when pupils of similar academic strength need to be grouped. Most teachers try to strike a balance between keeping friends together in situations where grouping does not rely principally on ability factors (such as in art work) and separating them where this is necessary because of the differentiated requirements of tasks and activities.

McNamara and Moreton (1997) refer to 'differentiation by organisation', suggesting a framework based on different types of tasks that present different types of risk of failure; thus:

1 High ambiguity/low risk: e.g. solving a complex maths problem.
2 Low ambiguity/high risk: e.g. constructing something as a group activity (perhaps using a set of instructions) while being observed by others.
3 High ambiguity/high risk: e.g. discussing a controversial issue in a large group with the teacher present.
4 Low ambiguity/low risk: e.g. routine addition sums.

McNamar and Moreton go on to say that certain learning situations are not complex but the risk factor is such that it hinders effective communication and efficiency in completing the task. For example, some children find it difficult to explain their thinking in front of classmates. The authors recommend that in organising learning, teachers create low risk environments by using pairs and small group work rather than exposing children to the whole class.

In addition, all schools now have a range of computers, interactive whiteboards and other equipment to support learning. If there is a computer suite situated away from the classroom, supervision of children to and from the room has to be considered. If computers are located in classrooms, managing fair access for all pupils is a priority, as more assertive children are inclined to dominate their use. Teaching assistants are frequently involved in supervising and advising children about effective use of technology, especially computers, so liaison with the teacher is essential. There are also practical factors to be taken into account if children require more space for wheelchair access or children with limited upper-body mobility require specially adapted working surfaces.

The provision of resources has to be appropriate to the tasks undertaken by pupils, though in enquiry-based activities (e.g. investigations in science, problem-solving in mathematics) sometimes a more diverse range of resources is required owing to the less predictable direction that learning might take. Consumable items (such as paper) must not only be readily available but pupils also have to be informed about when they can be used and for what purpose, as there are financial and practical implications if resources are abused. Incorrect use of tools can lead to expensive breakages and also deprive other pupils from the opportunity of using them. The higher the health risk factor, the more immediate the adult presence, high standard of discipline and training about the correct use of equipment needs to be.

Sources

Dean, J. (2008) *Organising Learning in the Primary School*, London: Routledge.
Hastings, N. and Chantrey Wood, K. (2002) *Reorganising Primary Classroom Learning*, Maidenhead: Open University Press.
McNamara, S. and Moreton, G. (1997) *Understanding Differentiation*, London: David Fulton.

OUT OF CLASS

See also: differentiation, integration, personalised learning, reading, self-esteem

Even if pupils benefit from specialised or individual instruction from an adult support assistant in a particular subject area in which they struggle (notably, literacy) it does not necessarily involve their removal from regular class activities and segregation from social activities, as there are stigmas attached to being seen as 'different'. The strategy of removing children from mainstream activities can also reinforce pupils' perceptions of their low status and may damage their self-esteem and confidence, though some pupils enjoy the exclusive attention. The move towards more integrative and inclusive practices that keep all children physically together as far as possible has become more evident in schools, while differentiating the work content appropriately. Nevertheless, being taken out of the classroom for specific teaching on a one-to-one basis or in very small groups is still commonplace for younger primary-age children who need extra support, especially in reading.

OUTDOOR EDUCATION

See also: discovery learning, environmental studies, forest schools, health and safety, relationships, self-esteem

Outdoor education means, in its simplest terms, learning that takes place outside the classroom door. A number of other definitions have been offered, including a strategy for curriculum enrichment in which the process of learning takes place out of doors and education takes place off the premises. Outdoor education may also be considered as an experiential method of learning ('discovery learning') with the use of all senses that takes place primarily but not exclusively through exposure to the natural environment to achieve personal, social, educational, therapeutic and environmental goals. Possible locations of outdoor learning for schools include schools' grounds, urban spaces, rural or city farms, parks, gardens, woodlands, coasts, outdoor centres and wilderness areas. The remit of the organisation *Learning Outside the Classroom* (www.lotc.org.uk) in England is that every young person should experience the world beyond the classroom as an essential part of learning and personal development, whatever their age, ability or circumstances. Similarly, the *Institute for Outdoor Learning* (www.outdoor-learning.org) encourages outdoor learning by developing quality, safety and opportunity to experience outdoor activity provision and by supporting and enhancing the good practice of those who work in the outdoors. Forest schools – literally, a school ('educational setting') in a forest – are a well-known example of innovative outdoor education.

Waite and Rea (2007) argue that working as a team to solve problems in a physical, experiential way in the British education system has been influenced by Lord Baden-Powell, who founded the Scouting movement, and the theories of Kurt Hahn, the originator of 'Outward Bound'. Both of these innovators were motivated by a belief that experiencing and overcoming challenges is an essential factor in character building. While recognising the considerable pressures on primary schools and the challenges they face in the context of parental expectations and national targets, Cramp (2008) insists that learning outdoors has many benefits, including behaviour modification, self-esteem, teamwork development, challenge and self-knowledge. However, he describes how the greatest benefit is learners' personal development, as pupils cultivate 'multidimensional views' of teachers, which lead to 'warmer personal relationships, a challenge to labelling and the potential for risk-taking back in the classroom' (p. 180).

Opportunities for outdoor education in the past were largely associated with study of a topic such as 'local studies', in which the geography, history and social fabric (such as leisure amenities) were studied in depth; and by science-orientated activities, such as observing and recording natural phenomena in the school grounds or a suitable nearby venue. In recent years, however, outdoor education has expanded its brief to include residential visits, opportunities for challenging physical education activities (e.g. canoeing, rock-climbing) and even overseas visits. One of the conclusions from an in-depth study of outdoor provision in Scotland by Nicol *et al.* (2007) is that outdoor education should no longer seen as being just about adventure or field studies or as the remit solely of geography or biology teachers. The younger the children, the more likely that the outdoor activities will take place locally; as children progress through the primary phase they are normally offered more challenging opportunities.

Fears about health and safety and litigation in the recent past had the effect of greatly reducing the extent and breadth of outdoor education in UK schools, as school governors, head teachers and teachers exercised considerable caution about ventures that involved above-average risk. More recently, the accreditation of outdoor centres and guidance from local authorities has had a reassuring influence on teachers planning outdoor activities. See Stagg *et al.* (2009) for comprehensive coverage of practical issues regarding forms of 'off the premises' educational visits.

Sources

Cramp, A. (2008) 'Knowing me, knowing you: Building valuable relationships outside the classroom', *Education 3–13*, 36 (2), 171–82.

Nicol, R., Higgins, P., Ross, H. and Mannion, G. (2007) *Outdoor Education in Scotland: A summary of recent research*, Perth: Scottish Natural Heritage (SNH) and Learning and Teaching Scotland (LTS).

Stagg, C., Thomas, A. and Smith, P. (2009) *Off the Premises Handbook*, London: Optimus Education.

Waite, S. and Rea, T. (2007) 'Enjoying teaching and learning outside the classroom', in Hayes, D. (ed.) *Joyful Teaching and Learning in the Primary School*, Exeter: Learning Matters.

P

P SCALES

See also: National Curriculum, special educational needs, tactile learners

Some pupils (notably those with special educational needs) struggle with regular work to such an extent that they are not even able to reach the first level of the National Curriculum, in which case there exist a set of indicators known as the P scales to record their achievement. The P scales are divided into eight levels from P1 (the lowest) to P8 (the highest) though the first three levels (P1, P2 and P3) are not subject-specific. In extreme cases, children may only have a tentative grasp of people, events and objects and rely heavily on tactile senses (e.g. through touching) to elicit a response, in which case P1 would be an appropriate level.

PAIRED WORK

See also: differentiation, literacy, phonics, reading, spelling, writing

Paired work in primary school classrooms is normally associated with the subject of English, specifically literacy work. Topping (1999) refers to three types of paired work: (1) reading, (2) writing, and (3) spelling. Paired reading is intended to be an enjoyable and easy to implement strategy in which a more able pupil or an adult (the 'tutor') helps a less able pupil (the 'tutee') to develop better reading skills. Initially, the pair read a section of text together at a pace that is comfortable for the weaker reader. If an error is made, the tutor pauses, repeats the word for the tutee to repeat, then they continue as before.

Paired spelling is also known as 'cued' spelling. The procedure is normally carried out several times per week, lasting for about fifteen minutes per session over a period of (say) six weeks. The tutee chooses some words in which he or she is interested, irrespective of complexity. The pair checks the spelling of the word in a dictionary and the tutor records it in a 'spelling diary'. The tutor and tutee then read the word out loud together and the tutee chooses cues (i.e. prompts/ reminders) to assist in memorising the written structure of the word. Cues can be phonic sounds (such as 'sh' in ship or 'ou' in loud); letter names; syllables (such as 'ing' in working; or 'con' in 'content') or other word fragments. The tutor encourages the tutee to select appropriate cues that make sense to the tutee and can be easily remembered. The pair says the cue out loud and the tutor records it; the process is then reversed as the tutor says the cue out loud and the tutee records it. Finally, the tutee says the cue and writes down the word at the same time. Typically, at the beginning of each week, children check which words on the list they can spell and ask their partner to give them a quick test. Every day from Monday to Thursday each child chooses one word from each column of the spelling sheet and writes it on their diary sheet. They use the ten steps and the cues to learn their five words each day. On Friday, partners review their twenty words from the week with a quick test. If any words are incorrectly spelt they repeat the procedure until they are spelt correctly.

Paired writing is a system that can be applied to any text and any form of writing ('genre'). The procedure consists of 6 steps: (1) ideas generation, (2) drafting, (3) reading, (4) editing, (5) best copy, and (6) evaluation. In a later study, Topping *et al.* (2000) concluded that the paired writing method proved practical and robust, adaptable to different classroom contexts and beneficial in affecting attitudes to writing and skill development. The authors suggest that its use during literacy sessions and across the curriculum is worth considering by teachers who are seeking methods to differentiate tasks and avoid mechanistic, prescriptive teaching approaches.

Sources

Topping, K. (1999) *Paired Reading, Writing and Spelling*, London: Cassell.

Topping, K., Nixon, J., Sutherland, J. and Yarrow, F. (2000) 'Paired writing: A framework for effective collaboration', *Reading*, 34 (2), 79–89.

PARENT COMMUNICATION

See also: head teacher, home–school, governors, parents' evening

Head teachers and governors are always anxious to ensure that parents are kept well informed about aspects of school life that impact upon their children's education. As Beverton (2005) rightly claims, 'the fact that parents nowadays have rights that mean that they can know quite a lot about their child's school and how it works means that schools have to make clear arrangements that allow these rights to be exercised' (p. 383). In addition, the move towards integrating education and social services in the UK and USA

has highlighted the importance of establishing and maintaining good relationships between all sectors of the community (see Allen 2007; McDermott 2007 for US perspectives). As an important part of the communication network, class teachers are often given the responsibility of ensuring that information reaches home and helping to ensure that parents don't receive conflicting or confusing messages about school life. Information is usually conveyed in one of four ways:

- printed correspondence, such as a school circular or letter, if the issues affect the whole group or class;
- verbal messages given to an individual child;
- handwritten notes;
- through electronic means (in a small number of situations).

Written messages often have to be produced in a variety of languages. Although the child may speak good English, parents do not necessarily do so. This situation makes the distribution of letters more time-consuming and has to be taken into account when organising sessions, so teachers tend to leave a few additional minutes at the end of the lesson and ensure that an assistant is on hand to help with the practicalities of distribution. Many schools have a special notice board for copies of important circulars, such as those from the school governors.

Teachers have to be very careful when relaying verbal messages. Although a child may nod when asked if a message from an adult has been understood, there remains a good chance that it will not have been or will not be remembered accurately. A special effort has to be made to communicate effectively with parents for whom English is not their first language. Use of a teaching assistant who speaks the same language is ideal but such a person is not always available.

Teachers do not often have the time or inclination to write notes to parents, but if they do so, parents expect high standards; untidy handwriting is viewed badly and spelling errors jump out of the page. The same is true of everything teachers write that is placed on public view, such as labels for displays or lists of words around the room. Teachers have to exercise particular care when sending home a handwritten note. Whereas an ill-advised, off-the-cuff remark can usually be smoothed over, a letter in the teacher's own handwriting is harder to dismiss and acts as primary evidence if a complaint is made. On the other hand, a note home is a wonderful opportunity for a teacher to compliment a child who has tried hard or made a special effort and parents and children are both delighted to receive those personal comments. In fact, studies suggest that this form of commendation is more important to most children than any number of house points or merit cards (e.g. Harrop and Williams 1992). In a large-scale study Shreeve (2002) found that in schools where pupils are motivated by an intrinsic desire to learn and achieve, formal systems of rewards and penalties are often unnecessary.

Electronic forms of communication with parents obviously rely on the availability of appropriate technology. The use of mobile phones (US, cell phones) makes it possible for schools to contact parents with information about events and details about pupil behaviour and performance. However, issues relating to confidentiality and the practicalities of dealing with technology limit the use of this form of communication in all but the largest and best-resourced schools.

The quality of communication with parents can help or hinder a teacher's attempts to build a good working relationship with home and may adversely affect the child's attitude towards school. One of the greatest challenges comes when a new teacher meets parents, often for the first time, in the formal circumstances of parent interviews, often known as the parents' evening. See Mariconda (2003) for advice about making positive, productive interactions with parents from the first letter home to the final conference.

Sources

Allen, J. (2007) *Creating Welcoming Schools: A practical guide to home-school partnerships with diverse families*, New York: Teachers College Press.

Beverton, S. (2005) 'Collaborating with parents', in Arthur, J., Davison, J. and Lewis, M. (eds) *Professional Values and Practice: Achieving the standards for QTS*, London: Routledge.

Harrop, A. and Williams, T. (1992) 'Rewards and punishments in the primary school: Pupils' perceptions and teachers' usage', *Educational Psychology*, 7 (4), 211–15.

Mariconda, B. (2003) *Easy and Effective Ways to Communicate with Parents*, New York: Scholastic.

McDermott, D.R. (2007) *Developing Caring Relationships Among Parents, Children, Schools, and Communities*, London: Sage.

Shreeve, A. (2002) 'Student perceptions of rewards and sanctions', *Pedagogy, Culture and Society*, 10 (2), 239–56.

PARENTAL INVOLVEMENT

See also: Every Child Matters, home background and learning, home–school, nurturing children, parents supporting learning, special educational needs

Parental interest and involvement in their children's learning is widely recognised as having a significant impact on the extent to which children realise their full potential. Pupils with parents who are involved in their education tend to have fewer behavioural problems, achieve better academic performance and are more likely to complete secondary school than pupils whose parents are uninvolved. The importance of parents in preparing children for learning in school was recognised long ago and has been written about at length. Some years ago Hurst (1987) emphasised that whoever is responsible for looking after young children becomes the 'chief resource' for different kinds of learning, which provide a child with the 'learning tools and resource to be used, adapted and developed as needed for all subsequent personal development and education' (p. 97).

The home or nurturing environment (nursery, child-minder, playgroup) offers a powerful medium for language development and other forms of communication on which the teacher can build once formal schooling is underway. There have been concerns expressed, however, over the speed with which the vibrant verbal exchanges that characterise the home environment, with children initiating the majority of questions, are replaced by teacher-directed talk and questions once the same children begin school (notably Tizard and Hughes 1984). Studies have also indicated that pupils with highly involved parents tend to receive greater attention from teachers, who are therefore more likely to identify problems that inhibit children's progress. Liaison with parents has become a necessary and important part of every teacher's role, especially those working with young children and pupils with special educational needs (e.g. Feiler 2003).

Warmth and affection in the parent–child relationship is related to positive outcomes for children, including higher self-esteem, better levels of communication and fewer psychological problems. Parental warmth is even found to encourage children's use of social support and proactive, problem-focused coping strategies. Conversely, insufficient levels of parental support foster feelings of alienation, expressions of hostility and aggression, low morale and antisocial behaviours. The publication *Every Child Matters* DfES (2005) suggests that 'The bond between the child and their parents is the most critical influence on a child's life. Parenting has a strong impact on a child's educational development, behaviour and mental health' (p. 39). Head teachers and governors/board members of schools are acutely aware of the need to maintain an open relationship with parents: engaging and involving them through newsletters; providing information about educational initiatives; canvassing their opinions about key issues where appropriate, and actively supporting parent–teacher association meetings. In fact all adults that work in primary school are required to help in promoting partnerships with parents and other

members of the community by acknowledging how experience and learning are shaped by cultural and linguistic heritage, gender, family and community. Most inspections of schools include a consultation with parents and (sometimes) a questionnaire to ascertain their satisfaction with the quality of education and school–home communication. The results of these various forms of data collection are included in the overall ranking of schools, so assume much greater significance than once they did.

Over the years, the number of parents working alongside teachers in the classroom and around the school has increased significantly. There are many reasons for this, including the publication of numerous reports stressing the importance of closer home–school links; a recognition of the useful skills possessed by parents; and the need to have more adult support in the classroom. Most schools will have a policy for parental involvement inside school and teachers have to work within these guidelines (Wood 2005). Voluntary parent helpers in the classroom can be a bonus or a problem depending on the care with which they are selected and the skill with which they are deployed. Good parent helpers provide an extra pair of hands and probably possess expertise that is invaluable in promoting learning (see Campbell and Fairburn 2005); poor ones can cause problems by being over-assertive, critical or casual in attendance. Grandparents in the classroom offer stability and a different perspective on matters of concern; they are often a calming influence for overstretched teachers (Kenner *et al.* 2004). Parents that are regularly in and out of a school and, perhaps, have reason to be in the staffroom, pick up a lot of information about individual children and internal affairs, so care about disclosing information is a key issue for staff.

Becta (British Educational and Technology Agency) is the government agency leading the national drive to ensure the effective and innovative use of technology throughout learning. One of its projects involves exploiting information technology to improve parental engagement, moving towards online reporting by providing a 'toolkit' for use in primary schools. The toolkit offers guidelines and a framework to help primary school teachers exploit ICT to promote and encourage the involvement of parents. It contains a DVD and three publications: *An introduction for primary schools*; *Getting started*; *Framework guide for primary schools*.

Sources

Campbell, A. and Fairburn, G. (2005) *Working With Support in the Classroom*, Maidenhead: Open University Press.

DfES (2005) *Every Child Matters: Change for children*, London: HMSO.

Feiler, A. (2003) 'A home visiting project for reception children predicted to experience literacy difficulties', *British Journal of Special Education*, 30 (3), 156–62.

Hurst, V. (1987) 'Parents and professionals', in Blenkin, G.M. and Kelly, A.V. (eds) *Early Childhood Education*, London: Paul Chapman.

Kenner, C., Arju, T., Gregory, E., Jessel, J. and Ruby, M. (2004) 'The role of grandparents in children's learning', *Primary Practice*, 38, 41–44.

Tizard, B. and Hughes, M. (1984) *Young Children Learning*, London: Fontana.

Wood, E. (2005) 'Managing other adults in the classroom', in Arthur, J., Davison, J. and Lewis, M. (eds) *Professional Values and Practice: Achieving the standards for QTS*, London: Routledge.

PARENTS SUPPORTING LEARNING

See also: curriculum, homework, parental involvement

Most parents are able to assist their children in various ways outside the school day, including support for assigned homework and talking about aspects of the curriculum that have been covered, their friendships and the sorts of activities that interest them. Older children in particular are surprisingly coy about sharing openly with a parent about details of the day unless an unusual incident or event has taken place. Nevertheless, unless parents talk naturally and without pressure to children they will find difficulty in helping them to set realistic goals, organise their schedule and check progress. Like a good teacher, parents should praise genuine effort but not be gushing about things that would be expected from the child; otherwise, the child's expectations are lowered. A number of parents feel unskilled in supervising homework, on the basis that the child knows more than them – which is sometimes true. Other parents may take some persuading that they should act as a surrogate teacher; however, as they were their children's first educators, supporting learning at home can be seen as an extension of this role.

PARENTS' EVENING

See also: behaviour, parents supporting learning, reputation of teachers

Face-to-face formal encounters with parents – often referred to as parents' evening or parent interviews – take many forms. Some schools operate a rota system, in which a set of appointment times is drawn up for parents to come in to the school during the late afternoon or evening. Other head teachers like to foster a less formal approach in which parents are encouraged to wander in and out of classrooms during the teaching day and chat to the teacher. Some schools have experimented by encouraging parents to have their children present during the discussion with the teacher as a means of giving the child some ownership of the process. A number of schools encourage parents to attend lessons and see first hand how the teacher fosters learning and how the children respond, though this option is not always successful because the adult presence impacts on pupil behaviour; in addition, young children may want to sit with their parents, creating logistical problems.

Whatever the form of parent interview adopted, all teachers find their first few formal meetings with parents rather nerve-racking and stressful. Over time, the experience becomes easier, but never easy. Teachers have variously described it as frightening, exhausting and exhilarating – sometimes all three – but ultimately very worthwhile. The groundwork for a parents' evening is done well in advance of the first parent entering the room. The teacher's personality, attitude to children in the classroom, pleasantness during informal contacts, willingness to take time finding out something of a child's interests and approach to learning will already have made a mark. Teachers are talked about regularly at home and at the school gate; their reputation goes before them and influences parents' reactions and inclination when they visit the school. Some parents are nervous about school and occasionally have a negative attitude towards teachers in general, which is often a reflection of their own unsatisfactory schooling or fear of adults when they were young. It is therefore unsurprising that the parent concerned finds it difficult to relax and act naturally. The vast majority of parents come into school because they are deeply interested in their child's education and want to find out more about their progress, both academically and socially. Teachers have access to this information and therefore something of genuine value to share with them.

PASSION IN TEACHING

See also: aims of education, caring teachers, curiosity, motivation for teaching, pedagogy and practice, teaching approach, teachers' beliefs

Although the use of the word 'passion' may sound a little out of place in primary education, it is easier to accept if passion is defined as something that someone loves and enjoys doing. Passion is the gold standard of teaching for the simple reason that it inspires and motivates teachers and learners alike. Some teachers expect that pupils will be enthralled by the work but fail to set the right example

or model a positive attitude. They are then disappointed that their teaching is having so little impact and may complain to pupils about their poor attitude. However, if adults show a sense of curiosity, inquisitiveness and wonderment, the children are quickly drawn into the learning and gradually develop the same approach. Showing excitement about discoveries and a sense of adventure are characteristics of a problem-solving pedagogy ('teaching approach'), rather than a bland 'get the right answer by using the standard method'.

Pupil curiosity is best satisfied when learning is presented in the form of issues to be resolved, as well as facts to be stored, so use of a range of 'open' and 'speculative' questions is essential in opening up children's eyes and minds to other possibilities. Adult interest should also be evident when children tell them something about their lives (such as a visit to a friend's house) or show them a precious photograph (of a visit to a theme park, for instance) or a possession (e.g. a birthday present). In this regard, adults have to learn to be childlike (as opposed to childish) and see life from their point of view.

Day (2004) regrets that passion is rarely acknowledged as being at the heart of intellectual endeavour and commitment. He highlights the fact that for many teachers, teaching is more than just a job or a management task but rather about education in its broadest sense, where emotional engagement and care are essential components. Day comments that these are teachers 'who are committed to service and who are or wish to be, passionate' (p. 10). Namblar (2008) is adamant that good teachers do not ply their trade for the money or because they have to, but because they truly enjoy it and want to do so. As a result, the majority of teachers cannot imagine doing any other job because they see teaching as the most powerful influence for social change and making the world a better place to live in. Education is not solely about feeding a mind with facts and figures but to evolve a mindset of being properly human.

Sources

Day, C.W. (2004) *A Passion for Teaching*, London: Routledge.

Namblar, S. (2008) *Teaching is a Passion*, on-line at www.razz-ma-tazz.net/2008/04/09/teaching-is-a-passion

PEDAGOGICAL FRAMING

See also: thinking

Pedagogical framing is an expression introduced by Siraj-Blatchford and Sylva (2004) in referring to an analysis about children's learning experiences, including planning, use of resources and the establishment of routines. The authors suggest that the educational settings that enhance children's development most effectively are those that incorporate pedagogical framing and interactions that orientate towards children's thinking and learning.

Source

Siraj-Blatchford, I. and Sylva, K. (2004) 'Researching pedagogy in English pre-schools', *British Educational Research Journal*, 30 (5), 713–30.

PEDAGOGY

See also: creativity, curriculum, gender (staff), humanities, instruction, literacy, numeracy, teaching approach, teaching methods, teaching profession

Pedagogy is variously defined as the art or profession of teaching; preparatory training or instruction (*Free Dictionary*); the art, science or profession of teaching (*Merriam-Webster*); the profession or function of a teacher; teaching or the art or science of teaching, especially instruction in teaching methods (*Your Dictionary*). Pedagogia uses the phrase 'content pedagogy' as referring to the pedagogical teaching skills teachers use to impart the specialised knowledge or content of their subject area(s).

There have been many attempts to describe and understand pedagogy and its impact on classroom practice. For example, Vic Kelly has written extensively about curriculum and pedagogy issues for many years. In the 2009 edition of his classic work (Kelly 2009), he focuses on the philosophical and political dimensions of curriculum, and especially on the implications for schools and societies of various forms of curriculum. The book outlines what form a curriculum should take if it is concerned to promote education for a genuinely democratic society. The author argues that the politicisation of the school curriculum has led to the establishment of policies and practices that demonstrate a failure to understand principles of curriculum theory and practice. In similar vein, Golby (1988) is critical of what he described as a means-end model of teaching in which:

> Teachers are viewed as operators of a 'delivery system' whose chief commodity is 'subjects'. Work and play are separated. Learning is regarded as something achieved through instruction … Children, insofar as they are seen at all, are seen as individual learners detached from the wellsprings of their social being in family and community. There is no conception of teaching as other than instruction and control and no account of the relation between the school and the outside world.
>
> (p. 36)

Moore (2001) claims that there are two broad areas in which official education policy impacts on teaching and learning. The first concerns the nature and content of imposed school curricula and syllabuses. The second concerns issues of enforced or 'encouraged' forms of pedagogy that impact upon class size, classroom organisation and guidance on appropriate teaching methodologies. Alexander (2004) raised some significant issues about pedagogy, creativity and curriculum. He describes pedagogy as

the act of teaching, together with its atten-
dant discourse. It is what one needs to
know, and the skills one needs to command, in order to make and justify the
many different kinds of decisions, of which
teaching is constituted. Curriculum is just
one of its domains, albeit a central one.

(p. 11)

One of the key points raised by Alexander
was that primary education now replicated
the two-track system introduced through the
elementary system that was abandoned in the
middle of the last century, with its high status,
protected and heavily assessed literacy and
numeracy curriculum and the low priority
given to non-assessed, vulnerable and even
dispensable curriculum of the arts and the
humanities. Alexander is particularly scathing
about what he perceives as a loss of teacher
autonomy and the imposition of externally
generated policy decisions:

> In tenor and purpose [the government's]
> preferred pedagogy deals with judgement
> rather than substance and justification; and
> with teaching rather than the wider sphere
> of morally purposeful activity, of which
> teaching is a part, which we call education.
> Teachers, in this characterisation, are tech-
> nicians who implement the educational
> ideas and procedures of others, rather than
> professionals who think about these matters
> for themselves.
>
> (p. 28)

Woods and Jeffrey in their book (2003)
describe a case study, 'Coombes School', in
which the teachers are constantly alert for
ways of providing uncommon interest, rous-
ing enthusiasm, demonstrating skills, advan-
cing achievement and stimulating thought
through an imaginative pedagogy in which
nothing is allowed to stagnate. The aim is
therefore 'creative learning', with children
coming to own their own knowledge and
skills, being enthused and changed by the
process, and having some control of the
learning process, but under teacher guidance.
Murphy et al. (2008) challenge practitioners

in every educational setting to reflect on
themselves as teachers and learners, and to be
reflexive about their own practices and contexts. The authors argue that learning
involves a 'transformation of identity' that
takes place through negotiation and reposi-
tioning, through new ways of relating and
through different ways of participating. They
argue for practices that create a bridge
between learners' worlds, their communities
and educational institutions.

Smedley (2006) raises an important issue
about whether pedagogical practices differ
between male and female teachers and particularly the adjustment that some men (as a
minority group in primary schools) have to
make in teaching younger children. In her
study of twenty-five teachers Ollin (2008)
suggests that many different types of silence
may be used productively in pedagogical
practice. She provides examples of questions
that might be asked when observing teachers'
uses of silence rather than talk and concludes
that teachers make conscious decisions to
abstain from intervention based on their continuous reading of what is happening in the
classroom. Clearly, pedagogy is a more complex enterprise than may be recognised by
those who formulaically reduce effective
teaching to 'what works' or 'best practice'
lessons downloaded from web sites.

Sources

Alexander, R. (2004) 'Still no pedagogy? Principle,
pragmatism and compliance in primary education',
Cambridge Journal of Education, 34 (1), 7–33.
Golby, M. (1988) 'Traditions in primary educa-
tion' in Clarkson, M. (ed.) *Emerging Issues in
Primary Education*, London: Falmer.
Kelly, V. (2009) *The Curriculum*, London: Sage.
Moore, A. (2001) *Teaching and Learning: Pedagogy,
curriculum, and culture*, London: Routledge.
Murphy, P.F., Hall, K. and Soler, J.M. (2008)
Pedagogy and Practice: Culture and identities,
Maidenhead: Open University Pres.
Ollin, R. (2008) 'Silent pedagogy and rethinking
classroom practice: Structuring teaching
through silence rather than talk', *Cambridge
Journal of Education*, 38 (2), 265–80.

Smedley, S. (2006) 'Listening to men student primary school teachers and some thoughts on pedagogy', *Changing English*, 13 (1), 125–35.

Woods, P. and Jeffrey, B. (2003) *The Creative School*, London: Routledge.

PEER COACHING AND REVIEW

See also: lesson management, professional development

Peer coaching is a system whereby colleagues work together supportively to develop personally and professionally to strengthen weaker areas of knowledge and expertise and enhance stronger ones. The coaching usually involves two teachers coming together regularly to share ideas, discuss current issues and refine their practice. The relationship is intended to be built on confidentiality and trust in a non-threatening, secure environment in which they learn and grow together; peer coaching should therefore not form part of the school's teacher appraisal scheme. Areas for attention might include scrutiny of a teacher's active classroom management; teaching effectiveness; pupils' learning; and the teacher's professional learning. Peer coaching helps colleagues to develop a shared vocabulary and gain insights into issues that might otherwise be restricted to private reflection. Peer *review* differs from peer coaching in that a more experienced or knowledgeable teacher is linked with a less experienced colleague or one who will benefit from that person's expertise.

PEER MEDIATION

See also: behaviour, bullying, falling out, learning climate

Peer mediation is a conflict resolution tool that schools can use to help pupils sort out some of their problems on their own or with minimal adult involvement. Children and young people are trained in the principles and skills of mediation to help disputants of their own age group and younger find solutions to issues that are causing friction between them. Baginsky (2004) claims that peer mediation has the potential to engender a more relaxed and positive learning climate and reduce staff time in dealing with pupil conflicts, brought about by a reduction in the incidence of behavioural problems and bullying – though some schools saw an initial increase in problems.

Source

Baginsky, W. (2004) *Peer Mediation in the UK: A guide for schools*, London: NSPCC.

PEER MENTORING

See also: playground, reading, self-esteem, social and emotional aspects of learning

Peer mentoring has increased in popularity after being introduced in a number of schools where it has contributed to the ethos ('feel') of the school and pastoral support systems. Peer support within schools has the potential to increase the opportunity for personal and social development within individuals; provide additional support and encouragement on aspects of schoolwork; help to build confidence and self-esteem; and foster positive participation in school life. An evaluation carried out by the National Foundation for Educational Research (NFER) showed that peer mentoring is beneficial to both mentors and pupils being mentored and can be helpful to young people by providing them with opportunities to improve their interpersonal skills (DfEE 2005). Schools use peer mentoring (child to child) or 'buddy' systems that enable older pupils to link with younger ones and support them in their learning (in reading, for instance) and general well-being (e.g. during break times) with an adult assistant having general oversight. Some schools initiate 'vertical tutoring' structures that are based on a mix of pupil ages, such that children can forge supportive relationships outside their own class and year group, a practice that reflects to an extent what happens in the playground and outside school. Bell (2009) provides advice to teachers who are training pupils in school to support their peers during playground problems by using conflict resolution and problem-solving approaches. The Department for Children, Schools and Families (DCSF) in England supports the Mentoring and Befriending Foundation to promote the development of peer mentoring for young people from 11–25 years of age.

Sources

Bell, L. (2009) *Peer Support in the Primary Playground*, London: Optimus Education.
DfEE (2005) *Peer Mentoring*, London: HMSO. Online at Teachernet, www.teachernet.gov.uk/teachingandlearning/socialandpastoral/mentoring/

PERSONAL EDUCATION PLAN

A personal education plan (PEP) is a document describing a course of action to help children reach their full academic and life potential, put together and completed at a meeting in which the designated teacher, social worker and carers for the young person in public care are present. The child is expected to participate or be consulted about the education planning, either at the PEP meeting itself or, particularly in the case of younger children, through discussions outside that meeting. The Plan is reviewed periodically to monitor its appropriateness and evaluate its effectiveness in assisting the child in question, socially and academically.

PERSONAL INTELLIGENCE

See also: emotions of teaching, intelligence, motivation for learning, motivation for teaching, multiple intelligences

The significance of emotions in the work and motivation of teachers has long been recognised; however, the theory that there is a separate type of social intelligence, unrelated to traditional abstract intelligence, is a relatively new idea. Drawing from the work on multiple intelligences by the American psychologist, Howard Gardner, the concept of emotional intelligence (EI), has been popularised by another US psychologist, Daniel Goleman. Emotional intelligence as defined by Goleman is basically another name for the 'personal intelligence' observed by Gardner (Gardner 1999). Personal intelligence includes two separate categories: *interpersonal* intelligence and *intrapersonal* intelligence. Interpersonal intelligence is concerned with the capacity to understand the intentions, motivations and desires of other people. Intrapersonal intelligence entails the capacity to understand oneself, to appreciate one's feelings, fears and motivation – factors highly relevant to the work of teachers and the emotions of teaching.

Source

Gardner, H. (1999) *Intelligence Reframed: Multiple intelligences for the 21st century*, New York: Basic Books.

PERSONAL, SOCIAL AND HEALTH EDUCATION

See also: citizenship, healthy eating, modelling behaviour, moral education, self-esteem, social learning

Personal, social and health education (PSHE) is a combination of taught elements that have been placed together for the purpose of curriculum organisation. Originally the area was described simply as personal and social education (PSE) and the 'health' dimension was added to stress the implications for individual well-being. The Department for Children, Schools and Families in England requires that PSHE should help pupils to lead confident, healthy and responsible lives as individuals and members of society and lists the following aims (modified; DCSF, on-line):

- To help pupils live healthily and safely and deal with the spiritual, moral, social and cultural issues they face as they approach adulthood.
- To reflect on their experiences and their implications for their lives.
- To understand and manage responsibly a wider range of relationships as they mature.
- To show respect for the diversity of, and differences between, people.
- To develop pupils' well-being and self-esteem, encouraging belief in the ability to succeed.
- To enable children to take responsibility for their learning and (eventual) future choice of courses and career.

The health education and citizenship education strands are brought together in a national framework and taught to children between the ages of five and eleven years. However, the comprehensive and wide-ranging nature of the subject raises issues about where parental guidance ends and school responsibilities begin; for example, in the area of ensuring that children receive a well-balanced diet. There are direct links between PSHE and the Every Child Matters requirements (DfES 2005), the elements of which include a need to be healthy, stay safe, enjoy life, reach one's potential, make a positive contribution to the community and avoid engaging in anti-social or offending behaviour. This extensive level of responsibility provides a considerable challenge for even the most diligent teacher. Needham (1994) memorably argues that everything teachers do comes under the gaze of the eyes of the children they are watching; is heard by the ears they encourage to listen; is analysed by the minds they encourage to evaluate; and can be – indeed, *will* be – interpreted and challenged by the voices they encourage to ask questions (see p. 162).

Sources

DCSF, *Personal, Social and Health Education*, on-line at www.teachernet.gov.uk/management/atoz/p/pshe

DfES (2005) *Every Child Matters: Change for children*, London: HMSO.
Needham, J. (1994) 'Personal and social education', in Pollard, A. and Bourne, J. (eds) *Teaching and Learning in the Primary School*, London: Routledge/Open University Press.

PERSONALISED CURRICULUM

See also: curriculum, curriculum leadership, knowledge, lesson planning, reading recovery, skills, teaching assistants, understanding

Every teacher has to take account of the resource and time implications of trying to develop too many tasks and activities for children in an attempt to cater for everybody's individual needs. Such a so-called 'personalised' or 'tailor-made' curriculum is impractical other than for classes numbered in single figures. Lesson planning must rely on a satisfactory grouping of children so that each group can cope with the demands of the work, and individuals can develop and enhance their own understanding, knowledge and skills in the subject. The allocation of teaching assistants to offer a child specific training or coaching in an area of difficulty (e.g. 'reading recovery') is usually determined by the head teacher or member of staff with responsibility for standards of attainment in that curriculum area (e.g. the curriculum leader with responsibility for literacy).

PERSONALISED LEARNING

See also: assessing children's learning, assessment for learning, learning, special educational needs, target setting (pupils)

The phrase 'personalised learning' was coined in 2004 by the then British prime minister, Tony Blair, and the then schools minister, David Miliband, and was intended to be the next big idea in education. The concept of 'personalisation' is posited on a philosophy that it is possible to assess children's progress accurately and tailor-make teaching such that it meets their needs and allows for regular 'assessment for learning' (AFL), thereby directly addressing identified learning needs rather than a 'one size fits all' philosophy. As evidence of the way in which the definition is changing and being interpreted, the Department for Children, Schools and Families (DCSF 2008) regards personalised learning as taking a highly structured and responsive approach to each child's and young person's learning in order that all are able to progress, achieve and participate. It means strengthening the link between learning and teaching by engaging pupils and their parents as partners in learning. Setting aside the politicised nature of the statement, it is a useful reminder to teachers and school leaders that a child's individual needs should not be overlooked in the process of whole-class teaching, maintaining pace or fulfilling the immediate curriculum requirements.

Bird (2006) helpfully suggests that models of a personalised education can be compared with assembling a motor vehicle. The first model is a version in which every pupil has an *identical* main chassis, frame, engine, body and wheels; however, each pupil has a *stylised* section, unique to each child. The second model is a version in which the basic composition of chassis, frame, engine, body and wheels, etc., are present in every vehicle but each pupil's education is stylised, while being superficially similar.

Personalised learning should not be confused with the 'individualised' learning of the past, characterised by each child engaged on solitary learning paths – often dominated by work sheets – or letting children choose what they want to do, which runs the risk of them selecting easy tasks that fail to stretch their minds. Rather, it is encouraging pupils to be involved in establishing their own medium-term targets for learning, while recognising that the ultimate target of success in national tests is already determined nationally. Hargreaves (2006) comments that public services have traditionally fitted the individual to the service rather than vice versa, but his research

revealed that a new view of the learner was central to personalisation, namely that instead of expecting pupils to adapt to the pre-ordained structures, practices and routines of the school, these could all be questioned and if necessary adapted better to meet the needs of learners (p. 16).

In a major study of the ways that schools use personalised learning, Sebba *et al.* (2007) describe how schools were using their personalised learning approaches to target specific interventions that were then developed more widely. Thus, literacy interventions, programmes and support initially aimed at pupils with identified special educational needs and provision for gifted and talented pupils could be targeted at one group of pupils and gradually extended across the school. The case study schools seemed to have developed activities that reflected greater involvement of the parents through review days and use of ICT for linking home to school.

Some schools have created leadership roles or teaching posts to manage and disseminate best practice in support of the personalised learning agenda, including information to parents and opportunities for them to receive advice about how they may better contribute towards their children's education. See a summary of key research and thinking into how school leaders can embed personalisation and high-quality learning within every aspect of their school in West-Burnham 2008. Schools now hold a lot of assessment information about children in their management systems that are available to staff and, in simplified form, to parents to provide information about measurable pupil attainment that can be valuable in planning for personalised learning.

Concerns have been raised about the implementation of personalised learning. First, that it is an unattainable ideal because no teacher, however, skilled and knowledgeable, can offer a bespoke education to each child. Second, learning does not depend solely on teaching methods, so even the most carefully designed programme cannot guarantee outcomes. Third, personalised learning can become unduly rigid in format and thereby constrain creativity and innovation. Finally, any approach to learning, regardless of its intentions, has to be cognisant of the need to achieve good pupil test results and satisfy inspection criteria.

Sources

Bird, R. (2006) 'Personalised learning', *Secondary Headship,* November, 11–20.

DCSF (2008) *Personalised Learning: A practical guide,* London: HMSO.

Hargreaves, D. (2006) *Personalising Learning 6: The final gateway – school design and organisation,* London: Specialist Schools Trust.

Sebba, J., Brown, N., Stewart, S., Galton, M. and James, M. (2007) *An Investigation of Personalised Learning Approaches Used by Schools,* DfES report RR843, Nottingham: DfES Publications.

West-Burnham, J. (2008) *Leadership for Personalising Learning,* National College for School Leadership, on-line via www.ncsl.org.uk

PHILOSOPHY FOR CHILDREN

See also: circle-time, curiosity, debating, dilemmas, discussion, enquiry, questions and questioning, teacher role, tests and testing, thinking, thinking skills

Philosophy for children is a distinctive approach to teaching that promotes questioning, reasoning and dialogue. The educational movement known as philosophy for children got its start in the early 1970s with the publication of Matthew Lipman's philosophical novel for children, *Harry Stottlemeier's Discovery,* where Harry and his friends discover several basic concepts and rules of logic and puzzle over questions about the nature of thought, mind, causality, reality, knowledge and belief, right and wrong, and fairness and unfairness. The story does not introduce any of the special vocabulary of philosophy – not even the word 'philosophy' itself makes an appearance – however, philosophical inquiry is initiated by the children in the story rather than by adults.

In facilitating philosophy for children, teachers allow their pupils to develop their own ideas and encourage children to think for themselves at the same time as thinking with other pupils. Teachers are not expected to provide or even have answers to all the questions; they can share uncertainties with their pupils, be open to unexpected responses to the questions they and the children pose and take pleasure in observing the exchanges that pupils have with each other. This approach means dispensing with the traditional role of teacher as information-provider and answer-giver and replacing it with one of facilitator.

Further work by Lipman (1991) was highly influential in promoting the popularity of this approach by offering a strategy for building on the inquisitiveness that children display. The dialogue between child and child, and between adult and child, is promoted by setting up the classroom in such a way that every person can see everyone else (a 'circle-time' approach) and a community of enquiry is fostered through oral (spoken) means. In this environment, all opinions are welcomed and the teacher discourages the concept of a 'right' or 'wrong' viewpoint. As a result, support is given to minority views as well as to mainstream ones and disagreements are presented as natural and tension-free, rather than as a source of conflict (Haynes 2007).

Teachers often use a stimulus to initiate debate or discussion; for instance, sharing an interesting picture book, relating a gripping story, reading a humorous or sad poem, showing an unusual or graphic image, presenting newspaper headlines, giving a personal account of a dilemma or difficult decision, or bringing in an item of interest. Children are then invited to respond – sometimes after giving them opportunity to sit quietly and think or discuss in pairs or small groups, making notes as appropriate if they wish to do so – before framing and sharing points and questions that have arisen. Teachers help children to express their ideas clearly without putting words into their mouths and encourage responses from other class members,

323

brokering the different perspectives and summarising key issues.

There is a growing body of evidence to support the claim that sustained participation in open-ended enquiry of this kind leads to growth in self-esteem and has a positive effect on pupils' cognition and their ability to reason. It is claimed that philosophy for children also has important social benefits, as children consider other viewpoints, concentrate hard, collaborate with others and treat their perspectives seriously. Huxtable *et al.* (2009) insist that we have an educational responsibility to enable our pupils to recognise the people they are and want to be, to grow in their understanding of a world worth living in and how they might contribute by living the best lives they can. Over time, pupils grow in confidence and develop skills of questioning, reasoning, evaluating evidence and articulating their thoughts in front of their peers.

Introducing a philosophy for children programme is not without its challenges, notably the pressures of an already crowded curriculum and the demands it places on teachers as they step aside from their more traditional role and have to inculcate children into unfamiliar practices and behaviour. In addition, teachers are required to demonstrate that their pupils are performing at satisfactory levels in the national tests, which do not incorporate philosophical reflection. Test results have implications for the school's reputation and funding, which is not an issue that teachers can take lightly, whatever their personal priorities and educational beliefs (Pritchard 2008). Supporters of the philosophy for children approach counter-argue by claiming that the development of reason, sound judgement, balanced argument and thinking skills positively influences academic work across the curriculum, so that time spent on philosophy for children is amply justified.

Sources

Haynes, J. (2007) 'Thinking together: Enjoying dialogue with children', in Hayes, D. (ed.) *Joyful Teaching and Learning in the Primary School*, Exeter: Learning Matters.

Huxtable, M., Hurford, R. and Mounter, J. (2009) *Creative and Philosophical Thinking in Primary Schools*, London: Optimus.

Lipman, M. (1974) *Harry Stottlemeier's Discovery*, Upper Montclair NJ: Institute for the Advancement of Philosophy for Children.

——(1991) *Thinking in Education*, Cambridge: Cambridge University Press.

Pritchard, M. (2008) *Philosophy for children*, Stanford University, on-line at http://plato.stanford.edu/entries/children

PHONICS

See also: alphabet, reading, spelling, synthetic phonics, writing

The phonics method is probably the best known and most widely used method to teach reading and writing in the English language. Knowledge of the sounds of letters and of the effect of the position of the letter upon its sound is an essential means of mastering the mechanics of reading and of enabling children to become independent readers (Williams 2008). It relies on children first being taught the alphabet and learning the names of the letters and the sounds they make. Once they have learnt the letter sounds, they begin to blend two letters together to make simple words, then three letters, then four and so on. Eventually the words combine to create simple sentences. Phonics is generally more applicable to teaching pupils during their first few years of formal education, though it is valuable in teaching an older primary child who has experienced learning difficulties. Approaches that use highly systematic phonics teaching may appear to be effective in the short term but must be embedded within meaningful and purposeful texts and reading activities.

Children first learn that words are constructed from phonemes – the smallest unit that is capable of conveying a distinction in meaning, such as the 'c' of cat and the 'p' of pin – and that phonemes are represented by graphemes – defined as all of the letters and letter combinations that represent a phoneme, as f, ph, and gh for the phoneme /f/ (e.g. fun, phone, laugh), and know a small selection of common consonants (all alphabet letters except a, e, i, o, u) and vowels (a, e, i, o, u, and sometimes y, as in 'hymn'). They are able to blend them together in reading simple consonant-vowel-consonant (CVC) words and segment them to support spelling.

Later, children can link sounds to letters, name and sound the letters of the alphabet, recognise letter shapes and know what each one sounds like. They learn to hear and say sounds in the order in which they occur in the word and sound out and blend the phonemes in the word from left to right. In time, they begin to recognise common digraphs – a pair of letters representing a single speech sound, such as the 'ph' in pheasant or the 'ea' in seal – and read some high-frequency words spontaneously. Children start to identify the constituent parts of two-syllable and three-syllable words, increase their skill in reading and spelling and create the capacity to attend to reading for meaning. Children eventually learn to apply their phonic skills and knowledge to recognise and spell an increasing number of complex words, such that they can read an increasing number of high- and medium-frequency words. The links between phonics and learning to spell are also significant (see, for example, Pinnell and Fountas 1998).

Even though children need to be read to in school and at home, and pick up familiar words and phrases from daily life, a programme of targeted tuition in reading is still necessary, of which phonics forms an integral part (e.g. Starrett 2007). Teachers use two broad approaches. In analytic phonics the teacher builds up the sounds to make a word, which is shown to the child at the same time; for example, a teacher might sound out the letters of 'f-l-a-g' and then ask the child to repeat the word. In synthetic phonics the children learn forty-four sounds of letters or groups of letters before being encouraged to look at books containing the words. Both analytic and synthetic approaches require the learner to have some phonological awareness (the ability to hear and discriminate sounds in spoken words) and can contribute to furthering children's development. Although most teachers use a balanced combination of analytic and synthetic approaches, the use of synthetic phonics has become the favoured method in most schools in the UK (Johnston and Watson 2007).

Whatever method of phonics teaching is favoured, there is agreement among educators that for young children to learn to read effectively they need access to books containing common words that are interesting to them and capable of being sounded out. Sometimes, children are so busy concentrating on sounding the words and blending the sounds that they don't think about their meaning, so teachers have to remind children about the significance of words, relate them to the accompanying pictures and use example sentences that include the word or words. Reading becomes more meaningful as children master the connection between different sounds and become familiar with the written words through stories, rhymes and songs.

The aim of systematic high-quality phonic work is to secure essential phonic knowledge and skills so that children progress quickly to independent reading and writing. Children therefore move from 'learning to read' to 'reading to learn' as they secure the alphabetic code, become confident in decoding and recognising words, and begin to read for purpose and pleasure. By the age of about seven years, the majority of children should be well on the way to becoming fluent readers and capable of decoding the words on the page automatically. Some reading specialists argue that the spelling-to-sound correspondences of English are so confusing that blending and sounding out is likely to lead to confusion rather than enlightenment; however, the majority of educationists believe that phonics has an important role to play in learning to read.

Sources

Johnston, R.S. and Watson, J.E. (2007) *Teaching Synthetic Phonics*, Exeter: Learning Matters.

Pinnell, G.S. and Fountas, I.C. (1998) *Word Matters: Teaching phonics and spelling in the reading/writing classroom*, New York: Heinemann.

Starrett, E.V. (2007) *Teaching Phonics for Balanced Reading*, San Francisco CA: Corwin Press.

Williams, L.M. (2008) *How to Teach Phonics*, on-line at www.BetterDaysBooks.com

PHYSICAL COMFORT

See also: circle-time, desks, displays, distractible children, interaction

Evidence from numerous studies and common sense are agreed on the principle that children learn best when they are physically comfortable and emotionally secure. Maslow's hierarchy of needs, consisting of five levels, is often used to explain this principle. The lowest level is associated with physiological needs (e.g. the availability of food and water), while the top levels are associated with psychological needs (e.g. security, friendship, self-confidence) – the higher needs are only attainable when the basic 'survival' needs are met. If a lower set of needs is no longer being met, the individual will temporarily focus attention on the unfulfilled needs, but will not permanently regress to the lower level. Thus, children who get hungry or uncomfortable or feel threatened when they are normally well fed will not be able to make adequate progress in learning until the position has been corrected. The message from Maslow's hierarchy is that adults have to take account of their own and their children's physical needs, security and comfort if learning is to proceed smoothly. For example to ensure that every pupil can see the teacher, the board/screen and visual resources without having to sit unnaturally.

Most interactive sessions with younger children take place 'on the carpet', with the teacher seated and the children clustered around her or his feet, whereas sessions with older primary children are often conducted with the children seated and the teacher standing. In the situation where children sit around the teacher, the teacher has closer physical proximity to the children, so that eye contact is easy and few problems exist in hearing what is said. However, children may become uncomfortable and there is always a temptation for restless, easily distracted children to move position, touch other children or make whispered comments, so some opportunity to stand and stretch is normally appropriate after ten or fifteen minutes. Some teachers of younger children in particular develop a regular system for gently stretching in time to a quiet song, rhyme or set of instructions. In the situation where children are at tables and the teacher is mobile, the physical distance across the room means that the person speaking needs to use a stronger voice in order to be heard. However, children can more easily view the teacher and are unable to 'hide' behind their classmates, as they can sometimes do when on the carpet.

Another important consideration is the comfort of pupils with specific physical limitations and learning needs. For instance, children with visual impairment will require good quality lighting; children with hearing problems need to sit where they can listen without strain and, perhaps, lip-read the teacher. Children who are confined to a wheelchair or have immobile limbs will almost certainly need modified table space and a specially adapted work surface. In addition, many pupils with special physical needs are assisted by an adult helper, who also deserves a comfortable working environment (e.g. an adult-sized chair). Leaman (2006) insists that tidiness, orderliness and bright energetic displays are inspirational; she warns, however, that classrooms need to be functional and physically comfortable as far as possible. Leaman also notes that it is important when anticipating and dealing with classroom behaviour to consider the fact that if a physical situation is irritating the teacher it is more than likely having a similar effect on the learners (see chapter 8).

Turner-Bissett (2003) provides an interesting historical perspective on the surroundings in which teaching takes place in relation to changing curricula and teaching methods down the years.

Sources

Maslow, A.H. (1943) 'A theory of human motivation', *Psychological Review*, 50, 370–96.

Leaman, L. (2006) *Classroom Confidential*, London: Continuum.

Turner-Bissett, R. (2003) 'On the carpet: Changing primary teacher contexts', *Education 3–13*, 31 (3), 4–10.

PHYSICAL EDUCATION

See also: communication, dance, gifted and talented, health and safety (physical activity), new entrants, sports

The programmes of study for key stage 1 (children aged 5–7 years) and key stage 2 (7–11 years) lay down six areas of physical education (PE) activity: dance; games; gymnastics; swimming and water safety; athletics; outdoor and adventurous activities. The majority of primary school teachers are non-specialists in physical education and there is, therefore, a particular need for information on appropriate planning and safe practice designed to meet their specific requirements. Safety is also a central issue in PE and as risk assessment is now a statutory part of health and safety at work requirements, it is essential that all staff have a clear understanding of their responsibilities (Severs 2003). PE has been a focus for government attention owing to the increase in obesity and poor diet evident among the population; a decree was issued in 2008 that all pupils in England should receive two hours high-quality PE and school sport each week.

Primary age children use movement as a means of self-expression and communication. Teachers have a responsibility to help pupils discover the entire range of bodily movements and develop ways in which sensitivity and awareness of the body can be fostered. Children gradually learn to appreciate different features of their movement and ways of 'using' space individually; in time, work in pairs and group activities can be developed. A variety of stimuli can be employed to assist movement types, notably the use of prompt words and phrases: skip, twist, stretch, and so forth. Careful teaching generates a growth of sensory perceptions ('the senses'), which will help children develop an understanding of themselves and others (Rose 1989).

Grey *et al.* (2000) describe how, when children first start school as new entrants, they can be taught how to link physical skills in short sequences or series of movements and learn to make simple judgements about their performance. Pupils build on their own creativity and enthusiasm for physical movement using indoor and outdoor environments. Very young children prefer to work alone but they gradually build the confidence and social skills to co-operate with a partner and assist one another. At the same time, they become aware of the changes that occur to their bodies as they exercise and recognise the effects on their bodies and minds.

Older children in primary school continue to develop their skills in dance, games and gymnastics, and become increasingly able to plan, perform and evaluate what they do. They are more able to work cooperatively but also become more competitive in a range of physical activities involving creative tasks, problem solving and decision-making. Teachers encourage the children to persevere in practising movements and sequences to improve and refine their performance – such as in ways of controlling and throwing a ball – and making judgements about their own and others' work. They are capable of sustaining energetic activity over appropriate periods of time and can understand the benefits of exercise, including swimming.

Although the profile of primary physical education is rising, the challenge for schools is to develop programmes that not only max-imise children's opportunities within school but also promote sport, dance and outdoor education opportunities beyond the school day (Jess 2002). One key to success is to help all children develop their so-called 'move-ment literacy' – the basic movement compe-tence that provides the building blocks for the more complex activities of late childhood and beyond. In addition, teachers have a respon-sibility to support less able pupils whose basic movement competence is a cause for con-cern, extend able pupils ('talented') who demonstrate mastery of their basic move-ments and offer additional opportunities for all pupils to practise and develop their basic movements.

Wright (2004) points out that one of the most significant benefits is the happiness that participation brings to children, as anyone who has witnessed a PE lesson will testify. Consequently, teachers must remain alert to the values that are enshrined in choice, play and links with other areas of the curriculum. Sime and Hayes (2007) refer to the need for children to run, leap and dance for joy. They comment that for many teachers 'the sheer pleasure of watching the children, red-faced and breathless, bounding around the play-ground or school hall, clearly exhilarated by the opportunity to explore their bodies, is unique, uplifting and truly joyful' (p. 68).

A report by the school inspectorate in England (OFSTED 2009) indicated that PE and associated physical activity is popular with primary-age children. Writing from a US per-spective, Graham (2008) provides comprehen-sive coverage of the principles and practices in developing a physical education programme and becoming an expert practitioner.

Sources

Graham, G. (2008) *Teaching Children Physical Education: Becoming a master teacher*, Champaign IL/Pudsey: Human Kinetics Publishers.

Grey, J., Hopper, B. and Maude, P. (2000) *Teaching Physical Education in the Primary School*, London: Routledge.

Jess, M. (2002) *Improving Physical Education in Primary Schools*, Edinburgh: Edinburgh University Press.

OFSTED (2009) *Physical Education in Schools 2005–8*, London: HMSO.

Rose, C. (1989) 'Physical Education for the early years of schooling', in Williams, A. (ed.) *Issues in Physical Education for the Primary Years*, London: Falmer.

Severs, J. (2003) *Safety and Risk in Primary School Physical Education*, London: Routledge.

Sime, E. and Hayes, D. (2007) 'Running, leaping and dancing for joy', in Hayes, D. (ed.) *Joyful Teaching and Learning in the Primary School*, Exeter: Learning Matters.

Wright, L. (2004) 'Preserving the value of happiness in primary school physical education', *Physical Education and Sport Pedagogy*, 9 (2), 149–63.

PIAGET, JEAN

See also: child development theories, intelligence, Intelligence Quotient, thinking

Jean Piaget (9 August 1896–16 September 1980) was born in Neuchâtel, Switzerland and began his career as a biologist. After completing his doctorate in science, he worked for a year in psychology laboratories and was introduced to the works of characters such as Freud and Jung. Piaget was unconvinced by intelligence tests and started interviewing boys at a local school to discover how chil-dren reasoned and thought. Later he observed how even very young children began to gain skills associated with the environment in which they were placed; he called these skills 'schema'. Piaget described cognitive structures as patterns of physical or mental action that underlie specific acts of intelligence and correspond to stages of child development.

Piaget called his general theoretical frame-work 'genetic epistemology' – epistemology is the study of the source, nature and limi-tations of knowledge (*Collins Dictionary*) – because he was primarily interested in how knowledge developed in human organisms. He proposed four levels of development in children: (1) infancy, (2) pre-school, (3) childhood, and (4) adolescence, each stage characterised by a general cognitive structure that affects all of a child's thinking. The application of Piaget's theory has implications for the education of children (Bybee and Sund 1990); for example, the provision of a stimulating environment for young children with numerous objects to play with, whereas learning activities for older children should involve activities such as classifying, ordering and conserving by using 'concrete' (i.e. three-dimensional) objects. Singer and Revenson (1998) provide a readable guide to Piaget's theories for teachers, students and parents. *The Psychology of the Child* by Piaget and Inhelder was reissued in 2000 by Basic Books.

Piaget was passionate about the education of children and claimed that only education was capable of saving our societies from possible collapse. Although he was not primarily an educational reformer, he provided the foundation for much of today's education structure, including the somewhat controversial idea that children need to be 'ready' to move on to the next developmental stage. Piaget published extensively, for example:

Piaget, J. (1929) *The Child's Conception of the World*, New York: Harcourt, Brace Jovanovich.
——(1932) *The Moral Judgement of the Child*, New York: Harcourt, Brace Jovanovich.
——(1969) *The Mechanisms of Perception*, London: Routledge & Kegan Paul.
——(1970) *The Science of Education and the Psychology of the Child*, New York: Grossman.
Piaget, J. and Inhelder, B. (1973) *Memory and Intelligence*, New York: Basic Books.

The Jean Piaget Society, established in 1970, has a membership of scholars, teachers and researchers who are interested in exploring the nature of the developmental construction of human knowledge (www.piaget.org).

Sources

Bybee, R.W. and Sund, R.B. (eds) (1970) *Piaget for Educators*, Prospect Heights IL: Waveland Press.
Piaget, J. and Inhelder, B. (2000) *The Psychology of the Child*, New York: Basic Books.
Singer, D.G. and Revenson, T.A. (1998) *A Piaget Primer: How a child thinks*, Madison CT: International Universities Press.

PLANNING

See *Lesson planning, Lesson planning (joint)*

PLAY

See also: body language, bullying, child development, creativity, discovery learning, drama fantasy, Foundation Stage, free play, home–school, imagination, motor skills, Piaget, play (older children), playfulness, playtime, skills

Play as an essential part of the educative process and a powerful learning agent. It serves as a development tool because it helps in the establishment of social relations, an understanding of natural and physical properties and the development of fine and gross motor skills. The creation of imaginary situations, characters, and events lays the foundation for abstract thinking (see Singer *et al.* 2006; also the editorial in *Play Therapy*, March 2008, www.a4pt.org). Play assists children in utilising spoken and other non-verbal forms of language ('body language') effectively. It offers pupils in school opportunities to converse meaningfully with other children and understand that their words and actions can evoke a variety of responses in their peers. There is a considerable body of evidence to support the view that play helps to develop a child's imagination and ultimately helps them to distinguish between fantasy and reality.

O'Hara (2004) suggests that there are four broad types of child play: structured, free, exploratory and social. Structured play is planned and initiated by the adult. Free play is spontaneous. Exploratory play is when children experiment with tools, equipment and materials (including sand and water). Social play provides 'opportunities to learn about and practise the rules, rituals and norms of society' (p. 79).

Orr (2003) presents a compelling argument for play as a vital agent in the development of children suffering from disabilities, and Garrick (2004) argues the importance of outdoor play. Chudacoff (2007) laments the increasing intrusion of parents into the play of their children, as free play stimulates the imagination and, allows for unstructured interaction between children that builds important social skills, such as taking turns, sharing, negotiating and compromising. He is also anxious about the commercialisation of toys that limit children's pretend and imaginative play potential.

Smidt (2006) offers four explicit characteristics that define the concept of play: (1) Play is something the child has chosen to do. (2) Play is often pleasurable and always deeply engrossing, and we tend to see children enjoying their chosen activity, except when the play is 'acting out' a traumatic experience. (3) In play there is no risk of failure, as the child simply changes the agenda. (4) The emphasis is on the process rather than on the product. Bruce (2001) maintains that play helps children to learn in a number of powerful ways: to become symbol-makers by making one item stand for another (such as using a stick to be a wand); to think in abstract ways that take them beyond the here and now; to develop theory of mind, an understanding of the way others think and feel, and relate to people; to make changes, transforming their lives and events, using imagination and creating alternative possibilities; and to be flexible thinkers, so that intelligence continues to develop throughout life. Robson (2006) argues that what she refers to as 'pretend play' may be 'particularly significant for the development of theory of mind' because in pretend play 'children step in and out of role, represent situations and transform objects, talk about mental states ... and have to negotiate meanings and actions with others' (p. 79).

The well-known psychoanalyst, Sigmund Freud, stressed the creative nature of play:

Might we not say that every child at play behaves like a creative writer, in that he creates a world of his own, or rather rearranges the things of the world in a new way which pleases him? It would be wrong to think he does not take that world seriously; on the contrary, he takes his play very seriously and he expends large amounts of emotion on it. The opposite of play is not what is serious but what is real.

(Freud 1908, p. 143)

The Swiss psychologist, Jean Piaget, has had a considerable impact on the way teachers perceive play in learning. In trying to classify how concept development takes place from early childhood to adulthood, Piaget argued that as children grow physically and intellectually, they expand the limits of their play in stages. The first stage is *sensorimotor play* in which infants and toddlers experiment with bodily sensations and motor movements involving objects and people. As children grow older and gain more motor skills (ability to manipulate objects and their own bodies) they also start to see the world in symbolic terms and begin to understand the social function of objects. Thus, they feed their teddy bears pretend food with a spoon or offer a grown-up an invisible drink in a cup. The second stage is *symbolic play* when children use simple objects to represent more sophisticated ones. A three- or four-year-old may use a coat as a superhero's cape and a cardboard roll as a light sabre. The space beneath a living-room chair becomes a cave and the stairs a mountain. By the age of four or five, children's ideas and experiences with the immediate family and the wider social world provide material for imaginative games. Many new entrants to primary school enjoy construction play, building and spontaneously exuberant games, such as chasing. Piaget refers to the next stage of play as *mastery* when children gain increasing control of their bodies and actions, while simultaneously incorporating imaginative forms of play. For example, mastery of riding a tricycle becomes a motorbike stunt in the child's mind. By the time they leave the Foundation Stage (for pupils aged 4–5 years) and enter the more formal period of primary schooling in key stage 1 (for pupils aged 5–7 years) children begin to develop an interest in formal games with rules, two or more sides and explicit activities in which issues of fairness become increasingly significant. As they mature children begin to think more abstractly, being dependent on what they can envisage and work out in their minds, rather than relying on visual stimuli and physical contact with resources. Thus, whereas a five-year-old boy may count on his fingers to work out an addition sum, an eight year old is likely to be able to calculate similar problems in his head without recourse to practical aids.

The place of play in the school day will depend upon the age of the children and the teacher's education philosophy. Very young children enjoy the freedom that comes from playing without restraint and a teacher may decide that this reason is justification in itself, in which case the children are offered the opportunity to play whenever it is practicable and desirable. Younger children, who are familiar with school routines and able to cope with more structure, may be allocated play opportunities on a rota basis or as a reward for working hard, though there is a tendency for children to rush to complete the formal task if they know that extra time to play is an incentive. Older children, too, need a chance to play, and although this normally has to be reserved for timetabled break times, the skilful use of improvisation and role-play in drama offers them the chance to relax and enjoy the spontaneity while performing an academically purposeful activity. The social aspect of play is useful in developing children's self-control, a consideration for other people and empathy with their situations. Children benefit from regular interaction with their peers in learning to share, negotiate and understand the world.

Adults responsible for young primary age children take account of the different forms of play when organising and monitoring activities. For instance, *parallel play* describes a situation where pupils play side by side, but with little or no interaction. A desire for isolation during play is normal, providing it is not excessive, as a balance of social and solitary play is necessary for all children. Pupils benefit from the social learning that is gained through sharing and co-operating with other children during *group play*, and it may signal a problem if children insist on playing on their own for most or all of the time (see Casey 2005 for suggestions about inclusive play). Elements of *imaginary play* are also significant for older primary pupils engaged in producing spontaneous drama sequences and acting out contrived scenes. Experienced teachers learn to judge when to become involved in children's play and when to observe and allow children to take the initiative (see Call, on-line). When left alone, children normally play unprompted and create imaginative situations out of the most ordinary conditions (Duffy 1998).

Drake (2003) provides advice about implications for the Foundation Stage. She offers suggestions about key areas of learning, resources, preparation, use of vocabulary and activities. Crucially, Drake refers to the role of adults and follow-up ideas that build on the basic play activity. The adult's principal role is to observe, and provide for the development and enrichment of play activities by introducing resources, suggesting different perspectives to the children and encouraging co-operation between them (Broadhead 2004). Sometimes the adult decides to join in with the proceedings; on other occasions she or he observes and makes a mental note of how to enhance learning through extending the vocabulary, pointing out links with other areas of knowledge and thinking aloud.

Break times in primary schools are often referred to as 'playtime', during which time children are free to 'go and play'. This timetabled form of play, with the uncertainties of climate and physical hazards, contradicts the notion that play should always be spontaneous, stress-free and valuable for learning. Unlike school playtimes, the time, place and location of the play that occurs outside school hours is normally chosen by the children and not by adults (Thomson 2003).

The significance of play has sometimes caused disagreements between teachers and parents, and even between teachers. Expressions such as 'She went to school but only played' and 'We didn't do any work, we only played', indicate the way in which play is perceived: that is, as a time-filling activity without educational value that has no place in the school curriculum. The majority of teachers, on the other hand, view play as an essential part of the educative process and a powerful learning agent.

Sources

Broadhead, P. (2004) *Early Years Play and Learning*, London: Routledge.

Bruce, T. (2001) *Learning through Play*, London: Hodder & Stoughton.

Call, N.J. (1999) *The Importance of Play*, on-line at www.acceleratedlearning.co.uk

Casey, T. (2005) *Inclusive Play: Practical strategies for working with children aged 3 to 8*, London: Paul Chapman.

Chudacoff, H.P. (2007) *Children at Play: An American history*. New York: NYU Press.

Drake, J. (2003) *Organising Play in the Early Years*, London: David Fulton.

Duffy, B. (1998) *Supporting Creativity and Imagination in the Early Years*, Maidenhead: Open University Press.

Freud, S. (1908) 'Creative writers and day-dreaming', in Strachey, J. (ed.) (1953–74) *The Standard Edition of the Complete Works of Sigmund Freud*, vol. 9, London: Hogarth Press, p. 143.

Garrick, R. (2004) *Outdoor Play in the Early Years*, London: Continuum.

O'Hara, M. (2004) *Teaching 3–8*, London: Continuum.

Orr, R. (2003) *My Right to Play*, Maidenhead: Open University Press.

Robson, S. (2006) *Developing Thinking and Understanding in Young Children*, London: Routledge.

Singer, D.G., Golinkoff, R.M. and Hirsh-Pasek, K. (eds) (2006) *Play Equals Learning: How play motivates and enhances children's cognitive and social-emotional growth*. New York: Oxford University Press, USA.

Smidt, S. (2006) *The Developing Child in the 21st Century*, London: Routledge.

Thomson, S. (2003) 'A well-equipped hamster cage: The rationalisation of primary school playtime', *Education 3–13*, 31 (2), 54–59.

PLAY (OLDER PUPILS)

See also: assembly, drama, play

Teachers of older primary pupils tend to encourage play within the confines of a planned and closely controlled learning environment (notably through drama). Play is used as a vehicle to explore issues and confront life choices through improvisation. Many teachers structure the play in such a way that there is an end product in the form of a presentation to classmates or to the whole school and parents during an assembly.

PLAYFULNESS

See also: creativity, humour, imagination, play, problem solving

All children and many adults love to play. It releases tension, excites interest and stimulates ideas. Being 'playful' is a related but different concept. Playfulness requires a willingness to take a gently 'sideways' look at life, to keep events in proportion and be willing to engage with the softer side of a child or colleague's personality. Humour has an important part to play in oiling the wheels of learning and is different from merely being funny or 'playing to the gallery' in a vain attempt to remedy other problems by recourse to an immature and embarrassing jokiness. Being playful allows a teacher to see the lighter side of situations; to be serious but not grim; to be dedicated without becoming obsessive; and to aim high while ensuring that there is a comfortable outcome when things go wrong. Children describe most 'playful' adults as 'good fun' or similar but beneath the good humour is a deep-rooted determination and professionalism. Teachers who can both 'dance and sing' as well as provide much-needed expertise and knowledge are every pupil's and parent's dream.

Work by Cohen (2006) suggests, however, that if learning is to occur, it is necessary for play to translate from the 'pretend' (or 'playful') state to a 'serious' state. The author argues that play is not is always beneficial, such as when 'messing about' initially can turn into something more threatening; adults need to be alert to occasions when children's natural liveliness deteriorates into bullying. Cohen views all play (adults as well as children) as a state of mind rather than a series of behaviours. He distinguishes between a playful state of mind, in which the individual is able to explore and elaborate a variety of skills and test them to the limits in a free and imaginative way and a serious state of mind, which is goal-orientated. Cohen claims that in the playful state, the child is able to build up a stockpile of habits, skills and knowledge that is more extensive than it would have been in the goal-orientated state alone. When in the 'serious' state, a child selects from this playful agenda and begins to articulate the ideas. The synergy between the two states is where learning takes place. In other words, it is not sufficient to simply let pupils play freely, but to do so in the expectation that the repertoire of skills and insights that they gain will be transformed into a better understanding of the world, increase self-confidence, develop new ideas, reduce anxiety and reinforce social relationships.

Parker-Rees (1999) emphasises the importance of playfulness and argues that it is a foundation for creativity, imagination and problem solving in adults as well as children. Pollard and Collins (2005) note that playfulness makes a significant contribution to children's intellectual development capacity, particularly when they are younger. In the light of Parker-Rees' assertion, Pollard and Collins ask whether playfulness should actually be a criterion for becoming a teacher.

Sources

Cohen, D. (2006) *Social Skills for Primary Pupils*, Birmingham: Questions Publishing.

Parker-Rees, R. (1999) 'Protecting playfulness', in Abbott, L. and Moylett, H. (eds) *Early Education Transformed*, London: Falmer.

Pollard, A. and Collins, J. (2005) *Reflective Practice: Evidence-informed professional practice*, London: Continuum.

PLAYGROUND

School playgrounds (sometimes known as 'yards' in North America) are typically limited to combinations of asphalt, turf and some large structures (such as low-level climbing equipment), although schools and local authorities have directed a lot of money and effort towards improving the play environment, not least because poorly designed and maintained play areas are unattractive and depressing venues for children. There is some evidence to suggest that a richly provisioned outdoor area reduces the level of aggressive play. Many schools and local authorities have made serious efforts to combat the problems that occur during break time through reorganising the layout of the play area to include quiet zones where children can sit uninterrupted by ball games and activities.

PLAYTIME

See also: break time, bullying, friendships, play

The concept of having an enforced break from lessons is so engrained in our primary schools that it is accepted largely without question and little thought is given to its wider role. The fact that the break is often referred to as 'playtime' ('recess' in North America) in primary schools is significant, as it reflects an ideology that play will happen spontaneously once the break begins and can be curtailed once it is over. A playtime may coincide with the formal break time or may be at the discretion of the teacher; sometimes playtimes occur inside the classroom or – in the case of the youngest children – in a designated area adjacent to the classroom. Blatchford and Baines (on-line) argue that playtime contrasts with other parts of the school day in that there is little discussion or agreement about its value and function.

Whatever the issues attached to playtimes and their purpose, it is typical during this period to see children disappear into the frantic world of games, chasing, arguments, intensive relationships, erratic behaviours and unpredictable weather. Playtime is a time when children can make friends from other classes and create imaginative activities in a relatively safe environment. It is an occasion when important social networks are formed; when children can fall out but can also develop strategies for avoiding and resolving conflict. Playtime is an opportunity to enjoy a larger degree of freedom from adult supervision and develop a social life outside the formal learning environment, in which they can formulate their own rules of conduct and initiate their chosen activities.

Breaks from lessons are not without their challenges, not least because children have to be organised to move out of their working environment into the open space of the playground and be supervised by a small number of adults. Inclement weather may oblige the break to take place indoors ('wet playtime'), with all the associated frustration for pupils of being denied a chance to go outside. On the other hand, some children dislike being outside in a large space and find all sorts of reasons for being allowed to stay in the classroom or library. The attractions of staying inside when at home – sophisticated technological equipment, large-screen televisions, comfortable rooms and the need to complete work – can also act as a disincentive for some pupils to leave the comfort of the building.

When the playtime is over, adults have the task of settling the children back down to work; there may be unresolved disputes that arose during the break time to be resolved or practical issues such as wet clothing, minor injuries and lost possessions. Children may be physically in the classroom but with their minds still focused on the fun they were enjoying a short time before (Blatchford and Sharp 1994). Due to a larger number of physically disabled children being educated in mainstream schools, adults have to be sensitive to their particular needs and the organisational, social and physical barriers that might affect their inclusion. These issues are likely to be brought to the fore in the playground area when there is lighter adult supervision (Woolley 2007).

Many schools employ a variety of strategies to foster positive play: boxes of dressing-up clothes and toys freely available; brightly coloured motifs to stimulate children's imagination; and the promotion of traditional co-operative games and quiet corners for those who simply want to relax and chat to their friends. It has also become popular to promote a policy of ensuring that no child is left out by creating cross-age groupings of children who 'look out' for one another, and the promotion of 'never say no' behaviour whereby it is not permitted to refuse a child entry to an existing playground game if requested.

Sources

Blatchford, P. and Baines, P.K. *Breaktime Project*, on-line at www.breaktime.org.uk/background. htm

Blatchford, P. and Sharp, S. (1994) *Breaktime and the School*, London: Routledge.

Whitney, I. and Smith, P.K. (1993) 'A survey of the nature and extent of bullying', *Educational Research*, 35 (1), 3–25.

Woolley, H. (2007) *Inclusion of Disabled Children in Primary School Playgrounds*, National Children's Bureau, as part of the series, *Understanding Children's Lives*, Joseph Rowntree Foundation Report, London: National Children's Bureau.

PLENARY

See also: assessment of learning, lesson planning, lesson plans, lesson review, metacognition, mistakes and misconceptions, summative assessment

A plenary is, strictly speaking, a coming together of everyone concerned in the learning process or 'a gathering'. In practice it is a period of time – often taking place at the end of a session as part of a lesson review – when formal activities are suspended and teachers reflect with pupils on what has taken place during the session or sessions or unit of learning. In lesson planning it has gradually become the term to describe the period of time that is used in one or more of four ways: (1) To encourage pupils to raise key points from their learning during the session. (2) To summarise the lesson content, in which the teacher gives an overview: 'Today we have been learning about/trying to explain/discussing the reasons for … ' (3) To explore possible confusion and a lack of understanding about key aspects of the lesson. (4) To encourage pupils to reflect on their own learning and, especially, to consider how they learned (a process sometimes known as 'metacognition'). If during the plenary it becomes clear that the children have failed to understand something properly, it is likely to take one or other of two forms: (a) a genuine misunderstanding that can easily be corrected by the teacher's careful explanation; or (b) misconceptions, where pupils have simply 'not caught on' or become muddled, in which case remediation is usually more prolonged and is often followed up in subsequent sessions.

A plenary can be highly beneficial but also makes considerable demands of the teacher. Thus, they have to ensure that pupils are paying attention and not finishing off their work; monitor comments and encourage them to be affirming and constructive; field the comments and contributions from pupils; summarise what a pupil may be struggling to say without being patronising or embarrassing the pupil. A well-conducted plenary should help teachers to modify their future lesson planning and teaching approach in the light of having gained a better understanding of what pupils have and have not grasped. For example, the teacher may realise that she needed to use more visual material and do less talking or to give pupils more time for the task or extend the more able pupils with challenging tasks. By listening carefully to children's responses, comments and grasp of the lesson content, a plenary can also provide the teacher with important assessment information about pupils ('assessment of learning' or 'summative assessment').

PLOWDEN REPORT

See also: child development, discovery learning, gifted and talented, home–school, infants, Intelligence Quotient, learning context, literacy, mixed ability teaching, Piaget, teaching approach, teaching assistants

By the late 1950s evidence pointed to the need for a new approach to how primary schools organised teaching and learning; research findings favoured the informal methods that most infant school teachers were already using. In August 1963 the then minister of education, Sir Edward Boyle, asked the Central Advisory Council for Education (England) to consider all aspects of primary education and issues relating to the transition from primary to secondary education. The Council, under the Chairmanship of Lady Bridget Plowden, presented its report to the secretary of state for education and science in October 1966, with the final publication of the 'Plowden Report' in 1967 (Central Advisory Council for Education 1967). In Wales, the Central Advisory Council for Education, under the leadership of Professor C.E. Gittins, produced a similar report.

The Plowden Committee met during the 1960s when the process of 'streaming' – i.e. sorting children into classes on the basis of ability or overall intelligence – was being replaced by mixed-ability teaching. At the same time, comprehensive (non-selective) schools and middle schools were being established (see Tidd 2007). The final report contained a number of significant statements, the best known of which include: 'at the heart of the educational process lies the child' and 'the [best] school lays special stress on individual discovery ("discovery learning"), on first hand experience and on opportunities for creative work'. Further, Plowden's team promoted the notion that knowledge does not fall into neatly separated compartments, and that work and play are not in opposition but complement one another. The report emphasised the need to see children as individuals and stressed that even an apparently homogeneous group of pupils contained children of differing abilities and aptitudes. It also warned that IQ (Intelligence Quotient) scores should not be treated as infallible predictors of potential. Plowden placed great faith in Piaget's theory of developmental sequence – events that are fixed in their order but varying in the age at which the sequence begins, such that it is pointless trying to teach a child something until he or she was 'ready' for this. One of the unintended consequences of promoting this philosophy was that some children were left 'treading water' and not making the progress of which they were almost certainly capable.

Plowden broadly supported teachers' curriculum freedom but expressed some concern that schools were slow to embrace change and use children's interests and enthusiasm as a basis from which they could learn for themselves in an affirming context. Individual learning, flexibility in the curriculum, the centrality of play, the use of the environment, learning by discovery ('finding out') and the importance of the evaluation of children's progress were all emphasised as significant in learning, while the Report warned that teachers should not assume that only what is measurable is valuable – a message that many politicians in the twenty-first century appear to ignore. The report was imaginative in its recommendations, such as:

- class size not to exceed a given maximum;
- lessons structured to incorporate individual, group and class work, with a greater emphasis on individual learning;
- recruiting more teachers' helpers and assistants;
- studying the needs/achievements of gifted children and providing an appropriate curriculum;
- flexibility in the school day and year;
- training to use technology;
- giving teachers more say in what is taught;
- creating a working partnership between parents and teachers (at a time when schools routinely had notices saying 'no parents beyond this point').

Opposition to Plowden's philosophy of primary education grew from the start of the 1970s, when there was a good deal of unease about some of the teaching and curriculum programmes in primary schools. In due course, Plowden began to be blamed for what was perceived as a lowering of educational standards. In truth, there was little evidence to support the view that this was the case; indeed, all the evidence suggested that standards, especially in English (literacy) and mathematics, had been rising steadily since the end of the Second World War.

Despite all the criticism and hostility that has been directed towards the Plowden Report, there is still considerable interest in many of its conclusions. For instance, there are signs that the educational pendulum is beginning to swing away from the sterility of the National Curriculum and back to a greater awareness of the importance of creativity and spontaneity in children's learning (Gillard, on-line). Aylen (2007) describes the changes in the role of classroom assistants over the past forty years and argues that the Plowden Report's recommendations for greater responsibilities, better training opportunities and an increase in the number of teaching assistants in schools are finally being implemented.

Sources

Aylen, M. (2007) 'From teacher aides to teaching assistants: How Plowden promoted parental participation in our primary schools', *Forum*, 49 (1), 107–14

Central Advisory Council for Education (1967) *Children and Their Primary Schools* ('The Plowden Report'), London: HMSO.

Gillard, D. 'The Plowden Report', *The Encyclopaedia of Informal Education*, on-line at www.infed.org/schooling/plowden_report.htm

Tidd, M. (2007) 'Whatever happened to Plowden's middle schools?' *Forum*, 49 (1), 135–40.

POETRY

See also: drama, English, literacy, reading aloud

Poetry provokes a variety of reactions in children and adults. Part of the ambivalence is probably due to the trend towards analysing and interrogating text instead of merely enjoying and relishing it for its own sake. The teaching of poetry has suffered as a result, being relegated to a body of print to be utilised in the pursuit of technical language competence. By contrast with this instrumental view of poetry, the UK Poetry Society (www.poetrysociety.org.uk) insists that poetry plays a powerful role in improving literacy skills. They argue that unless literacy starts with 'goosebumps, laughter, or contemplative silence, none of us would bother to read anything but bills, instructions and road signs'. The Society advises that when teaching the reading of poetry the key words to guide the approach should be immersion, leisure, enjoyment and fun. By associating poetry with pleasure we allow children to make a connection with the minds of these thinkers and continue this tradition.

Carter (1998) claims that a child is born with a 'poetic voice' that is brought into the classroom. Consequently, teachers should not be introducing their young pupils to poetry but 'letting loose each child's poetic voice into a poetic environment' (p. 2). He argues that poetry should start with the children's own language such that the teacher needs to respond to the child as much as the child to the teacher. Carter also expresses concern

about the suppressing effects of the over-regulation of poetry and emphasis on written forms at the expense of self-expression through oral means. Pagett (2007) warns that teachers are sometimes nervous about using this medium because of fears about their own ability to teach it; however, she is dismissive of such attitudes and argues that:

> Poetry can be powerful – not if it is locked in the pages of an unopened book but if it is read and engaged with. It can enable us to look afresh at fairly mundane things, affect our emotions and make us think. Many texts can do this, but poetry is more memorable and so we have it to hand more easily. It is often figurative and so creates pictures in the mind; the rhythms stay with us and resonate around our heads, so poetry is a form where both visual and aural aspects explore the way that meaning is created.
>
> (p. 89)

Pagett offers a variety of practical suggestions about promoting poetry, including: (a) learning a favourite poem by heart; (b) placing poetry posters around the school with sections of poems for children to read; (c) reading poems aloud and imaginatively to children; (d) using existing models of poems to write one of the same style; (e) incorporating musical instruments into a performance; and (f) supporting children's engagement through drama and art. See also Foale and Pagett (2008) for creative ideas for the use of poetry, including links with other subject areas.

Despite finding that poetry teaching was generally impressive, inspectors from the Office for Standards in Education (OFSTED) reported late in 2007 that children in England were studying too many 'lightweight poems' in primary school. Schools were invited to list ten poems they believed all pupils should read and results indicated that many teachers, especially of younger children, did not appear to know enough about poetry. As a result, younger pupils were being exposed to a limited range of work from poets such as Spike

Milligan, Lewis Carroll and Edward Lear. The list also revealed that a small number of poems, including Alfred Noyes' *The Highwayman*, Walter de la Mare's *The Listeners* and Roald Dahl's *Revolting Rhymes* dominated the primary curriculum. Inspectors concluded that while these poems were worth studying, too few of them seemed genuinely challenging. Popular classic poems used in primary schools included William Blake's *The Tyger*, with a small minority of teachers also using poems such as *Daffodils*, *The Ancient Mariner* and *The Pied Piper of Hamelin*. Poems by Benjamin Zephaniah were the most likely contributions to understanding poetry from other traditions. The survey revealed that the top ten poems used in primaries were as follows:

1 *The Highwayman* by Alfred Noyes
2 *On the Ning, Nang, Nong* by Spike Milligan
3 *Jabberwocky* by Lewis Carroll
4 *The Owl and the Pussycat* by Edward Lear
5 *From a Railway Carriage* by Robert L. Stevenson
6 *The Listeners* by Walter de la Mare
7 *The Magic Box* by Kit Wright
8 *The Sound Collector* by Roger McGough
9 *Revolting Rhymes* by Roald Dahl
10 *Dog in the Playground* by Allan Ahlberg

The Poetry Society (see earlier) argue that it would be sad to deny a young person the chance to read a poem just because they don't grasp its complete meaning, as this sort of restriction would be denying them the opportunity over the coming months and years to experience flashes of understanding and insight that have come about through their intellectual maturity. Thus, just as the pencilled lines on a doorframe show a child's growth in height, more challenging poems can be used to mark the child's growth in relation to ideas and use of language.

An indication that poetry is assuming greater importance for educators was a competition organised by the British Broadcasting Corporation (BBC) in 2009 as a means of helping primary school pupils to engage with learning and reciting poetry. Every primary school in the UK was invited to enter a child aged 7–11 years to represent their school and region and compete for the title of UK Poetry Recital Champion.

Sources

Carter, D. (1998) *Teaching Poetry in the Primary School*, London: David Fulton.
Foale, J. and Pagett, L. (2008) *Creative Approaches to Poetry for the Primary Framework for Literacy*, London: David Fulton.
Pagett, L. (2007) 'The joy of learning poetry off by heart', in Hayes, D. (ed.) *Joyful Teaching and Learning in the Primary School*, Exeter: Learning Matters.

POLITICAL INVOLVEMENT

See also: breakfast clubs, curriculum, English, Every Child Matters, extended schools, mathematics, National Curriculum, new entrants, nurturing, professionalism, teaching approaches

Political conviction that there is a right way to educate all children in maintained primary schools has had two consequences – one positive, the other much less so. The positive consequence has been a strengthening of the continuity and coherence of educational provision across the country. Nearly all schools, especially at primary level, now follow a broadly similar curriculum in comparable ways. Teaching approaches, especially in English and mathematics, are constrained by the powerful presence of government advice, which although ostensibly non-statutory for schools, have been embraced by the majority of head teachers. The outcome is that there is not only consistency of curriculum provision within single schools, but also between schools – though there are concerns that consistency is bringing about a lack of distinctiveness and 'sameness'. The *adverse* consequence has been that some teachers have felt that the structured curriculum and lesson format has constrained their ability to exercise professional judgements about what is appropriate for their pupils. There has been some resentment among teachers about the way in which the climate of testing and inspecting, with its inevitable winners and losers, has been at the expense of attending to the social needs of young children and their nurture.

The rate of change in school policy and practice in the twenty-first century has maintained its bewildering pace, as primary schools have had (amongst other things) to implement two revised versions of the National Curriculum, a structured approach to teaching mathematics and literacy, and an inclusive policy to accommodate disabled and emotionally vulnerable pupils. Schools have also had to increase substantially the number of teaching assistants, provide highly detailed reports to parents about pupil progress, play a greater role in training new teachers and demonstrate a commitment to employing 'creative approaches' to teaching and learning. New initiatives include expanding opportunities for physical exercise, breakfast clubs and after-school clubs for children requiring pre- and post-school supervision, out-of-school extension classes for children deemed in need of additional tuition in English, and homework clubs. The re-elected Labour government in the UK (May 2005) promised that there would be no slackening in the pace of reform and they have certainly kept their promise. The pace of change has scarcely lessened in the last few years, with initiatives such as Every Child Matters to fuse education and social services provision, and major changes in the structure of secondary provision.

One may be forgiven for believing that the tsunami of educational reform is as much about political expediency as educational merit, as all political parties claim that the NHS, homeland security and education are priorities for them. However, as Brehony (2005) points out, it is now becoming difficult for educators to distinguish between 'symbolic policies designed primarily to gain electoral advantage, from those that genuinely seek to address problems' (p. 41).

Source

Brehony, K. (2005) 'Primary schooling under New Labour', *Oxford Review of Education*, 31 (1), 29–46.

PPA TIME

See also: assessing children's learning, lesson planning, modern foreign languages, teaching assistant, workforce reforms

The workforce reforms guarantee teachers in maintained schools 10 per cent of their timetabled teaching to be set aside as preparation, planning and assessment (PPA) time during the school day. The aim of this allocation of time is to encourage collaborative professional activity in the preparation of high-quality lessons and to increase the work/life balance of teachers. A teaching assistant or supply (substitute) teacher usually supervises the teacher's class during the PPA time. Although PPA time has freed up teachers from some teaching responsibility, it has also placed on them an onus to be more thoroughly planned and carry out more detailed assessments than was hitherto the case. By providing appropriate training and support, some schools have been able to redeploy existing support staff in roles which build on under-utilised skills; for example, modern foreign language ability or computer expertise. Although originally welcomed by most staffs, concerns have been expressed that PPA time has, contrary to intentions, created additional paperwork for teachers as they try to justify their non-contact time.

PRAISE

See *Encouragement and praise*

PRIMARY NATIONAL STRATEGY

See also: English as an additional language, literacy strategy, numeracy strategy, Primary National Strategy, professional development

Charles Clarke, then secretary of state for education, launched the Primary National Strategy (PNS) document in the UK in May 2003 and incorporated the existing national numeracy and national literacy strategies in England. The PNS set primary schools seven challenges:

- To re-examine the curriculum, timetable and the organisation of the school day and week as a means of developing and enriching children's learning experiences.
- To set a trajectory for continuous and sustained improvement for standards of attainment in literacy and numeracy.
- To commit to a programme of staff professional development.
- To look beyond their own school and learn from practices in other educational settings.
- To review their strategies for involving parents in their children's education.
- To embed positive behaviour into the fabric of learning and teaching in the school.
- To review the way in which they use all the resources available to the school.

An 'English as an additional language' (EAL) programme within the Primary National Strategy was introduced, involving work with schools in developing an intensive professional development programme for mainstream staffs. The aim of the programme was to support improvement in the standards of attainment of bilingual learners in English and mathematics.

PRIMARY REVIEWS

See also: Alexander, arts, citizenship, creativity, curriculum, emotions of learning, geography, history, imagination, literacy, mathematics, numeracy, oracy, reading, science, writing

Two 'primary reviews' on the present state of primary education and recommendations for future policy were published in 2009. The first, a three-year study known as the 'Primary Review' and entitled *The Condition and Future of Primary Education in England* was an independent study led by Sir Robin Alexander on behalf of Esmée Fairburn Trust and the University of Cambridge. The Primary Review identified the purposes that the primary phase of education should serve, notably the values it should espouse; the curriculum and learning environment it should provide; and the conditions necessary to ensure the highest quality education and address the future needs of children and society. The report claimed that inadequacies in the primary curriculum stemmed from a mistaken belief that breadth in the curriculum is incompatible with improved standards in the basics of mathematics, literacy and numeracy. As a consequence, history, geography, science and the arts had been 'squeezed out'. The review recommended that the primary curriculum be re-conceived with twelve specific aims, arranged in three groups:

1 The needs and capacities of the individual: wellbeing; engagement; empowerment; autonomy.
2 The individual in relation to others and the wider world: encouraging respect and reciprocity; promoting interdependence and sustainability; empowering local, national and global citizenship; celebrating culture and community.
3 Learning, knowing and doing: knowing, understanding, exploring and making sense; fostering skill; exciting the imagination; enacting dialogue.

These aims would be achieved through eight domains: (1) arts and creativity, (2) citizenship and ethics, (3) faith and belief, (4) language, oracy and literacy, (5) mathematics, (6) physical and emotional health, (7) place and time, (geography and history), and (8) science and technology.

The second report was the *Primary Curriculum Review*, a UK government-sponsored report led by Sir Jim Rose, which was less explicit about professional attributes but advised on how the primary curriculum should change to ensure all children gain a good grounding in reading, writing, speaking, literacy and numeracy; offer schools greater flexibility of choice about content and delivery; allow time for a foreign language; place greater emphasis on personal development; support a smoother transition from play-based learning to formal learning; and encourage creativity. The Rose Review proposed six 'Areas of Learning' as the basis for a national curriculum, as follows:

1 human, social and environmental understanding;
2 understanding physical health and well-being;
3 understanding the arts and design;
4 understanding English, communication and languages;
5 mathematical understanding;
6 scientific and technological understanding.

Each Area of Learning contains a statement about its significance for learning; key ideas to identify understanding; skills and processes to identify what children need to learn to do; progression in learning and curriculum opportunities essential to a child's development. However, whereas Alexander's Primary Review commented on the damaging effects of national testing on children and recommended a major rethink, Rose's Primary Curriculum Review did not take account of assessment issues in producing its report. Both reports – especially the Rose Review – are likely to have a continuing influence on primary policy, curriculum and practice in the coming years.

Sources

Alexander, R. (2009) *The Condition and Future of Primary Education in England* ('The Primary Review'), Cambridge: University of Cambridge/ Esmée Fairburn Trust.
Rose, J. for the DCSF (2009) *Primary Curriculum Review*, London: HMSO.

PRIMARY SCHOOL

See also: elementary education, key stages

The name 'primary school' is derived from the French *école primaire* and describes an educational institution where children receive the first stage of compulsory education. In England and Wales it refers to a school for children between the ages of 5 and 11 years of age, also referred to as 'key stages 1 and 2'. In Scotland, Australia and New Zealand 'primary school' is the name given to a school for children between the ages of 5 and 12 years of age. In the USA and Canada 'primary' is a school equivalent to the first three or four grades of elementary school for children aged 4–8 years (*Collins Dictionary*).

PRIVATE EDUCATION

Private primary and secondary schools in the UK, also referred to as 'non-public' schools (USA) or independent schools, do not receive government funding from taxation and are operated for profit. In Britain, private schools are often referred to as 'public schools', though the term tends to be used for the secondary phase of education. By contrast, in North America, 'public schools' describes those that *are* maintained through taxation.

The principal source of funding for private schools is from tuition fees. They operate their own admissions policies, though in recent years questions about the appropriateness of their charitable status has led to some relaxation of the rules and a trend towards a more inclusive approach. Private schools continue to be a contentious issue for many educationists, and down the years there have been a number of unsuccessful moves to have them eradicated. Private schools are required to offer the use of their resources for community use; in practice, this allows local state schools to use their sporting facilities. As a footnote, before the advent of public education towards the end of the nineteenth century, all schools were private.

PROBATIONARY YEAR

See also: General Teaching Council (Scotland), induction of teachers

All newly qualified teachers in Scotland are required to complete a period of probation to show that they meet 'The Standard for Full Registration' to ensure that all new teachers are able to take on the demands and responsibilities of teaching. There are two ways in which new teachers can complete their probationary period: (a) through the *Teacher Induction Scheme*, and (b) through the *Alternative Route*. The teacher induction scheme provides a guaranteed one-year training post to every eligible student graduating with a teaching qualification from one of Scotland's universities. The General Teaching Council Scotland (GTCS), in partnership with the Scottish government's Education Department, is responsible for the administration of the scheme. The scheme is not compulsory but it allows probationer teachers to be considered for full registration within one school year (190 teaching days). Probationer teachers not completing their probationary service on the teacher induction scheme or who decide to opt out of the scheme may complete their probation via the 'Alternative Route' (lasting 270 days), which enables teachers who cannot commit to a full-time post to complete their probation on a part-time basis, and also enables teachers to complete their probation in the independent sector or outside of Scotland.

Source

General Teaching Council Scotland (GTCS), *Probation*, on-line at www.gtcs.org.uk/Probation/probation.aspx

PROBLEM SOLVING

See also: collaboration in learning, discovery learning, enquiry, information technology

A distinction can usefully be made between a collaborative venture in which there is a *problem to be solved* (i.e. a single solution) and *an investigation* in which there are likely to be a variety of solutions. Problem solving necessitates that members provide a pool of suggestions, conjecture about the outcome, trial the different propositions and experiment until the solution to the problem is found. Investigation follows a similar pattern but results in a set of possibilities rather than single solution; some investigations begin as a collaborative venture but end with individuals or pairs of children pursuing their favoured option. Both problem solving and investigating require that children are involved in the process of 'discovery learning'. It is estimated that work-related collaborative interaction between primary-age pupils accounts for less than 15 per cent of the total time they spend on learning, and much of the collaboration takes place in pairs rather than in larger groups (see General Teaching Council for England 2004). With the onset of information technology in schools there are many opportunities for children to share ideas and offer solutions via electronic communications.

Source

General Teaching Council for England (2004) *Grouping Pupils and Students: What difference does the type of grouping make to teaching and learning in schools?* On-line at www.gtce.org.uk/research/abilityhome.asp

PROFESSIONAL DEVELOPMENT

See also: excellent teachers, head teachers, pedagogy, professionalism, reflection

Teachers are required to undergo continuous professional development (CPD) from the moment they enter a course of training until they retire. Qualified teachers commonly refer to 'in-service training' or INSET to indicate that they are developing expertise 'on the job'. CPD can be defined as the systematic maintenance, improvement and broadening of knowledge and skill, together with the development of personal qualities necessary for the execution of professional and practical responsibilities throughout a working life. As teachers gain experience, they are expected to enhance their knowledge, improve their classroom practice, learn new skills and increasingly contribute to the school's academic performance and attractiveness to parents. One of the greatest challenges for teachers is that there is no universally agreed definition of a progressive pedagogy (science of the art of teaching) on which to base CPD, other than one that refers to pupils' formal test scores.

Teachers not only persevere to improve their competence through self-evaluation at the end of a lesson or series of lessons (reflection *on* action) but are also constantly evaluating their practice during their teaching (reflection *in* action). Newly qualified primary teachers tend to use the teaching approach that they developed during training or modelled on an experienced teacher whom they admired, but change occurs during their careers as they gain promotion and encounter new challenges. Teachers gradually extend the reaches of their intellect, focus their energies more efficiently and, for the most part, become more caring, wise and sanguine. Many take advantage of the internal promotion opportunities and a small number become head teachers. See Neil and Morgan (2003) and Bubb (2004) for an overview of issues attached to professional progression across a career. A feature of early twenty-first century Britain is that the number of teachers remaining in the classroom until retirement age has fallen sharply.

The need for teachers to provide verifiable evidence that children have benefited directly from their teaching has been integral to career advancement, so teachers have to be able to point to measurable and verifiable aspects of pupil learning. The implementation of a pay 'threshold' scheme for internal promotion to 'Advanced Skills' status, intended to keep excellent practitioners in the classroom, has had mixed results, as the vast majority of teachers applying for enhancement have been successful, thereby casting doubt on the principle of advancement on the basis of excellence. The establishment of a 'National College for School Leadership' (NCSL, www.ncsl.org.uk) in England – from September 2009 known as 'National College for School and *Children's* Leadership' to include leaders of children's services – for preparing and training aspiring subject leaders, deputy head teachers and head teachers is a clear signal that professional advancement is increasingly dependent on external verification. Mullen (2007) explores the concepts of curriculum and leadership in experiential learning contexts to promote democratic action and critical thinking.

Sources

Bubb, S. (2004) *The Insider's Guide to Early Professional Development*, London: Routledge.

Mullen, C. (2007) *Curriculum Leadership Development*, London: Routledge.

Neil, P. and Morgan, C. (2003) *Continuing Professional Development for Teachers*, London: Kogan Page.

PROFESSIONALISM

See also: General Teaching Councils, modelling behaviour, professional development, teaching assistants, values

Arguments about whether or not teaching, and primary teaching in particular, is a profession comparable with (say) doctors and lawyers have raged for many years. Only a generation ago, secondary teachers were paid more than primary teachers in the belief that their superior subject knowledge justified the differential. Contrarily, new secondary teachers were not required to possess a qualified teacher certificate until 1972 – some years after this stipulation applied to primary teachers. Since that time, all new members of the teaching profession are expected to have a minimum level of teaching ability, formally recognised by a teacher-training provider.

Teachers' professional values and practice includes having high expectations of all pupils, respecting their social, cultural, linguistic, religious and ethnic backgrounds, being committed to raising educational standards and showing concern for their development as learners. The establishment of standards for qualified teacher status and what amounts to a national scheme for teacher training (in the UK) helps to safeguard overall competence. More recently, the increase in numbers of teaching assistants in primary schools and the arguments about their role as substitute or ancillary teachers has re-ignited a debate about professional status.

The establishment of a professional code of conduct through the national General Teaching Council (GTC) not only takes into account factors such as the teachers' levels of expertise, knowledge and skills and minimum qualifications, but also their behaviour. The need for an acceptable standard of behaviour is necessary because primary teachers act as models or examples to their pupils and local communities. Welcome attributes include being positive about life in general, avoiding the temptation to moan and giving due consideration to other people's ideas. Practical considerations for teachers necessitate arriving in good time for school, relating well to other members of staff, using their time productively during the day and earning a reputation as an effective practitioner. Codifying acceptable behaviour for members of the teaching profession involves transparent monitoring and appraisal by an external body such as the local authority or inspectors to ensure consistency of practice and interpretation of legislation amongst its members.

To safeguard and enhance their professional knowledge, all practitioners are expected to take responsibility for their own professional development, keep up to date with significant education research and innovations in teaching, and understand their role in relation to agreed school policies and practices, including pastoral responsibilities, personal safety matters and bullying. Teachers have had to develop their skills in relating to and empathising with the aspirations of different client groups – parents, governors, head teacher, local authority and even central government – about key issues such as standards of reading, healthy living, environmental issues and pupil behaviour. As such, teachers have had to be well informed about the social, legal and cultural expectations within and beyond the school perimeter.

Sources

General Teaching Council websites
England, www.gtce.org.uk
Northern Ireland, www.gtcni.org.uk
Scotland, www.gtcs.org.uk
Wales, www.gtcw.org.uk

PROGRESSION IN LEARNING

See also: knowledge, learning, skills, tests and testing

Progression in learning refers to the need for children to build upon their existing knowledge, skills and understanding in a systematic fashion so that they build upon their previous learning. One measure of such progression is through formal tests to provide a numerical indicator ('grades') of attainment, though deep learning requires repetition, rehearsal of ideas and opportunity to explore concepts to achieve full and lasting understanding.

PROJECT WORK

See also: collaboration in learning, skills, thematic learning, topic work

Project work is an approach to learning that engages pupils in an extended process of enquiry structured around their authentic interests or in response to their questions. The project might vary from one of one to two

weeks' duration, located in a single subject –
also referred to as 'thematic' learning – to an
interdisciplinary study that crosses numerous
subject boundaries and involves wide-ranging
investigation, data collection and the production of a sophisticated end product.
Project work often involves collaboration
between pupils, organising and managing
time and resources, mastering specific skills
(including the use of computer software),
solving problems and summarising findings.
Project work is sometimes referred to as
'topic work'.

PUNISHMENT

See also: educational visit, gender, motivation
for learning, parents, relationships, rewards,
sanctions, teachers' beliefs

Despite every effort to ensure that pupils learn
in a stable, supportive environment, situations
inevitably arise from time to time when
deliberate and wilful wrongdoing invites
punishment through the use of a recognised
sanction, such as withdrawing privileges.
Some educators are uneasy with the use of
the word 'punishment' and many teachers
feel that the need to punish a child says as
much about their own failure to maintain
order or motivate pupils as it does about the
child's behaviour. Teachers normally give
children a number of warnings before punitive action is taken (akin to receiving yellow
cards in football), which offers the offender
opportunity to exercise self-constraint and
redirect their efforts more constructively.
Ultimately, children have to learn to take
responsibility for their own actions.

The intentional use of force as a form of
punishment was abolished in all maintained
schools in most of the UK 1986 and corporal
punishment was terminated in independent
schools in 1996 to be replaced by the *Schools
Standards Framework Act* 1998 (operational
from September 1999). No member of a
school staff is entitled to administer a physical

punishment, even if parents have said they are
happy for it to happen. Any teacher who did
so would not only be in breach of contract
but possibly of the Human Rights Act 1998.
Corporal punishment not only includes the
use of the cane, strap or slipper but also
slapping, rough handling, shaking, pinching,
prodding, pulling children's hair, pushing,
tying pupils up, taping their mouths and
throwing missiles at or towards a child.

Although the use of force is sometimes
required to deal with aggressive behaviour or
protect a child from harm, it must be done
with due regard to the circumstances and not
be excessive. However, teachers are not permitted to use threatening language at any
time, regardless of the provocation. Any teacher using unreasonable physical force against
pupils may be liable to a civil action for
assault, face internal disciplinary action or
even be referred to the General Teaching
Council (GTC), so teachers are understandably
reluctant to take risks.

In a study by Shreeve (2002) it was noted
that girls are punished less often than boys.
However, both the boys and (especially) girls
agreed that after-school detentions, a letter or
phone call home, extra work and detentions
at break were the most effective sanctions.
Girls in particular rate warnings and moving
class as the least effective penalties. See
Goldstein *et al.* 2003 for other perspectives.
A similar pattern emerged in a study of
rewards and punishments by Harrop and
Williams (1992) when teachers' and pupils'
views about the most effective punishments
were compared. Whereas pupils ranked parents being informed, being prevented from
going on a school trip ('educational visit') and
being sent to see the head teacher as the three
most powerful sanctions, teachers selected
being told off publicly, informing parents and
being told off in private as the top three. The
most significant contrast between teachers'
and pupils' views about punishment concerned the significance of school trips, which
pupils ranked second and teachers placed
ninth.

Teachers have to be perceptive of the impact that their decisions have on pupils, allow children to explain and to ask questions of clarification. All teachers are faced with the challenge of balancing sensitivity about children's feelings with decisiveness in curbing inappropriate behaviour. Willick (2006) warns against the 'over-reliance on sanctions that can create an atmosphere of distrust, fear and resentment, as well as having a negative effect on relationships' (p. 72). Unintended infringements and silliness are best resolved through dialogue with the child and establishing a target for rectifying the situation.

Sources

Goldstein, S.E., Tisak, M.S. and Brinker, S.R. (2003) 'Children's judgements about common classroom punishments', *Educational Research*, 45 (2), 189–98.

Harrop, A. and Williams, T. (1992) 'Rewards and punishments in the primary school: Pupils' perceptions and teachers' usage', *Educational Psychology*, 7 (4), 211–15.

Shreeve, A. (2002) 'Student perceptions of rewards and sanctions', *Pedagogy, Culture and Society*, 10 (2), 239–56.

Willick, S. (2006) *Emotional Literacy at the Heart of the School Ethos*, London: Paul Chapman.

PUPIL NUMBERS

Pupil numbers are important because a large percentage of a school's budget depends upon the number of children attending the school. The loss of just a few children, especially in a small school, can make a substantial difference to the overall financial position and put pressure on governors and staff to cut resources. Establishing harmonious relations with parents and the community is not simply a matter of good educational practice; it is necessary to ensure that parents are sufficiently satisfied to keep their children at the school and recommend it to others.

PUPIL PERSONALITY AND ATTAINMENT

See also: behaviour, stereotyping

Adult expectations can be influenced by pupil personality and even lead to stereotyping of children because teachers can develop expectations about achievement (and behaviour) that are related to their perceptions of a pupil's apparent willingness to learn rather than a child's true capability. Thus, the child with a bright personality who volunteers to do tasks and errands and who is comfortable chatting with the teacher, may or may not be a capable, committed learner. On the other hand, shy, passive children can be perceived as less capable than they really are. This description is, of course, also in danger of becoming stereotypical. Some articulate children with a bright personality are also clever. Some under-confident, diffident types struggle academically – which is part of the explanation for their timidity. Awareness of these interwoven factors suggests that it is foolish to jump to conclusions about children's abilities and potential. The outgoing child may, despite an apparently carefree approach to life, be concealing a deep unease that leads to underachievement. The shy child may be lacking self-confidence or may be an uncomplicated and contented person who does not feel the need to be assertive. Adults have to learn how to observe carefully and get to know the children before making a judgement about their attitude and potential. A single formal test is unlikely to yield such in-depth knowledge.

PUPIL PERSPECTIVES

See also: child development, core subjects, early years, school council

Although a considerable amount of evidence has been gathered about the views of secondary-age pupils (e.g. Woods 1990; Wood 2003; Harris and Haydn 2008) and an occasional publication about secondary and primary pupil perspectives (e.g. Rudduck and Flutter 2004), there have been relatively few research studies canvassing the views of primary-age children and almost none from an early years perspective. Individual primary schools do, however, often involve children through internal pupil forums or 'school councils', consisting of a cross-section of pupils from across the school – normally consisting of class representatives selected by their peers or volunteers – that meet from time to time to raise and discuss issues.

One of the key figures seeking to promote the primary pupil perspective in the UK is Cedric Cullingford. In one of his many articles on the subject, he describes how primary children usually respond to questions thoughtfully and on more than one level; for instance, he explains how they have the ability to understand the concepts of truth and falsehood at an earlier age than some child development educators have formerly claimed possible (Cullingford 2006). The same author also claims that children want to learn and 'listen to experts, enthusiasts, specialists, anyone who is not put into a position of authority. From their point of view the best teachers are the best people, not the best managerial performers' (p. 220). In similar vein, Hood (2008) set out to discover what a group of young learners might understand by an *identity as learner* under the acronym PPIL, standing for pupils' perceptions of their identities as learners, thereby moving from pupils as sources of data to pupils as agents of change. The eight- and nine-year-old mixed ability group of children demonstrated that they were

> very capable of talking and writing about their perceptions of a variety of aspects of being a learner, that they respond well to probes which ask for simple opinions or decisions about their lives in the classroom and are willing then to think more deeply in response to supplementary questions which may demand greater reflection.
>
> (p. 149)

Robinson and Fielding (2007) for the Primary Review under the leadership of Sir Robin Alexander (the final report was published in 2009) concluded from their study of primary children's voices that the Every Child Matters (ECM) ideal of equipping learners for life in its broadest sense appeared to conflict with the current emphasis on target setting and academic achievement in a narrow range of subjects. Consequently, further consideration needs to be given to the prime purposes of primary schooling and how these purposes are conveyed to pupils, families and the communities they serve. The authors also claimed that pupils agree with the view held by many teachers that there is a loss of breadth in the curriculum with the emphasis on the nationally tested core subjects.

It is noteworthy that a report compiled by Harlen and Tymms (2008) for the Wellcome Trust about primary science, published at around the same time as the Primary Review findings, concluded that children's interest in science and their understanding of it were being crushed by the compulsory tests they sat at primary school. The Robinson and Fielding report also raised issues about the considerable variation between schools in the level of pupil participation and the seriousness with which their views were accommodated. The authors drew attention to the fact that consideration must be given to the existence of a degree of staff apprehension about the possible loss of control or erosion of professionalism as pupil perspectives are sought. Importantly, however, the authors assert that fostering a learner identity depends in large measure on the relationship between pupils and their teachers. The government introduced legislation in 2009 to stop testing pupils in England in science at age 11 years and replace it with teacher assessment.

Sources

Cullingford, C. (2006) 'Children's own vision of schooling', *Education 3–13*, 34 (3), 211–21.

Harlen, W. and Tymms, P. (2008) *Perspectives on Education: Primary science*, for the Wellcome Trust, on-line at www.wellcome.ac.uk

Harris, R. and Haydn, T. (2008) 'Pupil and teacher perspectives on motivation and engagement in high school history: A UK view', on-line at http://eprints.soton.ac.uk/50812/

Hood, P. (2008) 'What do we teachers need to know to enhance our creativity?' *Education 3–13*, 36 (2), 139–51.

Robinson, C. and Fielding, M. (2007) *Children and their Primary Schools: Pupils' voices*, Primary Review Research Survey 5/3, Cambridge: University of Cambridge Faculty of Education.

Rudduck, J. and Flutter, J. (2004) *How to Improve Your School: Giving pupils a voice*, London: Continuum.

Wood, E. (2003) 'The power of pupil perspectives in evidence-based practice: The case of gender and underachievement', *Research Papers in Education*, 18 (4), 365–83.

Woods, P. (1990) *The Happiest Days? How pupils cope with school*, London: Routledge.

PUPIL QUESTIONS

See also: curiosity, listening, literacy, questions and questioning, skills

On the occasions when pupils initiate a conversation with an adult about learning, they tend to do so by asking one or other of two types of work-related questions. By far the most type of common question is about work procedures to clarify what they are meant to be doing. However, less confident children sometimes prefer to struggle on uncertainly or ask a friend rather than risk a teacher's exasperation by asking about an aspect of the work that they feel they should already have grasped. The second type of query that children frequently raise is uncertainty about how to work something out or the way to employ essential skills in completing a task. Teachers are regularly faced with a choice about whether to tell children, encourage them to try and find a solution for themselves or give them general guidance in the expectation that they will gradually make sense of the problem with which they are grappling without being told explicitly what to do.

Nearly all children are extremely curious and will, if their interest is aroused, ply adults with queries and questions about how and why. Teachers sometimes need to understand the reason for a child asking a question. An apparently innocent question from a five-year-old about 'Where did I come from?' may be the first sign of a wish to understand the wonders of human reproduction but is far more likely to relate to the fact that her friend said that she came from Birmingham! Interpreting children's questions is time-consuming but essential if teachers are to help them in finding answers to things that are of real interest to them (Baumfield and Mroz 2004). Whatever the age of pupils, teachers need to capture their curiosity, encourage a questioning attitude, engage with issues that concern young minds and provide enough stimuli to arouse fresh interest. Commeyras and Sumner (1998) found from their study of seven- and eight-year-old children in literacy classes that children were eager to pose questions that addressed what they needed and wanted to understand about literature and life. When given the opportunity to write, they generated numerous and varied questions; they listened carefully to each other and willingly discussed all questions presented. The authors noted the tendency of teachers to impose their own ideas about what constitutes a suitable discussion question, when in fact children are capable of generating appropriate discussion questions when they have opportunities to ask about anything they find interesting, curious or confusing.

Sources

Baumfield, V. and Mroz, M. (2004) 'Investigating pupils' questions in the primary school', in Wragg, E.C. (ed.) *Teaching and Learning*, London: Routledge.

Commeyras, M. and Sumner, G. (1998) 'Literature questions children want to discuss', *The Elementary School Journal*, 99 (2), 129–52.

Q

QUALIFICATIONS AND CURRICULUM AUTHORITY

See also: key stages, National Curriculum, tests and testing

The Qualifications and Curriculum Authority (QCA) in England is a public body, sponsored by the Department for Children, Schools and Families (DCSF). Its role is to maintain and develop the National Curriculum and associated assessments, tests and examinations in England. It is governed by a board drawn from leaders in the field of education, training and business. The QCA's close association with testing at the end of key stages means that it has struggled with an 'image problem', despite publishing a lot of on-line curriculum material to support classroom practitioners. In April 2006, the Welsh equivalent of the QCA – the ACCAC – merged with the Welsh Assembly Government's new Department for Education Lifelong Learning and Skills (DELLS) under the Department for Education, Lifelong Learning and Skills. In Scotland the national body is known as the Scottish Qualifications Authority (SQA) and is responsible for the development, accreditation, assessment, and certification of qualifications other than degrees. The majority of examinations sat, and education plans followed, in Northern Irish schools are set by the Council for the Curriculum, Examinations and Assessment (CCEA).

QUESTIONS AND QUESTIONING

See also: answering questions, body language, closed questions, fantasy, imagination, interactive teaching, memory, open questions, pupil questions, self-esteem, teachers' beliefs, teaching skills, thinking skills

The use of questions is at the heart of the interactive process between teacher and pupil as a means of enhancing children's learning. The questioning technique is widely used by teachers in both whole-class and group situations. Wragg and Brown (2001) claim that teachers ask thousands of questions in a year and may ask between 200 and 400 questions in a single day. The ability to ask intelligent and searching questions, to use questioning for different purposes and to know what to do with the answers is therefore crucial to teachers of all subjects and age groups.

Questions can be variously categorised, though are commonly divided into 'lower' and 'higher' order questions, the former requiring little active thinking. Another categorisation divides questions into 'open' or 'multi-answer' types and 'closed' types: open questions inviting a variety of answers; closed questions requiring a single or narrow range of answers. Yet another division is into 'spontaneous' questions ('say the first thing that comes to mind') and 'speculative' questions ('imagine if this be the case'). Speculative questions encourage children to make informed guesses and often employ the imagination (see Hayes 2009, chapter 4). Thus, the teacher might ask the children to imagine how language would change if the words 'then' and 'so' were not used. Again, children may be encouraged to put themselves in the shoes of a historical character and imagine how life would be different from today. In their uniquely comprehensive book focusing entirely on asking a fuller range of questions, Morgan and Saxton (1994) listed an extensive typology of question types as a means of stimulating teachers to consider the varied ways in which they use the technique.

The key skill in asking questions is for adults to help children think more carefully about the work and its practical implications. A teacher may wish to discover what facts they remember, to rehearse previous learning, to reinforce ideas, to probe an issue or even to rouse a sleepy bunch of children. Ideally, the effective use of questions encourages children to ponder and reflect on issues and problems as a means of aiding their understanding, opening up fresh areas of the topic for consideration and stimulating pupil initiative, creativity and innovation. See Stock (2004) for a book about questions for children intended to extend their thinking and imaginations.

Questions can be of low cognitive level designed to funnel pupils' responses towards the desired answer rather than promoting higher levels of interaction and cognitive engagement. Failure to consider the purpose for asking questions can lead to a lack of continuity and progression in the questioning; a surfeit of superficial questions that do not enhance children's understanding; a large proportion of single-answer questions and what may be termed 'question fatigue' on the children's part. Teachers sometimes 'shoot' a question from pupil to pupil until someone answers correctly, which is great fun for competent learners, but many children need to consider their answers and time has to be allowed for the pauses' increase in length as pupils grapple with more demanding higher-order questions.

To promote a 'thinking' climate, teachers share their interests with pupils and reveal their own doubts when they are unsure of an answer. They stimulate pupil interest by bringing into school unusual items and fascinating books that foster a sense of mystery and wonder, and encourage children to do the same. As a way to promote higher self-esteem and recognition, some teachers urge older primary children with knowledge about a hobby or pastime to act as experts among their peers by being in the 'hot-seat': talking to the class about their interest and handling questions that are put to them. One way and another, the types of questions used by teachers reflect their own beliefs about their appropriateness (Bullock et al. 2002).

When dealing with a wide ability range, teachers find that it is preferable to start with more straightforward questions as a means of involving all pupils, rather than beginning with conceptually challenging ones that limit the number of children that can participate. However, questions that are too simple may be perceived by the children as babyish, create a lacklustre atmosphere and even invite ridicule. The excessive uses of factual (right or wrong) questions that end abruptly and have no connections with the work that follows are educationally limiting. Teachers of young children have to be cautious about using too many rhetorical questions, especially when dealing with young children, who tend to offer verbal responses when the teacher is merely thinking out loud.

As with all verbal exchanges, the use of inappropriate vocabulary – whether too advanced, too vague or too specialised – confuses and puzzles children. A common failing among inexperienced teachers is to express questions poorly; include subsidiary questions within the main question and the use of double negatives. More experienced teachers avoid framing questions in a way that alarms pupils; instead, they employ a bright tone of voice and open body language to reassure the children. There is also a temptation to use a question-and-answer approach as a substitute for direct teaching when it would be better to tell the children rather than spend time asking large numbers of undemanding questions to tease out the answers. In making decisions about the balance between 'ask them' and 'tell them', teachers have to take account of the fact that although questions are an important teaching tool, they are more akin to grains of pepper than lashings of gravy, so fewer and better questions are preferable to numerous perfunctory ones.

For children to answer questions successfully, they need rapid access to what they already know and the confidence to risk being incorrect. However, a child who appears unable to answer may have stored the knowledge away and, in the pressure of the moment, been unable to draw it out of the memory bank or may be weighing up other options rather than offering a predictable response. Teachers have to be alert to the fact that a pupil who is always enthusiastic about answering questions is not necessarily more able or intelligent than a timid child who is reticent about offering a response.

A question may appear simple but have implications for children that would never occur to an adult. For instance, a class of ten-year-olds might be asked how the Pilgrim Fathers felt when they landed in America. The teacher would hope for a variety of responses that mention feelings of relief, celebration, happiness or apprehension. In their minds, however, children from Western Europe might associate America with theme parks, hurricanes, Indians and cowboys, and struggle to dissociate fantasy from the grim realities of fatigue, disease, fear and homesickness that the early settlers experienced. Questions that explore feelings and emotions, especially those that require empathy rather than personal disclosure, inevitably require more time and thoughtful consideration than questions that deal with facts.

Sources

Bullock, K., Stables, A. and Sahin, C. (2002) 'Teachers' beliefs and practices in relation to their beliefs about questioning at key stage 2', *Educational Studies*, 28 (4), 371–84.

Hayes, D. (2009) *Learning and Teaching in Primary Schools*, Exeter: Learning Matters.

Morgan, N. and Saxton, J. (1994) *Asking Better Questions*, Markham, Ontario: Pembroke Publishers.

Stock, G. (2004) *The Kids Book of Questions*, New York: Workman Publishing Company.

Wragg, E.C. and Brown, G. (2001) *Questioning in the Primary School*, London: Routledge.

R

READING

See also: accelerated learning, alphabet, dyslexia, English as an additional language, literacy, motivation for learning, parental involvement, phonics, reading aloud, reading recovery, reading schemes, slow learners, synthetic phonics

The ability to read is essential for children growing up in the twenty-first century, as the printed word, as well as information provided through computer programs and the Internet, dominates the way that society operates. In many ways there is no such thing as 'having learned to read' because reading cannot be defined in terms of a 'can do' or 'cannot do' skill; there is a continuum that stretches from people who read fluently and with understanding to people who struggle to say the words or extract meaning from the text.

Reading is a multifaceted process involving word recognition, comprehension and fluency – as well as requiring high levels of personal motivation – and is the foundational skill for all school-based learning (Poskiparta 2003). One of the most comprehensive reports on English in the UK, evocatively titled *A Language for Life* and popularly referred to as the 'Bullock Report' after the Chairman, Sir Alan Bullock, was published in 1975 by the then Department for Education and Science (DES). At the commencement of the chapter dedicated to reading (chapter 6), the authors express plainly that: 'There is no one method, medium, approach, device or philosophy that holds the key to the process of learning to read' and stress that although the teaching of reading can be improved, the solution 'does not lie in the triumphant discovery or rediscovery of a particular formula' (p. 77).

About 5 per cent of pupils learn to read effortlessly and one quarter learns to read without any great difficulty when they are given systematic and regular instruction. Twist *et al.* (2003) compared the reading habits of ten-year-old children in thirty-five countries and found that British children were third in terms of reading achievement but below average in terms of having a positive attitude (see also Shenton 2007). For a minority of pupils, reading is one of the most difficult tasks they will have to master, not least if they are struggling with dyslexia (so-called 'word blindness') or where English is not their first language (see, for example, Graham and Kelly 2000; Bell 2007). Experience shows that pupils who are poor readers when they first attend primary school are still likely to be struggling three or four years later.

The most important period for literacy development is during the early childhood years from birth to eight years, where regular exposure to books and stories is a crucial factor in learning to read. Parents can prepare their children to read by spending time with them, talking to them about interesting things in the world, telling and reading stories, and asking and answering their questions. As a result, by the time most children start the reception year in school at age five years they will have learned a lot about spoken and written forms of language; played, explored and made discoveries at home and in other settings; and watched, listened to and interacted with adults and other children. See Wyse (2007) for advice to parents, and Nation and Snowling (2004) for information about the importance of developing language skills.

There are four universally recognised approaches to reading. (1) The 'look and say' method, where children learn to recognise whole words or sentences rather than individual letter sounds. (2) Phonics, that relies on children learning the names of the letters of the alphabet and the sounds they make, then blending two letters together to make simple words, followed by three letters, four letters and so on. (3) An 'experiential' approach using the child's own words to help him or her read. The child provides a word or sentence for the adult to write down and in due course reads the words aloud and writes them independently. (4) The 'context' method that involves using books selected by children; this approach is based on the belief that they will be more enthusiastic about reading a relevant text that interests them than books that are chosen for them. Although there is no single reading programme that meets all the learning needs of pupils, the most effective ones focus on the mastery of word recognition and on comprehension, as the former (recognition) without the latter (comprehension) results in what has been described as 'barking at print'; that is, children sounding out words without properly understanding their meaning or significance.

A slightly different model of the reading process has been characterised as the *Dual Route Model*, based on the principle that skilled readers not only recognise words but also are capable of working them out. The 'working out' process involves analysing ('parsing') the printed word into units – known as graphemes – which translate into equivalent sounds known as phonemes. For example, the word 'sport' consists of three graphemes: 'sp', 'or' and 't'; if these graphemes are sounded out consecutively they approximate to the way the word sounds; this is a principal underpinning the so-called 'synthetic phonics' approach to reading and spelling.

To learn to read, children must normally be familiar with the spoken language of the written word because the purpose of reading is to help them receive messages from print that are similar to the messages already being received through their ears. This tenet means that children for whom English is not the first language may struggle to read until their verbal skills have improved; contrarily, however, there are many instances of such children who arrive with little knowledge of the language but rapidly match and even overtake the indigenous first-language speakers. Accelerated learning of this kind is almost certainly due in large measure to the high level of motivation and parental support that some ethnic minority children receive.

Children must also learn to dissect spoken words into component sounds, which requires familiarity with the alphabet in its various printed forms: lower case, capitals, printed script and cursive (joined-up) script. Gradually, new readers have to understand that a left-to-right principle operates in reading English (which is not true of all languages), not only governing word order but also in reading individual words. A child learns that there are patterns of highly probable correspondence between letters and sounds and recognises printed words from a variety of clues, notably the letters and sounds that represent them, but also their configuration and the meanings suggested by the context. For example, words such as 'aeroplane' and 'puppy' have very distinctive shapes; a series of words that read: 'Tom likes to play ... ' is almost certainly followed by the name of a sport if there is a single concluding word; or by a phrase 'with his friends' if there are several concluding words. Reading requires children to explore different options, invent and 'read between the lines' to analyse what is *not* being said as well as what is being said (Mills 1994). Teachers in school regularly share books with children, including so-called Big Books (physically big, with large print so that a group of pupils can see the words and read in unison).

The majority of poor readers are capable of increasing their reading skills to average levels through intervention programmes that combine knowledge of phonics, fluency development and reading comprehension strategies. For example, in England the 'Every Child a Reader' initiative was designed and introduced to reduce the 5.5 per cent (approximately) of children who leave primary schools each year without basic skills in English. The initiative funds so-called 'reading recovery' teachers in inner-city schools to provide intensive help for children who are most in need. The vision is that every child who needs early literacy support receives it such that the numbers of children experiencing long-term literacy difficulties are severely reduced. The UK government announced in December 2006 that Every Child a Reader would be rolled out nationally, affecting around 30,000 children year on year from 2010–11. The scheme began in September 2008, managed through the Primary National Strategy, working in partnership with the Reading Recovery National Network at the University of London's Institute of Education. Pupils receive one-to-one tuition for 30 minutes a day over about 6 weeks to help them catch up with their peers. About 60 per cent of the pupils are socially disadvantaged boys. Early results suggest that the scheme has the potential to be very successful, as reading ages increase by nearly 2 years on average after less than 6 months of regular help.

Sources

Bell, S. (2007) 'Factors affecting the integration of adult dyslexics in workplace environments in England', in *Proceedings of The International Conference on Education Research*, Latvia.

Department for Education and Science (1975) *A Language for Life*, London: HMSO.

Graham, J. and Kelly, A. (2000) *Reading Under Control*, London: David Fulton.

Masha, B. (2007) *Learning to Read*, Cambridge: Pegasus Elliot Mackenzie.

Mills, C. (1994) 'Making sense of reading', in Bourne, J. (ed.) *Thinking Through Primary Practice*, London: Routledge/Open University.

Nation, K. and Snowling, M.J. (2004) 'Beyond phonological skills: Broader language skills contribute to the development of reading', *Journal of Research in Reading*, 27 (4), 342–56.

Poskiparta E. (2003) 'Motivational-emotional vulnerability and difficulties in learning to read and spell', *British Journal of Educational Psychology*, 73 (2), 187–206.

Shenton, A. (2007) 'The joyful teaching of reading', in Hayes, D. (ed.) *Joyful Teaching and Learning in the Primary School*, Exeter: Learning Matters.

Stainthorp, R. (1996) 'Teaching reading in the primary classroom', in Croll, P. and Hastings, N. (eds) *Effective Primary Teaching*, London: David Fulton.

Twist, L., Sainsbury, M., Woodthorpe, A. and Whetton, C. (2003) *Reading All Over the World*, Slough: NFER.

Wyse, D. (2007) *How to Help your Child Read and Write*, New York: Prentice Hall Life.

READING ALOUD

See also: brain function, imagination, listening, literacy, oracy, poetry, reading, speech, stories

Reading aloud is beneficial for both children and adults because it is fun and assists children's growth as readers and learners. It also nurtures a child's love of both the written and spoken word, and gives adults a chance to rediscover their favourite stories and find new ones. Importantly, reading aloud assists children in developing essential language skills that help them to become independent readers. Reading aloud helps children develop the language skills that they will use in school and throughout their lives (RIF 2008, on-line). Stories and oral communications ('oracy') play an important part in some cultures as a means of ensuring that traditions and moral norms, as expressed through the events of the stories, are passed from one generation to the next. Studies about reading aloud to children conclude that it assists their neural (brain) development, increases their knowledge of the world, extends their vocabulary and familiarity with written language and generally enhances their interest in reading. It also builds listening skills and the ability to concentrate at length. It is extremely useful when working with children for whom English is not the first language, as it exposes them to new forms of vocabulary and allows them to 'tune' their ears to rhythm and inflections that characterise spoken English. See Coltheart *et al.* (2002) for a sophisticated analysis of reading and reading aloud issues.

Hislam and Lall (2007) write that oral storytelling appeals primarily to children's creative imaginations and 'breaks free from the stranglehold of the formulaic and prescriptive agenda that sadly characterises much literacy teaching' (p. 88). Reading aloud also has the potential to help children to gain exposure to a variety of writing styles and structures, explore social and moral issues and behaviour, discover which authors and writing styles they like and be motivated to read on their own. Reading picture books helps to promote a younger child's appreciation for the arts through exposure to different styles of pictures and illustrations. Pupils should continue to associate reading with a happy experience; learn about words and language; build listening skills; expand vocabularies; talk about characters, settings and plot; relate the events to things happening in their own lives; and gain knowledge about a variety of topics. A skilled storyteller entrances children, and the pleasure they gain as the story unfolds is obvious for all to see. Reading aloud to children will not, in itself, create readers, but it contributes to a book-loving culture and establishes an enthusiasm for the printed word because children associate it with intimacy, enjoyment and an opportunity to exercise their imaginations. A useful example of an accessible book with practical hints about reading aloud is Trelease (2006).

Reading poetry aloud is useful in teaching a variety of important skills and enthusing children. Linking poetry with other areas of the curriculum (such as drama) and increasing pupils' confidence through public speaking and choral speaking – a technique whereby children speak in unison and echo each phrase or line as spoken by the teacher, including imitating the intonation and volume – all help to enliven this area of the curriculum. Innovative use of poetry also involves memorising, interpreting the written text, giving consideration to the author's purpose in writing the poem and imitating the style in their own writing. Imagination has been described as a muscle in the mind; it needs proper feeding and regular exercise to help it grow – and oral traditions of reading aloud play an important role in nurturing it. Vardell (2006) offers advice about choosing suitable poems and developing presentations that will captivate children.

Sources

Coltheart, M., Curtis, B., Atkins, P. and Haller, M. (2002) 'Models of reading aloud', in Cohen, G., Johnston, R.A. and Plunkett, K. (eds) *Exploring Cognition: Damaged brains and neural networks*, Hove: Psychology Press.
Hislam, J. and Lall, R. (2007) 'Leaping oceans and crossing boundaries: How oral story can develop creative and imaginative thinking in young children and their teachers', in Moyles, J. (ed.) *Beginning Teaching, Beginning Learning in Primary Education*, Maidenhead: Open University Press.
RIF (Reading is Fundamental) (2008) *Tips for Reading Aloud with Elementary School Children'*, on-line at www.rif.org/parents/readingaloud/default.mspx
Trelease, J. (2006) *The Read-Aloud Handbook*, London: Penguin.
Vardell, S.M. (2006) *Poetry Aloud Here!* Chicago, IL: American Library Association (ALA) Editions.

READING DEBATE

See also: memory and memorising, phonics, reading, reading schemes, real books, synthetic phonics, teaching methods

Opinions about the best way to teach reading are as divided today as in the past. Many children who are now in middle to later life probably learned to read through the medium of phonics, together with a whole-word recognition look-and-say approach; that is, the child has to memorise words from their 'shapes' and through recognising letters and their sounds from the alphabet. However, use of word-recognition disadvantages children with poor visual memory and recall. Similarly, the sole use of phonics means that a lot of concentration is needed to sound out the letters or phonemes (parts of words), such that the fluency of reading and comprehension ('understanding') may be lost. A 'whole language' approach was introduced to offset some of these problems – incorporating reading, writing, speaking and listening ('oracy'), and focusing on 'real books' rather than using a reading scheme – an approach sometimes associated with a child-centred philosophy of education. Unfortunately, neglect of phonics in a whole language approach was found to be a problem in deciphering longer words with multiple syllables, and towards the end of the twentieth century there were concerns about a substantial number of children who lacked even basic reading skills.

Educators are striving for a balance of approaches, though presently in the UK there is considerable emphasis on the use of phonics, especially synthetic phonics. Understandably, practitioners tend to be suspicious of claims about 'foolproof' methods for effective teaching of reading, as over the years there has been no shortage of such claims. There is no question that training in phonics occupies an important place in reading, as does much of the thinking behind a 'whole language' approach, which emphasises the importance of contextualised learning. In addition, establishing cross-curricular connections and providing advanced reading opportunities for gifted pupils and 'reading recovery' for those that have fallen behind have to be incorporated. Most teachers have a short daily session of teaching phonics,

enthuse about reading at every opportunity and use a mixture of methods and strategies to try and encourage children to become enthusiastic and competent readers.

READING RECORDS

See also: modelling behaviour, parental involvement, reading, rewards

The reading record is a log in which pupils, parents and teachers record what the child has read aloud and, where appropriate, writes a comment about the quality of the reading and particular points of difficulty. The purpose of keeping reading records is to create a desire and interest in reading, such that reading has personal value and is a purposeful activity. The 'reward' must be reading in itself, as any extrinsic rewards will tend to diminish the goal of reading with desire and purpose. Adults have a responsibility to 'model' good practice by reading and enjoying books themselves, celebrating achievements and encouraging rather than pressurising children to read (Price, on-line). Many schools use a system of each child having a 'book bag' or folder, which is used exclusively for transporting the reading book and record to and from school. Parental support is important, such that they: (a) encourage their children to read at home, (b) listen to their children reading aloud, (c) offer constructive help, (d) complete the reading record, and (e) ensure that the book bag is taken each day to school.

Source

Price, R. *Reading Records*, on-line at www.egg plant.org

READING RECOVERY

See also: reading, writing

Reading Recovery (http://readingrecovery. ioe.ac.uk) is an early literacy intervention programme designed for children who have literacy difficulties at the end of their first year at primary school. It involves reading and writing in a daily one-to-one lesson with a trained teacher for a period of between 15 and 20 weeks. At the end of that time, most children have caught up with their classmates and can read and write at a level appropriate for their age.

READING SCHEMES

See also: motivation for learning, phonics, reading, real books

Reading schemes consist of a set of books, usually in story format and graded in terms of difficulty, that are designed to facilitate reading by systematically building on the vocabulary employed in the previous books in the series. Even so, each story has to engage the reader and not merely consist of 'suitable' vocabulary, so use of visual images and the occasional inclusion of a difficult word are justified because they increase pupil motivation and add to the interest.

Schemes provide a core structure for reading but are normally used in conjunction with other books outside the scheme, such as non-fiction reference books and having 'free choice' from a wide range of titles – the so-called 'real books' approach – and ongoing attention to phonics. Many schools have moved away from a reliance on reading schemes and use a more flexible approach. Some educationists object to reading schemes in that vocabulary is heavily controlled within the scheme, such that children appear to progress but experience difficulties in transferring their skills to books which are not part of the scheme (Solity 2002).

Source

Solity, J. (2002) 'Reading schemes versus real books revisited', *Literacy Today*, 31, 20.

REAL BOOKS

See also: phonics, reading, reading schemes

Real books is a 'whole language' teaching method, whereby children experience a range of vocabulary (written and spoken) and word-structures, rather than being introduced to sets of words systematically. Children are encouraged to select books that appeal to them, as opposed to moving on to the next book in the scheme. Solity (2002) recommends the use of real books because children need to encounter a wide and diverse range of books that reflect the literary structures they will experience as their reading progresses and help to ensure that they can apply their skills to books varying in style and difficulty. In addition, children are more likely to learn the distinctive and critical features of individual words when they are encountered in different contexts. Solity concludes by asserting that the use of reading schemes can only be justified if their structure is different from and easier than that of non-reading scheme books. Other educators argue that the use of a 'real books' approach must be combined with the systematic teaching of phonics, which might incorporate use of a core reading scheme.

Source

Solity, J. (2002) 'Reading schemes versus real books revisited', *Literacy Today*, 31, 20.

RECEPTION

See also: imagination, listening, literacy, nursery schools, play, singing, social and emotional aspects of learning, stories

The reception year is the name given to the first year of formal schooling in England and Wales. It is an exciting time for both the parents and the children as they contemplate the start of 'big school' as new entrants with the new challenges and opportunities. If children begin when they are still four years old but approaching their fifth birthday, they are popularly referred to as 'rising fives'. Many children start in the reception class at the start of September, while others start in January or April as rising fives and will complete only one or two terms in the class before moving to Year 1 (for children aged 5 to 6 years of age) during their second year of school. In some schools, the children start at weekly intervals across the year: autumn/winter-born first, then spring-born, then summer-born. In other schools, children born between September and 31 December attend full-time in September; children born between January and Easter attend only in the morning during the autumn term and then full-time from the start of January; children born after Easter only go to school in the mornings and then attend full-time during the summer term. Another system frequently used by schools is for all the rising fives to attend during mornings until Christmas and then full-time during the final two terms. Most children attend nurseries or playgroups prior to commencing school, which are sometimes incorporated into the school itself. With such young children and a diverse range of ages and educational and social experiences, teachers need to use a variety of strategies and teaching approaches, some of which are based on play activities and extensive use of the imagination.

Becoming literate depends on developing confidence and positive attitudes towards listening, speaking, reading and writing in children, and encouraging them to be keen to learn. The reception year is a critical time for building on children's literacy, which has been developing from birth and, some would argue, prior to birth. There has been an increasing acknowledgement that attention to children's personal and social and physical development, as well as good teaching, is necessary for a complete education. Such a rounded approach is seen as vital for establishing and nurturing reception children's ability to concentrate on their work, co-operate with peers, share the teacher's time and attention and become independent. Reception classes are also organised to promote both the social skills and the mathematical understanding of young children by using stories, songs, rhymes, board games, sand and water, construction on a large and small scale, imaginative play, outdoor play and games, cooking and shopping, two- and three-dimensional creative work with a range of materials, as well as by observing numbers and patterns in the environment and daily routines (DCSF 2008a).

The *Framework for Teaching* (DCSF 2008b) describes literacy objectives for the reception year, specified through the 'Desirable Outcomes for Children's Learning'. The outcomes emphasise early literacy, numeracy and the development of personal and social skills that contribute to children's knowledge, understanding and skills in other areas of the curriculum. Presented as six areas of learning, the goals provide a foundation for later achievement; thus: (1) personal and social development, (2) language and literacy, (3) mathematics, (4) knowledge and understanding of the world, (5) physical development, and (6) creative development. The abilities to speak competently and to listen with understanding are seen as particularly vital to the early and continuing development of literacy skills. Children whose achievements exceed the 'desirable outcomes' are given opportunities to extend their knowledge, understanding and skills.

Pre-school education and learning used to be exclusive to nurseries, playgroups, childminders, children's centres and special pre-schools, but some primary schools in England are able to take pre-school aged children in their reception classes. All children aged from three to five years old are recommended to be enrolled in some form of pre-school learning and education, not least because they are entitled to 12.5 hours a week free of charge. Reception classes are not allowed to have more than thirty children in them, but often there is only one qualified teacher and one or two regular classroom assistants. Many early years educators and parents of young children have expressed unease about the formalising and close monitoring at the expense of spontaneous play and natural curiosity. Others point out that establishing a firm foundation, especially in reading, offers the children the best chance of success later. For further details, see information provided by 'Get the Right School' (on-line).

Sources

DCSF (2008a) *Framework for Teaching Mathematics: How can we work in Reception?* London: HMSO.
——(2008b) *NLS Framework for Teaching: Additional guidance for children of reception age*, London: HMSO, on-line at www.standards.dfes.gov.uk/primary/publications/literacy
Get the Right School, *Reception Classes that Take Pre-Schoolers*, on-line at www.gettherightschool.co.uk/reception-classes-take-preschoolers.html

RECESS

See *Break time* and *Playtime*

RECORDING

See also: assessing children's learning, attendance, monitoring, nursery schools, observing children, questions and questioning

In the none-too-distant past, the only records that teachers had to keep were those relating to pupil attendance and the results of in-class tests, such as children's knowledge of multiplication tables. Today, the demand upon all staff to maintain detailed and accurate records of each aspect of pupil progress and achievement has become a national obsession in the UK (see DCSF 2008). Attendance records of both authorised and unauthorised absence are required from schools and local authorities

The Education (Pupil Information) (England) Regulations 2005 require all maintained schools other than nursery schools and some special schools to keep a curricular record for each pupil and disclose pupils' educational records to their parents if requested to do so. A *curricular* record means a formal record of a pupil's academic achievements, other skills and abilities and progress in school. The

record must be transferred free of charge and must not include the results of any assessments of the pupil's achievements. Upon request, head teachers must send a copy of a pupil's curricular record to the head teacher of another school (including an independent school) or an institution of further or higher education, where a pupil is under consideration for admission. Schools also have a duty to transfer a pupil's educational record to their new school, though this practice was standard practice long before it became a legal requirement. Primary teachers complain that the time they spend on detailed records can be wasted, as secondary teachers in the receiving schools take little or no account of them when allocating pupils to groups or classes, preferring to use evidence from their own internal tests instead.

There has to be a close relationship between teachers' observations of children – how they respond to questions, approach tasks, express their ideas and so forth – the assessment of what they have achieved and recording the outcome in a manageable form (see, for example, Cavendish and Underwood 1997; Ditchfield 2007). Assessments of pupil progress for the purpose of academic records are carried out in one or more of six ways: (1) asking specific questions and noting the children's responses to them; (2) monitoring the way that children undertake their regular work; (3) talking individually to children about their work, a process known as 'conferencing'; (4) giving groups of children problems or investigations to solve collaboratively; (5) marking/grading work completed in class; and (6) setting specific tests/tasks under formal conditions. However, it tends to be data from the last two categories that are formally recorded, and teachers are faced with decisions about precisely what should be written down and in what detail. Managing elaborate recording systems and storing large amounts of material is time-consuming and teachers have to be careful that the effort they expend is not at the expense of lesson preparation and other responsibilities. Hall and

Sheehy (2006) recommend that portfolios of children's work offer a useful means of keeping evidence of children's learning. The authors suggest that pupils might have 'an individual literacy portfolio into which they put lists of books read, written responses to stories, non-fiction writing, drawings or paintings in response to literature' (p. 348).

Storage and security of sensitive records is handled through the school's central administrative system. Ideally a record file should contain copies of reports, which have already been sent home, results of classroom tests and copies of any complaints parents have made, together with the action taken as a result. However, record keeping varies greatly from school to school, so while some schools only keep copies of test results and reports, others include far more information. Legally, the only type of bullying schools *must* record is racist bullying.

When considering what aspects of a child's progress to record, teachers have to bear in mind that parents are interested in their children's social as well as academic progress. This balance of interests is particularly well expressed through the *Foundation Curriculum* for children aged 4–5 years, that attends to the emotional well-being of children, their attitude and disposition to learning, socialising, concentration and persistence, as well as the more obviously academic achievements. A child's personal characteristics are much more difficult to record than measurable attainment, and teachers have to ensure that their disposition towards individual pupils (favourable or otherwise) does not cause them to be biased in the way they express their views.

A parent or legal guardian has a right to a copy of his or her child's school record if they put a request in writing to see it and on payment of photocopying costs. It is illegal for parents to be told that there are conditions to meet before they get a copy of the record, such as attending a formal meeting to receive it. The record must be supplied within fifteen days, not including weekends and holidays

(see Bullying UK 2008). Apart from records that disclose information about another pupil, records that parents are *not* entitled to see include:

- A teacher's record kept solely for his or her personal use.
- Occasions when the holder of the record believes that disclosure would be likely to cause serious harm to the physical, mental or emotional health of the pupil in question or any other person.
- Where the holder believes the record is relevant to whether the pupil is, or has been, a victim of child abuse or may be at risk of it.

Sources

Bullying UK (2008) *Access to Pupil Records*, on-line at www.bullying.co.uk/parents/pupilrecords.aspx
Cavendish, S. and Underwood, J. (1997) 'Keeping track: Observing, assessing and recording in the learning relationship', in Kitson, N. and Merry, R. (eds) *Teaching in the Primary School*, London: Routledge.
DCSF *School Attendance and Parental Responsibility*, on-line at www.dcsf.gov.uk/schoolattendance
——(2008) *Pupil Records*, 'Teachernet', on-line at www.teachernet.gov.uk/management/atoz/p/pupilrecords/
Ditchfield, C. (2007) 'Assessment, recording and reporting on children's work', in Jacques, K. and Hyland, R. (eds) *Professional Studies: Primary phase*, Exeter: Learning Matters.
Hall, K. and Sheehy, K. (2006) 'Assessment and learning: summative approaches', in Arthur, J., Grainger, T. and Wray, D. (eds) *Learning to Teach in the Primary School*, London: Routledge.

REFLECTION

See also: questions and questioning, thinking, thinking skills

It is generally acknowledged that the concept of reflection originated with John Dewey when he studied the actions involved in learning new skills. Reflection is not to be confused with fantasising or daydreaming – though there may be a place for both in education. Dewey concluded that there are two basic sorts of actions, the first type being *routine* action, governed by habit or expectations; the second type being *reflective* action, involving flexibility and self-appraisal, influenced by the social conditions. Dewey's original publication in 1910, *How We Think*, made a unique impact on education. He wrote this book for teachers and the first edition became the 'bible' of progressively minded educators. In more recent years, Donald Schön's work is often quoted as seminal in stimulating interest about reflective practices. In his 1983 book *The Reflective Practitioner: How teachers think*, Schön argued that professionals who receive coaching and encouragement to think carefully about what they do, while they do it, learn in a more profound way than those who fail to do so. Although such an assertion would not cause any surprise today, it was a thought-provoking statement a generation ago. Schön has also made a significant contribution to our understanding of the theory and practice of learning. His innovative thinking around notions such as 'the learning society', 'double-loop learning', and 'reflection-in-action' and 'reflection-on-action' has become part of the language of education.

In the UK, Andrew Pollard and Sarah Tann popularised the concept of teacher reflection by means of their much-acclaimed publication *The Reflective Practitioner* (Pollard and Tann 1987), by suggesting that there are four characteristics of reflective teaching. The first characteristic implies an active concern with the aims and consequences of an action, as well as with means and technical efficiency. The second characteristic combines implementation skills with attitudes of open-mindedness, responsibility and whole-heartedness. The third characteristic is a cyclical or spiralling process, in which teachers continually monitor, evaluate and revise their own practice on the basis of what they perceive to be its strengths and shortcomings. The final characteristic of reflective teaching is based on teacher judgement, partly by self-reflection and partly by insights extracted

from other areas of education. Since the 1987 publication, Pollard has continued to publish extensively, notably through a substantial work, *Reflective Teaching* (2005). Ghaye and Ghaye (2004) provides a model of the teacher as a reflective learner, with enlightenment and empowerment as central themes.

Despite the fact that 'reflection' is normally used as a noun (the reflection) it can also be viewed in the form of an adverbial clause (i.e. behaving reflectively). That is, an intelligent consideration of existing practice should be a continuous process (reflecting *during* practice) as well as a later event (reflecting *on* practice). The principle benefit attached to reflecting during and on practice is that it is a contributing factor towards teaching effectiveness. It is also an antidote to an instrumental (clinical/technicist) view of improvement that is characterised by the systematic enhancement of individual teaching skills; an approach well represented in the pages of competence checklists currently used in schools and teacher training institutions.

The process of reflection acknowledges that it is important for teachers to think hard about their work and exercise professional judgement about classroom practice, rather than meekly complying with externally derived priorities. Teachers may improve in implementing a national strategy or new initiative but be hindered in reaching their potential if they are not given opportunity to think, comment on policy decisions, challenge the status quo, negotiate their working conditions and exercise professional autonomy with regard to teaching methods and discipline.

The end result of a regulated curriculum and objectives-driven lessons, policed through national testing, may be a generation of children that feel disengaged from learning and fail to see its relevance for their lives. Teachers play an important part in promoting reflection in their pupils by asking open-ended and speculative questions that cause children to think, analyse, make suggestions and offer alternative perspectives.

Sources

Dewey, J. (1910/1997) *How We Think*, New York: Dover Publications.

Ghaye, A. and Ghaye, K. (2004) *Teaching and Learning Through Critical Reflective Practice*, London: David Fulton.

Pollard, A. (2005) *Reflective Teaching*, London: Continuum.

Pollard, A. and Tann, S. (1987, 1993, 1997) *The Reflective Practitioner*, London: Continuum.

Schön, D. (1983, 1991) *The Reflective Practitioner: How teachers think*, New York: Basic Books.

REGGIO EMILIA

See also: children, curriculum, early years, instruction, interaction, parents, play, playfulness, reading, writing

One of the reasons that teachers and assistants enjoy working with pre-school and reception children is because they are at a stage when they are changing daily and their eagerness to learn is almost guaranteed. Many practitioners are attracted to the Reggio Emilia approach to early childhood education, a system that has attracted worldwide attention. The 'Reggio' vision of the child as a competent learner has produced a strong child-directed curriculum model in which teachers follow the children's interests and do not provide focused instruction in reading and writing. Children learn through interaction with parents, staff and peers in friendly settings, where a great attention is given to the look and feel of the classroom in an atmosphere of playfulness. The Reggio approach has been adopted for children under the age of six years in the USA, UK, New Zealand, Australia and many other countries.

RELATIONSHIPS

See also: adult behaviour, behaviour, caring teachers, happiness, interaction

Building a relationship with children takes time and perseverance. No teacher can claim the automatic right to be respected; it has to be earned and has to be achieved as quickly as possible. Haydn (2007) claims that teachers place a high premium on 'getting on' with their pupils, which

> was felt to derive in part from their skills of interaction with pupils but also the degree to which they developed an understanding of the pupils they were teaching in terms of their attitude to being in the classroom, learning a school subject and to the enterprise of education.
>
> (p. 107)

Teachers can rarely claim say that they are liked by every pupil, but they have a duty to try and ensure that personality issues do not stop the children in their care from receiving a good standard of education. Similarly, teachers can never say that they equally like every pupil they teach, but it is essential that such feelings do not hinder the way they assist and respond to each child. The relationship between children and their teachers is helped if parents emphasise to their children that teachers are there to benefit them in their education and help safeguard their futures. It is also fair to say that how a child behaves at home in the presence of their parents also impacts on how they behave with adults in school (Get the Right School 2008).

Some teachers wonder why the standard of children's behaviour deteriorates when life is most stressful in school. In fact, it is easily explained. Children are extremely sensitive to mood and atmosphere, so as teachers become strained and less able to cope, the children pick up on the edginess. Each relationship therefore contributes to the sense of ease or restlessness in school, and to contentment or fractiousness among pupils.

New teachers become despondent when their attempts to establish good relationships with the children are initially rejected. Yet it may be that the class has had some unpleasant experiences with adults and takes some convincing that they can be trusted. Or perhaps they were very happy with their previous teacher and are less certain about the new teacher's ability to take her place. It may be that certain children are shy or fearful and can't respond naturally, so they adopt a passive or aloof posture until they feel more secure. In a small number of cases, mischievous children use a form of emotional blackmail, such that, 'I will give you the satisfaction that comes from seeing me happy and responsive in exchange for staying off my back and not expecting too much from me.' It is tempting for teachers to allow themselves to enter into this kind of unspoken agreement with a child; however, Wright (2006) describes the consequences attached to being a 'passive' teacher:

> The passive teacher is characterised by efforts to be popular that include ingratiating herself. She will have fragile feelings and will take criticism badly. She will plan her lessons in great detail but is not a forward planner in terms of managing the behaviour of her class. She ends up having to react to incidents and usually does it badly because she has not worked out her responses.
>
> (p. 58)

Demonstrating integrity and consistency in dealing with problems convinces most pupils that a good relationship with a teacher is worth the effort, though there may be one or two children who are dismissive of teachers' overtures. In such cases, teachers have to persevere to establish a working relationship with the children by being natural, showing flair in their teaching and being clear about where the boundaries of acceptable behaviour lie. Paradoxically, children who are initially reluctant to reciprocate are sometimes the ones with whom the teacher ultimately develops the closest bond.

Macgrath (2000) suggests that on the whole, most children, most of the time respond well when treated firmly but kindly and with respect; they want to feel valued and respected; they want to please; and they respond better to encouragement and praise

than to criticism. They also apply themselves to the task when the work is interesting and fun. The vast majority of children are intrinsically honest and trustworthy when they are not frightened of the consequences, but they also like to have boundaries that are firmly and kindly maintained by caring adults.

Sources

Get the Right School (2008) *Relationship Between Child and Teacher*, www.gettherightschool.co.uk/TheRelationshipbetweenyourChildandtheirTeachers.html
Haydn, T. (2007) *Managing Pupil Behaviour*, London: Routledge.
Macgrath, M. (2000) *The Art of Peaceful Teaching in the Primary School* London: David Fulton.
Wright, D. (2006) *Classroom Karma*, London: David Fulton.

RELIGIOUS EDUCATION

See also: assembly, awe and wonder, Qualifications and Curriculum Authority, moral development, spiritual education, voluntary aided schools

Religious education (RE) is a component of the basic curriculum in England and Wales and is taught to all pupils unless withdrawn from these lessons by their parents. All schools are required by law to provide a daily act of collective worship, of which over the course of the academic year at least 51 per cent must be Christian in basis, though the number of schools fully complying with this statute is unclear. In October 2004, the first non-statutory national framework for teaching RE was launched. Developed jointly by the Qualifications and Curriculum Authority (QCA), the Department for Children, Schools and Families (DCSF), major UK faith groups and RE professionals, the framework endorses the entitlement and explains the expectations for teaching and learning in RE, together with guidance for teachers. Proposals for future modifications to RE provision include a suggestion from the National Union of Teachers (NUT) in 2008 that parents should have a right to have specific schooling in their own faith, and that imams, rabbis and priests should be invited to offer religious instruction to pupils in all state schools.

In Scotland, religious education is called *religious and moral education* for pupils aged 5–14 years, and *religious, moral and philosophical studies* for students aged 14–18 years. Its national guidelines also state pupils' learning expectations. RE is a compulsory part of the Northern Ireland curriculum, though parents have the right to withdraw their child from part or all lessons and/or from collective worship. Schools have to provide RE in accordance with the core syllabus drawn up by the four main churches and specified by the Department of Education. The centrality of RE in primary schools requires that new teachers are properly prepared for teaching the subject but also that account is taken of their own beliefs and dispositions (see McCreery 2005; McCreery *et al.* 2008).

In the case of community and voluntary-controlled schools, school-based planning in RE is approached using the local agreed syllabus. In the case of voluntary-aided schools with a religious character, the approved policy of the governors is the starting point, though it is common practice for the head teacher and staff to present recommendations to the governors for approval. Standing Advisory Councils on Religious Education (SACREs) and other bodies may provide planning in the form of units of work that are consistent with the non-statutory national framework and nationally produced schemes of work. From ages 5–7 years (key stage 1), children explore Christianity and at least one other major religion, encounter and respond to a range of stories, artefacts and other religious materials, learn to recognise that beliefs are expressed in a variety of ways and begin to use specialist vocabulary. Pupils are encouraged to ask relevant questions and develop a sense of wonder (previously referred to as 'awe and wonder') about the world by using their imaginations. Typically, RE covers themes as diverse as what different people believe about God and the world; festivals, stories from different religions; celebrations; the meaning of different symbols (e.g. a cross in Christianity); the uniqueness of each person.

Most agreed syllabuses for children aged 7–11 years provide pupils with opportunities to learn about and from Christianity and at least two other major religions. Some agreed syllabuses offer the additional possibility of studying a religious community with a significant local presence, as well as a secular world view where this is deemed appropriate. Through a wide range of themes, children begin to use sources (e.g. the Internet) and experiences (e.g. visits to places of worship) to consider moral and ethical issues and better understand their places in the world. Older pupils learn about topics such as pilgrimages; inspirational figures; religion, family and community; the journey of life and death; and the links between belief and global issues such as human rights, justice and care for the environment. See Bastide (2006) for practical advice for primary teachers about the teaching of RE at the foundation stage; children aged 5–7 years; and children aged 7–11 years.

Sources

Bastide, D. (2006) *Teaching Religious Education 4–11*, London: Routledge.

Department for Children, Schools and Families, *Religious Education*, on-line at www.teachernet. gov.uk/teachingandlearning/subjects/re/

McCreery, E. (2005) 'Preparing primary school teachers to teach religious education', *British Journal of Religious Education*, 27 (3), 265–77.

McCreery, E., Palmer, S. and Voiels, V. (2008) *Teaching RE: Primary and early years*, Exeter: Learning Matters.

National Curriculum for England and Wales, *Religious Education*, on-line at http://curriculum. qca.org.uk/key-stages-1-and-2/subjects/religious-education

REPORTING

See also: parents' evening, target setting (pupils), tests and testing, visual aids

Reporting pupil progress in written or verbal form is a key issue for primary educators. It is often mistakenly believed that reporting is principally for the benefit of parents when the main recipients are the pupils, who require feedback from teachers about their progress. Younger children are not always able to grasp the implications of adult comments, so some teachers use visual aids, such as stickers or stars to reinforce their approval. Reporting to children of all ages is best carried out as a dialogue, where they can ask questions, clarify what the teacher is saying and discuss ways for improvement. In some upper primary classes, pupils keep a 'targets book' in which to record agreed areas for attention, though maintaining them is laborious.

All teachers are required to provide a report on pupils' progress to their parents or the person caring for them (the 'carer') on at least one occasion per year at the parents' evening (also known as the 'open evening'). The process of reporting is principally by means of a written set of comments sent directly to the parents and through an organised face-to-face meeting with them. With the advent of national tests and levels of pupil attainment, parental interest in scores and grades has been heightened. Whereas at one time it was adequate to inform parents about progress in general terms (excellent/good/satisfactory, etc.), quantifiable measures are now of considerable significance, accentuating differences in attainment between children. The individual results of any national tests that have been administered are confidential to the pupils, parents (or carers) and teachers; however, results for a class and the school as a whole are made available to all parents.

The best reporting systems provide up-to-date and accurate information about school attainment so that conscientious parents also have a clearer idea about the assistance they can offer at home. Primary school teachers have to strike a balance between providing sufficient information to satisfy the curiosity and 'need to know' of parents and overloading them with detail. Some reports are many pages long and saturated with facts about curriculum coverage, raising suspicions that such actions are an exercise in vanity on the part of the school rather than providing what most parents have any interest in seeing. Parents are also interested in social development, friendship patterns and attitudes towards learning.

Accurate recording and reporting pupil progress is also important for the teacher who will next teach the group or class and therefore interested in receiving information about the children's academic achievements to help plan and prepare work of suitable challenge for them. On transfer to secondary education, the reporting procedures must be sufficiently rigorous to assist the receiving teachers in allocating pupils to the most appropriate group or ability set, though again there is a common perception among teachers of the top class (about to transfer school) that their colleagues in the receiving schools pay limited attention to such data.

REPUTATION (TEACHERS)

See also: beliefs teaching and learning, courage (teachers), dress code, good teachers, parents, professionalism, relationships

It is said that a reputation is what others think of us and a character is what we are really like, so the heading for this section might just as easily be 'character' as 'reputation'. Nevertheless, every new teacher in school has to build a reputation quickly: with colleagues and parents to earn respect; among children to earn affection, even love. Teachers have to recognise that reputations grow as a result of their responses to situations over a period of time. Factors such as having appropriate relationships with children, preparing adequately for lessons and portraying a positive persona are all relevant factors in enhancing reputation. Style of dress and conduct, tone of voice, reaction to challenges and attitude to other adults also contribute to the sort of

impression that is created. Although inexperienced teachers in particular are more concerned with lesson planning and the
mechanics of teaching than about how they
are perceived by others, the advantages
gained through building a good reputation
are considerable:

- Children are proud of their teacher and
develop a healthy attitude towards
learning.
- Children talk positively about the teacher
at home, thereby encouraging their
parents and constructing a climate of
confidence.
- Gossip at the school gate about a teacher's competence is passed from parent
to parent so that they are eager for their
children to be taught by that person.
- Colleagues feel confident in the teacher
and respond positively.
- Parents and children look forward to
being in that teacher's class.
- The head teacher is able to speak of the
teacher in warm terms to governors,
visitors and prospective parents.

Although a good reputation is not easily
established, it is easily tarnished, and teachers
have to be sensibly vigilant to ensure that they
avoid situations and comments that might
invite accusations of inappropriate behaviour.
For instance, it is essential to avoid coarse
speech, threats and giving excessive attention
to individual pupils (especially of the opposite
sex). On the other hand, a sunny disposition,
friendliness and an obvious concern to be
helpful and co-operative with people of all
ages all assist in securing a positive reputation.

RESTORATIVE JUSTICE

See also: behaviour, bullying, discipline,
misbehaviour, sanctions

Restorative justice is a radically different
approach to school discipline and classroom
management that emerged from a different
approach adopted in the judicial system
during the 1980s as an alternative or adjunct
to the punitive sentencing of young people
for crimes against the person. At its core,
restorative justice is about helping to 'right
wrongs', and helping the perpetrators to learn
about the effect of wrongdoing on the victims
and reintegrating the aggressor into community life. In a school situation, the emphasis is
on resolution rather than merely imposing
sanctions, though these may be appropriate.
Miscreants have to be assisted to understand
the impact of their actions, seeing it as a consequence of making an unwise decision and,
in discussion with the victim and an adult
arbitrator, deciding how to put things right.
Restorative justice can be used with children
of all ages, though some children are too
emotionally immature to cope with a formal
procedure; they can, however, be helped to
comprehend the way that others are adversely
affected. Like all discipline strategies, restorative justice is not the sole answer to behaviour
problems and has to be used in conjunction
with other methods.

RETENTION IN LEARNING

See also: attention-deficit hyperactivity disorder, body language, brain function, knowledge, memory and memorising, motivation for
learning, teaching approach, visual auditory
and kinaesthetic learning

It is a puzzle why the brain so quickly deletes
apparently important information that was
supposedly learned in school a short time ago
when it easily recalls (say) the words to a song
from months or years ago after only hearing a
few notes. The answer to the conundrum is
closely related to the emotional reaction that
is triggered when particular issues, events or
subjects are raised. For example, it is surprising
how many people experience a 'blank' mind
when they are asked a mathematical question
because they fear the subject. By contrast, the
mere mention to a child of a key event such as
a birthday party will trigger a stream of talk and

physical exuberance. Understanding the importance of emotion upon memory and retention is therefore important to make better use of the brain's seemingly limitless learning ability.

Children who genuinely suffer from attention-deficit syndrome or are simply disorganised, as opposed to a refusal to concentrate or idleness, are likely to have problems in transferring knowledge from their short-term memories to longer-term memory, and in 'recovering' the knowledge (Stein and Chowdhury 2006). Rathvon (2004) also notes that such children 'may be especially likely to have poor reading comprehension because of deficits working memory, executive functioning and other related skills that interfere with their ability to attend to what they are reading and monitor their own understanding' (p. 160). The use of physical gestures ('body language') during the learning process appears to have a positive influence in increasing memory retention.

Choice of teaching methods also strongly influences the effectiveness with which children retain facts and, most importantly, gain understanding. There is little point in children mechanically regurgitating information without understanding its implications; it is for this reason that a child may be capable of spelling a word correctly in a test but fails to do so when using the word in a sentence. There have been many authenticated claims that some knowledge can be better retained if it is used in conjunction with a mind picture or word association techniques.

Koshy (2000) refers to the fact that different teaching approaches in mathematics have markedly different outcomes in terms of retention rate. Thus, whereas only about 5 per cent of the information presented in a formal lecture is retained, the figure increases with other strategies:

- 10 per cent retention when the same words are read;
- 20 per cent retention when audio-visual aids are used;
- 30 per cent retention for a demonstration;
- 50 per cent retention for a discussion group;
- 75 per cent retention for practising by doing;
- 90 per cent retention when teaching others the immediate use of the learning.

Although retaining facts is only one dimension of learning and the above figures are approximations, they suggest that direct transmission of information to children is unlikely to be effective if it is the sole teaching approach. The opportunity to read relevant text, listen to sounds or see images, watch an adult showing how something is done, discuss the lesson content with others, engage in practical activities and make use of peer tuition, can all enhance the quality of learning.

In addition, children learn best in different ways, often simplified to 'visual, auditory and kinaesthetic' or VAK. Thus, some children find it easy to understand written information; others prefer to hear it explained verbally; others like pictorial representations; and yet others benefit from something in diagrammatic form. Most children benefit from a combination of these approaches. Although the VAK categorisation of learning styles (and similar models) is somewhat arbitrary, it can be helpful to allow children a degree of choice in the way they present their answers or findings. For example, the teacher might have to consider the value of employing alternative pictorial and spoken means for children who are averse to writing things down.

It almost goes without saying that retention is enhanced when children (and adults) have the motivation for doing so. It is surprising how a reluctant learner can be transformed into a keen and determined individual if the incentive is sufficiently strong. Children who are apparently 'hopeless cases' will, if enthused, display high-quality articulation, memory and inventiveness.

Sources

Koshy, V. (2000) *Teaching Mathematics to Able Children*, London: David Fulton.

Rathvon, N. (2004) *Early Reading Assessment*, New York: Guilford Press.

Stein, S.M. and Chowdhury, U. (2006) 'The disorganised child', in Stein, S.M. and Chowdhury, U. (eds) *Disorganised Children: A guide for parents and professionals*, London: Jessica Kingsley Publishers.

REWARDS

See also: encouragement and praise, motivation for learning, parents, primary school, punishment

The concept of rewards is deeply embedded in pupils and adults working in primary schools, and its use is rooted in a belief that behaviour can be altered through the use of external stimuli. Pupils become dependent on pleasing an adult in order to gain favour and satisfaction, and the pattern of behaviour is thereby established. The limitation of this approach is that over time children view success largely in terms of pleasing the teacher rather than satisfying themselves. One basic need all children have is to be loved unconditionally, to know that they will be accepted even if things go wrong or they fail to reach the target (Kohn 2006). Kohn argues that conventional approaches to parenting such as punishments (including 'time-outs'), rewards (including positive reinforcement) and other forms of control teach children that they are loved only when they please us or impress adults and earn their approval.

Education psychologists Harrop and Williams (1992) carried out a study into rewards and punishments in the primary school and found that primary pupils' views about suitable rewards were different from those of teachers. Out of ten options, teachers selected being praised in front of other pupils (which the children placed seventh), giving merit or house points (which the children placed ninth) and mentioned in assembly (which the children placed fifth) as the top three incentives. By contrast, pupils' top three options were: their parents being informed about good behaviour (which teachers placed eighth), good written comments on work (which teachers placed fourth), and good marks (which teachers placed ninth). The Harrop and Williams study showed that whereas teachers tend to believe that adult approval *within* school – such as public praise and merit points, constitute the most powerful reward – children value adult approval *outside* school (notably, parental satisfaction). Thus:

Pupils' perceptions about rewards in school in rank order:

1 parents informed about good behaviour
2 good written comments on work
3 good marks
4 having work on display
5 mentioned in assembly
6 private praise
7 praised in front of other pupils
8 whole class praised
9 merit/house points given by teacher
10 praised by other pupils.

Teachers' perceptions about preferred rewards in school in rank order:

1 praised in front of other pupils
2 merit/house points given by teacher
3 mentioned in assembly
4 good written comments on work
5 private praise
6 having work on display
7 whole class praised
8 parents informed about good behaviour
9 good marks
10 praised by other pupils.

In a large scale study of eleven- and twelve-year-olds, Shreeve (2002) found that in schools where the pupils are motivated by an intrinsic desire to learn and achieve, formal systems of rewards and penalties are often not unnecessary. Good teachers were able to motivate pupils and manage their behaviour without the use of a formal system of rewards and penalties. Behaviour management was established and maintained by means of positive relationship between the teacher and pupil, good lesson planning and interesting work. Penalties were rarely used by teachers to signal disapproval.

Incentives and rewards place pupils into a relatively passive role. Too much incentive reduces the internal drive to achieve self-satisfaction; too little incentive creates a staid learning climate. The most effective teachers first encourage children to be proud of their achievements and then affirm the quality of their success through the use of external rewards if it is necessary – though Marshall (2001) emphasises the importance of pupils gaining personal satisfaction without being dependent on rewards (see chapter 2). A common practice is for the teacher's approval for an individual piece of work to contribute towards a whole-group or whole-class reward, thereby promoting a sense of teamwork and mutual endeavour.

Adults also value rewards, not only financial and certificated ones but those that help to fulfil their 'calling' through fostering a love of learning in their pupils. Consequently, the rewards that teachers and assistants most value are firmly rooted in successful classroom practice and the knowledge that they have contributed towards children's academic and social development. The sight of happy and contented children enjoying their schoolwork and getting on well with their peers provides the most powerful incentive for everyone associated with primary education.

Sources

Harrop, A. and Williams, T. (1992) 'Rewards and punishments in the primary school: Pupils' perceptions and teachers' usage', *Educational Psychology*, 7 (4), 211–15.

Kohn, A. (2006) *Unconditional Parenting: Moving from rewards and punishments to love and reason*, New York: Atria Books.

Marshall, M. (2001) *Discipline Without Stress, Punishments or Rewards: How teachers and parents promote responsibility and learning*, Los Alamitos CA: Piper Press.

Shreeve, A. (2002) 'Student perceptions of rewards and sanctions', *Pedagogy, Culture and Society*, 10 (2), 239–56.

RISING FIVES

Parents and guardians are obliged by law to send their children to school at the beginning of the term after their children reaches five years of age. However, if the school has sufficient accommodation to accept children before the statutory age of five, they may do so, in which case the pupils are referred to as 'rising fives'. They then begin their school lives in the first class ('the reception class'). Norman Nicholson (1914–87) wrote a poem entitled 'Rising Five' in which the character in the poem begins by insisting, *I'm rising five, not four!*

ROSE CURRICULUM REVIEW 2009

See *Primary reviews*

ROTE LEARNING

See also: alphabet, memory and memorising, multiplication tables, poetry, singing, understanding

Rote learning is a technique that does not necessitate understanding of a subject but instead focuses on memorisation of the content, notably through repetition. The principal that underpins rote learning is that children will be able to quickly recall the meaning of the material the more they repeat it. Rote learning is sometimes linked with the derogative expression, 'parrot fashion' because, though accurately reproducing the information, children may not have understood what they were saying.

In the primary classroom the use of rote learning is most commonly seen in chanting multiplication 'tables', reciting the alphabet or poetry, calling out the word held up on a 'flash card' by the teacher, singing the same songs until word-perfect and, in schools with a religious foundation, speaking out creedal statements or similar forms of words in unison. In recent years there has been more emphasis on fostering understanding rather than merely memorising information. Opponents of rote learning insist that children should no longer be forced to memorise facts and figures because such information is readily available on the Internet and through other technologies. However, there is some dispute among primary educators about the wisdom in abandoning all forms of rote learning.

RULES

See also: behaviour, educational visits, health and safety, learning climate, relationships, rewards

Rules are statements that translate principles about appropriate conduct and behaviour into practice. Good rules can be understood by pupils and adults and provide a shared understanding of what is permissible and what is unacceptable. Most schools develop a set of rules that apply to all pupils, regardless of where they are on the premises. Accordingly, pupils are governed by the policies and regulations set out in a school's code of conduct and discipline procedures. Individual teachers establish additional rules that are specific to the classroom in which the children spend the majority of their time, often drawn up after discussion with them (see, for example Rogers 2002; Rogers and McPherson 2008). Further rules cover conduct on educational visits and other trips outside the school grounds, with particular reference to health and safety issues.

Although rules can be expressed in terms of what children are not allowed to do, the most influential seem to be ones that are expressed in terms of what *should* be done and the type of behaviour and conduct that is expected. For instance, a rule that states 'walk along the corridor' is considered more effective than one that states 'do not run along the corridor'. Pollard (2005) refers to 'rule frames' that vary in strength according to different situations. Thus, a strong rule-frame is required at the start of a lesson when the teacher is sharing information and explaining what will be happening; on the other hand a less strong rule-frame is needed (say) during a child-initiated play session, and a weak rule-frame may be applied during a 'wet break' when children are kept indoors to read, play board games and draw. Pollard goes on to say that teachers influence the nature of the rule-framing by the way they act and behave; for instance, entering the room in a brisk, purposeful manner indicates 'down to business and no messing' with a tightening of the rule-frame (see Pollard 2005, pp. 123–28).

The renowned primary educator, the late Ted (E.C.) Wragg, noted that school life without any rules would be chaotic and dangerous (Wragg 2004). He draws attention to the breadth of rules that commonly govern school life and categorises them under nine headings: movement, talking, work-related, presentation, safety, space, materials, social behaviour, clothing/appearance. Wragg also argues that rules should not be viewed separately from relationships because the question of rules is closely bound up with, but also distinct from, that of interpersonal issues. He states that the relationship between two or more people is to some extent affected by the rule conventions under which it is operating. The problem with strictly applied rules and accompanying sanctions is that they fail to take account of specific circumstances. Thus, a normally placid child who throws a tantrum and bursts into tears requires a different response from the miscreant who tries to manipulate a situation by contrived fits of temper and exaggerated crying. Experienced teachers regularly discuss and clarify with children the importance and implications of self-control and do not allow themselves to be emotionally blackmailed by defiant or devious pupils.

Many schools use a system to reward positive behaviour; for example, well-behaved children are allowed a period of free choice activities during Friday afternoon (sometimes referred to as 'golden time'). Children that continue to misbehave may lose golden time or its equivalent and spend the time discussing with an adult what they did wrong and setting themselves targets for improving their behaviour. A continued infraction of the rules usually means that the child's parents are contacted and asked to come into school to discuss the situation with the class teacher or head teacher and initiate an agreed plan of action to remedy the situation.

Sources

Pollard, A. (2005, 2008) *Reflective Teaching*, London: Continuum.

Rogers, B. (2002) *Classroom Behaviour*, London: Paul Chapman.

Rogers, B. and McPherson, E. (2008) *Behaviour Management with Young Children: Crucial first steps with children 3–7 years*, London: Sage.

Wragg, E.C. (2004) 'The two Rs: Rules and relationships', in Wragg, E.C. (ed.) *The Routledge Reader in Teaching and Learning*, London: Routledge.

S

SANCTIONS

See also: punishment, relationship, stereotyping, teacher–pupil interaction

The word 'sanction' is preferred to 'punishment' by most teachers, as it does not convey any sense of being punitive. A sanction is seen as a response to the *misbehaviour* of the child (i.e. the action), as opposed to a punishment, which carries an implication about the inadequacies of the *person* and might reinforce negative stereotyping of individuals. Consequently, a sanction is supposed to foster the principle of 'this wrong action results in this outcome' and avoid damaging the basic relationship between adult and child, while maintaining an orderly learning climate.

SATS

See also: assessment for learning, key stages, literacy, numeracy, problem solving, tests and testing

SATs originally stood for 'standard assessment tasks' but was quickly changed to 'standard assessment tests'. A more accurate name for the tests is 'National Curriculum tests'. In England, the tests are given towards the end of end of key stage 1 in year 2 (seven-year-olds); towards the end of key stage 2 in year 6 (eleven-year-olds); and towards the end of key stage 3 in year 9 (fourteen-year-olds).

SATs are used to show a child's progress compared with other children born in the same month. SATs take place after Easter and are more formal and significant for pupils at the end of key stage 2 than key stage 1. Teacher assessment forms an integral part of tests in year 2. Depending on their attainment each child is given a 'level':

Level W = working towards level 1
Level 1 = the average for a typical five-year-old
Level 2 = the average for a typical seven-year-old
Level 3 = the average for a typical nine-year-old
Level 4 = the average for a typical eleven-year-old
Level 5 = the average for a typical thirteen-year-old
Level 6 = the average for a typical fourteen-year-old
Level 7 = the above average for a typical fourteen-year-old
Level 8 is only available in mathematics

Despite these 'average' levels, there is an expectation that a proportion of children in year 6 will achieve level 5. In England, league tables of school performance are published annually, which creates considerable pressure for teachers in year 2 and year 6 to prepare pupils for the test and ensure that they gain the highest possible grades. Wales and Scotland do not publish league tables. Wales abolished SATs but ten-year-olds are tested

373

on number skills ('numeracy'); how well they read and write; and problem solving. The curriculum in Scotland is far less rigid and centrally controlled, and allows teachers and local councils autonomy to decide if and when a child will be tested, as children work through a series of six levels, known as A to F.

The issue of SATs has been the source of considerable debate and unease among teachers and head teachers, many of whom dislike the narrowing of the curriculum in the months running up to the tests and the pressure placed upon children to succeed. See www.satsguide.co.uk for further details of the system in England.

SCHEMES OF WORK

See also: curriculum, key stages

Schemes of work set out the organisation and content for each subject of the curriculum across a full year and each key stage. The scheme for individual subject areas consists of curriculum units and supporting information about planning and teaching the subject. Each scheme indicates the likely progression that children will make in their learning, ways to include pupils with special learning needs and links with other subjects and areas of the curriculum. Many schools identify links between subjects and combine units from two or more schemes of work to consolidate pupils' learning and provide a more rounded learning experience.

SCHILLER, CHRISTIAN

See also: art, child-centred education, Plowden Report, Primary reviews, professional development

Christian Schiller (20 September 1895–11 February 1976) was an important promoter of progressive ideals and child-centred teaching in primary education. He was educated at Tyttenhanger Lodge Preparatory School near

St Albans and then at Gresham's School, Holt, from 1909 to 1914, where he became head boy, excelled at sprinting and won a mathematics scholarship to Sidney Sussex College, Cambridge. After World War I (1914–18) he took up his place at Cambridge University and briefly read mathematics there from 1919 to 1920. He later studied for a teachers diploma at the London Day Training College (1923–24). He became a member of His Majesty's Inspectorate of Schools in Liverpool and Worcestershire and was Staff Inspector for Primary Education, 1946–55. He was senior lecturer in primary education at the Institute of Education, University of London, 1955–63, where he established an influential one-year course for heads and senior teachers and ran residential courses for teachers.

In 1946 Schiller was appointed as the first staff inspector for primary education, following the reorganisation brought about by the 1944 Education Act. Schiller spent time pursuing his interest in the primary teaching of maths and his enthusiasm for art and movement in education grew. He continued to run courses for teachers, often with the collaboration of Robin Tanner, who became a good friend, where he promoted progressive ideals and practice.

After leaving the Ministry of Education, Schiller took up the post of senior lecturer to run a new course for primary head teachers at the University of London Institute of Education. The one-year course ran between 1956 and 1963 and many of those who attended it would go on to become influential figures in the field of primary education themselves, such as Leonard Marsh, John Coe, Connie Rosen and Arthur Razzell. Schiller left the Institute of Education in 1963 but remained actively involved in education lecturing, advising, visiting schools and acting as an external examiner and assessor. While at Goldsmiths College he also served on the Plowden Committee, which reported its findings in 1967.

In the early 1970s Schiller was instrumental in establishing a postgraduate course in primary education at Goldsmith's College, University of London. Schiller continued to work at his home in Kenton, London, up to his death on 11 February 1976. He had several articles published and worked on a book about numbers (which was never completed), but it was through his lectures and his involvement in courses for teachers that he reached such a wide audience and made such an impact on thinking. Schiller is now acknowledged as a pioneer in the field of primary education.

Sources

Griffin-Beale, C. (1979) *Christian Schiller: In his own words*, London: A&C Black/NAPE.

Institute of Education, University of London, *Papers of Louis Christian Schiller*, GB/366/DC/CS, on-line at www.ioe.ac.uk/library/archives/cs.html

——*Schiller, Louis Christian (1895–1976)*, GB 0366 CS, on-line at www.aim25.ac.uk/cgibin/frames/browse2?inst_id=5&coll_id=2333&expand

SCHOOL ATTENDANCE

See *Absenteeism*

SCHOOL CLIMATE

See also: head teacher, inspection, learning climate

Anyone who spends time in schools quickly discovers how one school – indeed, each classroom – can feel markedly different from another. 'School climate' is a general term that refers to the feel, atmosphere, tone, ideology or milieu of a school and just as individuals have personalities, so a school climate may be thought of as its personality (State University 2009). Inspectors of schools comment how much the atmosphere varies from one educational setting to another and the importance of the head teacher or principal in setting the tone. To emphasise this point, when a school has a change of leader, the school climate can change rapidly, as every teacher and visitor will testify.

Source

State University (2009) *School Climate*, on-line at http://education.stateuniversity.com/pages/2392/School-Climate.html

SCHOOL COUNCILS

See also: decision-making, job interviews, pupil perspectives, special educational needs

A school council consists of a group of pupils, normally elected by their peers, to represent the views of all the children in a school or educational establishment as a means of informing decision-making. School councils exist in a variety of forms but basically describe a school-based group run principally by pupils and in the case of the primary phase, assisted by teachers. Alternative names for the school council include 'pupil forum' and 'youth parliament'.

In 2005, the Innovation Unit (then called the DfES Innovation Unit) funded a project led by Geoff Whitty, Emma Wisby and Anne Diack (University of London, Institute of Education) to produce materials for primary schools to set up and run school councils. This project was part of the Innovation Unit's programme of work on so-called 'personalised learning'. A document was published in 2008 called *Real Decision-making? School Councils in Action*, which contained examples of good practice and opportunities for schools to share ideas. The authors made a number of recommendations, including the following (amended) list:

- Schools need to have a clear understanding of why they are introducing provision for pupil voice in general and establishing a school council in particular.
- Schools need to be willing to change their ethos and structures where necessary.
- Teacher support for pupil voice is crucial if its influence is to move beyond environment and facilities issues to the heart of teaching and learning.
- Schools must endeavour to include all pupils in their provision for pupil voice, not just those actually on the school council

or who are most comfortable expressing their views in a school context.

- Pupils with special educational needs may require particular support to participate in school councils.
- Training and support for pupils is essential if they are to contribute effectively to decision-making.

The Education and Skills Act became English law in 2008, an element of which requires that schools will have to listen to pupils on major decisions that affect them. Governing bodies are charged to invite and consider the views of its pupils on a variety of issues. As it is not practical to ask all pupils individually about every issue, an effective council can submit ideas on their behalf. One means of organising the process is the establishment of *class councils* (i.e. one council per class) to offer each child the opportunity to express a view or to vote for a particular preference from a range of options. If a good structure exists for feedback to governors and teachers, children can feel confident that their points of view have been heard and taken seriously. Issues for consideration can range from (say) discussion about altering the school uniform to a consideration of lunchtime arrangements to choosing a wall colour. A carefully selected panel of pupils may also be part of the interview process in appointing candidates for staff positions, though it is not usually appropriate for the youngest children to be involved in the formal mechanism and many teachers remain sceptical about this aspect of participation.

Amongst the many union responses to the move towards giving pupils a greater voice in decision-making, the Association of Teachers and Lecturers (ATL 2009) notes that school councils are not the only way of developing pupil participation. Schools can use pupil surveys and questionnaires on particular issues, or regular general consultation across the school, as well as formal meetings between pupils and staff, pupils and the head, and pupils and governors. ATL concludes that despite the useful role they play, school councils on their own are not the single answer to greater pupil participation.

Sources

ATL (2009) *Taking Pupils Seriously: Involving pupils in decisions that matter*, accessible on-line through www.atl.org.uk

Schools Council UK: on-line at www.schoolcouncils.org

Whitty, G., Wisby, E. and Diack, A. (2008) *Real Decision Making? School councils in action*, London: Innovation Unit, Institute of Education, University of London for the DCSF.

SCHOOL LIBRARY

See also: information technology, reading

The Chartered Institute of Library and Information Professionals (CILIP) recommend in their publication *The Primary School Library Guidelines* (CILIP 2002) that the main library should ideally be a single-use area, and a whole-school resource that is centrally located within the school and easily accessible to all classes and all children, whatever their particular needs. The library should not only contain the central fiction and non-fiction collection but also access to ICT (notably the Internet, Intranet and CD-ROMs), study space, enough seating for a whole class and informal reading areas. The Guidelines address the library needs of pupils aged between 4 and 11 years as independent learners and imaginative readers, thereby embedding the school library in the teaching and learning culture of the whole school.

Source

CILIP (2002) *The Primary School Library Guidelines*, on-line at www.cilip.org.uk

SCHOOL LIFE

See also: modelling behaviour, playtime, special events, teaching approach, teacher–pupil interaction

School life falls into well-defined categories for children and they sometimes confuse them. The energetic playtime behaviour can be brought into the classroom; the anticipation of going home can result in premature excitement; the tedium of sitting still during a long school assembly can lead to lethargy when work commences. Teachers have to adjust their teaching approach and temperament to allow for these vagaries without losing the smooth flow of classroom routines or neglecting basic standards and attitudes by being unnecessarily strict or grumpy. Some inexperienced teachers over-react to these unexpected situations and become nervy and edgy, cross and agitated. Wiser ones learn to take circumstances in their stride, to discriminate between sabotage and exuberance, between insolence and informality, between hostility and high spirits.

In some classrooms there is a notable co-operative spirit and children are generally courteous and kind to one another; in others, there seems to be an underlying tension and unhealthy rivalry that leads to sullenness and resentment. The ideal situation is one in which pupils are mutually supportive and celebrate other children's success as well as their own. Teachers who achieve this happy state do so through perseverance, modelling an appropriate attitude to their pupils and valuing children over and above their ability to attain academically.

Every educator must assume that children are capable of being 'shaped and moulded' by learning in school; if this were not so, teaching as an agent of change would not have any point to it. Learning involves the modification of behaviour by experience, and the pupil's participation and deliberate engagement with the process is essential if progress is to be made. The idea that children make progress in their learning is posited on the assumption that they change and develop in ways that are broadly orderly and predictable. However, every teacher knows that occasionally a child makes unexpected and rapid progress, much to the delight of all concerned.

SCHOOL SECRETARY

The first person a visitor or parent meets when coming to the school is the school secretary – sometimes known as the 'administrator'. In addition to acting as receptionist, secretaries work in school offices and visit other parts of the school as necessary. Their clerical duties include organising files, answering the telephone, typing letters, reports and memoranda for the head teacher; sorting and distributing mail; doing printing and photocopying; and keeping records of pupils and staff. A modern-day secretary is likely to spend a considerable amount of time using a computer and will probably be responsible for handling money. Some secretaries are responsible for statistical returns to government departments. In medium to large primary schools it is likely that duties will be shared among more than one 'secretary'. Everyone in school appreciates a good, competent school secretary with a pleasant personality.

SCHOOLYARD

See also: break time, play, playground, recess

A schoolyard is the word used in North America and elsewhere to denote the ground adjacent to the school building that is used as a play area during break times (sometimes called 'recess') and games that require a hard surface. In the UK, the term 'playground' is more commonly used for the main play area and 'field' for any grassed area.

SCIENCE

See also: creativity, cross–curriculum, discovery learning, enquiry, environmental studies, healthy eating, kinaesthetic learners, SATs

Most primary-age children are enthusiastic about science in school, not least because of the opportunities it affords for them to enjoy plenty of 'hands on' (kinaesthetic) experiences and make decisions during their enquiries.

Unfortunately, in recent years pupils have been steered towards a rather formulaic and prescriptive approach to doing science, in which the teacher provides children with closely defined tasks and activities with pre-determined outcomes. As a result, children learn to think systematically but not scientifically. That is, they complete experiments and can talk and discuss outcomes and findings but fail to grasp the scientific principles that control the phenomena. For example, they may correctly wire a circuit to illuminate a light bulb yet be unable to grasp the concept of electric current or circuits.

The best form of primary science is relevant to the children and their everyday lives because scientific concepts that relate to familiar and concrete contexts are easier for a child to comprehend than those set in unfamiliar or obscure ones. In addition, learning is most effective if children are offered opportunities to observe, to experiment and to gain practical experiences. Primary teachers often use science as a platform for establishing cross-curricular links with other subject areas. For example, a project about healthy eating might incorporate making nourishing sandwiches, designing lunch box motifs, conducting a survey of food preferences and a web-based investigation of the nutritional value of different fillings (Bennett *et al.* 2004).

Scientists place a high premium on particular modes of thought characterised by dispassionate observation, rational analysis, logical deductions, the formulation and testing of hypotheses and, by all these means, the generation of theoretical statements about the natural world (Brawn 2000). As well as teaching children to think in these classic ways, however, teachers also have to encourage them to think intuitively and imaginatively. The history of science contains numerous instances of great discoveries resulting from a combination of a painstaking step-by-step analysis *and* a creative and imaginative approach to finding solutions and suggesting alternatives. Experience suggests that children use their science knowledge intuitively most effectively

when the associated concepts and skills are first of all securely and firmly embedded. From 2010 in England, science ceased to form part of the annual National Curriculum tests (SATs).

Sources

Bennett, K., Crowther, P. and Johnston, J. (2004) 'Is there still a place for primary science?' in Johnston, J., Chater, M. and Bell, D. (eds) *Teaching the Primary Curriculum*, Maidenhead: Open University Press.

Brawn, R. (2000) 'The formal and the intuitive in science and medicine', in Atkinson, T. and Claxton, G. (eds) *The Intuitive Practitioner*, Maidenhead: Open University.

SCOTTISH CURRICULUM

See also: assessing children's learning, curriculum

In Scotland there are national, non-statutory guidelines for Scottish local authorities and schools. They cover the structure, content and assessment of the curriculum in primary schools and in the first two years of secondary education (ages 5–14 years). The curriculum is divided into five broad areas: language, mathematics, environmental studies, expressive arts, and religious and moral education. For each curricular area there are broad attainment outcomes, each with a number of strands or aspects of learning that pupils experience. The aim of the 5–14 programme is to promote the teaching of a broad, coherent and balanced curriculum that offers all pupils continuity and progression as they move through school. Scottish Gaelic may be taught to a small minority of pupils in Scotland, since it is not a core subject and is studied by choice. The curriculum in Scotland is not set by law but is flexible in that it places responsibility on individual education authorities and schools. National guidelines advise teachers by describing the subject areas that are to be covered; it does not, however, give detailed instructions about exactly what and how these areas should be taught.

Scotland is developing 'A Curriculum for Excellence' to set out the values, purposes and principles for education from 3 to 18 in Scotland, in harmony with the National Priorities, such that all children and young people should be valued by being safe, nurtured, achieving, healthy, active, included, respected and responsible. The single curriculum 3–18 is supported by an assessment and qualifications structure with the aim of providing the right pace and challenge for young people, particularly at critical points like the move from nursery to primary and from primary to secondary school (Curriculum Review Group 2004). In the Scottish 5–14 curriculum, most strands have attached to them attainment targets at five or six levels: A–E or A–F. Assessment to attain these target levels can be taken by individuals or groups as and when their teacher considers them ready. Whole classes or year groups do not sit tests; they are designed such that teachers can use them as a confirmation of the progress that pupils have made.

Source

Curriculum Review Group (Scotland) (2004) *A Curriculum for Excellence: Purposes and principles for the curriculum 3–18*, London: HMSO, on-line via www.scotland.gov.uk/Publications

SCOTTISH CURRICULUM FRAMEWORK 3–5

This document provides advice and guidance on the learning and development needs of young children in Scotland. It applies to centres involved in the education of children aged 3–5 years. The new 'Curriculum for Excellence' guidance will eventually replace the Framework and extend the approaches used in pre-school into the early years of primary.

SEATING ARRANGEMENTS

See also: computers in school, didactic teaching, group work, invisible children, physical comfort, teacher–pupil interaction, teaching approach

The way in which furniture and facilities are arranged within a teaching space sends out signals about the teacher's preferred teaching approach. Tasks that require a high degree of social interaction, such as play, drama, discussion and collaborative problem solving can only take place when the seating arrangement is conducive to that format. Similarly, it makes little sense for pupils to be clustered around a nest of tables when the activity is one requiring close concentration and individual work.

Although there has been a degree of standardisation in architecture, furniture and facilities over recent years, it is nonetheless true that classrooms differ in size, resources, numbers of pupils, position of radiators, windows, and so forth. Seating arrangements can make an educationally important difference to the quality of learning. For instance, seating pupils in rows rather than grouping them tends to foster an improvement in children's concentration levels and work output, though it does not facilitate group activities (Bennett and Blundell 1983).

Decisions about seating arrangements also have to be made with regard to the teacher's preferred teaching style. Some teachers – especially those teaching older children – tend to use a lot of direct (didactic) teaching and prefer that pupils are facing forward; other teachers – especially those teaching younger children – tend to favour children sitting in groups being supervised by an adult: teacher or assistant or parent helper (see Hastings and Chantrey Wood 2002). With the advent of national strategies for teaching literacy and numeracy there has been an emphasis on a mixed approach: direct ('didactic') teaching at the start and conclusion of the session, with group activities forming the heart of the lesson. It is common practice for teachers to bring pupils forward to sit 'on the carpet' around their feet for the introductory and concluding phases to generate intimacy and improve communication, though the room size and shape, as well as the children's physical size, sometimes militates against this practice.

Teachers tend to arrange the classroom furniture in one of three ways for the majority of the time: in rows, in nests of tables, or like a 'squared' horseshoe. However, innovative teachers take a pride in their willingness to change the pattern to suit the circumstances; for instance, if children are producing several large murals for display, tables may be pushed together to create a large area for painting the background, whereas during a formal test, the tables may be strictly in rows with sufficient room between them to allow the teacher to patrol the room. Classrooms for younger pupils normally incorporate a variety of additional facilities for practical activities; some rooms have movable screens that permit greater flexibility. The location of computing facilities in classrooms may also have to be taken into account in ensuring ease of access and allowing for the additional space it occupies. See Proctor *et al.* (1995, chapter 2) for a useful overview of some of the key factors.

Studies show that when a teacher is interacting with a class or large group, including the use of question-and-answer, the level of pupil concentration rises when social contact between children is minimised. The least helpful situation is where children are seated around a nest of tables and have either to swivel on their chairs to see the teacher or physically move the chair to face the front. With individual tasks occupying a significant proportion of classroom time, the practice of seating children in groups irrespective of the activity may work against effective teaching and learning. Changing seating arrangements from one activity/learning experience to another is rarely straightforward as it creates noise and opportunities for minor disruption.

Although a formal seating arrangement strongly influences the 'time on task', it does not necessarily correlate with quality of learning. Children may sit passively and obediently, yet learn little and lack motivation;

on the other hand, they may be quite lively, even noisy, yet be deeply involved in their work and gaining a thorough understanding through talking and discussing issues.

Teachers have to achieve a balance between competing factors in deciding about seating. First, they need to decide what pupils should be learning and how this can be facilitated. Second, they need to weigh the academic and discipline benefits against the social benefits accrued through group work. Third, they have to take into account the fact that greater pupil–pupil interaction inevitably leads to heightened adult intervention to bring pupils back on task and redirect their energies. This last point is significant because it is the less self-controlled children who invite most correction, which can spiral into repeated negative behaviour.

Sources

Bennett, S.N. and Blundell, D. (1983) 'Quantity and quality of work in rows and classroom groups', *Educational Psychology*, 3 (2), 93–105.

Hastings, N. and Chantrey Wood, K. (2002) *Reorganising Primary Classroom Learning*, Maidenhead: Open University Press.

Proctor, A., Entwistle, M., Judge, B. and McKenzie-Murdoch, S. (1995) *Learning to Teach in the Primary Classroom*, London: Routledge.

SECURITY

See also: break times, health and safety

In recent years, anxiety about child molestation; highly publicised instances of violence in schools, and strongly held concerns by school governors and staffs about their legal responsibilities has led many schools in Western Europe and North America to implement protective measures for children within the school grounds. The use of security locks, passwords, closed-circuit television (CCTV) and uniformed patrols have become commonplace during the early years of the twenty-first century. In addition, fears about touching children, worries about administering first-aid and a societal culture of litigation has led to a plethora of measures in schools to ensure physical and psychological safety for pupils and adults during break times as well as at all other times of the day.

SELF-ESTEEM (CHILDREN)

See also: deep learning, encouragement and praise, motivation for learning, pupil personality, success

Self-esteem is a state of mind controlled by what a person believes about the way that others view him or her. The associated terms, 'self-belief' and 'self-concept' and 'self-efficacy' indicate a state of mind controlled by how a person views himself or herself and are considered by some educationists to be more useful terms than self-esteem as they can be linked to verifiable achievement rather than opinion (Maclellan 2005). Nevertheless, high self-esteem contributes to a state of what is referred to as 'relaxed alertness' in learning, which in turn allows pupils to evaluate their strengths and weaknesses and increases the likelihood that learning will be deep rather than superficial.

Children are not born with a particular view of themselves or their level of worth; it is shaped through their relationships with others and the nature of their social experiences at home (initially) and increasingly with a wider circle of friends and associates. Some children seem to be naturally anxious and tentative; others express confidence from an early age and develop a higher level of self-esteem than their timid contemporaries (see Collins 2001). Pupils' responses to fear of failure may cause them to regress to a more infantile and helpless type of behaviour or vent their frustrations on a weaker child. Inexperienced teachers may assume that children with a bright and breezy personality have high self-confidence and that quiet, passive children struggle with feelings of self-worth; in fact, there is no simple correlation the two factors (Merry 1998).

Adults play an important role in influencing children's self-esteem. For example, two teachers monitor children's work and offer suggestions for improvement: the first teacher depresses the pupil by focusing solely on errors; the second brings about the desired change by the use of carefully chosen words, precise guidance and setting suitable targets for achievement. It is obvious which of the two approaches is more likely to bring about enhanced learning. However, some concerns have been raised that too much emphasis on self-esteem may result in pupils becoming too narcissistic ('self-absorbed') if over-praised.

Pupils with low self-esteem are less willing to take risks in learning and may spend their time and energy completing straightforward tasks that lead most directly to the reward of adult praise and a tangible record of success (such as a tick, a positive written comment, a house point). Although this strategy brings about a temporary boost in self-esteem, it can also lead to a situation where children avoid difficult tasks and rely heavily on external stimuli to boost their sense of well-being. Less confident children require careful nurturing if they are to break free from doing and saying only those things that they believe will elicit support and approval from others.

The renowned American educationist, Lilian Katz, suggests that parents and teachers can strengthen and support a healthy sense of self-esteem in children in at least seven ways: (1) Help them to build healthy relationships with peers. (2) Clarify their own values and those of others that may differ. (3) Offer them reassurance that support is unconditional. (4) Appreciate rather than merely praise their interests; and avoid flattery. (5) Offer them opportunities to face challenges as well as to have fun. (6) Treat them respectfully, take their views seriously and offer meaningful feedback. (7) Help them to cope with setbacks and use the information and awareness they gain to future advantage (Katz 1995).

Sources

Collins, M. (2001) *Because We're Worth It: Enhancing self-esteem in young children*, London: Lucky Duck/Paul Chapman.

Katz, L.G. (1995) *How Can We Strengthen Children's Self-Esteem*, University of Illinois, ERIC Clearinghouse on Elementary and Early Childhood Education, on-line at www.kidsource.com/kidsource/content2/Strengthen_Children_Self.html

Maclellan, E. (2005) 'Should we raise pupils' self-esteem?' *Education 3–13*, 33 (1), 7–12.

Merry, R. (1998) *Successful Children, Successful Teaching*, Maidenhead: Open University Press.

SELF-ESTEEM (TEACHERS)

See also: aims of education, effectiveness, motivation for teaching

Self-esteem (or 'self-worth') is significant for teachers, as confidence is a vitally important ingredient for effective teaching. Teachers' self-worth affects their attitude to the job and behaviour, which then influences pupil learning. When teachers feel secure in their ability to do the job effectively, this assurance is translated into a belief that pupils will respond appropriately; as a result, pupils sense the teacher's authority and are more likely to be cooperative and persevering.

Primary teachers tend to judge their own worth as persons in terms of their success at work; perceived inadequacies affect every aspect of their lives, both outside as well as inside school. Interestingly, there are numerous publications about ways in which teachers can boost the self-esteem of pupils but a dearth of material addressing specifically issues associated with the teacher's own self-confidence.

There appear to be a number of factors influencing a teacher's self-worth: (1) general competence and skills, (2) gaining approval from significant others (e.g. parents), (3) receiving support from colleagues, (4) being convinced that teaching makes a positive difference to children's lives, and (5) strong moral convictions, including religious faith. A mysterious contradiction exists in that teachers often seem to be complaining about the unreasonable demands placed on them yet they continue to remain in the job, which suggests that altruism and motivation generally outweigh self-doubt.

SENCO

See also: Code of Practice, Every Child Matters, external agencies, parents, special educational needs, statementing

A special educational needs coordinator or SENCO has responsibility for coordinating special educational needs (SEN) provision in the school. In a small school the head teacher or deputy may undertake the role. The SENCO's status was defined in the SEN Code of Practice (1994) where four major areas of responsibilities were listed: (1) working with, advising and contributing to the training of other teachers; (2) teaching and maintaining records for children with special educational needs; (3) liaising with the parents; and (4) working with 'other agencies', such as the educational psychology service, medical and social services and voluntary bodies. SENCOs have to take close account of the Every Child Matters legislation (DfES 2004a; see also Cheminais 2005). The SENCO works closely with colleagues to offer support and advice for children who exhibit special needs, both educational and behavioural, especially in the implementation of the SEN Code of Practice and the drawing up a statement of children's needs ('statementing'). SENCOs should be a member of the school's leadership team.

On the basis of what appeared to be inconsistencies and uncertainties about the SENCO role, new regulations were introduced from September 2009 prescribing the qualifications and experience needed, governing bodies' associated functions and plans for national accredited training. Cowne (2008) provides information and advice in relation to three key government publications, namely, *Removing Barriers to Achievement* (DfES 2004b), *Every Child Matters: Change for children* (DfES 2004a) and the *Disability Discrimination Act* (DfES 2005), particularly the disability equality duty and accessibility plan.

Sources

Cheminais, R. (2005) *Every Child Matters: New role for SENCOs*, London: David Fulton.

Cowne, E. (2008) *The SENCO Handbook*, London: Routledge.

DfES (2004a) *Every Child Matters: Change for children*, London: HMSO.

——(2004b) *Removing Barriers to Achievement*, London: HMSO.

——(2005) *Disability Discrimination Act*, London: HMSO.

SETTING AND STREAMING

See also: ability, English, gender, group work, mathematics, minority ethnic group underachievement

It is unusual to hear primary teachers using the terms 'setting' and 'streaming'; staffs in secondary schools much more commonly employ them. A 'set' refers to a group of pupils of similar academic kind that belong together; for example, pupils may be placed in the upper, middle or lower set for mathematics or English according to their scores from a formal test. A pupil may belong (say) to the upper set for English and the middle set for mathematics. Movement between sets is meant to take place if pupils are clearly wrongly placed; for example, pupils may be moved from the lower set to the middle set for mathematics if they demonstrate the ability to cope with the more demanding work. In practice, movement between sets does not happen often owing to practical difficulties. Pupils that struggle to make headway in a subject are sometimes allocated to a set with far fewer pupils per adult. The term 'stream' is rarely used because of its association with the fixed notion of being allocated to an A, B or C-stream for all subjects, with the associated status (for the A-stream) and stigma (for the C-stream). Traditionally, allocation to a stream was based on competence in reading, writing and arithmetic and was more or less fixed; passage of pupils between streams was unusual.

The advantages and disadvantages attached to mixed and 'comparable' ability grouping ('setting' or 'streaming') have been debated at length. While it seems sensible to put pupils of similar academic development in a particular subject together and adjust the teaching appropriate to their needs, it is the case that even within a single-ability group there can be considerable diversity. Grouping children in this way may have the potential to raise standards as measured by formal tests, but there is no known way of grouping pupils that will benefit all pupils equally. Gifted and talented pupils are believed to make more progress in a separate ability group, but putting slow learning children together in a 'low ability' group can result in teaching a narrower curriculum (notably 'the basics'), resulting in lower pupil motivation, lower teacher expectations, associated discipline problems and poor progress.

Ability setting also tends to reinforce divisions along lines of social class, gender, race and age; as a result, low ability classes often contain disproportionately large numbers of pupils from working-class background, boys, minority ethnic groups and summer-born children. Teachers try to plan lessons and activities in such a way that every pupil engages at his or her own level of competence and achieve optimum learning, but this apparently simple practice is far from easy to implement.

SEX EDUCATION

See also: children, curriculum, home–school, moral development, parents, personal social and health education, primary reviews, science, topic work

Sex education in primary schools in England formed part of the science curriculum until

2008, informing primary-age children about the main body parts and explaining that reproduction is one of the life processes common to all animals, including humans. In 2008 the government in England followed the approach in Northern Ireland and Wales, arguing that a review of sex lessons had identified the need to challenge the perception that sex and relationships education happened in a moral vacuum. Parents and schools are now encouraged to work together to decide how best topics should be taught. In primary schools, Sir Jim Rose looked at how personal, social and health education (PSHE) should best be delivered as part of his ongoing review of the curriculum (Rose 2009).

There is a broad body of opinion that primary school children not only need age-appropriate information about the biological processes of sex and reproduction but also that adult conversations with children need to include topics such as puberty, sexual responsibility, feelings and relationships. In this way, caring adults can begin to prepare children for what will become an important part of their adult life. Laying the groundwork early on may also help keep the lines of communication open during the child's teenage years (Victoria State Better Health, on-line). Children's interest in sexual issues is normal and typical behaviours include:

- becoming modest and embarrassed about being naked in front of their parents;
- gravitating towards same-sex friends;
- complaints about 'girl germs' or 'boy germs' when speaking of the opposite sex;
- games with other children that include kissing games and marriage role-play;
- curiosity about gender differences, sexual intercourse and pregnancy;
- discussion among themselves about sexual matters, with varying degrees of accuracy;
- sex play, such as 'playing doctor'.

Although the school has responsibility for a child's sex education, parents are the most important role models; if they prove to be unapproachable, the child will turn to other, less reliable sources, such as friends. Ideally, talking about sex and sexual issues should form a natural part of everyday family life and be open, relaxed and occasionally funny. Older children may think they already know everything there is to know about sex; asking careful questions allows the adult to identify the gaps in their knowledge. Reading age-appropriate books on sex together can also provide information as well as acting as a platform for further discussion.

From 2009, sex education for children in maintained schools in England became compulsory for all children aged 5 years and over. In the prescribed curriculum, pupils aged 5–7 years learn about themselves, their differences, their friendships and how to manage their feelings. This foundation facilitates learning about puberty and the 'facts of life' for pupils aged 7–11 years. If parents are unhappy about the curriculum content, they have the right to withdraw their children from certain lessons. Opponents argue that the government wants to sidestep traditional morality and assert its control over children of all ages, to the exclusion of parents, thereby extinguishing what remains of childhood innocence. The strongest criticisms claim that there is a fanaticism about government-sponsored social engineering that corrupts the minds of children through premature sexualisation.

The *Sex Education Forum*, which forms part of the National Children's Bureau (NCB) for England and Wales, is the national authority on sex and relationships education (www. ncb.org.uk/sef). It believes that good quality sex and relationships education (SRE) is an entitlement for all children and young people and is working with its member organisations – including religious, children's, parents, governors, health and education organisations – to achieve this aim. Martinez and Cooper (2006) provide information and advice on developing SRE policy and practice, including an outline of legislation and guidance, and sample lesson plans that tie into curriculum requirements.

Sources

Martinez, A. and Cooper, V. (2006) *Laying the Foundations: Sex and relationships education in primary schools*, London: NCB Publications.

Rose, J. for the DCSF (2009) *Primary Curriculum Review*, London: HMSO.

Victoria State Better Health (2008) *Sex Education: Primary school children*, on-line at www.better health.vic.gov.au

SHARED READING

See also: English as an additional language, interaction teaching, literacy strategy, modelling behaviour, poetry, reading, stories

Holdaway (1979) is credited with the 'shared reading' model, in which teacher and pupils simultaneously read aloud from a large format text. The model builds from research indicating that storybook reading is a critically important factor in young children's reading development. Oversized books (referred to as Big Books) are often used with enlarged print and illustrations to ensure that children can actively participate. As the teacher reads the book aloud, the children can see and enjoy the print and illustrations. The texts used need to be those that appeal to the children; chant and song can be used to maintain the feelings of involvement among pupils. This interactive teaching and learning approach to reading can be developed when revisiting favourite poems, jingles, songs and stories, giving close attention to specific words, letters and sounds. A new story can be used to explain how to work out unfamiliar words, such that shared reading is a springboard for independent and group reading.

The use of the phrase 'shared reading' in the literacy strategy for England and Wales involves teacher and pupils reading a single text together as a whole group or class. Wyse et al. (2007) suggest that the key features of such a shared reading experience include:

- a text pitched at or above average attainment level;
- a shared text, such as a 'big book' or other enlarged print or multiple copies of the text in normal size;
- high-quality teacher interaction;
- discussions about the text, focusing on meanings and on words and sentences;
- the modelling of the reading process;
- teaching that is informed by lesson (learning) objectives;
- preparation for main activities.

(See pages 88–89)

The success of shared reading for second language learners (English as an additional language) lies in its simplicity because the children don't need to be able to read fluently initially. The more often a teacher is seen and heard reading for pleasure in a meaningful way, the greater the chances of the listener modelling the behaviour when they are invited to join in. Shared reading advocates claim that it provides social opportunities, enabling the young second language learners to gain confidence, share knowledge, self-correct and construct meaning co-operatively with other pupils rather than struggling along alone. Teachers have to be wary, however, of imagining that all the children are participating in the active reading experience when, in reality, some of them are merely opening and shutting their mouths without saying anything or grasping their implications. When leading the group or class in reading in unison, inexperienced teachers tend to read aloud too fast and leave behind all but the most capable readers; with experience, they read aloud at half the normal speed to facilitate fuller pupil participation.

Sources

DCSF (2008) *Shared Reading*, on-line at www.standards.dcsf.gov.uk/nationalstrategies

Holdaway, D. (1979) *The Foundations of Literacy*, Sydney: Ashton Scholastic.

Houghton Mifflin Company (1997) *Shared Reading: An effective instructional model*, on-line at www.eduplace.com

Hyland, F. (2005) *The Concept of Shared Reading*, on-line at http://archive.gulfnews.com

Wyse, D., Jones, R. and Bradford, H. (2007) *Teaching English, Language and Literacy*. London: Routledge.

SHARED WRITING

See also: creative writing, learning objectives, literacy, literacy hour, phonics, writing, writing frames

Shared writing is a process by which a teacher and pupils jointly compose a piece of writing, with the teacher acting as scribe by recording ideas on a fixed board or interactive white board. It was an element of the original and now controversial 'literacy hour', conceived by the UK government and applied in England and Wales from 1999 as a means to improve national standards of literacy. Teachers use shared writing to teach children how to translate the writing plan they have constructed into a conventionally written piece of text. As such, the plan acts as a bridge between children's thinking and the formal process of writing. Attention is placed on how written language sounds (phonic awareness) and is structured (syntactical awareness) in order to transform speech into sentences; select appropriate vocabulary (words and phrases); choose from a range of connectives (words like 'but' and 'so') to sequence and structure the text; and use style and 'voice' appropriate to the type of text, its purpose and audience. For example, a different language is used in a formal business letter and on a holiday postcard.

Most shared writing sessions begin with a demonstration by the teacher, who models how the text is composed while maintaining a clear focus on the principal learning objectives. The teacher might begin by gathering the children around and starting a discussion about a shared experience, such as a recent event in school or a popular television programme. The teacher asks questions to stimulate talk, and pupils share their ideas and insights while the teacher records them both in story and/or (where practical) written

form, often making use of computing facilities. As teachers write they verbalise the skills they want the children to practise during the writing session that follows. The teacher thinks the process through aloud, rehearsing the sentence before writing it, making changes to its construction or word choice and explaining why one form or word is preferable to another. After allowing children to offer their suggestions, the sentence is rewritten, read out loud again and altered further if necessary.

As writing is used to convey ideas that can be read and understood, the process of 'shared writing' helps to demonstrate and explore aspects of the writing process and establish direct links with reading. In addition to focusing on the decoding aspects of reading, shared writing has the potential to expose children to a variety of different texts and genres (styles of writing). Shared writing encourages collaboration and is useful for exploring pupils' memories of (say) a class outing or an exciting incident. As pupils create their own text with adult support, they gradually assume greater ownership of the material and tend to be more enthusiastic about the work. It is particularly useful for inexperienced writers and children who struggle with literacy. However, it is fair to say that many primary teachers have instinctively used this method of teaching in the past, howbeit without necessarily comprehending the underlying principles.

Source

DCSF (2008) *Shared Writing*, on-line at www.standards.dcsf.gov.uk/nationalstrategies

SINGING

See also: assembly, music, voice care

The ability to use our voices effectively is one of the most basic and yet essential music skills. Children need to learn to control the vocal mechanisms to accurately reproduce or manipulate elements of beat, rhythm, pitch, tempo, dynamics, tone and colour. As children become more experienced, they can develop the skills and confidence to improvise while singing and even to compose their own songs. Correct use of the voice facilitates healthy vocal expression. Strain on the voice is alleviated if pupils are taught to stand and breathe correctly and warm up the voice before extended periods of singing. Ideally, children should be encouraged to sing every day and enjoy the group dynamics of being part of a music group.

Smith (2006) suggests that children may need help in singing for a variety of reasons, including a lack of confidence, auditory processing difficulties, hearing impairments and other physical impairments such as a chronically hoarse voice. She claims that all humans sing to express emotions that are beyond mere words, so that even very young children can, and do, express inexpressible feelings in song. Singing can become a source of joy, comfort and emotional sensation and is the birthright of every child with a normal speaking voice. As singing is a teachable skill, the more opportunity children have to sing, the better they sing and the more they enjoy singing and making music of different kinds. In turn, these experiences can result in richer and more emotionally satisfying experiences throughout their lives. The Montessori Educational Institute in the UK (www.mariamontessori.org) offers the following advice for inculcating a love for singing in children, a modified version of which is listed below:

- Try to have some group singing everyday.
- Don't force children to join the group or to sing as some children prefer to listen from a distance for some time before feeling comfortable enough to join in.
- Choose only a few songs and keep the session short (about five minutes).
- Be an enthusiastic teacher, who obviously enjoys the sessions.
- Avoid correcting the children or allowing negative comments.

- Quickly and quietly close the session if the children aren't paying attention or are being unruly.
- Look the children in the eye and talk as little as possible.
- Keep the children busy singing and eliminate pauses.
- Always respond positively to children's suggestions.
- Teach a song step by step and through repetition.
- Sing the songs unaccompanied if possible.
- Always involve the children by asking if anyone remembers a song that was sung the day before or remembers the words.
- Make singing the sole object of the gathering.
- Put tapes of the songs children are learning in a music library for the children.

In setting up a programme for children, teachers have to consider its purpose and what abilities children are being helped to develop, so that they acquire the knowledge and skills necessary to feel comfortable and successful in singing with others. However, it is commonly the case that older boys in particular are sometimes reluctant to participate in singing, regarding it as inappropriate for males, and opting for sport instead. Teachers have to take great care over the type of music used and the image presented of singing such that all children – boys as well as girls – will feel comfortable in participating. Special productions, such as at Christmas and the end of the school year, provide opportunities for children to enjoy being part of larger enterprise performing in front of an audience. However, wise teachers ensure that children first experience performing in front of their fellow pupils regularly (e.g. during assembly), rather than being pitched into a major production once a year.

At the start of 1997 a £10 million package of measures to boost singing and music education in primary schools in England was announced. The extra money was used to promote and organise a national singing campaign led by composer Howard Goodall, who was named as a new 'singing ambassador'. One of the purposes of the initiative was that schools with established choirs should work closely with other local schools to promote singing. A new songbook with a top-thirty of songs for whole-class singing was compiled, with teachers and children nominating songs for inclusion. *Sing Up* is the name of the national singing programme, which is an agenda to ensure that singing is at the heart of every primary school child's life in the belief that singing has power to change lives and help to build stronger communities.

Sources

Sing Up: on-line at www.singup.org

Smith, J. (2006) 'Every child a singer: Techniques for assisting developing singers', *Music Educators Journal*, 93 (2), 28–34.

SKILLS

See also: collaboration in learning, emotional intelligence, information technology, oracy, physical education, problem solving, reading, thinking skills, writing

The term 'skills' is used to describe a wide range of abilities that children need to function effectively in their lives. A skill can also be described as the capacity to do something well and perform certain tasks competently, normally acquired through training and experience. Skills may be considered under two broad headings: (a) abilities that children need so that they can find out things for themselves and enhance their existing knowledge and understanding; (b) abilities and attributes that children will need to acquire if they are to take learning forward. Skills can also be thought of in terms of those that are principally cerebral (i.e. mainly to do with active thinking) such as the skill required to present an opinion, and those that are manual (i.e. mainly to do with physical coordination) such as throwing a ball accurately or kneading

a ball of clay. This distinction is not to suggest that manual skills do not require thought and judgement, but that the predominant form of learning is represented by an immediate outcome in such cases.

Skill acquisition often involves the mastery of a variety of abilities that combine to create the key skill that is being mastered. Thus, the skill of accessing information through the Internet requires that pupils have first gained the ability to use a computer mouse, select from menus, and so on. Skills may also relate to a natural ability that is refined through study, practice and expert tuition; for example, a child may improve a natural ability in drawing or running or number work through coaching and adult guidance. Thinking skills can also be developed in pupils by promoting discretion, judgement, understanding and sensitivity through the use of individual and group activities designed for the purpose (Quinn 1997; Haynes 2007).

Most learning requires the application of both general and specialised skills. These may be of a practical kind (such as knowing how to use equipment) or problem-solving kind (such as knowing how to orientate a map or manipulate data) or social kind (such as collaborating as a team member). In a lesson plan, skills are listed under: (a) those that pupils have already mastered that are needed to complete the tasks and activities; (b) those that are being introduced, developed or revised through the activities.

Mastery of skills is of little use apart from their application. For instance, there is little to be gained from a child being able to open a book and find the index, but then being unable to use it effectively. Similarly, it is interesting to study the trajectory and flight of a ball in the air, but this does not ensure that the child will hit the target. Application of skills involves judgement, decision-making and evaluation as to the effectiveness of the procedure and the quality of the end result. In addition, many skills need to be exercised in conjunction with discernment or wisdom if they are to be most effective; for instance, as part of 'emotional intelligence' the skill of communicating verbally has to be done sensitively, with awareness of the impact on listeners.

The National Curriculum for England and Wales originally used the word 'skills' to denote transferable abilities in areas as diverse as communication, numeracy, problem-solving, personal and social relations, and information technology. These skills are intended to be used across the curriculum and apply to every subject area. For example, children should be able to express themselves in speech across the whole curriculum and use computer software to produce visual representations of findings. There are also six 'key skills' that are intended to help learners to improve their learning and performance in education, work and life as follows:

1 Communication, using speaking and listening ('oracy'), reading and writing. Skills required include the ability to take account of different audiences, to understand what others are saying and to participate in group discussions.
2 Application of number, including the development of a range of mental calculation skills and their application. The use of mathematical language to process data, solve problems and explain the reasoning behind solutions also forms part of this skill.
3 Information technology, developing the ability to use a range of information sources and ICT tools, and to make critical and informed judgements about when it is appropriate to use ICT to access information, solve problems and for creative expression.
4 Working with others, including the ability to contribute towards small group and whole class discussion, and to work collaboratively. The interaction requires the development of social skills and an awareness of other people's needs and perspectives (see Cohen 2006). The importance of identifying and understanding their own and others' emotions has assumed

greater urgency in recent years following unwelcome violent trends in society.
5 Improving own learning and performance, involving pupils in reflection and critical evaluation of different aspects of their work, assessing their own performance and establishing targets for learning. Most schools involve pupils in establishing and monitoring their own progress, both through setting targets and assessing outcomes.
6 Problem solving, including identifying and understanding problems, planning ways to solve them, monitoring progress and reviewing solutions.

One of the key decisions for teachers is whether mastery of basic skills should take place prior to the main task; or that competence in the skills should emerge from doing the task and mastering each skill as required. For example, pupils may be taught how to access a dictionary, but only regular use to discover the meaning of words allows a child the opportunity to come to grips with the complexities of the procedures. At the other extreme, a skill with a potential safety risk must be securely mastered before exploiting it; for example, it would be reckless to allow a young child to discover how to use a saw purely by experimenting with it. Teachers are constantly making decisions about the extent to which they monitor each step of the pupils' experiences and how much they step back and permit children to negotiate their own pathway through the work.

Sources

Carter, J. (2002) *Just Imagine: Creative ideas for creative writing*, London: David Fulton.
Cohen, D. (2006) *Social Skills for Primary Pupils*, Birmingham: Questions Publishing.
Haynes, J. (2007) 'Thinking together: Enjoying dialogue with children', in Hayes, D. (ed.) *Joyful Teaching and Learning in the Primary School*, Exeter: Learning Matters.
Quinn, V. (1997) *Critical Thinking in Young Minds*, London: David Fulton.

SLOW LEARNERS

See also: attention span, intelligence, memory and memorising, reading, self-esteem, special educational needs, target setting (pupils)

The slow-learning child or 'slow learner' is difficult to identify because he or she is not usually different in appearance from other pupils (i.e. does not have outward physical disabilities) and can function competently in the majority of life situations – outside formal academic study. Slow learners usually possess normal physical dexterity, adequate memory and as much common knowledge and sense as classmates but still struggle to keep up with their schoolwork. The measured intelligence of slow learners is 75–90 per cent of the average child; the ability to read competently can be up to a year later than their peers and the rate at which they learn is, perhaps, 80–90 per cent of the normal rate. They find it hard to work things out themselves, especially if given multiple-step instructions, and score consistently lower on achievement tests.

Abstract thinking (i.e. 'in the head', without visual aids or supporting equipment) is difficult for most slow learners; attention span tends to be shorter than expected for children of their age; they react more slowly to situations and in answering questions; they may struggle to express themselves in speech; and self-esteem is (understandably) rather fragile. Slow learners are able to learn like other children but understanding and mastery of skills comes more gradually. Unlike children who are deemed to possess 'special educational needs' (SEN), slow learners do not usually have specialist resources or adult assistance, though they may enjoy extended access to computers. Owing to the prevalence of timetabled sessions in schools, slow learners are disadvantaged in being expected to meet general lesson learning targets within the same time frame as their more capable peers. Despite the prevalence of 'slow learner' as a modern substitute for the rejected alternative, 'remedial learner', books with slow learner in

the title were largely published in the 1970s and 1980s.

SOCIAL CONSTRUCTIVISM

See *Constructivism*

SOCIAL DEVELOPMENT

See also: health and safety, new entrants, nursery schools, nurturing, parents, social and emotional aspects of learning

Social development occurs in stages and relies on emotional maturation. By the time they attend school, all children should have learned how to share with and support others, and understand the importance of health and safety. It is unquestionably true that parents' efforts to nurture and guide their children during the first few years of life have considerable implications for the work of adults in school with new school entrants. Such an important reality also reinforces the need for teachers of nursery and reception-age children in particular to engage with parents and encourage them in their demanding and vital work of childrearing.

SOCIAL AND EMOTIONAL ASPECTS OF LEARNING

See also: affective dimension of teaching, assemblies, emotional literacy, emotions of learning, friendships, motivation for learning

Helping pupils become emotionally aware and secure is an important part of a teacher's role. The national Social and Emotional Aspects of Learning (SEAL) programme was introduced to improve children's behaviour and attendance in schools in England. SEAL uses small group work to boost pupils' personal development and develop their relationships with others by improving their self-awareness and motivation. SEAL is a comprehensive, whole school approach to promoting the social and emotional skills that are said to underpin effective learning, positive behaviour, regular attendance and emotional well-being (DfES 2005) and is currently used in more than 80 per cent of primary schools across England (Humphrey *et al.*/DCSF 2008).

SEAL is delivered in three 'waves of intervention'. The first wave focuses on whole school development work designed to create the ethos and climate within which social and emotional skills can be most effectively promoted. Wave 2 involves brief, early interventions in small groups for children who are thought to require additional support to develop their social and emotional skills to assist children in five ways:

- facilitating personal development;
- exploring key issues in depth;
- practising new skills in a safe environment where they can take risks and thereby learn more about themselves;
- developing methods of relating to others;
- promoting reflection.

(DfES 2006, amended)

The final wave of the SEAL programme (wave 3) involves intervention on a one-to-one basis with children who have not benefited from the whole school and small group provision. Children at risk of or experiencing mental health issues are likely to be included in this phase.

The five key dimensions of SEAL are (1) empathy, (2) managing feelings, (3) motivation, (4) self-awareness, and (5) social skills. The Emotional Literacy (EL) curriculum works towards helping children to make the link between their emotional feelings, their thinking and their behaviour, based on the premise that the way children feel affects the way that they think, and vice versa. Thus, children's thoughts and feelings combine to have a strong impact on the way they react and respond. For example, if a child's best friend, as team captain, does not select her first, and the child decides that the friend's action is due to the fact that she doesn't want to be friends any more, the child is certain to feel hurt and critical. On the other hand, if

the child attributes her friend's actions to some other cause (such as the friend having chosen a new girl first to be kind to her) the child may feel disappointed but much less aggrieved. If the child is emotionally mature, she may also recognise the fact that she herself has acted in similar ways in the past.

Haddon *et al.* (2005) argue that emotional literacy should be seen as a potential existing in everyone, contingent on the interaction between a person and their social context, rather than as a capacity that is either present or absent in the individual. As such it is possible to develop emotional sensitivity and effective ways to communicate with others by using real scenarios and discussing actual circumstances, rather than theorising. A common way that head teachers begin the process of implementing SEAL across the whole school is through assemblies. Books such as that by Spendlove (2008) provide teachers with strategies and classroom activities to help them develop their pupils' emotional literacy.

Sources

DfES (2005) *Excellence and Enjoyment: Social and emotional aspects of learning (guidance)*, Nottingham: DfES Publications.
——(2006) *Excellence and Enjoyment: Social and emotional aspects of learning – Key Stage 2 small group activities*, Nottingham: DfES Publications.
Haddon, A., Goodman, H., Park, J. and Deakin Crick, R. (2005) 'Evaluating emotional literacy in schools: The development of the school emotional environment for learning survey', *Pastoral Care in Education*, 23 (4), 5–16.
Humphrey, N., Kalambouka, A., Bolton, J., Lendrum, A., Wigelsworth, M., Lennie, C. and Farrell, P./DCSF (2008) *Primary Social and Emotional Aspects of Learning (SEAL): Evaluation of small group work*, Research Report DCSF-RR064, University of Manchester.
Spendlove, D. (2008) *Emotional Literacy*, London: Continuum.

SOCIAL LEARNING

See also: collaboration in learning, interaction, moral development, relationships, social and emotional aspects of learning, social development

Not all learning leads to academic outcomes. For example, learning is enhanced when children work co-operatively and show a willingness to persevere and concentrate. The prevailing norms and expectations of the school and classroom are significant in promoting or inhibiting effective learning. Social learning – getting on with others, coping with relationships and responding to societal norms and expectations – is essential if children are to understand the significance and application of empathy, sympathy and the courage of their convictions ('moral development'). Both as part of the formal curriculum and informally through regular interaction, teachers encourage pupil collaboration and help children to learn a variety of strategies that can be applied to daily living.

SPATIAL-TEMPORAL REASONING

See also: visual learners

Spatial-temporal reasoning is the ability to visualise spatial patterns and mentally manipulate them over a time-ordered sequence. *Spatial* means pertaining to, involving or having the nature of space. *Temporal* means of, relating to, or limited by time. In practice, it means an ability to envision and rotate images in the mind. Visual learners (i.e. people who benefit from seeing pictures, diagrams and other visual forms to assist their learning) are most likely to be efficient in spatial-temporal reasoning.

SPEAKING AND LISTENING

See *Oracy*

SPECIAL EDUCATIONAL NEEDS

See also: Code of Practice, external agencies, kinaesthetic learning, learning difficulties, SENCO, teaching assistants, visual learning

The education of children with special educational needs (SEN) has assumed an increasingly high profile in primary education and had an impact on the work of every practitioner. At the same time it is unfortunate that the acronym SEN has become a label for children, rather than a means of focusing on their specific needs; consequently, unsatisfactory expressions such as 'SEN children' have found their way into the lexicon. Pupils are considered to have special educational needs if they display a learning difficulty or possess a disability that either prevents or hinders them from making use of educational facilities that are normally provided in schools for children of their age. It is estimated that around 20 per cent of all pupils suffer from a special educational need at some time in their school careers. The need may be temporary and have minimal impact on the child's education, or be more serious and chronic.

Every maintained school must have a member of staff who acts as a special education needs coordinator (SENCO) and a responsible person (usually the head teacher or a governor) who acts as a point of reference for the process (see Szwed 2004). A school governing body has a sub-committee to take a particular interest in such educational provision; it is obliged to report to parents about policies for children with SEN and their implementation. While the education of pupils with SEN, whether in special or in ordinary schools is broadly similar to that which is provided for other children, they are more likely to require access to specialist provision, teaching techniques and facilities. If pupils' needs necessitate formalised intervention, the Code of Practice for SEN is activated (DfES 2002).

There have always been and always will be some children who struggle with certain aspects of school work or suffer from some condition which prevents them from fulfilling their potential (see, for instance, Heeks and Kinwell 1997). Arthur *et al.* (2006) remind us that 'teaching in a primary school is a self-giving enterprise concerned with the betterment of [all] pupils' (p. 3).

Learning can be made more enjoyable and challenging if teachers respond to the range of preferred learning styles (e.g. pupils who learn more effectively through use of visual stimuli or by practical 'hands-on/kinaesthetic' application) in their teaching approaches. The richness of the experience is further enhanced when teachers make links across the curriculum and invite children to be partners with them in learning by inviting their comments, taking their views seriously and providing specific and constructive feedback. However, Claxton (2004) alerts us to the danger of taking learning styles too seriously, as a rigid attitude can be to the pupil's detriment.

The Code of Practice (England) is a document with which every teacher should be familiar. An equivalent code operates in Wales but not in Scotland, which has different procedures. The law dealing with special education in Northern Ireland is contained in the The Education (Northern Ireland) Order 1996 as amended by The Special Educational Needs and Disability (Northern Ireland) Order 2005 (SENDO). It contains detailed information about the identification of children with SEN and suggestions for appropriate action.

Provision for children with SEN emphasises *preventative* rather than remedial action, taking account of the following principles:

- having high but realistic expectations for all pupils;
- offering greater support for parents through information, advice about learning at home and liaison with outside agencies (such as educational psychologists);
- extending the inclusion of pupils in mainstream schools by providing appropriate resources, including staffing;
- promoting close liaison between schools and the support agencies, ensuring that parents are informed at all times except in cases where child abuse may be involved.

The increase in teaching assistants to support children with SEN now involves teachers in more sophisticated patterns of classroom management and organisation as they take account of the additional adult help and a wider ability range of pupils (see Jacklin *et al.* 2006, pp. 99–103). Spooner (2006) emphasises the fact that adult attitudes to pupils with special needs is a key factor in governing the way in which they respond to them and their expectations of them. The greatest challenges for teachers come from pupils whose educational problems are rooted in their emotional instability and antisocial behaviour.

The importance of oral ('spoken') work for children with special educational needs in a group or paired context is important. McNamara and Moreton (2001) offer many examples of good practice, arguing that the best way to learn something is to have to teach it. Teachers can provide children with the experience of being 'the expert' in at least one small area of the curriculum, as this is a powerfully affirming experience for a child used to being labelled a 'slow learner'. The most appropriate place to begin is with an area that interests the individual and to allow him or her to share informally with the group or whole class as appropriate.

NASEN is probably the leading organisation in the UK to promote the education, training, advancement and development of all those with special and additional support needs. Until 1992 it known as the National Association for Special Educational Needs, at which point the National Association for Remedial Education amalgamated with the National Council for Special Education. In Spring 2001, NASEN launched an electronic journal on the Wiley-Blackwell Publishing site called the *Journal of Research in Special Educational Needs*.

Sources

Arthur, J., Davison, J. and Lewis, M. (2005) *Professional Values and Practice: Achieving the standards for QTS*, London: Routledge.

Claxton, G. (2004) *Burning Issues in Primary Education Teaching*, no. 11, Birmingham: National Primary Trust.

DfES (2002) *Special Educational Needs Code of Practice*, Annesley: DfES Publications.

Heeks, P. and Kinwell, M. (1997) *Learning Support for Special Educational Needs*, London: Taylor Graham Publishers.

Jacklin, A., Griffiths, V. and Robinson, C. (2006) *Beginning Primary Teaching*, Maidenhead: Open University Press.

McNamara, S. and Moreton, G. (2001) *Changing Behaviour*, London: David Fulton.

Spooner, W. (2006) *The SEN Handbook for Trainee Teachers, NQTs and Teaching Assistants*, London: David Fulton/NASEN.

Szwed, C. (2004) 'The developing role of the primary SENCO', *Primary Practice*, 37, 36–42.

SPECIAL EVENTS

See also: collaboration (staff), collegiality, festivals, parents' evening

School life passes through many phases in a year (Brandling 1982; Sedgwick 1989, Smith and Lynch 2005) such as swapping the latest card collections, skipping, dances, songs, hairstyles, humour, plus the quirkiness of the latest electronic gadget and the 'must have' fashions. Preparations for festivals, open evenings, sports days, educational visits and other special events require planning and a great deal of hard work; they take place, of course, in addition to the regular teaching and learning programme. If well organised and managed, however, they act to increase collaboration between adults, strengthen collegiality and enhance the sense of community. Not least, they create eagerly anticipated highlights for children throughout the school year.

Sources

Brandling, R. (1982) *A Year in the Primary School*, London: Ward Lock.

Sedgwick, F. (1989) *Here Comes the Assembly Man: A year in the life of a primary school*, Lewes: Falmer.

Smith, J. and Lynch, J. (eds) (2005) *The Primary School Year*, London: Routledge.

SPECIAL SCHOOL

A special school is a school catering for pupils who have special educational needs due to learning difficulties or physical disabilities and whose learning needs cannot be met by a standard school curriculum.

SPECULATIVE QUESTIONS

See also: closed questions, literacy, numeracy, open questions, questions and questioning

Speculative questions are a form of open question – that is, without a simple 'yes-no' answer – in which the pupil is asked to consider the implications and likely outcomes from a scenario. The questions tend to be of the 'What would you do if … ?' or 'What might happen if … ?' types; for example, 'What would you do if you saw smoke coming from a building?' Teachers tend to employ this type of question to probe pupils' ability to employ logic, sequence events and use their imaginations. Myhill and Dunkin (2002) found that speculative questions were far more frequent in literacy than in numeracy. In literacy, 21 per cent of all questions asked were speculative, compared to 6 per cent in numeracy. In literacy, there were very few occasions when children were asked to articulate their thinking processes or their understanding (5 per cent of the total questions); by contrast, these were more frequent in numeracy (23 per cent of the total).

Source

Myhill, D.A. and Dunkin, F. (2002) 'What is a good question?' *Literacy Today*, 33, 8–9.

SPEECH

See also: stories, voice care

Some teachers have mellifluous, natural voices that sound like a mountain stream: clear, cool and smooth. Other teachers sound more like an old steam engine whistle: shrill, scratchy and hard on the ears, which is particularly hard on the children obliged to listen to them all day. Most teachers' voices lie somewhere between these extremes, but all practitioners need to improve their voice quality and technique by learning to relax when they speak, inhaling naturally and standing or sitting comfortably. A simple strategy – such as relaxing the shoulders and breathing deeply into the lungs to a count of five, then exhaling slowly to a count of five, then ten, then fifteen – has a remarkably beneficial effect if practised regularly. Wise teachers aim to use their voices less – by employing hand signals, for instance – and encouraging pupils to contribute their ideas. Listeners use the quality of speech as an indicator of a speaker's competence and sincerity. Some teachers gradually slip into using an unnatural tone when addressing children and parents, which can sound patronising and false. See Cera and Jacoby (2005) for advice about successfully interacting with parents.

It is not necessary to have a very loud voice for effective delivery, though teachers with quiet voices have to work hard on diction to ensure that all the children can hear what is said. To have a voice that carries well and provides sufficient volume, teachers must use their natural resonators: the voice box, the mouth and the nose. The voice is produced at the vocal chords and then amplified in the facial mask around the lips and nose. To develop a natural voice and project it without strain, air must be pushed from the lungs (i.e. breathing must be down into the chest rather than 'snatched' in the mouth) to give sufficient power for the voice resonators in the mouth and nose to operate efficiently. Teachers with strong dialects, who work in schools out of their home area, may need to improve the roundness of vowels and the crispness of consonants (see Berkley, on-line).

Effective teachers vary their speech pattern by occasionally slowing, accelerating or changing pitch as a means of emphasising key words, heightening interest in a phrase or adding character to the voice tone. The impact of slight changes in speech pattern can be increased by the use of strong eye contact and, where appropriate, adopting a fresh physical stance. Variation in speech pattern is particularly important during the opening phase of a lesson when seeking to maintain the children's attention and engage their enthusiasm, and take account of their propensity to listen and academic prowess. Teachers vary their voice tone by injecting expression during storytelling; speaking slowly, firmly and deliberately to emphasise points; showing enthusiasm when introducing a topic; and explaining things with precise and accurate phrasing.

Studies show that physical fatigue has a negative effect on the voice. Some voice specialists recommend a diet that includes whole grain, fruit and vegetables, as these foods contain important vitamins A, E and C, which help to keep the mucus membranes that line the throat healthy.

Sources

Berkley, S. (2002) *Soft Speaker RX: Top 4 ways to let yourself be heard*, on-line at www.ljlseminars.com/SOFT_SPEAKER_RX.htm, extracted from *The Voice Coach*, www.greatvoice.com
Cerra, C. and Jacoby, R. (2005) *Teacher Talk: The art of effective communication*, San Francisco CA: Jossey-Bass.

SPEECH CLARITY

See also: assembly, poetry, speech, voice care

It goes without saying that slurred or muttered speech affects the quality of communication and causes frustration among children, most of whom are genuinely interested in what adults or their peers are trying to convey to them. Poor speech compounds problems for children who are already disaffected with learning or feel uninspired, and can lead to misbehaviour and restlessness.

Improvement in clarity is achieved by avoiding casual ('informal') language and taking particular care over the use of consonants (letters of the alphabet except vowels). In particular, the loss of the letter 't' and 'd' from words, together with a failure to open the mouth widely leads to a muffled form of speaking that makes it more difficult for children to grasp what is being said. In turn, the children spend more effort attempting to follow the words than absorbing their meaning and implications. A teacher will sometimes rebuke a child who requests further explanation for not listening when, in truth, the child was not only confused by *what* was said but *the way* in which it was communicated.

In Hayes (1998) I emphasise the importance of correct breathing; good breath control depends upon approaching the task in a positive frame of mind to minimise tension and anxiety. Correct posture avoids cramping the lungs and careful control of the flow of air from the lungs to the mouth are important in supporting clear speech. Many children are reluctant to offer a comment publicly for fear of being ridiculed; the problem is compounded if children also have problems expressing themselves. Adults can encourage children to organise their thoughts beforehand, so that they can speak with greater confidence; use simple 'loosening' techniques (such as gentle humming and making the lips vibrate); and practise choral speaking of a poem or piece of text in unison, stressing good articulation. Public performance (e.g. during assembly) can be nerve-wracking for children but it builds confidence if preparation is thorough and the outcome successful.

Source

Hayes, D. (1998) *Effective Verbal Communication*, London: Hodder & Stoughton.

SPEED OF WORK

See also: ability, collaboration in learning, deep thinking, integrated day, mistakes

Children work on individual tasks at widely different paces. Co-operative and collaborative activities involving several pupils tend to proceed at the rate of the fastest rather than the slowest workers because the more assertive and speedier dominate. A small number of capable children are slow and methodical in their work, not because they lack the ability but because they are highly conscientious and anxious to avoid making mistakes. Some less able children complete work quickly because they can only engage with the concepts at a relatively superficial level and need to be encouraged to tackle tasks more thoroughly. More able children need to be given time and opportunities to extend their thinking ('deep thinking'), rather than merely repeating 'more of the same' type of work, which, though it guarantees a high success rate, ultimately leads to stagnation in learning. Creative children, who experiment with ideas and like to pursue their own interests, often take longer to complete a task than their more prosaic classmates. Strict adherence to timetabled sessions disadvantages slow and conscientious workers, who may benefit from working within an integrated day system.

SPELLING

See also: alphabet, literacy, paired work, phonics

It is not uncommon to hear a person admit to being 'useless at spelling'. Employers and even university lecturers are often quoted as complaining that students are weak in spelling and other basic areas of literacy. There are three basic approaches to teaching spelling: whole-word, phonemic, and morphemic. Each method has its advantages and disadvantages (for a very helpful analysis see 'Teach Me NZ' in the Sources section below and as follows). The *whole-word* approach requires pupils to memorise the spelling of individual words, which are sounded out loud. There are no rules involved; children just receive rote information such as being told that (say) the word 'rabbit' is spelled r-a-b-b-i-t. The advantage of whole-word spelling is in teaching words that cannot be spelled by applying simple spelling rules in words such as 'tomb'. The disadvantage of whole-word spelling is that each word or small set of similar words (e.g. ride, side, hide) has to be taught separately, so it is very time-consuming and, for busy teachers and assistants, a rather inefficient method.

A 'phoneme' is the smallest unit of meaningful sound, of which there are forty-four in English, including the five vowels and twenty-one consonants of the alphabet. Phonemic awareness is concerned with hearing and recognising the different phonemes within a word (Mallett 2008). The *phonemic* approach to spelling is therefore based on sound–symbol relationships. It involves teaching children the letters for various sounds, e.g. the sound /p/ is spelled 'p'. The main advantage of the phonemic method is that it offers generalisations for spelling many words and word parts that benefits less confident pupils. The phonemic approach is less appropriate when it is applied to words of more than one syllable; this is particularly true for words containing an unstressed vowel that sounds like 'uh' and could be spelled with any vowel letter. For example, the 'uh' in the word 'relative' (rel-uh-tiv) could be spelled with any of the five vowels.

A morpheme is the smallest unit of meaning. A word might be one morpheme as in 'hand' or contain two or more morphemes, as in 'handstand' (hand and stand). Prefixes and suffixes are also morphemes; for instance *sub*human and comfort*able*. The *morphemic* approach to spelling therefore teaches children to spell morphemes and put the units together to form words. The main advantage of using morphemes (also known as 'morphographs') is that a small number of them can be combined to form a large number of words, so the approach is most efficient for multi-syllabic words (e.g. con/tent/ed). The disadvantage of a morphemic approach is that learning to spell morphemes may depend on tricky sound–symbol and whole-word analyses.

Young (2008) suggests that collated research studies provides a broad consensus that children pass through stages of understanding in spelling, though there is disagreement about the precise nature of the stages:

1 random symbols to represent word
2 some sounds in words represented
3 all sounds in words represented
4 awareness of orthographic patters
5 application of syllable rules
6 application of derivational/meaning knowledge
7 generally accurate spellings.

(p. 128)

Jones (2002) advises that there are five basic rules to help improve spelling. (1) practice makes perfect; (2) avoid trying to learn all the words at once; (3) review repeatedly; 4) practise spelling as if you expect to spell the words correctly; and (5) use the words you have practised. To practise spelling a word, children can trace, copy and recall the word or speak it out loud then write it down, saying each letter expressively. The word is then written a second time but the last letter is omitted; then the last two letters; then the last three letters and so on. For longer words (e.g. 'understanding'), the same procedure can be followed except that syllables (under/stand/ing) instead of individual letters are omitted one by one.

Some words, like 'separate' have one difficult element; in this example, whether the letter 'e' or 'a' is in the middle of the word Such words may be correctly spelled in a test but cause uncertainty in a sentence a short time later. A technique used by teachers to aid pupil learning is to write the word boldly on paper or on the computer screen and make the 'difficult part' a different colour from the rest of the word. Once the pupil has made a mental picture of what has been written, the word is read aloud and then spelled aloud, with an emphasis on the hard part (e.g. saying it softly or using a different voice pitch).

In the 1990s a technique called 'paired' or 'cued' spelling became well-established in the

UK, promoted by enthusiasts such as Topping (1995; 1999) in which children work in pairs to master identified sets of words. Based on a study of cued spelling used in regular classroom practice, Marlin (1997) concluded that it was a procedure that is easily learned and flexible for a wide range of ages. He also claimed that it benefits from being relatively failure-free, as progress is measured against self-target setting and therefore enables pupils to develop less teacher-dependent methods for improving their spelling. An additional advantage of the cued method is that it encourages pupils to take risks and attempt to spell difficult words rather than giving up or using an adult or peer or information source to find the answer. Enthusiasts claim that cued spelling relies on a close level of co-operation learning and invites pupils to use more descriptive language, using a more elaborate and extended vocabulary to enhance their written work.

Sources

Jones, S. (2002) *Five Guidelines for Learning Spelling and Six Ways for Practising Spelling*, on-line at www.ldonline.org/article/6192

Mallett, M. (2008) *The Primary English Encyclopaedia*, London: Routledge.

Marlin, R. (1997) *Improving Written Vocabulary Through Paired Spelling*, London: Teacher Training Agency, on-line at www.tda.gov.uk/upload/resources/pdf/t/tta22.pdf

Teach Me NZ, *Spelling*, on-line at www.teachme nz.com/spelling/index.html

Topping, K. (1995; 1999) *Paired Reading, Writing and Spelling*, London: Cassell.

Young, K. (2008) 'Don't just look, listen: Uncovering children's cognitive strategies during spelling-related activities', *Education 3–13*, 36 (2), 127–38.

SPIRAL CURRICULUM

See also: ability, Bruner, child development, constructivism, curriculum, retention in learning

Ideas about a 'spiral curriculum' came to public attention when Jerome Bruner, then a professor at Harvard University, proposed the concept to facilitate structuring a curriculum around the great issues, principles and values that a society deems worthy of the continual concern of its members (Bruner 1960). Over succeeding decades educators attempted to implement the principles into their curriculum planning. Bruner first illustrated his theory in the context of mathematics and social science programmes for young children (see Bruner 1973) but later focused on language learning in young children (Bruner 1983). Bruner argued that in order to enable the transfer of thinking processes from one context to another, children needed to learn the fundamental principles of subjects rather than just master facts. He advocated learning through enquiry, with the teacher providing guidance to accelerate children's thinking, and recommended that the early teaching of any subject should emphasise grasping basic ideas intuitively. After that, he believed, the curriculum should revisit these basic ideas, repeatedly building upon them until the pupil understands them fully – the 'spiral curriculum' (GTC 2006). Sometimes the reinforcement will take place within a single session, but more commonly over a greater time span. For example, a teacher may be trying to explain to a class of six-year-old children about the change of state from a tadpole to a frog and later attempt the same explanation to a class of eleven-year-olds. Although the broad learning intention would be similar for both sets of children ('understanding the process of change') the level of detail and complexity would differ greatly and the ideas planted when children are six can be revisited and better understood as the learners construct new concepts based upon their original knowledge – from which the name 'constructivism' is derived.

Reinforcement of previous learning is most effective when children are offered the chance to engage with a variety of stimulating tasks through which they can develop, practise and rehearse their ideas. The reinforcement is facilitated when teachers use the introduction to each lesson as an opportunity to remind children of what has gone before, ask questions to stimulate thinking, point out the implications of previous learning and so forth. Similarly, the end of sessions can be used to rehearse the key points of the lesson and draw together the threads from across a series of lessons. As teachers provide opportunities for reinforcement and the development of new ideas through more demanding work and challenges, more able pupils can forge ahead by using their initiative to explore fresh avenues of thought and build upon their existing knowledge. Less able pupils can gain confidence and raise their self-esteem by dealing with familiar concepts in novel ways, such as using diagrams instead of extended writing.

Sources

Bruner, J. (1960, 1977) *The Process of Education*, Cambridge MA: Harvard University Press.
——(1973) *Going Beyond the Information Given*, New York: Norton.
——(1983) *Child's Talk: Learning to use language*, New York: Norton.
GTC (2006) *Jerome Bruner's Constructivist Model and the Spiral Curriculum for Teaching and Learning*, on-line at www.gtce.org.uk/research/romtopics/rom_teachingandlearning/bruner_may06

SPIRITUAL EDUCATION

See also: children's questions, foundation schools, moral education, religious education, Steiner–Waldorf, teachers' beliefs

Spiritual education has been described as learning and transformation through having direct contact with a form of reality, which can be interpreted in many ways. Some authors emphasise spirituality as the quest for peace and inner contentment that can only be found in a 'deity' or 'transcendent one' or 'God'. Erricker *et al.* (2001) argue that spiritual education needs to be taken seriously because it can radically reshape our educational vision and practice and have a significant effect on religious and moral education. The authors insist that teachers should address spiritual, moral, social, cultural, and emotional and religious education as interwoven and interdependent factors.

Yob (on-line) claims that spiritual education proposed by different writers reconnects pupils with the world, the needs of its peoples, its ecological concerns, its social justice issues, its distribution of goods and its peace. It does so indirectly by first reconnecting the pupil, personally and reciprocally with something other than their material selves: God, transcendence, ultimate destiny, truth or inner power.

Coles (1990) described children as seekers after truth and young pilgrims. The author asserts that children across cultures and ethnic/religious boundaries are soulful, spiritual beings who create representations of God to help them make sense of their experiences and the world. Teachers have to tread a careful path between helping their pupils to address and come to terms with the things that puzzle and fascinate them without overtly presenting their own view of life in a way that may be interpreted by parents or colleagues as indoctrination. In addition to religious foundation schools, Steiner–Waldorf schools also place considerable emphasis on children's spiritual development.

Sources

Coles, R. (1990) *The Spiritual Life of Children*, Boston MA: Houghton Mifflin.
Erricker, C, Ota, C. and Erricker, J. (2001) *Spiritual Education: Religious, cultural and social differences*, London: Routledge.
Yob, I.M. *Spiritual Education: A public school dialogue with religious interpretations*, on-line at www.ed.uiuc.edu/eps/PES-Yearbook/94_docs/yob.htm

SPORT

See also: asthma, competition, health and safety (physical activity), parents, physical education, self-esteem, success

All schools in the UK have been urged to increase pupil participation in physical activity.

Primary schools in England are required to ensure that pupils aged 5–16 in maintained schools in England participate in at least 2 hours of high-quality physical education (PE) and school sport each week (2008 figure). Critics have pointed out that for younger pupils in particular, half or more of that time is spent changing, listening to the teacher or observing other children demonstrating good practice. Pupils with disabilities or health problems can be further disadvantaged; for example, Asthma UK (www.asthma.org.uk) warned in 2005 that up to one third of children with asthma miss out on sport once a week in Wales.

There tends to be a distinction in teachers' minds between non-competitive curriculum physical education lessons – usually taking place in a school hall – involving use of specialist equipment (e.g. climbing frames) or small games equipment (e.g. balls, quoits) and 'sports' – normally outdoors and competitive in nature. Most UK schools organise a 'sports day' in the summer, to which parents and visitors are invited. Sports days have been the subject of considerable debate in recent years; some head teachers are uneasy about making them too competitive; others foster good-natured competitiveness by putting pupils into different teams as opponents, where points are allocated on the basis of finishing position, with a final rank order.

In the sports domain, the influence of parents on their children's self-esteem may be even greater than in the academic domain because parents have many opportunities to participate directly and 'thereby provide them with immediate, interpretive and evaluative feedback' (Brustad et al. 2001, p. 621). Children who are low achievers in the sporting arena may experience inadequacy and failure; they will also grow increasingly aware of their parents' and friends' carefully cloaked disappointment. In addition, the high stakes attached to commercial sporting success and its extensive media exposure often has an inflated impact upon young people's view of its significance for their personal status and life achievements. Children who excel in sport are likely to have many admirers among their peers, whereas non-sporty children are sometimes the subject of taunts and scornful comments from their classmates.

As children get older, some of them become obsessed with success in the sporting field – often aided and abetted by parents – and even in some cases fall prey to a variety of injuries at an early age. In particular, children who specialise in a single sport, play year-round or do the same sport for a variety of teams, are especially susceptible to detrimental effects on joints and growth plates, which are the areas of developing bone tissue that are the weakest parts of a child's skeleton. Common injuries include shin splints, bone fracture, knee damage, heel injury and inflamed elbows (Bryant and McElroy 1997). It is a worrying trend to note that when children are old enough to belong to a competitive sports team, health concerns tend to become of less concern and winning becomes all-important. The situation is particularly acute in North America where sporting prowess assumes a high profile; however, the televised Olympic Games has engendered a climate of 'must win' throughout the world.

Children don't normally start out with a win-at-all-costs mentality; they get involved in sports because they love to play the game. According to Coakley (2000) the consensus among youth sports experts is that some children reach the social and cognitive maturity that is required for successful participation in organised sports as early as the age of eight; however, they are unlikely to understand the complexities of game strategies until they are twelve years or older. In addition to promoting sport as an element of a healthy life style and antidote to obesity, the UK government initiatives concentrate on fostering and enhancing talented pupils to excel in sport, not least because of the London Olympic Games in 2012.

Inter-school sport competition at the primary level can be seen as an extension of a competitive achievement model, in which the emphasis is on the product and on winning, rather than on the process or on equal access and learning (Hellison and Templin 1991). Enjoyment increasingly resides in coming first rather than competing fairly. As such, the phrase 'sporting behaviour' is associated with a lack of determination, rather than as a positive view of competitiveness. For a helpful discussion of related issues, see Frankl (2003). Similarly, Cassidy and Conroy (2006) and McMahon (2007) offer insights into the impact of parental influence on children's self-esteem.

In England there exists the English Federation of Disability Sport (www.efds.co. uk). Scottish Disability Sport can be contacted through www.scottishdisabilitysport. com. Sports Council Wales has links to policies and activities for disabled young people. DSNI (Disability Sports Northern Ireland) claims to be the country's main disability sports organisation and can be contacted via www.dsni.co.uk

Sources

Brustad, R.J., Babkes, M.L. and Smith, A.L. (2001) 'Youth in sport: Psychological considerations', in Singer, R.N., Hausenblas, H.A. and Janelle C.M. (eds) *Handbook of Sport Psychology*, New York: John Wiley.

Bryant, J.E. and McElroy, M. (1997) *Sociological Dynamics of Sport and Exercise*, Englewood CO: Morton.

Cassidy, C.M. and Conroy, D. (2006) 'Children's self-esteem related to school- and sport-specific perceptions of self and others', *Journal of Sport Behaviour* (Red Orbit on-line) accessed through www.redorbit.com

Coakley, J. (2000) *Sport in Society: Issues and controversies*, Toronto: Times Mirror/Mosby.

Frankl, D. (2003) 'Should elementary school children take part in inter-school sports competition?' *The New PE and Sports Dimension*, January edition, on-line at www.sports-media.org/sportapolisnewsletter16.htm

Hellison, D.R. and Templin, T.J. (1991) *A Reflective Approach to Teaching Physical Education*, Champaign IL: Human Kinetics.

McMahon, R. (2007) *Revolution in the Bleachers*, New York: Gotham Books.

SPORTS DAYS

See also: competition, sport

In British schools, sports day is a period of time – normally a morning or afternoon, though occasionally a full day – when pupils compete in athletics contests and related events, such as racing, negotiating an obstacle course and the high jump. It is a convention that parents are invited to come and watch the proceedings. In recent years there has been considerable debate among educators about the appropriateness of using an adult model of competitive games for children. As a result, the competitive element of the day has been greatly diminished in a number of schools and replaced by co-operative events in which team effort is rewarded. Sports day is sometimes part of an 'open day', where parents can walk around the school, observe a special display, chat to members of staff and, perhaps, purchase items for sale that have been donated for that purpose.

STAFFROOM

The staffroom (sometimes known as the teachers' room) is a room used by adult members of staff in a school for relaxation during breaks, marking children's work, completing records and other administrative tasks. Most modern staffrooms have facilities for beverages and many contain a refrigerator and dishwasher. In a very large school there may be separate rooms for teachers and support staff. Other than in unusual circumstances and with special permission, pupils are not permitted to enter the staffroom.

STARTING SCHOOL

See also: citizenship, fantasy, friendships, healthy eating, home-school, induction of pupils, interaction, new entrants, nursery schools, primary school, reading, social and emotional aspects of learning, social development, speech

Children begin formal schooling at different ages in different countries. Whereas children England, Wales and Scotland begin at five years of age or as 'rising fives' (approaching their fifth birthday) those in Northern Ireland commence at age four years; children in the US and many other countries start by their sixth or seventh birthday – though the pattern of early educational provision is different. Some rising fives begin school part-time, depending on when they were born; summer-born children may be disadvantaged by starting school later than their autumn-born peers.

It is normal for children to make at least one visit to the school before the first day; sometimes the pre-school setting is on the same site as the main school, making visits straightforward. Either way, it is important for children to have opportunity to look around the school and, especially, their new classroom, and to meet their teacher and adult assistants. Knowing where they will put their coat and lunch box, where they will sit and the location of toilets are significant issues for new entrants. Very young children may not have been used to the procedure of raising an arm and receiving permission to ask a question. During the preliminary visit, parents and children are told about the daily routine and what to expect; for example, what happens at the start of the day and during break times (playtime/recess).

Parents are often anxious about 'losing' their children to school but are normally quickly reassured and relieved. With so many parents going out to work and an increase in child-minders and pre-school provision in the form of nurseries, the separation of parents and child on the first day at school is less traumatic than in former years but still a time of great significance for all concerned. The importance of the event is emphasised by Curtis (1998) when he claims that the transition from pre-school to compulsory schooling is 'one of the most important changes that will occur in a child's life'. Curtis goes on to say that 'the attitudes adopted by both children and parents to the new environment are

likely to have far-reaching effects upon later educational progress' (p. 147).

All bodily able four- and five-year-olds are learning to hop, skip, jump, throw and catch a ball, and to climb stairs effortlessly. For the most part, children are capable of both tying their own shoes and handling buttons before they finish their first year in school. New entrants also begin to grasp harder concepts represented by words such as under, over, because, why, before, and after, and generally increase their vocabulary – though the extent to which language acquisition is linked to home situation is a contentious issue. A typical school beginner has a vocabulary of more than 2,000 words and a five-year-old's speech should be intelligible, consisting of well-structured sentences and correct use of verb tense. Between 10 and 20 per cent of children at this stage will have a speech or language difficulty (e.g. lisping) that may necessitate specialist support. The majority of five-year-olds can write most or all of the letters of the alphabet and identify the sounds that correspond with many of them. Although a few pre-school children are elementary readers, the first year in school is a crucial time to make serious inroads into mastering the skill.

Children at this age begin to not only tell right from wrong, but also start to care more about doing what is right, though they are still prone to telling tales and being naughty. However, young children are still learning to distinguish between fantasy and reality, so some confusion is almost inevitable. Establishing friendships is a challenge for some children, who may suffer from personality disorders or simply lack social skills. In the UK a great deal of time and attention has been invested in programmes such as SEAL (social and emotional aspects of learning) and citizenship to promote harmony and tolerance, though evidence of their impact offers only a limited endorsement of their success.

Young children love to play but the physical and interactive skills needed for team sports are not usually fully mastered by most of them for some years; however, they are open to being taught the rules of a game and helped to enjoy team sports. Many parents and educators believe that it is preferable to begin with activities such as swimming, skating or dancing where children can compete against themselves rather than competing against others. Recent evidence has shown that regular outdoor exercise and diet is very important in a young child's well-being, and teachers and care assistants are highly aware of their responsibilities to promote healthy eating and exercise.

Sources

Curtis, A. (1998) A Curriculum for the Preschool Child, 2nd edn, London: Routledge.
Disney Family, Child Development, http://wondertime.go.com/learning/child-development/stages

STATEMENTING

See also: learning support assistant, SENCO, special educational needs, teaching assistants

If a child's special learning needs have been formally identified through involving the parents, head teacher, educational psychologist and local education authority, and are deemed to require specialist help within mainstream schooling, a formal statement is issued by the local authority. The statement describes the nature and parameters of the support, which frequently means receiving help from a teaching assistant (also referred to as learning support assistants, LSA).

Owing to the additional cost incurred, the 'statementing' process is often protracted. Pupils for whom a statement of special needs has been drawn up have attracted the label of 'statemented children', though the statement refers to concerns the nature of the educational provision and is not intended to be a description of the child. Ideally, if there is a pupil who has been formally identified as having special needs, a teaching assistant should become available to support the child for part or all of the day, depending on the nature and severity of the need. However, the concept of

one adult remaining in very close proximity to a single needy child throughout the day is becoming outmoded, unless the child's needs are so extreme (e.g. blindness) that such a continued adult presence is necessary.

STEINER WALDORF

See also: aims of education, child development, curriculum, educated child, festivals, foundation schools, inclusion, nurturing, religious education, spiritual education

Although the majority of state-funded schools are concerned principally with enhancing academic standards, two specific types of school are also closely associated with promoting a spiritual dimension in education. First, in the UK, schools within the Church of England or Roman Catholic traditions provided an elementary education for underprivileged people during the nineteenth century; these 'foundation' schools retain close control over the teaching of religious education. In recent years other denominations and world faiths have established schools that reflect their own spiritual and moral priorities. The second type is schools associated with the person of Rudolf Steiner, known as Steiner or Waldorf-Steiner or Steiner-Waldorf schools. In 1913 Steiner built a 'school of spiritual science' in Switzerland, which was the forerunner of the present-day schools. The name Waldorf is derived from the school that Steiner was asked to open in 1919 for the children of workers at the Waldorf-Astoria cigarette factory in Stuttgart, Germany. The first US Waldorf School opened in New York in 1928 and there are now more than 600 Waldorf schools in over 32 countries with approximately 120,000 pupils of primary and secondary age (Carroll 2003).

Steiner designed the curriculum of his schools to emphasise the relation of human beings to nature and natural rhythms, including an emphasis on festivals, myths, ancient cultures and various celebrations. He was driven by a conviction that practical skills, such as playing a musical instrument, weaving, wood carving, knitting and painting were an essential part of a child's education. He believed that each human being is comprised of body, spirit and soul and that children pass through three seven-year stages from birth to the age of twenty-one, so that the education provided at each stage should be appropriate to the 'spirit for each stage' (see Edmunds 2004). As Steiner believed that it is the spirit that comprehends knowledge and the spirit is the same in all people, regardless of mental or physical differences, he was a pioneer in educating the mentally and physically handicapped (as people were then described), which today is referred to as a policy of inclusion.

One of the more unusual parts of the course of study involves something Steiner called 'eurythmy', an art of movement that tries to make visible what he believed were the inner forms and gestures of language and music. Advocates of Steiner Waldorf education claim that as children grow up, they gain the characteristics that make them human because seeds of experience are sown that germinate, grow strongly through nurturing and later come to fruition. Education is therefore concerned with the whole person and not merely the growth of the intellect (Clouder and Rawson 2003).

Sources

Carroll, R.T. (2003) 'Anthroposophy, Rudolf Steiner, and Waldorf Schools', *The Skeptic's Dictionary*, on-line at http://skepdic.com/steiner.html

Clouder, C. and Rawson, M. (2003) *Waldorf Education*, Edinburgh: Floris Books.

Edmunds, F. (2004) *An Introduction to Steiner Education*, Vancouver: Sophia Books.

STEPPING STONES

See also: Early Years

For children in England, early learning goals have been identified within six areas of learning, with 'stepping stones' of progress towards those targets.

STEREOTYPING

See also: ability, assessing children's learning, behaviour, boys, encouragement and praise, expectations, gender, home background and learning

Stereotyping or 'labelling' is to attribute characteristic behaviour to a child in such a way that the description is intricately bound up with the person of the child. Negative labelling and stereotyping children can have a lasting effect that not only damages their self-esteem but can also affect their adult lives. It can take a number of different forms. Most commonly a child is labelled according to the level of conformity and quality of behaviour; for example, using expressions such as: *He's a waste of space* or *She is such a sweet kid* or *He's nothing but trouble*. Second, labelling can refer to academic potential; for example: *That child is really bright* or *Don't expect too much from him* or *She hasn't got a clue*. Labelling can also be socially orientated, such as: *The whole family is the same* or *His brother was just as clever*. Children can also be stereotyped on the basis of gender: *She's a typical girl, hopeless at maths* or *He's a typical boy, untidy and disorganised*. Teachers have to distinguish between accurate assessments of children's achievements and capability, as opposed to making unhelpful generalisations that can attach themselves throughout the school career and beyond. Even commending labelling may not always be helpful; for instance, a child referred to as 'bright' may be capable in some areas of learning but not in others.

STORIES

See also: attention span, auditory sources, awe and wonder, body language, imagination, reading aloud, tactile learning

All children love to hear good stories and children's literature abounds with tales of heroes, villains, elves, fairies, goblins, monsters and sea devils. In addition, a variety of 'touch-feel' tactile books are published, including those with numerous colour pictures and features (e.g. soft wool for a lamb picture; rough texture for a scaly creature). All sorts of stories have the potential to contribute to pupils' understanding of narrative, including 'classics' of the *Tom Sawyer* (Mark Twain 1876) and *Wolves of Willoughby Chase* (Joan Aiken 1963) variety, plus the 'love them or hate them' types of books by authors such as Enid Blyton, and even comic books – all of which can be rich educational resources. The best examples of them relate stories in a unique way and also provide an opportunity for a close examination, from a fresh perspective, of character and plot (Duncan 2009).

Reading stories aloud with enthusiasm while using a hand to articulate exclamations, pauses, concerns and happiness has the potential to enthral and enthuse children, which is important for at least five reasons. First, children may find routine and mundane reading tedious. Second, creative reading is more likely to engage the children's interest and help them to follow the story from start to finish, rather than daydreaming through parts of it. Third, it allows the reader to use tonal variation to emphasise key words and phrases that need to be impressed on the listeners. Fourth, it is likely to encourage pupil participation, including suggestions about possible endings, views of characters and celebrating the triumph of good over evil. Fifth, story sessions act as a bonding opportunity between adult and child and between child and child.

Stories have the potential to create memorable and comprehensible structures with devices such as cause-and-effect to help the child listener understand a plot, engage with the issues or be drawn into the awe and wonder of how seemingly impossible situations can be resolved. Storytelling also assists with transmitting world cultures as children hear about how others live; reinforcing learning experiences as they understand the implications of people's actions and decisions; helping the emerging ego as they grasp the fact that the world does not revolve solely around them; and enjoyment of oral literature for its own sake. Mallett (2008) argues that storytelling by both teachers and children is not only enjoyable but 'plays a significant role in the development of children's oral [i.e. spoken] language. It contributes particularly to children's ability to use narratives [i.e. an account or a story] as a way of organising ideas and experiences' (p. 317). Mallett also offers numerous suggestions about appropriate texts and other ways to enhance and exploit storytelling for learning.

The majority of pupils listen attentively and remember what is said, though younger children in particular usually need help to grasp the fuller implications of a plot and teachers may use questions after the story ends to tease out key points, set children thinking and encourage speculation about the feelings experienced by the main characters and what might happen, which is particularly useful in history studies. Stories not only fire pupils' imaginations but also offer them models for living, alert them to avoid foolish decisions and might even inspire them to take action; for example, a story about the plight of deprived children can lead to fund-raising initiatives.

Egan (1986) argues that it is possible to abstract from the basic form of the story a framework that can then be used in teaching the content of any curricular area, be it mathematics, science, language arts or social studies. One result of using such an approach is that teachers come to see lessons and units as 'good stories to be told' rather than as sets of objectives to be attained. The author suggests that teachers might invest some of their planning energy into considering how features of the 'story form' might shape their lessons, which involves bringing to the forefront of consciousness the *emotional importance* of the content as well as its information content. Egan offers a framework within which a story can be used in this way:

1 *Identifying importance.* What is important about this topic? Why does it matter? What is affectively engaging about it?
2 *Finding binary opposites.* What binary opposites best express and articulate the importance of the topic? (Note: examples of 'binary opposites' include good/bad; hot/cold; cultured/wild.)
3 *Organising content in story form.* What content most dramatically articulates the binary opposites, in order to provide access to the topic? And what content best articulates the topic into a developing story form? (For example, heat can be beneficial or injurious, depending on its application.)
4 *Conclusion.* What is the best way to resolve the dramatic conflict inherent in these binary opposites? What degree of mediation of the opposites is it appropriate to seek? (For example, nuclear power is a source of energy and of highly destructive weapons. Again, air travel facilitates political and trade links but also pollutes the atmosphere.)
5 *Evaluation.* How can one know whether the topic has been understood, whether its importance has been grasped, and whether the content was learned?

Children usually have firm views about the kinds of stories they like and dislike (Hislam and Lall 2007). They talk with their friends about their favourite characters; they laugh freely at amusing tales; they sit spellbound during tense moments. Although pupils love to see the pictures in a book and will often ask the teacher to show them, some children react more positively to stories being told orally than being read from a book and are capable of repeating the story to friends and people at home with a surprising degree of accuracy, even embellishment. The reason for such enthusiasm lies in the fact that without the additional responsibility of holding the book, turning the pages and allowing younger

pupils to see the illustrations, oral storytelling allows the reader to use more eye contact and a greater range of facial expressions, hand movements and physical gestures than is possible when handling a book.

Sources

Amit Gandhi, J. (2008) *Telling Stories to Children*, on-line at http://ezinearticles.com/?Telling-Stories-to-Children&id=1145062
Duncan, D. (2009) *Teaching Children's Literature*, London: Routledge.
Egan, K. (1986) *Teaching as Story Telling: An alternative approach to teaching and curriculum in the elementary school*, Ontario: Althouse Press.
Hislam, J. and Lall, R. (2007) 'How oral story can develop creative thinking', in Moyles, J. (ed.) *Beginning Teaching, Beginning Learning*, Maidenhead: Open University Press.
Mallett, M. (2008) *The Primary English Encyclopedia*, London: Routledge.

SUBJECT LEADERSHIP

See also: collaboration (staff), communication, curriculum, effectiveness, excellent teachers, head teachers, professional development

All teachers in primary schools apart from newly qualified teachers are expected to be subject leaders, though sometimes a new teacher might volunteer to undertake a subject leadership role, especially in a small school. The role has changed from one of being a subject coordinator responsible for ordering resources and maintaining a general overview of what was being taught in the school to one of subject leader, actively managing the subject. Subject leaders have a role in helping to improve standards of teaching and learning throughout the school and involving other interested parties, notably parents. Bell and Ritchie (1999) note that the notion of a subject leader is not a new concept, tracing its development as far back as a Board of Education Handbook from 1905 through to the 1990s when the need for a whole-school perspective was identified by school inspectors. The authors also distinguish between the original preferred descriptor 'subject coordinator' and the present 'subject leader' by claiming that the latter term indicates a more proactive approach and a willingness to monitor and evaluate standards across the school with a view to promoting change. By contrast, the coordinator 'tends to imply a position that is passive and reactive to the responsibilities and opportunities that present themselves' (p. 10). In other words, effective subject leadership is intended to contribute to 'school improvement' (Buster *et al.* 2000).

The National Standards for Subject Leaders (TTA/TDA, on-line) state that subject leaders should aim to provide professional leadership and management for a subject (or area of work) and to secure high-quality teaching, effective use of resources and improved standards of learning and achievement for all pupils. The standards are in five parts:

1 core purpose of the subject leader
2 key outcomes of subject leadership
3 professional knowledge and understanding
4 skills and attributes
5 key areas of subject leadership.

Subject leaders are said to be effective if they possess a wide range of competencies, including:

- a high level of curriculum knowledge;
- ability to relate the subject to the curriculum as whole;
- a secure grasp of the strategic development needs of the school and the subject;
- model good practice for colleagues;
- lead staff by inspiring them to believe pupils can achieve better results;
- communicate effectively and build good relationships with staff, pupils and parents;
- know how to plan and implement change;
- manage resources effectively;
- monitor staff and pupil performance and give objective feedback whenever possible.

The stated aims of the standards claim to be designed to guide the professional development of teachers who are aiming to increase their effectiveness as subject leaders or those aspiring to take responsibility for doing so. While the standards apply to all schools, they need to be applied and implemented differently in schools of different type, size and phase. For example, they will need to be used selectively in smaller primary schools where head teachers may retain more of the defined roles than in larger primary schools where the head teacher does not need to be involved. Ideally, training and development for subject leadership should provide a good grounding in many of the leadership and management skills necessary to take on broader and more senior leadership and management roles at a later stage (see Dean 2003; Burton and Brundrett 2005).

Sources

Bell, D. and Ritchie, R. (1999) *Towards Effective Subject Leadership in the Primary School*, Maidenhead: Open University Press.

Burton, N. and Brundrett, M. (2005) *Leading the Curriculum in the Primary School*, London: Paul Chapman.

Buster, H., Harris, A. and Wise, C. (2000) *Subject Leadership and School Improvement*, London: Paul Chapman.

Dean, J. (2003) *Subject Leadership in the Primary School: A practical guide for curriculum coordinators*, London: David Fulton.

Routledge 'Subject Leadership' series, on-line at www.routledgefalmer.com/series/frameloader.html?http%3A//www.routledgefalmer.com/series/slh.asp

TTA/TDA: *National Standards for Subject Leaders*, on-line at www.tta.gov.uk/php/read.php?resourceid=1708

SUCCESS

See also: competition, feedback, happiness, motivation for learning, rewards, self-esteem (pupils), slow learners

Every educator wants children to succeed; defining success is, however, far from easy.

407

General definitions might include statements such as, 'when things turn out as well or better than expected' or 'achieving what you aim to do' or 'growing, developing, improving and getting better'. Pupils in school often equate success with the pleasant sensation of getting good grades, ticks on a page, commending comments or tangible rewards such as stickers and house points. Some children find fulfilment in completing a piece of academic work accurately; others in solving practical tasks; yet others in sealing and affirming personal friendships. Part of a teacher's job is to help children to appreciate that happiness and contentment can be created through small achievements: a letter shape correctly made for the first time; a thoughtful answer to a question; a valid contribution to a discussion; a helpful comment to a classmate; a creative and imaginative response to a task; perseverance in tracking down information, and so forth.

Effort alone does not guarantee success. One child works hard and achieves little; another makes minimum effort and achieves a lot. A teacher's attitude to each child will reveal a great deal about the criteria that the teacher is using to evaluate success; for example, praise for the latter and rebuke for the former will send a signal that attainment is singularly important as a measure. It is all too easy for teachers unintentionally to make children feel that their worth as a person is directly linked to their success in their schoolwork – brainy children are treasured; slow learners are tolerated. Some children like to experiment and do things in a non-conventional way. As a result, they make more mistakes than their conventional peers but enjoy a richer learning experience. Teachers have to be careful to credit children for showing initiative as well as achieving the correct results. It is said that the great inventor, Thomas Alva Edison, asked his teacher so many questions that the teacher became exasperated and Thomas was branded as 'impossible' and had to be taught at home.

His mother exposed him to books at a far higher level than anyone of his age, so that Edison's horizons of knowledge included subjects such as philosophy, English, and history. By the time he was aged eleven, he established his own laboratory in his basement and via this he would acquire yet more of his skills. Not bad going for a so-called 'school failure'! (See Guthridge 1986 for a straightforward account of Edison's childhood experiences.)

Perseverance is an important constituent in finding success and most children are willing to persevere with their work for one or more of three reasons: (a) to achieve something worthwhile for their own satisfaction, (b) to compete with their classmates, or (c) to please the teacher. Some children are strongly self-motivated and gain enormous satisfaction through achieving something by their own efforts. They show a relentless determination to do well and relish the opportunity to demonstrate their competence publicly. Some children are highly competitive and view every task as a challenge to outperform everyone else. It is not possible or desirable to prevent children from being single-minded and it can act as a spur to achievement; but if it becomes the dominating factor it can lead to an unhealthy situation in which individuals are vying with each other simply to complete work quickest or gain the best mark. The majority of children want to please their teachers; in the majority of cases this is because they like them; in a minority of cases because they fear them.

While it is obviously desirable for children to want to seek an adult's approval, it is even more important for a child to seek *self-fulfilment* – see an engaging and warm-hearted book for parents by Paul Zucker (1996). Adults therefore play an important part in encouraging children to feel proud of their achievements; to allow a degree of competitiveness without tolerating rancour; and to acknowledge their successes warmly and wholeheartedly. Osguthorpe and Osguthorpe

(2008) argue that education becomes exciting and successful when both learners and teachers accomplish what they previously thought to be impossible. Educators have the responsibility of creating new expectations for learners and infuse them with new energy and motivation by encouraging individuals to go beyond familiar goals and take manageable risks.

Teachers have to exercise fine judgement when offering feedback to children about their work and effort. At one level there is a need to explain to the child how the work can be improved. At another level there is a pressing need, especially with children who have experienced limited academic success in the past, to encourage, praise and celebrate achievement. Katz (1995) suggests that parents and teachers can strengthen and support a healthy sense of self-esteem in children in at least seven ways (amended list):

- Helping them to build healthy relationships with peers.
- Clarifying the educator's own values but accepting that others may differ.
- Offering them reassurance that adult support is unconditional.
- Appreciating, rather than merely praising their interests, and avoiding flattery.
- Offering them opportunities to face challenges as well as to have fun.
- Treating them respectfully, taking their views seriously and providing meaningful feedback.
- Helping them to cope with setbacks and use the knowledge they gain to advantage in the future.

Sources

Guthridge, S. (1986) *Thomas A. Edison: Young inventor*, New York: Aladdin Books (Simon & Schuster).

Katz, L.G. (1995) *How Can We Strengthen Children's Self-Esteem?* Illinois: ERIC Clearinghouse on Elementary and Early Childhood Education, on-line at www.kidsource.com

Osguthorpe, R.T. and Osguthorpe, L. (2008) *Choose to Learn*, Thousand Oaks CA: Corwin Press.

Zucker, P. (1996) *Loving Children, Loving Ourselves*, Canada: Global Life Enterprises.

SUITABILITY FOR TEACHING

See also: induction of new teachers, motivation for teaching, professionalism

The belief that it is possible to 'spot' a good teacher is deeply engrained in the profession; heads, induction tutors and governors quickly conclude whether a new teacher has a promising future. The influence of subjective opinions (as opposed to using set criteria) to assess a teacher's potential is relevant from the beginning of the training process. Thus, in determining whether candidates are suitable to begin training, interviewers have to make an initial assessment of their suitability with regard to whether someone has the academic and personal qualities to succeed, relate well to children and have the tenacity and temperament to cope with the continuous pressures of classroom life. See Connelly and Clandinin (1999) for a series of case studies about 'shaping a professional identity'.

Source

Connelly, F.M. and Clandinin, D.J. (eds) (1999) *Shaping a Professional Identity: Stories of educational practice*, New York: Teachers College Press.

SUMMATIVE ASSESSMENT

See also: assessing children's learning, assessment of learning, formative assessment, tests and testing

Assessments that take place at the end of a definable period of time such as the end of a day or half term or year are referred to as 'summative assessments' or the now favoured expression, 'assessment of learning' (AOL) if at the end of lessons. The outcomes from summative assessments are intended to confirm the teacher 's opinion of what children have learned and what progress has been made in different subject areas. Summative assessment may take the form of a written or verbal test carried out under specified conditions or a series of small tasks with which children have to engage in order to show their level of competence. The most significant type of summative assessment is through national tasks and tests, the results of which must be made available to the parents of each child. Some schools provide parents with the teacher's assessment of the children's progress in all the curriculum subjects once a year.

SUPERFICIAL LEARNING

See also: deep learning, spiral curriculum, writing

It is difficult to believe that pupils can spend years in school listening to the teacher, doing the work set for them and even gaining high grades or marks in formal tests, yet have only a superficial understanding of the areas of learning with which they have engaged. It is even possible for teachers to convince themselves that children are 'making good progress' when what is *really* happening is that they are complying with adults' wishes and completing tasks as requested – but never being immersed in learning. For instance, children may be taught how to compose and set out a formal letter to someone important, yet might fail to realise that the letter: (a) will be read by a 'real' person, (b) may be shared with others, (c) will have to be interpreted by the reader, and (d) may effect change, such as inducing a written or verbal response from the recipient. In this example, the technical ability to write and compose the letter can be achieved successfully (with the appropriate tick on a record sheet) but the implications have not been fully explored. Superficial learning must not be confused with cyclical learning ('spiral curriculum'), in which ideas are revisited in greater depth as children grow and mature.

SURE START

See under *Excellence in Cities*

SUSPENSION AND EXCLUSION

See also: attendance, behaviour, external agencies, home background and learning, home–school agreement, home schooling, misbehaviour, parental involvement

Kyriacou (2003) refers to three types of exclusions: (1) fixed-period – also known as 'suspensions'; (2) permanent – also known as 'expulsions'; and (3) hidden – involving an informal arrangement between school, pupil and parent. The main purpose of suspension is one of corrective support rather than punishing pupils for misbehaviour. Suspension allows pupils the time, under the supervision of their parent/guardians to reflect on their unacceptable behaviour, accept responsibility for the behaviour that led to the suspension and change their future behaviour to meet the expectations of the school. Expulsions from primary school are very infrequent.

Head teachers are extremely reluctant to exclude children from school for disciplinary offences (excessively bad behaviour) and initiate exclusion procedures for at least two reasons. First, it is perceived as a sign of failure on the school's part. Second, the procedures are lengthy and unsettling for all concerned. However, there are occasions when all other means of remedying a situation have been exhausted and the pupil in question poses a danger to others or is interfering with the education of the other pupils that removal from the situation is necessary. Reports of an increased number of attacks on teachers have been widely reported and there is a concern that an emphasis on 'rights' has led to a diminution in respect for authority generally, including teachers. Furthermore, there have been claims that the pressure on schools to raise academic attainment has contributed to the number of suspensions and exclusion

410

because there is less time to attend to the needs of disruptive individuals.

Short-term exclusion (suspension) might be during a lunchtime, when the child is not allowed on school property; at the end of the exclusion time period, the pupil must return to school. If a child is excluded or suspended from school for more than one day, the teacher normally sets work to avoid a situation of 'falling behind' In the case of a *permanent* exclusion, schools have a responsibility to provide pupils with an alternative education, through ensuring the child is registered at another school or being educated at home through the provisions of a Pupil Referral Unit or receiving other home tuition. Government figures suggest that children in the poorest parts of the country are much more likely to be excluded from primary school than those in wealthy areas. In poor areas, pupils as young as five years of age are receiving thousands more suspensions each year than children who live in the most affluent neighbourhoods.

Source

Kyriacou, C. (2003) *Helping Troubled Pupils*, London: Nelson Thornes.

SYNTHETIC PHONICS

See also: literacy, phonics, reading, spelling

Synthetic phonics comes from the concept of synthesising, putting together or blending. What is synthesised/put together/blended in reading are the sounds prompted by the letters on the page, so the process involves the development of phonemic awareness (phonemes are the smallest units of sound). As part of the decoding process, the reader learns up to forty-four phonemes and their related graphemes (the written symbols for the phoneme). One phoneme can be represented by various graphemes, e.g. 'oa', 'ow', 'ough'. This sort of complication is, of course, one of the reasons that the English language is so

difficult to learn to read and spell. The reader is expected to recognise each grapheme then sound out each phoneme in a word, building up through blending the sounds together to pronounce the word phonetically.

Johnston and Watson (2005) are often credited with drawing attention to the value of synthetic phonics in teaching reading and spelling when they presented the findings of a seven-year study in which they examined the effects of teaching synthetic phonics on literacy attainment. In an earlier publication (2004) they had found that five-year old children getting a supplementary synthetic phonics programme had better word reading, spelling and phonemic awareness skills than children receiving a supplementary analytic phonics programme. (See also Johnston and Watson 2007.) Some of the most popular synthetic approaches involve a highly systematic whole-class teaching programme started very early in a child's school career. The sounds and their corresponding written symbols are taught in quick succession, up to five or six sounds per week. A multi-sensory approach is included where children see the symbol, listen to the sound, say the sound and accompany this by doing an action. This multi-sensory approach appears to support most learners in remembering many of the sound–symbol relationships.

There is no one way that works best for the decoding or spelling of all words in the language for all learners and there are powerful arguments for the inclusion of both approaches in any teaching programme. Each approach involves and develops a different set of skills, each of which is important to achieve the effective and efficient development of reading and spelling. There is some evidence to suggest that boys can emulate girls at reading and even do better on some tests if they are taught using more traditional phonetics-based lessons, thereby stopping some children from needing special forms of schooling. It also seems the case that synthetic phonics suits children from disadvantaged backgrounds, as well as those from more affluent homes.

411

Sources

Johnston, R.S. and Watson, J.E. (2004) 'Accelerating the development of reading, spelling and phonemic awareness skills in initial readers', *Reading and Writing*, 17, 327–57.

——for the Scottish Executive (2005) *The Effects of Synthetic Phonics Teaching on Reading and Spelling Attainment*, issue 17, on-line at www.scotland.gov.uk/library5/education/ins17-00.asp

——(2007) *Teaching Synthetic Phonics*, Exeter: Learning Matters.

Learning and Teaching Scotland, *5–14 Curriculum: Synthetic v analytic phonics*, on-line at www.ltscotland.org.uk/5to14

T

TACTILE LEARNERS

See also: attention span, design and technology, kinaesthetic learning, motor skills

The tactile learning style is almost always associated with kinaesthetic learning because both styles involve bodily movement. However, the tactile style is more constrained and involves the sense of touch and fine motor movements, rather than the large, whole-body movements observed in the kinaesthetic learning style. Children who are disposed towards tactile learning often have difficulty learning simply by reading about the subject or sitting through a formal talk or being given a verbal explanation on how to perform a particular task without exploring how it works in practice. Instead, tactile learners benefit from opportunities where they can actually do something physically with the information they are to learn with activities such as art-related activities – drawing, painting and sculpting; constructing models ('design and technology'); designing diagrams and creating mind maps; collecting items such as rocks, flags, stamps; folk dancing, singing and rhythmic movements. The tactile learner absorbs information through the sense of touch and feeling. Children generally have good eye–hand coordination and can be described as having 'active fingers'. That is, they enjoy fiddling with parts of objects, manipulating things and generally dabbling. Younger children with a tactile disposition love activities like finger-painting and building models by fusing a variety of materials. Some tactile learners have a difficult time in school because they have a low attention span and cannot sit still or concentrate without moving for long periods of time, so tend to irritate teachers. As with all forms of learning, children's tendency towards the tactile means should not be taken to imply that they are unable to learn in other ways.

TALK

See also: collaboration in learning, communication, curiosity, debating, dialogue for learning, discussion, imagination, interaction, intervention, learning context, oracy, questions and questioning, rules, speculative questions, speech

Acquiring speech is probably the single most important skill that people need. Learning to talk helps children to make sense of the world, to ask for what they need and to socialise. Children gradually learn to adjust their language to the situation they are in; for example they talk differently to their parents from the way they do to their friends. When children start school most of them can say their name, age and (sometimes) their address; hold conversations with their friends and parents; ask lots of questions; talk about imaginary situations; confuse truth and make-believe; tell true and pretend stories; make

413

up pretend words; and use 'naughty' words for fun.

Although the vast majority of children arrive in school with the capacity to talk, discuss and contribute ideas, to ensure that talk is effective and useful for learning, they have to be taught how to speak meaningfully to one another and listen carefully to what others are saying. Such skills do not always come easily to younger children, who are often over-eager to express their own views and share their own ideas. By posing interesting and speculative questions, inviting children to think aloud and offering alternative explanations for events and phenomena, teachers gradually foster a more inquisitive attitude and thirst to discover more.

The importance of promoting speaking and listening in school ('oracy') has received close attention in recent years after being allocated a marginal position in the curriculum. For example a booklet produced by DfES (2003) promoted a more systematic approach to oral ('spoken') work by showing how objectives for speaking and listening can be built into a teaching programme. The booklet contains learning objectives for teaching speaking and listening from year 1 (5–6 year-olds) through to year 6 (10–11 year-olds), arranged by term and by year to guide planning and by 'strand' to highlight pupil progression. Concerns that children are unable to express themselves clearly have also been given greater urgency by studies that suggest that parents are talking less to their children at home due to working long hours and the isolating influence of television and electronic games. Three structured opportunities for talk are commonly used in primary schools: (1) dialogue (between two persons), (2) discussion (involving several persons), and (3) debate (a formal discussion with clear rules).

Although rules of grammar govern sentence structure, people often use forms of verbal shorthand when talking to each other on the assumption that the listener is capable of decoding the messages and accommodating them within their existing understanding.

Mercer (2000) draws attention to the fact that human beings possess a unique facility for joining up their minds in a sophisticated way that no other living things can match, so that most great achievements are arrived at by teams of people rather than by individuals. Throughout this complex social and intellectual process, children gradually come to acknowledge that views other than their own exist and understand that their own opinions and judgement are open to scrutiny and, perhaps, criticism. Within a collaborative problem-solving session or investigation, all forms of speaking can be accommodated within the group discussion; even the occasional frivolous comment can provide a useful diversion from the intensity of the formal exchanges and 'oil the wheels' of the talk. See Eke and Lee (2005) for a range of practical ways that teachers can develop their interactions with primary school pupils.

Adults have an obligation to socialise children into school culture and thereby marshal the discourse, decide who will speak and when and what about, as well as communicating acceptable forms of behaviour (Hobday-Kutsch and McVittie 2002). Contrarily, the prevailing school culture and even the physical environment ('learning context') can also constrain the way that the teacher speaks, acts and behaves; for instance, the head teacher may insist that classrooms are quiet and calm places, which a naturally extrovert teacher is likely to find difficult to maintain. Children also have to submit to adult expectations about speech and use of language, such that if children fail to understand or conform they may be labelled as troublesome and rebuked. In practice, there is a negotiation of power between pupils and other pupils, and between adults and pupils. If the teacher intervenes too much, the flow of conversation becomes fragmented; if intervention is minimal, the talk may stray too far from the intended topic or dissolve into a series of trivial comments (Black 2004). To make classroom talk purposeful, children must understand the rules for taking turns and offering their opinions and learn strategies for expressing ideas openly (see Myhill *et al.* 2006).

Sources

Black, L. (2004) 'Teacher–pupil talk in whole-class discussions and processes of social positioning within the primary school classroom', *Language and Education*, 18 (5), 347–60.

DfES (2003) *Speaking, Listening, Learning: Working with children in KS1 and KS2*, Annesley, Nottingham: DfES Publications.

Eke, R. and Lee, J. (2005) *Using Talk Effectively in the Primary Classroom*, London: Routledge.

Hobday-Kutsch and McVittie (2002) 'Just clowning around: Classroom perspectives on children's humour', *Canadian Journal of Education*, 27 (2/3), 195–210.

Mercer, N. (2000) *Words and Minds: How we use language to think together*, London: Routledge.

Myhill, D., Jones, S. and Hooper, R. (2006) *Talking, Listening, Learning: Effective talk in the primary classroom*, Maidenhead: Open University Press.

TARGET SETTING (ADULTS)

See also: professional development

Teachers employ targets as a means of monitoring their own professional development and addressing them through adjusting their teaching approach, gaining advice from colleagues and attending appropriate training courses. Targets tend to consist of immediate ones associated with success in classroom practice (as deemed by an observer) and end product ones in demonstrating long-term outcomes (as determined by formal test results). Teachers have to provide evidence of specific achievements (e.g. courses successfully completed) and contributions to school life (e.g. close liaison with parents) if they apply for salary enhancement or promotion.

TARGET SETTING (CHILDREN)

See also: achievement, aims of education, annual meeting, individual education plan, special educational needs, tests and testing

There are three sorts of targets commonly used in primary education. The first type is quantitative, relying on numerical data from test scores, both internal and external to the school. Bremner and Cartwright (2004) found in their research that target setting seemed to be valuable in contributing towards 'school improvement' but pointed out that pressure on pupils to achieve more highly could be detrimental if used to excess. The second type of target is qualitative, based principally on a teacher's subjective evaluation of pupils' work, together with factors such as behaviour. For example, the target might be for pupils to master the use of particular computer software concerning healthy diet; or to walk quietly inside the building. The third type of target is based on pupils' evaluations of their own progress and ways to improve it. These targets are internal to the classroom, negotiated between the teacher and pupil, and sometimes recorded formally by the teacher, though older children are encouraged to maintain their own records.

Primary schools in England are required to set aggregate targets for pupils' attainment in literacy and numeracy for children aged 7–11 years, write targets for pupils in their annual report to parents and produce targets for pupils with special educational needs as recorded in their Individual Education Plan (IEPs). Despite the ubiquitous presence of targets in education, it is fair to say that target setting is certainly not a panacea for the improvement of schools, as many other factors have to be considered (Hewett 1999).

Muschamp (1994) refers to the need to distinguish between 'long-term aims' and 'short-term targets'. She notes that the challenge of sharing the teacher's understanding and expectations with young children necessitates an examination of learning aims that would otherwise not necessarily occur. Short-term individual targets for learning are in addition to the general targets set by the teacher for the whole group or class. Wyse (2001) asserts that a focus on children's individual needs through formative assessment (i.e. evaluating children's present learning to inform future learning) and oral discourse is greatly beneficial for children as it involves them closely in the process, rather than being passive recipients.

All targets must be realistic, manageable and challenging, based on evidence of previous attainment and informed by regular assessment of attainment and gaps in knowledge. However, owing to the pressure of time, targets have to be very clear, simple, few and easily recorded, which can lead to them becoming oversimplified. The wording of the targets can also give a child the impression that they are teacher commands (things that must be done) rather than learning ambitions (things for which to aspire).

There are three other factors associated with effective target setting of which teachers have to take account. First, targets that are too general are difficult to monitor because it is hard to know when they have been achieved. Second, targets that are too specific tend to narrow children's perspectives and lead to rote learning. Third, some targets are more to do with improvement than with mastery. This third point is significant because the concept of lifelong learning implies that although there may be identifiable stages in the process, there is no ceiling to the extent of improvement. In fact, many aspects of learning for primary-age children involve 'getting better' rather than 'concluding the learning'. For example, all pupils need to persevere constantly to improve their spelling and presentation, so a target expressed as 'get better at spelling' is unsatisfactorily vague; a more helpful target would be to identify a specific set of words that have to be mastered by a given date.

Sources

Bremner, I. and Cartwright, D. (2004) 'Target setting in primary schools: The big squeeze', *Education 3–13*, 32 (1), 4–8.
Hewett, P. (1999) 'The role of target setting in school improvement', in Conner, C. (ed.) *Assessment in Action in the Primary School*, London: Routledge.

Muschamp, Y. (1994) 'Target-setting with young children', in Pollard, A. and Bourne, J. (eds) *Teaching and Learning in the Primary School*, London: Routledge/Open University Press.
Wyse, D. (2001) 'Promising yourself to do better? Target setting and literacy', *Education 3–13*, 29 (2), 13–18.

TAYLOR REPORT

See also: annual meeting, governing body, governors

During the 1970s and 1980s, a new role for parents and governors began taking shape. As an important element of this initiative, the Secretary of State for Education and Science and the Secretary of State for Wales jointly instigated an enquiry under the chairmanship of Mr Tom Taylor – subsequently popularly known as the 'Taylor Report' (DES/Welsh Office 1977). One of the key proposals made by the report was that parents serve as governors, a decision that was later formalised in the 1980 Education Act. The 1986 Education Act included the requirement for an annual meeting of parents with governors; the 1988 Act extended parent power through open enrolment – parents able to express a preference for the schools they wish their child to attend – and the opportunity for parents to vote for their school to leave local authority control and be funded centrally.

Source

DES/Welsh Office (1977) *A New Partnership for our Schools* ('The Taylor Report') London: HMSO.

TEACHER BEHAVIOUR

See also: General Teaching Councils, reputation of teachers

Society has high expectations of teachers. Although there are a variety of General Teaching Councils in England, Wales, Scotland and Northern Ireland to monitor and advise about appropriate standards of teacher behaviour, it is noteworthy that very few teachers are ever formally called to account for their actions. Although accusations against teachers from pupils and parents have increased over recent years, it is rare for one to be substantiated. From time to time a head teacher has to answer charges about financial irregularities or unfairly manipulating national tests, but such incidents are so uncommon as to make headline news. The numbers of teachers officially reprimanded, suspended indefinitely or dismissed from post remains extremely low.

TEACHER LEARNING ACADEMY

See also: coaching, General Teaching Councils, professional development, teaching skills

The Teacher Learning Academy (TLA) is led by the General Teaching Council for England (GTCE) and was created to help teachers improve their own classroom practice while gaining formal recognition for doing so. An important element of the GTCE is to improving professional learning opportunities for teachers, of which the TLA forms a part in providing them with a framework to test out a newly learned approach or skill within the classroom. The TLA is suitable for registered teachers at all levels of experience and aims to help teachers broaden their teaching skills 'on the job' by learning from peers and eventually sharing their findings with others in their own school and schools in their area. Teachers begin by identifying an area in their classroom or school where they want to bring about a change or improvement, then each teacher works with a colleague (the 'coach') to plan his or her 'learning journey'. The teacher uses the TLA framework to carry out a small-scale, classroom-based piece of research at the school or learning centre that offers insights into the chosen area of investigation. Teachers are invited to report on their findings and where possible share the results of their learning with a wider audience. Some schools have members of staff trained as TLA leaders or verifiers. Further details can be found on-line at www.teacherlearningacademy.org.uk

TEACHER–PUPIL INTERACTION

See also: answering questions, assessing children's learning, daydreaming, interaction, interactive whiteboard, mistakes and misconceptions, questions and questioning, relationships, teaching assistant

Ingersoll and Kleucker noted as far back as 1971 that teacher–pupil interaction is an integral part of most classroom instruction, whereby the teacher initiates an interaction by making a statement or by asking a question about the lesson, followed by a pupil response. The overarching purpose during active pupil–teacher interaction consists of two parts: first, to encourage well-regulated pupil involvement; second, to offer insights into pupils' understanding and grasp of issues. Dean (2001) provides a helpful summary of an effective teacher–pupil relationship:

> It is evident that the teacher likes children and enjoys their company, respecting them as individuals without dominating them. The ideas and suggestions they offer are received in a positive and encouraging way because the teacher has the ability to see things from the point of view of each individual child and is thus able to motivate children and match work to each one.
> (p. 248)

The ability to ask probing questions as a means of eliciting and encouraging responses from pupils is important in ascertaining the depth of a child's knowledge and understanding. It is a common experience that high-achieving children tend to dominate learning interactions, while underachievers are more likely to be passive, daydream or behave inappropriately. Pupil passivity does not create a climate for deep learning unless

417

accompanied by opportunities for children to grapple with issues and concepts in subsequent tasks and activities (Coultas 2007).

Adult–child interaction facilitates an assessment of pupil progress as well as inspiring interest and reinforcing learning. Judging the usefulness of pupils' responses depends partly on the adult's instinct and experience (i.e. exercising an ability to see beyond a child's words) and partly on the learning objectives (i.e. the extent to which the response is located within the parameters of the lesson purpose). In this regard the teaching assistant can be of considerable help as she or he watches the proceedings and makes notes about particular children's responses and actions, with particular reference to misconceptions and misunderstandings. After the lesson, the teacher and assistant discuss significant responses, which may require careful interpreting; for instance, a child who keeps thrusting a hand in the air may be indicating enthusiasm rather than exhibiting understanding or accurate knowledge.

In gauging the quality of pupils' responses, teachers take account of the fact that working closely with a *group* of children raises different issues from working with the *whole class* (see Baines *et al.* 2008). Group work is more intimate and intensive and tends to invite spontaneity, so teachers must make it clear to what extent they welcome such behaviour. They watch that children don't have their hands up for too long and look for other ways of eliciting a response other than an individual pupil answering, such as suggesting, 'whisper what you think to a friend' or giving an either/or and asking children to select from the options by using a simple voting technique.

Because interactive whiteboards (IWBs) are widely used as a pedagogic tool for promoting interactive whole-class teaching, Smith *et al.* (2006) set out to investigate their impact on teacher–pupil interaction in the teaching of literacy and numeracy with children aged 7–11 years of age. The project looked specifically at the interactive styles used by a national sample of primary teachers over a two-year period by observing 184 lessons. The findings suggest that IWBs have some impact on the extensiveness of teacher–pupil interaction in whole-class teaching but that this impact is not as extensive as that claimed by the advocates of the technology. Nevertheless, lessons that incorporate the use of IWBs go at a faster pace, with less time spent on group work and more on whole-class involvement.

In their in-depth study of what makes a good primary teacher, Gipps *et al.* (2000) reported how some primary teachers perceived that 'it was hard for some children to ask the teacher questions while other children were listening, for example in a whole class situation' (p. 143). Teachers aimed to ensure that pupils felt safe in that they did not fear being humiliated by the teacher or their classmates. The more lively and interactive the exchanges, the more chance that a few pupils will get overexcited and act or speak inappropriately. Teachers are usually willing to exchange a degree of orderliness for the benefits gained from the interaction and explain calmly why a particular attitude is unhelpful rather than becoming agitated and irritable.

Sources

Baines, E., Blatchford, P., Kutnick, P., Chowne, A., Berdondini, L. and Ota, C. (2008) *Promoting Effective Group Work in the Primary Classroom*, London: Routledge.

Coultas, V. (2007) *Constructive Talking in Challenging Classrooms*, London: Routledge.

Dean, J. (2001) *Organising Learning in the Primary School Classroom*, London: Routledge.

Gipps, C., McCallam, B. and Hargreaves, E. (2000) *What Makes a Good Primary School Teacher*, London: Routledge.

Ingersoll, G.M. and Kleucker, J. (1971) *Analysis of Teacher-Pupil Interaction: Reacting to pupil responses*, Washington DC: Office of Education (DHEW).

Smith, F., Hardman, F. and Higgins, S. (2006) 'The impact of interactive whiteboards on teacher-pupil interaction in the national literacy and numeracy strategies', *British Educational Research Journal*, 32 (3), 443–57.

TEACHER RETENTION

See also: motivation for teaching, workforce reforms

The retention of teachers is considerably more problematic than their recruitment; the number of teachers that withdraw during training or who qualify but fail to remain in teaching for more than a few years has created a considerable challenge for governments. Surveys carried out during the early years of the twenty-first century indicate that around one third of trainee teachers qualify but do not enter teaching; a further one fifth leave the profession within three years. In total, almost one half of new teachers leave the profession within five years, though the reasons are varied and many. A mismatch between the aspirations of teachers and the external demands placed on them is the most common reason offered for leaving. In particular, the plethora of paperwork tasks, the closely prescribed curriculum, scrutiny of teaching methods and the testing regime have been cited as principal reasons for disillusionment.

While legislators and politicians accept that primary teachers in particular have borne the brunt of new legislation in recent years, objections to the programme of change have generally been dismissed as a sign of teachers' unwillingness to embrace twenty-first-century realities. However Kivi (1998) was among those who warned at an early stage that 'any new initiative that involves more paperwork or extra commitment out of hours is doomed to fail' (p. 67), and advocated that all new initiatives should be presented with an estimate of how much extra work would be involved in their implementation. Such warnings were swept away in the hysteria of 'raising standards' and the then British prime minister's mantra of 'Education, education, education' during the late 1990s. Recent surveys of newly qualified teachers suggest that burdensome paperwork now ranks alongside pupil indiscipline as the principal cause of dissatisfaction. Gorard *et al.* (2006) provide a detailed treatment of issues relating to the recruitment, quality, training and retention of teachers throughout the developed world, with recommendations for the future. Menter *et al.* (2002) offer an in-depth analysis of projects designed to improve recruitment into the teaching profession in England, showing which are effective and why. Podsen (2002) suggests strategies for retaining teachers of different status and at different stages of their careers in the USA.

Sources

Gorard, S., Huat See, B , Smith, E. and White, P. (2006) *Teacher Supply: Key issues*, London: Continuum.

Kivi, M. (1998) *Take Care Mr Blunkett*, London: Association of Teachers and Lecturers.

Menter, I., Hutchings, M. and Ross, A. (eds) (2002) *Crisis in Teacher Supply: Research and strategies for retention*, Stoke-on-Trent: Trentham.

Podsen, I.J. (2002) *Teacher Retention: What is your weakest link?* Larchmont NY: Eye on Education Publishers.

TEACHER ROLE

See also: busyness, collaboration (staff), collegiality, health and safety, home–school, monitoring, motivation for teaching, planning, relationships, teaching assistants, time management

The teacher's role – more accurately, roles – has many facets but is dominated by functional aspects, including curriculum implementation, planning lessons, assessing pupil progress and compiling reports. Motivating factors such as altruism, compassion, love for children, and the fulfilment of working in a school environment sometimes have to be subordinated to these pragmatic concerns. For most practitioners, little more than a half of their time is spent actively teaching; the remainder is absorbed in attending meetings, administration and other school duties. A teacher also has to be influential beyond the classroom door in areas of personal relationships with

419

support staff, contact with parents and visitors, demonstrating initiative with respect to health and safety issues and being a positive presence around the school.

Six key influences affect a primary teacher's work. First, the intense pace of life in school, lack of opportunity for thoughtful reflection and the need to constantly prioritise tasks due to heavy workloads. Second, coping immediately with daily occurrences such as resolving disputes between pupils, responding to parental concerns, caring for injured children and carrying out running repairs on equipment. Third, offering support to colleagues in an effort to maintain staff harmony and promote collegiality. Fourth, the shortage of time to achieve all that needs to be accomplished, regardless of how long and hard they work. Fifth, owing to the busyness of school life, the disconnection and reduced opportunities for liaison with colleagues that sometimes occurs. Sixth, the organisational demands that result from the combined impact of meetings with colleagues, contacts with parents, harnessing and managing resources, planning the teaching programme, sorting out visits and special events and liaising with teachers in other schools.

All teachers exercise the role of guardian by setting and maintaining a rule framework, making their expectations about behaviour clear to pupils and encouraging them to accept responsibility for their own actions. Using 'teacher manner' as a proxy for the moral development activities of teachers, Fenstermacher (2001, 2004) emphasises that teachers have a responsibility to foster moral development in their classrooms. The social dimension of the teacher's role is crucial to success in developing a positive attitude by convincing children that they have more to gain than to lose by behaving well. The guardian role means dealing with infringements in a way that reflects their level of seriousness, anticipates potential sources of disruption and takes pre-emptive action, using sanctions according to agreed procedures rather than randomly. Teacher as guardian

also involves protecting weaker and more vulnerable children from harm (such as bullying) and helping them to develop strategies to become more self-sufficient and confident.

Despite the many other calls on their time, classroom teaching lies at the heart of teachers' work. All teachers have the considerable responsibility of helping pupils to process information in ways that will help them to develop both a range of intellectual skills – notably thinking strategies – and develop conceptual understanding around which children can organise new experiences and gradually grasp their implications. Pupils are expected to assimilate a wide range of information and knowledge, so adults in school have to help them to devise systems for organising and sorting it all for later retrieval and application to new situations.

Monitoring pupil progress has become an essential aspect of the teacher role. Every teacher has to become expert in diagnosing the extent of children's understanding, the areas where they lack comprehension and the best methods for remedying the situation. All monitoring depends on close observation of children, careful listening to what they say, and skilful questioning to gain insight into their beliefs and ideas. The best teachers don't merely discover where children's problems lie but also investigate why they have occurred and how to remedy them.

External demands issuing from central government and keeping pace with the latest initiative from education policy-makers have heaped responsibility onto teachers that can make it difficult for many of them to keep pace. The network of responsibilities that comprise the teacher role mean that the successful management of the multiplicity of demands requires teachers to be vigilant in evaluating and adjusting each day's differing priorities, while maintaining the regular timetable of teaching and associated duties. The variety of demands has also reduced some teachers to a state of permanent exhaustion and stress, exacerbated by studies that strongly point to the teacher himself or herself as the chief factor governing pupil progress (see Carlyle and Woods 2002; Woods and Jeffrey 2002). Nevertheless, the teacher role provides a considerable amount of personal and professional satisfaction in doing a job that nearly all primary teachers view as being worthwhile and making a difference to children's lives. See Day *et al.* (2007) and Hayes (2009, chapter 2) for an in-depth description of teachers' work and lives.

Sources

Carlyle, D. and Woods, P. (2002) *Emotions of Teacher Stress*, Stoke-on-Trent: Trentham Books.

Day, C., Sammons, P., Stobart, G., Kington, A. and Gu, Q. (2007) *Teachers Matter: Connecting work, lives and effectiveness*, London: McGraw-Hill International.

Fenstermacher, G.D. (2001) 'On the concept of manner and its visibility in teaching practice', *Journal of Curriculum Studies*, 33 (6), 639–53.

——(2004) 'The concept of manner and its visibility', in Wragg, E.C. (ed.) *The Routledge Reader in Teaching and Learning*, London: Routledge.

Hayes, D. (2009) *Primary Teaching Today*, London: Routledge.

Woods, P. and Jeffrey, B. (2002) 'Teacher identities under stress: The emotions of separation and renewal', *International Studies in Sociology of Education*, 23 (1), 89–106.

TEACHERS' BELIEFS

See also: child-centred education, children, motivation for teaching, play, teaching approach

An interesting insight into primary teachers' views of teaching was exposed by Taylor (2002) who found that out of a group of fifty-five experienced teachers, over 80 per cent of them opted for an approach that can be broadly defined as 'child-centred' (Doddington and Hilton 2007), defined as follows:

- Learning comes naturally to pupils.
- Children/students learn because they want to learn and not because they are told to do so.

- Play and work are indistinguishable.
- Learning is a communal activity rather than individual.
- The main aim of teaching is to develop the whole person (academic, social, spiritual).
- The curriculum should be related to the child's or student's needs.
- The teacher should encourage children to develop their own mode of learning.
(See p. 34)

Taylor notes that these beliefs are almost identical to those of primary teachers some twenty-five years earlier (citing Ashton *et al.* 1975). Only about one fifth of the teachers in Taylor's sample group aligned themselves with the prevailing government view encapsulated in an ideology that (a) learning is never easy; (b) children must be made to work; (c) play is not work; (d) learning is an individual thing; (e) the main aim of teaching is to develop the intellect; (f) the curriculum should relate to societal needs; and (g) the teacher's job is to motivate and direct learning. Instead, Taylor's findings about teachers' child-centred orientation reflect research carried out (for instance) among aspiring primary teachers in England by Hayes (2004) and secondary students in Australia (Manuel and Hughes 2006), who confirmed that *altruism* and a *desire to care for children* provided the most powerful incentives for a large majority of trainees to pursue teaching as a career. Indeed, Manuel and Hughes conclude that many prospective teachers enter teaching 'with a sense of mission to transform the lives of young people and open opportunities for growth through learning and connecting' (p. 21).

Sources

Ashton, P., Kneen, P. and Davies, F. (1975) *Aims into Practice in the Primary School*, London: Hodder and Stoughton.

Doddington, C. and Hilton, M. (2007) *Child-Centred Education*, London: Sage.

Hayes, D. (2004) 'Recruitment and retention: Insights into the motivation of primary trainee teachers in England', *Research in Education*, 71, 37–49.

Manuel, J. and Hughes, J. (2006) 'It has always been my dream: Exploring pre-service teachers' motivations for choosing to teach', *Teachers Development*, 10 (1), 5–24.

Taylor, P.H. (2002) 'Primary teachers' views of what helps and hinders teaching', *Education 3–13*, 31 (2), 34–39.

TEACHING APPROACH

See also: assessment of learning, child development, didactic teaching, discipline, discovery learning, discussion, effectiveness, enquiry, information technology, lesson review, motivation for learning, organising for learning, plenary, relationships, social and emotional aspects of learning, speed of work, target setting (pupils), teaching methods, teaching strategy

A teaching approach consists of the methods and strategies that teachers employ to help pupils learn effectively, and reflects the beliefs that they hold about the nature of education and learning. Every teaching approach is based upon an understanding of child development and also a grasp of learning theory and its practical implementation. The best teaching approaches provide for the flexibility to change a lesson's direction if it becomes apparent that this is necessary, accommodate the needs of faster and slower workers and draw the lesson or session to a satisfactory conclusion.

In determining what constitutes an appropriate teaching approach, the teacher has to determine whether, in striving to be effective, it is necessary to be authoritarian or autocratic, or to engender a sense of trust and familiarity and be a 'leading friend' to children. A teaching approach is not rigid (as with a teaching method) but allows for and accommodates changes in opinion over time and depending on the pupils being taught. Thus, one teacher may believe that pupils learn best when they are motivated by opportunities to explore ideas as a group, while another teacher may be convinced that they learn best when working alone with tasks closely targeted to their individual needs. One teacher may employ a considerable amount of direct teaching, utilising question-and-answer supported by repetition of facts, while another teacher employs a problem-solving method in which children are encouraged to raise their own questions and seek their own solutions. One teacher's style may be informal and strongly interactive, using humour and repartee, while another teacher might adopt a more detached approach, eschewing familiarity. Compare, for instance, the 'assertive discipline' approach advocated by Canter and Canter (2001) with the 'art of peaceful teaching' advocated by McGrath (2000).

Paterson and Escarte-Sarries (2003) noted from their interviews with classroom teachers that rather than emphasising simple 'one way' didactic practice, reciprocal communication was preferred, which relied on feedback or contributions from pupils. The attempt to 'negotiate understandings' and 'dig deeper into meaning' drew attention to 'the important link ... between reciprocal communication and the presence of an appropriate classroom climate or environment, and thus implicitly the social and emotional needs of pupils' (p. 90). Most primary teachers place considerable emphasis on their relationship with pupils as a way to enhance the quality of teaching and learning, but do so on the understanding that the ultimate arbiter is the adult, not the child. Although primary teachers are commonly heard to say that they want their pupils to be responsive and offer their own opinions, the pressure to cover the curriculum and achieve good test results (especially for older pupils) can hinder such aspirations.

One of the most marked ways in which teaching approaches differ is in the use of discipline. The best teachers speak naturally to children and not at them; take a sincere interest in what the children say; respond strongly when necessary but do not shout or humiliate a child; place explanation ahead of sanctions and publicly acknowledge good behaviour. Children are given space to grow and develop and encouraged to express doubts, uncertainties and reservations. Adults offer advice and suggestions and promote a learning ethos in which children are convinced that nothing is beyond their reach if they try hard enough. In this regard, an experienced and highly successful former primary head teacher in England, Sir David Winkley, compares a successful teaching approach to good jazz, claiming that good teaching is both structured and improvised, making use of the finest instruments and themes available, but deploying them in personal, original ways (Winkley 2002). Egan (2005) insists that stimulating learners' imaginations and emotions is a fundamental prerequisite to effective learning. However, the recommended teaching approaches relating to literacy have colonised other areas of teaching such that many lessons now follow a similar pattern: a teacher-led introduction to the whole class, followed by specific teaching; guided and independent tasks for groups of children; and a summary of key lesson points in the lesson review (so-called 'plenary').

Adopting a teaching approach also involves fundamental questions about classroom organisation and class management. At one level teachers find that it pays to teach the whole class together as much as possible, as it saves time and avoids the need to repeat the same set of instructions and explanations to different groups of children. On the other hand the wide ability range and maturity level within a class means that teachers need constantly to be sensitive to the differences that exist in pupils' concentration span, grasp of concepts, vocabulary and previous learning experiences. Consequently, teachers normally use a mixture of whole-class, group work and individual work according to circumstances and what they are seeking to achieve. Ultimately, all teachers have to respond to the individual needs of children, but for organisational purposes they tend to group pupils in ways that facilitate ease of working. In English and mathematics the grouping is normally on the basis of pupil attainment. In other subjects it is on a social or practical basis (such as access to resources).

Teachers of younger and older primary children tend to adopt a different teaching approach. Teachers of young children rely a lot on visual images, story, repetition and guidance during closely monitored task completion; the very youngest children are provided with plenty of opportunities to play. Pupils are encouraged to explore, investigate and experiment with tangible objects, such as building materials ('discovery learning'). As children go up through the school, teachers use more direct whole-class teaching, question and answer, information technology and class discussion. Pupils are encouraged to grapple with and think deeply about issues, dilemmas and problems. Tasks tend to be used as a means of ascertaining pupil understanding through end-loaded assessment (assessment of learning, AOL). Older children are also more likely to be involved with the teacher in establishing their own targets for learning.

Sources

Canter, L. and Canter, M. (2001) *Assertive Discipline*, Santa Monica CA: Canter & Associates.

Egan, K. (2005) *An Imaginative Approach to Teaching*, San Francisco CA: Jossey-Bass.

McGrath, M. (2000) *The Art of Peaceful Teaching in the Primary School*, London: David Fulton.

Paterson, F. and Escarte-Sarries, V. (2003) 'Digging deeper: A typology of interactive teaching', in Moyles, J., Hargreaves, L., Merry, R., Paterson, F. and Escarte-Sarries, V. *Interactive Teaching in the Primary School*, Maidenhead: Open University.

Winkley, D. (2002) *Handsworth Revolution: The odyssey of a school*, London: Giles de la Mare.

TEACHING ASSISTANTS

See also: coaching, educational visits, higher-level teaching assistants, learning support assistant, planning, reading, reading recovery, statementing, workforce reforms

There has been a considerable expansion in the use of teaching assistants (TAs) in primary schools over recent years. TAs have been employed in larger primary schools over many years for general duties but they are gradually assuming more responsibility for pupils' learning, and the large increase in their numbers is to support the work of class teachers in boosting standards of achievement. Employment of TAs is intended to lead to more flexible models of teaching and learning. Being freed from more routine tasks means that teachers can concentrate on the more specialised elements of their role, especially the planning, preparation and assessment (referred to as PPA time) of pupils' learning. The application of this strategy necessitates that assistants are suitable trained to ensure that they possess the appropriate skills to complement the work of teachers (see Kerry 2005).

Adult assistants can be used in one or more of seven ways in primary school: (1) being involved as a genuine participant in pupils' activities; (2) as a detached observer of how pupils cope with tasks; (3) as a scribe for pupils who struggle with writing; (4) doing a variety of menial tasks; (5) checking what pupils are doing; (6) listening to what pupils want to read to them, tell them about and discuss; and (7) helping pupils to review their work. Typically, the regular responsibilities for a full-time teaching assistant include:

- Hearing children read orally and maintaining reading records.
- Assisting with a maths extension group.
- Working one-to-one with identified children.
- Mounting and displaying children's work around the room and corridor.
- Producing some resources for teaching as requested by the class teacher.
- Taking children to the library to select books and other general library duties.
- Assisting the teacher when children are moving around the school and being taken outside the premises.
- Keeping accident report records and overseeing health and safety requirements.

- Designing and producing scenery for school plays.
- The collection and distribution of refreshments, including drinking water.
- Voluntarily running an after-school craft club.

Some teaching assistants are responsible for the needs of one child, for whom the title *learning support assistant* (LSA) was frequently used in the past. However, assistants are now graded as a TA or as a higher-level teaching assistant (HLTA), so labels like LSA tend to be associated with their role rather than their status. HLTAs in particular are likely to work more closely with the teacher with respect to teaching and learning, though all adult assistants can be used in one or more of a variety of ways (Burnham 2006). *Special needs assistants* are also subsumed under the general title of 'learning support assistant' and undertake a specialist role in working alongside children whose learning needs are sufficiently acute to have been formally identified through a 'statementing' procedure that involves the parents, school, educational psychologist and local education authority (see McVittie 2005). The statement is a formal document in which the child's needs and an action plan to support these needs are identified. However, the concept of a TA clinging to a single needy child throughout the day is becoming outmoded; rather, the child works intensively with an adult for short periods of time, either inside or outside the main classroom base.

Although assistants have a job description and hold their own clear view of what they are and are not prepared to do, it is up to the teacher to be specific about expectations from day to day, and from session to session. The need for clarity is especially relevant in early years' classes where additional adult support is often interwoven into the fabric of the teaching day. With older children the TA may be involved in intensive coaching of children who have fallen behind or struggling; they may be allocated to supervise a group of children and guide them in task completion.

Whatever the specific responsibility, the principle of a teacher working closely with the TA and valuing her expertise is fundamental to a healthy working environment. One of the quickest ways to damage a TA's dedication is to make unjustified assumptions about her capability and level of responsibility or to take advantage of her goodwill (see contributors to Hancock and Collins 2005).

Suitably skilled TAs might be involved in assisting with using information technology, providing 'reading recovery' or even acting as counsellor in conjunction with the school's child advocate – the named person responsible for dealing with children who wish to share a particular concern or grievance, especially if it concerns an adult. It is a poor use of a TA's time to wash paintbrushes when she could (say) be leading a group of able children in mathematical problem solving.

Increasingly all paid assistants possess a qualification and nearly all attend additional in-service courses to develop their expertise (see Watkinson 2003a, 2003b; Cousins *et al.* 2004). However, for those assistants wishing to pursue further study there are career routes into teaching; indeed, it is estimated that about 10 per cent of teaching assistants are trained teachers. The need for developing expertise becomes even more essential when higher-level teaching assistants (HLTAs) take responsibility for teaching a group of children or even the whole class under the general guidance of the teacher. See for example, Rose 2005; Cullingford-Agnew 2006. However, in assuming greater responsibility, part of their essential skills' training is to gain more experience in behaviour management for those occasions when they are directly responsible for a group of children or the whole class (Bentham 2005). Teaching assistants also have an important role in supporting the teacher during additional learning opportunities, such as the visit of a theatre company, outdoor pursuits, educational trips and school productions.

Detailed information can be found through Teaching-Assistants.co.uk, a web site dedicated to those working as TAs and those who may seek to recruit and employ them, such as recruitment agencies, schools, nurseries and after-school clubs (www.teaching-assistants.co.uk).

Sources

Bentham, S. (2005) *Teaching Assistants' Guide to Managing Classroom Behaviour*, London: Routledge.

Burnham, L. (2006) *101 Essential Lists for Teaching Assistants*, London: Continuum.

Cousins, L., Higgs, M. and Leader, J. (2004) *Making the Most of your Teaching Assistants*, London: PfP.

Cullingford-Agnew, S. (2006) *Becoming a Higher Level Teaching Assistant: Primary SEN*, Exeter: Learning Matters.

Hancock, R. and Collins, J. (eds) (2005) *Primary Teaching Assistants*, London: David Fulton.

Kerry, T. (2005) 'Towards a typology for conceptualising the roles of teaching assistants', *Educational Review*, 57 (3), 373–84.

McVittie, E. (2005) 'The role of the teaching assistant', *Education 3–13*, 33 (3), 26–31.

Rose, R. (2005) *Becoming a Primary Higher Level Teaching Assistant: Meeting the HLTA standards*, Exeter: Learning Matters.

Watkinson, A. (2003a) *The Essential Guide for Competent Teaching Assistants*, London: David Fulton.

——(2003b) *The Essential Guide for Experienced Teaching Assistants*, London: David Fulton.

TEACHING METHODS

See also: discovery learning, feedback, instruction, mistakes and misconceptions, reading scheme, visual learning

Teaching methods are concerned with the principles of instruction in educating or activities that impart knowledge or skill. The use of the word 'method' implies that there is a specific and systematic way of doing something that involves an orderly logical arrangement, usually in identifiable steps. Pupils are expected to master the information and specific outcomes are attached to each step or stage of the instruction process at roughly equivalent levels. Teachers break down course material into manageable units and create formative tests for pupils to take on

425

completion of each of the units. It is likely that such teachers follow the textbook and curriculum to the letter; they avoid prompting discussion by asking questions and guiding pupils to understanding. A teaching method is unlikely to favour learning by 'doing' (i.e. discovery learning) and places more emphasis on visual means (use of pictures, diagrams, etc.) and auditory means (pupils learn by listening).

In Bloom's model (Bloom 1976), teaching method is based on the premise that learners receive individualised instruction as appropriate, so they all master the course material. However, Keller's *Personalised System of Instruction* or PSI (Keller 1968) has four distinguishing characteristics. First, instead of presenting information orally, teachers select and/or create appropriate reading materials, learning objectives and study questions, and prepare multiple forms of tests to measure progress and provide feedback. Second, pupils finish assignments at their own pace, stemming from a recognition that people learn at different rates. Third, pupils must demonstrate mastery in tests or correct deficiencies before they move on to the next stage in their work. Finally, resources are devoted specifically to helping pupils deal with their identified learning needs, whether lack of knowledge, misconceptions or misunderstandings. The first, third and fourth characteristic are reflected in many externally imposed requirements about acceptable teaching methods; however, the second characteristic (finishing at own pace) is constrained by the rigidity of set lesson times. A teaching method is most likely to be used by primary educators with regard to something like an early years reading scheme in which mastery of the word content of one book is necessary before progressing to the next book in the series. Similarly, children may be given systematic instruction about the use of technology software.

Sources

Bloom, B. (1976) *Human Characteristics and School Learning*, New York: McGraw-Hill.

Keller, F. (1968) 'Goodbye teacher ... ', *Journal of Applied Behaviour Analysis*, 1, 79–89.

TEACHING PROFESSION

See also: General Teaching Councils, professional development, professionalism

Ornstein (1977) suggests that for a job to be called a profession it requires a defined body of knowledge that is beyond the grasp of people outside the job; control over licensing standards and/or entry requirements; autonomy in making decisions about selected spheres of work; and high prestige and economic standing. Teachers have long held that the job is a profession in much the same way as (say) a lawyer or a doctor; however, primary teachers have had more of a struggle than secondary teachers to be accepted as 'professionals' for two principal reasons: (1) because they deal with young children, who are viewed as 'easier' to educate than older pupils; and (2) there is a blurring of subject boundaries in the primary curriculum and teachers are not identified as 'subject experts' in the same way as, for instance, a specialist geography teacher in a secondary school might be. It was only during the second half of the twentieth century that primary teachers received pay and merit awards on an equal basis to their secondary colleagues; nursery and 'foundation' teachers of children five years of age and under were not regarded as 'real teachers' until relatively recently. There are still anomalies existing in terms of status and promotion opportunities, but governments of all persuasions have been keen to foster the belief that all teachers are professionals. Sceptics claim that such enthusiasm is more a means of exercising control than admiration, expressed through the dictum that 'a true professional conforms to the system and priorities that we promote', which effectively suppresses individuality and silences dissent (see, for example, Richards 2001; Silcock 2002).

Gordon *et al.* (1983) and commentators such as Kizlick (on-line) suggest that professions are occupationally related social institutions established and maintained as a means of providing essential services to the individual and the society – an identifiable characteristic of teaching. Other characteristics of being a profession include concern with an identified area of need or function; possessing a body of knowledge and a repertoire of behaviours and skills; and the fact that members of the profession are involved in decision-making on behalf of the client – in the case of teachers, on behalf of pupils and parents.

The profession must be based on one or more undergirding disciplines (e.g. child development in the case of teachers) from which it builds its own applied knowledge and skills; organised into one or more professional associations that within broad limits of social accountability are granted autonomy in their work and the conditions that surround it – most commentators would agree that primary teachers have less autonomy than in previous generations. Systems must exist for the preparation for and induction into the profession – again, strongly evident in teaching. There are also General Teaching Councils for each country of the UK to monitor and help to maintain professional standards.

There must be a high level of public trust and confidence in the profession and in individual practitioners, who are characterised by a strong service motivation and lifetime commitment to competence – as witnessed by teachers' continuous professional development (CPD). There should be relative freedom from direct on-the-job supervision and from direct public evaluation of the individual practitioner – clearly the high level of scrutiny under which teachers are placed does not accord with this point. Remuneration should reflect the level of job demands and responsibilities and forms of professional knowledge required to successfully fulfil the various roles associated with the job – teaching is reasonably well paid at higher levels of responsibility.

In the UK the increase in teaching assistants to relieve teachers of various repetitive and routine tasks has sharpened the focus of 'professional' to refer to someone who plans, teaches, assesses and records pupil progress to ensure that children are making optimum progress, both academically and socially. In the twenty-first century, arguments about whether primary teaching is a profession have been superseded by questions about the characteristics of effective/good teachers and school improvement with respect to national test and examination results.

Sources

Gordon, P., Perkin, H., Sockett, H. and Hoyle, E. (1983) *Is Teaching a Profession?* Bedford Way Papers 15, London: Institute of Education.

Kizlick, B. 'Characteristics of a profession', on-line at www.adprima.com/profession.htm

Ornstein, A.C. (1977) 'Characteristics of the teaching profession', *Illinois Schools Journal*, 56 (4), 12–21.

Richards, C. (ed.) (2001) *Changing English Primary Education: Retrospect and prospect*, Stoke-on-Trent: Trentham.

Silcock, P. (2002) 'Under construction or facing demolition? Contrasting views on English teacher professionalism from across a professional association', *Teacher Development*, 6 (2), 137–55.

TEACHING SKILLS

See also: answering questions, discipline, interactive teaching, questions and questioning, rules, teacher–pupil interaction, visual aids

Kyriacou (1998) claims that developing skills as a teacher is as much about developing and extending the *type* of decisions made about teaching as about executing them. He suggests that teaching skills can usefully be considered in terms of three key features:

- they involve purposeful and goal-directed behaviour;
- their level of expertise is evidenced by the display of precision, smoothness and sensitivity to context;

427

- they can be improved by training and practice.

(See p. 2).

Teachers have to be clear about the appropriate teaching skills to employ for each occasion, though these intentions have to be tempered by a willingness to modify them in the light of what takes place during the session. Direct transmission teaching (DTT) involves imparting knowledge and understanding to pupils. How successfully this transmission is achieved depends upon teachers presenting the information in an orderly manner, using appropriate vocabulary, engaging the children by using varied tones of voice and speed of delivery, and employing visual aids where appropriate.

A second teaching skill is interactive transmission teaching (ITT) that is also based on direct transmission of information but includes interludes for interactive questions and answers with children. ITT is a more difficult teaching skill than DTT because the teacher has to switch between imparting information and handling pupils' answers as they respond to the questions that arise. Good teachers make sure that children can distinguish between genuine questions and rhetorical (think aloud) questions that do not require a response from them. Without such safeguards teachers have to handle a large number of unsolicited answers, especially from younger pupils.

The third teaching skill that teachers employ is participative teaching (PT) where they encourage active pupil participation, not only in answering questions but also in providing insights, suggestions and examples. PT requires a considerable amount of teaching skill because it provides the most opportunities for disorder, as pupils may not possess the experience or self-discipline to wait for their turn, listen to the ideas of classmates and maintain a suitable noise level. Teachers have to work hard to clarify the rules about when and how the pupils can make contributions and how they should respond courteously to the views of others.

Regardless of the skills involved, teachers have to take account of pupils' abilities, experience and speed of working, offering them the opportunities to employ familiar skills in different learning contexts or to grapple with relevant and challenging new ones. If pupils are asked to investigate or solve problems, the range of skills has to be identified beforehand by the teacher to ensure that pupils can make an earnest attempt to tackle the challenge without being hampered by ignorance of the skills needed to succeed. For example, if pupils were asked to produce designs for a proposed school garden, they would need to be equipped with skills that enabled them to plan, draw and measure, and the thinking skills necessary to envisage possibilities, in addition to knowledge of plants and soil conditions. See Watkin and Ahrenfelt (2006) for ideas about teaching skills needed to design challenging lessons, keep pupils interested and on-task, and organise teaching in order to control challenging behaviour.

Sources

Kyriacou, C. (1998) *Essential Teaching Skills*, Cheltenham: Nelson Thornes.
Watkin, N. and Ahrenfelt, J. (2006) *100 Ideas for Essential Teaching Skills*, London: Continuum.

TEACHING STANCE

See also: health and safety (adults), learning climate, learning context, physical comfort

Maintaining a set position from which to speak to the children is useful in that it gives them a single focal point on which to concentrate and does not cause any distractions that constant movement back and forth tends to invite (the 'tennis match' syndrome). At the other extreme, a rigid pose does little to transmit a message to the children that the lesson is going to be exciting or worthy of close attention. By deliberately changing physical position and occasionally adopting a fresh stance, however, teachers are encouraging pupils to follow their movements closely and this will help to keep them on their toes. If the change of position is accompanied by a slight adjustment to another feature of the physical environment (such as adjusting the position of a chair), the impact on children's concentration levels is even more pronounced. Speaking from the back of the class when pupils are looking ahead is a powerful strategy in helping to maintain an orderly learning climate; however, the use of technology in teaching sometimes means that the teacher is obliged to remain close to the controls for practical and safety reasons.

TEACHING STRATEGY

See also: attention span, body language, discipline, interactive teaching, learning contexts, motivation for learning, professional development, speech, teacher–pupil interaction, teaching skills

A teaching strategy is a device for employing teaching skills effectively. For instance, the skill of maintaining attention may involve strategies such as using pauses; engaging children in the lesson might involve use of a familiar example from the children's experience; explanation of learning objectives might involve translating the formal language of a textbook into child-friendly terms. Again, achieving quality of voice might incorporate the strategy of lowering the voice to a whisper or increasing the volume; articulation can be varied by deliberately stressing consonants; eye contact may vary from narrow eyes to wide eyes; one-to-one adult–child contact may involve physically moving slowly towards the child in a non-threatening way. A strategy to make better use of tangible visual apparatus might include selecting different children to hold the item; introducing a 'surprise' photograph may enhance use of technology; a teaching assistant can be asked to select children to answer questions, and so on.

Teachers use various strategies to maintain discipline and motivate children. They use systems of rewards for those who try hard and exceed expectations; they also use a variety of sanctions for pupils who refuse to attend to their work or behave inappropriately. For instance, if children become restless, one teacher may use the technique of making them read in silence or institute a few minutes of shared reading (in unison) or chanting a well-known rhyme to restore order, while another teacher might choose to use a short physical activity to act as a diversion and then quickly direct pupils back to work. Experienced teachers learn which techniques are most effective and can pass them on to colleagues, though every teacher has to find what works best for him or her with the children.

A lot of in-service training (also referred to as continuous professional development, CPD) courses and workshops that teachers attend offer strategies (colloquially known as 'tips') – activities and actions – that teachers can use to achieve certain goals in the classroom. In recent years there has been more emphasis on promoting strategies that are supported by research evidence rather than teacher instinct and hard-won experience. Even so, researchers do not always agree on what is efficacious, so teachers are still left to determine the best strategies for the learning contexts in which they are situated. Governments of all persuasions are keen to offer 'advice' about teaching strategies, though when teachers are alerted to these 'recommendations', they usually interpret them as requirements and incorporate them into their practice – few teachers have the confidence to do otherwise.

TEAMWORK

See under *Collaboration in learning, Collaboration (staff),* and *Collaborative problem solving*

TELEVISION

See also: attention span, communication, fantasy, home background and learning, imagination, interaction, literacy, mathematics, modelling behaviour, play

Television (TV) is used in nearly all primary schools to transmit knowledge and information, expose children to a variety of social contexts and develop literacy and mathematical concepts (Huston 1992). The provision of sounds, images and narratives from different perspectives, especially those beyond the child's immediate world, has the capacity to liberate and empower pupils. Children may view the programme in their own classrooms or in a room dedicated to that purpose. Some schools use TV programmes in conjunction with other technologies.

The idea that television can educate effectively is subject to considerable debate and scrutiny. Five reasons have been proffered to support a negative view of television's educational influence (Casey *et al.* 2002). First, TV is largely perceived as recreational and not educational. Second, TV viewing is considered to be a passive activity, requiring minimal intellectual engagement. Third, TV consists of a one-way flow of information; the child has little or no control over its pace and delivery. Fourth, TV depends largely on oral and visual modes and neglects the printed word. Finally, TV productions edit and reorganise material and, in doing so, deprive children of the skills attached to making decisions about extracting, prioritising and organising complex information so as to be manageable. Some programme makers have responded to this kind of criticism by introducing ways in which children can interact with the content, respond to points (perhaps using IT) and develop ideas in class.

A fifteen-year longitudinal study by Huesmann *et al.* (2003) about children's viewing of violent TV showed that their identification with aggressive same-sex TV characters and their perceptions that TV violence is realistic were all linked to later aggression as young adults, for both males and females. The authors claim that these findings hold true for any child from any family, regardless of the child's initial aggression levels, their intellectual capabilities, their social status as measured by their parents' education or occupation, their parents' aggressiveness or the mother's and father's parenting styles. Other studies offer a different perspective about the impact of the media on behaviour; nevertheless, there are concerns that children model themselves more readily on fantasy characters than on other adults. Small children who are still learning to discriminate between fact and fantasy will sometimes confuse the two states and bring inappropriate behaviour into the classroom. The extent to which children model themselves on different adults (parents, friends, teachers, celebrities, heroes and so on) is far from clear; the only certainty is that every adult has a degree of influence on children and should be constantly aware of this responsibility.

In *Selling Out America's Children*, Walsh (1995) examined the extent to which essential morals and values were absent in young people. He noted that in the days before television and video games, children learned primarily by observing and imitating parents, other family members and members of the community. By contrast, television and video games have become more prevalent in our society over the past few decades and many children spend more time watching television and playing video games than reading, playing or communicating on one-on-one basis with their parents. Consequently, much of what children are learning comes through the media, notably television; teachers and parents have the difficult task of protecting children from the potentially harmful effects of TV viewing without depriving them of the undoubted exposure to ideas and information that TV makes available.

Media can be entertaining and educational; however, the goal is not principally to raise or educate the nation's young people but rather to make money by holding the viewer's attention and keeping them absorbed in the programme until the next commercial break, including the use of violence, sexual innuendo and humour. It has also been estimated that children witness an average of 200,000 acts of violence on television before they are eighteen years old. Though watching acts of violence and committing them are two different things, studies indicate that there may be a connection between violent entertainment and antisocial behaviour, which has obvious implications for maintaining a stable environment in schools and other learning centres (Ozmert *et al.* 2002).

In an interesting study of nine- and ten-year-old German children by Heins *et al.* (2007), 28 per cent reported going to bed after 9 p.m. on week nights; 16 per cent reported watching television for more than three hours daily; and 11 per cent played computer or video games for more than three hours daily. Assuming that primary schoolchildren need to be awake at 7 a.m. on weekdays, only one in four of the children had a full ten hours sleep on weekdays. Such lifestyle factors were considered to be negative influences on their present development and future habits. The authors of the research concluded that the need for children to enjoy sufficient sleep necessitates less television viewing and computer leisure time. Furthermore, parents and guardians of primary school pupils need to be made more aware that the consequences of lack of sleep include diminished school performance.

Sources

Casey, B., Casey, N., Calvert, B., French, L. and Lewis, J. (2002) *Television Studies: Key concepts*, London: Routledge.

Heins, E., Seitz, C., Schüz, J., Toschke, A.M., Harth, K., Letzel, S. and Böhler, E. (2007) 'Bedtime, television and computer habits of primary children in Germany', *Gesundheitswesen*, 69 (3), 151–57.

Huesmann, L.R., Moise-Titus, J., Podolski, C.L. and Eron, L.D. (2003) 'Longitudinal relations between children's exposure to TV violence and their aggressive and violent behaviour in young adulthood', *Developmental Psychology*, 39 (2), 201–21.

Huston, A. (1992) *Popular Television and Film*, London: BFI/Open University Press.

Ozmert, E., Toyran, M. and Yurdakok, K. (2002) 'Behavioural correlates of television viewing in primary school children evaluated by the child behaviour', on-line at www.archpediatrics.com

Walsh, D. (1995) *Selling Out America's Children*, Fairview TN: Fairview Publishers.

TESTS AND TESTING

See also: ability, creativity, effectiveness, English, inspections, key stages, mathematics, political involvement, SATs, science, teachers' beliefs

A regime of testing has emerged in recent years whereby pupils' knowledge and understanding has been closely scrutinised and teachers' efficiency has been measured in terms of examination outcomes. One outcome has been that the primary curriculum has become more narrowly focused in a bid to raise attainment scores in mathematics and English. There is ample evidence to show that this emphasis has been at the expense of more creative and innovative approaches. Nevertheless, it is argued that when used carefully and appropriately, testing has the potential to stimulate greater effort and be useful for measuring the effectiveness of teaching.

Nearly all primary-age pupils in mainstream schools in England are required to undertake national tests during year 6 (aged 10–11 years). The tests are popularly referred to as SATs, based on the concept of a standard assessment task when national testing was first introduced in the early 1990s. However, they are more correctly referred to as National Curriculum tests, NCTs, though the acronym is rarely used. A few children are exempt from the requirement to take SATs because of their exceptional learning difficulties.

In England children were also formally tested at 7 years of age at the end of key stage 1 (KS1) in year 2. However, since 2005, teachers' own judgements of how pupils are progressing form the principal source of evidence. Children still sit the KS1 National Curriculum tests in English and maths, but not at a fixed time and with an emphasis on work that is carried out throughout the year. Key stage 1 national tests in English and mathmatics are marked within each school and each school's results are then made available locally. By contrast, key stage 2 (KS2) national tests in English, maths and (until 2010) science are marked externally and the school's results are published nationally. In a few areas, tests of various types for those seeking grammar school places are marked externally but the results are kept confidential. Key stage 2 national tests in English and Welsh, maths and science became optional in Wales between 2002 and 2005, though new skills tests in numeracy, literacy and problem solving became mandatory from 2008.

In Northern Ireland, transfer tests in English or Irish, maths and science and technology for those seeking grammar school places were marked externally and the results kept private; however, these tests ended 2008. In Scotland, national tests in English and maths are given, corresponding roughly to key stages 1, 2 and 3 (age 14 years). Pupils are tested at the discretion of teachers when they consider the children ready. However, unlike the system in England, the tests are marked internally and the results are not made known publicly.

The results of the KS2 tests in England contribute to national league tables of school performance; however, many head teachers strongly oppose the enormous significance attached to them with regard to a school's reputation, teachers' morale and future scrutiny from inspectors. Although parents undoubtedly take a great interest in the position in the table of local schools, numerous surveys suggest that many parents feel that their children are under too much stress because of the excessive numbers of tests, the accompanying expansion of homework and the impact of schoolwork on family life. Others argue that the tests, while imperfect, provide the fairest means for parents to compare schools and show whether a school is providing children with a good education.

An article in the *Independent* newspaper (8 February 2008) commenting on preliminary findings from the Primary Review (chaired by Robin Alexander) that were highly critical of the 'testing regime' in England, suggested that the heart of the problem is the fact that the testing culture appeared to be politically, rather than educationally, driven. Government ministers like tests and the constant stream of results they produce because it enables them, in their dealings with the media, to point to what they claim to be a rise in educational standards. Teachers of ten- and eleven-year-old children complain that they are required to spend far too long preparing and rehearsing for them, at the expense of more interesting and innovative activities (see, for example, Reardon 2004). After surveying over 100 secondary teachers in summer 2008, Civitas found that only 10 per cent of the teachers surveyed found pupil ability reflected their test results from primary school, taken a year earlier. Notably, nearly 80 per cent had found up to a third of their pupils' true abilities to be lower, and the main source of 'grade inflation' was reported to be the amount of time that primary teachers spent preparing pupils for the test. These sorts of criticisms led to a provisional decision in 2009 for schools in England that pupils would be tested when teachers believed they were ready, rather than together at a fixed age.

From an American perspective, Kohn (2000) is a staunch critic of testing, claiming that standardised testing has swelled and mutated, like a creature in one of those old horror movies. In support of his argument, he asserts that while previous generations of American students have had to sit through tests, never have the tests been given so frequently or played such a prominent role in schooling. He also suggests that factors lying *outside* a teacher's control explain most of the variance in test scores; thus, a combination of the number of parents living at home and their educational background, type of community and poverty rate accounts for a large percentage of the variations. Kohn also insists that norm-referenced tests were never intended to measure the quality of learning or teaching; rather, they encourage shallow forms of thinking. Noddings (2004) argues that high-stakes testing may be incompatible with many laudable aims, among them, critical thinking. She also questions whether the goals of the 'No Child Left Behind Act' (USA) are reasonable and contends that, if they are not, there may be no justification for imposing punishments and sanctions on children and schools unable to meet them.

Sources

Independent newspaper (2008) 'An oppressive system that is failing our children', 8 February, on-line at www.independent.co.uk/opinion/leading-articles

Kohn, A. (2000) 'Standardised testing and its victims', *Education Week*, 27 September, on-line at www.alfiekohn.org/teaching/edweek/staiv.htm

Noddings, N. (2004) 'High stakes testing: Why?' *Theory and Research in Education*, 2 (3), 263–69.

Reardon, T. (2004) 'Key stage 2 reading tests: What the teachers really think', *Education Journal*, 79, 28–30.

TEXTBOOKS

See also: curriculum, English, geography, mathematics, teacher–pupil interaction

A textbook is a standard book or manual of instruction relating to a specific subject area of the curriculum, produced in response to the perceived needs of teachers and other educators. The most common forms of textbook found in primary schools are in the subjects of mathematics, English and geography. Mathematics textbooks tend to contain examples of computations and exercises related to the area of study (e.g. two-dimensional shapes); a book might relate to a specific topic and contain problems of increasing difficulty, or each book in a set be separately numbered on the basis of level of difficulty. The most common English textbooks are dictionaries, spelling lists and comprehension exercises for

use by older and more capable younger pupils. Some teachers find that although textbooks provide a useful framework for teaching and learning, they can become a 'substitute teacher' and reduce the amount of direct engagement ('teaching interaction') with pupils. Books are also costly and need repairing and replacing regularly. Although most textbooks are only published in printed format, many are now available as on-line electronic books and increasingly in scanned format.

THEMATIC LEARNING

See also: citizenship, collaborating for learning, cross-curriculum, group work, learning styles, mathematics, organising for learning, reading, science, topic work

Thematic teaching is a method of organising teaching around themes or topics, thereby making it possible to integrate instruction across core areas such as reading, writing, mathematics, history, science and the arts. Thematic units are designed to encourage children to delve more thoroughly into topics to develop their awareness and understanding of connections between areas of learning. Thematic instruction integrates basic subjects like reading, mathematics and science with the exploration of a broad subject, such as life cycles, rain forests, the circus, the use of energy, and so on. It is commonly the case that one subject dominates a theme more than others; for instance, a theme based on 'the local community' is likely to emphasise history, map work (geography) and citizenship, whereas the theme of 'creepy-crawlies' is likely to be science-based. Terry (on-line) suggests that there are ten reasons to use thematic units; their use

1 increases effective use of computers and information technology;
2 compacts the curriculum;
3 demonstrates the interdisciplinary nature of learning;

433

4 increases student interest in learning and time engaged;

5 expands your assessment strategies;

6 utilises collaborative and cooperative learning;

7 focuses the learner on the mastery of objectives;

8 integrates word processing skills into creative activities;

9 models for students the resources used in research;

10 controls web access for students.

By using thematic units, teachers offer their pupils a way to root the different subject areas in real life issues; thus, social studies, science, environmental education and personal growth and development are all concerned with ideas about how the world operates and functions. Because thematic teaching integrates different subject areas, it allows long-term memory to retain concepts that apply across the curriculum, rather than specific subject-related facts. If properly organised and managed, the wide-ranging nature of a theme gives pupils more choice about where they focus their attention and allows for different learning styles and methods of teaching. For example, because children often work in small groups, they are exposed to collaborative learning (i.e. every member contributing towards the same outcome) and team responsibility; similarly, teaching tends to facilitate learning by providing resources and guidance, rather than being didactic (i.e. 'the teacher telling').

One of the reasons that thematic teaching is not widely used is due to three factors. First, the present focus on core subjects (notably literacy and mathematics) and the crowded curriculum has reduced the time available to explore and investigate a theme fully. Second, an emphasis on measurable outcomes sits uneasily alongside a form of teaching that offers pupils choice in selecting where they focus their energies. Third, thematic work has been tainted by poor practice that sometimes took place under its predecessor, referred to as 'project work'. The Rose Review of primary

education in England (Rose 2009) avoided using the word 'theme' but suggested that there could be six broad 'areas of learning' rather than individual subjects. Rose claimed that there had been a false distinction between teaching individual subjects and teaching across topics ('cross-curricular') and that it was possible to do both. The Review advocated that key ideas might overlap subjects; such as the way that learning about human settlements can incorporate both history and geography.

Sources

Rose, J. for the DCSF (2009) *Primary Curriculum Review*, London: HMSO.

Terry, P.J. *Using the Net to Create Thematic Units*, on-line at www.techtrekers.com/Thematic.htm

THINK-PAIR-SHARE

See also: discussion, problem solving, questions and questioning, thinking

Think-pair-share is a structure first developed by Professor Frank Lyman at the University of Maryland in 1981 for college students, and adopted by many educationists in the field of co-operative learning over succeeding years (Lyman 1981). The approach introduces into the peer interaction element of co-operative learning the idea of 'wait and think' time, a procedure that has been demonstrated to be a powerful factor in improving pupils' responses to questions. The procedure begins when the teacher poses a problem or asks an open-ended question. Children are then given opportunity to think independently about the issues involved before turning to face their partners, after which they share ideas, discuss, clarify and challenge each other's ideas. After an appropriate amount of time, each pair joins with another pair to exchange and interrogate their views and conclusions. Think-pair-share is more likely to ensure a high level of engagement and can feel more secure than speaking publicly in front of a large group of classmates. The strategy is particularly valuable for work with older primary-age pupils and encourages less confident children to offer an opinion and be involved in discussions.

A variation on think-pair-share called *Formulate-Share-Listen-Create* was developed by Johnson *et al.* (1991) as a strategy to use with problems or questions that invite a variety of solutions. Pupils formulate an answer or response to the question individually; share with a partner; listen carefully to the partner's answer, noting points of agreement and disagreement; and create a final response that synthesises all the ideas. The 'create' step allows pupils to synthesise their ideas and offer a consensus about the best solution to a problem.

Sources

Johnson, D.W., Johnson, R.T. and Smith, K.A. (1991) *Active learning: Cooperation in the college classroom*, Edina MN: Interaction Book Company.
Lyman, F.T. (1981) 'The responsive classroom discussion: The inclusion of all students', in Anderson, A. (ed.) *Mainstreaming Digest*, College Park: University of Maryland Press.

THINKING

See also: brain function, curiosity, imagination, multiple intelligences, new entrants, philosophy for children, problem solving, thinking skills

Over recent years there has been a surge of interest about the use of thinking as a means of improving the quality of learning in classrooms in the belief that the direct teaching of strategies to aid thinking helps to develop pupils' abilities in problem solving, investigations and forms of enquiry that can be applied across all areas of learning and are relevant to the needs of every child. From when they arrive in primary school as new entrants, children can be introduced to complex ways of thinking, provided that ideas and concepts can be introduced in straightforward and imaginative ways (see Fisher 2005). Costello (2000) argues that teaching thinking skills should be an essential requisite of early childhood education (aged 3–5 years), facilitated by enabling them to speak in a variety of situations and contexts. Thinking skills and strategies also open new avenues for intellectual growth that allow academically capable children to be acknowledged for developing ideas and ways of working that are complex, original and insightful.

Robert Fisher has also produced a series of books about poems, games, stories and first stories for thinking to assist teachers to help building thinking and learning communities (Fisher 1996, 1997a, 1997b, 1999). Simister (2004) studied the effects of teaching a twenty-five-lesson 'thinking skills' syllabus to a group of ten-year-old pupils and suggested that pupils' curiosity, inventiveness, discussion skills, ability to think laterally about given situations and understanding of the decision-making process can all be enhanced through specific skills teaching. Simister proposed a two-pronged approach in which thinking skills are taught initially in a child-friendly, test-free context and then integrated throughout the curriculum. Frangenheil (2006) emphasises that thinking should and can be fun for children as well as necessary for learning.

Thinking as a means of strengthening learning presents challenges for primary teachers who work within a predetermined timetable and school-wide agreement about learning objectives. Teachers may want to promote children's capability as creative thinkers but feel constrained by the limitations imposed by a need to conform to the timetable requirements. A teacher may be anxious to offer pupils more opportunities to grapple with ideas, think hard about their implications and produce innovative solutions, but hesitate to do so for fear of falling behind in covering the curriculum and distorting the plans agreed jointly with colleagues or detracting from preparing pupils for formal tests.

Primary-age children have to understand the difference between constructive arguing and quarrelling. Victor Quinn, a specialist in critical thinking, suggests that there are four central kinds of arguments that teachers and parents need to promote in children: (1) *empirical* arguments about matters of fact; (2) *conceptual* arguments about what words mean and how ideas relate; (3) *evaluative* arguments about attitudes and judgements and moral concerns with the needs and interests of others; and (4) *logical* arguments about making connections and disciplined thought (Quinn 1997; see also Haynes 2007).

Steve Higgins and Jennifer Miller from the University of Newcastle (Higgins and Miller 2005) classify thinking skills programmes and approaches into three broad categories. The first they refer to as a *philosophical* approach, where there is an emphasis on questioning and reasoning, particularly when this is undertaken by a group of children or the whole class. Thus, an issue or question is identified by the teacher and/or pupils, which can be solved or elucidated through discussion where the teacher takes the role of facilitator and supports or challenges the pupil reasoning. The leading proponent of thinking in this category is 'philosophy for children', an approach to learning developed in the United States by Matthew Lipman in the 1960s. The second approach to thinking is through so-called *brain-based learning*, drawing on research into how the human brain works and its implications for teachers and schools. Two of the more famous names associated with brain-based learning are Edward de Bono and Eric Jensen, both of whom claim that teaching approaches in schools have not sufficiently utilised information about the brain's functioning. Ideas about accelerated learning and multiple intelligences draw on brain research to inspire techniques or activities that can be used in the classroom. The third approach is *cognitive intervention*, where teaching strategies to promote pupils' thinking are based on activities and techniques for the purpose that the teacher devises.

Most educators agree that the approaches and techniques associated with thinking skills

need to be integrated or 'infused' into lessons rather than taught as separate skills or through lessons that are solely for the purpose. However, circle-time, an approach by which children have an opportunity to express considered views openly and without censure is one occasion when thinking skills can be specifically developed within a non-threatening and familiar setting. Sedgwick (2008) reinforces the point that a teacher will struggle to inculcate thinking and philosophical enquiry without support through a 'whole school' policy. He argues that treating children as the thinking human beings they are will fail if the teacher next door is treating children as 'empty vessels' to be filled or clean slates on which to write the teacher's ideas. As such, the development of thinking skills invites pupils to become partners in learning rather than passive recipients of it.

Sources

Costello, P.J.M. (2000) *Thinking Skills and Early Childhood Education*, London: David Fulton.

Fisher, R. (1996) *Stories for Thinking*, Oxford: Nash Pollock.

——(1997a) *Poems for Thinking*, Oxford: Nash Pollock.

——(1997b) *Games for Thinking*, Oxford: Nash Pollock.

——(1999) *First Stories for Thinking*, Oxford: Nash Pollock.

——(2005) *Teaching Children to Think*, London: Blackwell.

Frangenheim, E. (2006) *Reflections on Classroom Thinking Strategies*, London: Paul Chapman.

Haynes, J. (2007) 'Thinking together: Enjoying dialogue with children', in Hayes, D. (ed.) *Joyful Teaching and Learning in the Primary School*, Exeter: Learning Matters.

Higgins, S. and Miller, J. for the DCSF (2005) *Thinking Skills in Primary Classrooms*, on-line at www.standards.dfes.gov.uk/thinkingskills

Kelly, P. (2004) *Using Thinking Skills in the Primary Classroom*, London: Paul Chapman.

Quinn, V. (1997) *Critical Thinking in Young Minds*, London: David Fulton.

Sedgwick, F. (2008) *100 Ideas for Developing Thinking in the Primary School*, London: Continuum.

Simister, J. (2004) 'To think or not to think', *Improving Schools*, 7 (3), 243–54.

THINKING SKILLS

See also: creativity, deep learning, imagination, thinking

Robson (2006) claims that thinking 'is a fundamental human characteristic, an activity in which we all engage, from the moment we are born and even before' (p. 1). Five thinking skills are also identified as important in assisting children to know 'how', as well as knowing 'what': (a) information-processing, (b) reasoning, (c) enquiry, (d) creative thinking, and (e) evaluation skills. Information-processing skills enable pupils to locate and collect relevant information, to sort, classify, sequence, compare and contrast, and to analyse part/whole relationships. Reasoning skills enable pupils to give reasons for opinions and actions; to draw inferences and make deductions; to use precise language to explain what they think; and to make judgements and decisions informed by reasons or evidence. Enquiry skills enable pupils to ask questions; to pose and define problems; to plan what to do and how to research the problem; to predict outcomes and anticipate consequences; and to test conclusions and improve ideas. Creative thinking skills enable pupils to generate and extend ideas; to suggest hypotheses; to apply imagination; and to look for alternative outcomes. The key word attached to creativity is imagination, where the children are actively encouraged and liberated into fresh modes of thought and activity (see, for example, Carter 2002 for ideas for creative writing; Craft 2005 for a more comprehensive review of issues). Evaluation skills enable pupils to evaluate information, to judge the value of what they read, hear and do, to develop criteria for judging the value of their own and others' work or ideas, and to have confidence in their judgements. These critical skills are considered to be amongst the most difficult for children to grasp, as they require considerable experience and maturity if they are to be anything more than superficial, spontaneous responses (Quinn 1997).

It is vital for children to possess and develop their thinking skills, as the application of practical skills that involve only a small amount of thinking leads to inertia and passivity, limiting children's capacity to think more widely and imaginatively. Thus, knowledge, understanding and skills are mutually dependent. Wenham (1995) graphically expresses the relationship between the three elements: 'Without understanding, experience is blind; but without experience, knowledge and understanding are empty; and without skill, all of them are dumb' (p. 133).

Sources

Carter, J. (2002) *Just Imagine: Creative Ideas for creative writing*, London: David Fulton.

Craft, A. (2005) *Creativity in our Schools: Tensions and dilemmas*, London: Routledge.

Quinn, V. (1997) *Critical Thinking in Young Minds*, London: David Fulton.

Robson, S. (2006) *Developing Thinking and Understanding in Young Children*, London: Routledge.

Wenham, M. (1995) 'Developing thinking and skills in the arts', in Moyles, J. (ed.) *Beginning Teaching: Beginning Learning in the Primary School*, Maidenhead: Open University Press.

THREE WISE MEN

See also: child-centred education, expectations, inspections, learning outcomes, teaching approaches, topic work

In the late 1980s, so-called progressive, child-centred teaching, allegedly promoted by local education authorities (LEAs) and teacher training colleges, was under strong attack by government ministers who wanted a return to formal whole-class teaching, based on subjects, with children sitting in rows rather than grouped around tables. Three people were appointed – subsequently to be referred to as the 'Three Wise Men' – Jim Rose, chief primary HMI, Robin Alexander, an education professor and Chris Woodhead, chief executive of the National Curriculum Council. Their brief was to examine research and inspection evidence, and make recommendations. The then education secretary, Kenneth Clarke, was keen to promote a 'back to basics' agenda and hoped that the final report would recommend wholesale changes in the direction of primary education and see the end of topic work and individualised learning. In fact, the report urged a balanced approach, with high expectations of children and a focus on (measurable) learning outcomes. The trio also challenged the prevailing classroom practice and curriculum organisation and counselled teachers to interrogate the prevailing practice with an open mind. The Three Wise Men report said teachers should be equipped and free to choose the best method for the particular purpose of a particular lesson but, with hindsight, it opened the way for unprecedented government intervention in teaching that is still strongly evident today.

TIME ALLOCATION IN LESSONS

See also: learning objectives, lesson planning, lesson plans, monitoring, time management, time on task

Schools are highly time-sensitive institutions as a means of maintaining routines, ensuring orderliness and fitting in all the necessary teaching and learning experiences, particularly timetabled sessions. During lessons the teacher has a plan of action that involves introducing the content, reminding children of previous learning, explaining the lesson purpose ('objective'), allocating tasks, monitoring progress, bringing the session to a conclusion, reviewing what has taken place and dismissing the children in an orderly fashion. Outside of lesson time, teachers and their assistants have to liaise with colleagues, deal with administrative tasks, fulfil their supervisory obligations (such as playground duty) and incorporate short periods of relaxation.

In a classic study of time allocation during lessons, Alexander (1997) cites three examples of time usage in a teaching session of just less than one hour. The first involves a class of no fewer than thirty-eight five- and six-year-olds. (Note that classes of more than thirty children of this age are now rare in the UK.) The amount of time spent on each phase was broadly as follows:

> 2 minutes: teacher settles class down after playtime.
> 2 minutes: allocates tasks.
> 2 minutes: works with one language group.
> 1 minute: gives a task to an unsupervised number group.
> 16 minutes: works with the language group.
> 2 minutes: monitors a group completing a jigsaw.
> 5 minutes: works with writing group whose supervisor has been called away.
> 5 minutes: supervises changeover of free choice activities and then monitors maths group and two language groups.
> 3 minutes: supervises tidying up.
> 3 minutes: children sit and sing in the book corner.
> 9 minutes: teacher tells a story.
> 5 minutes: informal activities to conclude the session (e.g. clapping a rhythm).

Whereas the time allocation for the class of young children consisted of numerous short episodes, those for a class of thirty-six seven- to eight-year-olds consist of rather fewer and lengthier ones:

> 8 minutes: teacher takes register and then describes and allocates tasks.
> 14 minutes: monitors the work of all groups and deals with individuals who seek help.
> 7 minutes: works with language group.
> 8 minutes: works with science group.
> 2 minutes: monitors work of language and maths groups.
> 7 minutes: gives new task to maths group.
> 11 minutes: works with science group and deals with individuals needing help.

And the pattern for a class of twenty-nine eight- and nine-year-olds reveals that the trend towards shorter episodes continues, reflecting the increased attention span:

> 3 minutes: teacher talks with class about a Victorian penny brought in by a child and about penny-farthing bicycles.
> 7 minutes: sorts out the group choices for the afternoon session.
> 11 minutes: allocates tasks for current session.
> 11 minutes: works with maths group.
> 16 minutes: monitors the work of all groups and responds to individuals seeking help.
> 7 minutes: supervises tidying up.

In recent years there has been an emphasis on the importance of teacher-led sessions, use of information technology and closely structured lessons in which every minute is accounted for in the planning. However, there has been a growing acknowledgement that while learning needs to be reasonably systematic and structured, it cannot always be fitted neatly into slots. Some years ago Pinder (1987) asked readers to imagine 'the frustration experienced by a young learner who is on the verge of solving a problem, on the verge of *understanding*, when ordered by the teacher to pack up the work, hand it in or leave it to be finished at another time' (p. 120). More time is taken up when children are encouraged to offer their ideas, discuss options and explore issues than when the teacher does most of the talking ('didactic teaching'), sets tasks for pupils to complete as quickly as possible and is highly controlling about what is done.

Sources

Alexander, R. (1997) *Policy and Practice in Primary Education*, London: Routledge.
Pinder, R. (1987) *Why Don't Teachers Teach Like They Used To?* London: Hilary Shipman.

TIME MANAGEMENT

See also: attention span, effectiveness, emotions of teaching, teacher–pupil interaction, teacher role

Being able to organise and manage their time effectively and efficiently is a characteristic of successful primary teachers. Every teacher finds that unless priorities are established and acted on decisively, the hours slip past and essential things remain untouched, while trivial issues that emerge unexpectedly take precedence (Papworth 2003). Well-ordered routines contribute to higher standards in learning and help to reduce teacher stress levels; consequently, making optimum use of the time available benefits both children and adults. The best teachers seem to achieve more than their colleagues and produce work of a higher standard despite being busier (Timperley and Robinson 2000).

A detailed study of some 326 primary teachers in the early 1990s showed that less than three fifths of the teacher's working day was spent in direct contact with classes; 15 per cent of the day was spent in school but without class contact, and a quarter of the day was spent entirely outside school hours (Campbell and Neill 1994). Work overload was seen as a problem residing as much in the teachers as in externally imposed demands, as teachers did not spare themselves in meeting what they perceived as ever-changing and heavy demands made of them by way of government policy decisions. Campbell and Neill also noted the amount of time that teachers spent at the start and end of lessons on trivial tasks and on activities that did not require high-level graduate skills. The recruitment of large numbers of teaching assistants through the British government's workplace reforms in 2004 is intended to relieve these sorts of pressures on teachers and allow them to concentrate on what is perceived as the 'real job' of teaching.

Marty and Stephen Swaim (1999) wrote a book for teachers, parents and administrators in the United States about what they describe as the most fundamental, basic element in any school, namely, the time of a good teacher. They argue that learners need more of each teacher's time and teachers need more time to spend on each learner to plan, grade work and make decisions about resources. Paradoxically, such positive change would only come about if teachers had fewer classes to teach, though it is worth noting that the amount and length of adult–child contact time does not necessarily equate with quality of learning, not least because children's attention spans are often quite short.

To avoid being overwhelmed, teachers tend to mentally categorise tasks under a series of headings, such as not urgent and minor; urgent but minor; urgent and significant; and not urgent but significant. It is not sensible for teachers to spend time on doing things that are neither urgent nor significant, even if they are interesting; on the other hand, urgent tasks that are relatively unimportant still have to be dealt with as quickly as possible. If tasks are urgent and significant they obviously assume the highest priority. If too many tasks are pressing and significant, it acts as a warning that too little time has been left before the deadline, so use of a planning schedule with interim targets helps to avoid last-minute panics.

The intensification of work practices and increasing societal expectations of educators has placed further time pressures on practitioners and exacerbated feelings of helplessness and being unable to cope. Day *et al.* (2007) warn how such conditions 'lead to reduced time for relaxation and re-skilling, can cause chronic and persistent work overload [and] can reduce quality of service' (p. 26). It is possible for teachers to *feel* that they are doing a good job because of the effort that they are making when in fact the belief is illusory. Senior teachers and the head teacher in particular have to be careful that they do not get submerged in mechanical administrative tasks at the expense of being active around the school.

Sources

Campbell, R.J. and Neill, S.R. St John (1994) *Primary Teachers at Work*, London: Routledge.

Day, C., Sammons, P., Stobart, G., Kington, A. and Gu, Q. (2007) *Teachers Matter*, Maidenhead: Open University Press.

Papworth, M. (2003) *Every Minute Counts*, London: Continuum.

Swaim, S.C. and Swaim, M.S. (1999) *Teacher Time*, Lebanon IN: Redbud Books.

Timperley, H. and Robinson, V.M.J. (2000) 'Workload and the professional culture of teachers', *Educational Management and Administration*, 28 (1), 47–62.

TIME-ON-TASK

See also: attention-deficit hyperactivity disorder, attention span, brain function, collaborating in learning, daydreaming, dialogue for learning, interaction, motivation for learning, time allocation in lessons

Time-on-task is defined as the amount of time that pupils spend directly involved in curriculum activities, and Croll (1996) argues that it is important to teachers for a variety reasons. First, time-on-task is one of the factors that influences academic achievement, though there are, of course, many other factors such as pupil and adult motivation, relevance of the work, behaviour and discipline, health and so forth. The second reason is a practical one, in that children with 'time on their hands' usually find unhelpful distractions that make discipline more challenging to maintain. Put simply, busy children won't have as much opportunity for mischief as those who are meandering. Third, high levels of time-on-task are equated with high levels of whole class interaction; engagement with the work leads to heightened enthusiasm and responsiveness from across the class rather than from isolated pockets of keen children. Furthermore, when teachers interact with the whole class – as opposed to children being an audience with the teacher doing all the talking – through questions, inviting suggestions, offering feedback, summarising conflicting opinions and showing lively interest in children's ideas, not only are high rates of time-on-task maintained during the interactive phase but also during the individual work that often follows. In other words, where teachers spend more time in whole class interaction, children are also more on-task when they work on their own.

While there is a limited period that children can concentrate for, teachers know that it is better to err in giving them more rather than less time, particularly in an enquiry-based lesson (finding out/exploring a problem) or one in which teamwork plays an important part. There is little point in a teacher making a lot of effort to organise an activity and then curtailing it before pupils can achieve anything of value and telling them to 'pack away'. Pupils need to receive a time warning some five minutes and one minute before they have to complete what they are doing. A further minute or two of flexibility has also to be included to allow for slower workers and a few children so desperate to finish what they are doing that they are prepared to face the teacher's anger rather than conclude prematurely (Hayes 2009).

It is popularly claimed that extensive exposure to television and computer games develops brain systems that tend to *deflect* attention rather than *focus* it. It is essential that children receive active practice in thinking and learning to build increasingly stronger neural (brain) connections for the simple reason that a mature attention span comes with a mature brain (Healy 1991). Forms of active practice might include practical work involving the creation of a 3D or 2D product, verbal responses and decisions that involve selecting from a range of options. Children's brains continue to develop throughout the school years and attention span is determined in large measure by the type of 'programming' received from external stimuli. Studies suggest that an average child's formal attention span (in minutes) is approximately as long as the age of the child; in other words a five-year-old can normally only manage five minutes of uninterrupted concentration and thereby 'time-on-task'.

It is interesting to contrast the *external* control of visual stimuli used by the media to bombard children's senses, with the *internal* control and discipline required by children in class. A constant stream of interruptions (especially visually captivating ones) disengages the *inner dialogue*; that is, the talking that takes place inside the child's head. As a result, concentration and sustained attention become more and more fragmented; the more hyperactive pupils jump from one activity to another, restlessly seeking the next stimulus and unable to persevere to complete a task. Consequently, children's attention span diminishes, as they increasingly become spectators as opposed to being active participants in learning. On the other hand, nobody can concentrate continuously and a little daydreaming must be allowed for, especially with children suffering from attention-deficit syndrome.

Sources

Croll, P. (1996) 'Teacher–pupil interaction in the classroom', in Croll, P. and Hastings, N. (eds) *Effective Primary Teaching*, London: David Fulton.

Hayes, D. (2009) *Primary Teaching Today*, London: Routledge.

Healy, J. (1991) *Endangered Minds: Why our children don't think and what to do about it*, New York: Simon and Schuster.

TIME-OUT

See also: autism, behaviour, discipline, inclusion, statementing, teaching assistant

Time-out is a disciplinary measure used to describe a process whereby children are removed from mainstream classrooms or educational settings into a secure, calm and safe environment when they are unable to cope, become distressed or cause other children to become distressed. The time-out area may be a separate room, quiet open space or with a different adult/teacher in another functioning classroom. Time-out is intended to help children to recover their composure, receive appropriate adult attention and be reintroduced to their own classroom as soon as appropriate. As such, it is a constructive strategy and not a punishment, though Readdick and Chapman (2000) found that the very young children in their survey expressed largely negative self-attributions, such as feeling alone, being disliked by the teacher and ignored by one's peers, together with feelings of sadness and fear. Contrary to adults' intentions, young children often perceive time-out as a punishment.

Some parents and educators have questioned the usefulness and acceptability of time-out procedures. Some educators say the strategy is being used with increased frequency to discipline children with behavioural disorder – and probably doing more harm than good. There is particular concern over the appropriateness of time-out for disabled and disadvantaged children, as separating them from the positive aspects of the classroom merely highlights that they are different from other children. In particular, isolating an autistic child – characterised by underdeveloped communication skills – can be extremely counterproductive for the simple reason that one feature of autism is a desire to be separated from other people and the child might deliberately increase negative behaviour in the hope of being removed from the classroom.

Time-out may be part of the strategy for children in England and Wales for whom a formal statement of special needs has been agreed between the school and parents – so-called 'statementing'. If so, it is likely that the teaching assistant allocated to the pupil will accompany him or her to the designated area to monitor the situation.

Source

Readdick, C.A. and Chapman, P. (2000) 'Pre-schoolers' perception of time out', *Journal of Research in Childhood Education*, 15, 81–87.

TOPIC WORK

See also: deep learning, foundation subjects, free play, imagination, information technology,

meta-learning, motivation for learning, non-core subjects, play, problem solving, project work, religious education

Pinder (1987) helpfully describes a topic as 'something under discussion or a subject under investigation, and the word is, of course, related to *topical*' (p. 124). The curriculum in primary schools requires teachers to provide pupils with a breadth and depth of learning, giving adequate time and attention to the teaching of core subjects (English/ literacy, mathematics and science) while still providing sufficient attention to a worthwhile study of other subjects ('non-core'), information and communication technology (ICT) and religious education (RE). Some schools choose to organise the teaching of history, geography, art and design, and (sometimes) physical education within 'topics' or subject-related themes that incorporate knowledge and information from a cross-section of subjects. Unlike the regular teaching of single subjects, a topic approach is based on the principle that learning does not need to be confined within subject boundaries but is more eclectic and wide-ranging.

Although topic work can be closely regulated and monitored by the teacher, an ultimate form of it is found in child-directed learning, notably imaginative ('free') play. However, even at a time when topic work was commonplace in British schools, Gunning *et al.* (1981) warned that organising learning on the basis of children's interests could be deceptive, as teachers 'find in children what they hope and expect to find' (p. 21). Furthermore, it is unlikely that all the children in a class or group will share common interests; consequently, teachers 'may seize upon the interest of one child but be unable to find any expressed interest in particularly apathetic and unresponsive children who are not prepared to initiate activity' (p. 22).

Katz and Chard (2000) argue that teachers should strive to create a learning environment that offers diverse experiences, excites children's interest and, wherever possible, builds on their enthusiasm. By its very nature, a topic can cover any area of learning but common examples include themes such as road safety, homes, exploring the school grounds, mini-beasts (small creatures) and colours. Thus, a topic on road safety with eight-year-olds might involve aspects of geography (road layouts, planning routes), mathematics (speed and direction), ICT (creating maps), drama (acting out road-crossing scenes) and art/design (designing warning posters). A topic based on a colour (green, say) with reception-age children might incorporate science (natural and artificial objects), art (painting an imaginary scene based on shades of green), literacy (talking about scary green monsters), geography (the shape of hills) and science (wildlife in fields).

Although topics incorporate a variety of subject areas, most of them are weighted towards a particular subject, commonly history, geography, science or RE. Pupils explore the theme using art, design, dance, drama and IT as tools to explore and create links across the subjects. Thus, eleven-year-olds might use ICT to reproduce a historical event; dance and movement to examine the cultural factors that impinged on the event; and discussions about issues associated with conflict through religious education and citizenship.

Topic work is closely associated with the concept of an *integrated day* where the conventional timetable is set aside in favour of a more flexible way of organising learning. Topic work frequently involves group work and the production of displays and performances as means of presenting findings.

Critics of the topic approach express concerns over children careering from one thing to another and gaining only a superficial grasp of content and failing to sharpen their learning skills ('learning how to learn' or 'meta-learning') in their eagerness to find the next point of interest. However, children are almost invariably motivated by the freedom to explore and creativity that topic work offers; one important role for the teacher is to ensure that work is completed satisfactorily

and not allow children's enthusiasm to dominate at the expense of deep learning. In practice, the demands of following a national curriculum and covering the prescribed curriculum content places time limitations on the extent to which a teacher can respond to children's preferences, though in England and Wales the 'Rose Report' on behalf of the Department for Children, Schools and Families (Rose 2009) recommended the introduction of 'areas of interest' to replace strictly defined single subjects. Wise teachers ensure that the set curriculum is covered, while offering pupils a degree of choice about which elements they pursue in greatest depth.

Sources

Gunning, S., Gunning, D. and Wilson, J. (1981) *Topic Teaching in the Primary School*, London: Croom Helm.

Katz, L.G. and Chard, S.C. (2000) *Engaging Children's Minds: The project approach*, Stamford CT: Alex Publishers.

Pinder, R. (1987) *Why Don't Teachers Teach Like They Used to?* London: Hilary Shipman.

Rose, J. for the DCSF (2009) *Primary Curriculum Review*, London: HMSO.

TRAINEE TEACHERS

See also: caring teachers, General Teaching Councils, induction of new teachers, motivation for teaching, workload reforms

In England and Wales, a trainee primary teacher – also referred to as a 'student teacher' – is someone following a recognised route into teaching ('initial teacher training') to gain qualified teacher status (QTS) or its equivalent. QTS as such does not exist in Scotland or Northern Ireland. However, like in England and Wales, all teachers in Scotland and Northern Ireland are required to register with either the General Teaching Council for Scotland or the General Teaching Council for Northern Ireland; the GTCs will only consider graduates with teaching qualifications (such as the PGCE or PGDE – Professional Graduate Diploma of Education) for registration. In Scotland a one-year probationary period (equivalent to induction in England and Wales) must be completed. In the UK, the Bachelor of Education (B.Ed.) is a recognised degree in education during which the trainee undertakes teacher training during the course and gains qualified status on graduation. The B.Ed. degree is normally over three or four years full time or around five years part-time. The Bachelor of Arts (B.A.) and Bachelor of Science (B.Sc.) is where a main degree subject is combined with teacher training so that on graduation the trainee receives a B.Sc. or B.A. 'with QTS'.

For entry to *Postgraduate Initial Teacher Training* a trainee requires a relevant degree or equivalent qualification. It usually takes a year to complete a postgraduate programme and achieve qualified status; trainee primary teachers spend at least 18 weeks of the year in school, compared with 24 weeks for trainee secondary teachers. Less commonly, the *Graduate Teacher Programme and Registered Teacher Programme* enable schools to employ people who are not yet qualified to teach to undertake an individual training schedule. The Graduate Teacher Programme involves up to one year of postgraduate training, whereas the Registered Teacher Programme requires that trainees have successfully completed two years of higher education and complete a relevant QTS degree while they train over a period of at least two years.

The age profile of trainee teachers shows that the majority of students pursuing a first degree begin the course in their late teens or early twenties; postgraduate trainees tend to be in their twenties or thirties. However, cohorts include a significant proportion of more mature students, especially in early childhood studies courses (for children aged 3–5 years) and early years courses (for the lower primary age range); see, for instance, Duncan (1999) for case studies about mature women entering teaching.

All trainee teachers in England have to pass 'skills tests' in literacy, in numeracy and in information and communication technology (ICT) before they can be recommended for the award of QTS by their provider of initial teacher training. They also have to conform to ('meet') the *QTS Standards*, which comprise a list of outcome statements about the things that a trainee teacher must know, understand and be able to do, with a particular emphasis on classroom practice. Training providers are permitted a reasonable degree of autonomy in deciding how they organise and respond to the needs of individual trainee teachers, though these programme features are closely scrutinised during institutional inspections.

Studies show that trainee teachers want a career that offers variety and fulfilment, opens up avenues for learning and is intellectually and practically engaging. Studies by Smethern (2007) and by Manuel and Hughes (2006) confirm that altruism and a desire to care for children provide the most powerful incentives. The authors claim that many prospective teachers enter teaching 'with a sense of mission to transform the lives of young people and open opportunities for growth through learning and connecting' (p. 21). Browne and Haylock (2004) set out some of the professional demands made on primary school teachers by parents, the children themselves, government agencies, society and the profession. Despite these pressures, there is general agreement among all teachers that even though working in school is difficult, emotionally draining and exhausting, the job is eminently worthwhile.

Research by Smithers and Robinson (2009) found that more than a quarter of all trainee teachers never work in the classroom and may experience a 'culture shock' of such intensity that 40 per cent leave after just a few years, citing poor behaviour among pupils and excessive workload as the main reasons. On the other hand, one of the greatest thrills of being a teacher is to see the fulfilment that successful teaching and learning engenders in children (Hayes 2009).

Sources

Browne, M. and Haylock, D. (2004) *Professional Issues for Primary Teachers*, London: Paul Chapman.

Duncan, D. (1999) *Becoming a Primary School Teacher: A study of mature women*, Stoke-on-Trent: Trentham.

Hayes, D. (2009) *Learning and Teaching in Primary Schools*, Exeter: Learning Matters.

Manuel, J. and Hughes, J. (2006) 'It has always been my dream: Exploring pre-service teachers' motivations for choosing teaching', *Teacher Development*, 10 (1), 5–24.

Smethern, L. (2007) 'Retention and intention in teaching careers: Will the new generation stay?' *Teachers and Teaching*, 13 (5), 465–81.

Smithers, A. and Robinson, P. (2009) *Good Teacher Training Guide 2008*, Buckingham University, Centre for Education and Employment Research.

TRANSITIONS

See also: bullying, citizenship, friendships, homework, primary school, relationships

Moving on to another class and particularly to another school is a major event for pupils, and as well as being exciting can be extremely unsettling for children, who become restless and sometimes less co-operative as the transition time approaches. When they move up to a new class at the start of the year, children tend to look back wistfully to the time they spent in their previous class and it is not uncommon to hear them complain that they don't like the new teacher as much as the old one. It takes time for the adult–child relationship to stabilise and for the new teacher's methods, preferences and ideas to be communicated to the children. It is also possible for *teachers* to look back wistfully at the last class they taught and compare them favourably with the new one. The transition time during early encounters between a teacher and new class is therefore full of hope and expectancy but also creates a degree of uncertainty and tentativeness. The Teachernet web site offers insights into the effect that moving school can have on a child, especially if it takes place mid-year (due to moving location) without the ameliorating impact of end-of-year rites of passage, farewells and 'separation' routines.

Every change, therefore, generates the excitement of new horizons and potential for new friendships, but also strong emotions, not least the grief felt about lost friendships and the fear generated by the unknown. In addition to maintaining and making friends, there are practical considerations for pupils to consider, such as adjusting to a new timetable, remembering when to bring in a games kit and making sure homework is completed. Children whose families have had to leave their country at short notice owing to persecution or fear will have to overcome a suspicion of authority as well as learning a new language. The standard of work and expectations of behaviour in the new school may be different from the previous situation, creating further uncertainty and requiring time for adjustment. Guidelines as part of key stages 1 and 2, Citizenship in the UK, entitled 'Moving On', is a resource for exploring transition issues with pupils and includes themes such as 'buddying' (making a special close friend), welcoming new pupils, exploring and coping with change, on-line at www.standards.dfes.gov.uk/schemes2/ks1-2 citizenship/cit12/

Zeedyk and Gallacher (2003) undertook a survey to ascertain the views of primary pupils, secondary pupils, parents and teachers in regard to the transition process. They found that bullying was a major concern for all groups, followed by fears of getting lost, increased workload and peer relationships. The authors argue that the views of both primary pupils and their parents need to be considered if the experience of transition is to be improved. Finally, it was noted with some concern that teachers focused on institutional initiatives and rarely identified children's individual abilities as making a difference to the transition process, which carried the risk of creating a degree of helplessness for individual children.

Pupils' experiences in changing school also appear to vary according to their socio-economic backgrounds. In a major study of primary–secondary transition in state schools in England, data from over 12,000 primary schools, more than 2,000 secondary schools and about 400,000 pupils indicated that the experiences of poor pupils at age eleven may be quite different from their peers not classified as poor (Burgess *et al.* 2008). Results from the study show that poor pupils' peer groups in primary schools are more fractured at the age of eleven years; furthermore, these pupils subsequently find themselves concentrated within lower-performing secondary schools. The authors claim that 'within primary school' differences in secondary school destination provides one of the study's most significant findings.

A lot of work goes into making sure that the transition from school to school takes place as smoothly as possible. Teachers from the 'feeder' primary and 'receiving' secondary school are supposed to liaise closely, though practice is variable; primary teachers pass on information about children's academic achievements and some indications of their social skills, friendship patterns, behaviour and attendance. Governments are most concerned about the communication of pupils' formal levels of attainment to the receiving schools – principally information about national test scores – but secondary teachers are just as interested in each pupil's character and attitude to learning. It is not uncommon for secondary schools to administer their own internal tests to new pupils as a means of organising ability groups, causing primary teachers to complain that their secondary colleagues fail to utilise sufficiently the data they have passed on to them about the children.

Sources

Burgess, S., Johnston, R., Tomas, K., Propper, C. and Wilson, D. (2008) 'The transition of pupils from primary to secondary school in England', *Transactions of the Institute of British Geographers*, 33 (3), 388–403.

Teachernet (2007) *Individual Pupil Transition*, on-line at www.teachernet.gov.uk/teachingand learning/library/individualpupiltransition

Zeedyk, M.S. and Gallacher, J. (2003) 'Negotiating the transition from primary to secondary school', *School Psychology International*, 24 (1), 67–79.

TRUST

See also: children's questions, morality, parents, relationships, teachers' beliefs

Trust underpins every relationship, not least between parents, children and school staffs. Children love to tell the adults they trust about key events and moments from their private lives, especially if the adult responds enthusiastically. However, adults have to be careful to distinguish between being *personable* (likeable and charming) and *personal* (intimate) in their exchanges with pupils. Children are fascinated by teachers' private lives, particularly their sporting and musical achievements, and are delighted if a teacher shares something of their interests and (perhaps) family situations with them. On the whole, however, teachers are cautious about disclosing too much personal information in the early stages of meeting a new class or group. Gradually, teachers can release snippets of information about their lives outside school to enhance their reputation, stimulate curiosity and foster intimacy. Those who talk too freely about their situations may be perceived as naïve by colleagues and, perhaps, considered a bore by pupils.

If children ask an adult for an opinion about a controversial or sensitive subject, wise practitioners lay out the options first. Thus, 'Some people believe (this) and some people believe (that) but I believe … ' or admit that they are still making up their minds. They then follow up by asking the child who made the initial request what he or she thinks. In the case of a moral issue, the child's comments probably reflect what the parents believe. Sensitive teachers accommodate all viewpoints, regardless of how odd they may seem, as a sensitive child may be reluctant to offer one again if rebuffed and many are simply grappling with difficult issues. Parents trust teachers to treat their children fairly and sympathetically and to give them every opportunity to reach their potential and be happy in school.

U

UNDERSTANDING

See also: curiosity, deep learning, home background and learning, knowledge, questions and questioning, spiral curriculum, teaching skills

One of the most common questions that teachers ask their pupils is whether they understand something. In the majority of cases, the children chorus 'yes' and the teacher, pleased at her skill in explaining, proceeds to the next stage of the lesson. But teachers have to have ways to ascertain whether or not the children really understand, which first requires clarity about what 'being able to understand' means.

Understanding comes initially through raising awareness, as many children simply do not properly realise what needs to be understood. Raising awareness is followed by increased interest levels based on a belief that children are naturally inquisitive, a characteristic which needs to be exploited by the teacher through posing relevant questions or wondering out loud about a situation. A heightening of inquisitiveness should result in children offering their own questions, and this is the point at which the teacher's skill in explaining is important, as pupils' queries are dealt with and their misconceptions are corrected. Subsequently, children should have opportunity to explore, discover and test propositions, experiment with ideas and raise fresh issues. This cycle from raising awareness and interest, leading to further questions being raised by the children as well as by adults, can be continued until pupils reach the limits of their understanding.

Howe (1999) makes the point that teachers devise various ways of helping children to understand materials that are new and unfamiliar: 'they ask questions, demonstrate their own curiosity, assist children to predict what will happen next in a story, and try to activate children's background knowledge' (p. 126). Children gain understanding gradually because it operates at a variety of conceptual levels and requires considerable reinforcement and testing out in real contexts before a thorough grasp of the issues can been achieved.

Vosniadou (2001) asserts that when information is superficially memorised it is easily forgotten but when something is understood it is not forgotten easily and can be transferred to other situations. In order to understand what they are being taught, pupils must therefore be given opportunity to think about what they are doing, to talk about it with others, to clarify it and to understand how it applies in a variety of situations. The author suggests that teachers can use the following strategies:

- Ask pupils to explain a phenomenon or a concept in their own words.
- Show pupils how to provide examples that illustrate how a principle applies or how a law works.
- Give pupils opportunities to solve characteristic problems in the subject-matter area.

449

- Teach students how to abstract general principles from specific cases and generalise from specific examples.

Knowledge and understanding are inextricably entwined. For instance, young children may know through systematic observation that seeds grow into plants with roots and a stem under certain conditions. As they proceed through school, children not only understand the significance of the root system and the influence of different types of soil but can also offer explanations as to *why* it happens. The five-year-old who gazed in wonder at the bean plant's speed of growth and talked about it excitedly becomes the eleven-year-old who can not only describe what is happening but also use evidence to suggest underlying principles about the effect of light, warmth and soil conditions. The steady progression from the five-year-old who wonders at what she sees happening, to the eleven-year-old who can provide insights about the unseen biological processes at work, is testimony to the different levels of understanding that children can attain if given sufficient guidance and opportunity (cf. the *spiral curriculum*, Bruner 1973). Examples of this progression can be found in every area of the curriculum. The development of understanding therefore involves a combination of intellect, maturity (the ability to think abstractly) and the opportunity to explore ideas and 'play' with alternatives. Higher levels of understanding come through experimentation and opportunities to explore ideas, to discuss findings and to investigate possibilities. See under **Bloom's Taxonomy** elsewhere in this book.

Robson (2006) stresses the social, cultural and emotional contexts of thinking and learning ('social understandings') that are conditioned by the cultural contexts in which they take place. In addition, 'the ways in which children see themselves as thinkers and learners is dependent upon their self-image, self-esteem and view of themselves as part of their surrounding social world' (p. 39).

Robson goes on to emphasise the important role that is played by other people in the development of social understandings; thus, 'the key seems to lie in children's relationships with family and friends. It is within the arena of young children's relationships with parents and carers, siblings and friends that their understanding is both developed and revealed' (p. 45).

Sources

Bruner, J. (1973) *Going Beyond the Information Given*, New York: Norton.
Howe, M.J.A. (1999) *A Teacher's Guide to the Psychology of Learning*, London: Blackwell.
Robson, S. (2006) *Developing Thinking and Understanding in Young Children*, London: Routledge.
Vosniadou, S. (2001) *How Children Learn*, Educational Practices 7, Geneva: International Bureau of Education.

UNIFORM

See also: dress code

Over recent years there has been a trend towards schools insisting on pupils wearing the school uniform, though at primary level the emphasis is on simplicity to ease problems for younger children when they change for games and physical education. Most uniforms consist of a 'top', possibly with the school name and logo, and grey or black trousers/skirt. The small percentage of schools that include the use of a tie increasingly favour those that 'clip on' rather than knot, owing to concerns about health and safety. Advocates of the school uniform argue that it looks smart, saves a lot of arguing about what is and is not suitable clothing for school and emphasises school membership and group identity. Opponents insist that uniforms interfere with parents' and pupils' rights to self-expression, create an unnecessary expense, and engender an atmosphere of compliance, which is ultimately counter-productive. Opinion polls suggest that the majority of parents favour the uniform, not least because it avoids an area of conflict about what to wear each morning.

UNITED KINGDOM LITERACY ASSOCIATION

See also: communication, literacy, reading, teaching assistants, writing

The United Kingdom Literacy Association (UKLA) was formerly known as UKRA, the letter R standing for 'Reading'. It is a registered charity, which has as its sole object the advancement of education concerned with literacy in schools and out-of-school settings throughout all phases of education. Members of UKLA include classroom teachers, teaching assistants, school literacy coordinators, literacy consultants, teacher educators, researchers, inspectors, advisors, publishers and librarians. UKLA's stated aim is to be a lively and inclusive subject association whose activities include conferences and professional development activities, publications, research and international projects. UKLA can be contacted on-line at www.ukla.org

V

VALUE-ADDED

See also: effectiveness, good teachers, home background and learning, inspections, parents, teacher role, teaching strategy

National criteria for teacher effectiveness rely heavily on what is referred to as the 'value-added' factor; namely, the measurable improvement that pupils make from the time they enter a teacher's influence to the point at which they leave it. Though logical in principle, the value-added approach to judging effectiveness is crude and has severe limitations, as progress in learning cannot be itemised and checked off like a shopping list. Furthermore, an instrumental view of teaching, in which skills and strategies are identified, isolated and implemented as part of a seamless robe, belies the complex nature of the job and the many other influences outside the teacher's control that influence attainment (notably, home circumstances). Nevertheless, a belief that attainment is directly attributable to the effectiveness of teaching underpins the production of the numerous competence statements that have characterised the teacher's role in recent years (e.g. Muijs and Reynolds 2005). Parents are greatly influenced by schools that are officially pronounced good or excellent by inspectors, reflected in the house prices in areas where school test results are strong and the clamour to get their children into schools perceived to be the best.

Source

Muijs, D. and Reynolds, D. (2005) *Effective Teaching: Evidence and practice*, London: Paul Chapman.

VALUES

See also: behaviour, caring teachers, educated child, Every Child Matters, moral development, morality, relationships, social and emotional aspects of learning, spiritual education, teachers' beliefs

Values are fundamental beliefs or principles that determine attitudes towards human behaviour. They guide judgements about what is right or wrong and focus attention on what is important. Sridhar (2001) argues that all good education is, in essence, a process of developing the human personality in all its dimensions – intellectual, physical, social, ethical and moral. Great thinkers in every period of recorded history have devoted a lot of attention to understanding the significance of character and values in life and the role of various agencies of education in promoting these values in young people. According to Thornberg (2008) values education is most often reactive and unplanned, embedded in everyday school life with a focus on pupils' everyday behaviour in school and partly or mostly unconsciously rather than deliberately performed. In schools, values reflect the personal concerns and preferences that help to frame relationships between pupils and adults.

453

There are five key values in which education is grounded: spiritual, cultural, environmental, aesthetic and political. These values are expressed in terms of personal values with relation to self; moral values with respect to others; and social values with regard to the impact on the community. Eaude (2006) argues that a person who is a teacher cannot be dissociated from that teacher who is a person. Consequently, the values that individuals bring to the classroom with regard to relating to others' expectations and the things they espouse, influence children at least as much as when they are directly teaching them.

A generation ago, a leading education writer (Jeffreys 1971) claimed that teachers must combine personal morality with impartial justice, as freedom of thought does not mean the right to hold any sort of random viewpoint. Consequently, the values that teachers bring to the classroom should not be casual beliefs but the result of careful consideration and informed thinking. More recently, Richards (2009) refers to the teacher as a frighteningly significant person whose teaching helps to shape attitudes to learning at a most sensitive period in children's development' (p. 20). Rossano (2008) argues, however, that while most children grow up to develop competent moral skills, a small number of them fail to do so and few develop them to a sophisticated level. Consequently, deliberate moral practice is necessary for the acquisition of expertise, and religious participation appears to provide the basic elements to facilitate it (Rossano 2008, Abstract).

As the prime satisfaction for primary teachers is the pleasure of interacting with children and affecting their young lives, rather than a desire for monetary reward or status, their value position is rooted in a need to love and care, to serve, to empower and to benefit their pupils. Consequently, primary teachers are constantly evaluating their work through interrogating the fundamental purpose of what they are doing as educators. The teacher's own values and ideas about what is acceptable in education, as well as in life

generally, are strong determining elements in shaping classroom practice. In effect, teachers view the classroom to be a microcosm of what wider society should become, where pupils develop the capability to analyse, synthesise, evaluate, communicate effectively and demonstrate compassion towards others. Arthur *et al.* (2006) provide wide-ranging coverage of the practical implications of many of these key issues.

Sources

Arthur, J., Davison, J. and Lewis, M. (2005) *Professional Values and Practice: Achieving the standards for QTS*, London: Routledge.

Eaude, T. (2006) *Children's Spiritual, Moral, Social and Cultural Development*, Exeter: Learning Matters.

Jeffreys, M. (1971) *Education: Its nature and purpose*, London: Allen and Unwin.

Richards, C. (2009) 'Primary teaching: A personal perspective', in Arthur, J., Grainger, T. and Wray, D. (eds) *Learning to Teach in the Primary School*, London: Routledge.

Rossano, M.J. (2008) 'The moral faculty: Does religion promote moral expertise?' *International Journal for the Psychology of Religion*, 18 (3), 169–94.

Sridhar, Y.N. (2001) 'Value development', *National Council for Teacher Education (NCTE)*, Value Orientation in Teacher Education conference, New Delhi.

Thornberg, R. (2008) 'The lack of professional knowledge in values education', *Teaching and Teacher Education*, 24 (7), 1791–98.

VISUAL AIDS

See also: speculative questions, visual auditory and kinaesthetic learning, visual learners

When employing visual means a teacher might decide to use a large, interesting photograph or a relevant object or a number of unusual items to stimulate curiosity and engage children's interest. It is often the case that when a teacher produces something strongly visual it elicits a spontaneous and active response from pupils; an explosion of remarks, laughter or gasps of wonder. The teacher might point out features relating to the visual aid or invite the children to contribute suggestions, or ask specific questions about the object that children can answer through close observation. A teacher might encourage the children to speculate about the item's uses, origin or potential or to express their feelings about its qualities. As the lesson unfolds, teachers are required to make numerous other decisions about whether to:

- retain control of the equipment or pass the items around the group for children to touch and feel;
- send the children to tables and speak to them about the task once they are seated; or organise everything before they sit down or provide written instructions for children to use with a teaching assistant;
- provide a closely predetermined structure for working (such as an activity sheet) or leave the task more open-ended and introduce a problem-solving approach, such as to investigate how many ways the object might be useful in the home – in which case a longer period of time will be needed.

VISUAL, AUDITORY AND KINAESTHETIC LEARNING

See also: auditory learners, kinaesthetic learning, learning, learning styles, reading, speech, tactile learners, visual aids, visual learners, writing

Visual, auditory and kinaesthetic modes or styles of learning, which for simplicity are referred to as VAK, are defined as *visual* (learn best by seeing); *auditory* (learn best by hearing); and *kinaesthetic* (learn best by doing). Some authors add a further category: *read/ write (R)* – indicating a preference for information displayed as words – to create the acronym VARK (see Fleming and Mills 1992). Not surprisingly, more academic pupils have a strong preference for the read-and-write modality, emphasising text-based input and output expressed through reading and writing in their various forms.

Advocates of the VAK model assume that every child will, of necessity, be required to read and write, so do not include it in the description of styles. Other theorists (e.g. Cook 2008) separate 'kinaesthetic' from 'tactile', the former characterised by 'experiential' activities, such as games, models and outdoor activities; the latter involving direct hands-on experiences, such as working with clay or gardening. It should be noted that researchers such as Sharp *et al.* (2008) claim that developments in neuroscientific knowledge hold great promise for our understanding of the learning process, but as yet do not offer practical suggestions for teaching. The authors note that many proponents of VAK are evasive and uncritical about their evidence base and that other 'weak' models of learning styles do little or nothing to demonstrate their validity.

Visual learners are often characterised by rapid speech and comments such as 'it looks fine to me'; they enjoy writing, seeing and drawing diagrams and imagining possibilities. Franklin (2006) argues strongly that every pupil can benefit (for example) from visual images. *Auditory* learners prefer to have information presented to them and enjoy explaining things to other people; they have a tendency to sit upright and look directly ahead; they may also make comments such as 'I hear what you are saying'. There are claims that *kinaesthetic* (tactile) learners often exhibit a restless temperament, with short concentration spans; they like to make things and 'fiddle' around with items; they also tend to avoid eye contact and get inspired by colour, movement and practical task completion.

Children who are not disposed to learn visually may daydream when asked to observe something and fail to spot important details. Children who are not disposed towards auditory learning may become easily distracted and start whispering, doodling or communicating with a friend. Children who don't rely on kinaesthetic learning may stand back when invited to volunteer, allow others in the group to dominate the resources and (in the case of young children) may resist doing messy activities.

In practice, children learn best when teachers use a combination of learning approaches and organise teaching in such a way that it takes account of each individual's learning tendencies as far as possible. It is a mistake to label children as fitting snugly into one of the VAK categories, as labelling of any kind is usually unhelpful and can artificially limit a child's potential for learning.

There are numerous practical considerations to consider when teachers determine the best VAK-related teaching approach to adopt. For instance, if the visual aid is small, children furthest away may struggle to see or simply not bother to attend. Again, computerised images on a large screen are useful in many teaching situations but they do not allow the children to learn by first-hand experience – touching, testing, smelling and so forth. Crucially, in every situation it is vitally important that the adult's speech is consistently clear and easy on the ear, as careful articulation of words and a measured pace are essential features of effective teaching, whatever mode of learning is targeted.

Sources

Cook, S.L. (2008) *Learning Styles*, on-line at www.learningabledkids.com/home_school_info/learning_styles.html

Fleming, N.D. and Mills, C. (1992) 'Not another inventory, rather a catalyst for reflection', *To Improve the Academy*, 11, 137.

Franklin, S. (2006) 'VAKing out learning styles', *Education 3–13*, 34 (1), 81–87.

Sharp, J.G., Bowker, R. and Byrne, J. (2008) 'VAK or VAK-uous? Towards the trivialisation of learning and the death of scholarship', *Research Papers in Education*, 23 (3), 293–314.

VISUAL LEARNERS

See also: imagination, reading, visual auditory and kinaesthetic learning, writing

A great deal of learning is supported by visual aids and representations such as diagrams and charts. So-called 'visual learners' prefer to see ideas presented in pictures, slides and other. Consequently, visual learners benefit from the use of graphs, concept maps (a web diagram for presenting knowledge in a visual form) and illustrations such as Venn diagrams, to enhance their thinking and learning skills. Strong visual learners can also use their imaginations to reconstruct a scene or situation from a description. Some educationists prefer to separate visual learners into two categories: first, learners who are *visual-linguistic* learn best through written language, such as reading and writing tasks; second, learners who are *visual-spatial* have more difficulty with written language and prefer charts, demonstrations, videos and other visual materials.

VOICE CARE

See also: communication, healthy eating, speech

The voice is probably a teacher's single most valuable resource, so it pays to take good care of it (Hayes 1998; Kovacic 2005). Similarly, Grant-Williams (2002) insists that as the voice is the body's powerhouse, it must be treated with the utmost respect. As such, teachers should avoid placing undue pressure on their voices by sudden switches from a normal speaking tone to a fierce or forced one. In addition to avoiding smoke and polluted atmospheres, there is benefit in breathing carefully through the nose (and out through the mouth) avoiding unsuitable foods (such as very spicy ones) and using alcohol and dairy products sparingly. General health is improved through humming quietly before speaking (making the lips vibrate), standing upright and taking regular pauses for breath. Teachers should also keep to a minimum the amount that they clear the throat, which causes the vocal cords to collide and causes wear and tear; and avoid talking too quickly – which leads to inadequate breathing and increases chest tension – or an unnatural pitch or forced whisper. Caring for the voice requires that teachers attend to a range of issues when addressing the class, including controlling the volume to avoid getting progressively louder; learning to hear themselves; and avoiding shouting – speaking strongly is a different matter; controlling the tone and not being controlled by it.

The basic classroom technique of gaining pupil attention before commencing reduces the likelihood that teachers have to raise their voices. Teachers also minimise the need to raise their voices by getting physically closer to pupils when addressing them. Teachers can help themselves by sipping water, breathing deeply into the furthest recesses of the lungs and making a determined effort to preserve the voice when it is tired or hoarse by relaxed rather than forced speech.

Sources

Grant-Williams, R. (2002) *Voice Power*, New York: AMACOM.
Hayes, D. (1998) *Effective Verbal Communication*, London: Hodder & Stoughton.
Kovacic, G. (2005) 'Voice education in teacher training', *Journal of Education for Teaching*, 31 (2), 87–97.

VOLUNTARY AIDED SCHOOLS

See also: faith schools, governing body, religious education, voluntary controlled schools

Voluntary aided schools are usually called religious schools or faith schools. The land and buildings are normally owned by a charity – often a religious organisation such as a church – but the governing body is responsible for running the school. The school is funded partly by the local authority (Education and Library Board in Northern Ireland), partly by the governing body and partly by the charity. The governing body employs the staff but the local authority provides support services. The admissions policy is determined and administered by the governors in consultation with the local authority and other relevant schools in the area and, as with voluntary controlled schools, pupils have to follow the nationally agreed curriculum.

VOLUNTARY CONTROLLED SCHOOLS

See also: governing body, religious education, voluntary aided schools

A voluntary controlled school can also be called a religious or faith school and is distinctive in that the land and buildings are owned by a charity – often a religious organisation such as a church – that appoints some of the members of the governing body. The local authority (Education and Library Board in Northern Ireland) is responsible for running and funding the school, employing the staff and providing support services. The admissions policy is usually determined and administered by the local authority and pupils are obliged to follow the nationally agreed curriculum.

W

WARNOCK REPORT

See also: Code of Practice, inclusion, special educational needs, statementing, teaching assistants

The Warnock Report of 1978, followed by the 1981 Education Act, radically changed the concept of special educational needs (SEN) in England, Scotland and Wales by introducing the idea of an inclusive approach, based on common educational goals for all children regardless of their abilities or disabilities, offering them independence, enjoyment, and understanding. The 1981 Act requires schools and local authorities to identify and meet the requirements of all children with SEN. Vaughan (on-line) notes that the landmark report is famous for giving weight to the importance of parental views about suitable educational provision for their disabled children in mainstream schools. The report certainly created a turning point in public and professional opinion by declaring that parents of disabled children had vital information about their offspring that must be incorporated and used in the assessment, placement and educational process. In practice, an increasing number of children who were formerly educated in special schools are now integrated into mainstream life with the support of an adult assistant. Though Lady Warnock herself has expressed concerns about what she perceived to be the negative aspects of the report that bears her name (Warnock 2005), there is no doubt that her contribution to the legislation surrounding SEN pupils is still making a positive impact on their lives today.

Sources

Vaughan, M. *Milestones on the Road to Inclusion*, on-line at http://inclusion.uwe.ac.uk/inclusion week/articles/milestones.htm

Warnock, M. (2005) *Special Educational Needs: A new look*, London: Philosophy of Education of Great Britain.

WELCOMING ENVIRONMENT

See also: body language, communication, learning climate, minority ethnic children, teaching stance

Teachers and support staff make every effort to show pupils that they are pleased to see them and glad to have them there. The use of 'soft' eye contact, smiles and encouraging comments is deemed especially important for new entrants. Chaplain (2003) suggests that eyes transmit two types of information. First, they indicate that the adult is prepared to receive information by showing that the lines of communication are open. Second, they demonstrate an interest in the other person or persons. In particular, children from families of asylum seekers or immigrants (often referred to as 'migrant' families) require close support as they are integrated into the class. The use of allocated assistants and, ideally, coupling with another child with the same language, are frequently used strategies.

In practice adults go into the playground or take up a position near the door to welcome children as they arrive. Close physical proximity and, in the case of younger children especially, a willingness for adults to place their head at the same level as the child's, also acts to enhance the quality of communication by blurring the formal adult–child or teacher–parent boundaries, while maintaining the core of the relationship. The concept of 'blurring the formal boundaries' with children means that the privileged adult status is eased, while 'maintaining the core' means that despite the blurring the adult retains the right at any given moment to revert to a formal relationship if a child tries to take unreasonable advantage. Teachers are sometimes nervous about being too friendly with pupils for fear of losing control and encountering bad behaviour; however, an insistence on courtesy and reasonable behaviour minimises the chances of any unwanted consequences. An attractive, colourful and 'child-friendly' environment – perhaps with soft background music – assists in reassuring anxious children that they are going to enjoy their time in school.

Source

Chaplain, R. (2003) 'Managing classroom behaviour', in Arthur, J., Grainger T. and Wray D. (eds) *Learning to Teach in the Primary School*, London: Routledge.

WET PLAYTIME

See also: playground, teaching assistants

Wet playtime is a phrase commonly used in primary schools to describe occasions when the weather is unsuitable for children to play outdoors during the timetabled breaks. Children normally remain in their own classrooms or congregate in the school hall, supervised by teaching assistants and at least one qualified

teacher. Some schools use wet playtimes as an opportunity for children to play board games and use computers. There are various publications with ideas for keeping children usefully occupied during a wet playtime; for example, see Mosley and Sonnet (2005).

Source

Mosley, J. and Sonnet, H. (2005) *Wet Playtimes Games*, Trowbridge: Positive Press.

WILLIAM TYNDALE CONTROVERSY

See also: arts, discovery learning, free play, head teacher, home–school, Office for Standards in Education, teaching methods

William Tyndale Junior School was located in Islington, north London and in 1974 was the focus for a high level of media attention after some of the staff espoused an extreme form of liberal behaviour, which eventually resulted in the breakdown of order and considerable antagonism in the local community. Davis (2002) writes that the school was paralysed by internal arguments over teaching methods, partly as a product of the pressures prevalent in the then Inner London Education Authority (ILEA) at the time and partly through poor management. Deference to the autonomy of teachers by the ILEA led to the adoption in the school of adventurous and extreme teaching methods, including giving pupils considerable autonomy in the classroom and school, which many parents found unacceptable.

The affair exposed divisions between so-called radical (new teaching methods) teachers and traditional teachers, between teachers and school managers (the forerunners of governors), between teachers and parents, between different groups of parents and between the local authority (ILEA) and the London Borough of Islington. The William Tyndale controversy was complex but the outcome was blamed on an apparent failure of 'progressive' methods in the school that ultimately triggered a more interventionist government approach to the curriculum, teaching methods and standards of discipline in schools. One unforseen consequence was a diminution of the power and autonomy of local authorities across the country.

The 'William Tyndale affair' gave critics a powerful source of evidence on which to base what they perceived as the failure of progressive methods. However, the report on the affair shows that it was as much a case of mismanagement in the system and inside the school as it was to do with teaching methods. It was unreasonable to suggest, as some people claimed, that this unsatisfactory state of affairs was the inevitable outcome of liberal progressive education policies arising from recommendations made in the Plowden Report (Central Advisory Council for Education 1967). A more considered view indicates that the problems were probably due to an ineffectual head teacher, weak school managers ('school governors') and an impotent local authority. William Tyndale Junior School became the touchstone for controversy over what constitutes effective teaching methods and how education policy and practice are monitored. These issues are still being debated and it is interesting to note that some of the so-called 'progressive' methods used and criticised at William Tyndale – such as discovery learning and exploratory ('free') play – are today espoused for younger primary pupils in particular.

It is worth noting that the contemporary William Tyndale is now (as at 2009) a primary school for children aged 3–11 years and has been described as a great school that specialises in teaching the arts. It consistently receives positive OFSTED reports and pupils perform higher than the national average. The school is presently over-subscribed.

Sources

Central Advisory Council for Education (1967) *Children and their Primary Schools* ('The Plowden Report'), London: HMSO.

Davis, J. (2002) 'The Inner London Education Authority and the William Tyndale Junior School Affair, 1974–76', *Oxford Review of Education*, 28 (2–3), 275–98.

WORKFORCE REFORMS

See also: higher-level teaching assistants, teaching assistants, teaching profession, time management

In January 2003 a government policy document called *Raising Standards and Tackling Workload: A national agreement* was signed by most, though not all union leaders and local government employers to introduce a series of significant changes to teachers' conditions of service and so-called workforce 'remodelling'. These changes became part of the *School Teachers' Pay and Conditions Document* in three annual phases, commencing in September 2003. The reforms also opened the way for enhanced roles for school support staff, notably teaching assistants. Key elements of the workforce reforms included reducing the number of hours that teachers worked and introducing new work/life balance clauses. From September 2005 there has been what is described as 'guaranteed professional time' for teachers to undertake preparation, planning and assessment (commonly referred to as PPA time). In practice, the reforms have altered the responsibilities undertaken by teaching assistants; it is not uncommon for assistants to supervise a class while the teacher is absent from the room, though only higher-level teaching assistants (HLTAs) are supposed to actively teach children, howbeit under general guidance from the teacher. See Burgess (2006) for an evaluation of this policy.

A report in 2008, *Deployment and Impact of Support Staff in Schools and the Impact of the National Agreement*, from the University of London's Institute of Education on the deployment of the wider workforce in schools, from teaching assistants to administrative support staff, has shown that 88 per cent of teachers felt that support staff had a positive effect on their job satisfaction; 77 per cent felt they have helped to reduce levels of stress; 59 per cent believed that they had led to decreases in their workload. Teachers valued the specialist help that support staff brought to aid pupil learning, together with their capacity to free teachers to teach and not spend excessive amounts of time on relatively trivial tasks.

Source

Burgess, H. (2006) 'The butterfly effect: Teaching assistants and workforce reform in primary schools', in Webb, R. (ed.) *Changing Teaching and Learning in the Primary School*, Maidenhead: Open University Press.

WRAGG, TED

See also: misbehaviour, mixed ability teaching, political involvement, reading schemes, teaching strategies, television, trainee teachers

Edward 'Ted' Conrad Wragg was born on 26 June 1938 and died suddenly on 10 November 2005. He was educated at King Edward VI Grammar School in Sheffield and achieved a first class degree in German at Durham University. He taught in Wakefield and then Leicester, and took an M.A. in education at Leicester University. After five years as professor of education at Nottingham in the early to mid-1970s, Wragg returned to Exeter as a professor in 1978, where he directed numerous research projects on topics such as classroom processes, teaching strategies, curriculum evaluation, assessment, good and incompetent teaching, and performance-related pay. Throughout his academic career he made as much time available as possible to teach a class of children each week so that he would remain in touch with the profession at the 'chalkface'. Wragg was an excellent communicator as broadcaster and journalist, championed teachers' rights and argued strongly to protect their professionalism from political interference.

Wragg strongly objected to what he viewed as government interference in education, preferring to let individual professionals decide what worked for them. He was largely scornful of the school inspection regime that had been imposed by a succession of governments during the 1980s and 1990s and into the new millennium. He wrote columns for the *Guardian* and the *Times Educational Supplement* (*TES*) over three decades, in which he offered amusing and often barbed comment on issues such as mixed-ability teaching and phonics. However, Wragg was also a passionate advocate of spreading best practice and the 'Teacher Education Project', directed by him from the late 1970s, remains one of the largest studies of teaching styles ever conducted in the UK. He was knowledgeable about education theories but never lost sight of the realities of practical classroom implementation.

Wragg served on the board of the Qualifications and Curriculum Authority from its inception in 1997 until 2003, where colleagues say his understanding of the curriculum and pedagogy was invaluable. He wrote more than fifty books on a wide range of educational topics, as well as producing a 120-book reading scheme, two CD-ROMs, a DVD on teachers' questions, and many videos and audiotapes. Wragg attracted new audiences on *Teachers TV* and notably in the Channel 4 series, *The Unteachables*, where he led a team of experts in a bold attempt to engage a group of disruptive pupils. Despite being on first-name terms with senior politicians, Wragg remained an independent, charismatic figure to the end of his life. Tedd Wragg was undoubtedly one of the most influential education figures of the late twentieth century.

Sources

Wikipedia: http://en.wikipedia.org/wiki/Ted_Wragg
Woodward, W. (2005) 'Obituary: Ted Wragg', *Guardian*, 11 November.

WRITING

See also: creative writing, English, handwriting, information technology, literacy, writing frames

Writing is one of the elements of literacy, together with reading and speaking and listening (oracy). At one time children spent a lot of time in writing about topics that interested them or producing fictional stories. In recent years, there has been more emphasis on 'writing with a purpose' and 'writing frames' – structuring writing according to a prescribed format to help children in gathering, organising and recording their thoughts. Teachers use computer technology to support children in drafting and re-drafting their ideas to produce a more polished final product. Writing is often undertaken with an audience in mind, such as producing simple stories to share with younger pupils or writing letters to counsellors about local issues affecting the school. Criticisms have been raised about the strong emphasis on functional writing at the expense of opportunities for children to undertake imaginative writing for pleasure. Mallett (2008) provides an in-depth analysis of writing and the development of writers (see pp. 351–58).

Source

Mallett, M. (2008) *The Primary English Encyclopaedia*, London: Routledge.

WRITING FRAMES

See also: creative writing, feedback, literacy, teaching methods, writing

Writing frames are formats that provide an outline of the overall text structure with additional support provided through headings, phrases and sentences. The use of writing frames is a method to combat a child's apprehension when faced with having to write something down on a blank piece of paper. It may also benefit pupils to attempt writing in the more challenging writing genres ('forms'). Each completed writing frame provides useful experience of the writing process and is a step towards independent planning and writing of extended pieces. The teacher may 'model' the process by working through the structure with children, offering examples and showing how to organise information. Alternatively, the children can be given the frame and asked to produce a piece of writing, for which the teacher subsequently offers feedback that includes suggestions for modification and improvement. Writing frames are said to benefit pupils in that they offer a framework on which to 'hang' their ideas; less able and confident children can also make use of suitable sentence starters.

Critics of writing frames claim that they can lead to monotonous lessons that fail to stretch more able pupils, and create an artificial system that bears little resemblance to everyday writing tasks. There is now general agreement among teachers that the use of a frame is helpful, especially as an initial prompt and scaffold for developing the writing, but should not act as a constraint or suppress a pupil's creativity and flair.

Y

YEARLY CLASS SYSTEMS (UK)

See also: infants, juniors

England and Wales have an identical system of naming classes in each year group. Children aged 4–5 years are in Reception (R); aged 5–6 in Year 1 (Y1); aged 6–7 in Year 2 (Y2); aged 7–8 in Year 3 (Y3); aged 8–9 in Year 4 (Y4); aged 9–10 in Year 5 (Y5); aged 10–11 in Year 6 (Y6). Sometimes years 3 and 4 are colloquially referred to as 'lower juniors' and years 5 and 6 as 'upper juniors'. The first year of secondary education is in Year 7 for children aged 11–12.

Northern Ireland uses 'P' plus a number to indicate the year group in the primary phase. The nomenclature changes to 'Year' once secondary education commences; for example, Year 8 is for children aged 11–12. Thus, P1/2 is broadly equivalent to Reception/Year 1 in England and Wales; P2/3 = Year 1/2; P3/4 = Year 2/3; P4/5 = Year 3/4; P5/6 = Year 4/5; P6/7 = Year 5/6; and P7/Year 8 = Year 6/7.

Scotland's primary schooling terminates at age 12 years (as opposed to 11 years in England, Wales and Northern Ireland). The descriptor for the year system is the word 'Primary'; thus, Primary 1 for 4–6 year-olds, Primary 2 for 5–7 year-olds … ending with Primary 7 to describe children in the final year of primary school, aged 11–12 years (i.e. equivalent to the first year of secondary schooling elsewhere in the UK).

Z

ZONE OF PROXIMAL DEVELOPMENT

See also: interaction, intervention, learning, monitoring, thinking skills

An important element of a teacher's role is to ascertain the extent and depth of children's learning. The influential Russian psychologist, Lev Vygotsky (1896–1934) maintained that a child follows the adult's example and, after initially receiving a lot of help, advice and support, gradually develops an ability to do the task or activity without help or assistance. His most famous work, *Thought and Language* (Vygotsky 1986 [1934]) – published shortly after his death – developed for the first time a theory of language development that described the development of language and logical thinking in young children in the course of their interactions with adults and the world around them; one of his tenets is that thought and language are inextricably linked.

Vygotsky famously referred to the difference between what children can achieve with help from a more knowledgeable teacher (adult or child) and what they can do without guidance as the 'zone of proximal development' (ZPD). The active intervention and support of adults in children's learning as they try to narrow the ZPD is equivalent to scaffolding placed around a house as it is constructed. As a child grasps the concept and gains the necessary understanding, the amount of 'scaffolding' (i.e. adult support) can be reduced. Once the child is in a position to progress independently, the support is removed completely. Consequently, it is essential that teachers be aware of children's existing knowledge and understanding and able to identify their limitations to know what support mechanisms to put in place such that the child can become an independent thinker and learner.

Source

Vygotsky, L.S. (1986 [1934]) *Thought and Language*, ed. A. Kozulin, trans. E. Hanfmann and G. Vakar, revised edn, Cambridge MA: MIT Press.